lonely planet

Korea

Ann Babe, Marco Ferrarese,
Simon Richmond, Phillip Tang

OSCAR ESPINOSA/SHUTTERSTOCK

Sinheung-sa (p163), Seoraksan National Park

CONTENTS

DS3ANN/IMAZINS/GETTY IMAGES

Jeju Olle Trail (p322), Jeju-do

KOREA

THE JOURNEY BEGINS HERE

Growing up as a Korean in the US, I could never have imagined that South Korea would someday be as cool around the world as it is now. A tiny peninsular country with an outsized cultural impact, Korea is as small as a singular US state and as big as a global tidal wave where K-Pop, K-Beauty and Korea's league of K-hyphenates feel all but inescapable. But this country is much more than that. Korea is home to endless wonders, from the slick cityscape of Seoul to the quiet countryside beyond; the swathes of green parkland rising in precipitous peaks and falling in mist-filled valleys; the rivers winding through, little villages nestled in their bends; the craggy coasts and wild seas dotted with hundreds and thousands of islands. I've lived in Seoul and in one-third of the country's nine provinces, and still I'm astounded at the multitudes it contains. Experiencing even a fraction of them is a gift.

Ann Babe

𝕏 *@ann_e_babe*

Ann is a Korean-American writer who covers Korea and beyond. She wrote the introductory and Jeju-do chapters.

My favourite experience is hiking the **Jeju Olle Trail** (p322), greeting folks along the way and collecting stamps in my Olle passport.

WHO GOES WHERE

Our writers and experts choose the places that, for them, define Korea.

SEONDEOK OH/SHUTTERSTOCK

Perched like a dragon above the Geum River, the ancient ramparts of **Gong-sanseong** (p338; pictured) are an open-air bastion to Gongju's regal past as a Baekje capital. Today, you can hike a scenic 2.6km circuit and feel history rising from its great walls and floodlit stonework. You'll hardly see a foreign tourist and will have time to yourself among the pines.

Phillip Tang

hellophillip.com, @mrtangtangtang

Phillip has spent over a decade traversing Korea for Lonely Planet. He wrote the Chungcheong-do chapter.

KOREA TOURISM ORGANIZATION - KANG MYEON-GU

If you want to experience a unique side of Korea, rent a car or start bikepacking from Mokpo and head west to the **Shinan Archipelago** (p292; pictured). Sea bridges make it a breeze to reach several of the main islands that remain well off the beaten track even to locals. You'll enter a world of endless beaches, small villages and *getbeol* mudflats.

Marco Ferrarese

marcoferrarese.com

A Malaysia-based writer and journalist, Marco discovered Korea as a teen through the Italian dub of Oldboy. He wrote the Gyeongsang-do, Busan and Jeolla-do chapters.

KOREA TOURISM ORGANIZATION - PARK EUNKYOUNG

I love the work of architect Tadao Ando. His designs for **Museum SAN** (p157; pictured) provide a wonderful setting for an extraordinary collection of contemporary-art sculptures and installations. My favourite space at the museum is Ground, his 2025 collaboration with British artist Anthony Gormley.

Simon Richmond

@simonrichmond

An award-winning travel writer, Simon has been visiting Korea and writing about it for more than 25 years. He wrote the Gangwon-do, North Korea and History in 15 Places chapters, and curated the Seoul chapter.

CONTRIBUTING WRITER

Charles Usher

charles-usher.com, @charlesreclausher

Charles lived in Seoul for a decade and is the author of a book about the city's neighbourhoods. He contributed to the Seoul & Around chapter.

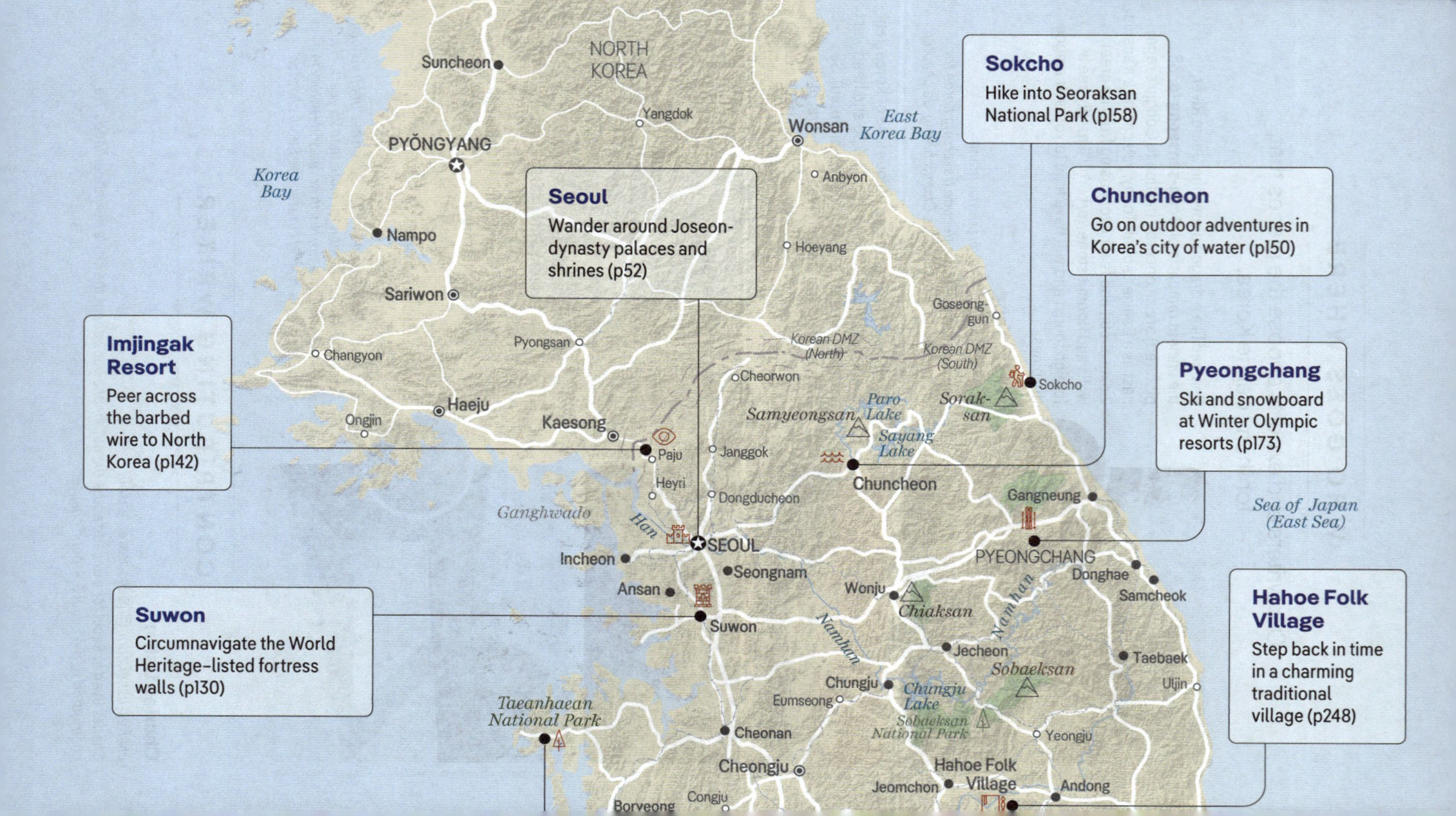
Sokcho
Hike into Seoraksan National Park (p158)
Chuncheon
Go on outdoor adventures in Korea's city of water (p150)
Pyeongchang
Ski and snowboard at Winter Olympic resorts (p173)
Hahoe Folk Village
Step back in time in a charming traditional village (p248)
Seoul
Wander around Joseon-dynasty palaces and shrines (p52)
Imjingak Resort
Peer across the barbed wire to North Korea (p142)
Suwon
Circumnavigate the World Heritage–listed fortress walls (p130)
NORTH KOREA
Suncheon
Yangdok
Wonsan
East Korea Bay
PYŎNGYANG
Korea Bay
Anbyon
Nampo
Hoeyang
Sariwon
Goseong-gun
Korean DMZ (North)
Korean DMZ (South)
Pyongsan
Changyon
Cheorwon
Sokcho
Sorak-san
Paro Lake
Samyeongsan
Sayang Lake
Haeju
Ongjin
Kaesong
Paju
Janggok
Heyri
Chuncheon
Dongducheon
Gangneung
Ganghwado
Han
SEOUL
Sea of Japan (East Sea)
Incheon
PYEONGCHANG
Seongnam
Donghae
Ansan
Samcheok
Wonju
Chiaksan
Suwon
Namhan
Jecheon
Taebaek
Sobaeksan
Chungju
Chungju Lake
Uljin
Eumseong
Taeanhaean National Park
Sobaeksan National Park
Cheonan
Yeongju
Cheongju
Hahoe Folk Village
Jeomchon
Andong
Borveong
Congju

Taeanhaean National Park
Discover coastal sand dunes and more than 100 islands (p350)
Jeonju
Stroll a neighbourhood of beautiful wooden *hanok* (p256)
Gwangju
Marvel at art exhibits and learn about recent history (p266)
Daegu
Explore Korea's oldest herbal-medicine market (p235)
Gyeongju
Tour temples, tombs and palace ruins (p222)
Busan
Savour fresh seafood at a buzzing market (p176)
Jeju-do
Take it slow on the island's Jeju Olle Trail (p309)
Daejeon
Yeongdeok
Nakdong
Seocheon
Gunsan
Iksan
Jeonju
Gimcheon
Deogyusan
Daegu
Yeongcheon
Pohang
Gyeongju
Ulsan
Yellow Sea
Namwon
Chirisan
Jinju
Changwon
Busan
Gwangju
Suncheon
Samcheonpo
Tongyeong
Geojedo
Mokpo
Boseong
Yeocheon
Yeosu
Jangheung
Hongdo
Heuksando
Haenam
Goheung
Dolsando
Jindo
Yeondo
Korea Strait
Hajodo
Oenarodo
Wando
Cheongsando
Bogildo
Geomundo
East China Sea
Jeju
Hallim
Hallasan
Jungmun
Seogwipo
JAPAN
0 100 km
0 50 miles

TASTE OF KOREA

Get ready for an unforgettable gastronomic experience. The flavours and textures of Korean cuisine run the gamut from tangy kimchi and irresistible *jjigae* (stews) to tempting *tang* (soups), crispy *jeon* (pancakes) and moreish *mandu* (dumplings). There are noodles to slurp, quality beef and pork to barbecue and a bounty of seafood to devour. Wash it all down with some local drinks, including quenching craft beers, regional *makgeolli* (rice wine) and shot glasses of soju.

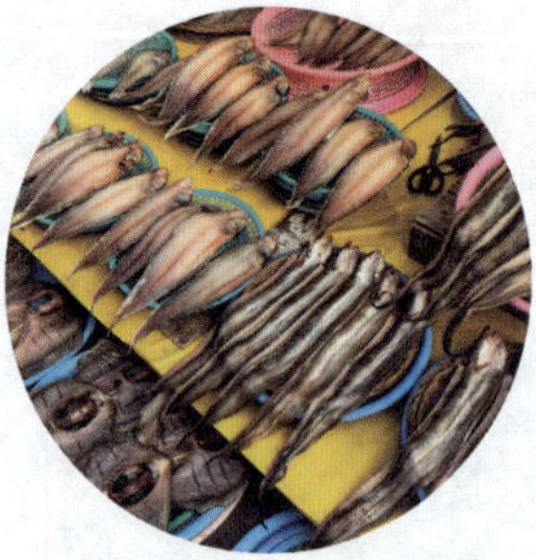

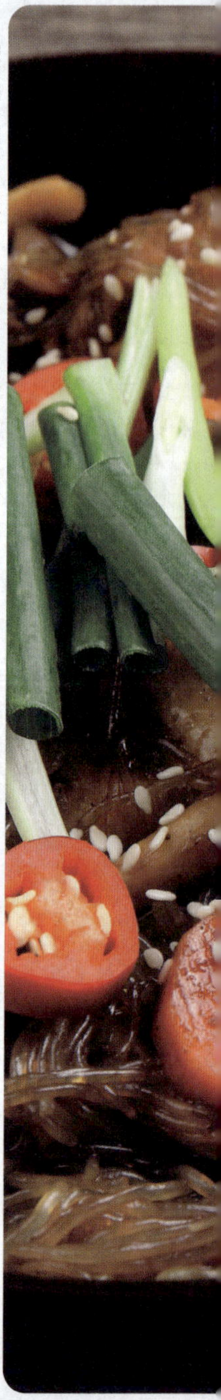

FROM LEFT: IMAGEBROKER.COM/ALAMY, MASOVAIDA MORGAN/LONELY PLANET, KYTAN/SHUTTERSTOCK

Temple Food

Vegetarian shines at Buddhist temples across the country, such as **Baegyang-sa** (p275) in Jeolla-do where Jeong Kwan (pictured above), who appeared on Netflix's *Chef's Table*, cooks her vegan food.

Fish Markets

Sample some remarkable seafood, buying direct from vendors at **Jagalchi** (p184; pictured above) in Busan and **Noryangjin** (p105) in Seoul.

Michelin Guide

South Korea has 253 Michelin Guide restaurants, 39 of them with stars – all located in Seoul and Busan.

Jjimdak, Jjimdak Alley (p245), Andong

BEST CULINARY EXPERIENCES

Tuck into tasty street food, including *bindaetteok* (crispy mung-bean pancakes), in Seoul's busiest *meokjagolmok* (food alleys) at ❶ **Gwangjang Market** (p59).

Try fiery *dakgalbi*, Chuncheon's cherished pan-fried chicken and rice-cake dish, on ❷ **Myeongdong Dakgalbi Street** (p152).

Savour *jjimdak*, a soy-braised chicken and vegetable dish, on Andong's ❸ **Jjimdak Alley** (p245), where it's a time-honoured local speciality.

Feast like Joseon royalty on a banquet of *hanjeongsik* (a multicourse menu that would have graced tables of Korean palaces) at ❹ **Goong** (p261) in Jeonju.

Dig into a fresh seafood feast and sample local delicacies such as *abai sundae* (sausages) and *dak gangjeong* (fried and glazed pieces of chicken) at ❺ **Sokcho Tourist Fish Market** (p158).

FROM LEFT: NATIONAL MUSEUM OF KOREA/WIKIMEDIA/PUBLIC DOMAIN, PHOTO_JEONGH/SHUTTERSTOCK, TRABANTOS/SHUTTERSTOCK

FROM DYNASTY TO DEMOCRACY

With 17 World Heritage sites in South Korea and three in North Korea, an abundance of history and heritage awaits you on the peninsula. Korean culture stretches back thousands of years, into prehistoric times. On your travels, you'll encounter everything from funerary monuments of the Neolithic and Bronze Ages to the beautifully decorated Joseon-dynasty palaces of Seoul and museums that tackle some of the most traumatic Korean events of the 20th century.

National Museums

Seoul's **National Museum of Korea** (p86; pictured above *Portrait of Yi Haeung*) is Korea's most visited museum, but there are also national museums in Cheongju, Chuncheon, Gongju, Gyeongju, Jeju, Jeonju and more.

Museum Without Walls

Scattered with heritage, the Silla capital of Gyeongju includes astonishing tumuli, ancient royal tombs and the ruins of **Hwangnyong-sa** (p225; pictured above), Korea's largest-ever temple.

World Heritage-Listed Fortress

Korea's fortress walls serpentine around Cheongju, Gongju, Seoul and, most notably, Suwon, where its restored 18th-century **Hwaseong** (p132) encloses the city's historic heart.

Changdeokgung (p62), Seoul

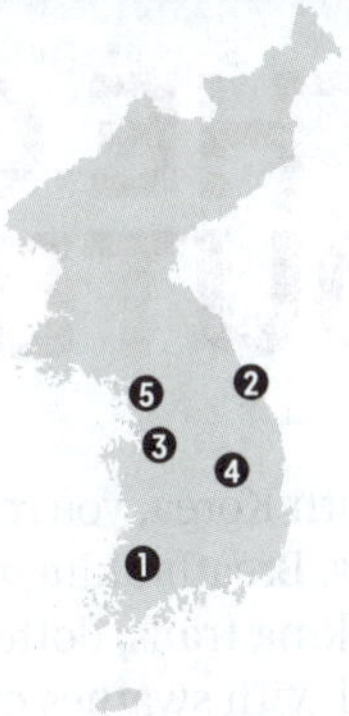

BEST HISTORICAL EXPERIENCES

Witness the bullet holes and learn about violent 1980 clashes between citizens and military in Gwangju at the ❶ **Jeonil Building 245** (p268).

Step back in time at ❷ **Ojukheon** (p169), one of the oldest Joseon-dynasty homes in Korea, located in a beautifully landscaped park in Gangneung.

Get an overview of Korean history and the country's struggle to free itself from Japanese colonisation at the ❸ **Independence Hall of Korea** (p345) in Cheonan.

Admire centuries-old rural architecture and a practically unchanged way of life in ❹ **Hahoe Folk Village** (p248), one of the most authentic such villages in Korea.

Imagine life in the Joseon court at World Heritage–listed ❺ **Changdeokgung** (p62), the beautiful Seoul palace that includes the serene Secret Garden.

THE GREAT OUTDOORS

In South Korea, you're never too far from the big outdoors. Breathtaking mountain landscapes are cut with hiking trails, dotted with ancient temples and covered with swathes of forest. There are beautiful lakes and mighty rivers. The crinkly coastline is indented with beaches, dunes, craggy cliffs and extensive mudflats. Human-made landscapes in the shape of gorgeous gardens, tea plantations and fields of grain are also part of the pretty picture.

FROM LEFT: CAVAN IMAGES/GETTY IMAGES, SUEUY SONG/GETTY IMAGES, INSUNG JEON/GETTY IMAGES

UNESCO Biosphere Reserves

South Korea is home to 10 biosphere reserves, including the entire island of **Jeju-do** (p299), as well as **Seoraksan National Park** (p162; pictured above), **Suncheon** (p276) and the **Wando** (p296) archipelago.

The Korean Archipelago

With more than 17,000km of careening coastline, South Korea has 3382 islands, 2918 of them uninhabited (Sodeung Island pictured above).

Korea's National Parks

Among the country's 23 national parks, a vast majority are mountainous, but four are marine and coastal, and one, lone Gyeongju, is historical.

Chungju-ho (p364)

BEST OUTDOOR EXPERIENCES

Climb 1915m ❶ **Cheonwang-bong** (p283), Korea's second-highest mountain and one of a dozen peaks that form a 40km-long ridge through Jirisan National Park.

Boat hop or sail your way through ❷ **Hallyeohaesang National Park** (p210) off the charming port town of Tongyeong.

Summit South Korea's highest mountain, ❸ **Hallasan** (p310), a dormant volcano crowned by a crater lake.

Canoe on and camp beside ❹ **Chungju-ho** (p364), Korea's largest artificial lake, a scenic area with vistas of Woraksan National Park.

Cross ❺ **Moaksan** (p263) west to east, stopping at ancient temples en route.

SEASONAL SPECTACLES

South Korea hosts various festivals and events throughout the year, many of which are worth building your travel plans around. The changing of the seasons also brings delightful outbursts of colour to both town and countryside, from the sugary pink of cherry blossoms in spring to the fiery blaze of maple and ginkgo trees in autumn.

Buddha's Birthday

Each May, temples across the country are festooned with decorations to mark the Buddha's big day. The largest celebration is Seoul's **Lotus Lantern Festival** (p67; pictured above).

Floral Festivities

In spring, Korea erupts in blooms at the **Jinhae Cherry Blossom Festival** (p203), **Suncheon Bay National Garden** (p276; pictured above), **Taean World Tulip Exhibition** (p353) and more.

Happy New Year!

Be awed by fireworks lighting up the sky over Busan's **Gwangalli Beach** (p194), or hike up Jeju-do's World Heritage–listed **Seongsan Ilchul-bong** (p309) to see the first sunrise of the year.

FROM LEFT: JULY7TH/GETTY IMAGES, ST_TRAVEL/SHUTTERSTOCK, CSTRIKE/SHUTTERSTOCK

Taebaeksan Snow Festival (p174), Taebaeksan National Park

BEST SEASONAL EXPERIENCES

Head to Taebaek town and the foothills of ❶ **Taebaeksan National Park** (p173) in January for the annual snow festival featuring giant snow sculptures and other wintery activities.

Celebrate Gyeongsang-do's famous ceramic tea bowls at the ❷ **Mungyeong Chasabal Festival** (p250), with contests, exhibitions, performances and more.

Splash about in sludge at the ❸ **Boryeong Mud Festival** (p348) in July – it's fun and said to be good for your skin.

Commemorate styles and music from decades past at Gwangju's ❹ **Chungjang Street Festival of Recollection** (p271) in October.

Gaze at thousands of lanterns and fireworks reflecting in the Nam River at the ❺ **Jinju Namgang Yudaeng Festival** (p220) in October.

SACRED & SPIRITUAL KOREA

There are about 20,000 Buddhist temples scattered across Korea, many located in beautiful mountain and forest settings. To fully experience their serenity and peacefulness, opt for a templestay and set forth on an inward journey. More spirituality comes in the form of ancient sites of shamanism, Confucian shrines, World Heritage-listed *seowon* (academies for teaching Confucianism) and relatively modern churches.

FROM LEFT: YLLYSO/SHUTTERSTOCK, MIRKO KUZMANOVIC/GETTY IMAGES, JINROO/SHUTTERSTOCK

Shamanic Sites

Shamanic sites dot Korea, centering on natural features such as the Zen Rocks on the west side of Seoul's sacred mountain **Inwangsan** (p126; pictured above), said to help women become pregnant.

Christian Spaces

Admire the stained glass at **Myeongdong Cathedral** (p78; pictured above) and the spiritually inspired art at **Seosomun Shrine History Museum** (p78), both in Seoul, and see the historic churches of Daegu.

Confucian Academies

Once flush with Confucian academies, the state destroyed many of them in the late 1800s. **Oksan Seowon** (p232) in Gyeongju is one of the prettiest to remain.

Haein-sa (p242), Gayasan National Park

BEST TEMPLE EXPERIENCES

Admire the skills of the carpenters and painters who crafted Gyeongju's ❶ **Bulguk-sa** (p228), an outstanding example of Shilla architecture.

Explore World Heritage–listed ❷ **Haein-sa** (p242), in a beautiful forest setting and home to one of the world's largest Buddhist woodblock scriptures.

Stand beneath the compassionate gaze of the 16m-tall statue of Gwaneum at ❸ **Naksan-sa** (p164), a temple with perhaps the most spectacular coastal location in Korea.

Enjoy a free vegetarian meal or an overnight templestay at ❹ **Guin-sa** (p367), wedged into a forested valley in Sobaeksan National Park.

Squeeze between boulders to reach ❺ **Hyangir-am** (p284) Buddhist hermitage, halfway up a mountain at the tip of Dolsando, an island connected to Yeosu by a bridge.

OFF THE BEATEN PATH

Urban Korea bristles with human activity and it's rare to find yourself alone, anywhere. This said, it is possible to find pockets of calm, even in Seoul, and very easy to get off the beaten track in rural parts of the country and the bigger national parks. Bridges and ferries connect the peninsula to thousands of islands, many of which are perfect for finding a beach and dropping off the radar.

FROM LEFT: HITSUJIKUMO33/GETTY IMAGES, KOREA TOURISM ORGANIZATION · JEON HYEONGJUN, CHO GYO SANG/SHUTTERSTOCK

Stone Island

On the island of stones, **Jeju Stone Park** (p317; pictured above) displays an incredible collection of rocks and stones, some shaped by nature, others by humans.

Furthest South

Ride the monorail to **Ttangkkeut Observation Deck** (p295; pictured above) at the southernmost tip of the peninsula, and the ferry to **Marado** (p332), the southernmost point in all of Korea.

Alternative DMZ

Peer into North Korea from less-visited points along the 250km border, such as **Cheorwon Peace Observatory** (p156) or **Tongil Security Park** (p165).

Ulleungdo (p234)

BEST REMOTE EXPERIENCES

Take the ferry to ❶ **Ulleungdo** (p234), the tip of an extinct volcano 135km east of the Korean Peninsula that offers spectacular scenery.

Drive over super-scenic sea bridges to the islands of ❷ **Shinan Archipelago** (p292).

Climb Gitdae-bong for panoramic views across remote ❸ **Hongdo** (p294), a beautiful island rising precipitously from the sea west of Mokpo.

Wander around charming ❹ **Sangdomun** (p160), on the outskirts of Seoraksan National Park, and see how many animals and birds you can spot painted on the stones of the village's low stone walls.

Walk around the island of ❺ **Gapado** (p332) on route 10-1, Jeju Olle Trail's shortest course at just 4.2km.

KOREA NOW

Hallyu, the Korean Wave of pop culture, is readily on tap in Korea. Attend K-Pop concerts, festivals and dance classes, and visit locations where your favourite K-Movies and K-Dramas were filmed. Korea also delivers big time on cutting-edge technology and visionary architecture and art, with major festivals devoted to what's new. Plus there's 'newtro', a trend that celebrates touchstones of the analogue era, such as listening to vinyl records, with a contemporary spin.

Big in Busan

In June, the **Busan One Asia Festival** *(bof.or.kr)* showcases a range of *hallyu* content, while in October the latest K-Movies are screened at **Busan International Film Festival** (p183; pictured above).

Korea's Biennales

Gwangju's **arts festival** (p268) is Korea's most famous biennale, but also look out for **Cheongju Craft Biennale** (p357; pictured above) and Seoul Biennale of Architecture and Urbanism.

Stars in Seoul

Performing arts take centre stage at the autumn **Seoul Performing Arts Festival** (p67), a month of theatre, dance and music at Sejong Center and other venues.

FROM LEFT: WOOHAE CHO/GETTY IMAGES, KOREA TOURISM ORGANIZATION - KIM JIHO, SANGA PARK/SHUTTERSTOCK

Suncheon Open Film Location (p277)

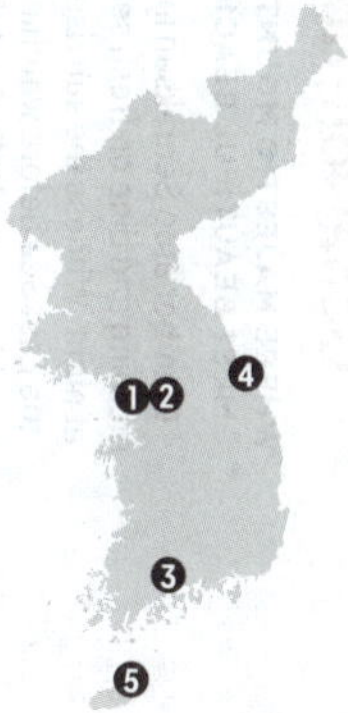

BEST CONTEMPORARY EXPERIENCES

Be dazzled by the space-age architecture of ❶ **Dongdaemun Design Plaza & Park** (p93). Seoul Fashion Week is held here in February.

Saunter along Seoul's ❷ **Hongdae Street** (p97), which is a chaotic confluence of bright lights, K-Pop and a window onto Korea's current mainstream fashion trends.

Travel back in time at the ❸ **Suncheon Open Film Location** (p277), a series of movie sets where famous K-Dramas, including *Gangnam Blues* and *Pachinko*, were filmed.

Follow the BTS ARMY of fans to golden ❹ **Cheongsihaeng Beach** (p170) in Gangneung, the location of the K-Popsters' *Spring Day* album cover.

Head to Hado-ri and its ❺ **Haenyeo Museum** (p315) to see where some scenes of the hit Netflix show *When Life Gives You Tangerines* were set in Jeju-do.

REGIONS & CITIES

Find the places that tick all your boxes.

North Korea

REPRESSIVE DICTATORSHIP AND NUCLEAR POWER

Occupying more than half of the Korean Peninsula, the Democratic People's Republic of Korea (DPRK) is one of the strangest and most unsettling places on Earth. A pariah state, in the dangerous grip of a personality cult to a dictator, it's also a nation rich in natural beauty.

Seoul & Around

CITY OF PALACES, PARKS AND K-POP

South Korea's dynamic capital is fashion- and technology-forward, but also deeply traditional. Take in palaces, temples, cutting-edge design and mountain trails, all to a nonstop K-Pop beat. Leave time to explore the surrounding province of Gyeonggi-do and neighbouring metropolis of Incheon, offering everything from ski resorts to remote islands.

Gangwon-do

WHERE MAJESTIC MOUNTAINS MEET BEAUTIFUL BEACHES

Clamber atop Seoraksan in the morning and dine on fresh seafood at night. Witness the sun rise over the East Sea before watching for rare birds in the DMZ. Don't forget snow sports, surfing and suspension bridges. It's all possible in this beautiful, wild wonderland.

Gyeongsang-do

CULTURAL HERITAGE AMID ASTONISHING SCENERY

Korea's southeastern expanse encompasses the country's fourth-biggest city, tiny harbour towns and secluded villages. In Gyeongju, things quieten amid all the antiquities, but not too much, with a hip 'hood of converted *hanok*. Andong has the soul, and yesteryear folk villages in which to show it. Then there are the islands – oh, the islands.

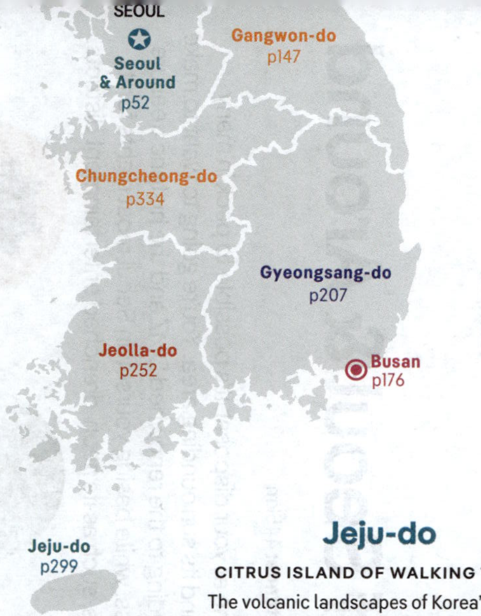

Chungcheong-do

UNEXPLORED COAST, HISTORY & LAKE WONDERLAND

From the Yellow Sea to Chungju's Lakeland, Chungcheong-do is an offbeat gem. Besides natural bounty – think remote beaches, Korea's oldest pine forests and its largest lake – the region holds the ancient fortresses and tombs of the Baekje dynasty and gave birth to the world's first block-printing system.

Jeolla-do

CULTURE, MYSTIC PEAKS AND INFINITE ISLANDS

Korea's southwestern corner offers a fascinating history of rebellion and rewards explorers with never-ending adventures. Start from its artistic and green cities, cruise endless kilometres of coastline, hop between hundreds of islands and climb the mystic peaks of some of the country's best national parks.

Busan

SOUTH KOREA'S HERITAGE-MODERN COASTAL CITY

Hemmed between mountains to the north and spread thin along kilometres of glistening beaches and jagged coastline, South Korea's second-largest (and second most visited) city is a rollicking port town with tonnes to offer. Home to one of Asia's most important film festivals, it has fantastic seafood, enticing shopping districts and some of the country's best craft-beer scenes.

Jeju-do

CITRUS ISLAND OF WALKING TRAILS

The volcanic landscapes of Korea's largest island are so special that it's listed as a UNESCO Global Geopark. Its culture, distinct from that of the mainland, is unique, too. Come to hike up South Korea's tallest mountain, amble along its Jeju Olle Trail and dive walls of spectacularly colourful corals.

OZONE FOTO/SHUTTERSTOCK

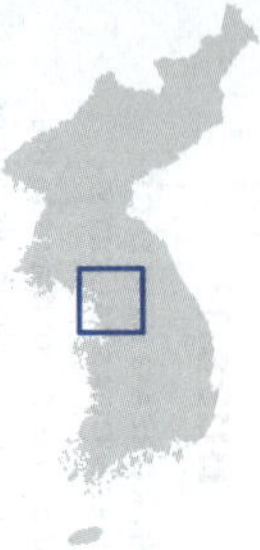

Seoul (p52)

ITINERARIES

Best of Seoul & Around

Allow: 7 days **Distance:** 445km

Even with a short time at your disposal, it's possible to pack in many highlights of Seoul and its surrounding area. You're going to want to make a few day trips, including to the renowned DMZ and the historic treasure of Hwaseong fortress, while basing yourself in Seoul most nights for its after-dark diversions, such as its neon-drenched entertainment districts.

1 SEOUL 2 DAYS

In the **capital** (p52), prioritise sights north of the Han River, focusing on the royal palaces, picturesque *hanok* neighbourhoods (doors pictured above) and brightly lit, perpetually busy Myeong-dong for its shopping and street food. Head up Namsan, the most central of Seoul's four guardian mountains, for great views of the metropolis. Treat yourself to neo-Korean cuisine in Gangnam, and sample the nightlife in Hongdae.

2 DMZ 1 DAY

Arrange a full-day tour to the **DMZ** (p142; museum pictured above), where you'll go to Imjingak Resort, walk into the Third Infiltration Tunnel and, if it's open at the time, step into the Joint Security Area's Freedom House. Wrap up the day with a graze at the street-food stalls in Gwangjang Market before having a nightcap at a speakeasy-style bar in nearby Euljiro.

3 SUWON 1 DAY

Home to World Heritage–listed Hwaseong (pictured above), an 18th-century fortification of stone and brick, **Suwon** (p130) is also famous for its take on KFC (Korean fried chicken) and its beef *galbi* (ribs). Return to Seoul to dine and drink your way through Itaewon.

***Detour:** A trip to **Korean Folk Village** (p131) near Suwon is a fascinating step back in time.*
3 hours.

FROM LEFT: AARONCHOI/GETTY IMAGES, KOREA TOURISM ORGANIZATION - GANGWON OFFICE, MOMENT

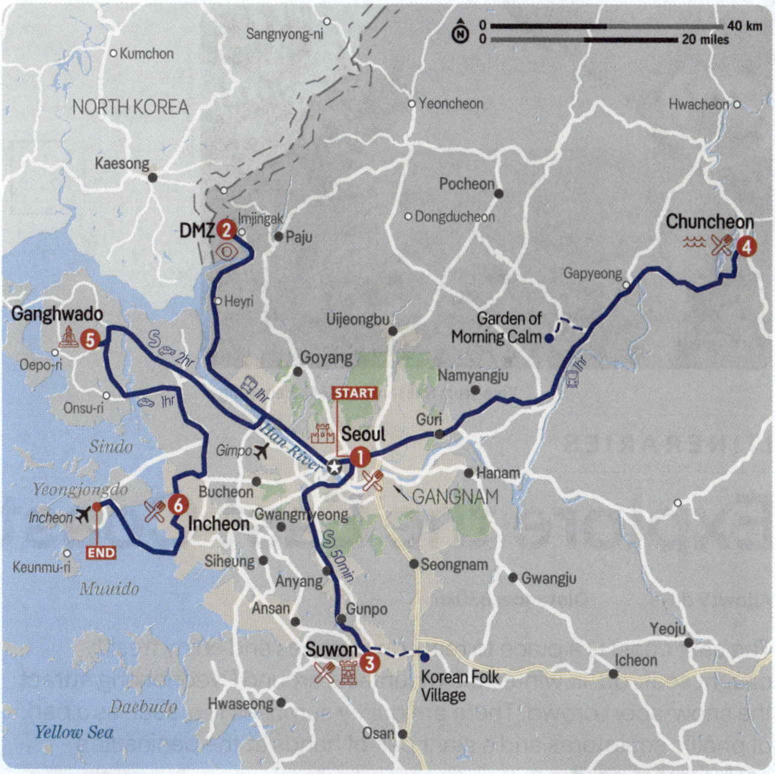

4

CHUNCHEON 1 DAY

Popular as a weekend getaway from Seoul, the provincial capital **Chuncheon** (p150) is known as the City of Water for its proximity to lakes. Cycle alongside Uiam Lake (pictured above), drop by LEGOLAND and sample the town's famous spicy chicken and rice-cake dish, *dakgalbi*.

Detour: *If you're driving, consider going via the gorgeous* ***Garden of Morning Calm*** *(p134) in Gapyeong or nearby* ***Nami Island*** *(p155).* *3 hours.*

5

GANGHWADO 1 DAY

Pick up a rental car at Gimpo Airport to drive to the historic island of **Ganghwado** (p138), home to a couple of impressive temples, beaches and a chance to hike up Manisan to the stone altar (pictured above) said to have been used by the mythical first Korean, Dangun.

6

INCHEON 1 DAY

Incheon (p135; pictured above), South Korea's third-biggest city, certainly deserves exploring before you leave. Eat delicious Chinese food and visit a *jajangmyeon* (noodles in a black bean sauce) museum in Incheon's historic and colourful Chinatown. Hang out in cool cafes such as COSMO 40 and wander the hip 'hood of Gaehang-ro before dropping off your rental at the airport.

STUDIO, CHANNARONG LUECHA/GETTY IMAGES, THOMAS MCCOMB/GETTY IMAGES, PHILIP80/SHUTTERSTOCK, NOOMNA NAKHONPHANOM/SHUTTERSTOCK

View from Naksan-sa (p164), Yangyang

ITINERARIES

Explore the East Coast

Allow: 9 days **Distance:** 830km

The east coast is a place to relax on beaches and enjoy freshly caught seafood. In winter, the mountains around Pyeonchang attract the snow-sport crowd. There are quirky surprises too, such as a park of phallic sculptures and a giant pair of hands at the peninsula's easternmost point.

1

SOKCHO 2 DAYS

From this charming **coastal city** (p158, pictured above), organise a trip into Seoraksan National Park, a UNESCO Biosphere Reserve. In Sokcho itself, stroll around two portside lakes, walk the beautiful Bada Hyanggi trail and visit the village of Abai Maeul to sample North Korean cuisine. A 15-minute drive away, the Goddess of Mercy looks out to sea at Naksan-sa and surfers ride the waves at Yangyang.

2

GANGNEUNG 1 DAY

A place of wind-twisted pines, **Gangneung** (p167) is popular in summer for its string of beaches (Gyeongpo Beach pictured above) and in winter as an access point to Pyeongchang's ski resorts. See Joseon-dynasty architecture and sip your way around the coffee spots of Anmok Beach and the historic neighbourhood of Chilsadang. An hour south is seaside Haesindang Park, studded with more than 50 phallic sculptures.

3

ULLEUNGDO 2 DAYS

It can be a rough three-hour ferry ride from Gangneung to **Ulleungdo** (p234), but it's worth it for the chance to experience the extraordinary landscapes (pictured above) and nature of this island that's the tip of a volcano. Hike through lush forest to the 986m summit of Seongin-bong, tramp along the spectacular Haengnam Coastal Walkway and gaze across the ocean to the politically disputed island of Dokdo.

FROM LEFT: PURIPAT LERTPUNYAROJ/SHUTTERSTOCK, THOMAS MCCOMB/GETTY IMAGES, SANG WOON/SHUTTERSTOCK

4

POHANG 1 DAY

Catch the ferry back to **Pohang** (p232). The HQ of POSCO, Korea's largest steel manufacturer, may not seem like somewhere to linger, but it does have fun features. Tackle Korea's largest walkable art installation, Space Walk, for bird's-eye views of the city. Stand at the Korean Peninsula's easternmost point beside a giant pair of hands (pictured above), then explore a converted Japanese colonial district.

5

GYEONGJU 2 DAYS

There's a lot to see in this lovely **city** (p222), once the capital of the Silla kingdom, including tombs, temples, rock carvings, pagodas, Buddhist statuary, palace ruins and traditional *hanok*. Highlights include Bulguk-sa, a temple considered the crowning glory of Silla architecture, and the Gyeongju National Museum (pictured above). Save time to stroll along the trendy shopping and cafe street, Hwangnidan-gil.

6

DAEGU 1 DAY

Korea's fourth-largest city, **Daegu** (p235; pictured above) is packed with heritage-activist sites, historic churches and missionary residences and the country's oldest medicine market. Contemporary diversions include pretty parks, fine eating, shopping and entertainment. Another option is to base yourself in Daegu for a trip to Haein-sa, housing a World Heritage–listed library of more than 80,000 14th-century woodblocks.

KOREA TOURISM ORGANIZATION - KIM JIHO, THE MARINER 4291/SHUTTERSTOCK, SANGHWAN KIM/GETTY IMAGES

ST_TRAVEL/SHUTTERSTOCK

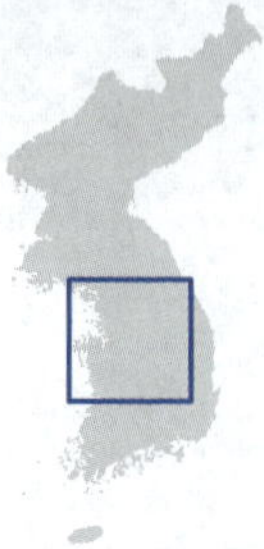

Baekje Cultural Land (p343), Buyeo

ITINERARIES

West & Central Korea

Allow: 8 days **Distance:** 635km

South of Seoul and north of the mountain ranges of Jeolla-do, Chungcheong-do is an easy-to-reach part of the country where few domestic Korean tourists bother going. Along the west coast are fine beaches and islands, while inland are ancient sites, temple-studded mountains, charming folk villages and Korea's largest artificial lake.

1

GONGJU 2 DAYS

Gongju (p338), the ancient capital of the Baekje dynasty, is just over an hour by express train south of Seoul. Highlights include the commanding hilltop fortress of Gongsan-seong and the nearly 2000-year-old tomb of King Muryeong (pictured above). Make a day trip to compact Gyeryongsan National Park, where there are three temples offering templestays.

Detour: *Stop off at Cheonan to visit* ***Independence Hall of Korea*** *(p345). 3 hours.*

2

BUYEO 1 DAY

More Baekje sites are located in **Buyeo** (p341), including a five-storey stone pagoda. Baekje Cultural Land is a full-scale replica of what a Baekje palace and attendant village may have looked like. Drop into one of town's museums and take a romantic evening stroll at Seodong Park (pictured above). Alternatively, Mansusan, west of Buyeo, is home to several significant historic sights, including the temple of Muryang-sa.

3

TAEANHAEAN NATIONAL PARK 2 DAYS

Underwater tunnels and bridges make it possible to drive to **Taeanhaean National Park** (p350) via the beach resort of Daecheon and the islands of Wonsando and Anmyeondo. The park covers 130 islands and islets, more than 30 beaches and a panoply of hiking and cycling trails. Places not to miss include Sinduri Coastal Sand Dunes (pictured above) and Anmyeondo Recreational Forest.

FROM LEFT: STOCK FOR YOU/SHUTTERSTOCK, PHOTOI / IMAZINS/GETTY IMAGES, ISEO YANG/GETTY IMAGES

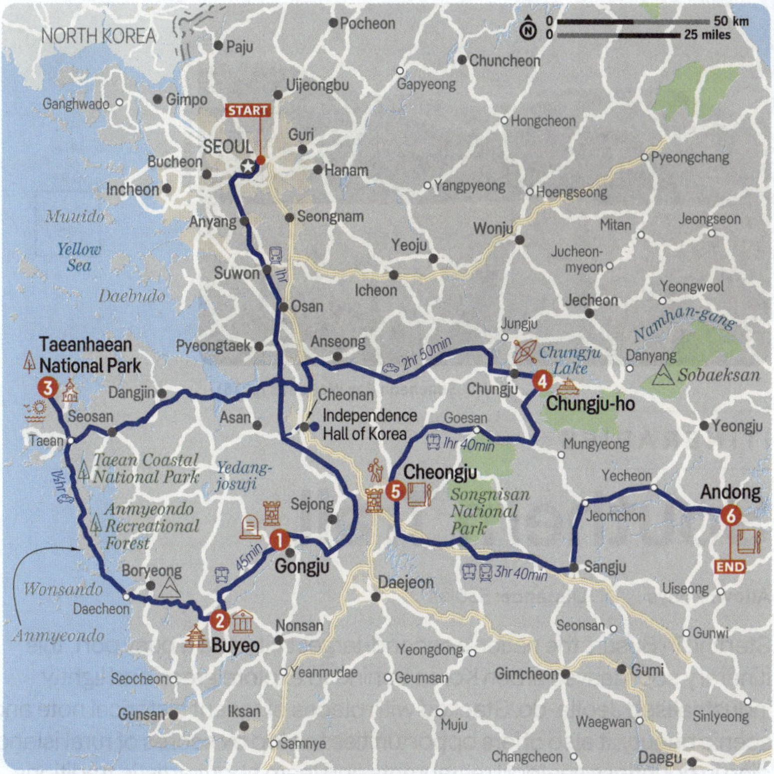

4

CHUNGJU-HO ⏱1 DAY

Stretching from Chungju in the west to Jecheon and Danyang eastward, massive **Chungju-ho** (p364) is a scenic spot to spend a day. There are cruises on the lake (pictured above), or you can rent a kayak or canoe to paddle around yourself. Drop by the Cheongpung Cultural Heritage Complex to understand the complicated history behind the creation of the lake.

5

CHEONGJU ⏱1 DAY

Cheongju (p355) is where the world's oldest book made with movable metal type was created in 1377 (78 years before Gutenberg's Bible); learn all about it at Cheongju Early Printing Museum (pictured above). Contemporary arty locations in the city include the Culture Factory in a revamped tobacco factory. For hiking, head to the fortress of Sangdang-sanseong and the trails in Songnisan National Park.

6

ANDONG ⏱1 DAY

With a strong commitment to preserving Korean culture (and an even stronger local soju to imbibe), **Andong** (p243) is an excellent base for heading to nearby Hahoe Folk Village (pictured above), a picturesque UNESCO World Heritage site listed for its commitment to preserving its rural architecture and way of life.

SNOWTIGERMAN/GETTY IMAGES, KEN ECKERT/WIKIMEDIA/CC BY-SA 4.0, PHOTO_JEONGH/SHUTTERSTOCK

SANGA PARK/SHUTTERSTOCK

Suncheon Bay Wetlands (p278)

ITINERARIES

Southern Trail

Allow: 9 days **Distance:** 530km

Starting in Busan, the nation's second-largest city and a busy port, this itinerary soon leaves urban Korea behind to explore green and lightly industrialised Jeolla-do. Stacked with places of recent historical note and scenic beauty, it also offers opportunities to stop by scores of rural islands, dine in countless seafood restaurants and learn about artistic traditions.

1

BUSAN 2 DAYS

With international transport connections, **Busan** (p176) is a vibrant port peppered with majestic mountains, glistening beaches and steaming hot springs. Its Jagalchi Fish Market (pictured above) teems with every marine species imaginable. Escape the city at the beautiful temple of Beomeo-sa. Rejoin the party at popular Haeundae beach and arty Gamcheon Village, which began as a refugee shantytown during the Korean War.

2

TONGYEONG 2 DAYS

At the southern tip of Goseong Peninsula, **Tongyeong** (p210) offers a pretty harbour lapped by cerulean seas. Come to dine on the freshest seafood and sail to an incredible collection of islands. Ride the cable car (pictured above) to near the top of Mireuksan for jaw-dropping coastal views. The coastal drive around the island of Namhaedo to the west is one of most scenic routes in Korea.

3

SUNCHEON 1 DAY

Immerse yourself in nature at **Suncheon** (p276), a green city of gardens. The biggest floral fest of all is Suncheon Bay National Garden (pictured above), where entry also includes access to Suncheon Bay Wetlands, a top location for bird-watching. Or use Suncheon as a base for visiting Yeosu, where attractions include an aquarium, the hillside Hyangir-am temple and immersive digital art at Arte Museum.

FROM LEFT: NIIIMAGE/SHUTTERSTOCK, STOCK FOR YOU/SHUTTERSTOCK, EUNKYUNG PARK/GETTY IMAGES

4 MOKPO 1 DAY

Move on to the port of **Mokpo** (p287; pictured above), where you can ride Korea's longest and highest marine cable car. The port's old core is a web of charming little alleys snaking behind Japanese-colonial-era buildings, while the coastal Gatbawi Cultural District hosts several fascinating museums. If you have more time, ferries shuttle from here to the western islands of Dadohae Haesang National Park.

5 GWANGJU 2 DAYS

In Jeolla-do's largest **city** (p266), learn all about the 1980 democracy uprising (5.18 Archives pictured above) and visit mind-blowing art exhibits. Set out hiking in Mudeungsan National Park in search of the majestic Seoseokdae Colonnade, then wend your way through the bamboo forest of Juknokwon. Alternatively, you can walk the hills surrounding **Gochang** (p273) to view World Heritage–listed tombs.

6 JEONJU 1 DAY

Jeonju (p256) has a fascinating *hanok* village (pictured above) crammed with more than 700 traditional houses and buildings and a couple of cool mural-art neighbourhoods. It's also where the classic rice dish bibimbap was invented and is a place to enjoy the milky rice wine *makgeolli*. Another option is to base yourself here for hiking in Maisan Provincial Park or Deogyusan National Park.

SIMON RICHMOND

Jusangjeolli-dae (p328)

ITINERARIES

Around Jeju-do

Allow: 7 days **Distance:** 210km

Located 85km off the southern tip of the peninsula, Korea's largest island offers fascinating volcanic landscapes, the country's tallest peak and dozens of sandy beaches. One of the best ways to experience the island's beauty and distictive culture is to walk one or more of the Jeju Olle Trails.

1 JEJU-SI ⏱ 1 DAY

The island's **capital** (p302), where you'll arrive either by flight or ferry, is a big city with plenty of places to eat and shop, not least its atmospheric Dongmun Market (pictured above). Arario Museum of contemporary arts is fantastic and both Jeju Folklore & Natural History Museum and Jeju National Museum are worth seeing to understand a bit more about the island's culture and history.

2 SEONGSAN-RI ⏱ 1 DAY

Seongsan-ri (p309) is the base for climbing Seongsan Ilchul-bong (pictured above), a spectacular extinct volcano that rises straight out of the ocean. Climb it in the early hours of the morning and greet the dawn at the edge of its forested crater. Nearby attractions include Tadao Ando–designed architecture on Phoenix Island and Seongeup Folk Village, where you can get a feel for how islanders have lived for centuries.

3 UDO ⏱ 1 DAY

The largest of 62 islets surrounding Jeju-do, and supposedly shaped like a sprawled-out cow, **Udo** (p316; pictured above) is clearly visible from Seongsan-ri. Attracting throngs of day-tripping tourists, particularly on weekends and holidays, it's a beautiful place with lovely beaches and a friendly vibe. To best appreciate its rural charms, follow the Jeju Olle Trail around the island and plan to stay overnight.

FROM LEFT: DANIEL FUNG/SHUTTERSTOCK, TONOITOO/SHUTTERSTOCK, SANGA PARK/SHUTTERSTOCK

4

SEOGWIPO 2 DAYS

The commercial hub of the island's southern half, **Seogwipo** (p318) is the best all-round base for touring this part of Jeju-do. Blessed with two lovely waterfalls (Jeongbang Pokpo pictured above), one of which cascades into the sea, the city provides access to some of Korea's best diving and walking trails along a spectacular coastline that culminates in the rectangular rock columns of Jusangjeolli-dae at nearby Jungmun Resort.

5

SAGYE-RI 1 DAY

Hugging Jeju-do's southwest corner, the seaside community of **Sagye-ri** (p329) offers dramatic coastlines with incredible rock formations and the craggy Sanbangsan outcrop. On this volcanic hill's slopes is a colourful temple (pictured above) and, at the top of a short hike, a cave dripping with water that shelters a stone Buddha staring out to sea.

***Detour:** Ferries from Unjinhang can connect to the lovely southern islands of **Gapado** and **Marado** (p332). 4 hours.*

6

HALLASAN NATIONAL PARK 1 DAY

Devote a day in this **park** (p310; pictured above) to hiking up Hallasan – it's a strenuous climb to the 1950m summit, but worth the effort. There are also some alternative short, easy climbs through the park, which is the world's only habitat for Korean firs and remains beautiful throughout the seasons, with flowering azaleas in April and May being a particularly notable sight.

ADVENSHOTER/SHUTTERSTOCK, PANGJEE_S/SHUTTERSTOCK, SIMON RICHMOND

WHEN TO GO

Visiting Korea is wonderful in either late spring or early autumn, when the weather and nature can both be ideal.

Korea is a pleasure to visit throughout the year, with each season having something to offer. Early April is when areas of the peninsula turn pink in a transient flurry of delicate cherry blossoms. There's more flower viewing in early May, with wisteria and azaleas peaking near the same time as the spectacular nationwide celebrations around Buddha's birthday. Although you need to be prepared for sticky heat, monsoon rains and high humidity throughout summer, this is also a great time to hit Korea's beaches and islands. The amazing autumnal leaf colours make October and early November peak season for hiking in national parks. As the temperatures start to drop and the snow falls, the nation's ski resorts crank into action and outdoor ice rinks, such as the one in Seoul Plaza, open up. The coldest season is also a great time to get cosy in a traditional Korean sauna.

I LIVE HERE

JEJU, CITRUS ISLAND

Soojin Ivy Lee is the director of brand management for the Jeju Olle Trail. *jejuolle.org*

By November, mainland South Korea is getting cold, but on Jeju it's still mild and it's the least windy season for the island. This is why we schedule our Jeju Olle Trail Walking Festival each November. Jeju's scenery feels rich at this time of year, with fruits such as tangerines ripening and silver grass blowing in the breeze on the *oreum* (parasitic cones).

***Pajeon* (spring-onion pancake) and *makgeolli* (milky rice wine)**

FROM LEFT: BONCHAN/SHUTTERSTOCK, SITI AISHAH/SHUTTERSTOCK

MONSOON SEASON

During the monsoon season of *jangma*, lasting from mid-June to the end of July, Koreans like to eat *pajeon* pancakes and drink the rice alcohol *makgeolli*. Both boost serotonin, a chemical that elevates emotion and appetite.

Weather Through the Year Seoul

	JANUARY	FEBRUARY	MARCH	APRIL	MAY	JUNE
Avg. daytime max:	1°C	4.5°C	10°C	19°C	23°C	27°C
Days of rainfall:	7	6	6	7	7	10

TYPHOON SEASON

Typhoons can hit the peninsula any time between May and November, with the majority impacting South Korea between July and September. Be flexible with your travel plans during these months, especially if they include taking ferries to the islands.

Korea's Big-Three Holiday Periods

The exact dates of the following traditional holidays are based on the lunar calendar and so vary slightly each year.

Seollal During the Lunar New Year, Koreans visit their hometowns to honour ancestors and eat traditional foods over this three-day national festival. Cultural events geared towards families are held at Seoul's royal palaces and places such as **Namsangol Hanok Village** (p74). **Late January or early February**

Buddha's Birthday Temples are hung with brightly coloured lanterns for this celebration best experienced at Seoul's Lotus Lantern Festival, which culminates in a spectacular evening lantern parade. **Late April or May**

Chuseok **The Harvest Moon Festival** is another major three-day holiday when families gather, eat crescent-shaped rice cakes and visit their ancestors' graves to make offerings of food and drink. **Mid- to late September or early October**

Mud, Mimes & Masks

Chuncheon International Mime Festival (p152) Wordless indoor and outdoor shows feature at one of the world's top mime fests. **End of May**

Boryeong Mud Festival (p348) On Daecheon's seafront, millions of visitors come to coat their bodies in mineral-rich grey gloop trucked in from the Boryeong mudflats. **July**

Andong Mask Dance Festival (p246) Watch performances by dancers donning *tal* (Korean traditional wooden masks), as well as other global masked dances. **Late September to early October**

Tamna Cultural Festival (p303) Jeju's flagship event celebrates the history and heritage of Tamna – the ancient kingdom of Jeju-do – along with its mythical demigod founders at Samseonghyeol and venues across Jeju-si. **October**

I LIVE HERE

SEVEN GARDEN SEASONS

Kim Minjeong is public relations officer for the Garden of Morning Calm. *morningcalm.co.kr*

At the garden, we observe seven seasons: early spring (April), mellow spring (May), early summer (June), midsummer (July and August), early autumn (September), late autumn (October and November) and winter (December to March). My favourite time is October, when our maple and larch trees are at their very best. April and early May is also beautiful for tulips and azaleas.

Tulips, Garden of Morning Calm (p134)

24 SEASONS

Korea's traditional lunar calendar was measured in *jeolgi* – 24 different seasons of weather and climate, each spaced approximately 15 days apart. The observance of these *jeolgi* was crucial to agricultural cycles and the practice of other seasonal rituals.

JULY	AUGUST	SEPTEMBER	OCTOBER	NOVEMBER	DECEMBER
Avg. daytime max: **29°C**	Avg. daytime max: **30°C**	Avg. daytime max: **25°C**	Avg. daytime max: **20°C**	Avg. daytime max: **12°C**	Avg. daytime max: **3°C**
Days of rainfall: **15**	Days of rainfall: **13**	Days of rainfall: **9**	Days of rainfall: **6**	Days of rainfall: **7**	Days of rainfall: **6**

FROM LEFT: JACKTAMRONG/SHUTTERSTOCK, BARAM PICTURES/PAN ENTERTAINMENT/ALBUM/ALAMY

Man wearing *hanbok* (Korean traditional clothing)

GET PREPARED FOR KOREA

Useful things to load in your bag, your ears and your brain.

Clothes

Waterproof jacket and shoes Be prepared for rain during your visit to Korea and pack apparel that you're sure will keep you dry in the worst conditions, especially in late summer.

Trainers Comfortable walking shoes will make on-foot explorations of Korea's sights a pleasure.

Hanbok Don't be shy about dressing up in rental *hanbok* (Korean traditional clothing). It's encouraged when visiting historical landmarks such as Seoul's palaces.

Hiking gear On mountain trails, you'll see locals kitted out with the latest high-tech performance gear as if they're about to scale Everest. You don't need to follow suit – basic hiking gear will suffice – but do if you want to!

Manners

A quick, short bow is most respectful for meetings and departures. Give or receive any object using both hands, especially name cards, money and gifts.

Remove your shoes before entering a Korean home, guesthouse, temple or Korean-style restaurant.

Potentially awkward remarks or scenes should be quickly smoothed over. An argument or embarrassing situation should be avoided at all costs.

READ

Kim Jiyoung, Born 1982 (Cho Nam-joo; 2020) Fictional account of a woman's mental breakdown living in a misogynistic society.

I Want to Die But I Want to Eat Tteokbokki (Baek Se-hee; 2018) Best-selling memoir that helped normalise mental-health conversations in Korea.

Human Acts (Han Kang; 2014) Novel that provides a multidimensional examination of the 1980 Gwangju uprising.

Korea: A New History of South and North (Victor Cha & Ramon Pacheco Pardo; 2023) Excellent overview of the peninsula's modern history.

Words

An·nyong·ha·se·yo (안녕하세요) Hello.

An·nyong·hee·gye·se·yo (안녕히 계세요) Goodbye (if leaving).

An·nyong·hee·ga·se·yo (안녕히 가세요) Goodbye (if staying).

Ne/Ye (네/예) Yes.

A·ni·yo (아니요) No.

Yo·bo·se·yo? (여보세요?) Hello? (on the phone)

Shil·le·ham·ni·da (실례합니다) Excuse me.

Jway-song-ham-ni-da/ Mi-an-ham-ni-da (죄송합니다/미안합니다) Sorry.

Gam·sa·ham·ni·da (감사합니다) Thank you.

Go·map·seum·ni·da (고맙습니다) Thank you.

Gwaen-cha-na-yo (괜찮아요) It's fine/It's alright/It's no problem.

Ne. An·nyong·ha·se·yo? (네. 안녕하세요?) Fine, thanks. And you?

Song-ha-mi ot-to-ke dway-se-yo? (성함이 어떻게 되세요?) What is your name?

Je i·ru·mun ...·im·ni·da (제 이름은 ...입니다) My name is ...

Yong·uh hal su iss·seum·ni·kka? (영어 할 수 있습니까?) Can you speak English?

Mot a·ra du·ross·o·yo (못 알아 들었어요) I didn't understand.

Gwaen·cha·na·yo (괜찮아요) It's OK.

Jam·kkan·man·yo (잠깐만요) Just a moment, please.

Ot·to·ke? (어떻게) How?

On·je (언제) When?

O·di (어디) Where?

Wae (왜) Why?

WATCH

When Life Gives You Tangerines (Kim Won-seok; 2025; pictured above) Award-winning Netflix series about a love story that blooms on Jeju-do.

Peppermint Candy (Lee Chang-dong; 1999) One man's demise told in reverse chronological order, set during the Gwangju uprising and Asian Financial Crisis.

Little Forest (Yim Soon-rye; 2018) After failing her teacher's test in Seoul, a young woman returns to her countryside village.

Parasite (Bong Joon-ho; 2019) Oscar-winning drama set in Seoul about a poor family infiltrating the life of a wealthy family to devastating effect.

Squid Game (Hwang Dong-hyuk; 2021) Hit TV series in which players risk their lives in a deadly game for a ₩45.6-billion prize.

LISTEN

Born Pink (BLACKPINK; 2022) The K-Pop quartet's definitive international breakthrough album, cementing their global superstardom.

Map of the Soul: 7 (BTS; 2020) The Bulletproof Boy Scouts' most popular album, which broke all-time domestic sales records at the time.

FML (Seventeen; 2023) South Korea's best-selling album of all time, with more than 6.2 million copies sold.

The Korea Society Podcast Covers a fascinating range of topics – everything from politics and contemporary arts to history and cooking.

FROM LEFT: RAINER HESSE/SHUTTERSTOCK, JEAN CHUNG/GETTY IMAGES

Joint Security Area

TRIP PLANNER

VISITING THE DMZ

One of Korea's top tourist attractions, the Demilitarized Zone (DMZ) is a fearsome frontier splitting the peninsula into the two Koreas: an authoritarian dictatorship on one side, an economically successful democracy on the other. A place of high military tension, it's also somewhere to come for historical sights and to view pristine nature.

LIVING IN THE DMZ

Created on 27 July 1953, when the Korean Armistice Agreement was signed, the DMZ is not the no-man's land it's often characterised as.

On the South Korean side, **Daeseong-dong** (Freedom Village) is where less than 200 people live in modern houses with high-speed internet connections. Residents don't pay tax and don't have to do military service. Soldiers stand guard while the villagers work in ricefields and tend their ginseng plants. On the North Korean side is **Gijeong-dong**. The North calls it Peace Village, while the South calls it Propaganda Village because virtually all the buildings are believed to be empty or just facades – the lights all come on and go off here at the same time each night. The village's primary feature is a 160m-high tower flying a flag that weighs nearly 300kg – it's markedly larger than the one on the South Korean side. These DMZ villages have always been off-limits to tourists.

On the demarcation line is **Panmunjeom** (Truce Village), home to the **Joint Security Area** (JSA). At the time of research, it was expected that visitors would soon be able to access Freedom House at Panmunjeom, but not the blue conference buildings that actually straddle the border.

DMZ DESTINATIONS

Most visitors join a guided tour that goes via the park at **Imjingak Resort** (p142) into the South Korean buffer zone, visiting the **Third Infiltration Tunnel**, **Dora Observatory** and **Unification Village**.

DIY OR GUIDED TOUR?

Most visitors join a guided tour. Booking one of these tours is easy to organise in Seoul and Cheorwon. The tours take care of transport logistics and include an English-speaking guide.

There's also the option of travelling to Imjingak on your own and joining a DMZ tour there, if tickets are available. These tours may not have an English-speaking guide.

Alternatively, you can get yourself to any of the observatories and other tourism sites dotted along the DMZ, such as Goseong, Ganghwa Peace Observatory and Hwagae Garden and Observatory. Be sure to bring your passport with you.

On the island of Ganghwado, there's **Ganghwa Peace Observatory** (p141) and, on the neighbouring island of Gyodongdo, **Hwagae Garden and Observatory** (p141).

In Gangwon-do, there is **Cheorwon** (p156), a key battleground during the Korean War, and Goseong, where the **Tongil Security Park** (p165) includes the Unification Observatory, the Korean War Exhibition Hall and the DMZ Museum.

DMZ PEACE TRAIL

Home to more than 2700 species of wild plants and animals, including 67 endangered species, there has long been a hope (at least in South Korea) of eventually turning the DMZ into a nature park. As a small step in that direction, and to bring tourism to additional areas of the buffer zone, the 510km **DMZ Peace Trail** with 35 routes has been launched. For details, see *durunubi.kr/dmz-introduction.do*.

Dora Observatory

DECODING THE DMZ

The DMZ is a complicated place with several acronyms to decipher.

- **DMZ (Demilitarized Zone)** The 4km-wide strip of no-man's land straddling the actual border between North and South Korea. Although small groups of troops from both sides patrol the DMZ, large troop concentrations, tanks and artillery are forbidden here.
- **MDL (Military Demarcation Line)** The border crosses the 38th parallel at an angle and is marked by 1392 metal signs placed at 200m intervals along a 250km stretch from the mouth of the Han River in the west to the coastal village of Myeongho-ri in the east.
- **CCL (Civilian Control Line)** Also known as the Civilian Control Zone (CCZ), this is a buffer zone on the South Korean side that's between 5km and 20km from the southern limit of the DMZ. The barbed wire and watchtowers that many visitors see and photograph belong to the CCL, not the DMZ.
- **NLL (Northern Limit Line)** The disputed maritime border between North and South Korea in the Han River estuary and out into the West Sea. Clashes between North and South Korean fishing boats and naval vessels have frequently occurred along the NLL.
- **JSA (Joint Security Area)** At Panmunjeom on the MDL, this is where military meetings between the two sides take place.

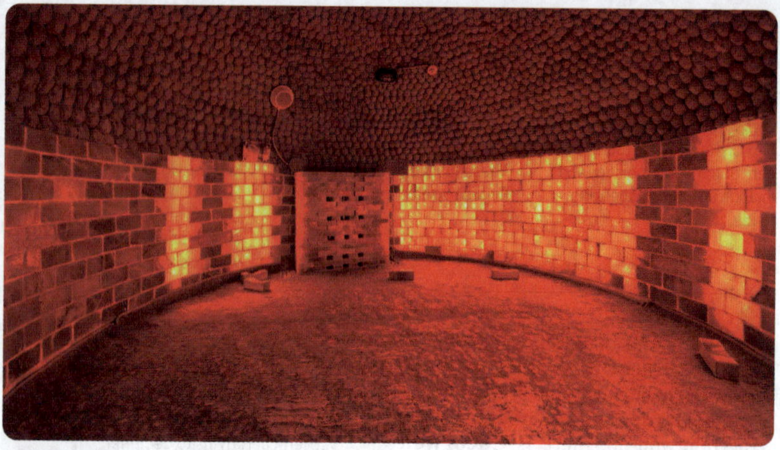

SUNSTOCK/SHUTTERSTOCK

HOW TO... Jjimjilbang

A fun way to experience an aspect of Korean culture is to visit a *jjimjilbang*. Meaning 'heated rooms', these traditional saunas are where Koreans unwind and engage in a host of health and beauty rituals. In some cases, they're combined with mineral-rich hot springs.

Korean Sauna

Don't confuse *jjimjilbang* with *mogyoktang* (public bathhouses), where people go for a wash and scrub, facilities are always gender segregated and bathing is nude. In addition to such baths, *jjimjilbang* have heated rooms and/or traditional stone or clay-kiln saunas (called *hanjeungmak*) of varying temperatures and properties. These are enjoyed by both sexes together, wearing loose pyjamas provided by the facility. Customers shower and bathe separately first, then head to the *jjimjilbang* to relax, sweat and socialise.

Preliminaries

Slip your shoes inside the lockers by the door and head to the front desk to pay the entry fee and hand over your shoe-locker key. In exchange, you'll be given a new locker key for the changing room (sometimes the first key is used for both), plus a towel and a pair of pyjamas.

Many *jjimjilbang* have electronic keys or wristbands, which are used to record the fees for any additional services, such as a full-body scrub (called a *seshin*) or massage. Otherwise, staff will note your locker-key number if you add any services and bill you at the end.

Be sure to shower *before* soaking in a tub.

Heat, Eat & Sleep

South Korea saunas are typically heated to between 50°C and 90°C and are really quite pleasant. As you lie on hemp mats (or sometimes salt or jade crystals), the heated stone gently warms your body. After about 15 minutes, you'll start to sweat. It's easy to fall asleep, but don't – you'll risk dehydration.

Relax after your sauna in the *jjimjilbang* common areas, where you can play computer games, watch TV or simply snooze (at many *jjimjilbang*, it's possible to stay overnight). Cap off a good steam by drinking *sikhye*, a fermented sweet rice drink usually sold at *jjimjilbang*, and eating hard-boiled eggs that have been steamed in the saunas.

TOP SPAS & JJIMJILBANG

Yulpo Haesu Nokchatang, Boseong (p286) Bathe in glorious green tea at Yulpo Beach.

Spa Land, Centum City, Busan (p199) Part of a huge shopping mall, with 18 different hot springs and 13 theme saunas.

Insadong Spa & Sauna, Seoul (p70) Good things come in small packages at this foreigner-friendly operation.

O'REVE Hot Spring & Spa, Seogwipo (p324) Unwind in outdoor hot pools looking up at blue skies at this Jeju-do resort spa.

SANGA PARK/SHUTTERSTOCK

Tongdo-sa (p204), near Busan

HOW TO... Templestay

Korea's temples are havens of calm and quiet reflection amid the country's often non-stop activity. The templestay program provides a chance for visitors to stay in these beautiful places – either for a few hours or a couple of days – and experience the life of a Buddhist monk.

Open to All

The templestay program is run by the Joyge Order of Korean Buddhism, Korea's largest Buddhist organisation. You can usually choose between a day program, lasting around three hours, and an overnight stay, including accommodation and meals. No attempt will be made to convert you to Buddhism. It's a wonderful way to experience Korean spiritual culture, spend time in historic and beautifully decorated buildings and visit some incredible locations.

One-Day Templestays

Sometimes referred to as a templelife program, the one-day stay is between two and three hours and will typically include a temple tour in which you'll learn about the architecture, decoration and daily rituals, a session of Seon (zen) meditation and a tea ceremony. There may be a chance to make a paper lotus-flower lantern or a string of prayer beads and/or chat with a monk.

Overnight Templestays

These usually last two days, but some extended periods are available. During any overnight stay, you'll be given a set of comfy cotton pyjamas to wear. Accommodation will be simple, traditionally Korean in style (*ondol* heated floors and *yo* floor mattresses) and usually shared. There'll be more time for meditation and you'll join the monks for the communal dinner and breakfast. Additional elements could include cleaning chores around the temple, or a mindful walk.

More Information

Visit *eng.templestay.com,* which lists the various programs available nationwide and where you can make a booking. Every year there's a special-event period during which the first 1500 applicants can book an overnight stay for as little as ₩30,000. For inspiration, read *webzine.templestay.com/en/main* and, if you're in Seoul, visit the Jogye-sa Information Center for Foreigners (p59) opposite Jogye-sa.

108 BOWS

Part of an overnight templestay is rising before dawn to perform the ritual of 108 bows. The Buddha taught that there are 108 delusions of the mind, so each bow aligns to an act of atonement for our various cravings and sources of suffering.

A video may be played to provide an English explanation of what each bows signifies. A bow starts by bending at the knees, hands in prayer at the chest, lowering the knees onto a meditation cushion, bowing the head to the floor, then standing again – to repeat this 108 times is physically demanding.

NOONBUSIN/SHUTTERSTOCK; FAR LEFT: AMANKGUPTA/SHUTTERSTOCK

Baechu kimchi

THE FOOD SCENE

Korean cuisine tastes fantastic, is visually appealing and has many health benefits – so dig in!

The most delicious part of the *hallyu* (Korean Wave) sweeping the world is Korean food culture. These days, kimchi, Korean fried chicken (the best kind of KFC) and the fiery *gochujang* chilli sauce are staples on supermarket shelves and need little explaining. A trip to Korea opens up a universe of flavoursome dishes, from moreish street foods such as sweet *hotteok* (sweet pancakes) to contemporary versions of royal cuisine.

Many Korean dishes are served boiling or sizzling-hot off the stove. There are many hearty main-course soups called *tang* or *guk*. *Jjigae* are stews for everyday eating, often spicy and served in a stone hotpot. Common ingredients are *dubu* (tofu), *doenjang* (fermented soy-bean paste) and kimchi, with seasonal vegetables, meat or fish. Centuries of Buddhism have also resulted in a decent vegetarian and vegan food scene.

There's creativity, too, with neo-Korean cuisine, though experimentation is nothing new. *Budae jjigae* ('army base stew'), for example, was concocted during the Korean War using leftover hot dogs, Spam and macaroni scrounged from American bases.

Say Kimchi

What began as a pickling method to preserve vegetables through Korea's harsh winters has become a cornerstone of its cuisine, making an appearance at every meal. High in fibre and low in calories, kimchi is said to lower cholesterol, fight cancer, supercharge gut health and prevent flu viruses. It also delivers a complexity of flavours: sour, usually but not always spicy, with a tang that often lingers.

Best Korean Dishes

SUNDUBU JJIGAE
Chunks of soft tofu and often seafood, simmered in a spicy stew.

BIBIMBAP
Rice topped with egg, vegetables and spicy sauce and then mixed.

SAMGYEOPSAL
Pieces of grilled pork belly wrapped with accompaniments in lettuce leaves.

The most common type is *baechu* kimchi, made from Chinese cabbage, but there are some 200 other varieties, including ones made with radish, cucumber, eggplant, leek, mustard leaf and pumpkin flower. Some are meant to be eaten in tiny morsels, while others, such as *bossam* kimchi, are flavour-packed packages containing vegetables, pork or seafood. Most are red, but some are white.

To make kimchi, vegetables are salted to lock in the original flavour, then seasoned with spices – which vary depending on the recipe, but typically include garlic, red-pepper powder, onions, ginger and fish sauce – and left in earthenware jars to ferment for hours, days or even years.

Rice & Noodles

A perennial favourite, bibimbap is a a tasty mixture of rice and vegetables (and sometimes meat) with a fried egg on top. The ingredients reflect the five primary colours of Korean food – white, yellow, green, red and black – which represent the five elements. Just stir everything up (go easy on the *gochujang* sauce if you don't want it too spicy) and eat. A variant is *dolsot* bibimbap, served in a heated stone bowl.

Gimbap are rolls of *bap* (rice) flavoured with sesame oil and strips of vegetables, egg and meat wrapped in *gim* (dried seaweed). *Samgak* (triangular) *gimbap* is filled with a savoury fish, meat or vegetable mixture.

There's also a wide variety of noodles to enjoy, including *ramyeon* (instant noodles made from wheat), *japchae* (made from sweet potato starch) and *naengmyeon* (buckwheat noodles served in an icy beef broth, garnished with vegetables, Korean pear, cucumber and half a boiled egg).

ELENA ERYOMENKO/SHUTTERSTOCK

Bulgogi

FOOD & DRINK FESTIVALS

Boseong Green Tea Festival

Yeongdeok Snow Crab Festival (p250; *crab.ydfesta.kr; late February, early March*) Dig into delicious *daege* (snow crab) at this celebration of the crustacean.

Boseong Green Tea Festival *(teafestival.kr; May)* Pick tea leaves, make tea and sample tea snacks in the birthplace of Korea's commercial tea industry.

Jeju Food & Wine Festival *(jfwf.kr; May)* A showcase of Jeju-do's unique culinary heritage, innovative cooking and fresh produce.

Ulleung-do Squid Festival (p250; *ulleung.go.kr; August*) Catch squid with your bare hands, see squid drying and taste squid dishes on this East Sea island.

Sunchang Fermented Food Festival *(jangfestival.co.kr; October)* Enjoy all kinds of fermented foods in the home of Korea's signature *gochujang* red-chilli sauce.

Gangneung Coffee Festival (p167; *coffeefestival.net; October*) A coffee-culture convention in the coffee capital of Korea.

KIMCHI JJIGAE	DAKGALBI	PAJEON	BULGOGI	SAMGYETANG
Spicy stew starring Korea's classic fermented cabbage, often with pork.	Chicken, veggies and rice cakes sautéed in a spicy sauce.	Crispy spring-onion batter pancakes.	Thin slices of meat marinated in sweetened soy sauce.	Chicken stuffed with rice, ginseng and jujube in a soup.

Gimbap

Vegetarians & Vegans

While Korean cuisine uses lots of vegetables, they're frequently pickled or cooked with meat or seafood ingredients. *Dubu jjigae* (tofu stew), for example, may be made from meat or seafood stock, and *beoseot deopbap* (mushrooms on rice) may contain a little meat or seafood as well. Kimchi, too, is often made with fish sauce or fermented shrimp. The only assuredly meat-free meals are those served at vegetarian or vegan eateries, or at Buddhist temples or restaurants.

The safest approach is to ask about ingredients, or order something such as bibimbap or *gimbap* without the ingredients you don't eat. Be as specific about your requirements as you can be – for instance, saying 'no meat' may not suffice to omit seafood. A useful phrase is 저는 채식주의자입니다 (*jeoneun chaesigjuuija imnida*; 'I am a vegetarian'), or simply say '*chaesigjuuija*' and point to yourself.

Tea & Coffee

Part of Korean culture for centuries, *cha*, or tea, is also used to describe drinks brewed without tea leaves. The most common leaf tea is *nokcha* (green tea), grown in Jeju-do and Jeolla-do. Non-leaf teas include the ubiquitous *boricha* (barley tea), *daechucha* (jujube tea), *omijacha* (five-flavour berry tea), *yujacha* (citron tea) and *insamcha* (ginseng tea).

It's said that King Gojong was the first Korean to taste coffee in 1896. Since then, the drink has really caught on and the number of gourmet coffee shops has multiplied exponentially in recent decades. In 2024, it was estimated there were more than 100,000 coffee shops across Korea, the equivalent of one cafe for every 500-or-so people.

Alcoholic Drinks

Korea's most popular *sool* (alcohol) is the spirit soju, an ethanol-based drink that, despite its alcohol content ranging from 12.5% to 45%, can go down easy while leaving you with a killer hangover.

Makgeolli is a traditional farmer's brew made from unrefined fermented rice wine. With a milky appearance and a sweetish yoghurt flavour, it's much lower in alcohol content than soju. While it's traditional to slug down *makgeolli* with a side of *pajeon* (green-onion pancake) on rainy days, the drink has also gained popularity at artisanal *makgeolli* bars serving quality drops.

A host of traditional spirits, brewed or distilled from grains, fruits and roots, include *bokbunjaju* (made from wild raspberries), *meoruju* (from wild fruit), *maesilju* (from green plums) and *insamju* (from ginseng).

Beer, or *maekju*, comes in bland mass-market brands such as Cass, Hite and OB, as well as more interesting microbrewery regional craft brews.

BANCHAN & JEONGSIK

A Korean meal is always accompanied by *banchan* (side dishes). Invariably including one or more types of kimchi, *banchan* are served to create balance in the meal through saltiness, spiciness, temperature and colour. Common *banchan* dishes include greens such as spinach, seaweed, bean sprouts and tofu. You are not expected to eat them all and, if you like a particular dish, you can ask for free refills (within reason).

Jeongsik is a set meal where all the dishes are served at once: fish, meat, soup, *dubu jjigae* (tofu stew), rice, noodles, shellfish and a bevy of *banchan*. The most elevated type of *jeongsik* is *hanjeongsik*, based on traditional royal-banquet spreads of 12 dishes or more, usually served on *bangjja* (bronze) tableware.

Specialities

Dare to Try

Gopchang Pork or beef intestines, popularly enjoyed with soju.

Beondegi Silkworm larvae boiled or steamed. Has both a soft and crunchy texture.

Dakbal Chicken feet seasoned with sesame and red-pepper paste.

Sundae Beef or pork blood sausage, similar to black pudding.

Jokbal Boiled pigs' trotters cooked with leeks, soy sauce, ginger, sugar and rice wine.

Sannakji Slices of live octopus.

Street Food

Tteokbokki Chewy rice cakes in a spicy *gochujang* sauce, often with fish cakes and boiled eggs.

Twigim Various batter-dipped and fried ingredients such as squid, shrimp, vegetables, sweet potatoes and even boiled eggs.

Dakkochi Skewers of chicken and spring onion with a smoky charred flavour, glazed in a sticky, tangy sauce.

Gyeranbbang Literally 'egg bread'; golden muffins with a whole egg baked on top.

Jjinbbang Soft, fluffy steamed buns with fillings that can include pork and kimchi.

Mandu Fried or steamed dumplings, often including a vermicelli-noodle and tofu or pork filling.

Odeng Fishcakes on a skewer, either long or folded over, simmered in vats of seafood or spring-onion broth.

Haemul pajeon Savoury batter pancakes with green onion and seafood such as squid and prawns.

Sweet Treats

Bungeobbang Fish-shaped waffles stuffed with sweet red-bean-paste.

Hotteok Pancakes filled with cinnamon, sugar and chopped nuts.

Patbingsu Shaved ice topped with red beans and condensed milk.

Ggwabaegi Sugar-covered twisted doughnuts.

Yakgwa Honey-flavoured, cookie-shaped confections.

Yanggaeng Sweet red-bean jelly.

Gotgamssam Persimmon-wrapped walnuts.

Dalgona Sugar candy made with baking soda.

MEALS OF A LIFETIME

Mishmash (p59) Korean-Danish fusion cuisine in a *hanok* overlooking Changdeokgung.

Mingles (p112) Innovative neo-Korean cooking with artful presentation in Gangnam.

Ggulggeok House (p194) Enjoy modern twists on Korean classics at this Busan restaurant.

Sujata (p268) A vegetarian all-you-can-eat feast prepared by monks in Gwangju.

House of Baekje (p344) Buyeo joint serving sensationally good meat wrapped in salad leaves.

Hachi (p320) Dine on chef Jeon's amazing Japanese seafood banquets in Jeju-do.

Myeongdong 1(il)beonji Dakgalbi (p152) Dig into Chuncheon's iconic chicken dish on Dakgalbi St.

Solbat Sikdang (p249) (솔밭식당) Hahoe Folk Village restaurant with excellent *jjimdak* and *godeungeo gui* (grilled mackerel).

THE YEAR IN FOOD

SPRING

Head to Korea's east coast to eat king crab at its most flavourful. Search out dishes with fresh spring greens such as *minari* (water dropwort), *ssuk* (mugwort), *gosari* (bracken; pictured) and *dalle* (wild chives).

SUMMER

Wheat-flour *kong-guksu* and buckwheat *naengmyeon* are two classic summer noodle dishes served in chilled savoury soups. Also try the rice-stuffed chicken dish *samgyetang* and refreshing *patbingsu* (shaved ice topped with sweet red beans; pictured).

AUTUMN

Sample the fish *jeoneo* (gizzard shad), best served salted and grilled, *gejang* (crab marinated in soy sauce) and jumbo prawns. Sweet orange-fleshed persimmons (pictured) and juicy Korean apples and pears are also at their best.

WINTER

Enjoy *hallabong* tangerines, warming bowls of *patjuk* (a red-bean porridge with rice cakes) and seafood such as scallops, oysters, *bangeo hoe* (yellowtail sashimi) and *gwamegi* (partly dried Pacific herring or saury; pictured).

PTERA/SHUTTERSTOCK, SOHOME JACARANDA LILAU/WIKIMEDIA/CC BY-SA 4.0, ACLJ/GETTY IMAGES, YEONGSIK IM/SHUTTERSTOCK

FROM LEFT: SURACHAT TREEKIDAKORN/SHUTTERSTOCK, SUNGMOON HAN/GETTY IMAGES

Muju Deogyusan Resort (p263)

THE OUTDOORS

South Korea's countryside, coastline and islands are a year-round wonderland for outdoor activities such as hiking, cycling, diving, skiing and surfing.

Korea's natural features invite adventure. More than 70% of the country is covered by mountains – great for hiking, rock climbing and skiing in winter. There are 23 national parks and scores more provincial parks and they are well patronised by Koreans, who have a penchant for hiking.

Thousands of kilometres of coastline and more than 3300 islands provide plenty of opportunities for hanging out on beaches, diving, snorkelling, sea kayaking and yachting. Abundant rivers and lakes are also good for canoeing, kayaking and swimming.

Hiking

If you're planning a major overnight mountain trek, making reservations in the national-park shelters at least two weeks in advance is recommended. For trail information and online reservations for all types of park accommodation, go to the website of the **Korea National Park Service** *(knps.or.kr)*.

Fancy a challenge? Korea has a several long-distance trails. The **Seoul Dulle-gil** *(gil.seoul.go.kr)* runs for 156.5km around the capital's outskirts. Each of its 21 routes starts and finishes beside a subway station.

The **Jeju Olle Trail** (p322) is 437km of footpaths that encircle Jeju-do and three other islands. The **Korea Dulle Trail** *(durunubi.kr)* is made up of four sections covering a whopping 4500km around the coastline of the peninsula and the southern edge of the DMZ buffer zone.

More Outdoor Activities

CYCLING
Spend a day pedalling around **Udo** (p316), the largest of the 62 islands surrounding Jeju-do.

KAYAKING
Take in the gorgeous scenery as you paddle across **Chungju-ho** (p364), South Korea's largest lake.

SURFING
Catch a wave at **Surfyy Beach** (p165) in Yangyang, one of Korea's most popular surfing spots.

FAMILY ADVENTURES

Fly 150m up into the skies in a tethered **hot-air balloon** (p132) for a bird's-eye view of Suwon's World Heritage–listed fortress walls.

Play at **LEGOLAND Korea Resort** (p153), Chuncheon's outdoor theme-park extravaganza of the famous interlocking bricks.

Venture inside Manjang-gul (p315), part of one of the world's largest lava caves, in Jeju.

Cycle along the Han River using Seoul's **Ttareungi** (p379) bike-sharing system.

Camp overnight at **Myeongsasim-ni** (p296), one of the southern coast's most beautiful beaches.

Explore the **Sinduri Coastal Sand Dunes** (p350); the Sinduri Sand Dune Center has a playground and a rooftop terrace.

Spiral your way up to the top of the 33m-high **Sky Observatory** (p173) for panoramic views of Taebaeksan National Park.

A great source of information is Roger Shepherd's **Hike Korea** *(hikekorea.com)*. Shepherd is one of the authors of *Baekdu-Daegan Trail,* a book that details the 1400km 'White Head Great Ridge' down the southern Korean Peninsula.

Skiing & Snowboarding

Korea's snow season runs from December to March. Package deals from travel agents include transport, tickets, rentals and, if required, lessons and accommodation. Weekends are often very crowded, especially at resorts near Seoul. Skiers and snowboarders alike are catered for. Many resorts run dedicated shuttle buses to/from pick-up points in Seoul, making for a long, but easy, day on the slopes.

Pyeongchang county in Gangwon-do hosted the 2018 Winter Olympic Games, with **Alpensia** (p173) serving as the main resort and the larger, nearby **Mona Yongpyong** (p173) hosting the slalom events. In the Taebaek Mountains, **High1** (p173) offers some of the best facilities and snow in Korea, as well as Korea's first ski school for skiers with disabilities. The **Muju Deogyusan Resort** (p263), the only ski area inside a national park, has the highest altitude and longest slope (6.1km) in Korea.

Bird-Watching

With some of the widest and most extensive tidal flats in the world, the Korean Peninsula is a natural magnet for birds. More than 500 species have been spotted in the country, including 34 threatened species. Most are on their migratory route between Siberia and Manchuria in the north, and Southeast Asia and Australia and New Zealand in the south.

Popular birding spots include **Suncheon Bay** (p278), a wetland park on Jeolla-do's south coast where hooded cranes winter, and **Bamseom Bird Sanctuary**, a pair of islets in Seoul's Han River where mandarins, mallards, spotbills and great egrets can be spotted from an observation platform in Yeouido Hangang Park. The **Demilitarized Zone (DMZ)** is another preferred stop for migrating birds and is a haven for rare white-naped and red-crowned cranes.

Black-faced spoonbill, Suncheon Bay Wetlands (p278)

DIVING
Dive around the islets of **Seopseom, Munseom** and **Beomseom** (p324) near Seogwipo to view polychromatic soft corals.

GOLFING
Pack your clubs for **Jeju-do** (p309), where popular courses include PINX Golf Club and Jungmun Beach Golf Club.

ROCK CLIMBING
Tackle some two dozen routes up granite Bagaji Bawi in **Gyeryongsan National Park** (p346).

ZIP-LINING
Fly along the **Seonyu Sky SUN Line** (p264) in Seonyudo, Korea's longest over-ocean zip line.

ACTION AREAS

Where to find Korea's best outdoor activities.

Skiing/Snowboarding

1. Alpensia Ski Resort (p173)
2. Muju Deogyusan Resort (p263)
3. High1 Ski Resort (p173)
4. Phoenix Park (p173)
5. Welli Hilli Park (p173)
6. Mona Yongpyong (p173)

National Parks

1. Seoraksan National Park (p162)
2. Hallasan National Park (p310)
3. Jirisan National Park (p282)
4. Bukhansan National Park (p128)
5. Songnisan National Park (p360)
6. Hallyeohaesang National Park (p210)
7. Sobaeksan National Park (p367)

Beaches

1. Geumneung Beach (p332)
2. Haeundae (p194)
3. Mallipo Beach (p351)
4. Sanho Beach (p316)
5. Daecheon Beach (p348)
6. Gyeongpo Beach (p169)
7. Sinduri Coastal Sand Dunes (p350)

Surfing
1 Jungmun Beach (p325)
2 Songjeong Beach (p197)
3 Yangyang (p164)
4 Woljeong Beach (p315)
5 Taeanhaean National Park (p350)
6 Mallipo Beach (p351)
Walking/Hiking
1 Jeju Olle Trail (p322)
2 Haengnam Coastal Walkway (p234)
3 Inwangsan, Seoul (p126)
4 Hwaseong, Suwon (p132)
5 Taebaeksan National Park (p173)
6 Gyeryongsan National Park (p346)
7 Taejongdae coast (p185)
Yellow Sea
East China Sea
Korea Strait
JAPAN
Boryeong
Congju
Daejeon
Hahoe Folk Village
Yeongdeok
Nakdong
Gimcheon
Seocheon
Gunsan
Iksan
Jeonju
Deogyusan
Pohang
Yeongcheon
Daegu
Gyeongju
Ulsan
Namwon
Chirisan
Jinju
Changwon
Busan
Gwangju
Suncheon
Samcheonpo
Tongyeong
Geojedo
Mokpo
Boseong
Yeocheon
Yeosu
Jangheung
Goheung
Dolsando
Yeondo
Oenarodo
Haenam
Jindo
Hongdo
Heuksando
Hajodo
Wando
Cheongsando
Bogildo
Geomundo
Jeju
Hallim
Hallasan
Jeju-do
Jungmun
Seogwipo
0 100 km
0 50 miles

KOREA

THE GUIDE

Chapters in this section are organised by hubs and their surrounding areas. We see the hub as your base in the destination, where you'll find unique experiences, local insights, insider tips and expert recommendations. It's also your gateway to the surrounding area, where you'll see what and how much you can do from there.

Deoksugung (p77), Seoul

JOHN W. BANAGAN/GETTY IMAGES

Researched by
Simon Richmond, Ann Babe and Charles Usher

Seoul & Around

CITY OF PALACES, PARKS AND K-POP

South Korea's dynamic, six-centuries-old capital is the source of the *hallyu* (Korean Wave) sweeping the world.

Fashion- and technology-forward, but also deeply traditional, Seoul is the beating heart and powerhouse of South Korea – home to more than 26 million people when you include surrounding Gyeonggi-do and Incheon (on its own, the country's third-largest metropolis). Split by the broad Han River (pictured), Seoul offers colourful Joseon-dynasty palaces, world-class museums and galleries, K-Culture centres and some of the world's most delicious cuisine. And that's just for starters.

Gaze down on the city from atop Namsan, the most central of Seoul's four guardian mountains, and you'll sense the powerful *pungsu-jiri* (feng shui) that has long nurtured and protected this location. When important buildings have been destroyed, as they so often have during centuries of conflicts, they've been rebuilt. Amid the skyscrapers, giant LED screens and elevated highways, you'll encounter tenacious fragments of the past such as World Heritage–listed Jongmyo shrine, the graceful *hanok* (traditional wooden homes) in Bukchon and the magnificent Seoul City Wall.

CSTRIKE/SHUTTERSTOCK

In recent years, Seoul has prioritised softening its industrial hard edges with more parks, improved cultural offerings and better design. Glass, concrete and steel are crafted into natural forms at the spectacular Dongdaemun Design Plaza and City Hall. For quick hits of nature, access beautifully landscaped parks, gardens and promenades such as those along the Han River, on the reimagined overpass Seoullo 7017, or beside the Cheonggye-cheon.

Whatever you want, at any time of day or night, Seoul can provide. Join locals shopping in stylish boutiques and drinking at cool cafes and convivial bars. Soju (a vodka-like drink) and snacks in a *pojangmacha* (street tent bar) will fuel you for browsing the buzzing Dongdaemun or Namdaemun night markets, partying in Hongdae or Itaewon, singing karaoke at a *noraebang,* or steaming at a *jjimjilbang* (sauna).

Public transport is brilliant, which makes day trips beyond the city limits a breeze. Options include Suwon, home to World Heritage–listed fortifications, and peering across the barbed-wire fences of the Demilitarized Zone (DMZ) into North Korea.

THE MAIN AREAS

GWANGHWAMUN & JONGNO-GU
Royal palaces, traditional houses, arts and crafts. **p58**

MYEONG-DONG & JUNG-GU
Shopping, nightlife and urban oases. **p71**

ITAEWON & YONGSAN-GU
Top museums, multicultural vibe, vibrant nightlife. **p81**

DONGDAEMUM & EASTERN SEOUL
Amazing architecture, marvellous markets, verdant parks. **p90**

For places to stay in Seoul & Around, see p144

BOTOND HORVATH/SHUTTERSTOCK

Left: Han River, Seoul; Above: Gyeongbokgung (p68)

WESTERN SEOUL
Youth culture, park life, hip neighbourhoods. **p97**

GANGNAM & SOUTHERN SEOUL
Luxe lifestyles reflect Seoul's meteoric rise. **p108**

NORTHERN SEOUL
Fortress wall, fine museums and mountain trails. **p119**

BEYOND SEOUL
Excursions to mountains, coast and the DMZ. **p130**

Find Your Way

Seoul's subway and buses, which generally run between 5.30am and midnight, are the best way to go. Taxis fill in the gaps, or you can rent one of the city's public bicycles. Naver Map will help you find the best route to get to your destination.

FROM THE AIRPORT

From Incheon International Airport, ride the A'REX Airport Express train to Seoul station. The express service (43 to 48 minutes) departs every 30 minutes; the more frequent all-stop train takes 55 minutes. Gimpo International Airport is 35 minutes from central Seoul by subway.

SUBWAY

Nine colour-coded subway lines are integrated with urban railway lines. You'll do a fair amount of walking up and down stairs and along corridors, especially when changing lines. Maps inside the stations help you figure out which of the subway exits to take.

BUS

Phone apps make it easy to work out which bus to take. Some bus stops have route maps in English. On most buses, you can't pay in cash, so have a Tmoney card loaded with credit to hand. Aboard, each stop is usually announced in English.

BICYCLE

Access Ttareungi, Seoul's bike-sharing scheme, via bikeseoul.com or its app – you'll be given a code, which is then keyed in on the bike to unlock it. The website and app have a live map of all docking stations and available bikes.

Plan Your Days

The enormous range of things to do and see in Seoul can feel overwhelming. To narrow down the options, consider the following itineraries that focus on the best of the best.

RICHIE CHAN/SHUTTERSTOCK

National Folk Museum of Korea (p68)

Day 1

Morning

- Arrive at **Gyeongbokgung** (p68) by 10am to watch the changing of the guard. Tour the palace grounds and the **National Folk Museum of Korea** (p68). Enjoy a coffee and sandwich at **Cafe Husbands** (p67), or a temple-cuisine banquet at **Balwoo Gongyang** (p64).

Afternoon

- Take in the views over *hanok* roofs on a walk around **Bukchon** (p60). Join the late-afternoon tour at the World Heritage–listed **Jongmyo** (p58).

Evening

- Stroll along the **Cheonggye-cheon** (p76) towards **Gwangjang Market** (p59) to dine on delicious Korean street food. Have a nightcap at **7.8 Makgeolli 2** (p69) or **Seoul Gypsy** (p69).

You'll Also Want to...

Beyond the grand palaces, top-tier museums and superb civic parks and gardens, there's plenty more to do in the greater Seoul metropolis.

LEARN HOW KOREA WAS DIVIDED

Visit the **War Memorial of Korea** (p84) and make a day trip to the **DMZ** (p142) splitting North from South Korea.

STROLL THROUGH A GARDEN

Wander in delight through World Heritage–listed **Changdeokgung** (p62), **Garden of Morning Calm** (p134) or **Seoul Botanic Park** (p106).

ENJOY CUTTING-EDGE ART

Admire creative and ambitious contemporary works at **MMCA Seoul** (p67), **Seoul Museum of Art** (p76) and **Seosomun Shrine History Museum** (p78).

Day 2

Morning

- Admire the many treasures of the **National Museum of Korea** (p86), or dip into contemporary art at the splendid **Leeum Museum of Art** (p81). Have lunch at **Honfleur** (p85) or **Morococo Café** (p84).

Afternoon

- Climb Namsan to **N Seoul Tower** (p75). It's not a difficult walk, but if you don't have the energy, there's a cable car or bus. It's romantic watching sunset over the city from atop this central mountain.

Evening

- Shop and graze on street food in **Myeong-dong** (p71), then hit the bars of **Euljiro** (p79) and the late-night haunts of **Itaewon** (p87).

Day 3

Morning

- Explore **Dongdaemun Design Plaza** (p93) and park. Check out the chic cafes, quirky galleries and arty boutiques of **Seongsu** (p95).

Afternoon

- Find some inner peace at the **Bongeun-sa** (p113) Buddhist temple. Discover Gangnam style as you window shop around **Apgujeong Rodeo Station** (p112).

Evening

- Dine at one of Gangnam's flash restaurants such as **Mingles** (p112). Catch a concert at **Seoul Arts Center** (p114), or enjoy coloured lights rippling on the Han River from **Some Sevit** (p116) cultural complex.

EXPERIENCE K-CULTURE

Stride out along **Hongdae St** (p97), snap selfies at **HiKR Ground** (p74) and pick up souvenirs at **Ktown4u** (p112).

DINE AT THE FISH MARKET

Marvel at the aquatic creatures on sale at Korea's largest fish market, **Noryangjin** (p105), where you can feast on delicious seafood.

HIKE UP A MOUNTAIN

Follow the Seoul City Wall to the summit of **Inwangsan** (p126), or hit the verdant trails of **Bukhansan National Park** (p128).

WALK AROUND MURAL VILLAGES

Enjoy the street art in **Ihwa Maeul** (p125) and **Mullae Arts Village** (p106).

Gwanghwamun & Jongno-gu

ROYAL PALACES | TRADITIONAL HOUSES | ARTS AND CRAFTS

GETTING AROUND

The best way to explore the densely packed streets of Bukchon, Seochon, Insa-dong and Ikseon-dong is on foot. To the north of Gyeongbokgung, hiking trails run up Bukaksan, while from Seochon you can access Inwangsan.

Subway Lines 1, 3 and 5 have stations in this area. Anguk is the best for Insa-dong and Bukchon, and Jongno 3-ga Exit 4 for Ikseon-dong. Gyeongbokgung station is the most convenient for the palace and Seochon.

TOP TIP

Anyone wearing *hanbok* (Korean traditional clothing) is granted free entry to the four main palaces and Jongmyo. It's an incredibly popular way to visit and there are loads of rental shops offering a wide range of outfits. Rentals start at ₩15,000 for four hours, but it's worth paying more for high-quality *hanbok*.

Jongno-gu, Seoul's regal heart, is defined by two major palaces: Gyeongbokgung and Changdeokgung. Both are worth a visit and take half a day each to tour fully. The area by Gyeongbokgung is commonly referred to as Gwanghwamun after the majestic gate to the main Joseon palace and the square in front of it, which has been Seoul's quintessential gathering place through the ages. Behind the palace rises Bukaksan, the tallest of the city's four guardian peaks.

Jongno-gu is the best place to view traditional *hanok* (Korean wooden homes). Bukchon is the most famous – and overtouristed – but there are some equally beautiful *hanok* in Seochon and Ikseon-dong. Many art galleries and craft shops can be found in Jongno-gu, particularly in Insa-dong, which is also home to Seoul's leading Buddhist temple, Jogye-sa. Other top sights include the Confucian shrine Jongmyo and Gwangjang Market, a celebrated spot for street food.

Shrine of Royal Spirit Tablets

MAP P60

Tour the wooded grounds of Jongymo

Dating to 1395, **Jongmyo** *(royal.khs.go.kr; adult/youth/child ₩1000/500/free)* is a World Heritage–listed Confucian shrine housing the 'spirit tablets' of Joseon royalty and loyal government officials. Korea is the only country in the world where a royal ancestral shrine is perfectly preserved and veneration rites continue to be conducted in the authentic manner according to Confucian tradition.

Jongmyo's buildings are simply decorated, befitting the shrine's solemn purpose. The main shrine, **Jeongjeon**, reopened in 2025 following its first major renovation since 1870, a project that replaced all 70,000 roof tiles with traditionally handmade ones. The shrine is closed Tuesdays. On other weekdays, you're required to join a guided tour group to enter. On weekends and public holidays, you can explore on your own.

Every May a major ceremony, Jongmyo Daeje, is held here.

VTT STUDIO/SHUTTERSTOCK

Gwangjang Market

Insights into Buddhist practice

MAP P60

Join a templestay program at Jogye-sa

The headquarters of the Jogye Order, the largest order of Korean Buddhism, **Jogye-sa** *(jogyesa.kr; free)* is a lively and attractive compound festooned with colourful paper lanterns. At the centre is the Joseon-dynasty-style **Daeungjeon**, a grand wooden prayer hall decorated with scenes from Buddha's life and carved floral latticework. Near the main entrance, the **Jogye-sa Information Center for Foreigners** is staffed by English-speaking guides. Drop by here to make a booking for a templestay program (from ₩10,000).

Tasty Treats & Vintage Finds

MAP P60

Feast on street food

Don't miss **Gwangjang Market** *(kwangjangmarket.co.kr)*. This atmospheric covered market, founded in 1905, is a place to buy textiles, *hanbok* and bedding. Head upstairs to hunt through the secondhand-clothing stalls, piled high with everything from flannel shirts, sweatshirts and army jackets to choice pieces of vintage and designer fashion.

continued on p64

WHEN SEOUL WAS HANYANG

Seoul, meaning 'capital' in Korean, has only been the city's official name since 1945. Before the Joseon dynasty, it was known as Hanyang; during the Joseon dynasty (1392 to 1910) it was named Hanseong – and both Hanyang and Hanseong were used interchangeably. Later, during Japanese rule, Seoul was also called Gyeongseong.

The centre of administration, arts and culture, Jongno-gu was the historic heart of Hanyang. Its name comes from the major east-west street, Jong-no, which means 'Bell St', where the **Bosingak** (p86) bell pavilion is located, from which the opening and closing of the city-wall gates were signalled. Today Bosingak is a popular gathering spot to ring in the New Year, when the bell (a replica) is tolled 33 times to wish for prosperity.

EATING IN JONGNO-GU: CONTEMPORARY KOREAN

MAP P60 & P66

Wooara: Near Gwanghwamun, *omakase* (chef's choice) meals are served in private rooms with impeccable presentation. *11am-3pm & 5-10pm* ₩₩₩

A Flower Blossom on Rice: Only organic, farm-fresh ingredients appear on the menu of this classy restaurant on an Insa-dong alley. *11.30am-3pm & 5.30-9pm* ₩₩₩

Onjium: Contemporary fine dining in a sophisticated setting. Open kitchen with counter seating and views of Gyeongbokgung. *noon-3pm & 6-10pm Tue-Fri* ₩₩₩

Mishmash: Delicious set lunches and dinners at this Korean-Danish fusion restaurant in a modern *hanok* with a view over Changdeokgung. *11am-3pm & 6-9pm* ₩₩₩

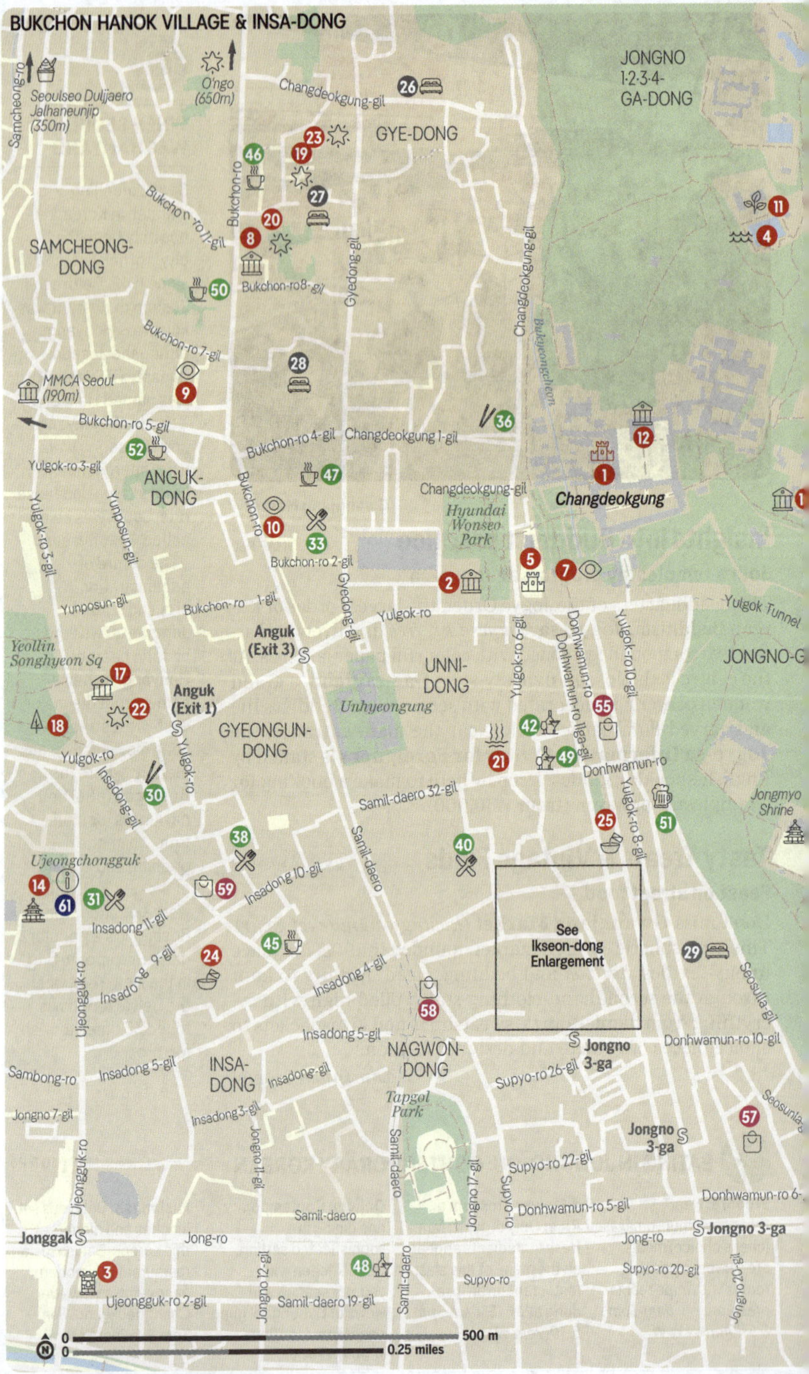
BUKCHON HANOK VILLAGE & INSA-DONG
Seoulseo Duljjaero Jalhaneunjip (350m)
O'ngo (650m)
MMCA Seoul (190m)
SAMCHEONG-DONG
GYE-DONG
JONGNO 1·2·3·4-GA-DONG
ANGUK-DONG
UNNI-DONG
GYEONGUN-DONG
INSA-DONG
NAGWON-DONG
JONGNO-G
Changdeokgung
Hyundai Wonseo Park
Unhyeongung
Yeollin Songhyeon Sq
Ujeongchongguk
Tapgol Park
Jongmyo Shrine
Anguk (Exit 3)
Anguk (Exit 1)
Jongno 3-ga
Jonggak
See Ikseon-dong Enlargement
Samcheong-ro
Changdeokgung-gil
Bukchon-ro
Bukchon-ro 11-gil
Bukchon-ro 8-gil
Bukchon-ro 7-gil
Bukchon-ro 5-gil
Bukchon-ro 4-gil
Bukchon-ro 2-gil
Bukchon-ro 1-gil
Changdeokgung 1-gil
Gyedong-gil
Bukyeongcheon
Yulgok-ro 3-gil
Yunposun-gil
Yulgok-ro
Yulgok Tunnel
Yulgok-ro 6-gil
Yulgok-ro 10-gil
Yulgok-ro 8-gil
Donhwamun-ro
Donhwamun-ro 11ga-gil
Donhwamun-ro 10-gil
Donhwamun-ro 6-
Donhwamun-ro 5-gil
Insadong-gil
Insadong 10-gil
Insadong 11-gil
Insadong 9-gil
Insadong 4-gil
Insadong 5-gil
Insadong 3-gil
Samil-daero 32-gil
Samil-daero
Samil-daero 19-gil
Seosulla-gil
Supyo-ro 26-gil
Supyo-ro 22-gil
Supyo-ro 20-gil
Supyo-ro
Ujeongguk-ro
Ujeongguk-ro 2-gil
Sambong-ro
Jongno 7-gil
Jongno 11-gil
Jongno 12-gil
Jongno 17-gil
Jongno 20-gil
Jong-ro
0 500 m
0 0.25 miles

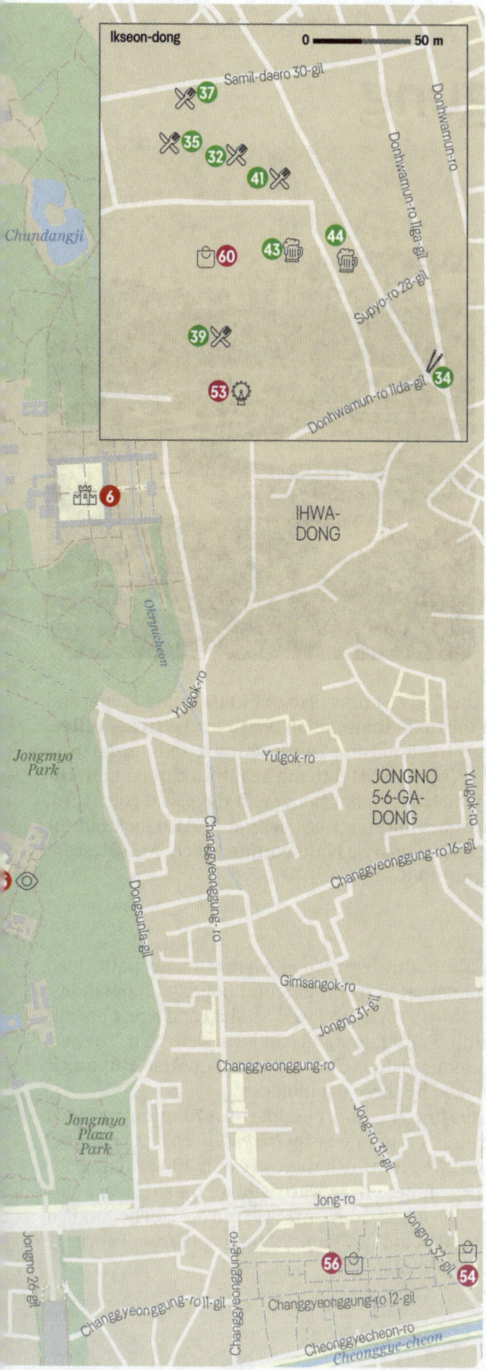

HIGHLIGHTS
1 Changdeokgung

SIGHTS
2 Arario Museum in SPACE
3 Bosingak
4 Buyongji Pond
5 Changdeokgung Ticket Office
6 Changgyeonggung
7 Donhwamun
8 Gahoe Minhwa Museum
9 Hanji House
10 Hansik Space E:eum
11 Huwon
12 Injeongjeon
13 Jeongjeon
14 Jogye-sa
15 Jongmyo
16 Nakseonjae
17 Seoul Museum of Craft Art
18 Yeollin Songhyeon

ACTIVITIES
19 Bukchon Traditional Crafts Center
20 Dong-Lim Knot Workshop
21 Insadong Spa & Sauna
22 Korean Temple Food Center
23 Kumbakyeon
24 Museum Kimchikan
25 Tteok Museum

SLEEPING
26 Bukchon Maru
27 Butler.Lee
28 Rak-Ko-Jae
29 Tongtong Hotel

EATING
30 A Flower Blossom on Rice
31 Balwoo Gongyang
32 Cheongsudang
33 Dotori Garden
34 Galmaegisal Alley
35 Jayeondo Sogeumbang
36 Mishmash
37 Oncheonjip
38 Osegyehyang
39 Soha Salt Pond
40 Vegan Insa
41 Zio Cucina

DRINKING & NIGHTLIFE
42 7.8 Makgeolli 2
43 Aledang
44 Art Monster
45 Dawon
46 Green Mile Coffee
47 Hollow
48 Ooze Whale
49 Orb of Light
50 Osulloc
51 Seoul Gypsy
52 Tea Therapy

ENTERTAINMENT
53 Saeseoul Com Com Play

SHOPPING
54 365 Iljang
55 Guiroe
56 Gwangjang Market
57 Jongno Jewelry District
58 Nakwon Musical Instruments Arcade
see 10 Sool Gallery
59 Ssamziegil
60 Teterot Salon

INFORMATION
61 Jogye-sa Information Center for Foreigners

TOP EXPERIENCE

Changdeokgung

If you only have time to see one of Seoul's palaces, make it Changdeokgung. Dating to 1405, it is the best preserved and most beautiful of the city's palaces. It's also World Heritage–listed because of its serene Huwon (aka Secret Garden), the epitome of Joseon-dynasty landscaping, which covers almost 60% of the palace grounds.

SAYAN URANAN/SHUTTERSTOCK

TOP TIPS

- Turn up to the ticket office at 9am and there's a good chance you'll be able to snag a Huwon tour ticket.
- Koreans say the garden should be visited throughout the seasons, so don't hesitate to go even if it's winter.

PRACTICALITIES

- royal.khs.go.kr
- adult/youth/child ₩3000/1500/free
- 9am-6pm Tue-Sun (to 6.30pm Jun-Aug, to 5.30pm Nov-Jan)

Guided tours in English are available at 10.15am and 1.15pm and depart from the main information board by the **ticket office**. Enter through the imposing **Donhwamun** and head across a stone bridge (built in 1414) to the beautiful throne hall, **Injeongjeon**, which sits in harmony with the paved courtyard, the open corridors and the trees behind it. Also look out for the austere Confucian-style **Nakseonjae**, where royal descendants lived until 1989.

Huwon

The Huwon is a naturalistic wood where sinuous paths lead into glades punctuated by ornamental ponds and pavilions. This is where Joseon royalty relaxed, studied and wrote poems, and where military exercises and banquets were held. The garden's most famous vista is that of the lotus-dotted **Buyongji Pond** overlooked by three pavilions.

Visiting the Huwon is only possible on a 70-minute guided tour and requires a separate ticket *(ticket.uforus.co.kr; adult/youth ₩5000/2500)*, of which there are only 100 available for each tour. Fifty of these tickets are held for on-site, same-day bookings, sold on a first-come, first-served basis. The English tour times are 10.30am, 11.30am, 2.30pm and, from February to November, 3.30pm.

ARTS & CULTURE IN BUKCHON

Stroll through Seoul's largest concentration of hanok – but be mindful of the visiting hour restrictions, as this is a real residential neighbourhood.

START	END	LENGTH
Onion	Kiwa Taproom	2.3km; 2hr

Begin at 1 **Onion**, housed in a large converted *hanok*. Drop by the 2 **Bukchon Traditional Culture Center**, which has a small exhibition about the area's history and its renowned architecture. See how the other half lived at 3 **Baek In-je House** (p65), a grand *hanok* that's now a museum. Nearby, luxe skincare brand 4 **Sulwhasoo** occupies an award-winning renovation of a 1930s *hanok*.

It's easy to see why 5 **Gahoe-dong Hill** is Bukchon's go-to selfie spot. From the top of the steep street, the clay-tiled roofs of *hanok* contrast with the modern towers of Seoul's city centre. Walk up to 6 **Jeongdok Public Library**, where the small, quiet park in front of the building is a prime spot for viewing cherry blossoms in spring and the yellowing leaves of ginkgo trees in autumn. From there, check out a few of the renowned contemporary-art galleries in the area, of which there are many, including the longstanding 7 **Art Sonje Center**, with a cafe and arthouse cinema on site, 8 **Kukje Gallery** and 9 **Hakgojae**, based in a *hanok* with a robot sculpture on the roof.

Tucked away on an alley east of 10 **MMCA Seoul** (p67) is 11 **Kiwa Taproom**, a *hanok* bar pouring ales from one of Seoul's best microbreweries, Euljiro Brewing, and serving tasty bites.

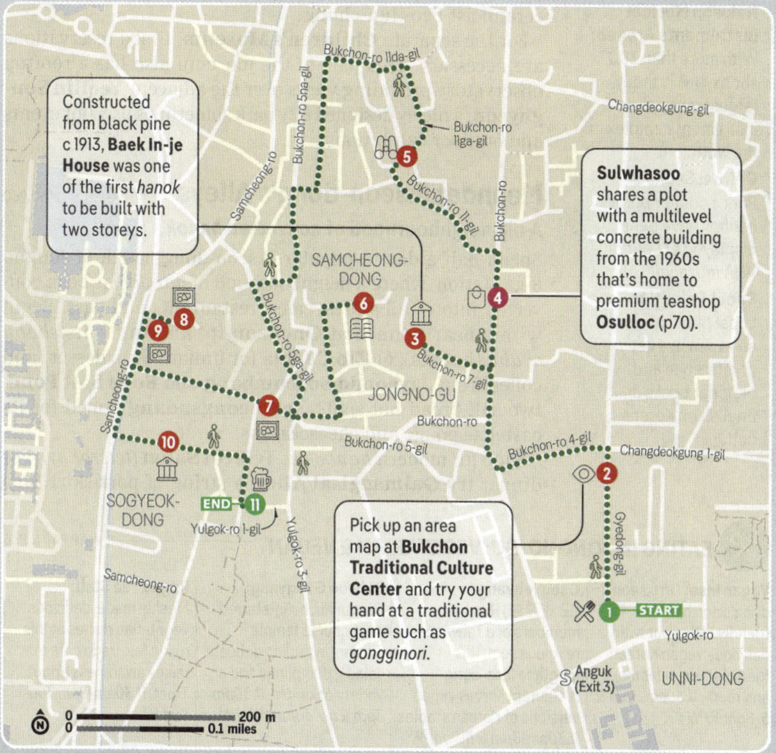

WHERE TO SHOP IN JONGNO-GU

Jongno Jewelry District: Since the 1960s, hundreds of jewellery shops have been concentrated in this district, selling discounted gold, silver and more.

Ssamziegil: Arty Insa-dong complex good for fashion, accessories and souvenirs.

Kyobo Bookshop: Stocks a wide range of English-language books and magazines, as well as stationery and electronics.

Nakwon Musical Instruments Arcade: With more than 300 shops, this is the largest musical-instrument complex in the world.

Guiroe: Seonock Park's contemporary *hanbok* have been displayed at London's V&A museum.

Seoul Selection: Local publisher with an expansive list of reference and pictorial books in English on Korean culture.

continued from p59

For many, though, the best reason for visiting Gwangjang is to eat. All manner of freshly made street foods can be sampled here, including *nokdu bindaetteok* (mung-bean pancakes), *mandu* (dumplings), *kalguksu* (hand-cut noodles), *jokbal* (braised pig's trotters) and *gimbap* (seaweed-wrapped rice rolls). There's an alley of stalls offering *yukhoe* (raw beef) and an ultra-popular *ggwabaegi* (twisted donuts) stall, near North Gate 2.

For cute souvenirs, including arty postcards, local craft beers and spirits and decal-covered purses, **365 Iljang** is near South Gate 1. To get directions and a printed market map, look for the 'Red Angel' Seoul Tourism guides who stand near the first cross alley from North Gate 1.

Decorative Arts Repository

MAP P60

Swoon over a superb collection of crafts

The splendid **Seoul Museum of Craft Art** *(craftmuseum.seoul.go.kr; free)* has a spectacular collection of 23,000 items, ranging from Joseon-dynasty ceramics, metalwork and mother-of-pearl inlaid chests to folding screens of delicately embroidered birds and flowers and beautifully decorated *bojagi* (traditional wrapping cloths). There are also works by contemporary Korean artists such as the internationally renowned ceramicist Lee Hun-chung.

For the separate **Children's Museum**, timed reservations are necessary. This part of the museum also has a rooftop observatory providing views over the adjacent **Yeollin Songhyeon**, a nicely designed city park sometimes used for events and outdoor exhibitions.

Meander Ikseon-dong's Alleys

MAP P60

A hip neighbourhood of converted *hanok*

Spend half a day in popular Ikseon-dong, north of Jongno 3-ga station, where a neighbourhood of *hanok* has been converted into retail stores, cafes, restaurants and bars. Begin with a hearty lunch at **Oncheonjip**, known for its *shabu shabu* (hot pot), or **Zio Cucina** for Italian. Grab dessert and coffee from **Jayeondo Sogeumbang** and **Soha Salt Pond**, two salt-bread hot spots, or **Cheongsudang** famed for its castella sponge and cheesecakes.

Shop for modern *hanbok* at **Teterot Salon** *(teterot.kr)*. For dinner try **Galmaegisal Alley**, a string of pork-skirt BBQ

EATING IN JONGNO-GU: VEGETARIAN & VEGAN

MAP P60 & P66

Vegan Insa: On Ikseon-dong's north side, a friendly little spot with delicious vegan Korean fried chicken, *bibimbap* and more. *11.30am-3pm & 5-8pm* **WW**

Osegyehyang: (오세계향) Run by members of a Taiwanese religious sect, this longtime Insa-dong restaurant serves vegan versions of Korean staples. *11.30am-3pm & 5-9pm* **W**

Balwoo Gongyang: Savour Michelin-starred multicourse temple cuisine, including delicate salads, dumplings and a variety of kimchi. *11.30am-3pm & 6-7.30pm* **WWW**

Rogpa Tea Stall: Freshly made, delicious vegetarian dishes at this rustic fair-trade cafe that raises awareness about Tibet. *11.30am-8pm Tue-Sun* **W**

WOOHAE CHO/BLOOMBERG VIA GETTY IMAGES

Tongin Market

joints with seating that flows out onto the street, followed by a pint at a craft-beer pub such as **Art Monster** or **Aledang**. Check out **Saeseoul Comcom Play** for retro arcade games and finish up with late-night street snacks and drinks at a *pojangmacha* (street tent bar) along Donhwamun-ro.

Explore Hanok-Studded Seochon

MAP P66

A pleasant place for casual wanderings

West of Gyeongbukgung, Seochon is a less touristed area that's home to some attractive *hanok* and other vintage buildings. Start exploring at **Tongin Market** pausing for lunch at the **Lunchbox Cafe**, where you can buy tokens *(₩5000 for 10)* to spend on helpings of dishes from the various food stalls. From here, keep going west until you hit Ogin-gil, an attractive street lined with cafes, bakeries, boutiques and oddities such as **Ogin Oraksil**, an old-school video-games arcade. Also in this area is **Park No-soo Museum**, the one-time home of the celebrated painter Park (1927–2013) that's still decorated with his art today.

Head south of Tongin Market to find the charming **Daeoh Bookstore** cafe. Opened in 1951, it's a bygone-days space, overflowing with books and memorabilia. Further south, you'll come to **Seochon Lounge**, a beautifully designed modern

HANOK ARCHITECTURE

Vessels of Korean architectural tradition, *hanok* are single-storey wooden homes, insulated with mud and straw and topped with clay-tiled roofs. Designed to blend with nature, they are typically left unpainted, their earthy tones providing a warm, intimate feel. All rooms have sliding doors, *ondol* (underfloor heating) and face onto a central *madang* (courtyard).

In recent years, many of the surviving *hanok* of Bukchon, Seochon and Ikseon-dong have been adapted to become guesthouses, restaurants, cafes, bars and boutiques, making it easy to appreciate this unique form of architecture. A few, such as **Baek In-je House** *(museum.seoul.go.kr; free)*, have been preserved in their original form – wander its grounds freely on your own, or join an English tour on Fridays at 2pm.

DRINKING IN WEST JONGNO-GU: OUR PICKS

MAP P66

Bar Cham: Inspired by Korea's different provinces, with drinks that showcase Korean traditional spirits and ingredients. *6pm-1am Mon & Wed-Sun*

Bar Pomme: Skilled bartenders concoct innovative seasonal cocktails, like the Crimson Foliage with rum, peanut and Aperol. *6pm-1am Mon & Wed-Sun*

Cobbler: Sophisticated *hanok* bar on an alley near Sajik Park, serving a complimentary piece of pie with your drink. *7pm-3am Mon-Sat*

Mutual Sound Club: Artfully presented cocktails in a cosy Seochon vinyl bar. If you like lemon and gin, get the Bee's Knees. *6-11pm, to 11.30pm Fri & Sat*

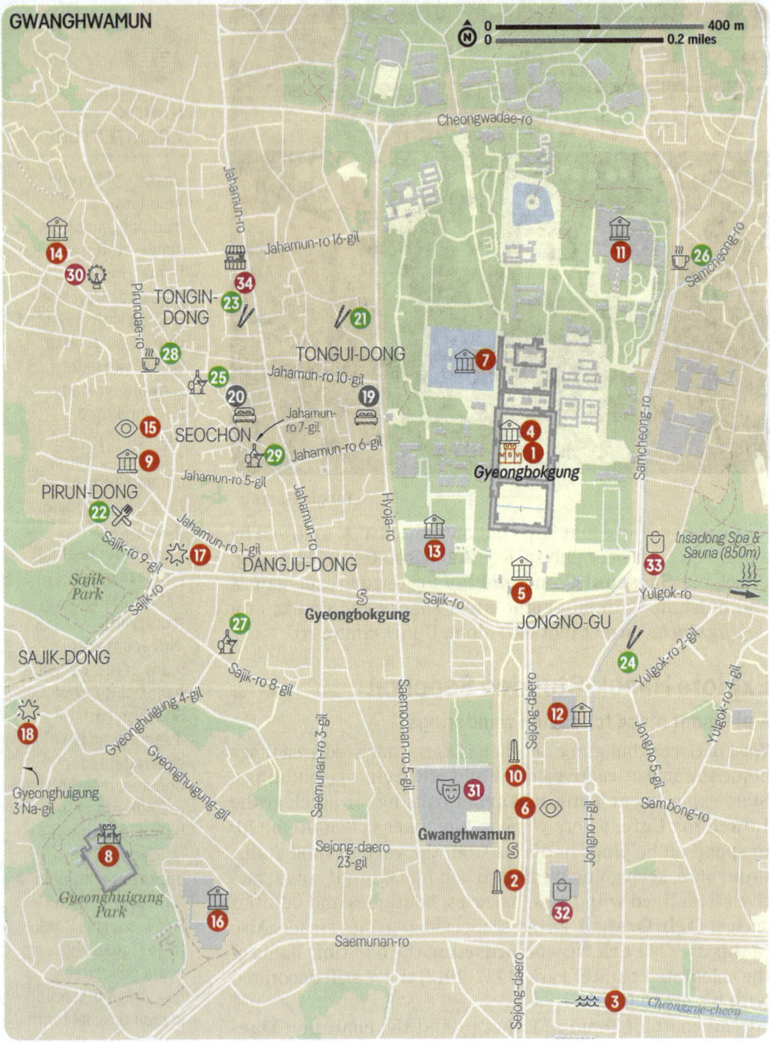

HIGHLIGHTS
1 Gyeongbokgung

SIGHTS
2 Admiral Yi Sun-sin Statue
3 Cheonggye-cheon
4 Geunjeongjeon
5 Gwanghwamun
6 Gwanghwamun Square
7 Gyeonghoeru
8 Gyeonghuigung
9 Hong Geonik's House
10 King Sejong Statue
11 National Folk Museum of Korea
12 National Museum of Korean Contemporary History
13 National Palace Museum of Korea
14 Park No-soo Museum
15 Seochon Lounge
16 Seoul Museum of History

ACTIVITIES
17 Food & Culture Korea
18 Seoul Kimchi Academy

SLEEPING
19 Boan Stay
20 Seochon Guesthouse

EATING
21 Onjium
22 Rogpa Tea Stall
23 Tongin Market Lunchbox Cafe
24 Wooara

DRINKING & NIGHTLIFE
25 Bar Cham
see 25 Bar Pomme
26 Cafe Husbands
27 Cobbler
28 Dae-oh Bookstore
29 Mutual Sound Club

ENTERTAINMENT
30 Ogin Oraksil
31 Sejong Center for the Performing Arts

SHOPPING
32 Kyobo Bookshop
33 Seoul Selection
34 Tongin Market

hanok hosting exhibitions of contemporary Korean craft and design. Further south still is **Hong Geonik's House**, the last *hanok* in Seoul with an *ilgakmun* (two-post gate), *binggo* (ice storage) and a well.

See the Palace of Shining Celebration

MAP P66

A makeover for Gyeonghuigung

Of Seoul's five major palaces, **Gyeonghuigung** *(museum.seoul.go.kr; free)* is the least visited and most peaceful. A ten-year project began in 2025 to transform the palace and its surrounding area into a history and culture park that's slated to cover 136,000 sq metres. Gyeonghuigung's entrance was revitalised with a traditional stone pathway newly installed between Heunghwamun and Sungjeongmun, as well as a garden planted with native trees.

The palace, closed Mondays, was completed in 1620, renamed in 1760 and largely destroyed during the Japanese occupation. Since then, three of its buildings (the main hall Sungjeongjeon, Jajeongjeon and Taeryeongjeon) have been restored. The history-park project will also rebuild Donuimun, the only one of Seoul's four major gates yet to be restored.

Korea's Dynamic Contemporary-Art Scene

MAP P60

Check out two major galleries

Cutting-edge works of art are displayed in the many spacious modern galleries of **MMCA Seoul** *(mmca.go.kr; price varies by exhibition)*, which partially occupies the repurposed red-brick buildings of the former Defense Security Command. To see all the temporary exhibitions here takes at least half a day. The well-stocked bookshop and gift store alone make it worth a visit. On Wednesdays and Saturdays the galleries are open until 9pm, with all exhibitions free after 6pm.

One of Seoul's best private art galleries, **Arario Museum in SPACE** *(arariomuseum.org; adult/youth/child ₩15,000/9000/6000)* showcases pieces from the collection of Korean business magnate Kim Chang-il. These include works by Nam June Paik, KooKang, Kōhei Nawa, Tracey Emin, Damien Hirst and Cindy Sherman.

The ivy-clad brick SPACE building (closed Mondays) is considered a seminal piece of early 1970s architecture. Its compact, low-ceilinged rooms and labyrinthine layout fit the art works like a glove. Also part of the complex are a *hanok* and a

LOCAL FESTIVALS

K-Royal Culture Festival: Ritual reenactments, exhibitions and other experiences unfold across Seoul's palaces and **Jongmyo** (p58) every spring and autumn.

Lotus Lantern Festival (Yeon Deung Hoe): In honour of Buddha's birthday, a weekend fete with cultural performances and a magical lantern parade down Jong-no to **Jogye-sa** (p59).

Jongno Hanbok Festival: At **Gwanghwamun Sq** (p69) in October, with *hanbok*-related fashion shows and festivities.

Seoul Performing Arts Festival: In autumn, a month of performances at the **Sejong Center** (p70), **National Theater of Korea** (p74) and more.

Seoul Lantern Festival: Fantastical lanterns illuminate Gwanghwamun Sq and **Cheonggye-cheon** (p76) each December and January.

Insa-dong Traditional Culture Festival: A celebration of the area's heritage, held in September.

CAFES IN BUKCHON: OUR PICKS

MAP P60 & P66

Hollow: In a neighbourhood of chaotic queues, this quiet cafe with serene rooftop seating is a welcome reprieve. *8am-9pm*

Green Mile Coffee: With a rooftop overlooking the surrounding *hanok* and a sleek warm-wood interior, this cafe is a stunner. *9am-5.45pm Mon-Fri, 10am-7pm Sat & Sun*

Dottori Garden: Whimsical Totoro-esque cartoon cafe serving acorn-shaped madeleines and creamy yoghurt bowls. *8am-11pm*

Cafe Husbands: Small, rustic spot with high-quality coffee and a killer grilled-cheese sandwich on the menu. *8am-7pm Mon & Wed-Sun*

TOP EXPERIENCE

Gyeongbokgung

Set aside the better part of a day to do justice to Gyeongbokgung, the hub around which Seoul has revolved since 1395. Much altered and rebuilt over its history, the largest and oldest of the city's royal palaces also offers two great museums and spectacular changing-of-the-guard ceremonies at its main gate, Gwanghwamun.

JI-IN/SHUTTERSTOCK

Gyeonghoeru

TOP TIPS

- The Changing of the Guard ceremony is at 10am and 2pm daily except Tuesday. The guard dispatch is at 11am and 1pm.
- In May to early June and September, Gyeongbokgung is also open 7pm to 9.30pm (last entrance 8.30pm) – check online for exact dates.

PRACTICALITIES

- royal.khs.go.kr
- adult/youth/child ₩3000/1500/free
- 9am-6pm Mon & Wed-Sun (to 6.30pm Jun-Aug, to 5pm Nov-Feb)

Meaning 'palace of shining brilliance', Gyeongbokgung was the principal royal residence until 1592, when it was destroyed during the Japanese invasion. It was rebuilt at enormous expense for King Gojong, who moved in during 1868. The palace's most impressive buildings are **Geunjeongjeon**, the ornate throne hall where kings were crowned, met foreign envoys and conducted affairs of state, and **Gyeonghoeru**, a large pavilion resting on 48 pillars that stands in an ornamental pond.

Museums

For context on what life was once like within the palace walls, spend some time exploring the **National Palace Museum of Korea** *(gogung.go.kr; free)*. The comprehensive exhibitions here highlight the artistic skills of the Joseon dynasty. Its Digital Library for Cultural Heritage includes a multisided video zone as well as interactive virtual-reality experiences.

Also within the palace grounds is the superb **National Folk Museum of Korea**, with a trio of creatively designed permanent exhibitions on aspects of Korean culture. Beside the museum is an open-air exhibition of historic buildings and structures, including an atmospheric street of buildings styled as they would have been in the 1970s and '80s.

five-storey glass annexe (added in 1997) housing cafes, restaurants and the free **Arario Gallery** *(arariogallery.com)*, closed Sundays and Mondays.

Delve into Seoul's History

MAP P66

From Joseon-dynasty Hanyang to modern megacity

For a comprehensive overview of the Korean capital's trajectory, from the dawn of the Joseon dynasty to the present day, visit the excellent **Seoul Museum of History** *(museum.seoul.go.kr; free)*. A highlight is the scale model of Seoul brought to life with lights and projected videos. The museum is closed on Mondays.

Over at the **National Museum of Korean Contemporary History** *(much.go.kr; free)*, get more context about the country from 1894 onwards. The museum offers engaging exhibitions on how far the Korean people have come in the decades since their fight for freedom from Imperial Japan, navigating the tumult of the Korean War, the democracy movement and ultrarapid modernisation. There's also an interactive gallery about intergenerational communication, imaginative art pieces and a rooftop that provides good views of Gwanghwamun Sq and Gyeongbokgung.

All about Korean Food & Drink

MAP P60

One-stop shop for hansik

A showcase for *hansik* (Korean cuisine), **Hansik Space E:eum** *(hansik.or.kr; free)* has exhibitions about the national food culture, a cafe, shop, library and a learning centre where you can take classes (₩11,000) on how to make seasonal dishes, desserts and more. Book ahead online; it's closed Mondays.

Also at Hansik Space is **Sool Gallery** *(thesool.com)*, which promotes Korean alcoholic drinks, from the milky rice wine *makgeolli* to the clear rice wine *cheongju*, as well as various fruit wines, medicinal liquors and distilled spirits such as soju. Sign up in advance for free tasting sessions of five different liquors and buy bottles from boutique producers across Korea.

Seoul's Most Iconic Public Plaza

MAP P66

Learn about Korean history in Gwanghwamun Sq

Over 500m in length, **Gwanghwamun Sq** provides a grand approach to Gyeongbokgung. This vast public space is used

COOKING CLASSES

Museum Kimchikan: Make different kinds of kimchi, from radish to cabbage, and taste savoury kimchi pancakes. *kimchikan.com*

Seoul Kimchi Academy: Hands-on courses near Gyeonghuigung to make and take away your own pouch of kimchi. *kimchischool.net*

O'ngo: Long-established operator offering a range of cooking classes and food tours. *ongofood.com*

Korean Temple Food Center: On Saturdays at 10am there's a class in English on cooking vegan dishes as traditionally served at temples. *koreatemplefood.com*

Food & Culture Korea: Prepare and sample various dishes, leaving with a certificate of attendance. *koreanrecipe.co.kr*

Tteok Museum: Learn how to make rice cakes, then steam, boil or fry them up for a tasting. *tkmuseum.or.kr*

DRINKING IN EAST JONGNO-GU: OUR PICKS

MAP P60

Ooze Whale: By Tapgol Park, a cosy basement bar serving pastas and other mains. It's not mandatory to order food, but it is necessary to order wine. *6pm-1am, to 2am Fri & Sat*

Orb of Light: Wine and cocktails in an intimate space on the edge of Ikseon-dong. Try the signature Florist. *6pm-2am Tue-Sun*

7.8 Makgeolli 2: Superb selection of *makgeolli*, including its own Not Applicable brand garnished with a squeeze of lemon. *5pm-midnight*

Seoul Gypsy: Near Jongmyo, an atmospheric *hanok* bar with 10 ales on tap, including a porter pilsner, Belgian white and lager. *4-11pm Tue-Sun*

CRAFT CLASSES

Bukchon Traditional Crafts Center: Join the program of the day, which ranges from needle and patchwork, to painting, dying, ceramics and beyond.

Kumbakyeon (금박연): Visit this gold-leaf-gilding workshop to create decorative pouches and other items inspired by royalty.

Dong-Lim Knot Workshop: Learn how to make knotted bracelets, necklaces and other ornaments using various threads.

Gahoe Minhwa Museum: View the special exhibition and try your hand at a one-day *minhwa* (folk art) painting class.

Hanji House: Browse this *hanji* (handmade paper) showroom run by the Korean Craft & Design Foundation and make your own *hanji* bookmark.

KOREA TOURISM ORGANIZATION - PARK SEONGGEUN

Gwanghwamun Square (p69), statue of King Sejong

for events such as the Seoul Lantern Festival (p67) in December and January.

Giant statues in the square celebrate two national heroes: **King Sejong** (1397–1450), a revered scholar who oversaw the invention and adoption of Korea's writing script *hangeul*; and 16th-century **Admiral Yi Sun-sin**, who had a series of victories over the much larger Japanese navy. An entrance at the base of Sejong's statue leads to an underground exhibition with sections on both the men (closed Mondays).

On the square's west side is the **Sejong Center for the Performing Arts**, one of the city's leading arts complexes, with several performance and exhibition spaces.

Soak, Steam & Body Scrub

MAP P60

Relax at a traditional sauna

Local bathhouses and saunas are known as *jjimjilbang* (heated rooms). A good one to sample, with English-speaking staff, is **Insadong Spa & Sauna**. In the same-sex bathing sections, get naked and soak in different baths and the steam sauna. Pay extra for a full-body scrub from one of the attendants – as dead skin is sloughed off, you'll feel reborn. Pyjamas are provided for the mixed-sex dry sauna and relaxation area.

TEAHOUSES IN JONGNO-GU: OUR PICKS

MAP P60

Dawon: In Insa-dong, sip your tea inside or in the garden. Try the *omija hwachae* (five-flavour berry punch). *10am-10pm*

Seoulseo Duljjaero Jalhaneunjip: (서울서둘째로잘하는집) Little has changed at 'Second Best in Seoul', a tiny medicinal tea cafe, since it opened in 1976. *11am-8.30pm*

Tea Therapy: Teas and herbal infusions for whatever ails you, and a chart to aid your selection. Footbaths outside the front door. *10am-9pm*

Osulloc: Enjoy a matcha latte, tea-based cocktail or green-tea sponge roll in this sleek Bukchon branch of the premium tea shop. *11am-8pm*

Myeong-dong & Jung-gu

SHOPPING | NIGHTLIFE | URBAN OASES

You could spend a lifetime exploring Seoul, but if you don't have that kind of time, a day in Myeong-dong and Jung-gu will do. Seoul's central district combines a bit of everything that makes this city special.

The Joseon dynasty's most interesting palace, Deoksugung, is here, but so is Myeong-dong, the bright neon bull's-eye for travellers coming to Seoul to shop, and Euljiro's eclectic bar scene, existing side by side with light industrial shops. 'Myeong' means 'light', which is apt for an area where Seoul's commercial razzle-dazzle reaches its apogee – the huge digital billboards wrapping around venerable department store Shinsegae are an attraction in themselves.

Just down the road, Namdaemun Market does business much the same way it has for centuries. It's a lot to take in, but if you need a breather, you'll also find two of the city's favourite escapes here: majestic Namsan and the restored Cheonggye-cheon stream.

GETTING AROUND

Jung-gu is quite compact and – Namsan excepted – flat, and interesting sites seem to pop up around every corner, making it easy and rewarding to explore on foot.

Subway Lines 1 to 5 run through the area, linking local neighbourhoods and providing connections to the rest of the city. City Hall, Chungmuro and Euljiro 3-ga are major transfer stations.

Being in the city centre, the area is well serviced by public buses. Buses 01A and 01B will take you to the top of Namsan.

Seoul's Oldest Market

Shop for bargain souvenirs

Sprawling **Namdaemun Market** *(namdaemunmarket.co.kr)* is nearly as old as Seoul itself. You can find pretty much anything here, from food and flowers to spectacles and camera equipment. Pick up a market map from the **tourist information booth** on the central alley near Gate 5 to get orientated.

The market is a great place to eat as well as shop. Just inside Gate 5 is **Kalguksu Alley**. Diners down bowls of noodle soup at counters lining either side. Not far from Gate 1 is **Hairtail Alley**, where tiny restaurants serve up clay pots of braised *galchi* (hairtail) and grilled mackerel. Next to Gate 2 you'll find a wildly popular **hotteok stand**. Along with the typical sugar-and-nut-filled version of these fried pancakes, it also does versions with vegetables and sweet red beans.

TOP TIP

Deoksugung-gil, the street that runs along Deoksugung's south side and that leads to SeMA, makes for one of the prettiest walks in Seoul, especially in autumn, when its ginkgo trees turn golden above the old palace walls. It's also frequently the site of flea markets and street festivals.

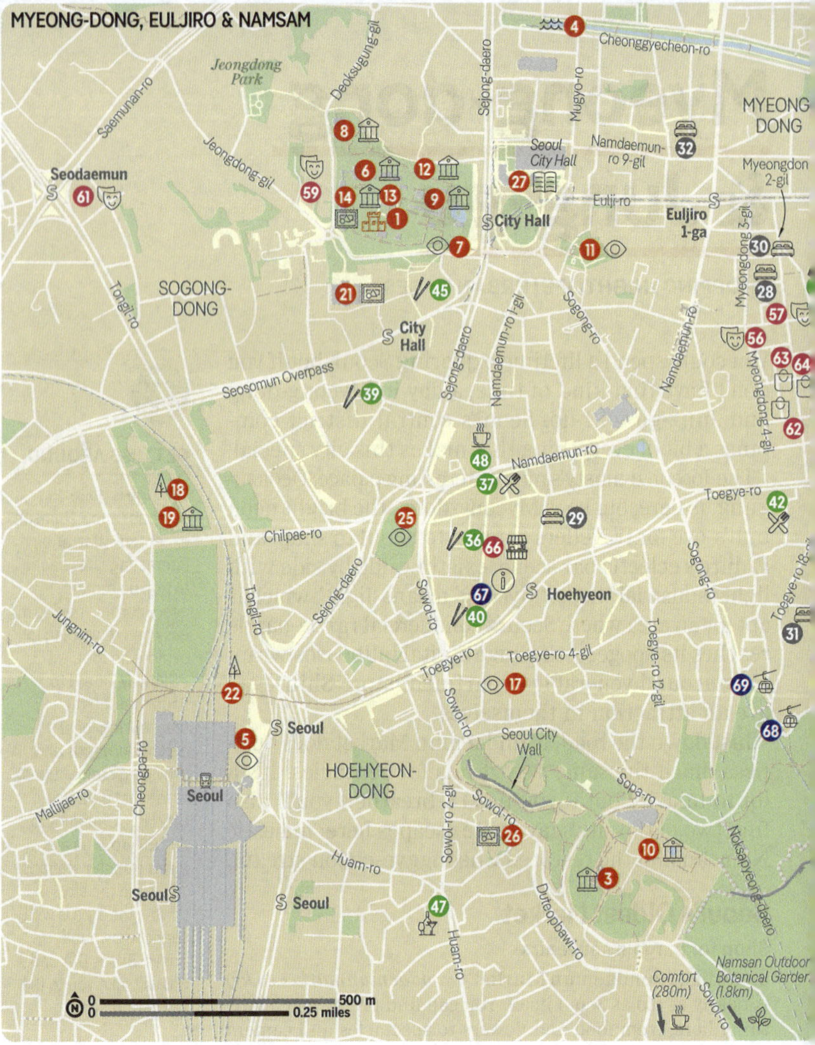

HIGHLIGHTS
1 Deoksugung
2 Namsan

SIGHTS
3 Ahn Junggeun Memorial Museum
4 Cheonggye-cheon
5 Culture Station Seoul 284
6 Daehan Empire History Museum
7 Daehanmun
8 Dondeokjeon
9 Hamnyeongjeon
10 Hanyangdoseong Historic Site Museum
11 Hwangudan
12 Jeonggwanheon
13 Junghwajeon
14 MMCA, Deoksugung
see 2 N Seoul Tower
15 Namsan Beacon Station
16 Namsangol Hanok Village
17 Piknic
see 6 Seokjojeon
18 Seosomun Historical Park
19 Seosomun Shrine History Museum
20 Seoul Film Center
21 Seoul Museum of Art
22 Seoullo 7017
23 Sewoon Electronics Museum
24 Sewoon Sangga
25 Sungnyemun
26 Whitestone Gallery

ACTIVITIES
27 Seoul Metropolitan Library

SLEEPING
28 Hotel28
29 L'Escape
30 Metro Hotel
31 Namsan Hostel Guest House
32 Small House Big Door
33 Zaza Backpackers

EATING
34 Euljiro Las Vegas
35 Hadongkwan
36 Hairtail Alley
37 Hotteok stand
38 Jangmanok
39 Jinju Hoegwan
40 Kalguksu Alley
41 Korea House
42 Mari Meokja
43 Menten
44 Woo Lae Oak
45 Yurimmyeon

DRINKING & NIGHTLIFE
46 Ace Four Club
47 Bar Jaerae
48 Cafe Gabaedo
49 Champ Coffee
50 Euljiro Brewing
see 49 Ggeek Beer Company
51 Leesar
52 Myeongdong Sookhee
53 Seendosi
54 Tabacchi

ENTERTAINMENT
55 Myeongbo Art Hall
56 Myeongdong Nanta Theater
57 Myeongdong Theater
58 Namsan Gugakdang
59 National Jeongdong Theater of Korea
60 National Theater of Korea
61 NH Arthall

SHOPPING
62 ÅLAND
63 Covernat
64 EMIS
65 JJMG
see 64 Matin Kim
66 Namdaemun Market
see 62 Nick Nicole

INFORMATION
67 Namdaemun Market Tourist Information Booth

TRANSPORT
68 Namsan Cable Car
69 Namsan Oreumi

CONTEMPORARY K-CULTURE HOT SPOTS

HiKR Ground: A showcase for *hallyu* (Korean Wave) content, with temporary exhibitions on the nation's dynamic pop culture and works of contemporary art. *english.visitkorea.or.kr/svc/sp/hikr*

Piknic: Combines exhibition halls, a roof garden, cafe, top-class design shop and the Michelin-starred Gigas Mediterranean restaurant. *piknic.kr*

Whitestone Gallery: Specialises in contemporary and emerging Asian artists. *whitestone-gallery.com*

Comfort: Hip space that includes a trendy streetwear and fragrance boutique, a small gallery and a cafe. *comfortseoul.com*

Seoul Film Center: Hosts film-related exhibitions and screens movies, with a focus on independent and art films. *seoulfilmcenter.com*

Seoul's Great South Gate

See the revamped Sungnyemun

Built in 1398, **Sungnyemun** – commonly called Namdaemun, or Great South Gate – is the oldest and largest of the historic city wall gates. Its two-storey pavilion underwent major reconstruction following a 2008 fire. Repairs were completed in 2013. Aim to visit at either 10am or 3.30pm, when costumed guards conduct gate opening and closing ceremonies. The plaza around the gate is closed on Mondays.

Joseon-era Village in the City

Tour Namsangol Hanok Village's homes

A great place to learn about traditional Korean culture, **Namsangol Hanok Village** *(hanokmaeul.co.kr; free)* is a collection of five Joseon-era *yangban* (aristocrat) houses that were relocated here from different parts of Seoul. Explore them by yourself or take a free 90-minute guided tour. On Fridays, Saturdays and Sundays from April to June and September to October, join cultural programs where you can make straw crafts, archery bows or medicinal foods, among other things. Reserve tour and activity spots on the village's website. The grounds also contain a lovely traditional garden and a teahouse. The village is closed Mondays.

The Arts of Old

Experience a traditional meal or show

Three performance venues specialising in traditional art forms cluster on Namsan's northern slope. Within Namsangol Hanok Village is the **Namsan Gugakdang** *(sgtt.kr)*, a 306-seat theatre that hosts music and dance performances, from *pansori* singing (p116) to *seungmu*, the monk dance.

Next to Namsangol is **Korea House** *(kh.or.kr)*, where you can indulge in an extravagant *hanjeongsik* (Korean table d'hôte), based on royal court cuisine, or a tea service with traditional sweets. The meals are often accompanied by performances.

Head to the **National Theater of Korea** *(ntok.go.kr)* to watch the national dance company, national orchestra or national *changgeuk* (Korean opera) company perform. Book tickets for events at all three venues through their respective websites.

EATING IN JUNG-GU: CLASSIC KOREAN RESTAURANTS

Yurimmyeon: Puts more than 50 years of expertise into its *memil guksu*, buckwheat noodles you dip in broth. *11am-8.30pm, to 7.30pm Sat & Sun* W

Jinju Hoegwan: First dished up its famous *kongguksu* (noodles in a chilled soybean broth) and stews in 1962. *11am-9pm Mon-Fri, to 8pm Sat* W

Woo Lae Oak: Renowned for the bulgogi and Pyeongyang *naengmyeong* (noodles in chilled broth) it's been serving since 1946. *11.30am-9pm Tue-Sun* WW

Hadongkwan: Open since 1939, this Myeong-dong eatery makes simple, perfect *gomtang* (beef and rice soup) seasoned with spring onions and black pepper. *7am-4pm Mon-Sat* WW

TOP EXPERIENCE

Namsan

When the Joseon dynasty established its royal capital, Namsan marked the city's southern boundary. Today it's smack dab in the middle of Seoul, and a perfectly placed escape where locals come to exercise and get some air. Join them on the 270m mountain's many trails to access nature, historic sites and N Seoul Tower for panoramic city views.

Seoul City Wall

N Seoul Tower

N Seoul Tower pokes 236m into the sky from Namsan's summit. The views from its observation deck are well worth the cost of admission. If you can, visit at dusk to watch the metropolis slowly light up as night descends. There are several souvenir shops and restaurants in the tower.

The most enjoyable way to reach the tower is aboard the **Namsan Cable Car** *(cablecar.co.kr; adult/child ₩12,000/9000)*. A free shuttle bus to its lower station departs roughly every half-hour from Myeongdong station, Exit 1. Alternatively, ride the free **Namsan Oreumi** inclined elevator, which trundles up to the station from Sogong-ro.

Historic Sites

On the plaza in front of N Seoul Tower, **Namsan Beacon Station** is a re-creation of a Joseon-era signal beacon used to relay messages via fire and smoke.

Sections of **Seoul City Wall** (p124) snake across the mountain. Learn about the wall at the **Hanyangdoseong Historic Site Museum**. Across a plaza is the **Ahn Junggeun Memorial Museum** *(ahnjunggeun.or.kr)*, dedicated to an independence fighter who was executed for assassinating Ito Hirobumi, the Japanese resident-general of Korea, in Harbin, China, in 1909.

TOP TIPS

- Lighting ceremonies of the Namsan Beacon are held from 11am to 12.10pm Tuesday to Sunday.
- Pick up a brochure with maps of Namsan's walking trails from the info centre opposite N Seoul Tower bus stop.
- On the mountain's southern flank, explore **Namsan Outdoor Botanical Garden**.

PRACTICALITIES

- nseoultower.co.kr
- free; N Seoul Tower observatory adult/child ₩26,000/20,000
- mountain 24hr, facility hours vary

BEST THEATRE FOR NON-KOREAN SPEAKERS

Myeongdong Theater: Home to the National Theater Company of Korea, it stages everything from Shakespeare to Korean dramas. English subtitles for some shows. *ntck.or.kr*

NH Arthall: Come here for *The Painters*, in which talented performers with K-Pop boy-band looks mix dance with live drawing and painting. *thepainters.co.kr*

Myeongdong Nanta Theater: The long-running *Nanta* show mixes drumming, cooking, *samulnori* folk music, comedy and audience participation. *nanta.co.kr*

National Jeongdong Theater of Korea: Well-regarded theatre specialising in contemporary stagings of traditional stories. English subtitles. *jeongdong.or.kr*

Myeongbo Art Hall: This Euljiro theatre hosts the popular nonverbal show *Jump*, a mashup of physical comedy and martial arts. *mbah.co.kr*

Art for the People

Enjoy the shows at Seoul Museum of Art

The **Seoul Museum of Art** (SeMA; *sema.seoul.go.kr)* holds superbly curated exhibitions, most of which are free. Many focus on the work of Korean creatives, but they run a thrilling gamut from retrospectives to group exhibitions. A permanent exhibition is devoted to the major 20th-century painter Chun Kyung-ja. Also notable is the building itself, a 1928 structure that once housed the Korean Supreme Court. The museum is closed Mondays.

Transport Transformation

Promenade along Seoullo 7017

Built in 1925, the original Seoul station is a stately Renaissance-style building. Replaced by a new, larger station in 2004, it reopened in 2011 as **Culture Station Seoul 284** *(seoul284.org)*, a space for art exhibitions and events. Shows here are reliably excellent, but what really sets the venue apart is the ability to explore the restored station as you peruse the art.

Seoullo 7017 is a 17m-high vehicle overpass from the 1970s that's been turned into an elevated park stretching nearly 1km from Seoul station's west side to Hoehyeon station. Watch trains pulling in and out of the station and stroll among potted trees and plants.

Stroll along a Revived Stream

Decompress beside Cheonggye-cheon

The **Cheonggye-cheon**, a 10.9km-long revitalised stream cutting through Seoul, starts just north of Myeong-dong. It provides a sunken pedestrian corridor with landscaped walkways and places to rest and enjoy the trickling water and wildlife that has returned to the heart of the city. The embankment walls and surroundings are graced with public art works, such as murals and the oversized pink-and-blue shell entitled *Spring* in **Cheonggye Plaza**.

DRINKING IN JUNG-GU: OUR PICKS

Myeongdong Sookhee: Slip through the secret door of this deliberately hard-to-find bar for Joseon-era ambience and excellent cocktails. *6pm-1am*

Bar Jaerae: This classy spot has a curated whisky selection and a wide array of Korean spirits to sample. *8pm-midnight Wed & Thu, to 2am Fri, from 6pm Sat*

Cafe Gabaedo: The Namdaemun Market branch occupies an early 20th-century commercial building with Sungnyemun views. *9am-9pm, from 11am Sat & Sun*

Leesar: Italian-style espresso bar that would get an approving nod from your *nonno*. Has several locations around the city. *7am-8pm, from 8am Sat & Sun*

TOP EXPERIENCE

Deoksugung

You can practically see the Korean world changing at Deoksugung, Seoul's most unusual and interesting Joseon palace. The complex embodies the country's tumultuous early 20th century (p398) with its mix of traditional wooden halls and Western-style buildings and its occasionally charming, often tragic, history. It also possesses an excellent art museum and one of the city's best nighttime scenes.

Seokjojeon

The Old Palace

What you see within the grounds today represents only a third of the palace at its height. The centrepiece is **Junghwajeon**, the stately throne hall engraved with dragons, befitting Gojong's status as emperor. To the east is **Hamnyeongjeon**, Gojong's private chambers. Gojong also had the Russian architect Aleksey Seredin-Sabatin build **Jeonggwanheon** as a pavilion where he could enjoy a cup of coffee and entertain guests. The building blends Romanesque designs and Korean motifs.

Western Influences

Facing a very European-looking fountain, and connected by a loggia, are the two wings of **Seokjojeon**. The neoclassical north wing, completed in 1910, served as Gojong's living quarters. It now houses the **Daehan Empire History Museum** and has been decorated to look as it would have in Gojong's time. You need to join a guided tour to see inside; English tours are held at 11.50am and 2.50pm. Sign up in advance inside the museum entrance.

Seokjojeon's west wing, built in 1938, hosts **MMCA, Deoksugung**. Exhibitions change every few months. Behind Seokjojeon is the striking brick **Dondeokjeon**, used as a banquet hall and accommodation for state guests – it's a replica, rebuilt in 2023.

TOP TIPS

- Free one-hour guided tours of the palace grounds are provided in English at 10.45am and 1.30pm.
- Changing-of-the-guards ceremonies take place outside **Daehanmun**, the main palace gate, at 11am and 2pm Tuesday to Sunday and last about 15 minutes. They're photogenic and lively affairs.

PRACTICALITIES

- royal.khs.go.kr
- adult/child ₩1000/free
- 9am-9pm Tue-Sun

LOCAL FASHION BRANDS

Among the local fashion brands with shops in Myeong-dong are:

EMIS: Cute sweats, T-shirts, bags and accessories. Its caps are seemingly everywhere in Seoul. Has clothes for pets, too.

Matin Kim: Men's and women's clothing basic enough to wear every day but with a bit of edge to stand out.

Covernat: A popular brand that plays it chill, with subdued workwear-inspired looks that won't go out of style.

ÅLAND: A lifestyle store that carries a wide array of trendy Korean and international labels. A good place to go exploring.

Nick Nicole: This womenswear line has a bit of the catwalk in its DNA and takes a more grown-up approach to its designs.

A Martyrs' Memorial & a Grand Cathedral

Pilgrimage to Korean Catholic sites

During the early 19th century, many Catholics were put to death for their beliefs (p258). **Seosomun Historical Park** and **Seosomun Shrine History Museum** *(seosomun.org)* form an extraordinary integrated complex that commemorates these religious martyrs.

Wander the park to view memorials and find the Executioner's Well, where the executioner washed his sword, then take the ramp down to the museum (closed Mondays) to learn about Catholicism's development in Korea and its conflict with Joseon's ruling Confucian ideology. Within the museum you'll also find religious artworks, the austere St Chong Ha-sang Chapel and the open-air Sky Square, where 44 statues made from railroad ties represent the 44 Seosomun martyrs who were canonised in 1984.

You can mark Catholicism's eventual acceptance at the grand, Gothic **Myeongdong Cathedral** *(mdsd.or.kr)*. Completed in 1898, it features soaring arches and lovely stained-glass windows. English mass is held on Sundays at 9am.

Civic Architectural Statement

City Hall, old and new

It's impossible to miss the symbolism of the giant tsunami-wave-shaped glass building of **Seoul City Hall**, looming over the old Japanese-built civic building (now the **Seoul Metropolitan Library**). Step inside the lobby to view a vertical garden rising seven storeys high. Adjacent to the verdant walls is a 24m-tall stack of white balloons forming Jeon Sucheon's striking *Metaseosa Seobeol* art installation. Take lift 11 to the 8th floor to find the **Sky Plaza Gallery**, which holds rotating, typically Seoul-themed art exhibitions.

The grassy plaza in front of both buildings is often used for events. In winter, it turns into a skating rink (skate rentals available), while on summer weekends in recent years, it has been a venue for the Seoul Outdoor Library, filled with beanbag chairs and bookshelves.

EATING IN JUNG-GU: INTERNATIONAL EATS

Menten: Serves just two ramen varieties: *shoyu* (soy-sauce broth) and *tantanmen* (spicy broth with minced pork), both delicious. *11.40am-2.30pm & 6-7.30pm Mon-Sat* **WW**

Mari Meokja: Malaysian favourites such as *nasi lemak* and chicken curry, plus halal versions of Korean food. *8am-4.30pm, 5.30-10pm* **W**

Euljiro Las Vegas: A lively Japanese *izakaya* with a menu including udon, dumplings and highballs. *4pm-midnight Mon-Thu, to 1am Fri & Sat* **W**

Jangmanok: Chinese small plates served up beneath red lanterns and a mirror ball in Euljiro's nightlife district. *4pm-midnight, from noon Sat & Sun* **WW**

JUNG-GU AFTER DARK

When the sun goes down, Jung-gu lights up. Experience its after-hours energy on a walk through Myeong-dong, Cheonggye-cheon and Euljiro.

START	END	LENGTH
Myeongdong station, Exit 6	Euljiro neon signs alley	4km; 2hr

Come out of Exit 6 of Myeongdong station and plunge straight into Myeong-dong's nighttime shopping scene. Squeeze through the crowds to Myeongdong-gil. Once there, take a quick detour east to leave behind earthly pleasures for a bit of spiritual sustenance at majestic 1 **Myeongdong Cathedral** (p78), illuminated against the dark. Double back and chow your way through 2 **street food stalls** cooking up lamb skewers, candied fruit and much more.

Cross 3 **Seoul Plaza** (p78), where the glass 4 **City Hall** (p78) looms over its predecessor. Head to 5 **Deoksugung** (p77) by 8pm so you can see its historic palace buildings lit up and forming a captivating contrast with the surrounding skyscrapers.

Head up Sejong-daero to 6 **Cheonggye Plaza** (p76) and start a stroll down the Cheonggye-cheon, watching Seoulites at play and seeing the city lights reflect in the water. If you get to 7 **HiKR Ground** before 7.30pm, pop inside to snap some selfies on its K-Pop stages. Watch one of the laser shows at 8 **Cheonggye-cheon Digital Canvas** between 7pm and 9pm before heading to 9 **Nogari Alley** for street beers. Finish by heading down Eulji-ro 12-gil, the centre of Euljiro nightlife. The night's always young here, so after you bask in the glow of an 10 **alley of neon signs**, stick around to explore Euljiro's bars and restaurants.

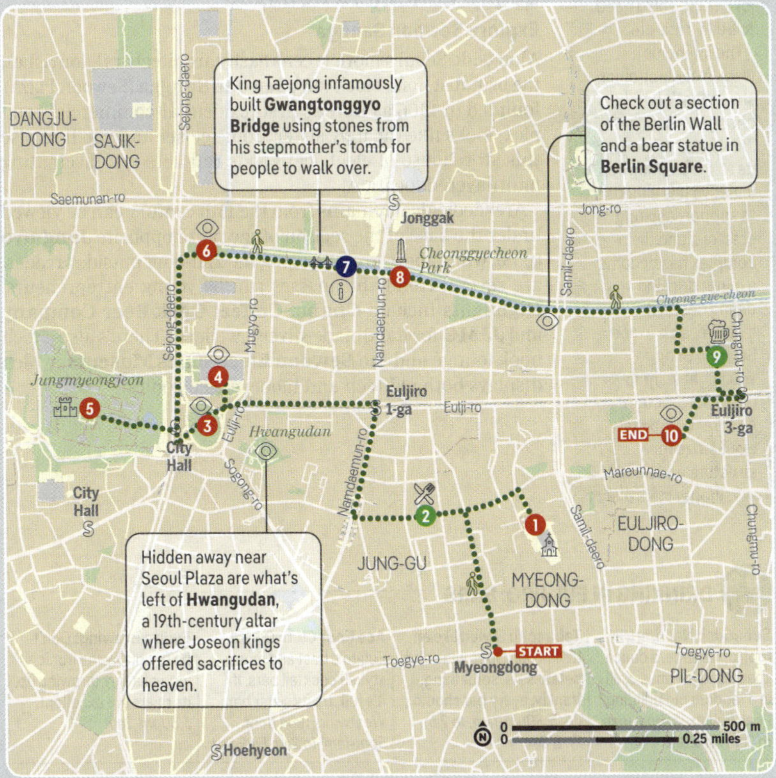

THE EVOLUTION OF SEWOON SANGGA

The concrete massif Sewoon Sangga is emblematic of Korea's 1960s development boom. It was designed by Korea's leading 20th-century architect, Kim Swoo-geun, who also designed Seoul Olympic Stadium. While it's now showing its age, Sewoon Sangga was in its day at the forefront of tech culture and a place where you could even find everything, as the joke went, you'd need to build a missile.

The interior is a warren of electronics shops that's barely changed since the '80s. More recently, its Makercity Sewoon initiative has aimed to support aspiring creators, and the complex has become a minor drinking and dining destination. If you're keen to see Sewoon Sangga, you might want to do it soon, though. A current proposal would raze the structure and build a skyscraper in its place.

CHARLES USHER

Sewoon Electronics Museum

Euljiro Landmark Remixed

Explore Sewoon Sangga

Alongside Seoul's more recent flashy architectural flourishes, the brutalist, four-block-long **Sewoon Sangga** (Sewoon Plaza), founded in 1968 as Korea's first residential-commercial complex, looks like the ugly sister. Come closer and you'll realise this storehouse of electrical-goods retailers is a fascinating multilayered location.

Archaeological remains from the 15th century can be viewed under the base of the section of the plaza opposite **Jongmyo** (p58), while above ground, along the 2nd-floor outside arcades, are several trendy businesses run by young entrepreneurs. Highlights include **Champ Coffee**, **Geek Beer Company** and **JJMG** for handmade silver jewellery . There's also a tech book lounge and the **Sewoon Electronics Museum**, which displays both old tech and modern electronics.

DRINKING IN EULJIRO: BARS

Seendosi: Neon, art, a rooftop terrace, a dance space and live music, all in a random old building? Peak Euljiro. *7.30pm-1am, to 2am Fri & Sat*

Tabacchi: Styled like an Italian bar. Does wine and gelato sets, something, frankly, every bar should do. *5.30pm-1am, to 2am Fri & Sat*

Ace Four Club: One of Euljiro's best and most stylish cocktail bars. If it's full, try its sister bar, Westwing, next door. *5pm-1am, to 2am Fri & Sat*

Euljiro Brewing: Don't be put off by the ironic logo of a guy throwing up. Its beers are excellent. *3.30pm-2am*

Itaewon & Yongsan-gu

TOP MUSEUMS | MULTICULTURAL VIBE | VIBRANT NIGHTLIFE

Boasting a multicultural restaurant scene, with a dynamism that extends to nightlife, arts, entertainment and beyond, Yongsan-gu is Seoul's ultimate district of diversity. Its most famous district is Itaewon, which has long been Seoul's most cosmopolitan neighbourhood, a place where the capital's LGBTQI+, Muslim and sex-worker communities rub shoulders.

The broader Yongsan district is dominated by the huge Yongsan Park, nestled around the country's top museum, the National Museum of Korea, and the former US Army Garrison, which is in the process of opening to the public as part of a project to revitalise the green space. The adjacent neighbourhoods of Gyeongnidan and Haebangchon (HBC for short) are diverse enclaves of laid-back restaurants, bars and cafes.

Heading east along the main drag of Itaewon-ro is the ultra-bougie Hannam-dong, the preferred neighbourhood of many a celebrity Seoulite. Over by Yongsan station is another hip pocket, Hangangno-dong.

GETTING AROUND

This is a hilly part of Seoul, but the best way to access the attractions scattered through the area is on foot.

Subway Line 6 is the best way to reach Haebangchon, Itaewon and Hannam-dong. Hangangjin is the closest station to the Leeum Museum of Art. For the War Memorial of Korea, get off at Samgakji; also transfer here to Line 4 for the National Museum of Korea and Yongsan Park, all a short walk from Ichon station. From Yongsan station, you can also access Korea's rail network.

TOP TIP

Book Park is beautiful multilevel reading lounge inside the **Blue Square** *(bluesquare.kr)* cultural space. For the price of entry (₩9900), you can browse and read a curated selection of books and enjoy a drink from the cafe. Also here is a theatre and concert hall that host big-time musicals.

Treasures from Leeum's Collection

MAP P82

Enjoy contemporary art alongside traditional crafts

Stunningly designed and arranged, the **Leeum Museum of Art** *(leeumhoam.org; adult/youth/child ₩12,000/6000/free)* balances traditional Korean works with modern and contemporary art across its three buildings, each designed by a different architect.

M1 is a fortress of terracotta bricks by Swiss architect Mario Bottal. Its exhibits focus on arts and craft from the Goryeo and Joseon dynasties and are free to view. At the bottom of a sun-drenched spiral staircase is *Gravity Stairs,* a light installation by Olafur Eliasson.

M2, a rusted stainless-steel structure designed by French architect Jean Nouvel, showcases early and mid-20th-century

continued on p84

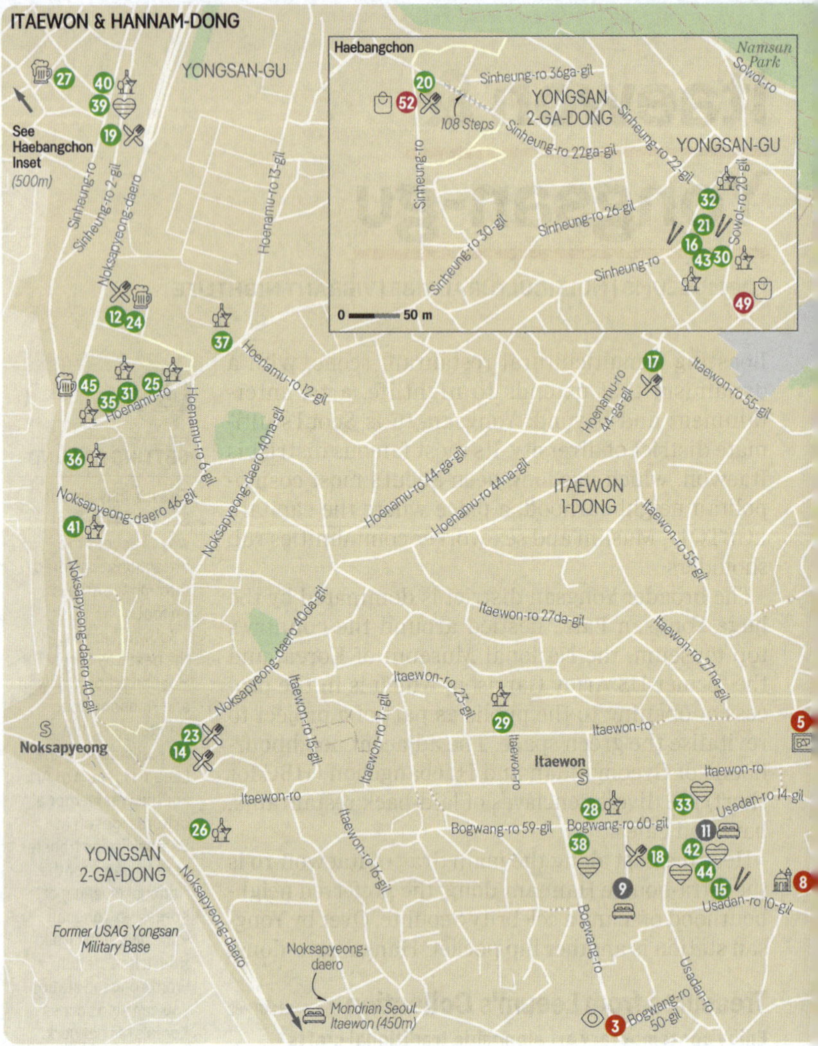

SIGHTS
1 FOUNDRY SEOUL
2 Gallery Joeun
3 Itaewon Antique Furniture Street
4 Leeum Museum of Art
5 Lehmann Maupin
6 Pace Gallery
7 Pipe Gallery
8 Seoul Central Mosque

SLEEPING
9 G Guesthouse Itaewon
10 Imperial Palace Boutique Hotel
11 Seoul Cube Itaewon

EATING
12 Baker's Table
13 Chakra
14 Crispy Pork Town
15 EID
16 Ginn-Laoo
17 Honfleur
18 Lazzat
19 Morococo Cafe
20 Normal Brunch
21 Pad Kapaw
22 Passion5
23 Petra Palace

DRINKING & NIGHTLIFE
24 Booth
25 Burn
26 Cakeshop
27 Dank Yard
28 Faust / Tanz Bar
29 Fountain
30 Gil Bar Dak
31 Jazz Garage
32 Karma
33 Kockiri
34 Lesvos
see 26 Lit Lounge
see 12 Magpie Brewshop
35 Mr Ahn's Craft Makgeolli
36 Namsan Sool Club
37 Pet Sounds

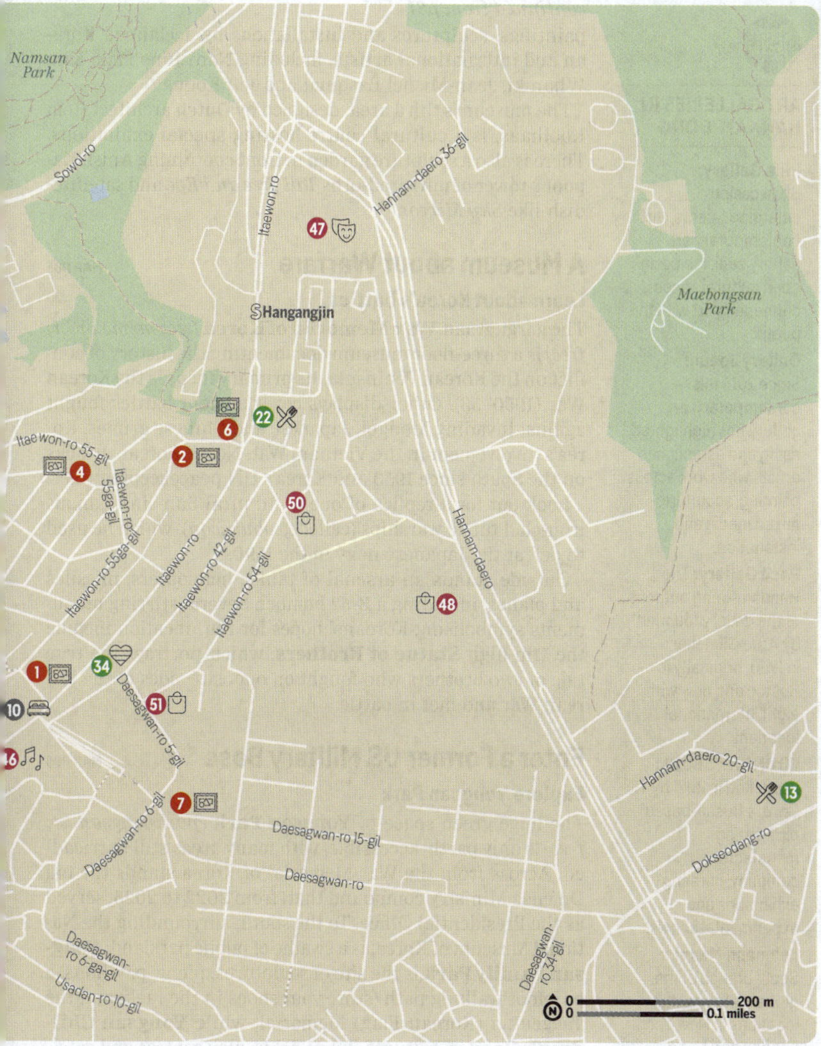

38 Queen
39 Rabbithole Arcade Pub
40 Social Haven
41 Southside Parlor
42 Trance
43 Vin Vin
44 Why Not
45 Woori Super

ENTERTAINMENT
46 All That Jazz
47 Blue Square
see 37 Boogie Woogie

SHOPPING
48 BOMARKET
49 Cat Allergy
50 Kinki Robot
51 MIMI Got the MUSEUM
52 Woori Bookstore

ART GALLERIES IN HANNAM-DONG

Pipe Gallery: Showcasing emerging talents, this contemporary art gallery seeks to be an open cultural space connecting art with the public.

Gallery Joeun: Since 2016 this contemporary-art gallery has highlighted rising and established artists who work across painting, sculpture, mixed media and installation.

Pace Gallery: The Hannam-dong outpost of the gallery founded by Arne Glimcher in 1960, originally in Boston and now with eight international locations.

FOUNDRY SEOUL: Launched in 2021 by TK Corp, a Busan-based pipe-fittings manufacturing company, curating exhibitions and experimental shows.

Lehmann Maupin: Seoul branch of the global gallery with locations in New York, London and Hong Kong. Appointment only.

continued from p81
paintings, sculptures and installations by acclaimed Korean and international artists, including Nam June Paik, Kim Whan-ki, Jean-Michel Basquiat and Jeff Koons.

The museum's third area, designed by Dutch architect Rem Koolhaas, is a cultural centre hosting special exhibitions. There is also a sculpture garden in front containing Anish Kapoor's tower of mirrored-orbs *Tall Tree and Eye* and satellite-dish-like *Sky Mirror*.

A Museum about Warfare

MAP P85

Learn about Korea's battles

The gargantuan **War Memorial of Korea** *(warmemo.or.kr; free)* is a three-floor museum documenting the history of conflict on the Korean Peninsula. Its primary focus is the Korean War (1950–53). Other displays cover ancient battles fought against invading Mongol, Japanese and Chinese armies, Korea's involvement in the Vietnam War, North Korean attacks on the South since 1953 and Korea's UN peacekeeping roles.

Look out for a replica of one of Admiral Sun-sin's famous iron-clad turtle warships (called *geobukseon*), which he used to defeat the Japanese navy in the 1590s.

Outside stands an arsenal of tanks, helicopters, missiles and planes, including a B-52 bomber. Several stirring monuments symbolising Koreans' hopes for reunification include the 11m-high **Statue of Brothers**, which portrays the true tale of two brothers who fought on opposite sides of the Korean War and met in battle.

Enter a Former US Military Base

MAP P85

Explore Yongsan Park

The huge green space of **Yongsan Park** *(parkyongsan.kr; free)* is only partly accessible, with many areas still barricaded. Across from the War Memorial of Korea stands the old Defence Ministry compound that, from 2022 to 2025, served as the Presidential Office. To the south, surrounding the National Museum of Korea, is a swathe of public parkland. **Yongsan Family Park** is the site of sculptures, picnic pavilions, a barefoot walking path (store your shoes in the rack) and the Taegeukgi (Korean Flag) Memorial, while **Yongsan Children's Garden** features sports fields, play centres and cafes.

EATING IN YONGSAN-GU: INTERNATIONAL CUISINES

MAP P82

Crispy Pork Town: Tacos and quesadillas served up in a colourful, casual setting. *noon-3pm & 5-10pm Tue-Sun* WW

Morococo Café: Spice-scented spot serving a small menu of dishes like chicken with preserved lemon and must-try 'Morocco Over Rice'. *noon-10pm Tue-Sun* WW

Petra Palace: Stop into this blink-and-you'll-miss-it joint for fresh, vibrant Middle Eastern dishes like tabouli, kebab and falafel. *11am-8pm Mon, Tue & Thu-Sun* WW

Chakra: Authentic Indian food in Hannam-dong, with a welcoming atmosphere and delicious curries, biryani and more. *11.30am-4pm & 5-10pm* WW

HIGHLIGHTS
1 National Museum of Korea

SIGHTS
2 Amorepacific Museum of Art
3 Baekbin Railroad Crossing
4 Ichon Hangang Park
5 Nodeul Island
6 War Memorial of Korea
7 Yongsan Children's Garden
8 Yongsan Family Park
9 Yongsan History Museum

Around Yongsan Children's Garden and at the **Partially Open Site**, in the park's southeast corner, you can see the former quarters of the US military. The area resembles a little America and offers a fascinating glimpse into a long-secretive space. Take a look inside the officers' complex, which displays exhibitions and art, and have a coffee at the cafe.

Textile Market Turned Hip Hangout

MAP P52

Eat and drink at Sinheung Market

The 1960s-era **Sinheung Market**, which once sold textiles, has been revived as a buzzy cultural space full of fine-dining restaurants, rooftop lounges and wine and cocktail bars with an intimate speakeasy vibe. **Ginn-Laoo** and **Pad Kapaw**, a

ITAEWON'S BEST LGBTIQ+ BARS

Lesvos: Since 1996, this lesbian bar has been a safe space for sexual minorities and women in Korea.

Rabbithole Arcade Pub: Located in Haebangchon, this basement venue offers weekly drag shows and a welcoming vibe.

Kockiri: A hip gay bar that plays disco and caters to a diverse clientele. A plus is its beautiful terrace.

Why Not: The perfect place to begin the night before hitting the clubs next door. Known for being foreigner-friendly.

Trance: Famed for its late-night drag shows, this small basement club has been a scene staple for almost three decades.

Queen: In a new location and popular among foreigners for its fun atmosphere that doesn't really get going until 2am.

EATING IN ITAEWON & YONGSAN-GU: BREAKFAST & BRUNCH

MAP P82

Normal Brunch: A normal name with an elevated menu, the food is scrumptious and presented beautifully. *11am-8.30pm Mon, Tue, Thu & Fri, 10am-8pm Sat & Sun* WW

Honfleur: Near the Grand Hyatt, a charming little restaurant with tasty pastas, smoothies and a brioche French toast that's out of this world. *9am-6pm Tue-Sun* WW

Baker's Table: Serves breakfast, sandwiches, schnitzels and bratwurst. Also bakes sweet and savoury pastries, and is generous with free samples. *8am-9pm* WW

Passion5: A pastry paradise, with more glistening, glazed treats than you can imagine, along with salads and sandwiches. *7.30am-10pm* W

TOP EXPERIENCE

National Museum of Korea

At the south end of Yongsan Park, at Ichon station, the National Museum of Korea occupies a mammoth marble-lined, modernist complex designed by architect Kim Chang-il. It's Korea's most popular museum – and one of its most accessible – and is home to a dazzling array of cultural treasures dating from prehistoric times to the Joseon dynasty

NATIONAL MUSEUM OF KOREA/WIKIMEDIA/KOGL TYPE I

Pensive Bodhisattva

TOP TIPS

- Hour-long English-language tours leave from the lobby at 10.30am and 1pm daily.
- The museum's app serves as an excellent audio guide.
- Special exhibits are half-price on Culture Day, the last Wednesday of the month.
- Virtual-reality experiences in Digital Gallery 2 require advance registration.

PRACTICALITIES

- museum.go.kr
- free
- 10am-6pm, to 9pm Wed & Sat

Collection Highlights

Among the 1st-floor galleries, don't miss the **Golden Treasures from the Great Tomb of Hwangnam**, a delicate 5th-century Silla Kingdom gold crown and belt dripping with jade gems; the **Baekje Incense Burner**, a decorative metal piece that's an extraordinary example of the artistry of the 6th- to 7th-century Baekje Kingdom, and the Goryeo-dynasty **Ten Storey Pagoda**, carved out of marble.

On the 2nd floor, the Room of Quiet Contemplation contains the 7th-century **Pensive Bodhisattva**. In the 3rd-floor sculpture and crafts gallery, view the lopsided beauty of the 18th-century **Moon Jar**, a white porcelain vessel from the Joseon dynasty. There are also several immersive digital galleries where you can see projections of paintings and 3D renderings of cultural artefacts.

Museum Grounds

Outside, the grounds are best appreciated in clear conditions, when the Great Hall is perfectly reflected in the large **Mirror Pond**. An outdoor exhibition area showcases pagodas, stupas, steles and other ancient stoneworks, such as a twin lion stone lantern from the Goryeo dynasty. The highlight is the original **Bosingak Bell**, near the picturesque **Dragon Falls**. There's also a pavilion and gardens.

duo of Thai restaurants run by Sriprateep Paw, serve authentic northeastern Thai fare, while **Vin Vin** is a sleek wine bar featuring a protein-forward menu of seafood, beef tartare and other beautifully presented plates. Follow up dinner with a cocktail at **Karma**, which boasts an impressive menu that includes nonalcoholic options, or **Gil Bar Dak**.

Riverside Revitalised

MAP P85

An artsy park plus an island

Enjoy the newly revived **Ichon Hangang Park**, undergoing restoration as part of the city's conservation efforts to regain the riverbanks' natural environment and increase its biodiversity. The redesigned park has more wetland and observations decks, and is a lovely place to have a picnic, rent a bicycle (₩3300 for one hour) and walk among the sculptures. Among the most impressive is the 8m-tall *Scroll-Flowing Stories*, a larger-than-life coil crafted out of steel and fibreglass.

Nearby, floating in the Han, **Nodeul Island** *(nodeul.org)* hosts festivals and musical and cultural performances. Check ahead to see what special events might be happening. There's also an art gallery, bookstore, lounge and several restaurants on Nodeul, closed Mondays.

Itaewon's Party Scene

MAP P82

Dance the night away

Itaewon is a top location for late-night drinking and clubbing. The lights are kept low at **Lit Lounge**, a hookah lounge known for its inclusive atmosphere and approachable staff. It's also great for dancing.

Cakeshop, a small club with a huge reputation, has been a mainstay of Itaewon's club scene for a decade. Listen to new and niche genres as well as visiting international acts.

Entertainment complex **Fountain** offers a dance floor that plays top-40 music on the 1st level, bar games on the 2nd and has a VIP lounge on the 3rd. It gets packed at peak hours.

For full-on techno, head to **Faust/Tanz Bar**, where the mood is welcoming and the party goes very, very late.

See Seoul's Little Arabia

MAP P82

Learn about the city's Muslim community

With its twin minarets rising high above 'Halal Hill', Seoul's only mosque anchors the city's Islamic community, standing

SHOPPING IN YONGSAN-GU

Kinki Robot: In Hannam-dong, wonderfully weird toys, art and lifestyle collectibles.

MIMI Got the MUSEUM: Vintage shop selling gorgeous art deco, modernist and other jewellery.

Cat Allergy: A cat-themed collectibles store brimming with all the weird and wacky trinkets you never knew you needed; it's sure to make you chuckle.

Woori Bookstore (우리책방): If dogs are more your thing, a bookstore dedicated to our beloved canine companions. Pet-friendly, of course.

BOMARKET: Kitsch, colourful kitchen and homewares shop selling vivid, modern designs.

Itaewon Antique Furniture Street: Go-to destination for antique furniture, vintage dishes, paintings, light fixtures, curios and other home decor.

DRINKING IN ITAEWON & YONGSAN-GU: OUR PICKS

MAP P82

Namsan Sool Club: Pick from more than 100 varieties of *makgeolli* and soju. *6pm-1am Mon & Wed-Fri, from 4pm Sat & Sun*

Mr Ahn's Craft Makgeolli: Sample different kinds of craft *makgeolli* paired with small plates. *6pm-midnight Sun-Thu, to 2am Fri & Sat*

Southside Parlor: A pioneer of Seoul's cocktail scene. Check out its new sister bar downstairs. *6pm-midnight Sun & Tue-Thu, to 2am Fri & Sat*

Social Haven: A mainstay of the HBC expat community, this bar specialising in Aperol spritz gets crowded after aperitif time. *6pm-2am Mon-Fri, 4pm-3am Sat, to 2am Sun*

THE ALLEYS OF HAEBANGCHON

Meaning 'Independence Village', Haebangchon is a former refugee shantytown, full of winding alleyways with plenty to reveal.

START	END	LENGTH
Undebt	Noksaypyeong station	2.2km; 1½hr

Kick off with a sugar high in Huam-dong at 1 **Undebt**, a unique cave-themed cafe converted from a Japanese colonial house. Setting the mood with stone walls and a warm-wood interior, it serves up a decadent menu of desserts. Next, come to a staircase of 2 **108 Steps**, another vestige of the occupation, which was built by the Japanese as a pathway to their Shinto shrine honouring Japanese war casualties. After liberation, the shrine was demolished but the stairs remain.

Not far beyond is 3 **Storage Book & Film**, an indie shop with an ambient playlist and some real treasures tucked within its tightly packed cases. Heading southeast to a web of alleyways, you'll stumble into 4 **Sinheung Market** (p85), which began by cooking North Korean food for war refugees and later became a centre of textiles. Today it's a hip dining and drinking sector. Just outside the market is a branch of 5 **Nuldam Space**, a small cafe chain special for selling letter-writing sets along with lattes.

Follow Sinheung-ro, the main Haebangchon street, passing a strip of international eateries and a stretch of kimchi pots stacked outside 6 **Hansin Pottery**, in operation since 1967. On the way to Noksaypyeong station, stop across the street at 7 **Coley**, a cosy corner bar with convivial vibes.

at the centre of its many Arabic restaurants, food marts and other businesses. Open to worshippers and visitors, the **Seoul Central Mosque** houses the Korean Muslim Association office on the 1st floor, the men's prayer hall on the 2nd floor and the women's prayer hall on the 3rd floor. In addition to being a place of worship, the mosque aims to educate Korea's broader public, less than 1% of whom are Muslim, mostly immigrants. Stop at the mosque (remember to wear modest clothes), then enjoy a hearty halal lunch nearby. Two recommended options: **EID** for Korean classics made halal, and **Lazzat** for halal Uzbek and Central Asian fare.

At Yongsan's Railway Crossroads

MAP P85

Hangangno-dong in transition

Hangangno-dong, the neighbourhood around Yongsan station, is an interesting pocket of central Seoul, where old town newtro vibes and futuristic smart city are colliding. Construction here of the Yongsan International Business District – a high-density vertical city with skyscrapers, some more than 100 storeys high, sky trails, green space and housing – is now underway.

For retro vibes, head first to the **Baekbin Railroad Crossing**, popularised by the K-drama *My Mister* and one of the few remaining active railroad crossings in the capital. Wait to see the trains rattling through, then wander the narrow surrounding streets, dotted with cute restaurants, bars, cafes and shops. Stop at the **Yongsan History Museum** *(museum.yongsan.go.kr; free)*, housed in a former railway station turned railroad hospital, for an overview of the area's past. The museum also has a lovely rooftop terrace.

Also check out the **Amorepacific Museum of Art** *(apma.amorepacific.com; price varies by exhibition)*, housing contemporary works on the bottom level of a corporate-office headquarters. Here you can also shop for Amorepacific beauty brands such as Sulwhasoo, Innisfree and Etude.

LIVE MUSIC IN ITAEWON

All That Jazz: A fixture on the Seoul jazz scene since 1976. There are usually two sessions of live music a night, the first starting around 7pm.

Jazz Garage: Live jazz, whisky and wine, along with barbecue, at this intimate Gyeongnidan lounge. The open-air patio spills music out onto the street.

Boogie Woogie: Get down at this neon-clad live-music den featuring local jazz acts and a smattering of blues, funk and hip-hop.

Pet Sounds: Named after Korean owner Jay's love affair with the Beach Boys' *Pet Sounds* album, this friendly upstairs rock bar features live local acts and DJs.

Burn: Blaze up a top-class Cuban, swirl your aged single malt and kick back in a leather club chair at this throwback cigar bar. Live jazz nightly (cover ₩7000).

DRINKING IN ITAEWON: CRAFT BEER

MAP P82

Woori Super: Browse the coolers, pick your poison and take a seat at a plastic table at this corner bottle shop with an amazing selection and a fun vibe. *2pm-2am*

Magpie Brewshop: Korea craft-beer pioneer pouring some of the country's finest brews. Pull up a stool at the tiny bar or duck into the pizza-pub basement. *3-11pm*

Dank Yard: A friendly HBC joint serving an excellent craft-beer selection and delicious *anju* (food eaten while drinking). *6pm-midnight Tue-Thu, to 1am Fri & Sat, 4-11pm Sun*

Booth: The original Booth brewpub looks the part with its pop-art murals and warehouse-chic interior, pouring craft suds and serving pizza since 2013. *11am-9pm*

Dongdaemun & Eastern Seoul

AMAZING ARCHITECTURE | MARVELLOUS MARKETS | VERDANT PARKS

TOP TIP
At 7pm every Thursday between April and December, there's a professional performance of traditional Korean music, dance or theatre at **Gwangmudae** (*@gwangmudae*), a theatre hidden away on the 10th floor of N building of Dongdaemun Shopping Complex.

Past and present Korean retail collide in areas around and east of Dongdaemun. Negotiate massive markets, hunt down the latest pop-ups and chill out in leafy parks.

In Dongdaemun, labyrinthine markets and malls, mostly selling fashion and fabric, orbit the spaceship-like Dongdaemun Design Plaza (DDP). Follow the Cheonggye-cheon east to Sindang, where cool cafes, hidden cocktail bars and offbeat boutiques are colonising the area's old rice warehouses near Jungang Market. Inevitably, it's been dubbed 'hip-dang'. The upmarket district of Jangchung-dong around Dongguk University subway station is also great for eats, drinks and contemporary art at Frieze House Seoul.

Further east is Seoul Yangnyeongsi Herb Medicine Market, Korea's largest herbal-medicine market, and Dapsimni, one of the best places in Seoul for antiques. The old shoemaking and light-industrial district of Seongsu-dong is now awash with trendy boutiques and cafes. It's also close to Seoul Forest, one of the city's best parks.

Historic City Wall Gate

MAP P91

Admire majestic Heunginjimun

Meaning 'Gate of Rising Benevolence', **Heunginjimun**, which is also known as Dongdaemun (Great East Gate), is one of the

GETTING AROUND

Dongdaemun or Dongdaemun History and Culture Park subway stations are best for the Dongdaemun area. Jegi-dong is the hop-off point for Yangnyeongsi Herb Medicine Market and Gyeongdong food market. Seongsu station is the main access point for trendy Seongsu, or go to Ttseukom or Seoul Forest for Seoul Forest Park.

Paths alongside the Cheonggye-cheon provide pleasant strolling between Dongdaemun and Seoul Yangnyeongsi. The market areas themselves and Seongsu are best explored on foot.

Buses are also handy for quick hops around these spread-out areas.

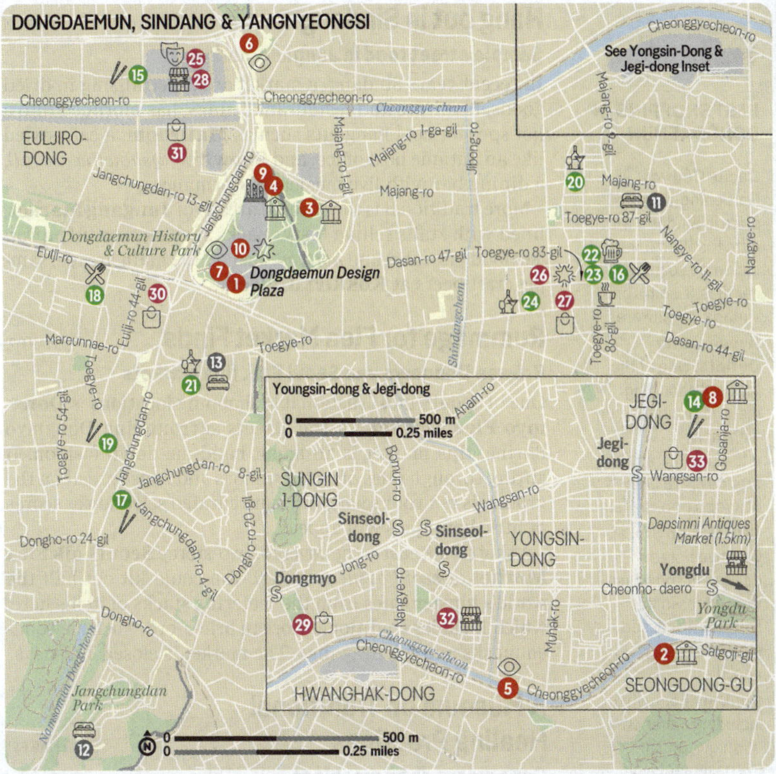

HIGHLIGHTS
1 Dongdaemun Design Plaza

SIGHTS
2 Cheonggye-cheon Museum
3 Dongdaemun History Museum
4 Dongdaemun Stadium Memorial
5 Former Pillars of Cheonggye Expressway
6 Heunginjimun
7 Oullim Square
8 Seoul K-Medi Center
9 Yigansumun

ACTIVITIES
10 Diki Diki

SLEEPING
11 ABP Sindang
12 Hotel Shilla
13 Mangrove Dongdaemun

EATING
14 Chamdajeong
15 Dongdaemun Grilled Fish Alley
16 Jungang Market
17 Soop Mama Kitchen
18 Star Samarkand
19 Woori Yeah Sool

DRINKING & NIGHTLIFE
20 Gu Seoul
21 Jean Frigo
22 Kokkiri Brewery
23 Mailroom
see 11 Manmool
24 Zoo Sindang

ENTERTAINMENT
25 Gwangmudae
26 Showflix

SHOPPING
27 Cécile Cédric
see 7 DDP Design Store
28 Dongdaemun Market
29 Dongmyo Flea Market
30 DunDun
31 Hyundai City Outlets
32 Seoul Folk Flea Market
33 Seoul Yangnyeongsi Herb Medicine Market

eight entrances through Seoul City Wall. First built in 1396, and rebuilt several times since (the last full reconstruction was 1869), the grand gate is the only one of the eight to feature an *ongseong*, a half-circle-shaped wall that's an added defence feature. Forming a traffic island, the gate is closed to pedestrians, but there are good photo ops of it from Dongdaemun Seonggwak Park to the north.

Hang out in Sindang

MAP P91

Sample street food in Jungang Market

In recent years Sindang, a market area specialising in dried goods, furniture and restaurant fittings, has morphed into a hot spot for cool hangouts such as **Mailroom**, a cafe styled like an antique post office, and **Showflix** *(@showflix_seoul)*, a dining bar with live musical performances.

More traditional is the covered arcade of **Jungang Market**, lined with stalls selling tasty snacks such as *haemul pajeon* (seafood pancake) and *hotteok*. Just off the main arcade, sample craft beers at **Kokkiri Brewery**.

Rummage for Flea Market Finds

MAP P91

Browse Dongmyo and Seoul Folk flea markets

One of Seoul's most sustainable shopping locations is **Dongmyo Flea Market**. In the streets surrounding Dongmyo Shrine, this market is all about hand-me-down fashion. If sifting through piles of clothes, shoes and bags spread on the ground is not your scene, the more curated selection at scores of little boutiques will appeal.

A short walk east is the covered, two-storey **Seoul Folk Flea Market** *(@seoulfolkfleamarket)*. You could kit out half the world's hipster cafes from the teetering stacks of items here, which includes traditional Korean bric-a-brac such as wooden masks and ink drawings. The market is closed Tuesdays.

A Museum on Traditional Healing Practices

MAP P91

Get a massage by machines

For insights into the weird and wonderful products sold at the surrounding **Seoul Yangnyeongsi Herb Medicine Market** (p94), swing by the museum at **Seoul K-Medi Center** *(kmedi.ddm.go.kr; adult/child ₩1000/500)*, which is housed in a multistorey building partly styled to resemble the Bojewon, a hospital from the early Joseon era. The centre also offers massages of hands, feet and back *(30 minutes, ₩5000)*, all done by machines! Between March and November, treat your feet to a herbal bath of mugwort and mint while sipping herbal tea *(20 minutes, ₩6000)*.

BEST SHOPPING IN DONGDAEMUN

Cécile Cédric: Gardening-themed store in Sindang with gifts for plant lovers, including scented candles, T-shirts and vintage housewares.

Hyundai City Outlets: One of the fanciest shopping malls in Dongdaemun, with many international fashion brands and a branch of Kyobo bookstore.

DDP Design Store: Creative Korean designers showcase their wares in this souvenir-focussed store stocking lots of cool items.

DunDun: For fashion, including a branch of Uniqlo, and in the basement a big 7-Eleven stocked with cosmetics and instant *ramyeon*.

Dongdaemun Market: For ready-to-wear (and made-to-measure) *hanbok* outfits, bedding and fabric accessories.

EATING IN DONGDAEMUN & JANGCHUNG-DONG: OUR PICKS

MAP P91

Dongdaemun Grilled Fish Alley: Small, no-frills restaurants specialising in tasty charcoal-grilled samchi (Spanish mackerel), plaice and other fish. *8.30am-8.30pm* ₩₩

Star Samarkand: Try *plov* (a rice and meat dish), *lagman* noodles, *manti* dumplings and freshly baked breads at this friendly Uzbek restaurant. *10am-11pm Wed-Mon* ₩₩

Woori Yeah Sool: (우리예술) Wash down plump, deep-fried prawns and delicious spicy pork ribs with house-made *makgeolli. 5-11pm Tue-Sun* ₩₩

Soop Mama Kitchen: Homemade Korean meals, including various bibimbap, as well as an all-day breakfast platter and craft beer from Jeju. *11am-8pm* ₩

TOP EXPERIENCE

Dongdaemun Design Plaza (DDP)

Designed by the late Zaha Hadid, DDP is a spaceship-like complex that's the largest 3D amorphous building in the world. An architectural landmark, it serves as a multipurpose cultural space for exhibitions, events, museums and retail and acts as a showcase for Seoul design and fashion. At night, the 222m silvery facade becomes a giant canvas for projected image and light shows.

Architecture Tours

Covered in 45,133 aluminium panels, no two alike, DDP has graceful curved walls both inside and out. Spread across five levels, it can be a confusing building to navigate – to fully appreciate its architectural ingenuity, join the free English tour at 1.30pm Tuesday to Sunday, starting from the complex's M3 entrance off Miraero Bridge.

Check the DDP website to see if rooftop tours *(₩38,000)* are running – they're well worth joining for an elevated perspective on the building and surrounds.

Dongdaemun History & Culture Park

In 2008, during the dismantling of Dongdaemun Stadium to make way for DDP, major archaeological remains were uncovered, including Seoul City Wall foundations going as far back as the late 14th century, as well other Joseon-dynasty buildings. The remains have been incorporated into Dongdaemun History and Culture Park and include the two-arched **Yigansumun** floodgate.

Dongdaemun History Museum provides the historical background to the ancient foundations preserved outside, while **Dongdaemun Stadium Memorial** presents the history of the sporting complex that occupied the site from 1925 to 2007. Two of the stadium's floodlight towers have been preserved.

TOP TIPS

- **Oullim Square** hosts an excellent farmers' and craft market *(@marchefriends)* on Sundays between April and November.
- Shop for local design products at **DDP Design Store**.
- **Diki Diki**, a fun play space for kids, is on the 4th floor of DDP Museum (closed Mondays).

PRACTICALITIES

● ddp.or.kr ● free ● 24hr

KOREAN MEDICINE MARKET

Plants form a large portion of the pharmaceutical ingredients of Korean medicine, and parts of plants that have medicinal uses are called *boncho*.

Jegi-dong, location of **Seoul Yangnyeongsi Herb Medicine Market**, has been associated with traditional medicine since the 17th century – that's when the Bojewon, providing lodging for travellers and free medical treatment for the sick and poor, was established here. It was outside the city walls to prevent the spread of infection.

Today the market has more than 1000 specialised traders and businesses. Shopfronts are piled with all manner of roots, seeds, barks, dried flowers, fruits and vegetables, from *youngji* mushrooms and cinnamon sticks to deer antlers and Korean red ginseng.

Across the central courtyard is **Chamdajeong**, a cafe serving herbal teas and traditional food such as pumpkin porridge or a lotus-leaf rice set meal.

Visit Cheonggye-cheon Museum

MAP P91

A stream through Seoul

The mammoth and costly effort to resurrect Seoul's long-buried east–west stream is detailed at **Cheonggye-cheon Museum** *(museum.seoul.go.kr; free)*. Learn how the stream evolved from a Joseon beauty spot to a sewer dubbed 'Seoul's cancer' to a beacon of urban regeneration. The museum, which is closed Mondays, is a fine starting point for a walk along the stream's banks. Head west to encounter the remains of **three concrete pillars** from the elevated highway that was dismantled before the stream's resurrection.

Treasure Trove of Korean Crafts

MAP P91

Browse Dapsimni Antiques Market

Antiques dealers have clustered in two buildings in **Dapsimni Antiques Market** since the 1980s. Here you can find a wealth of Korean arts and crafts – mostly old, sometimes new – ranging from silk tassel decorations for *hanbok* to fish-shaped wooden locks and stone carved Bodhisattva. It's a fascinating place to rummage for unique pieces. The selection of goods is also larger and prices tend to be cheaper here than at dealers in Insa-dong. The market is closed on Sundays.

Family-Friendly Parks

MAP P96

Eastern Seoul's green spaces

A hunting ground in Joseon times, **Seoul Forest** is one of Seoul's best parks. Among its attractions are an enclosure for sika deer, adventure playgrounds, butterfly and insect gardens, wetlands, a skate park and a sculpture garden.

Ttukseom Hangang Park is a base for kayak and stand-up paddleboard (SUP) operations, including English-speaking **Koa Travel** *(@koa.travel_kr)*. Paddling the Han, particularly around sunset with the light glittering off the soaring Lotte Tower and Gangnam's skyline, is especially memorable.

Enormous **Seoul Children's Grand Park** includes amusement rides, a free zoo, a botanical garden, a wetland ecology area, a giant musical fountain and a children's museum with plenty of hands-on edutainment.

DRINKING IN DONGDAEMUN & SINDANG: BARS

MAP P91

Jean Frigo: Push against a fridge door to find this chic cocktail bar hidden behind a day-time greengrocers. *6pm-1.30am Tue-Sat, 5pm-midnight Sun*

Gu Seoul: Chris Jang is the friendly, English-speaking mixologist running this spacious bar decorated with his own furniture designs. *6pm-1am Thu-Tue*

Zoo Sindang: Sip Chinese-zodiac-themed cocktails at this fun speakeasy decorated with a jungle of fake plants. *6pm-2am*

Manmool: Enjoy the retro vibes of this vintage-furnished cafe-bar serving coffee, wine, cocktails and desserts. *3pm-1am Tue-Sun*

SEONGSU STROLL

Spend a visually stimulating half-day cruising Seongsu's arty, surreal boutiques, cafes and pop-ups.

START	END	LENGTH
Onion	Seoul Brewery Seongsu	3.5km, 2hr

Fuel up on coffee and baked goods at ❶ **Onion**. Nearby, at ❷ **Amore Seongsu**, the flagship of beauty company Amorepacific, there's a lovely rock garden with grasses and trees. Further east is ❸ **Common Ground**, a hip shopping mall created from converted shipping containers.

❹ **LCDC Seoul** hosts a cute cafe, pop-up exhibitions and small stores championing Korean creatives and lifestyle brands such as Hanahzo for handmade soaps. Head south to marvel at the contemporary architecture and art at ❺ **Haus Nowhere** (p96).

A cavernous converted *changgo* (warehouse) is home to the long-running ❻ **Daelim Changgo** cafe and ❼ **Musinsa Store Seongsu@Daelim Changgo**, one of several physical branches of the major Korean online fashion platform. Gawp at the giant media globe rising three floors through ❽ **Blue Elephant Space Seongsu**. The ❾ **Dior** pop-up store has been such a hit it's likely to be around a few more years; across the way is another architectural and branding showpiece for cosmetics brand ❿ **Tamburins**.

Shop a superb range of stationery from Korea and overseas at ⓫ **Point of View**, then enjoy a beer and a bite at ⓬ **Seoul Brewery Seongsu** – you've earned it!

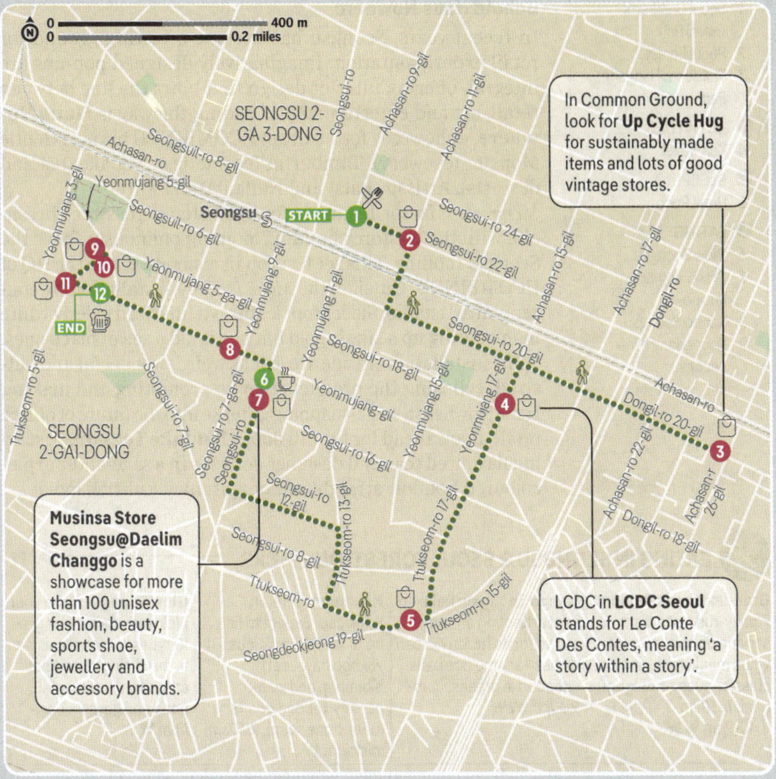

SIGHTS
1 Seoul Children's Grand Park
2 Seoul Forest
3 Ttukseom Hangang Park

ACTIVITIES
4 Koa Travel

SLEEPING
5 Hotel Poco

EATING
6 Glow Seongsu
7 Grandmother's Recipe
8 Nanpo Seongsu
9 Neungdong Minari Seongsu

Surreal Retail Playground

MAP P95

Behold Haus Nowhere

In recent years, Seongsu has become a testing ground for retail experimentation. Imaginatively designed pop-ups are integral, offering interior design that blurs the line between retail, art and entertainment. Leading the way is **Haus Nowhere**, a showcase for a suite of IICOMBINED brands: Gentle Monster (eyewear), Tamburins (cosmetics), Nudake (tea and desserts), Attissu (hats) and Nuflaat (tableware).

The wow factor begins before you step across the threshold, with the 14-storey building looming ominously above the Seongsu roofline. This sci-fi vision in concrete is also the HQ of IICOMBINED. Outside, the *More is More* installation by conceptual artist Max Siedentopf features a life-sized elderly white man holding up a single gold bin bag amid a sea of black ones.

The installations inside are just as weird, wonderful and outsized, eclipsing the products they're promoting and making Haus Nowhere a selfie-snapping glimpse into the future of offline retail. Book ahead for the 5th floor's **Nudake Teahouse**, serving flavoured teas and designer desserts in a sage-and-purple-coloured boudoir straight out of a Stanley Kubrick movie.

EATING IN SEONGSU & SEOUL FOREST: OUR PICKS

MAP P96

Grandmother's Recipe: Family-run restaurant serving delicious, great-value meals featuring classics such as bulgogi beef. *11.30am-3.40pm & 4.40-9pm* ₩₩

Nanpo Seongsu: Relaxed joint attracting a young crowd for its fusion Korean dishes – try the rice balls wrapped in greens. *11am-9.30pm* ₩₩

Neungdong Minari Seongsu: Expect to line up to sample delicious *yukhoe* (raw beef) bibimbap and water-parsley-topped *gomtang* (beef-bone soup). *9.30am-midnight* ₩

Glow Seongsu: Take your pick from stalls selling 10 types of global cuisine at this dining village set around an ornamental pond and garden. *11am-11pm* ₩₩

Western Seoul

YOUTH CULTURE | PARK LIFE | HIP NEIGHBOURHOODS

Hongdae, Seoul's principal student quarter, takes its name from resident Hongik University; it's also close by Yonsei, Sogang and Ewha Womans universities. This abundance of young people means the area has Seoul's best nightlife. Street performances by dance crews and busking musicians lend the district a perpetual carnival-like atmosphere. Nearby Yeonnam and Mangwon are hip quarters packed with cafes and boutiques.

On the Han River is Yeouido, a 3km-long and 2km-wide island home to international finance and investment firms, as well as the National Assembly. Yeouido's parks are lovely places to walk or go for a bike ride, particularly in mid-April when the cherry trees blossom. Not far away is Noryangjin, Seoul's premier fish market.

Other sights scattered across Western Seoul include Mullae Arts Village, where light industrial meets street art; lush Seoul Botanic Park; mountain hiking trails and an artificial waterfall on Ansan, and Eunpyeong Hanok Village.

TOP TIP

E-Land Cruise *(elandcruise.com)* runs an array of Han River pleasure cruises. Boats depart from a wharf just north of Wonhyo Bridge in Yeouido Hangang Park. Daytime, sunset and starlight cruises sail west to Seogang Bridge. Longer moonlight cruises sail east to Banpo Bridge's **Moonlight Rainbow Fountain** (p116).

Seoul's Fountain of Youth

MAP P98

Revel in Hongdae's nightlife

For decades, Hongdae has been at the forefront of Seoul's alternative culture. Its popularity has seen it gentrify in recent

continued on p100

GETTING AROUND

Paths along the Han River and several streams make this one of the best parts of town for cycling. Seoul Bike docking stations are ubiquitous.

Subway Line 2 loops through many popular areas, including Hongdae and Mullae. Lines 5, 6 and 9 connect Yeouido, Gongdeok and World Cup Park. The AREX provides easy access to the airports.

The hop-on, hop-off Mapo Tour Train Bus circulates through Mapo District tourist spots such as Hongdae, Gyeongui Line Forest Park and World Cup Park. Tickets are valid for a full day.

SIGHTS
1 Ansan
2 Eunpyeong Hanok Village
3 Eunpyeong Historical Hanok Museum
4 Gyeongui Line Forest Park
5 Hongdae Playground
6 Hongdae Street
7 Hongje-cheon Artificial Waterfall
8 Jingwan-sa
9 Myeongin Museum
10 Solhyangjae
11 Yeonhui Forest Rest Area

SLEEPING
12 Roi Guesthouse
13 RYSE
14 Time Travelers Relax

EATING
15 Chuncheonjip Dakgalbi & Makguksu
16 Gyeongju Sikdang
17 Hongik Sutbul Galbi
18 Joseon Sidae
19 Sinchon Hwangso Gopchang

DRINKING & NIGHTLIFE
20 Bar Da
21 Cafe Pokpo
22 Channel 1969
23 Club Ocean
24 Coffee Libre
25 d.still
26 Gopchang Jeongol
27 Irin Iljan
28 Manufact Coffee
29 MODECi
30 Morning Calm Coffee Lab
31 NB2
32 Sanullim 1992
33 Shinleedoga
34 Yri Cafe

ENTERTAINMENT
35 Club Evans
36 Club FF
37 Jebi Dabang
38 Luxury Su Noraebang

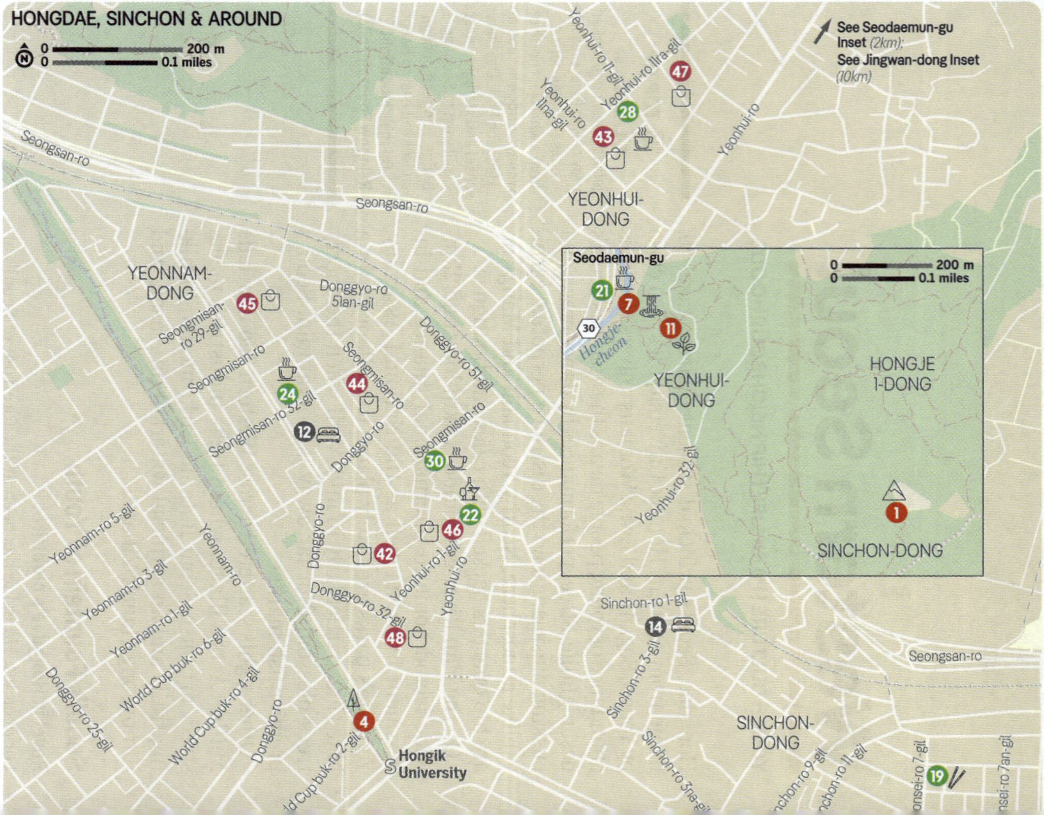

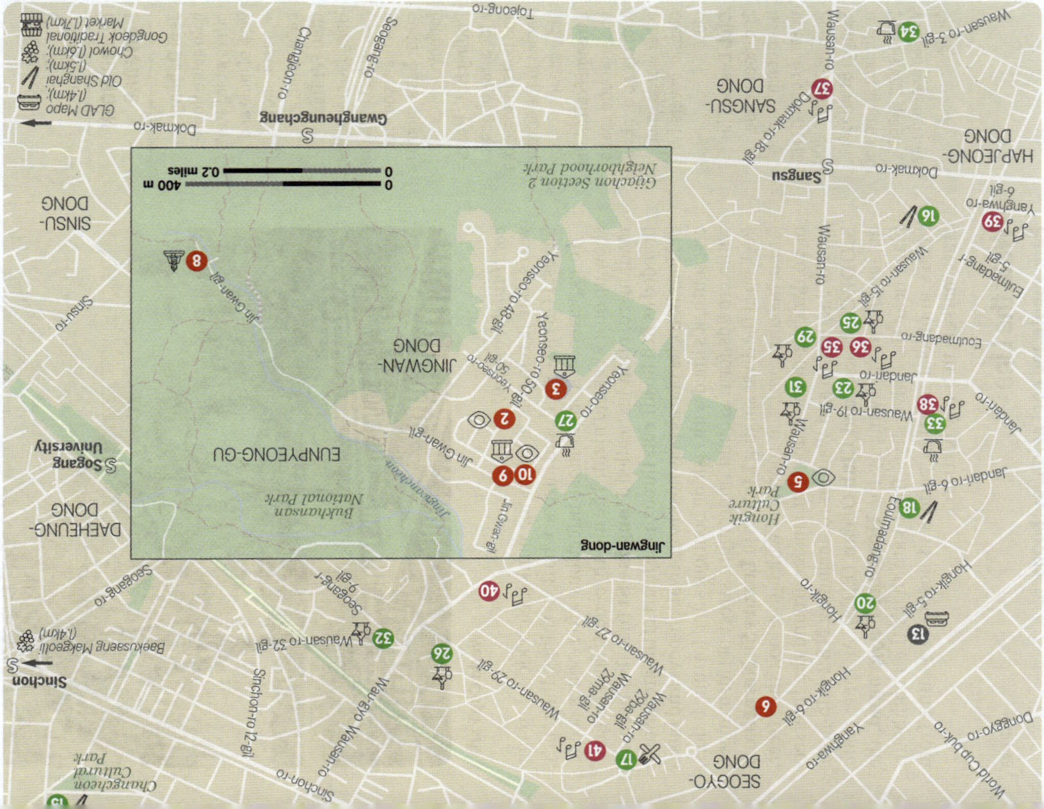

39 Rolling Hall
40 Senggi Studio
41 Strange Fruit
● SHOPPING
42 Acorn Caricature
43 Banul Story
44 Bowlow
45 Gravel
46 Juuneedu
47 YOUR-MIND
48 Youssoful

CLUBBING IN HONGDAE

Jebi Dabang: A hole in the floor offers a bird's-eye view of indie and acoustic shows in the basement.

Club FF: This Hongdae staple likes it loud. Mostly sticks to a tried-and-true guitar-bass-drums formula.

Rolling Hall: Hosts a wide array of genres and pulls in some big names in the Korean indie scene.

Strange Fruit: A tiny underground space with cheap drinks – in other words, your classic university club.

Club Evans: This 2nd-floor venue has been nurturing up-and-coming jazz musicians since 2001.

Senggi Studio: A recording studio and performing space with an experimental streak.

SANGA PARK/SHUTTERSTOCK

World Cup Park

continued from p97
years, but it remains a haven for punks, club kids, hip-hop heads, LGBTIQ+ youth and anyone who does things differently.

To experience Korea's most infectious after-hours scene, show up on a weekend night. The mostly pedestrianised Eoulmadang-ro, often just called **Hongdae St** (it's also been rebranded as Red Road), cuts through the heart of the area. North of Hongik-ro, its plazas play host to festivals, b-boys and buskers; south, it's lined with fashion boutiques and fortune tellers, while crowds form around impromptu street performances. Peek up at the divas singing karaoke in **Luxury Su Noraebang** *(sunoraebang.com)*, the rooms of which overlook the street, or go dancing in the clubs that cluster around the intersection of Jandari-ro and Wausan-ro, including **NB2** (hip-hop), **MODECi** (house) and **Club Ocean** (EDM). At some point during the night, swing by the **Hongdae Playground**, the plaza near the university's front gate that's the neighbourhood's unofficial meeting point and hosts everything from craft markets to b-boy battles.

Walk the Line

MAP P98

Park people and cool neighbourhoods

Built atop former railroad tracks, the 6.3km **Gyeongui Line Forest Park** extends from Hyochang Park station to Gajwa station. Its most popular stretch is right outside Hongdae University

EATING IN HONGDAE

MAP P98 & P102

Hongik Sutbul Galbi: A Hongdae institution popular for late-night pork barbecue that's grilled over charcoal for a richer flavour. *3.30pm-4am* WW

Spacca Napoli: Owner Lee Young-woo trained in Naples, and his cosy spot was recently named Korea's best pizzeria. *11.30am-3pm & 5-9.30pm Wed-Sun* WW

Gyeongju Sikdang: Grilled meat and Korean comfort food served in a house that feels like the chef's home. *11.30am-3.30pm & 5.30-11pm* WW

Joseon Sidae: A Joseon-dynasty-themed bar/restaurant done up to look like a traditional tavern. *4.30pm-2.30am Sun-Thu, to 4am Fri & Sat* WW

station, where it's a proper urban planner's dream. Maples and ginkgos flank patches of grass, locals walk dogs, photographers set up fashion shoots and visitors criss-cross the park on their way to the surrounding restaurants, photo booths and board-game cafes. Dive into the streets to the northeast to explore Yeonnam, a trendy neighbourhood bursting with small cafes and indie shops of the sort that used to fill Hongdae before its rents shot up. Keep angling northeast, across Seongsan-ro, to check out the Yeonhui area, which has similar, if slightly more upscale, vibes, with jewellery ateliers, gelato shops and the like.

Seoul's World Cup Showpiece

MAP P102

Soccer, spa and parks

Seoul World Cup Stadium was built for the 2002 FIFA World Cup, which Korea co-hosted with Japan. Its roof resembles a traditional kite. Today the stadium hosts national team matches and is the home ground of FC Seoul. Within the stadium you'll find **World Cup Spa Land 24**, a 24-hour *jjimjilbang* with hot baths and saunas, a department store and movie theatre.

World Cup Park was built atop what was once a giant landfill. The enormous green space is divided into five smaller parks. Across the bridge from World Cup Stadium, **Pyeonghwa Park** features a pond and is a popular picnic spot. Westwards, **Haneul Park** offers excellent views across the city, art installations and photo ops amid fields of silver grass. The adjacent **Noeul Park** is known for its hilltop campsites. To the north is **Nanji-cheon Park**, where wooden boardwalks cross the water and kids fly kites on a large lawn. To the south, along the river, **Nanji Hangang Park** has more campsites and boardwalks snaking through a marsh that's home to otters and waterfowl.

Out With Oil, In With Art

MAP P102

Explore a reimagined industrial space

Four giant fuel tanks have been reimagined as an exhibition pavilion, amphitheatre, culture complex and media hall, while a fifth has been preserved in its original form at

BEST YEONNAM & YEONHUI SHOPS

YOUR-MIND: An art bookstore that also stocks 'zines and stationery. Sometimes hosts local artist pop-ups.

Bowlow: This men's fashion brand sells *au courant* styles in muted tones, from jackets to bags.

Acorn Caricature: Get a cute K-Cartoon drawn of yourself.

Youssoful: Local cosmetics brand that makes perfume, hand cream and diffusers.

Juuneedu: Sells charming women's pyjamas that'll have you looking forward to Sunday mornings.

Banul Story: Shelves full of colourful yarn and other knitting supplies, plus knitted hats, scarves and sweaters.

Gravel: This vintage shop specialises in things like French work jackets and skateboard backpacks.

DRINKING IN HONGDAE: OUR PICKS

MAP P98 & P102

Bar Da: Largely unchanged over 20 years, this 2nd-floor hideout is a favourite of locals and expats alike. *7pm-2am Sun-Thu, 6pm-3am Fri & Sat*	**UniQorn Craft Beer & Wine:** Laid-back and LGBTIQ+-friendly, with vegan food options on a quiet side street. *5pm-2am Wed-Sun, 6pm-midnight Mon & Tue*	**Gopchang Jeongol:** Classic '60s to '90s pop occasionally inspires singalongs at this enthusiastically retro bar. *7.30pm-1am Tue-Thu, to 2am Fri & Sat*	**Shinleedoga:** A bit of Bukchon in Hongdae, this lovely *hanok* cafe has a courtyard with a small pond that becomes a firepit in winter. *11am-11.30pm*
d.still: Hongdae for adults. A low-key establishment serving elevated cocktails in a speakeasy setting. *7pm-2am, closed 1st Sun of the month*	**Sanullim 1992:** Sample some of 250 different traditional alcohols – *makgeolli*, soju and more – at this joint styled like a country *jumak* (tavern). *5pm-1am Tue-Sun*	**Seoul Brewery:** A sleek brewery making six year-round brews plus seasonal offerings and 'wild beers' fermented with wild yeast. *5pm-midnight, from 1pm Sat & Sun*	**Yri Cafe:** A neighbourhood staple, this boho cafe has packed bookshelves and sometimes hosts evening concerts or author talks. *11am-midnight*

SIGHTS
1 Haneul Park
2 Jeoldusan Martyrs' Shrine
3 Nanji Hangang Park
4 Nanji-cheon Park
5 Noeul Park
6 Oil Tank Culture Park
7 Pyeonghwa Park
8 Seoul World Cup Stadium
9 World Cup Park

ACTIVITIES
10 World Cup Spa Land 24

EATING
11 Spacca Napoli

DRINKING & NIGHTLIFE
12 Seoul Brewery
13 UniQorn Craft Beer & Wine

Oil Tank Culture Park *(parks.seoul.go.kr/culturetank)*. A sixth structure, a community space with a cafe and library, was constructed out of the dismantled pieces of two other tanks. Wander the grounds (open 24 hours) – once a designated national-security facility – stopping at the tanks (closed on Mondays) to appreciate the architecture and artwork and to snap some post-industrial pics.

DRINKING IN YEONNAM & YEONHUI: OUR PICKS

MAP P98

Coffee Libre: Look for the *lucha libre* mask to find this cafe, which helped kick-start Korea's craft-coffee revolution. *11.30am-8pm*

Morning Calm Coffee Lab: This very Zen place has a rock garden out back and a temple-like basement with a reflecting pool. *10am-10pm*

Channel 1969: Attracting a more mature crowd, this bar has DJs spinning anything from J-Pop to psychedelic, plus concerts. *7pm-midnight Wed, Thu & Sun, to 2am Fri & Sat*

Manufact Coffee: A sleek upstairs space with an industrial vibe and a bar and seating area that blend into one another. *8.30am-6.30pm*

Sign up for Some Makgeolli 101

MAP P98

Join a class or tasting

Makgeolli, an unrefined rice wine, is a uniquely Korean alcoholic drink. Long dismissed as a farmer's brew, it's now treated with the same seriousness as beer and whisky, and craft *makgeolli* breweries have sprung up all over the country. Learn how to make your own at **Baekusaeng Makgeolli** *(baekusaeng.com)*, a brewery in Ahyeon Market. If you don't have time for a full class, craft *makgeolli* brewer **Chowol** *(chowolhada.com)* offers short tasting sessions in its basement space near Mapo station.

A Waterfall in the City

MAP P98

Hike Ansan's mountain trails

A relatively easy climb, 296m **Ansan** is topped with a *bongsudae*, a beacon tower used to relay smoke signals during the Joseon dynasty. The mountain's numerous trails include the accessible Ansan Jarak-gil. On the northwest flank is **Yeonhui Forest Rest Area**, filled with flower beds, a herb garden and a babbling stream. From here, you might be able to hear the soothing sounds of **Hongje-cheon Artificial Waterfall**, which pours off the mountain's base and into Hongje stream. Admire the scene from a small beach, a beanbag chair or the large **Cafe Pokpo** across the stream.

Visit Eunpyeong Hanok Village

MAP P98

...and a prestigious Buddhist temple

Way up in Seoul's northwest corner is **Eunpyeong Hanok Village**, the city's largest neighbourhood of neo-*hanok* – two-storey structures that combine traditional materials and craftsmanship with modern technologies. The views of Bukhansan and the homes' tiled roofs from **Irin Iljan**, a cafe at the village's entrance, are breathtaking and as close to a Joseon landscape as you'll get in Seoul. To learn about *hanok* construction and local history, visit the adjacent **Eunpyeong Historical Hanok Museum** *(museum.ep.go.kr; adult/child ₩1000/500)*, closed Mondays. As you wander the village's charming streets, two more good places to drop in are **Myeongin Museum**, which displays a collection of masks from around Asia and Africa, and **Solhyangjae** a cultural space where you can partake in a tea tasting.

From the village it's a pleasant walk to **Jingwan-sa** *(jinkwansa.org)*, which dates to at least the first years of the 11th century.

continued on p106

SEASONAL EVENTS

Yeouido Spring Flower Festival: Crowds flock to Yeouido to view the many cherry trees and other flowers in full bloom. *April*

Hangang River Festival: Events in the riverside parks include outdoor movie screenings, concerts and circus acts. *July & August*

Seoul International Fireworks Festival: Spectacular displays of aerial artistry in the skies over Yeouido. *Late September/early October*

Red Road Festival: Buskers, art exhibitions, flea markets and more along Red Road in central Hongdae. *October*

Seoul Silver Grass Festival: Cultural and music festival against the illuminated backdrop of Haneul Park's silver grass. *October*

EATING IN WESTERN SEOUL: OUR PICKS

MAP P98

Sinchon Hwangso Gopchang: If you're keen to try *gopchang* (offal) barbecue, this decades-old joint in lively Shinchon is a good pick. *2pm-1.30am* ₩₩

Chuncheonjip Dakgalbi & Makguksu: Chuncheon-style *dakgalbi* (spicy stir-fried chicken) cooked at your table with add-ins like cheese and noodles. *11am-3pm & 4-10.30pm Tue-Sun* ₩₩

Old Shanghai: Stop here for a pot of beef or lamb *malajeongol* (spicy stew with numbing pepper). It also serves great dumplings. *4pm-1am* ₩₩

Gongdeok Traditional Market: A cluster of market restaurants specialise in *jokbal* (pork trotters) or *jeon* (savoury fried pancakes). *hours vary* ₩₩

TAKE A SPIN AROUND YEOUIDO

Flat terrain and pretty parks make Yeouido perfect for cycling. Hop on two wheels to explore the island's architecture and green spaces.

START	END	LENGTH
National Assembly station, Exit 3	KDB Bank Building	8km; 1½hr

Grab a public Seoul Bike from the docking station outside National Assembly station, Exit 3, and pedal in the direction of the domed 1 **National Assembly Building**. Soon after, you'll pass 2 **Yoido Full Gospel Church**, which boasts the biggest congregation of any church in the world.

Briefly pop into Yeouido Park to take a pedestrian tunnel to 3 **Mulbit Sq**, where kids splash in the fountains and shallow pool. Take your time pedalling through 4 **Yeouido Hangang Park**, stopping to take in the river views or slurping up some convenience-store ramen when the mood strikes.

The golden, 249m 5 **63 Square** used to be Korea's tallest building. It now hosts a branch of France's Centre Pompidou. Round the island's corner and you'll come upon a traditional Turkish vineyard house in 6 **Jamae Park**, which celebrates Seoul's sister-city relationship with Ankara.

Cross the street and head down into the beautiful 7 **Yeouido Saetgang Ecological Park**, where you'll find reed beds, ponds and waterfowl. Head back up to street level and ride to 8 **Yeouido Park**. Its trees, ponds and pavilions are a stark departure from the surrounding skyscrapers. When you're done, return your ride to the Seoul Bike docking station in front of the KDB Bank Building.

TOP EXPERIENCE

Noryangjin Fisheries Wholesale Market

Seoul's largest seafood market, Noryangjin Fisheries Wholesale Market, opened in 1927 and has occupied its current building since 2016. About 300 tonnes of marine products – half of all the capital's seafood – pass through here every day. Explore some 700 stalls to encounter sea creatures you've probably never seen before, tuck into the freshest fish in the city and stick around for the spectacle of late-night auctions.

Market Stalls

Noryangjin's stalls are spread across the building's 1st and 2nd floors. Wander the aisles to see crabs stacked like Frisbees, ribbony silver cutlass fish and rubber-booted fishmongers displaying some serious knife skills. It's fine to gawk and take pictures – vendors are used to it – but stay aware of your surroundings. The place is a hive of activity, with workers scooping fish out of tanks and rolling dollies through the aisles. For the liveliest action, come between midnight and 3am Monday to Saturday, when the fish auctions are held.

Eating at Noryangjin

For the full market experience, pick out a fish and eat it at one of the 2nd-floor restaurants. Haggling is expected at stalls, so have a calculator app at the ready. Many vendors partner with specific restaurants, in which case someone will lead you to the appropriate establishment. The most typical preparations include *hoe* (sashimi) and *maeuntang* (spicy fish soup). If you don't know where to start in the market, some restaurants, such as **Busan Ilbeonji**, can help with interpretation, or you can just order off a restaurant's menu. You can also buy presliced sashimi platters at many stalls. Feeling adventurous? Try *gaebul* (penis fish, a type of spoon worm), *sannakji* (sliced live octopus) or *hongeo* (fermented skate). Just be warned: there are no refunds.

TIPINGATO/GETTY IMAGES

TOP TIPS

- Wear close-toed shoes and clothes that can withstand an errant splash or two.
- You'll find more upscale restaurants on Noryangjn's 5th floor.
- Cross the 3rd-floor car park to find a deck with killer views of the golden **63 Square** (p104) building.

PRACTICALITIES

- susansijang.co.kr
- free
- 24hr

BEST OFF-THE-BEATEN TRACK SPOTS

Yangcheon Hyanggyo: Dating to 1411, this quiet complex is Seoul's only remaining *hyanggyo* (Joseon-era Confucian academy).

Daerim-dong Chinatown: The neighbourhood around Daerim station is home to a large Chinese population; accordingly, it has some of Seoul's best Chinese food.

Dongjak District Office: In 2025 the office unveiled a twisting three-storey slide called the D-Lide. Who says bureaucrats don't know how to have fun?

Pureun Arboretum: The city's first municipal arboretum, with a cafe, walking paths, several themed gardens, a pond and flower beds.

Gocheok SkyDome: If the game at Jamsil Baseball Stadium is rained out, you can still watch the Kiwoom Heroes play at their domed park.

continued from p97

Most of the complex was destroyed in a fire during the Korean War, but it's been beautifully rebuilt and enjoys a lovely setting in the Bukhansan foothills. Savour the atmosphere at a pleasant thatch-roofed teahouse, or take part in a three-hour templestay program.

A New Kind of Industrial Park

MAP P107

Witness Seonyudo's transformation

In the 1970s, a water treatment plant was built on Seonyudo, an island in the Han River. In the early 2000s, when the island was turned into **Seonyudo Park**, the redundant plant's infrastructure was incorporated into the park's award-winning design. Set aside a couple of hours to explore the island, where a former chemical settling basin has been turned into a multilevel aquatic garden, and other parts of the plant have been reborn as amphitheatres and play areas. To reach the island, walk across the footbridge north of Seonyudo station, disembark at the island's Seonyudo Park bus stop, or cycle across Yanghwa Bridge from one of the neighbouring stretches of Hangang Park.

Mullae's Creative Spark

MAP P107

Where art and industry coexist

In the area south of Mullae station, machine shops line the streets, filling the air with clanking and the acrid smell of hot metal. But dive into the alleys and you'll find yourself in **Mullae Arts Village**, where young creatives have transformed empty factories into visual-art studios. South of Dorim-ro, in particular, you'll come across numerous small galleries, ateliers, watering holes and restaurants serving everything from traditional Korean to upmarket Italian. It's a photogenic neighbourhood where street art abounds, so take your time poking around. Come on a weekday when the machinists are at work to get the full industrial-artistic experience, or show up at night or on a weekend to see the artworks on closed shop doors on display. Be sure to also drop by the small **Gong Gan Tou** *(gongcraft.net)* and **Seoul Art Space Mullae** *(sfac.or.kr)* to see what's showing in their galleries.

Heaven for Plant Lovers

MAP P107

Take a global botanic journey

Featuring plants from a dozen countries, **Seoul Botanic Park** *(botanicpark.seoul.go; adult/child ₩5000/2000)* feels a world apart from urban Seoul. The superbly designed park's unique concave greenhouse features multiple climate zones and a skywalk for up-high viewing. Eight exterior themed gardens include a 'meditative garden' designed according to traditional Korean aesthetics, and a 'windy garden' where you can listen to the sounds of swaying silver grass. Trails connect to a lake surrounded by irises and a wetland with a footbridge crossing to the Han River. Also here is a library, places to eat, a rooftop observatory and an aquaponics-powered smart farm.

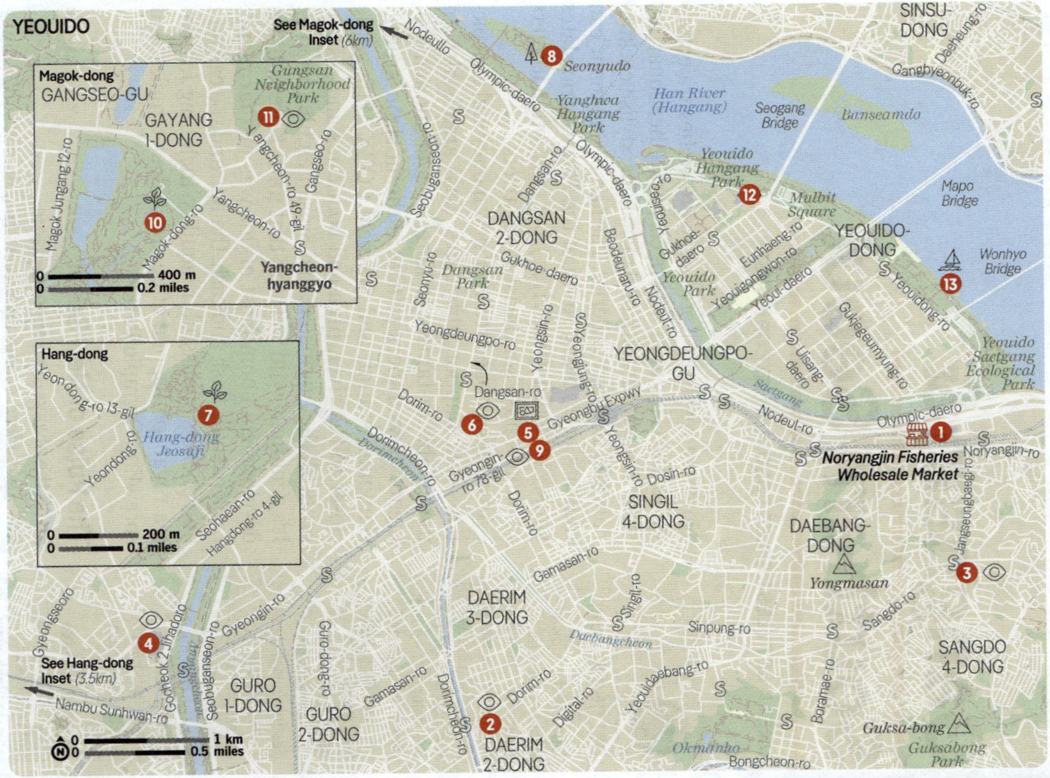

★ **HIGHLIGHTS**

1 Noryangjin Fisheries Wholesale Market

● **SIGHTS**

2 Daerim-dong Chinatown
3 Dongjak District Office
4 Gocheok SkyDome
5 Gong Gan Tou
6 Mullae Arts Village
7 Pureun Arboretum
8 Seonyudo Park
9 Seoul Art Space Mullae
10 Seoul Botanic Park
11 Yangcheon Hyanggyo
12 Yeouiseo-ro

● **ACTIVITIES**

13 E-Land Cruise

● **EATING**

see 1 Busan Ilbeonji

Gangnam & Southern Seoul

LUXE LIFESTYLES REFLECT SEOUL'S METEORIC RISE

GETTING AROUND

Line 2 of the subway connects several major stations, including Gangnam, Samseong and Jamsil. Line 3 and the Suin-Bundang Line are major north–south routes, while Lines 5 and 8 go to Olympic Park and Seoul's eastern reaches.

Buses reach destinations without immediate subway access, including the Seoul Arts Center (bus 406 to Seoul Arts Center) and Seorae Village (bus Seocho 13 to Seorae Village Entrance).

Gangnam is more car-centric than other parts of Seoul, but remains highly walkable within individual neighbourhoods. Apgujeong, Garosu-gil and Seorae Village are especially good areas to explore on foot.

Nowhere revels in Korea's rags-to-riches trajectory quite like Gangnam, where corporate headquarters share boulevards with designer shops, stylish cocktail bars and sleek art galleries. The name 'Gangnam' can indicate everything south of the Han (it translates simply to 'south of the river'), but most often it refers to Seoul's posh southeastern districts.

An oft-lampooned realm of new money and conspicuous consumption, this upper-class area is also an undeniable testament to Korea's economic achievements. Skyscrapers puncture the horizon around Gangnam station and Starfield COEX Mall, while closer to the river, high-end boutiques and restaurants fill the Apgujeong and Sinsa neighbourhoods. It's genuinely wild to think that until Korea's 1970s development boom most of this was just farmland. Look past the flash and cash, though, and you can still find pockets of blissful tranquility, including Joseon-era royal tombs, one of Seoul's oldest temples and sprawling Olympic Park.

The Pulse of New Seoul

MAP P110

Stroll the always-on Gangnam-daero

Korea's modern economic success is reflected in the shiny glass facades of skyscrapers lining Gangnam-daero between Gangnam and Sinnonhyeon stations. Headliners include the **GT Tower** near Gangnam station, its wavy blue form seeming to perpetually bake in a heat haze, and the aptly named **Urban Hive**, near Sinnonhyeon station. Designed by Kim In-Cheurl, its unusual honeycomb exterior helps support the building. Beneath the towers, shoppers and office workers pack the footpaths. Join the crowds filling their bags with makeup from **Chicor** *(chicor.com)* and clothing from **Musinsa** *(musinsa.com)*, or just soak up the K-Culture vibes: pop music pouring out of cosmetics stores, idols shilling contact lenses from giant video billboards and visitors still crossing their wrists and striking a pose at the **Gangnam Style**

Starfield COEX Mall, Starfield Library (p112)

'Horse Dance' Stage, a decade after Psy's satirical hit put the district on everyone's playlist.

Final Royal Resting Places

MAP P110

Contemplate the Seonjeongneung tombs

Amid the Gangnam skyscrapers, the earthen mounds of the **Seolleung and Jeongneung Royal Tombs** *(royal.khs.go.kr; adult/child ₩1000/free)*, often referred to as Seonjeongneung, cut a relatively modest figure. On the west side is Seolleung, the twin tombs of King Seongjong and Queen Jeonghyeon. Their son King Junjong's tomb, Jeongneung, lies to the east. At each tomb, pass through the red *hongsalmun* gate and follow the route later kings used when paying their respects. Keep off the upper path, the *sindo*, which is reserved for spirits. Also on site is a small history centre, while serene trails threading the forested premises take you past a tomb-keeper's house and royal kitchen. Seonjeongneung is closed on Mondays.

Mall That Has It All

MAP P110

Entertain yourself at Starfield COEX

The gargantuan **Starfield COEX Mall** *(starfield.co.kr/coexmall)* packs in enough to keep you occupied for an entire

continued on p112

SYMBOLS IN STONE

Joseon-dynasty royal tombs aren't mere mausoleums. They're elaborate arrangements, the elements of which are imbued with important symbolic meaning. Flanking the burial mounds are *seokho*, stone guardian tiger deities that protect the tomb, and *seogyang*, stone sheep that repel evil spirits and ensure the deceased's peaceful repose. Just in front of these are *mangjuseok*, towers meant to guide the soul home. Further forward are several *muninseok*, stone scholars and military officers who serve and guard the dead monarch, along with their stone horses. In front of these and near the building for memorial rites is the *bigak*, a monument engraved with the king's or queen's accomplishments, lest anyone forget.

EATING IN GANGNAM: KOREAN COMFORT FOOD

MAP P110

Muwol Table: An inviting eatery serving elegantly presented home-cooking classics like bulgogi and *bossam* (boiled pork belly) with cool barley tea. *11am-10pm* ₩₩

Gangnam Gyoja: Specialises in big bowls of *kalguksu* (handmade knife-cut noodles) and steamed pork dumplings. Has English menus with pictures. *10.30am-9pm* ₩

Neurin Maeul Brewery: The 'Slow Village' brewpub serves savoury pancakes and other filling faves alongside its own *makgeolli*. *5pm-midnight Mon-Sat, 4-11pm Sun* ₩₩

Mom Korean Bistro: In Seorae Village, Mom gives home cooking the French-bistro treatment. The bibimbap lunch specials are terrific value. *11.30am-3pm & 5-9pm Tue-Sun* ₩

GANGNAM-GU & SOUTHERN SEOUL

HIGHLIGHTS
1 Bongeun-sa

SIGHTS
2 'Dosan' Ahn Chang-ho Memorial Hall
3 Gangnam Style 'Horse Dance' Stage
4 GT Tower
5 Horim Museum
6 Jamwon Hangang Park
7 Ktown4u
8 Montmartre Park
9 Moonlight Rainbow Fountain
10 Seolleung and Jeongneung Royal Tombs
11 Seorae Village
12 Seoripul Park
13 Some Sevit
14 Urban Hive
see 5 White Cube Seoul

ACTIVITIES
15 Fold and Tie
16 Jenny House
17 SEA LIFE COEX, Seoul Aquarium
18 Spa Lei
19 Starfield Library

SLEEPING
20 H Avenue Hotel Yeoksam
21 Josun Palace
22 Owall Hotel

EATING
23 Gangnam Gyoja
24 Jeongdon
25 Jinmi Pyeongyang Naengmyeon
26 Jungsik
27 Mingles
28 Mom Korean Bistro
29 Monks Butcher
30 Muwol Table
31 Neurin Maeul Brewery
32 One Degree North
33 Orabang

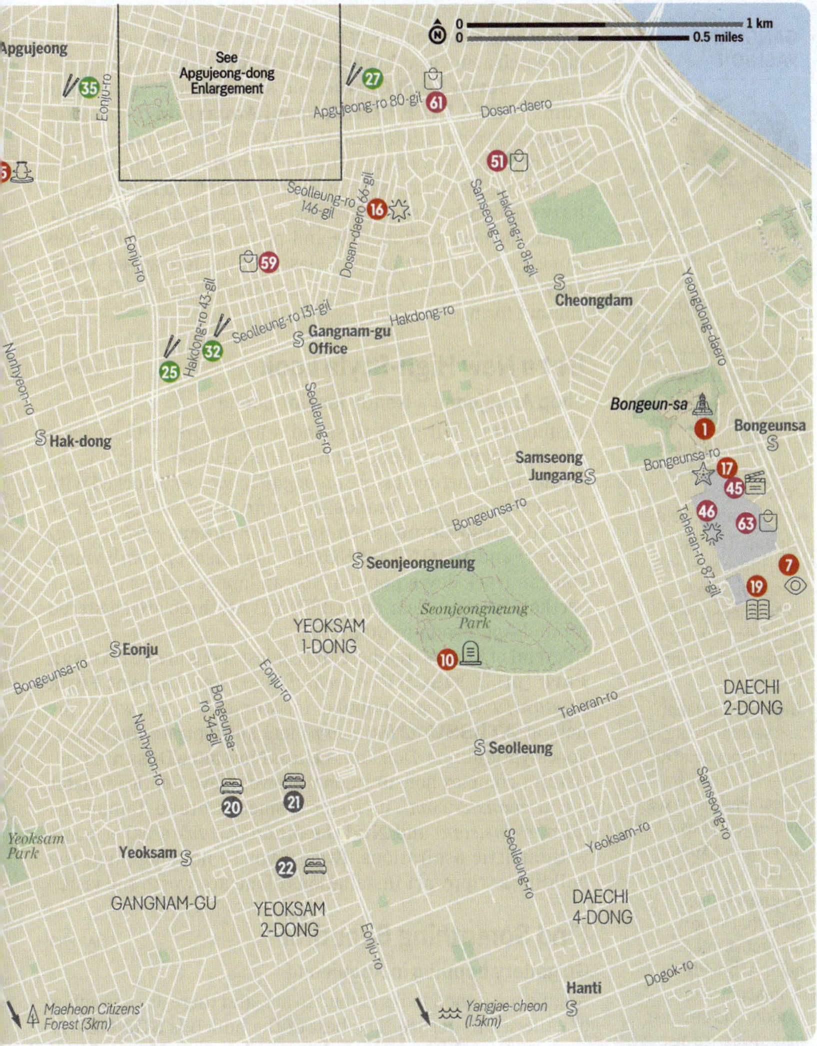

34 Ryunique
35 Samwon Garden
36 Soigné
37 Solsot
38 Yukgak Gogi

DRINKING & NIGHTLIFE

39 Alice Cheongdam
40 Bar Tea Scent
41 Maillet
42 Nudake
43 Pine&Co
44 Zest

ENTERTAINMENT

45 Megabox COEX
46 Seven Luck Casino

SHOPPING

47 10 Corso Como
48 ATiiSSU
49 Beaker
50 BOONTHESHOP
51 Brown Hat
52 Chicor
53 Fromagerie Le Meunier
54 Glowny
55 Instant Funk
56 Klairs
57 MSCHF
58 Musinsa
59 Notdam
60 Opener
61 Seoul House of Dior
62 Sinoon
63 Starfield COEX Mall
64 Sulhwasoo
65 Toudou

TOP TIP

Korea has become a major destination for medical tourism, and not just plastic surgery, which grabs most of the headlines, but for dental care, dermatology and plenty more. If you're considering treatment, the **Gangnam Medical Tour Center** *(medicaltour.gangnam.go.kr)* provides information, arranges consultations and offers interpretation support.

continued from p109

day or more. Beyond its 250-plus shops and restaurants, you can catch a movie at **Megabox COEX** cinema, test your fortune at **Seven Luck Casino** and see sharks, rays and penguins at **SEA LIFE COEX, Seoul Aquarium** *(visitsealife.com/coex-seoul; adult/child ₩35,000/31,000)*. Young ones will delight in the daily otter feedings and mermaid performances.

At the mall's centre is the eye-candy **Starfield Library** and its two-storey bookshelves. A must for K-Pop fans is **Ktown4u**, which includes a shop, cafe and photo zone. Aspiring idols can even take dance or voice classes at the **Ktown4u Academy** *(ktown4uacademy.com)*. Enquire using the website's contact form.

Get a New High-Style Look

MAP P110

Shop Apgujeong's trendy fashion scene

Fashionistas will want to spend a few hours in the streets around Apgujeong Rodeo station. Just outside the exit is the **Galleria** department store *(dept.galleria.co.kr)*, stocked with international luxury brands. For more street swagger, check out **10 Corso Como** *(ssfshop.com)*, **Beaker** *(ssfshop.com/beaker)* and **BOONTHESHOP** *(boontheshop.com)*, where you can track down popular Korean labels such as thisisneverthat, San San Gear and OPEN YY. All three are clustered around Apgujeong-ro 60-gil.

Several of Korea's trendiest and edgiest shops are near **Dosan Park** (p115). **MSCHF** *(mischief.co.kr)* and **Instant Funk** *(instantfunk.kr)* are popular for women's wear, while the hats at **ATiiSSU** *(atiissu.com)* feel appropriate for a post-apocalyptic anime. Don't miss **Haus Nowhere Dosan**, a multistorey complex housing global eyewear fave Gentle Monster *(gentlemonster.com)*, its sister cosmetics brand Tamburins *(tamburins.com)* and **Nudake** *(nudake.com)*, a bakery-cafe with artistic aspirations. Even if you're not shopping, the building's trippy art installations alone are worth the visit.

Find Something Beautiful

MAP P110

Go gallery hopping in Apgujeong

Apgujeong's good looks extend to art, and there are a number of galleries to peruse. The best of the bunch is **SONGEUN** *(songeun.or.kr)*, housed in a silver shard designed by the Swiss studio Herzog & de Meuron. Its rotating contemporary exhibitions can range from sound installations to explorations

GANGNAM FASHION

Kim Minji, stylist and owner of the fashion brand minjiena, shares where she goes to get the look in Gangnam. *@minjiena*

Brown Hat: Truly unique hats you won't find anywhere else. Its high prices are reasonable considering the unbelievable quality.

Sinoon: The flagship branch of this designer brand in Apgujeong is a must-visit if you love cute and charming things.

Glowny: The label has several locations, but I recommend its newest branch, by Dosan Park. It makes high-quality basic items with a Korean touch.

Opener: A select shop that imports distinctive international brands. A great place to explore and discover new styles. It's also a favourite with celebrities.

EATING IN GANGNAM: FINE DINING

MAP P110

Mingles: Chef Kang Mingoo is known for his innovative cookery with clean flavours and artful presentation. Book far in advance. *noon-3pm & 6-10pm Tue-Sat* **WWW**

Ryunique: French and Japanese influences combine in platings that incorporate wood and moss, reflecting a reverence for the natural world. *noon-3pm & 6-10.30pm Tue-Sun* **WWW**

Jungsik: Chef-owner Yim Jungsik serves neo-Korean food at its finest. Reservations for two-month periods open on the first of even-numbered months. *noon-3pm & 5.30-10pm* **WWW**

Soigné: Contemporary Seoul cuisine that tells a story of Korean culture in a chic, minimalist dining room. Book well in advance. *noon-3pm & 6-10pm Tue-Sun* **WWW**

TOP EXPERIENCE

Bongeun-sa

Wedged between the flashy Starfield COEX Mall and the ritzy Cheongdam-dong neighbourhood, Bongeun-sa stands in stark juxtaposition to the surrounding spectacle. Dating to 794, it's one of Seoul's oldest and most treasured temples, though it has stood in its present location only since 1562 and has undergone numerous reconstructions. Today, it provides not only religious sanctuary but a much needed reprieve from Gangnam's high-tempo lifestyle.

Shrines & Halls

Pass through **Jinyeomun** (Gate of Truth), where you encounter the four heavenly kings who protect the Buddha-Dharma by guarding the four cardinal directions. Beyond a small pond with a laughing Buddha is the large Beopwangru hall, where religious ceremonies are held at 10am each morning. Behind Beopwangru is the temple's main courtyard and Daewoong-jeon, its main Buddha hall. Inside is a trio of wooden Buddha statues that are a designated National Treasure. Surrounding Daewoongjeon are several smaller halls, including Panjeon, Bongeun-sa's oldest structure (1855), housing 3503 wooden blocks carved with the 81 volumes of the *Avatamsaka Sutra*. Next to Panjeon is the temple's most conspicuous feature, the 23m-high **Great Statue of Maitreya Buddha**, who, it's believed, will one day return to relieve people of their suffering.

Templelife & Templestay

If you can, visit Bongeun-sa on a Thursday to take part in one of its templelife programs – either a temple tour followed by a tea ceremony, or an experience that combines Buddhist crafts, sound meditation and sutra copying using golden ink. For a more in-depth experience, join an overnight templestay program. Held on the first Saturday of the month, these include *Seon* (Zen) meditation, monastic meals and a conversation with a monk. Both programs should be booked in advance online *(templestay.com; templelife/templestay ₩30,000/120,000)*.

TOP TIPS

- The peaceful Meditation Trail runs past bamboo and flowers on the hillside at the rear of the temple.
- The information centre at the temple entrance is open 10am to 4pm daily.
- Scan the QR code at the entrance for a mobile guide available in 10 languages.

PRACTICALITIES

- bongeunsa.org
- free
- 5am-10pm

BEST SELF-CARE SPOTS

Sulhwasoo: The flagship store of this esteemed cosmetics brand has a herbal medicine spa and a rooftop lounge.

Jenny House: Splurge on a K-Idol makeover at this top-tier salon, which has styled some of Korea's biggest celebrities.

Klairs: For Klairs, doing good equals looking good. All cosmetics at its Garosu-gil store are vegan and ethically sourced.

Spa Lei: A relaxing women-only spa with an open-air bath, sitz baths and saunas. Massages and facials, too.

Fold and Tie: Take a class to learn the Korean art of cloth gift wrapping so you can pay all that good feeling forward. *fold-tie.com*

Gangnam Medical Tour Center: Join one of its K-Culture programs to do a bit of yoga or discover your personal colour.

of links between Asian and African cultures. You're asked to reserve your visit in advance, but it's possible to just show up and register on site. A few blocks down Dosan-daero, **White Cube Seoul** *(whitecube.com)* has frequently changing shows, while the adjacent **Horim Museum**'s *(horimmuseum.org; adult/child ₩5000/3000)* collection consists of incense burners, Buddhist paintings and other centuries-old artefacts.

Seoul's French Connection

MAP P110

Be a Seorae Village flaneur

The charming **Seorae Village** neighbourhood took shape in 1981, when the Lycée Français de Séoul moved here and the city's French expats followed. You won't confuse it with the 8th arrondissement, but the enclave does have a distinct feel, more relaxed than the rest of the city, with little Gallic touches such as street signs in both Korean and French. Spend an afternoon casually exploring its bistros and wine bars, making sure to pick up some chocolates at **Toudou** and savour **Maillet**'s superb pastries – mille-feuilles, eclairs, lime tarts – in the cafe's leafy back garden. If the weather is nice, grab some cheeses from **Fromagerie Le Meunier** and picnic in **Montmartre Park**, Seorae's pleasant hilltop green space.

South Side Arts & Culture

MAP P110

Major museums and performance venues

Seoul's southern edge is home to a trio of important arts institutions along Nambusunhwan-ro. At **Seoul Arts Center** *(SAC; sac.or.kr)*, lovers of the performing arts can catch the national opera, ballet or orchestra in an opera house that resembles a traditional hat, listen to a piano recital in the music hall, or watch a play in a theatre dedicated to experimental works. Purchase tickets in person or at *interparkglobal.com*. Prefer the visual arts? The centre's **Hangaram Art Museum** has seven galleries with changing exhibitions that might display anything from furniture to French Impressionist works. Also here are **Hangaram Design Museum** and, in a separate building, **Seoul Calligraphy Art Museum**.

EATING IN SOUTH-CENTRAL SEOUL: OUR PICKS

MAP P110

Samwon Garden: Has been serving top-class *galbi* (beef ribs) amid a traditional garden for more than 40 years. *11.30am-9.30pm* ₩₩₩

One Degree North: Singaporean favourites like chicken rice and *char siu* pork transport you (almost) to the equator. *11.30am-10pm Mon-Sat* ₩₩

Solsot: Among the many rice-pot options at this chain restaurant are steak, salmon, freshwater eel and cheese *dakgalbi* (spicy chicken). *11am-9pm* ₩₩

Monks Butcher: The menu at this stylish vegan restaurant ranges from pastas and risotto to meatless burgers and cottage pie. *noon-10.30pm* ₩₩

Jinmi Pyeongyang Naengmyeon: Soothing Pyeongyang-style *naengmyeong* (noodles in a cold broth), plus dumplings, bulgogi and boiled pork. *11am-9.30pm* ₩₩

Orabang: This cosy joint brings the flavours of Jeju to Seoul. Try the *gosari yukgaejang*, a spicy beef soup with bracken. *11.30am-10pm Mon-Fri, from 1pm Sat & Sun* ₩₩

Yukgak Gogi: This barbecue restaurant has a unique location: on the roof of the old Express Bus Terminal. Great views. *11am-10pm* ₩₩

Jeongdon: Serves crispy, juicy Japanese-style pork cutlets. Fried chicken and fish cutlets are also on offer. *11.30am-9.30pm* ₩₩

WALK GANGNAM IN STYLE

Put on your best look and strut through Sinsa and Apgujeong, neighbourhoods synonymous with luxury brands and K-Pop swagger.

START	END	LENGTH
Sinsa station	SONGEUN	4km; 2hr

From Sinsa station, head to the blocks west of ❶ **Garosu-gil** to find photo booths, skincare shops and local streetwear favourite ❷ **ADERERROR**. Near the road's north end are the ritzy Hyundai Department Store and ❸ **Gangnam Medical Tour Center**, where you can learn about the latest medical procedures. South, the main drag of Nonhyeon-ro is filled with plastic-surgery clinics.

Follow Eonju-ro south to leafy ❹ **Dosan Park**, named after independence activist 'Dosan' Ahn Chang-ho (1878–1938), who is buried here. Exit the park's northeast corner and pop into ❺ **Haus Nowhere Dosan** (p112) for mind-bending art installations and the eyewear brand Gentle Monster. Break for coffee and sculptural baked goods at the basement-level Nudake cafe.

Window-shop through the boutique-packed roads north of the park, collectively known as ❻ **Apgujeong Rodeo Street**. Emerge in front of the west wing of the ❼ **Galleria** (p112) department store, which is covered in shimmering, scale-like glass discs that turn a psychedelic pink at night. Heading east, Apgujeong-ro is lined with luxury brand stores in architecturally audacious buildings. These blocks also make up ❽ **K-Star Road**, where cutesy bear sculptures erected in 2014 pay homage to OG K-Pop icons such as SHINEee and Kara. Around the corner is the ❾ **SONGEUN** (p112) gallery, where contemporary art offers a reprieve from the neighbourhood's commercial pressures.

TRADITIONAL MUSIC FORMS

Before there was K-Pop, there was *gugak*, Korea's traditional music. *Gugak* comes in a vast array of forms. These are some of the major genres you may hear at a National Gugak Center concert.

Jeongak: Formal music reserved for banquets and events such as Confucian ceremonies. It's performed by soloists or small ensembles.

Pansori: Epic dramas sung and acted out by a solo singer. Traditionally, a performance could last several hours.

Nongak: Lively, percussive songs performed in rural communities to accompany agricultural labour or scare off evil spirits.

Sanjo: Solo instrumental music, often played on a *gayageum* or *geomungo*, both types of zithers. Occasionally accompanied by a drummer.

Next to the SAC is **National Gugak Center** *(gugak.go.kr)*. Head to its **Gugak Museum** to view and hear traditional instruments and to try interactive features that take you on a listening journey through Korean music history. Free guided English tours are held on Saturdays at 2pm. At 3pm, the centre holds its weekly Saturday Gugak Concert, a medley of several different musical styles. Book tickets through the centre's website.

A short bus ride west, **Nam-Seoul Museum of Art** *(sema.seoul.go.kr)* occupies a stately red-brick and granite structure that once housed the Belgian consulate. An outpost of **Seoul Museum of Art** (p76), its permanent exhibition displays work by the 20th-century sculptor Kwon Jin-kyu, while rotating exhibitions change every three months. All three venues are closed on Mondays.

Somewhere Under the Rainbow

MAP P110

See an aqueous spectacle

Make your way to Banpo Hangang Park to see the wonderful water and light show put on by the **Moonlight Rainbow Fountain**. Running for 570m along both sides of the double-decker Banpo Bridge, it's the longest bridge fountain in the world – a spectacle of 380 water jets and 10,000 coloured lights pulsing in time to K-Pop recordings. The fountain operates daily from April to October at noon, 7.30pm, 8pm, 8.30pm and 9pm. There's an additional show at 9.30pm in July and August. Each performance lasts 20 minutes. There's no show when it's raining.

If the bridge fountain isn't playing, you can still enjoy coloured lights reflecting on the water at the adjacent **Some Sevit** *(somesevit.co.kr)*. The trio of floating artificial islands houses restaurants, a cafe, event spaces and a beer garden with a view of the Moonlight Rainbow Fountain that almost justifies its inflated prices. For fun on the water, charter a yacht, book a boat tour, or rent a kayak from Some Sevit's Golden Blue Marina, or take a spin on a round Tubester boat.

Korea's Tallest Skyscraper

MAP P117

Welcome to Lotte World

The chaebol's massive complex *(lotteworld.com)* is home to **Lotte World Tower** (Korea's tallest building), **Lotte World Adventure** amusement park, **Lotte World Mall**, **Lotte World Aquarium** and a slew of other 'Lotte' entertainment

DRINKING IN APGUJEONG: TOP COCKTAILS

MAP P110

Zest: Named one of the world's best bars, Zest focuses on upcycling ingredients like corn silk that would normally go to waste. *6.30pm-2am, from 3pm Sat & Sun*

Pine&Co: Creative concoctions riff on traditional Korean ingredients like shitake mushrooms, *omija* (five-flavour) berries and fermentation starter *nuruk*. *7pm-2am*

Alice Cheongdam: This *Alice in Wonderland*–inspired bar has more than a few surprises. Drinks might feature a flower pot or bubble tower. *6pm-2am, to 3am Fri & Sat*

Bar Tea Scent: Tea-based spirits and tea-infused cocktails like the Sencha Sonic (with green-tea gin) and Iron Daiquiri (oolong tea rum), presented with a flourish. *7pm-3am*

SIGHTS
1 Lotte Museum of Art
2 Lotte World Tower
3 Mongchon-toseong
4 Olympic Park
5 Seoul Baekje Museum
6 Seoul Olympic Museum of Art
7 World Peace Gate

ACTIVITIES
8 Lotte World Aquarium

SLEEPING
9 Lotte Hotel World
10 Seoul Olympic Parktel

EATING
11 Bangi Shabu Shabu Kalguksu
12 Bogil
13 Byeolmi Gopchang
14 Cafe Pepper

ENTERTAINMENT
15 Lotte World Adventure

SHOPPING
16 Lotte World Mall

options. Is it all rather corporate? Exceedingly. Is it a tonne of fun anyway? Absolutely.

The 555m Lotte World Tower's sleek design was inspired by Korean ceramics and calligraphy. A ticket to **Seoul Sky** *(adult/child ₩31,000/27,000)* whisks you up to an observatory that spans the 117th to 120th storeys and features a glass floor, outdoor terraces and epic views. Adventurous types can join a **Sky Bridge Tour** *(₩130,000)* to walk across an 8m-long bridge outside the 124th floor. Within the tower, exhibitions at **Lotte Museum of Art** *(lottemuseum.com; adult/child ₩20,000/13,000)* range from French street artist JR to up-and-coming Korean artists.

Giant Open-Air Sculpture Gallery

MAP P117

Enjoy the art of Olympic Park

Vast **Olympic Park** *(ksponco.or.kr/olympicpark)* combines Olympic landmarks and sports facilities with ample green space, interesting historic remains and several arts and culture centres. The park's striking entrance is **World Peace Gate**, with its red-and-blue winged arches and impressive murals.

The collection at **Seoul Olympic Museum of Art** (SOMA; *soma.kspo.or.kr; adult/student/child ₩5000/4000/3000*) includes several video artworks by Nam June Paik. Among them

BAEKJE KINGDOM

Most of Seoul's major historic sites date to the Joseon era, but it was the Baekje kingdom that first established the area as an important settlement. Baekje was one of several kingdoms to emerge from the collapse of the northern Gojoseon kingdom, and in 18 BCE it founded its capital in what's now the Songpa district. Its demise came in the mid-7th century, when it was conquered by the southeastern Silla kingdom.

JINTAK HAN/THE WASHINGTON POST VIA GETTY IMAGES

Jamsil Baseball Stadium

are *Golden Crown*, a piece inspired by Baekje culture, and *Coubertin*, a tribute to the father of the modern Olympics. SOMA is best known for its sculpture collection, which debuted five days before the '88 Olympics' opening ceremony. Nearly 200 pieces by artists from across the world are installed inside the museum and around the Olympic Park grounds.

The park contains the remains of **Mongchon-toseong**, a rammed-earth rampart surrounded by a moat, built in the 3rd century CE during the Baekje dynasty. At the park's **Seoul Baekje Museum** *(baekjemuseum.seoul.go.kr)* you can learn about this ancient Korean kingdom, the early capital of which, Wiryeseong, was located in this part of Seoul.

Cheer on the Home Teams

MAP P117

Catch a baseball match

Baseball is Korea's most popular sport and, even if you're not a fan, attending a game is a fun activity for people-watching alone. The 25,000-seat **Jamsil Baseball Stadium** is shared by two pro teams: the Doosan Bears *(doosanbears.com)* and LG Twins *(lgtwins.com)*. Buy tickets online or at the stadium up to 90 minutes before games. The baseball season runs from March to October.

BEST GREEN SPACES

Seorae Island: In spring, take the footbridge to this tiny Han River island to wander amid fields of yellow canola flowers.

Gwanaksan: Mountain on Seoul's southern edge serving up amazing city views. A hermitage sits atop.

Maeheon Citizens' Forest: Large park with lots of shady walking paths, a playground and a memorial to independence fighter Yun Bong-gil.

Jamwon Hangang Park: An outdoor pool, pink muhly grass and a Starbucks floating on the Han River (with views of Moonlight Rainbow Fountain).

Seoripul Park: Pedestrian bridges link Seoripul's two halves with Montmartre Park, creating a long green corridor amid apartment buildings.

Yangjae-cheon: Peaceful stream lined with paths that pass drooping willows, reed beds and rows of metasequoia trees.

EATING IN SOUTHEASTERN SEOUL

MAP P117

Bangi Shabu Shabu Kalguksu: Neighbourhood favourite serving *kalguksu* (knife-cut noodles) with mushrooms and sliced beef to cook in the broth. *11am-9.30pm Mon-Sat* W

Bogil: Abalone, eel and other superb seafood sourced from the south-coast island of Bogil-do, where the chef grew up. *11am-4pm & 5-10pm Tue-Sun* WW

Cafe Pepper: This adorable cafe makes gluten-free desserts such as strawberries and cream cake, pistachio cherry tarts and banana poundcake. *noon-9pm* W

Byeolmi Gopchang: Dishes up grilled beef intestines so popular it had to open a second location a block away. *11am-3am, to 5am Thu-Sat* WW

Northern Seoul

FORTRESS WALL | FINE MUSEUMS | MOUNTAIN TRAILS

It's hard to resist following the Seoul City Wall as it snakes across Naksan, Bukaksan and Inwangsan, three of the city's guardian mountains. Further north is majestic Bukhansan National Park, home to higher peaks, ancient temples and myriad hiking trails.

The university and theatre district of Daehangno lies at the western foot of Naksan. To the east and north are two hillside neighbourhoods: working-class Changsin-dong and affluent Seongbuk-dong. The upmarket neighbourhood of Buam-dong shelters northwest of Bukaksan, while some of the key sights of Seodaemun are at the foot of Inwangsan.

Learn about key episodes in Korean history at the Changgyeonggung (Changgyeon royal palace) and the sombre Seodaemun Prison History Hall. Visit museums devoted, among other things, to Korean furniture and stone carving. Here, too, lies an elegant late-Joseon villa and garden, the perfect escape from contemporary Seoul.

GETTING AROUND

Daehangno and Seongbuk-dong are easily accessed by Hyehwa and Hangsung University subway stations. For Seodaemun, alight at Dongnimmun. For trails into Bukhansan National Park, head to either Dobongsan or Bukhansan Ui subway stations.

Buses are handiest for reaching Buam-dong and for the further-flung sites of Seongbuk-dong. Hiking is the best way to access the Seoul City Wall and the city-centre mountains.

TOP TIP

Fans of contemporary architecture should seek out **Won Buddhism Wonnam Temple**, designed by Mass Studies, the practice of internationally acclaimed Korean architect Minsok Cho. Exposed concrete in sinuous curves encircles the temple, which includes an elegant *hanok* hall.

A Grand Palace & Greenhouse

MAP P120

Explore Changgyeonggung

Built in the 15th century by King Sejong for his father, **Changgyeonggung** *(royal.khs.go.kr; adult/child ₩3000/free)* is one of Seoul's five main palaces. The throne hall, Myeongjeongjeon, rebuilt in 1616, is a rare example of intact 17th-century Joseon architecture. Join free English guided tours at 11am and 3pm Tuesday to Sunday.

The smaller buildings beyond the main hall were where the kings and queens lived in their separate households. From here, paths lead through a forested garden to **Daeonsil** (Great Greenhouse), a European-style glasshouse stocked with Korean plants, including lovely examples of *bunjae* (bonsai). Between March and November, the Moonlight Lotus Show, an after-dark media art show, is projected across the garden's ornamental pond.

HIGHLIGHTS
1 Seoul City Wall

SIGHTS
2 Changgyeonggung
3 Changuimun
4 Daeonsil
5 Dongnimmun
6 Gilsang-sa
7 Hanyangdoseong
8 Hyehwamun
9 Inwang-sa
10 Inwangsan Guksadang
11 Korea Furniture Museum
12 Korean Stone Art Museum
13 Paik Ground SeMA
14 Seodaemun Independence Park
15 Seodaemun Prison History Hall
16 Seokpajeong Seoul Museum of Art
17 Seonbawi
18 Won Buddhism Wonnam Temple

ACTIVITIES
19 Bukaksan
20 Changsin Sungin Quarry Observatory
21 Inwangsan

SLEEPING
22 Glue Hotel
23 Original Backpackers

EATING
24 Chang Chang
25 Gyeyeolsa Chicken
26 Hyehwa Kalguksu
27 Jaha Sonmandoo
28 Neungra Bapsang
29 Olden Grey
30 Scoff
31 Solnamugil Deongjang Yesool

DRINKING & NIGHTLIFE
32 Club Espresso
33 Haero Coffee
34 Inwangsan Mountain Chosochaekbang
35 Okba
36 Suyeonsanbang

ENTERTAINMENT
37 Arko & Daehakro Arts Theater
38 Daehangno Information Center
39 Hongik University Daehakro Art Center

DAEHANGNO THEATRE DISTRICT

Daehangno's association with youth culture and the performing arts goes back decades. The district was the original home of Seoul National University and remains the base for Arts Council Korea. There are some 170 theatres in the area, the largest ones being **Hongik University Daehakro Art Center** *(artscenter.hongik.ac.kr)* and **Arko & Daehakro Arts Theater** *(theater.arko.or.kr)*.

At Marronnier Park, **Daehangno Information Center** has flyers for most of the shows playing. The staff here can point out ones that have subtitles in other languages or are occasionally performed in English, such as the long-running comedy-thriller *Hangover*. Tickets are typically around ₩15,000. The centre is closed Mondays.

SANGA PARK/GETTY IMAGES

Gilsang-sa stone tower

Explore Changsin-dong

MAP P120

Visit Paik Ground SeMA

Close by Dongdaemun's clothing markets, Changsin-dong was once home to small-scale sewing factories. Seoul Museum of Art has converted a 1960 *hanok* here into **Paik Ground SeMA** *(sema.seoul.go.kr; free)*. It's a small exhibition space (closed Mondays) with an attached cafe, but worth a visit for fans of Nam June Paik's groundbreaking artworks.

Weave your way up through the steep streets north of Paik Ground to eventually overlook a former granite quarry dating to the 1920s. Stone from here was used to construct buildings such as Seoul train station and old City Hall. The quarry is now a park and there's a splendid view over it from the cantilevered **Changsin Sungin Quarry Observatory**, which houses a cafe.

Stone Sentinels & Wooden Wonders

MAP P120

Museums dedicated to furniture and stone art

An army of centuries-old stone sentinels stands guard on the hillside overlooking Seongbuk-dong at the **Korean Stone Art Museum** *(koreanstonemuseum.com; ₩5000)*. Start by viewing the interior displays, mainly of *beoksu* (village guardians),

EATING IN DAEHANGNO & CHANGSIN-DONG: OUR PICKS

MAP P120

Solnamugil Deongjang Yesool: (솔나무길된장예술) Serves a veggie bibimbap with a tofu stew and many tasty side dishes. *10.30am-2.30pm & 3.30-9pm* ₩₩

Chang Chang: Retro-themed Cantonese restaurant serving warming bowls of beef-brisket noodles and stir fries. *11.30am-3pm & 5-9pm* ₩₩

Hyehwa Kalguksu: (혜화칼국수) Old-school eatery specialising in Andong *guksi* noodles in a milky-white beef-bone broth with leeks. *11am-9.30pm* ₩

Olden Grey: Trendy brunch restaurant close to Dongmyo, sharing premises with the Olden Brown cafe. Also has a rooftop garden. *11am-10pm* ₩₩

before emerging onto the museum's roof, which blends into landscaped, hillside gardens. Meander paths lined by enigmatic stone figures, elegant Buddhist deities and lanterns as you also take in the marvellous city views. The museum is closed Mondays.

The nearby **Korea Furniture Museum** *(kofum.com; ₩20,000)* is a gem. Advance reservation by email is necessary to tour the collection of traditional furniture, including chests, bookcases and dining tables made from wood such as persimmon, maple and paulownia. The museum is based in a series of elegant *hanok*, including a villa that was once part of Changdeokgung (p62).

Gift from a Gisaeng

MAP P120

Meditate at Gilsang-sa

In a leafy, hillside setting, **Gilsang-sa** *(kilsangsa.info)* was once a restaurant where *gisaeng* (female entertainers accomplished in traditional arts) performed. In 1995 the property was donated by its owner, Kim Yeong-han, to the venerable monk Beopjeong, who turned it into a Buddhist temple. A tiny museum dedicated to Beopjeong, who passed away in 2010, is at the top of the complex, beside the creek that flows down the mountainside. Gilsang-sa runs overnight templestays.

Charming Hanok Teahouse

MAP P120

Sip tea at Suyeonsanbang

Meaning 'a home in the mountains for reading and scholarly gatherings', **Suyeonsanbang** *(@sooyeonsanbang)* was the residence of the novelist Yi Tae-jun from 1933 to 1946. Today it is one of Seoul's most enchanting *hanok* teahouses. Sit inside the cosy, beautifully constructed wooden building or take a table on the verandah with a view of the garden to enjoy drinks and sweets, including matcha, honey ginger tea and pumpkin soup. It's open 11.30am to 6pm Wednesday to Friday and until 8pm Saturday and Sunday.

Historic Villa & Garden

MAP P120

Swoon at Seokpajeong Seoul Museum of Art

Your ticket for **Seokpajeong Seoul Museum of Art** *(seoul museum.org; adult/child ₩20,000/13,000)* will grant you access to at least two major exhibitions of modern and contemporary art and photography. On permanent display are a

continued on p126

A MOUNTAINSIDE RETREAT

When Yi Ha-eung's 12-year-old son Yi Myeongbok became King Gojong in 1863, his father gained the title Heungseon Daewongun and effectively ruled Korea as regent for his young son.

Up until this point the Andong Kim clan had been powerful in the Korean court. To exert his new authority, Heungseon Daewongun devised a plan to acquire Seokpajeong villa, which was built and owned by Kim Heung-geun, a member of the Andong Kims. Kim was reluctant to sell the villa, but allowed Heungseon Daewongun to stay a night. The wily regent took along his son, a shrewd move as vassals, such as Kim, could no longer own a property where an emperor had stayed. Thus the villa became royal property, and Heungseon Daewongun got his mountainside retreat.

EATING IN BUAM-DONG & SEODAEMUN: OUR PICKS

MAP P120

Gyeyeolsa Chicken: Dig into golden-fried chicken and crisp potato wedges. One basket serves two nicely. *noon-10.30pm Tue-Sun* ₩₩

Jaha Sonmandoo: Posh *mandu* (dumpling) house for heavenly dough parcels stuffed with veggies, beef and pork, served either boiled or in soup. *11am-9.30pm* ₩₩

Scoff: Lemon-drizzle sponge, Earl Grey scones and sausage rolls are among the many tempting bakes at this long-running cafe. *10am-8pm Mon-Fri, from 9am Sat & Sun* ₩

Neungra Bapsang: Famous North Korean restaurant serving specialities such as Pyongyang cold noodles and *gamja mandu* (potato dumplings). *11am-9pm* ₩₩

TOP EXPERIENCE

Seoul City Wall

Completed in 1396 during the reign of King Taejo, Hanyangdoseong (Seoul City Wall) was built to defend the capital. Today, the stone fortifications, which connect Seoul's four inner 'guardian' mountains of Bukaksan, Naksan, Namsan and Inwangsan, are a top visitor attraction. Hiking trails alongside the wall bring you up close to historic architecture and provide awesome views across the city.

CHANOO8/SHUTTERSTOCK

TOP TIPS

- A free map and walking guide is available at Seoul City Wall Museum.
- A night hike beside the illuminated wall up to Naksan is recommended so as to enjoy the twinkling panorama of city lights.

PRACTICALITIES

● seoulcitywall.seoul.go.kr ● free ● 24hr

Seoul City Wall Museum

To learn all about the 600-year history of the fortifications, visit **Seoul City Wall Museum** *(museum.seoul.go.kr; free)*. Feng shui principles were used in the wall's construction, which follows the city's natural topography. Joseon-dynasty builders carved their names on the stones of the original fortress – you can do likewise via an interactive display onto a video projection of the wall. The museum is closed Mondays.

Hiking the Wall

Between 5m and 8m in height, the wall runs for 18.6km around Seoul's city centre, with just under 80% of the structure restored. While it's possible to hike the entire route in a single (exhausting) day, it's better to split the circuit up over two days, or focus on one of the four sections.

The shortest and least strenuous route is 2.1km over **Naksan** between the sub-gate **Hyehwamun** and **Heunginjimun** (p90), one of the four original principal gates in the wall. Here the fortress wall cuts a graceful, sinuous curve through the city and provides beautiful vistas. The most challenging section is up and over **Bukaksan** (4.7km).

CLIMB NAKSAN

Follow the old fortress walls to the mural-covered alleyways of Ihwa Maeul and the summit of guardian mountain Naksan.

START	END	LENGTH
Heunginjimun	Hakrim	1.5km, 2hr

Admire 1 **Heunginjimun** (p90), the majestic Great East Gate, before learning all about the historic fortifications at 2 **Seoul City Wall Museum**. Follow the wall uphill for the brief, steep climb to 3 **Ihwa Maeul**. Take a rest at 4 **Gaebbul** bakery-cafe, near the top of the village.

Continue to 5 **Naksan Park**, which is bordered by more impressive sections of the wall and offers splendid urban views. Retrace your steps to Ihwa Maeul and head downhill, passing 6 **Ihwajang**, the historic home of Syngman Rhee, the first president of South Korea.

Drop into 7 **ithinkso Archive**, a design store selling bags, stationery and house plants. Continue to 8 **Marronnier Park**, where you can see what art is being exhibited at 9 **Arko Art Center**.

Along Daehak-ro, beside the entrances to Hyehwa subway station, are some tempting street food stalls, including a 10 **vendor** who prepares and sells *dalgona*, the honeycomb toffee that featured in the Netflix drama *Squid Game*. Step back in time at the classic 11 **Hakrim** *dabang* (cafe) and order a creamy Vienna coffee, its signature drink.

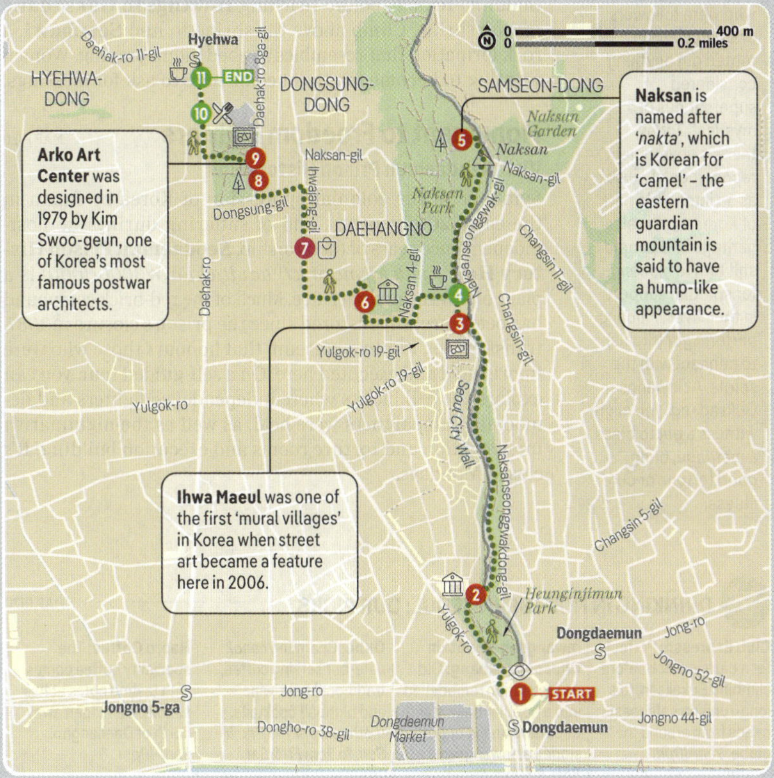

FOLK RELIGION

Musok is Korea's ancient, highly ritualised and somewhat taboo folk religion. Scholars believe it's not wholly correct to compare this belief system to shamanism, or call the *mudang* (often women who are said to have the skills to connect to the supernatural) shamans, but there are similarities.

The stigmatisation of *musok* goes back to the Joseon era, when the ruling class, who were followers of Confucianism, rooted out anything considered superstitious or mystical. Today, there is government recognition of *musok* as an intangible part of Korean cultural heritage and people still turn to *mudang* for spiritual support in their lives. *Mudang* perform *gut* (rituals) to connect with the spirits. At Inwangsan Guksadang, you might witness a *gut* to bless a marriage, bring good fortune or cure illness.

continued from p123
couple of works by Japanese artist Yayoi Kusama, including one of her famous polka-dot pumpkin sculptures.

The best reason for visiting, however, is hidden behind the museum buildings. Here you'll find **Seokpajeong**, an elegant late-Joseon villa. Paths meandering through the leafy hillside gardens lead to a resting pavilion and ancient carvings in the rocks. Themed exhibitions of sculpture and ceramics are held in the gardens and the villa's rooms, usually between June and November. The museum is closed Mondays and Tuesdays.

Climb Inwangsan

MAP P120

And visit a musok shrine

Inwangsan (339.9m) offers a sweeping vista of the city and the Seoul City Wall flowing over Bukaksan, Naksan and Namsan. The mountain is a strenuous, but relatively easy climb, with several different routes to the summit.

For the least amount of climbing start at **Changuimun**, the sub-gate in Buam-dong, and follow Seoul City Wall. Another popular route is the **Seonbawi Trail** from the historic **Dongnimmun** arch beside **Seodaemun Independence Park**. Along this trail, you'll pass **Inwang-sa** (인왕사), a Buddhist temple, before reaching **Inwangsan Guksadang** *musok* shrine. Climb above the shrine to find **Seonbawi**, a rock formation that resembles a robed monk praying. Women wanting to become pregnant come here to ask for blessings.

Monument to Freedom Fighters

MAP P120

Visit Seodaemun Prison History Hall

Symbolic of the colonial oppression of Korea by Japan in the early 20th century, and of suffering during the post-independence years of dictatorship, **Seodaemun Prison History Hall** *(sphh.sscmc.or.kr; adult/child ₩3000/1000)* is a place of tragedy and sacrifice. Much of the red-brick compound has been carefully restored since the prison's closure in 1987, transforming it into a museum that honours those who were imprisoned and executed here. On a self-guided tour, you can explore the cell blocks where independence fighters and democracy campaigners were held, as well as the nightmarish interrogation and torture rooms and execution building. It's closed Mondays.

DRINKING IN NORTHERN SEOUL: OUR PICKS

MAP P120

Club Espresso: Perfect for a caffeine kick before climbing Bukaksan, this long-running cafe roasts beans from around the globe. *9am-10pm*

Inwangsan Mountain Chosochaekbang: Old police station remodelled into a popular bakery and book cafe on the upper slopes of Inwangsan. *8am-9.30pm*

Okba: Charming *hanok* cafe-bar serving coffee, traditional teas, wine and highball cocktails. *11.30am-6pm Tue-Thu & Sun, to 9pm Fri & Sat*

Haero Coffee: The speciality coffee comes with tasting notes at this *hanok* cafe hidden away north of Daehangno. *11am-10pm*

★ **HIGHLIGHTS**
1 Bukhansan National Park

SIGHTS
2 Baegundae
3 Cheonchuk-sa
4 Daenammun
5 Eunpyeong Hanok Village
6 Insu-bong
7 Jaun-bong
8 Jingwan-sa
9 Jungheung-sa
10 Mangwol-sa
11 Samcheon-sa
see 7 Sinseondae
12 Yeong-bong

ACTIVITIES
13 Bukhansanseong Visitor Center
14 Dobongsan Visitor Information Center
15 Seoul Hiking Tourism Center
16 Uiryeong-gil

SLEEPING
17 Anto Resort
18 Ui-dong Family Camping Ground

DRINKING & NIGHTLIFE
19 Sunwoongak

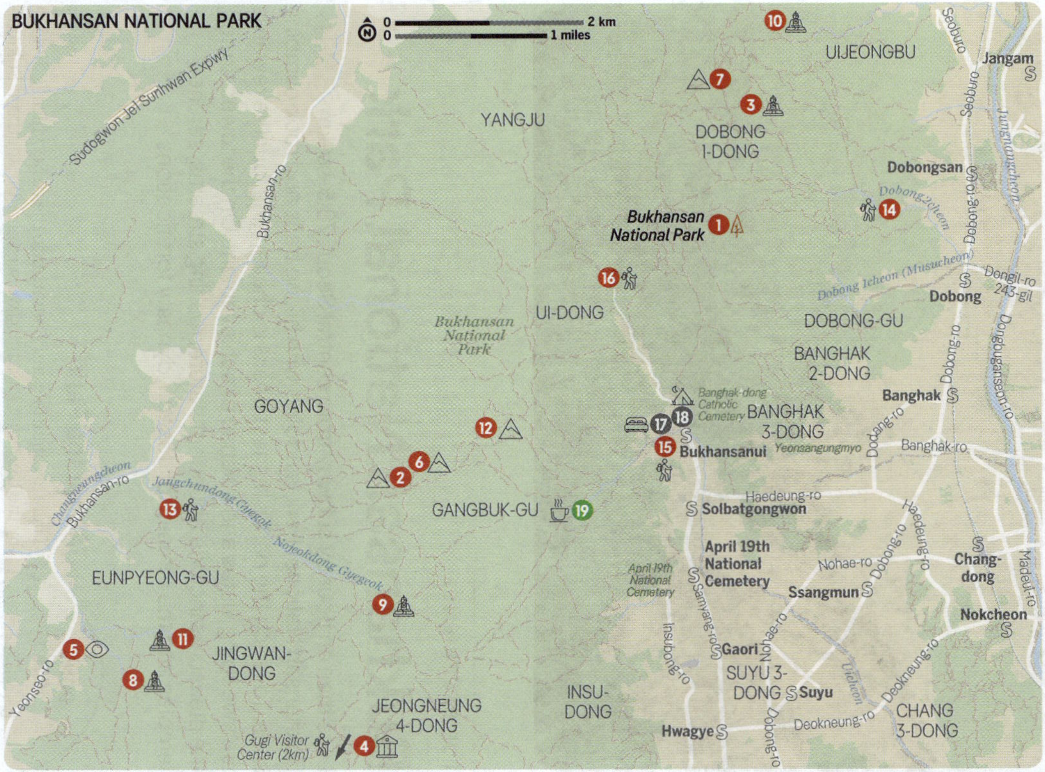

CJ NATTANAI/SHUTTERSTOCK

Baegundae

TOP EXPERIENCE

Bukhansan National Park

Less than an hour by subway from central Seoul, 78.5-sq-km Bukhansan National Park is riddled with hiking trails and rock-climbing sites. To reach the park's highest peaks is challenging, but the rewards are sweeping vistas and a sense of achievement. On the lower slopes, the pleasures include abundant nature, rushing streams, serene temples and the remains of Joseon-dynasty fortifications.

DON'T MISS

- Baegundae
- Insu-bong
- Samcheon-sa
- Jingwans-sa
- Sinseondae
- Cheonchuk-sa
- Mangwol-sa
- Uiryeong-gil

About the Park

MAP P127

There are multiple entry points into the park, which is divided by the Uiryeong Pass into two sections: the southern Bukhansan area, accessed via Bukhansan Ui subway station, and the northern Dobongsan area, reached via Dobongsan station.

Bukhansan Trails

Seoul's highest peak, **Baegundae** (836.5m) offers 360-degree views of the city and parts of Gyeonggi-do. The shortest route up the mountain (around 8km return, taking about four hours)

PRACTICALITIES

● knps.or.kr ● free ● 24hr

is the **Baegundae Ui Gugok Trail**. This starts and finishes at **Seoul Hiking Tourism Center**, a five-minute walk from Bukhansan Ui (Doseon-sa) station, the terminus of the Seoul LRT Ui Sinseol Line. Hiking shoes and gloves are necessary as parts of this trail are steep and can be slippery.

A short detour off the Baegundae Ui Gugok Trail takes you to the peak of **Yeong-bong** (604m). Opposite here is the granite outcrop **Insu-bong** (811m), which has some of the best multipitch rock climbing in Asia and routes of all grades.

The 10.2km **Bukhansanseong-Daenammun Trail**, between **Bukhansanseong Visitor Center** and **Gugi Visitor Center**, is a popular route. Along it you can visit **Jungheung-sa**, an old temple undergoing restoration, the remains of a temporary palace from the Joseon dynasty and **Daenammun**, a principal gate along the 11.6km Bukhansanseong Fortress wall built in 1711.

The **Samcheon-sa Trail** (7.33km, around 2½ hours) starts at **Samcheon-sa**, a temple founded in 661 CE, and ends at **Jingwan-sa**, a beautiful temple close to **Eunpyeong Hanok Village** (p103).

Dobongsan Trails

Jaun-bong (740.2m) is the tallest peak in the Dobongsan section of the park, but access to its steep rock cliffs is restricted. Instead, hikers aim for **Sinseondae** (726m), a 6.3km (2½-hour return) journey from Dobongsan subway station. Note that the final part of the ascent is very steep and the trail can get busy on weekends and public holidays.

An alternative is the 9.32km, six-hour **Dobongsan Main Ridge Trail** between Mangwolsa station and **Dobongsan Visitor Information Center**. It's physically demanding but offers panoramic views from the ridge. Along the route, take signed detours to visit the atmospheric, forest-surrounded **Cheonchuk-sa** and **Mangwol-sa** temples.

Bukhansan Dulle-gil

An alternative to scaling the park's exposed peaks is to hike the **Bukhansan Dulle-gil**. Split into 21 sections, with a total length of just over 75km, this gently undulating path circumnavigates the park through the forest on the lower slopes of Bukhansan and Dobongsan.

Section 21 of the trail is the **Uiryeong-gil**, an unsealed path over a high pass between the park's two mountains. Up until 2009, this 6.5km route was closed to the public for decades for security reasons, which has helped preserve the ecosystem. Reservations (via the park's website) are required from September to the end of November and every weekend throughout the year. Access is from 9am, with last entry at 4pm (3pm in winter). Bring photo ID as this will be checked at the trailhead.

EASY HIKING

If time is short, or you'd prefer an easy hike in the park, Cho Juhyon, a guide at Seoul Hiking Tourism Center, recommends the **Sogwicheon Trail** (7km return) to Daedongmun, one of the gates in the Bukhansanseong fortress wall. It's also possible to reach Yeong-bong along an easier 8.6km route that is moderately challenging and still provides fine panoramas of Seoul.

TOP TIPS

- Seoul Hiking Tourism Center (closed Mondays) offers free maps, guidebooks and gifts, as well as lockers and showers.
- Hiking boots and other gear can be rented from Seoul Hiking Tourism Center.
- Although not especially high, some of the park's peaks are physically challenging ascents, so choose hiking routes with care.
- Bring plenty of water and waterproof clothing.
- Peak hiking season is from the middle of October to the middle of November, when the autumn colours are at their best.
- For a short walk, aim for the *hanok* cafe **Sunwoongak** (closed Wednesdays).

Beyond Seoul

When you've had your fill of the city, the countryside and coast around Seoul are stacked with day-trip options.

Places

GETTING AROUND

The greater Seoul metro area is incredibly well connected by subway, buses and trains. With a bit of forward planning, and patience waiting for buses in more rural areas, most places can be comfortably accessed using public transport.

Renting a car is most useful to tour the more rural areas. If you pick up your car at Gimpo Airport, you can hop on highways and avoid having to drive through central Seoul.

Break free from the gravitational pull of Planet Seoul and you'll discover a fascinating mix of things to do, nearly all of them easily accessible by public transport. The surrounding region, which covers Gyeonggi-do and the port city of Incheon, is steeped in history, from Suwon's majestic Hwaseong Fortress, the apex of Joseon achievement, to the infamous Demilitarized Zone (DMZ), the heavily mined border with North Korea. Schedule kid-centric outings to Everland amusement park and the immersive Korean Folk Village, explore Incheon's Chinatown, or decompress on a rural break to Ganghwado island and the gorgeous Garden of Morning Calm. Whichever direction you go, a different world awaits.

Gwacheon

TIME FROM SEOUL: **30MIN**

Family fun in Seoul Grand Park

Just south of Seoul, the suburb of Gwacheon is home to the enormous **Seoul Grand Park** *(grandpark.seoul.go.kr)*, a favourite with local families. The park contains **Seoul Zoo** *(adult/student/child ₩5000/3000/2000)*, home to elephants, flamingos and many other animals; **Seoul Grand Park Botanical Garden**, which has a children's zoo where you can watch Border collies herd sheep, and the vintage **Seoulland** *(seoulland.co.kr; adult/student/child ₩52,000/46,000/43,000)* theme park, which has rides, stage shows and seasonal events.

Travellers without kids might be more drawn to the Gwacheon branch of the **Museum of Modern and Contemporary Art** *(mmca.go.kr; adult/child ₩3000/free)*. Begin on the top floor and work your way down to trace the history of Korean modern art. Besides these facilities, Seoul Grand Park also makes a great place for a picnic, with lots of walking paths and a large artificial lake.

Suwon

TIME FROM SEOUL: **1HR**

Art at a fortress' heart

If you're visiting Suwon to see **Hwaseong** (p132), it's worth popping in to **Suwon Museum of Art** *(suma.suwon.go.kr; adult/student/child ₩4000/2000/1000)*, located next to **Hwaseong Haenggung** (p132). The facility hosts rotating

PHOTO_JEONGH/SHUTTERSTOCK

Traditional kitchen, Korean Folk Village, Yongin

exhibitions of modern and contemporary art and has some large spaces that can be used for sound installations and the like. The museum is closed on Mondays and doesn't accept foreign cards, so bring cash.

Yongin

TIME FROM SEOUL: 1HR

Time travel at a folk village

The **Korean Folk Village** *(koreanfolk.co.kr; adult/child ₩37,000/30,000)* has been transporting visitors back to the Joseon dynasty since 1974. Its picturesque grounds are filled with 270 thatch-and tile-roofed buildings that have been relocated here from around the country. The village is realistic enough to have served as a filming location for some of Korea's most popular historical dramas, including *Dae Jang Geum* and *Kingdom*.

Much more than a collection of buildings, the village brings the past alive through daily performances and hands-on activities. Special events are held on Korean holidays, providing a rare opportunity to participate in traditional ceremonies that are fast disappearing in contemporary life. There's also a children's amusement park, should any kids you're travelling with start to get bored (doubtful).

SEOUL GRAND PARK TIPS

The most scenic way to reach the zoo and botanical garden is the **Skylift** *(skylift.co.kr)*, a chairlift that soars over the lake and zoo.

The **Elephant Train** *(₩2000)* runs in a loop between Seoul Grand Park station, Seoul Zoo and SeoulLand. A free bus runs in a loop around the zoo and botanical garden.

A free shuttle bus runs from Seoul Grand Park station to the MMCA, Gwacheon. To find the bus stop, make a U-turn from Exit 4. The MMCA also runs a free shuttle bus between its Seoul, Deoksugung and Gwacheon branches Tuesday to Friday.

Try to time your visit to the MMCA, Gwacheon for between 2pm and 4pm, when Nam June Paik's monumental video artwork *The More, the Better* is screened.

EATING IN SUWON: OUR PICKS

Bonsuwon Galbi: Suwon is famous for its beef *galbi* (ribs), and this is one of the best places in the city to sample them. *11.30am-8.30pm, to 8pm Sun & Mon* ₩₩₩

Yeonpo Galbi: Grills up mouthwatering beef *galbi*. For lunch, it also serves *galbitang*, a beef-rib soup that's a good option for solo diners. *11.20am-9pm* ₩₩₩

Yongseong Tongdak: Popular *chimaek* (chicken and beer) spot for juicy, golden chicken and cold, cheap brews. *11am-11pm Wed-Mon* ₩₩

Starfield Suwon: This large mall has a good range of dining outlets, including a big 7th-floor food court. *10am-10pm* ₩

TOP EXPERIENCE

Hwaseong

Completed in 1796, this majestic citadel represents the apex of Joseon achievement, combining mountain and lowland fortress design with Chinese and Western construction techniques. As well as being a defence installation, it was also a grand expression of filial piety – part of King Jeongjo's project to move his father's tomb from Seoul to a more auspicious location in Suwon.

BASTIEN ALTERMATT/GETTY IMAGES

Hwaseong Haenggung

TOP TIPS

- The **Hwaseong Fortress Tourist Trolley** circles between several of Hwaseong's main sites. It runs 9.40am to 5pm Tuesday to Sunday.
- Want to see Hwaseong from 150m up? **Flying Suwon** *(flyingsuwon.com)* operates a tethered hot-air balloon near Changnyongmun.
- Download the Suwon Museum Agency app to access English text and audio for Suwon Hwaseong Museum.

PRACTICALITIES

● swcf.or.kr ● free ● 24hr

Walk the Walls

The best way to experience **Hwaseong** is to set aside a day to walk its walls, which extend for 5.7km through central Suwon, running over the top of 143m Paldalsan and along the lowlands to the east. En route, you'll encounter four imposing gates, command posts, fire beacons and secret exits where troops could pass undetected. Hwaseong sustained considerable damage during the Japanese colonial period and Korean War, and much of what you see today is the product of reconstruction carried out in the 1970s. At the fortress' northern and southern points are **Janganmun** and **Paldalmun** gates. Janganmun, where Jeongjo would arrive, served as the main gate, while Paldalmun was a conduit for merchants from the south. There are still markets there today. In good weather, be sure to relax at **Hwahongmun**, a military facility/pleasure pavilion built directly over the Suwon-cheon stream.

Hwaseong Haenggung

At the centre of the fortress, **Hwaseong Haenggung** *(adult/student/child ₩2000/1500/1000)* was where Jeongjo stayed when visiting his father's tomb. With 600 rooms, it was the largest palace outside of Seoul. It's been meticulously reconstructed after all but two buildings (Nangnamheon and Noraedang) were destroyed during the colonial period. Learn more about the fortress and palace at nearby **Suwon Hwaseong Museum** *(adult/child ₩2000/1000)*.

Escape to (never-n)Everland

Korea's largest amusement park, **Everland** *(everland.com; from ₩46,000)* makes for a fun-filled family day out, but it's also a good time for anyone who likes thrill rides and sugary snacks. The park is split into several themed areas. Magic Land is mostly dedicated to kid-friendly rides, while American Adventure ups the adrenaline. Ride the T Express, a gargantuan wooden roller coaster, in European Adventure, and see elephants, tigers and the panda twins, Rui Bao and Hui Bao, in Zoo Topia.

The Everland complex is owned by Samsung, and selections from its founder Lee Byung-chull's extensive art collection feature in rotating exhibitions at the superb **Hoam Art Museum** *(leeumhoam.org; adult/student ₩25,000/13,000)*. Buddhist art, paintings by 18th-century master Gyeomjae Jeong Seon and international augmented-reality works are just some of what you might come across.

Korea's video art star

The father of video art, Nam June Paik was arguably Korea's most influential modern artist, and his works still feel fun and fresh decades after they were created. The **Nam June Paik Art Center** *(njp.ggcf.kr)* has regularly changing exhibitions of pieces pulled from Paik's archive, as well as by avant-garde creators who share his experimental approach. Viewing works by Paik, who died in 2006, you get the sense that no one understood the way video would come to shape our lives quite like he did.

In the adjacent park, handsome displays at **Gyeonggi Province Museum** *(musenet.ggcf.kr)* trace life in the region from Paleolithic to modern times. Special attention is paid to Gyeonggi-do's historic role as the gateway to the capital. The province produced most of Joseon's porcelain, and the exhibits related to the area's pottery are a particular highlight.

Gwangju

TIME FROM SEOUL: 1¼HR

Hike beside 17th-century fortress walls

The World Heritage–listed fortress of **Namhan-sanseong** once guarded Seoul's southern entrance and served as a backup capital in times of emergency. Today the fortress walls, of which 12.3km remain, are protected within a provincial park threaded with hiking trails that take you through beautiful pine and oak forests. The most popular route is a two-hour loop past three of the fortress' four gates that serves up sweeping panoramas along the way. Budget a full day to trek the wall's entire perimeter.

Just inside Namhan-sanseong's main entrance is a fine reconstruction of **Namhan-sanseong Emergency Palace** *(adult/child ₩2000/1000)*. Considering its beautiful setting, you have to imagine the Joseon king would have been tempted to make his residence here permanent. Outside the gate, you'll find a collection of

EVERLAND PRACTICALITIES

Purchase tickets online to access discount packages, or at the ticket booth dedicated to foreign visitors.

Caribbean Bay *(adult/child ₩45,000/39,000)* is the resort's separate water park. It has indoor and outdoor pools, an impressive assortment of rides, a lazy river and a not-so-lazy wave pool.

For both Everland and Caribbean Bay, its best to visit on a weekday, when crowds are more manageable. Avoid public holidays.

The Hoam Art Museum cafe is an architecturally eye-catching, if pricey, place for a meal.

Outside the art museum, the beautiful Heewon traditional garden has a lotus pond, plum trees and sculptures.

HOAM'S SISTER MUSEUM

See more art from Lee's collection at **Leeum Museum of Art** (p81) in Itaewon, where items range from a 1500-year-old gilt-bronze crown to works by Salvador Dalí, Louise Bourgeois and Bahc Yiso.

TEMPORARY PALACES

When Joseon's rulers travelled around Korea, they needed somewhere fitting to stay. In places where they often went, such as the tombs of ancestors or a regional fortress, a *haenggung* (temporary palace) was constructed. The Namhan-sanseong Emergency Palace was built in 1625 and proved useful to King Injo a decade later when he took shelter here from the invading Manchu armies from China. Unlike other temporary royal abodes, Namhan-sanseong was designed to be the hub of a temporary capital in times of crisis. Subsequent kings stayed here when visiting Yeongneung and Nyeongneung, the tombs of King Sejong and King Hyojong, respectively.

Other temporary palaces are located in Suwon, Ganghwa and Jeonju.

restaurants to fuel your hike and the informative **Namhan-sanseong Historical Museum**, where you can learn about the fort's construction and the warrior monks who defended it.

Guri

TIME FROM SEOUL: 1HR

Pay your respects at the tombs of Joseon royalty

Donggureung *(royal.khs.go.kr)* is the largest and most attractive of the World Heritage–listed Joseon royal tomb complexes scattered around Seoul and Gyeonggi-do. Spend a bit of time in the small **History Center** near the entrance to learn about the elaborate burial rites and pick up a site map before visiting the tombs of the seven kings and 10 queens that are buried here.

All the tombs are similarly arranged on large grassy mounds according to the precise rules of Confucianism and feng shui. The entrances are marked by a simple red-painted wooden gate, stone pathway and hall for conducting rites in front of the humped burial mounds decorated with stone statuary – typically a pair of civil officers and generals, plus horses and protective animals such as tigers and rams. Note the silver grass atop the tomb of Joseon-dynasty founder King Taejo, which comes from his hometown of Hamheung, North Korea. Plan on 1½ hours to explore Donggureung in its entirety.

Yangpyeong

TIME FROM SEOUL: 1¾HR

See where the waters meet

When the weather's good, few places make for a better outing than **Dumulmeori**, the spot where the northern and southern branches of the Han River meet before flowing through Seoul. You'll find cafes and restaurants catering to day-trippers, a regal 400-year-old zelkova tree and a traditional sailboat moored just offshore, a tribute to the time when this was an important merchant port. Be sure to try the Dumulmeori specialities of corn dogs and ice cream made with lotus leaves.

From Dumulmeori, you can cross a bridge built atop anchored boats to **Semiwon** *(semiwon.or.kr; adult/child ₩7000/4000)*, a garden that's particularly known for its many lotuses and water lilies. Peak bloom for the lotuses is early June, while the water lilies are at their best in July and August.

Gapyeong

TIME FROM SEOUL: 2HR

Surround yourself with horticultural beauty

Deep in the verdant hills of Gapyeong is the astonishing **Garden of Morning Calm** *(morningcalm.co.kr; adult/student/child ₩11,000/8500/7500)*, covering 33 hectares and including 20 different themed gardens, among them a traditional Korean garden, an English cottage-style garden and a bonsai garden. You could quite easily spend an entire day here, admiring the countless beautiful views and lingering in the garden's cafes and restaurants.

In spring, expect cherry blossoms and colourful tulips; in summer, hydrangeas burst into cheerful spheres and streams

CHIARA SAKUWA/SHUTTERSTOCK

Garden of Morning Calm, Gapyeong

offer respite from the heat; in autumn, ginkgos light up in gold, and pink muhly grass creates feathery pastel waves. Even in winter, the snow and an elaborate light display make the garden worth a visit.

Reaching the garden by a combination of train and bus is a time-consuming process, so you might want to consider renting a car for your visit. The surrounding valley has many good pensions and places to eat, including the **Kraemerlee** microbrewery, serving smoked-meat platters and over a dozen craft beers.

Incheon

TIME FROM SEOUL: 1HR

Ride the monorail to Wolmis

Jump on the **Wolmi Sea Train** *(wolmiseatrain.or.kr; adult/student/child ₩14,000/10,000/8000)* to Wolmido, a former island that was connected to the mainland after the Korean War. Leaving from near Incheon station, the monorail makes three stops around the island. You need a Korean phone number and bank card to book online. If you need assistance, try the **tourist info centre** at the station. Buses also make the trip.

On the 'island', a waterfront boardwalk has amusement parks, arcades, cafes and restaurants. The forested **Wolmi Park** contains an observatory for panoramic views and a large

KOREAN GARDEN DESIGN

Although it incorporates a wide range of styles, Garden of Morning Calm is part of a venerable tradition of gardens on the peninsula. Whereas gardens in the West often seek to shape and apply order to the natural world – think of all those trimmed lawns and clipped hedges – traditional Korean gardens seek to blend in with their surroundings. Garden locations are often chosen for their favourable *pungsu*, or feng shui, and follow the existing topography. When being laid out, Korean gardens typically factor the surrounding view (often mountains) into their design. Informality, simplicity and an unforced appearance are prized, thus strengthening the connection between people and the natural world.

EATING IN INCHEON'S CHINATOWN

Mandabok: Specialises in *hayan baengnyeon jajang*, a white *jajangmyeon* (noodles in black bean sauce) with pork, seafood and vegetables. *11am-9.30pm, from 10.30am Sat & Sun* ₩

Yanjing: An unmissable multistorey place cooking up *jajangmyeon*, *jjamppong* (spicy noodle soup with seafood) and Chinese classics like Peking duck. *10.30am-9.30pm* ₩

Taehwawon: Century-old restaurant making its own bean paste for its signature Incheon *hyangto jajang*. Also has an all-veg menu. *11am-9pm, to 8.30pm Sat & Sun* ₩

Sinseung Banjeom: Run by a granddaughter of the man whose restaurant invented *jajangmyeon*. Large menu runs from dumplings to *mapo tofu*. *11am-3pm & 4.45-9pm* ₩

NAVIGATING INCHEON OPEN PORT

Walk through Korea's early modern history as you traverse the Chinese, Japanese and Western settlements of Incheon Open Port.

START	END	LENGTH
Incheon station	Seokjeongnu Pavilion	1.3 km; 1½hr

Exit Incheon station and aim for the vibrant 1 **pai-loo gate** marking the entrance to 2 **Chinatown**. Snack your way through dumplings and noodles at the neighbourhood's restaurants, then learn about what you ate at 3 **Jajangmyeon Museum**, which tells the story of Incheon's most moreish invention.

Leaving Chinatown, walk to the collection of old warehouses that make up 4 **Incheon Art Platform** to see what's on in its galleries and performance spaces. At the complex's eastern end, take a left and go to Sinpo-ro 23beon-gil. You're now in the heart of the old Japanese settlement. On either side of the intersection are 5 **Incheon Open Port Modern Architecture Museum** and the domed 6 **Incheon Open Port Museum** Both occupy erstwhile Japanese banks from the turn of the 20th century. A few steps further on is 7 **Daebul Hotel Exhibition Hall**, site of Korea's first Western-style hotel.

Turn right and you'll arrive at a set of 8 **stairs** that once marked the border between the Chinese and Japanese settlements. Note the different styles of stone lanterns on either side. Before climbing up, break for *pat-bingsu* (shaved ice with sweet red beans) at 9 **Pot-R**, housed in a well-preserved *machiya* (Japanese wooden townhouse) from the 1880s. At the top of the stairs is 10 **Jayu Park**. Head to 11 **Seokjeongnu Pavilion** for views over the Port of Incheon.

traditional garden. On the park's southern edge is the fascinating **Museum of Korea Emigration History** *(incheon.go.kr)*, which chronicles the Korean diaspora starting in the early 20th century, when thousands emigrated to work on Hawaiian sugar cane plantations.

Re-inventing old Incheon

On the edge of the Incheon Open Port area is **Incheon Art Platform** *(inartplatform.kr)*, a grouping of squat red-brick warehouses from the 1930s and '40s that has been turned into a creative space and artist residency. Stop by to peruse its galleries, installations and performances. Most events are free. The structure housing IAP's offices is the country's oldest Western-style office building, dating to 1888.

In recent years, old commercial buildings in Incheon's Gaehang-ro area, close to Sinpo Market, have had makeovers. Drop by retro-chic cafes such as **Brown Hands** and other cool places to eat and drink.

For more industrial-artistic mashups, venture out to **COSMO 40**, near Gajaeul station. The former chemical factory is now a super-cool cafe/bakery/gallery/performance space. Wander Void Hall, where giant illuminated metal columns stretch two storeys high, play ping-pong on the 2nd floor and scramble around catwalks before settling in for a latte beneath dangling crane hooks.

Learn about the Korean War

The strikingly designed **Memorial Hall for Incheon Landing Operation** *(landing915.com)* commemorates the daring September 1950 attack, codenamed Operation Chromite, that was a turning point in the Korean War. Displays go into granular detail about the operation's planning and execution using archival newsreels, displays of weaponry and a room-sized scale model of the battle. Outside, amphibious landing vehicles and other materiel are on display.

Next door, **Incheon Metropolitan City Museum** *(incheon.go.kr)* has some good exhibitions on Joseon-era farming tools and Open Port history, though English info is limited.

See Korea's city of the future

After decades of development, the 'smart city' of Songdo, built on some 600 hectares of reclaimed land, is mostly complete. The planned neighbourhood lacks the soul of other Korean cities, but it's worth a visit to marvel at the engineering and see the future of Korean urbanism.

Songdo's highlight is **Songdo Central Park**, which is surrounded by glassy skyscrapers and has walking paths and a canal. Rent pleasure boats from the boat house at the canal's east end. There are several sights of note in and around the park. Most arresting is **Tri-Bowl** *(tribowl.kr)*, a curving, metallic arts and culture complex that seems to only be visiting our planet temporarily. It's especially stunning lit up at night. Inside are a concert hall and exhibition space.

KNOW YOUR NOODLES

One of Korea's favourite noodle dishes, *jajangmyeon* was invented in Incheon. Sometime around 1910, chefs in the Gonghwachun kitchen (the building now houses the **Jajangmyeon Museum**; p136) tweaked a Chinese recipe to create a dish of noodles in fermented bean sauce. Tasty, filling and cheap, it became a staple of Chinese dockworkers and bricklayers in Korea.

In the post–Korean War years, imported American wheat flour helped a taste for *jajangmyeon* spread among the public. By 2015, Koreans were slurping up some seven million bowls a day. Today, *jajangmyeon* is in every Chinese restaurant and sold in instant-noodle form. Two of the most common versions are *ganjajang*, a slightly drier, made-to-order style, and *hayan* (white) *jajang*, made with a lighter Chinese bean paste.

INCHEON HISTORY

Incheon's modern history began in 1883, when its port opened to international trade. Japanese, Chinese, American, French, Russian and other foreign merchants poured in, bringing their cultures and transforming the fishing settlement then known as Jemulpo into a major city.

Incheon's most famous chapter came during the Korean War. Pushed back to the peninsula's southeastern corner and in danger of losing the war only months after it began, South Korea and its UN allies plotted a daring raid behind enemy lines. In September 1950, some 75,000 troops and 261 naval vessels under the command of US General Douglas MacArthur landed at Incheon, overwhelming North Korean forces and advancing to retake Seoul.

Incheon Urban History Museum *(incheon.go.kr)* gives a good overview of the city's past 150 years, while across the canal, **National Museum of World Writing Systems** *(mow.or.kr)* is a captivating odyssey through the history of the written word, from Egyptian hieroglyphs to AI. Don't miss the Akkadian cuneiform tablet from at least 1600 BCE. On the park's south side, the **Songdo Hanok Village** is a collection of restaurants in newly built *hanok* – pretty, but not exactly rich in history.

Whatever you do in Songdo, make sure you visit the **G-Tower** observation deck. Take the elevator next to the info desk and you'll be treated to a 33rd-floor view of Songdo in all its hubris and accomplishment. From this vantage point, imagining that everything you see was once ocean is genuinely mind-boggling.

Ganghwado

TIME FROM SEOUL: 1HR

Tour historic island sites

When the Mongols invaded Korea in the 13th century, the Goryeo royal court hightailed it to this large island at the mouth of the Han River. **Goryeo Palace Site** *(adult/child ₩1200/900)* consists of reconstructions of Joseon government offices destroyed by the French in 1866. Most interesting is a royal library with displays on valuable records the French looted.

Just downhill are the 19th-century **Yongheunggung Royal Residence**, where King Cheoljong lived before ascending to the throne, and the **Ganghwa Anglican Church**. Built by a royal architect in 1900, its traditional Korean exterior and Western interior create a distinctive dissonance. View photos of early 20th-century parishioners and masses in the nave. Services are held on Sunday.

Ganghwado's location made it a frequent place of conflict, and the Joseon government built 53 defensive facilities around the island. The most impressive is **Gwangseongbo Fort** *(adult/child ₩1500/1100)*. Constructed in 1658, it was the site of an 1871 battle with the US Navy. Walk the walls to check out observation posts, bulwarks and the wicked currents in the strait below. Overlooking the primary bridge to the mainland is **Gapgot Dondae** *(adult/child ₩1200/900)*, which dates to 1679. Besides the fortress walls and cannons, there's a small war museum and a 400-year-old orange tree.

EATING ALONG INCHEON'S GAEHANG-RO

Sinpo International Market: Traditional market famed for *dakgangjeong* (fried chicken pieces in spicy sauce). Wonjo Sinpo and Channuri are hugely popular. *10am-9pm* ₩₩

Taxco Market: Skip the nachos, but do try its respectable *birria* and *carnitas* tacos. There's also a shelf of Mexican snacks for sale. *11.30am-3pm & 5-9pm Wed-Mon* ₩

Mekong Sarong: A stylish restaurant with checkerboard floors and lots of plants that serves Vietnamese staples like pho and banh mi. *11.30am-3pm & 5-9pm Tue-Sun* ₩₩

Gaehangro Tongdak: Old-fashioned fried chicken in a deliberately retro setting decorated with old photos and glass lamps. *5pm-midnight, from 4pm Sat & Sun* ₩₩

JUN HYUN/SHUTTERSTOCK

Ganghwa Dolmen Park, Ganghwado

Learn about textile history

In the 1900s, Ganghwado was known for its *sochang*, a light, breathable cotton fabric. You can encounter this legacy at a trio of Ganghwa-eup sites. Learn about the industry, watch a weaving demonstration and sew a *sochang* souvenir at **Sochang Fabric Experience Hall** (closed Mondays). You can also sample local *sunmu* radish tea in a 1938 *hanok* on site. Down the street, **Dongkwang Textile Living Culture Center** displays old *sochang* manufacturing machines in a former factory.

Also nearby is **Joyang Bangjik**, occupying another former textile factory. It's nominally a cafe and bakery, but mainly it's a fever dream that seems to have emptied out every antique store in a 100km radius. Amid preserved sections of the factory are carousel horses, phone booths, a camera collection, religious memorabilia and who knows what else. Order a coffee and embrace the ephemera.

Survey 5000 years of island history

The imaginative displays at **Ganghwa History Museum** *(ganghwa.go.kr; adult/child ₩3000/2000)* start with the island's ancient dolmen sites and continue up to the US Navy attack on the island in 1871.

Speaking of dolmens, you can view several of them in **Ganghwa Dolmen Park** just outside the museum. There are about 45,000 of these Bronze Age megalithic tombs around the globe, and close to 40% are on the Korean Peninsula, including 160 on Ganghwado. Most impressive is the park's **Bugeun-ri Dolmen** – three giant stones hefted into a megalithic tomb (the two 'door' stones are missing). The enormous capstone weighs 53 tonnes. With expansive valley views it's no wonder the site was chosen for its auspicious purpose.

ISLAND ESCAPES

Dozens of islands are accessible from Incheon by road or ferry. These are some of the best.

Yeongjongdo: Besides Incheon International Airport, this large island is home to a pair of glitzy casino resorts: **INSPIRE Entertainment Resort** and **Paradise City Casino**.

Sindo, Sido & Modo: Bridge-linked islands reachable via a 10-minute ferry from Yeongjongdo's **Sammok Port**. Aim for the sculpture park at Modo's end.

Jangbongdo: A 40-minute ferry ride from Sammok Port, this island is known for camping, strangely shaped rocks and fine sunsets.

Muuido: A bridge links Yeongjongdo to this small island with forested hiking trails and sandy **Hanagae Beach**.

Deokjeokdo: This laid-back island is a two-hour ferry ride from Incheon. Suntan on spectacular, 2km-long **Seopo-ri Beach**, backed by a thick grove of 200-year-old pines.

GANGHWADO HISTORY

Dangun – grandson of a god, son of a bear-woman – is said to have founded the Korean people in 2333 BCE. Whether you believe that or not, Gangwhado's history stretches back almost as far. Some 160 dolmens provide proof of a civilisation existing here by at least 1500 BCE.

Fast-forward to the 13th century CE, and Ganghwado had its 39 years of fame when King Gojong moved his Goryeo capital here while Mongols rampaged on the mainland. The island also played a major role in Korea's modern history, as the scene of a bloody 1866 skirmish with the French, who were seeking revenge for the execution of French Catholic missionaries, and an 1871 conflict with a US naval mission attempting to open Korea to trade.

Korean Buddhism beginnings

Established in 381 CE, **Jeondeung-sa** *(jeondeungsa.org)* is Korea's oldest temple. Located within the walls of Samnang Fortress in the island's south, it has a beautiful forested setting on the slopes of Jeongjoksan. Views reach all the way to the mainland. Take a couple of hours to soak up the vistas and the peaceful setting, making sure to seek out the temple's 900-year-old iron bell and a 700-year-old ginkgo.

The temple's marquee attraction is **Daeungjeon Hall**, built in 1681. Beneath a coffered ceiling decorated with dragons, mythical birds and lotus flowers, it holds a treasured gilded Buddha triad. Outside, carved wooden figures appear to hold up each corner of the roof. According to legend, they depict a barmaid who stole from the hall's carpenter. After you've toured the grounds, pause for a drink at the temple's charming teahouse, **Jungnim Dawon** You can also spend the night at Jeondeung-sa as part of the templestay program.

Sample some magkeolli

After leaving Jeondeung-sa, pop into nearby **Geumpung Brewery**, which has been making *makgeolli* since the 1930s. The original building has a shop and an upstairs exhibition space where you can watch a video about the brewing process

EATING ON GANGHWADO

Wangjajeong Mukbap: Next to the Goryeo Palace Site, specialising in *mukbap*, an acorn jelly and rice soup with diced cabbage. *10am-9pm Tue-Sun* W

Manisan Sanchae: Real country eatin'. Superb bibimbap with wild mountain vegetables, served with a rich soybean-paste soup. *9.30am-7pm, from 9am Sat & Sun* W

Toga: Soft tofu stew made with salted and fermented shrimp and sliced hot peppers. *9.30am-5pm Mon, Tue, Thu & Fri, 9am-7pm Sat & Sun* W

Wondumak Garden: Open since 1990. Try its signature soup made with *galbi* and salted shrimp (a Ganghwado speciality). *10am-2.30pm & 5-9pm Thu-Tue, 10am-9pm Sat & Sun* WW

CSTRIKE/SHUTTERSTOCK

Jeondeung-sa, Ganghwa-gun

and see artefacts from the brewery's history. Contact Geumpung in advance to join one of its brewing or tasting classes.

Hike to Dangun's altar

The peak of **Manisan** is crowned by Chamseongdan Altar, said to have been built by Dangun, the mythical first Korean. The views from here are phenomenal. Of the three different routes to the 472m summit, the shortest (4.8km, three hours return) starts at Hamheodongcheon campsite in Hwado-myeon village. Alternatively, follow a 6.4km route to the summit from Manisan Tourist Information Centre in the village of Sangbang-ri. After you descend, recover at the broad Dongmak Beach, where you'll find plenty of restaurants and convenience stores.

View North Korea from Gyodongdo

Rising from the northern tip of Ganghwado is **Ganghwa Peace Observatory** *(adult/student/child ₩2500/1700/1000)*. There are some information displays in Korean, but the main attraction is the views into North Korea, just on the other side of the Han River. Note the South Korean military facilities along the riverbank.

Another, prettier, place to spy across the border is **Hwagae Garden** *(ganghwa.go.kr/hwagae; adult/child ₩5000/3000)* on Gyodongdo, connected to Gangwhado by bridge. Divided into themed zones, the garden climbs a mountain slope – at the top is a glass-floored observatory that looks into North Korea and over a scattering of small islands. Come at sunset for the most drama. It's a 45-minute climb to the observatory, or you can ride the slow monorail up. Near the garden is the old-timey **Daeryong Market**, with retro cafes and places to eat.

GANGHWADO PRACTICALITIES

Buses from the mainland end up in the island's largest town, Ganghwa-eup, which is a handy base from which to explore. The town has numerous hotel options, while pensions dot the island's rural interior and cluster on its southern and western coasts.

You can reach all sites listed here by public transport, but Ganghwado is big and buses infrequent, so if you're aiming to visit numerous sites, consider joining an organised bus tour from Seoul or Incheon or renting a car. If you rent, do so from an agency at Incheon or Gimpo international airports. Rates there are considerably cheaper than at agencies in Seoul, and English-speaking staff are available to help.

TOP EXPERIENCE

The DMZ & Imjingak Resort

Less than 50km north of Seoul is the Demilitarized Zone (DMZ), the 4km-wide, 240km-long no-man's land separating North and South Korea. It's a sinister place where the tension is palpable, but it's also a major tourist attraction, fascinating and forbidding in equal measure. Join a tour to enter the DMZ, or travel independently to Imjingak to get as close as you can on your own.

GUILLAUME B/SHUTTERSTOCK

Dora Observatory

TOP TIPS

- At the time of research, DMZ tours were not permitted to visit the JSA. Check with tour operators to see if this changes.
- For all tours, you need to bring your passport. There are other rules to be observed – check with your tour company beforehand.
- You can reach Imjingak Resort from Seoul by bus or a combination of bus and train (2¼ hours).

PRACTICALITIES

- dmz.gg.go.kr
- tour prices vary
- Imjingak Resort 9am-6pm

DMZ Tours

The only way to access the heavily mined DMZ is on a tour. Most operators offer half- and full-day options. Both typically visit **Imjingak Resort**, the **Third Infiltration Tunnel** and **Dora Observatory**. Discovered in 1978, the tunnel is one of four that North Korea is known to have dug under the DMZ for a potential surprise attack. Creeping along 265m of this 73m-deep tunnel isn't for the claustrophobic, or the tall. At Dora Observatory, you can peer through binoculars into North Korea. On a clear day, you can make out the city of Kaesong. When geopolitical conditions permit, longer tours also visit the **Joint Security Area** (JSA), where the Military Demarcation Line separates the two countries and North and South Korean troops stand face to face.

Imjingak Resort

This park on the banks of the Imjin River makes for a surreal day. Solemn sites such as the **National Memorial for Abductees During the Korean War**, a bullet-riddled locomotive and the remains of a bridge that once connected the two countries share space with art installations, fast-food restaurants and an amusement park. Take the gondola across the river to visit an observatory and **Gallery Greaves**, a museum in a former US Army camp bowling alley.

Paju

TIME FROM SEOUL: 1HR

Visit a book city...

On the way to Imjingak Resort, soak up the literary vibes in **Paju Book City** *(pajubookcity.org)*, a collection of some 900 publishing houses, bookshops, bookbinders and related businesses that began to take shape in 1989. Many occupy architecturally striking buildings. Bibliophiles should visit **Book City Letterpress Museum** *(letterpressmuseum.co.kr;₩4000)*, which displays working presses, typewriters from around the world and a restoration of the office that published Korea's Declaration of Independence. The museum's collection of 35 million metal printing blocks, weighing a cumulative 25 tonnes, is truly...ahem...impressive.

Next door, the **Asia Publication Culture & Information Center** houses the Forest of Wisdom library and Booksori Bookstore. Both offer plenty of places to curl up with a good read from the towering shelves. Hunt around and you'll find some in English. If you've ever wished you could just live at the library, book a room at **Jijihyang** *(jijihyang.com)*, the centre's on-site guesthouse.

A short walk away is the contemporary **Mimesis Art Museum** *(mimesisartmuseum.co.kr; adult/student/child ₩10,000/8000/5000)*, a curvaceous concrete building designed by Portuguese architect Álvaro Siza.

...and an art village

Several kilometres north of Book City is **Heyri Art Valley** *(heyri.net)*, a cultural complex with dozens of museums, galleries, studios and performance spaces. It tends to offer more kitsch than culture – there are museums dedicated to Coca-Cola, dolls, dinosaurs etc – but there are also some gems, a good deal of interesting architecture and lots of charming cafes.

By far the complex's best site is the free **National Folk Museum of Korea, Paju** *(nfm.go.kr/paju)*, a branch of, and storage facility, for the main museum (p68) in Seoul. Two-storey glass cabinets showcase a fascinating range of artefacts, from ceramics and beer glasses to an amulet for cows meant to ward off misfortune. There are also interesting displays that take you behind the scenes of how the museum conducts its conservation work.

START THE PRESSES!

Paju is the centre of Korea's modern publishing industry, but printing has a long and storied history on the peninsula. People were producing woodblock prints of Buddhist texts by at least the first half of the 8th century, making Korea among the first cultures to adopt the technology after its invention in China.

While Johannes Gutenberg created the movable-type printing press in Germany in the mid-1400s, Koreans were using a form of movable metal type up to two centuries earlier. In fact, the world's oldest surviving book published using movable metal type is Korean. *The Anthology of Great Buddhist Priests' Zen Teachings*, also known as Jikji, was printed by Buddhist monks at Heungdeoksa Temple in 1377 – learn all about it at Cheongju's **Early Printing Museum.**

Places We Love to Stay

W Budget WW Midrange WWW Top End

Bukchon & Seochon

MAP P60 & P66

Seochon Guesthouse WW Charming *hanok* with mostly Korean-style rooms, run by kind hosts who offer a homemade breakfast and lots of neighbourhood tips.

Boan Stay WW Stylishly minimalist rooms featuring art and furniture by contemporary designers, On the 3rd and 4th floors of Artspace Boan 1942, overlooking Gyeongbokgung.

Bukchon Maru WW The *ondol* (heated-floor) rooms at this family-run *hanok* guesthouse are basic, authentic and comfortable. Only the family room has its own bathroom.

Tongtong Hotel WW Close to Ikseon-dong. Small rooms styled in a spare aesthetic, with a lovely rooftop overlooking a Buddhist temple next door.

Butler.Lee WWW Manages 20 different luxury self-catering *hanok* around Gyeongbokgung, some in historic homes and all gorgeously decorated.

Rak-Ko-Jae WWW Beautifully restored *hanok* with an enchanting garden and a mud-walled sauna. Second branch nearby has a culture lounge and cafe.

Myeong-dong

MAP P72

Zaza Backpackers W A top option in the enclave of hostels and guesthouses south of Myeongdong station, with nice design touches and friendly staff.

Namsan Hostel Guest House W Nice, no-frills place with some of the lowest rates you'll find this close to Myeong-dong. Has private rooms, a female-only dorm and a rooftop terrace.

Hotel 28 WW There's a Korean-cinema theme at this classy boutique hotel at the heart of Myeong-dong's action.

Small House Big Door WW Offers an excellent style-to-price ratio with modern furnishings and rooms decorated in *obangsaek*, Korea's traditional five primary colours.

Metro Hotel WW Splashes of style abound at this small, professionally run hotel with boutique aspirations. Room size and design vary.

L'Escape WWW The decor throughout this plush hotel channels *belle époque* Parisian glamour. The deep-red *amour* rooms are particularly striking.

Itaewon & Yongsan-gu

MAP P82

G Guesthouse Itaewon W Outstanding budget digs in the heart of Itaewon, ideal for meeting fellow travellers in the kitchen or on the rooftop.

Seoul Cube Itaewon W For people who like to party, this hostel at the doorstep of the local club scene offers free breakfast and communal facilities.

Mondrian Seoul Itaewon WW Chic contemporary hotel. Lots of facilities, including swanky indoor and outdoor pools, sauna and indoor virtual golf.

Imperial Palace Boutique Hotel WW This hotel, with comfortable rooms in a prime location, is easy to spot with its bright colour-block exterior.

Dongdaemun & Seongsu

MAP P91 & P96

Mangrove Dongdaemun W Co-working and living apartment block offering dorms and small apartments with self-catering kitchens, canteen and rooftop terrace.

Hotel Poco WW Perfect base for checking out the trendy Seongsu neighbourhood. Deluxe double rooms feature a dart board and mini ping-pong table.

ABP Sindang WWW Standing for A Better Place, with four stylishly designed self-catering units. Check-in at Manmool cafe-bar.

Hotel Shilla WWW Luxe digs on a hillside near Namsan. Highlights include an all-season outdoor pool and Michelin-starred Korean restaurant La Yeon.

Western Seoul

MAP P98

Time Travelers Relax W A choice of dorms or private rooms, quirky art, a library, lots of plants and a small courtyard make this Hongdae hostel a great budget option.

Roi Guesthouse W Budget-friendly guesthouse with larger rooms than most and a quiet location on a tree-lined Yeonnam-dong street.

GLAD Mapo WW This sleek hotel offers good value, with modern rooms, a gym and a work lounge, just steps from the well-connected Gongdeok station.

RYSE WWW Takes the surrounding Hongdae aesthetic and dresses it up with artsy rooms, a private cinema, on-site skate shop and 15th-floor bar with terrace.

Gangnam & Southern Seoul MAP P110 & P117

Seoul Olympic Parktel ₩₩ Within Olympic Park, this tower has tidy, basic rooms, some of which have lush views over the park's greenery.

Owall Hotel ₩₩ Six stunningly designed rooms that bring together Japanese and Scandinavian minimalism. All come with a private terrace; two have their own pools.

H Avenue Hotel Yeoksam ₩₩ Smartly furnished rooms in a high-rise. Two suites have access to small rooftop swimming pools, glamping tents and city views.

Lotte Hotel World ₩₩₩ Some rooms look directly onto Lotte World Adventure theme park's Magic Island. Also has cartoon character rooms.

Josun Palace ₩₩₩ A glamorous hotel with midcentury-modern touches and rooms in soothing shades of white and cream.

Daehangno & Changsin-dong MAP P120

Original Backpackers ₩ Superior design hostel with lots of cool facilities, including a 'AI' laundry and rooftop kitchen.

Glue Hotel ₩₩ Orange pillows, house plants and art elevate this boutique hotel. Some rooms have views across to Ihwa Maeul. There's a cafe-bar in the basement.

Bukhansan National Park MAP P127

Ui-dong Family Camping Ground ₩₩ Pitch your own tent or stay in a glamping tent with beds, air-con and cooking facilities. Its *ondol* makes it a year-round option.

Anto Resort ₩₩₩ Set in landscaped grounds on the park doorstep, the spacious, stylish rooms at this luxe resort feature timber decor.

Suwon & Yongjin

Hotel Dono ₩₩ Decent modern rooms at this pleasant hotel in the heart of the city and within easy reach of Hwaseong's main gate.

Golden Tulip Ever Yongin ₩₩ Family-friendly hotel near the entrance to Everland, should you want to get an early start on your theme-park fun.

Novotel Ambassador Suwon ₩₩₩ Spacious and contemporary in design, with an ideal location next to Suwon's subway and train station.

Gapyeong

Leikki Puisto ₩₩₩ Fantastic family accommodation with super-king-size four-person beds, separate self-catering kitchens, a big kid-friendly pool and charming children's play area.

Incheon

Harbor Park Hotel ₩₩ Plain but well-equipped rooms with views of the working harbour and Chinatown. Facilities include a fitness centre.

Gyeongwonjae by Walkerhill ₩₩₩ The palatial-style *hanok* rooms at this luxe hotel in its own landscaped plot next to Songdo's Central Park make for a memorable stay.

Ganghwado

Hotel Everrich ₩₩ Offering expansive views towards the mainland from its hillside perch, this contemporary-styled hotel has stylish rooms in a range of sizes.

Spoonbill Pension ₩₩ This south-coast pension provides nice views out to the ocean, and all rooms have enclosed verandahs and picnic tables with built-in barbecue grills.

KIKUJUNGBOY CC/SHUTTERSTOCK

Myeong-dong (p71)

For places to stay in Gangwon-do, see p175

LIMLIM/SHUTTERSTOCK

Above: Seoraksan National Park (p162); Right: Jukdo Beach (p165), Yangyang

Researched by
Simon Richmond

Gangwon-do

WHERE MAJESTIC MOUNTAINS MEET BEAUTIFUL BEACHES

South Korea's lightly populated and mountainous northeastern state is an adventure playground of superb national parks, soft-sand beaches and fascinating cultural attractions.

Glorious Gangwon-do offers some of South Korea's most stunning natural landscapes, up-close Demilitarized Zone (DMZ) experiences and laid-back coastal getaways. This is where many overworked Seoulites escape – to daydream on the beaches of Gangneung and Yangyang, chow down on Sokcho seafood and Chuncheon's spicy chicken, get lost in the hills of Odaesan and Taebaeksan and, come winter, to enjoy snow sports around Pyeongchang.

THE KIMMI/SHUTTERSTOCK

Seoraksan, the region's premier national park and a UNESCO Biosphere Reserve covering more than 150 sq km between Sokcho and Inje, is one of Korea's most beloved hiking locales. Atop Dinosaur Ridge, with rocky landscapes spreading out before you, there's no better feeling.

Contrast this with the barbed wire, war memorials and peace observatories along the DMZ. It's a bleak but beautiful border where the hope of reunification stays alive and wildlife thrives.

Inland, the provincial capital, Chuncheon, is a watery wonderland, surrounded by lakes and brimming with recreational activities, including Korea's longest cable-car ride. Use the city as a base for trips to amazing gardens and art galleries in magnificent natural settings. Along the East Sea are harbour towns, big and small, humming with fishing industry and lively seafood markets. Gangwon-do also celebrates its traditional culture with zest – from Gangneung's 400-year-old Dano Festival to Samcheok's park packed with phallic sculptures.

THE MAIN AREAS

CHUNCHEON
Recreational leisure in the city of lakes. p150

SOKCHO
At the foot of Seoraksan, a seaside delight. p158

GANGNEUNG
Korea's coffee capital on the shore. p167

Find Your Way

Large swathes of this province can feel very much off the beaten path, with looming mountains seeming to always block your path. Be patient, go slow and don't try to pack too much in.

Chuncheon, p150

The great outdoors in easy reach, a celebrated mime festival and an alley dedicated to delicious spicy stir-fried chicken.

Sokcho, p158

Appealing port city with scenic walks along the ocean and around lakes, plus North Korean eats and seafood treats.

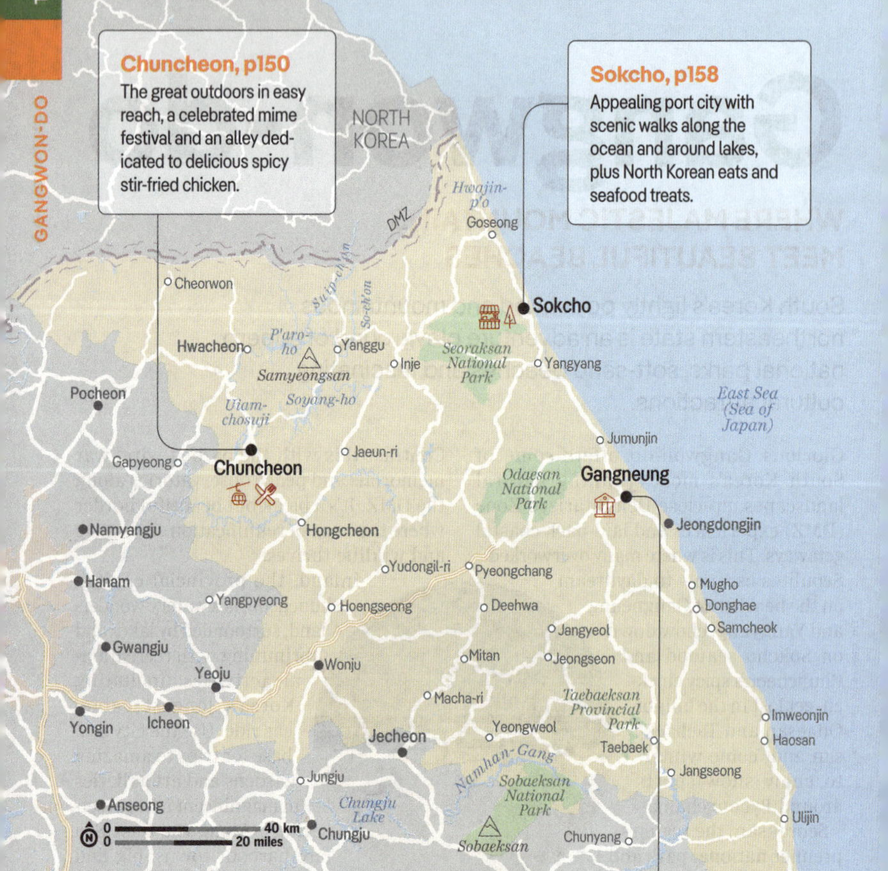

Gangneung, p167

Relax on sandy beaches dotted with wind-bent pines, and visit *hallyu* (Korean Wave) sites and cafe hot spots.

CAR

A car is your friend in Gangwon-do. Without one, you'll feel like you're spending more time travelling from place to place than ever settling in anywhere.

BUS

If you don't have a car, you'll mostly be travelling by bus, as there aren't many train routes out this way, save for the east-west lines that connect Seoul to Chuncheon and Gangneung, and a line extending south from Gangneung.

MIRKO KUZMANOVIC/GETTY IMAGES

Nami Island (p155)

Plan Your Time

Set your sights on Seoraksan National Park, but don't forget about the region's beaches and port towns.

Pressed for Time

- Start in **Chuncheon** (p150), spending a day around the lakes, riding the cable car and relishing spicy chicken. Make an excursion to beautiful **Nami Island** (p155), then proceed to **Sokcho** (p158). Here, walk along the beach and eat some fish by the sea before heading to **Seoraksan National Park** (p162), where you can ride the cable car and climb to Ulsan Bawi.

A Weeklong Stay

- Be dazzled by **Les Jardins de Médongaule** (p156) and **Museum SAN** (p157). Laze on the beaches of **Gangneung** (p167) and cycle around its lagoon. Tour the spectacular **Naksan-sa** (p164) seaside temple. Spend an evening in **Sokcho** (p158), then head as far north as you can go for beautiful vistas across the DMZ at **Goseong** (p165).

SEASONAL HIGHLIGHTS

SPRING
In Gangneung, cherry blossom fringes the **Gyeongpodae** (p170) lagoon in April, and Chuncheon celebrates its mimes (p152) in May.

SUMMER
Yangyang's beaches come alive with surfers and parties, and Gangneung gets into the Dano spirit (p169).

AUTUMN
Late October and early November is an ideal time to visit **Seoraksan** (p162), when it becomes a dazzling tapestry of autumn foliage.

WINTER
Hit the snowy slopes at Gangwon-do's ski resorts (p173), some of the best in Korea.

Chuncheon

CABLE CAR | LAKELAND | LEGOLAND

Cocooned by low-lying mountains and lapped by shimmering Uiam Lake, Gangwon-do's provincial capital is known as Korea's 'City of Water'. These inviting surroundings make the city an outdoor-activities hot spot, with everything from hiking and swan-shaped paddle boats to pedalling a 'railbike' and gliding high on Korea's longest cable car to the forested peaks of Samaksan on offer. It's this easy access to nature, combined with superb transport links to Seoul and a relaxed atmosphere, that make Chuncheon a popular weekend getaway for capital dwellers. Food lovers also flock here, thanks to the city's twin signature dishes: *dakgalbi* (spicy stir-fried chicken) and *makguksu* (cold buckwheat noodles). All this, plus playing host to a major international mime-performance festival, one of Korea's national museums and Asia's largest LEGOLAND theme park, makes Chuncheon an ideal base for exploring central Gangwon-do.

GETTING AROUND

Chuncheon is well connected to major South Korean locations by express and intercity buses, the terminals of which are beside each other south of the river, near **Namchuncheon train station**. Travellers coming from Seoul on the subway extension along the Gyeongchun Line or KTX trains can either alight here, or at Chuncheon, which is closer to the city centre area. Within town, buses or taxis are the best way to get around as attractions are fairly scattered.

TOP TIP

Keep your admission ticket when you visit some of Chuncheon's major attractions to qualify for a discount at another attraction, either on the same day or the following day. For full details, pick up a leaflet from the tourist information centres at Chuncheon and Namchuncheon train stations.

Ride Korea's Longest Cable Car

Aerial wonder

For breathtaking views of Uiam Lake and the surrounding mountains, the **Chuncheon Samaksan Mountain Lake Cable Car** *(samaksancablecar.com; adult/child from ₩23,000/17,000)* is not to be missed. Spanning 3.61km from Samcheon-dong across Uiam Lake to Samaksan, it's Korea's longest cable-car ride. For an additional thrill, pay extra to ride in a 'crystal cabin' with a transparent floor. From the top station, follow the 800m-long Skywalk path to the Skydeck observatory for more views. A round-trip takes around one hour. Note that there's no way to connect to Samaksan's trails at the top, so if you want to explore the mountain, plan on doing so separately.

HIGHLIGHTS
1 Chuncheon Samaksan Mountain Lake Cable Car
2 Myeongdong Dakgalbi St

SIGHTS
3 Chuncheon National Museum
4 Gongjicheon Sculpture Park
5 Literary Village of Kim You-jeong
6 Memorial Hall for Ethiopian Veterans in the Korean War
7 Samaksan
8 Soyang-gang Maiden

ACTIVITIES
9 Gangchon Rail Park
10 Soyang-gang Skywalk

SLEEPING
11 Chuncheon Stay
12 Hotel YAJA Namchuncheon

EATING
13 Byoldang Makguksu
see 2 Myeongdong 1(il)beonji Dakgalbi
see 2 Woomi Dakgalbi

DRINKING & NIGHTLIFE
14 Dancing Caffeine Baker
15 Gallery Cafe
16 Gamja Island
17 Yedam the Gallery Cafe

ENTERTAINMENT
18 LEGOLAND Korea Resort

TRANSPORT
19 Bicycle Rental
20 Chuncheon Train Station
21 Express & Intercity Bus Terminals
22 Namchuncheon

CHUNCHEON'S MIME CULTURE

At the end of May, the annual **Chuncheon International Mime Festival** takes the spotlight in Chuncheon, drawing mime artists from around the globe who perform in a collection of theatre and outdoor shows. Together with the London Mime Festival and France's Mimos Festival, Chuncheon's event is considered among the world's top three mime festivals, putting on a spectacle of movement set to water, lights and fire. Launched in 1989, the festival is the making of first-generation mime artist Yu Jin Gyu, known for putting a uniquely Korean spin on miming by creating Dokkaebi Nanjang, a playful and chaotic performance piece that invites audience participation.

KARAMAJOVA/SHUTTERSTOCK

***Dakgalbi* (spicy stir-fried chicken)**

Hike up Samaksan

Chuncheon's three-peaked mountain

Just 20 minutes from central Chuncheon by bus, **Samaksan** *(entry ₩2000)* is a convenient hiking choice. Named because of its three peaks – Yonghwa-bong (654m), Cheongun-bong (546m) and Deungseon-bong (632m) – the mountain offers incredible views of the surroundings, but don't be fooled by its relatively low altitude – Samaksan's trails are rocky and steep. It takes around two hours to climb to the highest peak from the Deungseon Falls' ticket booth, passing several temples and a fortress along the way.

Sample Chuncheon's Signature Dishes

Dakgalbi and *makguksu*

In the 1980s an alley in central Chuncheon was devoted to the city's signature spicy chicken dish – you can't miss it as there's a giant statue of a chicken at one end and a gate crowned with a chuck at the other. Around 20 restaurants line **Myeongdong Dakgalbi St**, all serving their variations on the classic. One of the longest-running is **Woomi Dakgalbi**, but if you want to eat here, come early as the food does sell out. Opposite, and just as good, is **Myeongdong 1(il)beonji Dakgalbi**.

At most *dakgalbi* restaurants you can also order another Chuncheon culinary staple – the buckwheat noodle dish, *makguksu*. A pile of noodles is topped with julienned vegetables and half a boiled egg. Pour over cold broth and add vinegar, sugar and mustard to your taste. Worth searching out is **Byoldang Makguksu**, which has been dishing up the noodles since 1972 in a *hanok*-style building close by the Gongjicheon waterway.

Marvel at the 500 Arhats

Digital art at Chuncheon National Museum

The excellent **Chuncheon National Museum** *(chuncheon.museum.go.kr; free)* showcases a beautiful collection of Gangwon-do's Three Kingdoms relics and Buddhist artefacts. A highlight is the 500 Arhats gallery, where you can wander amid mini stone monks, each one an individual character. Stick around for the dazzling digital-art films projected across a panoramic screen and the floor of the museum's cafe – they start on the hour and last around 25 minutes.

Cycle alongside Uiam Lake

Sculptures, war memorial and a skywalk

Take a stroll beside the Gongjicheon waterway to the **Gongjicheon Sculpture Park**, where the stream meets the river. Here, locals picnic beneath trees among the park's many art pieces.

Next to the **Memorial Hall for Ethiopian Veterans in the Korean War**, you can rent a **bicycle** to pedal the flat path around Uiam Lake. Aim for the **Soyang-gang Skywalk** *(₩2000)*. This 156m glass-floored pier is especially attractive at night when illuminated with multicoloured lights (note it closes at 5.30pm from November to March). Nearby stands a 7m-tall bronze statue of **Soyang-gang Maiden**, the heroine of the 1969 Korean hit song, who waits by the river for her lover to return.

Spend a day at LEGOLAND Korea

Plastic fantastic

Family fun is guaranteed at **LEGOLAND Korea Resort** *(legoland.kr; adult/child from ₩65,000/55,000)*, a multi-coloured theme park and hotel on Jungdo, an island in Uiam Lake. Korea's take on the LEGOLAND formula serves up an appealing mix of gentle fairground rides and a couple of small-scale white knucklers alongside scores of LEGO constructions and character models. Most amazing are the detailed reconstructions of Korean landmarks, including an 11m-tall replica of Seoul's Lotte Tower. Book online for discounted tickets.

BIRTHPLACE OF DAKGALBI

The origins of Chuncheon's most famous chicken recipe are thought to go back to the 1950s, though the dish most likely took on its current form as a stir-fry of spicy *gochujang*-marinated pieces of chicken, cabbage, sweet potato, spring onion and rice cakes in the late 1960s. Low on price but big on portions, *dakgalbi's* boom was in the 1980s when gas-fired skillets built directly into restaurant tables were introduced.

The traditional way to eat *dakgalbi* is to wrap a mouthful of cooked chicken in a lettuce or sesame leaf. An extra topping of cheese is recommended. If you're still not full, order some rice to be fried in the leftovers in the skillet.

DRINKING IN CHUNCHEON: OUR PICKS

Gallery Cafe: Tucked behind the MBC broadcasting building, with a good selection of drinks and desserts and views of Uiam Lake. *10am-10pm*

Dancing Caffeine Baker: Slump in a beanbag on the terrace of this cafe beside the KT&G Sangsang Madang arts centre, overlooking the lake. *9am-9.30pm*

Gamja Island: Craft brewery offering award-winning beers, including ones made with potato, corn and tomato. *5pm-1am Mon-Thu, noon-2am Fri & Sat*

Yedam the Gallery Cafe: Relax over a cup of Korean fruit tea and traditional rice-cake desserts at this charming *hanok* cafe hung with art. *10am-10pm Tue-Sun*

SIMON RICHMOND

Gangchon Rail Park

Pedal Along the Old Gyeongchun Railway

River views from Gangchon Rail Park

Gangchon Rail Park *(railpark.co.kr; 2/4-seater rail bikes ₩40,000/56,000)* provides an enjoyable way to take in Chuncheon's natural scenery. Startsing from next to Gimyujeong train station, it's a leisurely pedal on a rail bike for 6.5km past fields and through tunnels (jazzed up with soap bubbles, flashing lights and music) before emerging beside the Bukhan River. The final 2km to the Gangchon terminus is aboard the 'romantic train'. A bus returns you to Gimyujeong. It's popular – book online at least a day in advance to secure your time slot.

Tour the Literary Village of Kim You-jeong

House of a hometown hero

Also in Gimyujeong, the **Literary Village of Kim You-jeong** *(kimyoujeong.org; ₩2000)* showcases the brief life of an acclaimed literary talent. Born here in 1908, Kim died aged 29 from tuberculosis, leaving behind a collection of writing that sheds light on the life of 1930s peasants. Designed as a traditional Korean village, with thatched roof houses, the facility is closed Mondays.

Beyond Chuncheon

West of Chuncheon is the famed beauty spot Namiseom, an island in the Han River with soaring metasequoias, ginkgo trees and art.

Cheorwon, in the northwest corner of Gangwon-do and close to the DMZ, is a migratory sanctuary for cranes and eagles and one of Korea's premier bird-watching destinations. Also here is the Hantan River basin, a UNESCO World Geopark, offering spectacular landscapes sculpted by nature 60 million years ago.

Southward, around the city of Wonju, a world-class art museum unfolds gorgeously across a mountain, and Chiaksan National Park has a legend of nine lake-dwelling dragons. Set against such stunning scenery, camping is a wonderful way to experience the area and immerse yourself in its charms.

Places

Namiseom (Nami Island) p155
Cheorwon p155
Les Jardins de Médongaule p156
Wonju p157

Namiseom (Nami Island)

TIME FROM CHUNCHEON: **20-40MIN**

Zip to Nami Island

Gorgeous at any time of year, but particularly in autumn, **Nami Island** *(namisum-en.imweb.me; ₩19,000)* is a 430,000-sq-metre garden famous for its avenues of majestic metasequoias, ginkgos and pines. There are plenty of restaurants and scenic spots for a picnic. There's also plenty of sculptural art and various exhibitions, with a focus on the art of illustrated children's books.

Branding itself Naminara Republic, this half-moon-shaped island requires a 'visa' ticket to enter – the basic entry fee includes a return ferry ride. Thrill seekers will want to upgrade to the **zip line** *(zipwire.co.kr; ₩55,000 incl entrance)*, which whisks you to the island from an 80m-high tower in about 1½ minutes. Nami Island is super popular – to experience it without the day-trip crowds, stay overnight at its Hotel Jeonggwanru (p175).

Cheorwon

TIME FROM CHUNCHEON: **1¾HR**

DMZ tours and Cheorwon attractions are closed on Tuesdays. Also, whenever you pay for an attraction in Cheorwon, you'll get vouchers that can be used like cash at other attractions and businesses in the town.

Tour the border zone

Cheorwon endured some of the fiercest battles of the Korean War – their locations now lay within the Civilian Control Line (CCL), the buffer zone to the DMZ. This means that to visit

GETTING AROUND

Getting between Chuncheon and Wonju intercity bus terminals is easy. From Wonju, you can catch a bus to Chiaksan National Park with no problem. To other places, such as Museum SAN, it gets complicated, with very long wait times, so it's recommended to rent a car or take a taxi. If heading to Cheorwon, it's best to drive yourself.

AN ISLAND IN THE RIVER

Created as an island in the Bukhan River when the waterway was dammed in the 1940s, Namiseom is named after General Nami, who was executed in 1468, aged 28, after being falsely accused of treason. Nami's supposed grave is on the island, which was purchased in 1965 by the successful book publisher Minn Byeong-do.

Minn planted the island with flowers and trees and began to develop it into a tourism destination and a showcase for children's book art. Nami's popularity soared internationally after filming of the hit Korean TV drama *Winter Sonata* in 2002, both on the island and in nearby Chuncheon. There are statues of the drama's main characters on the island and in Chuncheon.

PLAN SHOOTING2 / IMAZINS/GETTY IMAGES

Cheorwan former Labor Party headquarters

them and other sites, including the **Second Tunnel**, dug by North Korea and discovered by South Korea in 1975, and the **Cheorwon Peace Observatory**, which offers a panoramic view of the DMZ, you'll need to join the **DMZ Peace Tour** *(cwg.go.kr; ₩4000)*, which departs four times a day from the **Goseokjeong Tourist Information Center** and lasts around three hours. If you have your own wheels, you can also join this tour at DMZ Peace Town for Migratory Birds.

Just outside the CCL is **Cheorwan History and Culture Park**, across from which stands the shell of the **former Labor Party headquarters** – when Cheorwon was part of North Korea, civilians were imprisoned and tortured here. The park itself evokes an early 20th-century Cheorwon (long since vanished) and includes a **monorail** *(adult/child ₩7000/4000)* up 362m **Soisan**, from where there are panoramic views across the Cheorwon Lava Plateau.

Admire the Hantan River scenery

Beautiful scenery is Cheorwon's trump card, with the Hantan River carving through basalt rock gorges. Look down on the river and a 10m-tall rock pillar from the historic **Goseokjeong** pavilion, then follow the steps to the river itself. Between April and November, **boat tours** *(adult/child ₩6600/3300)* along the river depart from here.

Another sweeping perspective over the Hantan is from the asymmetrical **Cheorwon Hantangang Milky Way Bridge**, which offers a prime view into **Songdaeso**, a basalt canyon. Cross the bridge to climb to the 53m-high torch-shaped **observatory tower** *(₩6000)*.

Les Jardins de Médongaule

TIME FROM CHUNCHEON: 1HR

Beautiful Korean and contemporary gardens

Taking inspiration from the philosophy of Friedrich Nietzsche, the extraordinary **Les Jardins de Médongaule** *(medongaule.com; ₩50,000)* are a balm to the soul. A must-see for lovers of horticulture and architecture, the complex (which is closed Mondays) includes extensive Korean gardens that reflect many aspects of the country's culture, and a dazzling set of Contemporary Gardens that include the striking Überhaus restaurant and Dionysos visitor centre. Be sure to stick around for the daily performances by an accomplished troupe of traditional Korean musicians and dancers.

The garden's French name is a nod to the designers, father and son team Yves and Guillaume Gosse de Gorre, creators of France's celebrated Les Jardins de Séricourt.

Wonju

TIME FROM CHUNCHEON: **1HR**

Appreciate art amid nature

An acronym for 'Space, Art, Nature', **Museum SAN** *(museumsan.org/eng; ₩23,000-59,000)*, designed by award-winning architect Tadao Ando, is a minimalist master-piece of concrete and stone that combines architecture, art and landscaping in ingenious ways. The basic entry fee gains you access to the outdoor gardens, studded with contemporary sculptures, as well as the complex's art and paper museums (SAN's owner is a paper-production company). It's well worth investing, however, in ticket packages that include attractions such as the Meditation Hall, the Space of Light, Ground (a collaboration between Ando and the sculptor Antony Gormley) and the James Turrell Hall, where you can view four works by the namesake American Light and Space artist. It's closed Mondays.

Traverse Sogeumsan Mountain Grand Valley

You can used thigh power to attain the heights of **Sogeumsan Mountain Grand Valley** *(cms.wfmc.kr; trekking course/cable car ₩10,000/18,000)*, with its views of the spectacular surrounding landscape, or you can take the easy route up on the cable car. Either way, you'll subsequently negotiate mountainside escalators, cliff-hugging walkways and two pedestrian suspension bridges – one of which is 404m in length – to cover the full circuit of the river valley in around two hours. It's a place you might want to linger as there's a glamping site and, on weekends and holidays between May and the end of October, a night light show and musical fountain.

Hike at Chiaksan National Park

Though the smallest of Gangwon-do's national parks, 175-sq-km **Chiaksan National Park** *(knps.or.kr)* still offers challenging hikes amid spectacular scenery. It's the site of several temples, the main one of which, **Guryong-sa** *(guryongsa.or.kr)*, has a templestay program. According to legend, the temple, which was founded in 668 CE, was built atop a lake where nine dragons lived. From the temple, a popular but strenuous 5km hiking route (three hours) ascends 1288m **Biro-bong**, passing the waterfall of **Seryeom Pokpo** en route.

CRANES AT THE DMZ

In Korea, cranes are a symbol of peace and longevity (you'll notice a crane on the ₩500 coin) and they've also come to symbolise hope for the reunification of North and South Korea. In the 70 years since the DMZ's formation, the inaccessible area has become a sanctuary for plants and wildlife, with more than 100 endangered species finding refuge at the border. Among them are the migratory white-naped and red-crowned cranes, both designated natural monuments by Korea.

At **DMZ Peace Town for Migratory Birds**, there's an exhibition on these magnificent birds, which can be spotted in the skies around Cheorwon between November and February. During these months, bird-watching tours are run out of the facility.

Sokcho

SEORAKSAN | NORTH KOREAN HERITAGE | WATERFRONT FUN

GETTING AROUND

Most travellers to Sokcho will arrive by bus at either the **express or intercity** bus terminals. There are also flights into **Yangyang International Airport**, 19km south.

Bus routes are plentiful around Sokcho and out to Seoraksan National Park, Naksan Provincial Park and Yangyang. It's easy to walk around town and along the waterfront to see the main sights.

TOP TIP

Following your hike in Seoraksan National Park, treat yourself to a soak and a scrubdown at **Choksan Spa & Hotel** *(choksan.co.kr; ₩11,000)*. Alternatively, go for a paddle in the hot-spring-filled pools of nearby **Cheoksan Foot Spa Park** *(free)*.

Sokcho is a launchpad for the spectacular mountain landscapes of Seoraksan National Park. But this coastal city also boasts its own charms, including sandy beaches, fish markets teaming with aquatic abundance and the chance to graze on fresh seafood with the tang of salt in the air. Sokcho's attractive lagoon, Yeongnang-ho, is an opportunity for pleasant strolls along tree-lined paths, while southward, Sokcho Beach is linked to the fish market of Deapo Port by the beautiful Bada Hyanggi Trail.

From 1945 to the end of the Korean War, the border between North and South Korea shifted around Sokcho, so the port carries a history of displacement. In Abai Maeul, a village on an island where refugees settled, view the murals that celebrate the North Koreans' culture and taste their food. You also won't regret visiting the beautiful low-stone-walled village of Sangdomun on the way to the national park.

Graze Sokcho Central Market

Packed with delicious edibles

Known as **Sokcho Tourist Fish Market** *(sokcho-central.co.kr)*, but selling all kinds of goods, this covered market on several levels is *the* place to consume local culinary specialities, from *abai sundae* (sausages) to *dak gangjeong* (fried and glazed pieces of chicken). There's a great selection of baked goods, too, including sponge-like breads made with *makgeolli* (milky rice wine) and rice flour.

Head to the basement to find the fish market with all kinds of seafood swimming in tanks, just waiting to be bought and eaten at the surrounding restaurants – a fresh snow-crab meal for two starts at around ₩150,000. The market is open 8am to 10pm.

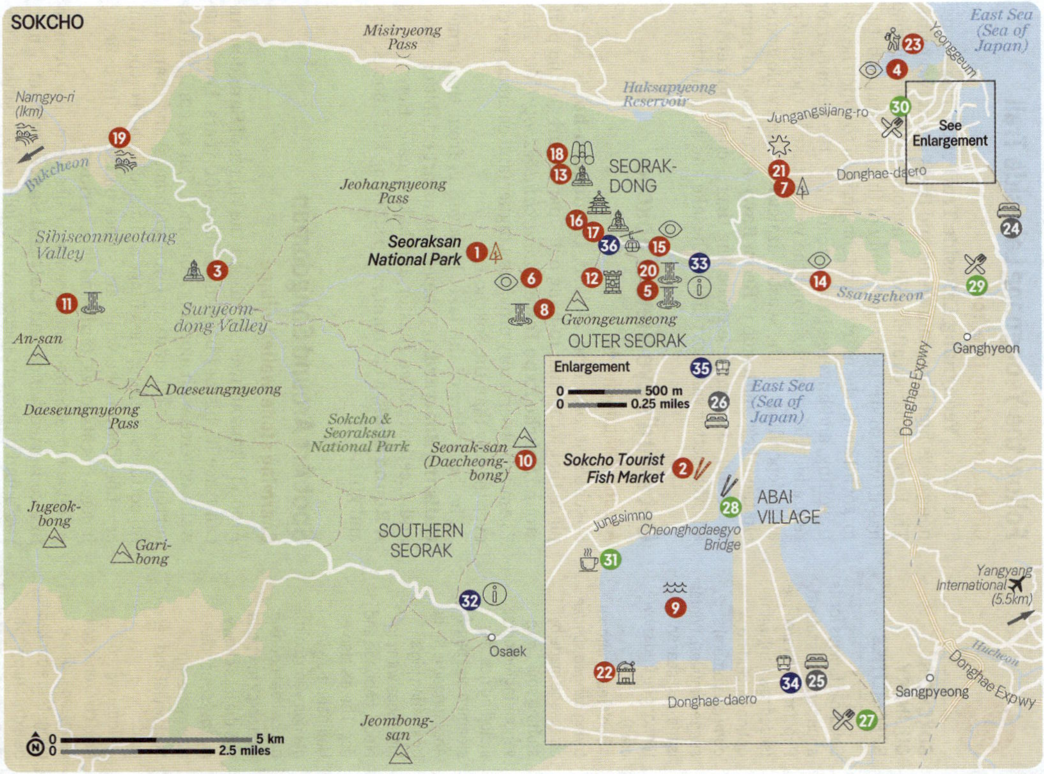

HIGHLIGHTS
1 Seoraksan National Park
2 Sokcho Tourist Fish Market

SIGHTS
3 Baekdam-sa
4 Beom Bawi
5 Biryong Pokpo
6 Biseondae Rock
7 Cheoksan Foot Spa Park
8 Cheondang Pokpo
9 Cheongcho-ho
10 Daecheong-bong
11 Dumun Pokpo
12 Gwongeum-seong
13 Gyejo-am
14 Hangmujeong Pavilion
see 13 Heundeul Bawi
see 14 Sangdomun
15 Seoraksan Cherry Blossom Tunnel
16 Sinheung-sa
17 Tongil Daebul
18 Ulsan Bawi
19 Yongdae-ri
20 Yukdam Pokpo

ACTIVITIES
21 Choksan Spa & Hotel
22 Sokcho Expo Tower
23 Yeongnang Lakeside Trail

SLEEPING
24 Cassia Sokcho
25 Good Morning Hotel
26 House Hostel

EATING
27 Bossa Nova
28 Bukcheong Abai Sundae
29 Matsu
30 Sokcho 751 Sandwich

DRINKING & NIGHTLIFE
31 Chilsung Boatyard
see 14 Cultural Space Doldam
see 14 Domun

SHOPPING
see 31 A Round Book

INFORMATION
32 Namseorak Visitor Center
see 36 Seorak-dong Park Information Center
33 Seoraksan National Park Visitor Centre

TRANSPORT
34 Express Bus Terminal
35 Intercity Bus Terminal
36 Seorak Cable Car

SOKCHO'S CULINARY SPECIALITIES

Sokcho is famous for its abundance of seafood. Popular are *hwareohoe* (sliced raw fish), with options including *domi* (sea bream) and *sungeo* (mullet). Winter is the best season for *hongge* (red snow crab).

Don't leave without trying *ojingeo sundae*, a sausage made by stuffing squid with various ingredients, including rice. It's steamed and pan-fried. *Abai sundae* is made by stuffing pig's intestines with pig blood, cabbage and rice. There's also Hamheung-style *naengmyeon* (cold buckwheat noodles with spicy raw pollack) and the less chewy *makguksu* noodles, also made with buckwheat and served cold.

A local twist on fried chicken is *dak gangjeong*, where nuggets are cooked to be extra crispy, coated in a sweet sauce and garnished with peanuts or *deodeok* root.

Follow the Yeongnang Lakeside Trail

Climb a crouching tiger rock

The 7.3km **Yeongnang Lakeside Trail** encircling Yeongnang-ho is highly recommended and takes about two hours. The lagoon is named after a Silla kingdom warrior who, legend has it, was so struck by the beauty of this landscape that he forgot all about the martial arts competition to which he was travelling, and lingered here instead. Walk the perimeter, or rent a bicycle, stopping along the way to take in the scenery and, depending on the season, azaleas or cherry blossoms. On the lake's south side is **Beom Bawi**, an outcrop of giant rock said to resemble a crouching tiger – climb up here for an even better vantage point of the lake and surroundings.

Get a Bird's Eye View of Sokcho

Around Cheongcho-ho

Sokcho's second central lake, **Cheongcho-ho**, is also a place that locals like to hang out – particularly in the park around **Sokcho Expo Tower** *(adult/child ₩2500/1500)*. This 73.4m-tall observatory provides a higher (and cheaper) perch over the city than the Sokcho Eye.

The best view of the lake, however, is from the former **Chilsung Boatyard**, revamped into an art exhibition space and excellent coffee roaster and bakery cafe. Here, too, is **A Round Book**, a charming shop stocking kids' books, toys and gifts.

Spot Art Around Sangdomun

Charming stone-walled village

Around 9km southwest of Sokcho, the village of **Sangdomun** can trace its history back more than 600 years. Low stone walls, covered with morning glory and other creeping plants, surround *hanok* (traditional wooden homes) and characterful cottages, making the village a visual delight. Perched on, or embedded in, the walls are stones painted with delicate images of cats, dogs, birds and other critters.

Rest at one of Sangdomun's several cafes, including **Domun** in a converted *hanok* and **Cultural Space Doldam**, where you'll find quirky art pieces. A path follows the banks of the Ssangcheon stream, providing views towards Seoraksan. Nearby is the serene **Hangmujeong Pavilion**, hidden in a grove of twisting pine trees.

EATING IN SOKCHO: OUR PICKS

Sokcho 751 Sandwich: Justly famous for its takeaway sandwiches, including ones packed with crab or egg and pollack roe. *8am-3pm Wed-Sun* ₩

Matsu: Head to the city's south for delicious homemade pasta dishes served in a charming pine-tree-themed setting. *11am-8pm Thu-Tue* ₩₩

Bukcheong Abai Sundae: (북청전통아바이순대) This friendly place specialises in squid-stuffed *sundae* and traditional North Korean-style *abai sundae*. *8am-9pm* ₩₩

Bossa Nova: Classy bakery cafe with a very tempting selection of pastries to go with its signature peanut butter latte. *8am-10pm* ₩

STROLL SOKCHO'S WATERFRONT

This walk along Sokcho's seafront connects two of the city's major fish markets.

START	END	LENGTH
Sokcho Tourist Fish Market	Daepo Port	4km; 2-3hr

Graze the food stalls of ❶ **Sokcho Tourist Fish Market** (p158), then hop aboard the ❷ **Gaetbae** *(adult/child ₩500/300)*, a ferry pulled by steel rope, to reach ❸ **Abai Maeul**. Beneath the flyover are art works celebrating the life and culture of the North Korean refugees who settled this island more than 70 yeas ago. Check out the village's restaurants, cafes and shops. Be sure to taste *abai sundae* and *naengmyeon*.

Cross the red-painted ❹ **Seorak-daegyo** bridge and continue south along seafront Cheonghohaean-ro. Pause for a drink and views across to the Jodo Islands from black-themed dessert cafe ❺ **SHLTR**. Keep on in the direction of the ❻ **Sokcho Eye** *(sokchoeye.imweb.me; adult/child ₩18,000/12,000)* – a ride in one of the Ferris wheel's 36 cabins lasts 15 minutes and takes you up to 65m above the ground.

Take a sip at local craft brewer ❼ **MontBeer**, then wander along pretty, pine-fringed ❽ **Sokcho Beach** towards the ❾ **Bada Hyanggi Trail**, a dirt path and elevated walkway that offers glimpses of the sea below – the trail's southern stretch is particularly scenic. Finish with a seafood feast at one of many restaurants in ❿ **Daepo Port**.

DMITRY RUKHLENKO/SHUTTERSTOCK

Ulsan Bawi

TOP EXPERIENCE

Seoraksan National Park

Translating as 'Great Snow-covered Mountain', Seoraksan National Park features nature-chiselled beauty unlike anywhere else in Korea. Covering 173.7 sq km, this UNESCO Biosphere Reserve is visually stunning, especially in autumn, and is home to thousands of species of plants and animals. The vast majority of visitors enter at the Oeseorak (Outer Seorak) gateway closest to Sokcho.

DON'T MISS

- Seorak Cable Car
- Sinheung-sa
- Ulsan Bawi
- Heundeul Bawi
- Daecheong-bong
- Yukdam Pokpo
- Biryong Pokpo
- Seoraksan National Park Visitor Center

Cable Car

Close to the Seorak-dong entrance is the **Seorak Cable Car** *(sorakcablecar.co.kr; adult/child ₩16,000/12,000)*. The five-minute ride whisks you to within a short climb of the natural fortress rocks of **Gwongeum-seong** (860m) for out-of-this-world views. Tickets are for specific timed departures – it's a good idea to book them as soon as you arrive in the park to avoid a wait for an available slot.

PRACTICALITIES

● knps.or.kr/seorak ● admission free, parking ₩6000 ● visitor centre 9am-5pm Tue-Sun

Sinheung-sa

About 700m beyond the cable car is the venerable **Sinheung-sa** *(sinheungsa.kr)* temple. Founded here in 652 CE, it's been destroyed and rebuilt many times. First you'll pass the 14.6m-tall bronze **Tongil Daebul** (Great Unification Buddha), dedicated to the hope of reunification between the two Koreas. A little further on, beside the stream and off to the right, is the temple's main prayer hall, its entrance gate guarded by polychromatic statues of the Four Heavenly Kings.

Ulsan Bawi

From Sinheung-sa it's a roughly three-hour round-trip hike (7.6km) to reach the park's iconic feature – **Ulsan Bawi**, a spectacular granite cliff with six peaks, the tallest at 873m. About 1km from the cliff, you'll arrive at **Gyejo-am**, a Buddhist grotto hermitage dating to 652 CE. Outside, balanced on a ledge, is **Heundeul Bawi**. Although *heundeul* translates as 'wobbly', hikers try in vain to shift this giant boulder. The final climb to Ulsan Bawi is hard-going (including an 808-step metal staircase), but well worth it for the stupendous views all the way to the coast.

Daecheong-bong

The ascent to the park's highest peak, **Daecheong-bong** (1708m), is a solid tramp of five to seven hours, traversing 10km to 14km, depending on the route you take. Hardcore hikers will want to follow **Dinosaur Ridge**, an up-and-down stretch with some of Korea's toughest trekking – and most jaw-dropping views. If you'd like to time your arrival at Daecheong-bong for sunrise, as many Korean hikers do, there are mountain shelters along the way.

The quickest way up Daecheong-bong is from the park's southern **Namseorak entrance**, though the climb is still very steep and difficult and goes through thick forest, so lacks the wow factor of the main route to the peak. Plan on four hours up and three hours down.

Inner Seorak

The relatively uncrowded valleys in the park's northwestern section are stunners to explore. From the park entrance near **Yongdae-ri**, take a shuttle bus, or hike 6.5km, to the serene temple of **Baekdam-sa**, which faces east and is best appreciated in the morning. From there, you can ramble along the Suryeomdong Valley for an hour or two, or even connect to Outer Seorak (seven hours, 14km).

Alternatively, from **Namgyo-ri** there's a splendid 2½-hour hike in the Sibiseonnyeotang Valley to the waterfall of **Dumun Pokpo**.

Seoraksan National Park Visitor Center

Fronted by a giant statue of Asiatic black bears, and about 1km before the park's main entrance, this well-conceived **visitor centre** has displays on Seoraksan's history, flora, fauna and geology. Closed Mondays, the centre is in a small village packed with accommodation and eating options.

HIKES TO WATERFALLS

Park Yongkyu, a volunteer interpreter at the **Seorak-dong Park Information Center**, recommends the following hikes: "I like the 3.5km course along the Cheonbuldong valley from the **Biseondae rock** to the **Cheondang Pokpo**. It's most beautiful in autumn. Another easy hike of around 2.5km is to **Yukdam Pokpo**, a series of six small falls, and the 40m-high **Biryong Pokpo**.

TOP TIPS

- Seoraksan's upper peaks are closed to visitors from 15 November to 15 December and 15 March to 15 May.
- Hiking gear, including boots, poles and small backpacks, can be borrowed for free from the Seorak-dong Park Information Center.
- Overnight shelters (₩13,000) fill up quickly, so it's crucial to make a reservation in advance via *knps.or.kr*. You'll need to bring your own bedding and food.
- Both Sinheung-sa and Baekdam-sa offer templestay programs. Apply in advance at *templestay.com*.
- Leading to the Outer Seorak entrance is the **Seoraksan Cherry Blossom Tunnel**, which is particularly beautiful when the trees are in spring bloom.

Beyond Sokcho

Seek serenity at a seaside temple, gaze across the DMZ into North Korea, learn to surf and breathe easy in a magical forest.

Places

Yangyang p164
Goseong p165
Inje p166

GETTING AROUND

From Sokcho, it's easy enough to take a direct bus to Naksan Provincial Park, Yangyang terminal or Inje terminal. Anywhere else, though, it's predictably inconvenient, with often extended waits, multiple transfers, long walks and unreliable timetables. It's far more convenient to rent a car, or to hire a taxi – to visit the DMZ sights in Goseong, it's mandatory.

Sokcho is an ideal base for trips north and south along the east coast, as well as inland to the beautiful white birch forest at Inje. As far north as you can get in South Korea, Goseong county was split into two after the Korean War armistice. This is where you can peer into North Korea from a unification observatory and learn about the war at a DMZ museum. Heavy military presence and barbed-wire-lined beaches remind you how potentially dangerous things could be along this gorgeous coastal landscape. South of Sokcho, surfing has emerged as a popular pastime in Yangyang county, which is home to lovely beaches and the stunning temple of Naksan-sa.

Yangyang

TIME FROM SOKCHO: **20MIN**

Buddhist beauty by the sea

Set amid Naksan Provincial Park's stupendous 24km stretch of coastline, **Naksan-sa** *(naksansa.or.kr)* enjoys a prime location overlooking the sea. Founded in 671 CE, it's a must-see Buddhist sight, with its towering effigy of Gwaneum, the Goddess of Mercy, and vividly decorated buildings amid serene, wooded grounds. This is a wonderful place to experience a templestay.

Most of the complex had to be rebuilt after a devastating forest fire in 2005. The majestic 16m-tall statue of **Gwaneum** presides over the East Sea from the temple's highest point. Also don't miss the **Uisangdae Pavilion** and the **Hongnyeonam Hermitage** (one of the temple's oldest buildings, dating to 1865), both of which overlook the crashing waves of the sea and are wonderful spots for watching sunrise (the temple opens at 6am). Relax in the arty **Daraeheon** cafe, which also has a gorgeous sea view. Free tea is offered in the **Binlru** and **Botarak** pavilions.

Once you're done with the temple, boost your bliss on **Naksan Beach**, one of the east coast's best stretches of sand.

Surf's up!

In recent years, Yangyang has become one of Korea's main surfing destinations, with cars full of urbanites escaping the weekday grind to unwind on the beach on weekends. The atmosphere along the Yangyang coast is hip and the summer waves are easy for beginners.

OSCAR ESPINOSA/SHUTTERSTOCK

Naksan-sa, Yangyang

Among the popular locations are **Jukdo Beach**, lined with surf shops, bars, cafes and guesthouses; **Seorak Beach**, where you can get surf lessons and hang out at the sandside **Meta Beach** *(@meta_beach_)* cafe-bar; and **Hajodae Beach**, home to **Surfyy Beach**, which is known for its after-surf parties as much as it is for its actual surf – its motto is 'Surf all day! Party all night!' and it's quite the selfie scene.

Come to join the sandy fun, whether it be with a surfing or stand-up paddleboarding (SUP) class in the sun, or with dinner and drinks after dark.

Goseong

TIME FROM SOKCHO: **55MIN**

Glimpse North Korea across the DMZ

Goseong was part of North Korea from 1945 to 1953, and today the area around its **Tongil Security Park** *(tongiltour.co.kr; adult/child ₩3000/1500, parking ₩6000)* is the closest you can get to the no-man's land of the DMZ and the border.

Note that from where you fill in the required forms and purchase your admission ticket, it's another 10km to the observatory – there's no shuttle bus, and pedestrians, bicycles and motorbikes are not allowed. If not driving yourself, come by taxi directly from Sokcho. At the ticket counter, be prepared to present identification, contact information and your (or your taxi driver's) licence plate number.

Once inside the security area, head straight to the **Unification Observatory** (pausing along the way is strictly forbidden). On a clear day, there are amazing views of Kumgangsan, a celebrated mountain about 20km northwest inside North Korea. The waves breaking along the jagged coast and the empty beaches make for a hauntingly beautiful scene. At the time of research, new viewing platforms and a suspension bridge were under construction as extra attractions.

GWANEUM, THE GODDESS OF MERCY

Go to enough Buddhist temples and you might begin to recognise a familiar face gazing back at you. There's the Buddha, yes, but there's also the Goddess of Mercy. In Korean, her full name is 관세음보살 (Gwanse'eum Bosal), the sounds of which derive from her Chinese name, 觀世音菩薩 (Guanshiyin Pusa), which means 'the Bodhisattva who observes the sounds of the world'. She lends a compassionate ear to those who come needing sympathy.

Naksan-sa's Gwaneum has been a commanding feature of the temple since 1971. Immediately below the statue's viewing platform is a small shrine, with a window strategically constructed so that a kneeling devotee can look up and gaze upon her kindly face.

MORE DMZ OBSERVATORIES

Besides the one in Goseong, there are also observatories into the DMZ in **Cheorwon** (p156), **Ganghwado** (p138), **Gyodongdo** (p141) and **Imjingak Resort** (p142).

GOSEONG'S BEST BEACHES

Hwajinpo Beach: Featuring monazite sands, along with an ecological museum, aquarium and a lodging once stayed in by Kim Il Sung and his family.

Songjiho Beach: Notable in the summer, when the ocean's currents form a sandy path that connects to the island of Jukdo.

Myeongpa Beach: Close to the Tongil Security Park, this small, quiet beach with barbed wire at its northern end offers camping and has a quirky hotel with rooms designed by artists.

Daejin Beach: An area known for its octopuses, with the nearby Daejin Port hosting a seafood festival every May.

Ayajin Beach: Shallow waters make this stretch of ocean a preferred swimming spot.

KOREAKHW/SHUTTERSTOCK

Wondae-ri Birch Forest, Inje

Also inside the security area, the **Korean War Exhibition Hall** provides a primer on the war (with some harrowing footage of the conflict), and the **DMZ Museum** has a good amount of English in its narration of the history of the Demilitarised Zone, as well as exhibits such as US POW letters and extensive photos. Despite the solemnity of the location, it's cluttered with restaurants, photo zones and shops selling products made within the CCL (Civilian Control Line) buffer zone.

Inje

TIME FROM SOKCHO: 1HR

Wander the Wondae-ri Birch Forest

Standing among the silvery trees of **Wondae-ri Birch Forest** *(forest.go.kr; admission free, parking ₩5000)* is an ethereal experience. The 25-hectare protected forest is a stark contrast from Korea's usual hiking landscapes, and particularly striking in winter when the branches are barren and the ground is covered in snow. From the entry point off the road, it's a roughly 3km hike uphill along one of two routes to the forest. Pick up a birch-branch hiking stick at the entrance and look out for quirky statues and wigwams made from birch logs.

The forest is best reached by car. If not self-driving, it's around a ₩25,000 taxi ride (20 minutes) from Inje bus terminal. Next to the forest car park is **Sanchae Iyagi** (산채이야기), where you can try the *sanchae* (mountain vegetable) bibimbap and local *makgeolli* – use your parking voucher for a ₩5000 discount.

EATING IN YANGYANG: OUR PICKS

Pibing: Popular pizza place at Jokdo Beach, also serving fried shrimp, wings and chips, along with draught beer. *11.30am-10pm Wed-Mon* ₩₩

Aloha Wave: Casual cafe overlooking Jokdo Beach, serving Hawaiian mains such as poke bowls and loco moco. *11am-10pm Mon-Thu, to midnight Fri-Sun* ₩₩

Surfyy Beach: The place to see and be seen at Hajodae. Burgers and pizzas on the shore – what more could you ask for? *10am-2am* ₩₩

Singlefin Aleworks: Hip craft brewery at Hajodae, where a good range of ales wash down Chicago-style deep-dish pizzas. *11am-10.30pm* ₩₩

Gangneung

CAFFEINE FIX | SHAMANIST TRADITION | DELIGHTFUL BEACHES

In 2018 Gangwon-do's largest coastal city hosted the ice-skating events of the Pyeongchang Winter Olympic (you'll notice the Olympic rings and Games' mascots outside Gangneung train station). That event bequeathed the city a zippy high-speed train line to Seoul, which makes it a popular getaway for urbanites looking to relax by the sea. The beaches of Gyeongpo, Anmok and Jungmunjin, fringed by wind-twisted pines, are a breezy delight, with endless stretches of sand on which to laze, picnic and daydream.

Gangneung's heritage attractions, such as the centuries-old shamanist Danoje Festival and the well-preserved Joseon-era buildings of Ojukheon, Seongyojang and Chilsadang, are matched by modern features that celebrate the city as a hot spot for quality coffee, stylish cafes and sweet escape. In spring, azaleas cover the town in gorgeous splashes of colour, while in summer, the shoreline really comes alive.

Get Your Caffeine Fix

Korea's coffee capital

Gangneung's reputation for good coffee has been building since the 1980s when canned coffee-vending machines were a feature of the city's beachside strips. Those vending machines are long gone, replaced by third-wave barista coffee shops. **Coffee Street** at the southern end of **Anmok Beach** is literally wall-to-wall cafes, each offering vistas of the wind-ruffled pines and waves rippling on the sands. There is also a **coffee festival** *(coffeefestival.net)* held every October.

The national success of hometown roastery **Terarosa** has set the bar high – sample its espresso and cold brew at several locations, including the library-themed **Gyeongpo Lake branch** *(terarosa.com)* that's a choice place to chill. It's open 9am to 9pm.

Coffee lovers shouldn't miss **Sinami Myeongju**, a low-key, historic neighbourhood close by the well-preserved **Chilsadang** complex of Joseon-era government offices. Here you'll

GETTING AROUND

KTX trains take just 90 minutes to reach **Gangneung station** from Seoul. From Gangneung, a slower seaside railway heads south to Donghae, where you can transfer onward. Gangneung's express and intercity bus terminals share the same location to the west of the city centre, with frequent routes going to other major cities across Korea. Around town, several buses go between the city centre and the beaches, or you can catch taxis.

TOP TIP

If the weather isn't playing ball for a beach day, a fun indoor option is to immerse yourself in the digital art of **Arte Museum Valley Gangneung** *(artemuseum.com; adult/child ₩19,000/12,000)*. Wander though 18 dazzling sections, many themed around nature and similar to Arte's other outposts in Busan, **Yeosu** (p281) and on **Jeju-do** (p331).

HIGHLIGHTS
1 Ojukheon

SIGHTS
2 Arte Museum Valley Gangneung
3 Chamsori Edison Film Museum
4 Chilsadang
5 Gangneung Dano Cultural Center
6 Gangneung Money Museum
see 6 Gangneung Municipal Museum
7 Gangneung Seongyojang
8 Gyeongpo Beach
9 Gyeongpodae
10 Gyeongpo-ho

SLEEPING
11 Brown Dot Hotel Gyeongpo
12 Gangneung Ojuk Hanok Village

EATING
13 Geumhak Kalguksu
14 La Cocina
15 Rui Kitchen

DRINKING & NIGHTLIFE
16 Bonbon Bangatan
17 Budnamu Brewery
18 Oh New World
19 Terarosa Gyeongpo Lake Branch

TRANSPORT
20 Express & Intercity Bus Terminals
21 Gangneung KTX Station

find charming cafes such as arty **Bonbon Bangatan**, open 10am to 9pm, in a former flour and chilli pepper mill, and **Oh New World**, open 11am to 6pm Tuesday to Saturday, in a converted *hanok* filled with mid-century modern furniture.

Visit Joseon-dynasty properties

Home to a revered mother and son

Ojukheon *(gn.go.kr/museum/index.do; adult/child ₩3000/1000)* is the birthplace of Sin Saimdang, the paragon of Korean womanhood, and her son, the philosopher and government official Yi Yulgok. One of the oldest surviving Joseon-dynasty homes in Korea, the property sits in an elegant park, with punctiliously maintained gardens, courtyards, lotus pools and the black-stemmed bamboo groves for which the complex is named.

Within the park, and covered by the entry fee, is the **Gangneung Municipal Museum**, with its displays of art, calligraphy and ceramics, and the **Gangneung Money Museum**, celebrating the fact that Sin Saimdang and Yi Yulgok are the world's first mother and son to feature on banknotes.

Nearby is the beautifully preserved **Gangneung Seongyojang** *(knsgj.net; adult/child ₩5000/2000)*, another Joseon-era complex. Dating from late in the dynasty, this national cultural property was the home of a *yangban* (aristocratic) family for more than 300 years. It was built for a descendant of the brother of King Sejong and has been restored in keeping with the original floor plan and architectural style. It's possible to stay overnight here in one of the complex's *hanok* – see the website for details.

Hang out at Gyeongpo Beach

Golden sands, pines and seafood

One of the largest beaches on Korea's east coast, **Gyeongpo Beach** has 1.8km of golden sand bordered by wind-twisted pine trees and pleasant waters. There are serene walking paths along the way, winding between benches, picnic spots and art works that range from interesting sculptures to Insta-minded photo-op sets. In the evenings, visitors launch fireworks from the beach and you can enjoy local buskers. The entire strip is lined with places to eat and drink, including many lively raw fish ('sushi') restaurants.

GANGNEUNG'S DANO FESTIVITIES

The **Gangneung Danoje Festival** *(danojefestival.or.kr)* is celebrated for one week starting on the fifth day of the fifth lunar month (usually in June). As the climax of a month-long series of shamanist ceremonies for peace, prosperity and bountiful harvests, it's one of the biggest traditional holidays in Korea and has been inscribed on UNESCO's list for Intangible Cultural Heritage. On the first day, there's a parade to welcome a mountain deity who unites with his 'wife', a village deity dwelling in Gangneung.

To implore their blessings, female shamans perform the *dano gut*, a rite of song, dance and sacrificial offering. On the final day, the male deity is sent back to the mountain.

To find out more about the festival, drop by the **Gangneung Dano Cultural Center** *(free)*.

EATING IN GANGNEUNG: OUR PICKS

La Cocina: Treat yourself to a tapas and Spanish-food feast, with an excellent-value set menu and a most delightful chef and staff. *11.30am-3pm & 5-9pm Fri-Wed* ₩₩

Rui Kitchen: Exceptionally good Japanese food at Gyeongpo Beach, including *tonkatsu* (breaded pork) and salmon rice bowls. *11am-8pm* ₩₩

Budnamu Brewery: Great craft beers, plus yummy pizzas and Mexican dishes that will have you calling, 'More napkins, please!' *noon-4pm & 5-11pm* ₩₩

Geumhak Kalguksu: Along a central alley, this noodle shop is the real deal. The broth is piquant and sprinkled with seaweed and sesame seeds. *10am-8pm* ₩

SIN SAIMDANG

Sin Saimdang (1504–51) was an accomplished poet and artist, and is traditionally regarded in Korea as a model daughter, wife and mother, according to Confucian ideals. Many of her paintings are in the collection of the **National Museum of Korea** (p389) in Seoul and some are on display at Ojukheon, including a delicate folding screen with eight studies of flowers and insects.

Sin's visage graces the ₩50,000 note, a move that irked some women's groups, who believed that it reinforced the idea that women should devote themselves to their children at home, as Sin did, teaching her son the Confucian classics. Her son, Yi I (1536-84), also known by his pen name, Yulgok, appears on the ₩5000 note, with Ojukheon on its front and back.

MIN GEUN CHO/SHUTTERSTOCK

BTS bus stop

Circumnavigate Gyeongpo-ho

Spring beauty spot for cherry blossoms

Behind Gyeongpo Beach is **Gyeongpo-ho**, a serene lake. A 4km pathway circuits the lake and it's the perfect jogging circuit early in the morning when you can understand why the lake's name translates as 'clean as a mirror'. Alternatively, you can rent a bike from any of the outfits at the north end of the lake.

Overlooking the lake is venerable and beautifully painted **Gyeongpodae**, a pavilion originally built in 1326 but relocated in 1508. It is poetically said that you can see five moons from the pavilion – the moon itself and its four reflections: one in the sea (now obscured by pine trees), one in the lake, one in your obligatory glass of alcohol and one in your mind.

Also beside the lake is the **Chamsori Edison Film Museum** *(@charmsori_museum; adult/child ₩18,000/10,000)*, three museums focussing on antique gramophones, music boxes, the inventions of Thomas Edison and film memorabilia. Closed on Tuesdays, it's the extraordinary collection of Son Sung-Mok, whom you may meet at the ticket desk.

The lake area is particularly beautiful in April, when the trees turn candy-floss pink and the **Gyeongpodae Cherry Blossom Festival** is held.

Search Out the BTS Bus Stop

K-Pop culture beach

Around 18km north of Gangneung, in Jumunjin, **Cheongsihaeng Beach** offers golden sand and a blue sea. At the beach's northern end is a **bus stop** created for BTS's *You Never Walk Alone* album cover, making it a popular photo op for the band's fans. Take some of your own snaps (there might be a queue), or just walk along the shore, splash around in the shallow waters, or stop at a nearby cafe. At the southern end of Jumunjin, there's another famous pop-culture site – the **breakwater** scene of the popular K-Drama *Goblin* was filmed here.

Beyond Gangneung

Serene sunrises over the East Sea, a pair of eclectic art spaces, a gigantic cave, mountains, waterfalls and more.

The sandy expanses south of Gangneung are as lovely as they are surprising, with one of the region's most visited New Year's Day sunrise spots at Jeongdongjin station, the quirky art sculptures and unique hotel stay of Haslla Art World and a 'penis park' with just about every phallic rendering you could imagine at Samcheok. Head inland to go deep into a cathedral-like cave, to contemplate the beauty of nature and the soul at the Romyzian Garden and to hike into the majestic mountains of the Odaesan and Taebaeksan national parks. The latter is home to a sacred altar to Korea's mythical founder and a major snow and ice festival every January.

Places

GETTING AROUND

From Gangneung, it's a quick direct train ride to Jeongdongjin, or an hour-long bus ride to Samcheok. There are also trains to and from Mungok, the closest station to Taebaeksan National Park. For Odaesan National Park, take the train or bus from Gangneung to Jinju, then transfer to a bus. Renting a car to reach most of these inland destinations is far easier.

Jeongdongjin

TIME FROM GANGNEUNG: **15MIN**

Ride the train to Jeongdongjin Beach

Jeongdongjin station holds the Guinness World Record for having the closest railway tracks to a beach. A popular location for Koreans to gather to watch the sun rise on New Year's Day, the beach draws visitors year-round. From Gangneung station, board the southbound train, sitting in a left-side window seat for gorgeous views of the coastline.

Once at the beach, hop aboard the **Jeongdongjin Railbike** *(railtrip.co.kr; 2/4 people karts ₩25,000/35,000)*. A round trip along the 3.5km of seaside track takes a hour. In a two-storey wooden cabin overlooking the sea, **Cafe Sun** serves sandwiches and pastries and roasts its own coffee beans.

A visual feast at Haslla Art World

Sitting atop a hill, **Haslla Art World** *(museumhaslla.com; adult/child ₩17,000/11,000)* is an art museum, hotel (p175) and sculpture park where you can immerse yourself in the extraordinary creations of artist couple Choi Ok Yeung and Park Shin Jung. First you'll venture through the museum's five galleries, one of which is devoted to sometimes creepy depictions of Pinocchio and other marionettes, before going outside to the sculpture garden, spread across 11 hectares and offering sweeping coastal views. Choi's giant works of art, including the Silver Wave and Ocean Square, made from more than 10,000 pieces of steel framing, are unique and visually stunning. It's easy to spend several hours here and there are two cafes and a fancy restaurant on site.

Samcheok

TIME FROM GANGNEUNG: **1HR 10MIN**

Korea's largest limestone cave

High up a mountainside at the southwestern edge of Samcheok is **Hwanseongul** *(adult/child ₩4500/2000)*, a cave measuring 6.2km in length. There are many steps to negotiate along the 1.6km of steel gantries that flow around the vast cavern's varied formations, each one given poetic names. Look out for a heart-shaped hole named Love's Oath and a difficult-to-spot stalagmite that resembles a tiny statue of the Virgin Mary.

From the car park, walk 750m uphill to the **monorail** *(one way/round trip ₩4000/7000)*, which is worth taking to save the effort of the very steep climb to the cave mouth. On the way to the monorail, you'll pass the entry path to another cave, **Daegeumgul** – only hardcore cave enthusiasts will want to see this after the cathedral-like splendour of Hwanseongul.

Phallus-packed park by the sea

Offering panoramic sea views, **Haesindang Park** *(samcheok.go.kr; adult/child ₩3000/1500)*, in the sleepy fishing village of Sinnam, is studded with more than 50 phallic sculptures, including an elaborate series representing the Chinese zodiac, along with penis-shaped benches and stools on which to rest. It's a cheeky, eye-opening 20- to 30-minute walk if you don't stop...but you will stop.

Penis worship is deeply rooted in ancient Korean spiritual culture. Samcheok's phallic preoccupation goes back to a legend about a drowned girl whose restless spirit was impeding the village's catch. One day, a fisherman discovered that after he peed into the sea, her spirit was appeased, so the village began carving wooden phalluses and putting them up to placate her.

The park also contains the **Fishing Village Folk Museum**, which presents a history of fishing and shamanist rituals in the region. Afterwards, buy some freshly grilled fish from the grannies manning the market stalls at the port and enjoy them on the pebbly beach watching waves crash on the jagged rocks.

Odaesan National Park

TIME FROM GANGNEUNG: **45MIN**

Visit two temples

Odaesan National Park *(knps.or.kr; parking ₩6000)* is a high-altitude massif, combining splendid hiking, superb views and two prominent Buddhist temples. **Woljeong-sa** *(woljeongsa.org)*, founded in 643 CE, has been rebuilt many times, yet one treasured structure that has survived from the Goryeo dynasty is the octagonal nine-storey pagoda in the main courtyard, with the figure of a kneeling Bodhisattva before it. Woljeong-sa offers templestays.

From Woljeong-sa, it's a 9km hike or a 25-minute bus ride to its sub-temple, **Sangwon-sa**. Look out for the bronze bell cast in 725 CE – it's the oldest temple bell in Korea. Another

CHOI'S WORLD

The land artist Choi Ok Yeung made his name by peppering the countryside with sculptures made from cow dung. In 2002, Typhoon Rusa – the deadliest such weather event to hit Korea in nearly half a century – destroyed Choi's studio and washed away most of his dung sculptures.

Undefeated, and together with his artist wife Park Shing Jung, Choi ploughed his efforts into creating Haslla Art World, where his land and sculptural art would take on monumental proportions and his choice of materials would broaden out into metal tubing, chunks of wooden scaffolding from shipyards, old rubber tyres and pine logs. Choi also designed the interior of the museum and attached hotel, with each guest room an individual artwork.

AARON CHOI/SHUTTERSTOCK

Odaesan National Park

of its prized objects is a wooden statue of the Bodhisattva of wisdom, Munsu, said to have been made in the 15th century on the order of King Sejo after the Bodhisattva cured his skin disease. Munsu Hall is hung with a galaxy of votive effigies of the Bodhisattva.

Trek to peaks and waterfalls

The park's main hiking trail begins at Sangwon-sa and is a fairly steep 6.5km climb to the park's highest peak, **Biro-bong** (1563m, three hours return). Avid hikers can continue from Biro-bong along a ridge to **Sangwang-bong** (1491m), then back down to the road to the temple (12.5km, five hours).

Another option is to take a bus from Gangneung to Odaesan's northeastern entrance and start hiking at **Sogeum-gang**. From here, a trail runs 13.3km (seven hours one way) to the **Jingogae pass**, going by several waterfalls, including **Guryong Pokpo** and **Nagyeong Pokpo**, up to the summit of **Noin-bong** (1338m) and down.

Taebaeksan National Park

TIME FROM GANGNEUNG: 1½HR

Climb Sky Observatory

Even if you're not hiking in the park, it's worth visiting the **Sky Observatory** *(free)*, accessed along a wheelchair-accessible trail from **Danggol Information Center**, the main entry point to the national park. A gently sloping spiral path makes it easy to reach the 33m-high platform for views of the surrounding mountains and forests. Along the way to the observatory is a campsite, a play zone for kids and the Wilderness Theater, featuring a digital artwork showing the four seasons and Taebaek's guardian tiger. A good place for a drink or something to eat here is **Gangnam Sajang** (강남사장), serving soup and pizza.

BEST SKI RESORTS

High1: At 1340m, with 18 slopes of varying levels, High1 has some of the country's top skiing facilities as well as a ski school for the disabled. *high1.com*

Mona Yongpyong: A perennial favourite, with 31 slopes and 15 lifts. It's possible to glimpse the East Sea on a clear day. *yongpyong.co.kr*

Phoenix Park: With 18 slopes, this is a great option for intermediate and advanced downhill skiers and snowboarders. *phoenixhnr.co.kr*

Alpensia: Used for the 2018 Olympics, this small but well-serviced six-run resort is good for families and beginners. Also has a water park. *alpensia.com*

Welli Hilli Park: Easily accessible from Wonju, this resort offers one of Korea's best freestyle hills, along with a half-pipe. *wellihillipark.com*

COAL MINING

Coal mining in the Taebaek range dates back to the Joseon dynasty. For many decades, mining here was on a small scale, but the 1973 oil crisis changed that. Taebaek became the biggest source of coal in the country during the 1980s, and the population of towns such as Taebaek and Gohan boomed.

As the profitability of coal mining fell and concern about its environmental impact grew, the mines shut down. The last state-run mine at Dogye, which opened in 1936, closed in 2025. To learn more about mining in the mountains, visit the **Taebaek Coal Museum** *(adult/child ₩2000/1500)*, which does a thorough job of explaining the industry and has a basement section that replicates the conditions in the mines.

Ancient mountaintop altars

From Danggol you can follow an 8.4km walking route up to **Janggun-bong** (1567m) and down to the **Yuilsa entrance** to the park – it takes around four hours. Along the way you'll see **Cheonjedan**, a trio of stone altars associated with Korea's mythical founder, Dangun, where people once performed rituals to the heavens.

Winter wonderland

Every January, the **Taebaeksan Snow Festival** *(taebaek.go.kr)* takes place at various locations around Taebaek town and the main entrance to the national park. Featuring giant snow sculptures and other wintry activities, including an igloo restaurant and musical performances, it's among the largest and most well-attended ice festivals in the country.

Jeongseon

TIME FROM GANGNEUNG: 1¼HR

Rest and revive at Romyzian Garden

There's a romantic story behind the creation of **Romyzian Garden** *(romyziangarden.com; adult/child from ₩10,000/7000)*, a serene destination in the alpine-like hills near Jeongseon. Built by industrialist Zin-ick Son (whose nickname is Zian) for his beloved but health-challenged wife Romy, the gardens cover around 330,000 sq metres and are imaginatively designed around the theme of self-reflection. They are marketed as a wellness retreat, and you can stay here in either upmarket glamping tents surrounded by woods, or in the hilltop Mountain House.

Jucheon-myeon

TIME FROM GANGNEUNG: 1HR 50MIN

Monumental colourful art

Artists Choi Ok Yeung and Park Shin Jung (p171) have given a radical makeover to Jucheon-myeon's Sulsaem Museum. **Youngwol Y Park** *(ypark.kr; adult/child ₩15,000/10,000)* includes the original museum, showcasing the history of the region and its production of a traditional liquor, but that's overshadowed by Choi's pavilions, galleries and monumental, interactive artworks. Similar to Haslla Art World (p171), it's a colourful, creative foil to the surrounding countryside, fun for kids to explore and a photography thirst trap. There's an on-site cafe, while luxurious accommodation at the **Hanok Heritage** is a 35-minute drive southeast.

Places We Love to Stay

W Budget WW Midrange WWW Top End

Chuncheon & Namiseom

MAP P151

Chuncheon Stay WW Part of the lakeside KT&G Sangsang Madang arts complex, this hotel offers pleasantly decorated, comfortable and modern rooms.

Hotel YAJA Namchuncheon WW Close to Namchuncheon station, this contemporary-styled property offers great value for its large rooms. Rates include breakfast.

Hotel Jeonggwanru WWW Nami Island's characterful hotel surrounded by greenery offers cosy rooms and cottages, either Western or Korean style, each decorated with different works of art.

Wonju

Oak Valley WWW Stay in luxe condominium rooms at this resort beside Korea's largest golf course and Museum SAN. Also a ski resort in winter.

Sokcho

MAP P159

House Hostel W Close to the intercity bus terminal, with simple, comfy rooms and eclectically decorated common areas that are great for meeting fellow travellers over breakfast or games.

Good Morning Hotel WW Views of Sokcho Beach (and the Sokcho Eye Ferris wheel) from a spiffy nine-storey hotel with good-looking rooms that have floor-to-ceiling windows.

Cassia Sokcho WW Three-tower complex at Deapo Port offering spacious rooms with kitchenettes, ocean views and good amenities, including a spa, infinity pool and indoor pool.

Seoraksan National Park

Red House W Hostel offering dorms and simple private rooms, kindly hosts and a convenient location not far from the park entrance.

Kensington Stars Hotel WW British-themed, old-fashioned hotel next to the park's Seorak-dong entrance, with a Routemaster double-decker bus outside and autographed memorabilia, including Beatles records.

Yangyang

Two-Y Hotel WW At Seorak Beach with stylish wood-furnished rooms offering ocean views and a sleek 7th-floor rooftop bar.

Naksan Beach Hotel WW Beside Naksan-sa temple, enjoying splendid sea vistas, this luxury hotel has modern rooms, a minimalist lobby and a fitness centre and sauna.

Gangneung & Jeongdongjin

MAP P168

Brown Dot Hotel Gyeongpo WW Overlooking Gyeongpo Beach. Rooms are spacious, contemporary-styled and great value.

Gangneung Ojuk Hanok Village WW Across the road from Ojukheon, this newly built village includes a superior range of modern *hanok*, sleeping between two and eight people in Korean-style rooms.

Haslla Museum Hotel WW Architectural one-off offering offbeat design – beds shaped like large wooden bowls and rooms furnished with quirky art pieces, plus great ocean views.

Pyeongchang

InterContinental Alpensia Pyeongchang Resort WW Offers a grand lobby lounge, a spa with heated indoor soaking pools and a Western-style restaurant. Rooms are spacious, with soft beds, flat-screen TVs and terraces.

Holiday Inn Resort Alpensia WW Spacious, comfy rooms with balconies and big bathrooms right next to the resort's slopes. The buffet breakfast will fill you up for the day.

Jeongseon

Village Hotel 18th St WW Community-run guesthouse along a charmingly revived street in the former mining town of Gohan, which is handy for High1 ski resort.

Romyzian Garden WWW Choose between Mountain House, offering Zen-calm duplexes and suites, or the safari-style glamping tents with proper beds surrounded by the forest.

Jucheon-myeon

Hanok Heritage WWW On a palatial scale, this luxurious property combines traditional wooden architecture with contemporary amenities and art. The setting is gorgeous and the food worth a trip alone.

Researched by
Marco Ferrarese

Busan

SOUTH KOREA'S HERITAGE-MODERN COASTAL CITY

Towering skylines, old neighbourhoods steeped in history and a backbone of wild nature...like its cinematic fame, Korea's southern culture capital is on the rise – fast.

Chances are, if you are bound for Korea, a ride south on the KTX train to Busan (부산) – sans the flesh-hungry zombies – should be on the cards for all the good reasons. Hemmed between mountains to the north and spread thin along kilometres of glistening beaches and jagged coasts, South Korea's second-largest (and second most visited) city is a rollicking port town with tonnes to offer. Home to one of Asia's most important film festivals, fantastic seafood, enticing shopping districts, one of the country's best craft-beer scenes and an almost endless array of diversions, eclectic Busan truly has something for everyone. You'll find casual pop-up tent bars next to chic designer cafes, coastal hiking trails and bicycle paths, well-executed global cuisine in restaurants in walking distance to an old-world fish market where every species imaginable wriggles on display behind glass tanks. Take your pick and have it cooked in front of your eyes.

ARTRAN/GETTY IMAGES

When the sun's out, swim at Haeundae, Songjeong and Gwangalli beaches, try out a water sport or two, or hop on the Haeundae Beach Train for a sunset coastal ride skirting 4.8km of dramatic seaside cliffs. If murals and hip cafes are your thing, you can witness everyday life at former refugee shantytowns turned trendy art attractions such as Gamcheon and Huinnyeoul Culture Village. Busan is also perfectly situated between sea and mountains, offering anything from casual city-park strolls to proper hikes along kilometres of rocky coast that's as wild as it is wonderfully accessible – think of the majestic sea boulders of Taejongdae, or striking out on all or part of Igidae, a popular 4.7km coastal route passing through forests and over bedrock. Hanging like a crown on the city's northern outskirts, rugged mountains beckon hiking enthusiasts to more scenic trails that offer a different perspective of the city's dramatic coastline. Then there's the Busan International Film Festival and several popular K-Drama filming locations, a calendar full of other festivities and the city's global appeal. It's all a pleasure to explore.

THE MAIN AREAS

SOUTH & CENTRAL BUSAN
Markets, museums, shopping streets and a green lung. p180

WEST BUSAN
Cable car, islands and an Insta-glorified village. p189

BEACHES & EAST BUSAN
Kilometres of soft sand right by soaring skylines and timeless temples. p193

NORTH BUSAN
Mountainous playground on the city's doorstep. p200

BEYOND BUSAN
Industrial cities and temple-studded nature reserves. p203

SEAN PAVONE/SHUTTERSTOCK

Left: Songdo Marine Cable Car (p189); Above: Busan skyline

Find Your Way

Packing 3.5 million people into 770 sq km, South Korea's second-largest city is not the kind of place you can visit on a rushed day trip from Seoul. Pick one handy base and explore the surroundings.

SUBWAY

Metro access in Busan is extensive, with four numbered lines covering 116.5km across 114 stations. Add the BGL line from Gimhae International Airport and the Donghae Line, and you have 205.6km of tracks served by 158 stations.

FROM THE AIRPORT

The BGL line is the cheapest option (₩1600) to travel from Gimhae International Airport to Busan city centre, requiring a transfer at either Sasang or Daejeo stations. Airport Limousine Buses (₩9500) to Haeundae or Seomyeon and taxis are more expensive options.

JAMESTEOHART/SHUTTERSTOCK

Gwangalli Beach (p194)

Plan Your Time

Don't rush your Busan visit: allow at least three full days to experience beaches, city life, spiritual temple getaways and even a bit of the northern mountains.

A Three-Day Sampler

- Walk in Nampo-dong from **Jagalchi Fish Market** (p184) to **Yongdusan Park** (p183), then catch a bus to **Gamcheon Culture Village** (p192) and cafe-hop until sunset. At night, eat and party at **Jeonpo and Seomyeon** (p186). Use a day to beach hop between **Gwangalli Beach** (p194) and **Haeundae** (p194), taking the **Blueline** at sunset. Spend your last day on Yeongdo, walking around **Huinnyeoul Culture Village** (p183) and hit the **Taejongdae coast** (p185).

A Week in Busan

- After the three-day itinerary, walk the **Igidae Coastal Trail** (p199) from Oryukdo to the city and catch a metro to **Songjeong** (p197) for surf spotting, and then catch sunset at **Haedong Yonggung-sa** (p197). Spend another day at **Songdo Marine Cable Car** (p189), **Amnam Park** (p190) and far-flung **Dadaepo Beach** (p191). Keep the **Geumgang Cable Car** (p200) or hiking to **Geumjeong Fortress** (p201) last, leaving the afternoon for exploring **Beomeo-sa** (p202).

SEASONAL HIGHLIGHTS

K-MOVIES

Visit **Busan Cinema Center** (p183) to access an enormous free library of Korean cinema magazines, memorabilia and sound scores for the use and joy of movie fans.

STAND-UP PADDLEBOARDING

Go to **Gwangalli** (p194) to enjoy the city's calmest sea and take a SUP class against a backdrop of gleaming high rises.

JJIMJILBANG

Few spas in Korea beat the luxe, labyrinthine experience provided at **Spa Land** (p199), one of the country's most famous saunas, set inside the world's largest department store.

MONORAIL

Join locals for a ride on the pastel-coloured monorail along the **Stairs of Wishes** (p186) and then visit offbeat **Dakbatgol Mural Village** (p186).

South & Central Busan

HARBOUR SWAGGER MEETS CINEMA STREETS, MARKET ALLEYS AND ROASTERS

TOP TIP

If you're planning to hit a lot of the city's top attractions, the **Busan Pass** *(visitbusanpass.com; from ₩45,000)* is good value. Choose from a 24- or 48-hour time span, or three or five attraction choices from among more than 30 sights.

The heart of Busan (Nampo-dong, Yeongdo, Busan Station, Seomyeon and Jeonpo) is chock-full of wildly different sights and is an ideal area for first-time visitors to base themselves – straight into the thick of the action, and yet in quick reach of the city's other places of interest. Grown during the Japanese occupation between 1940 and 1945, Nampo-dong's modern identity was shaped by refugees during the Korean War, a legacy that's still evident in famous markets such as Jagalchi and Gukje, within walking distance of cinema-centric BIFF Square and landmarks such as Busan Tower.

To the south, across the namesake bridge, is Yeongdo, the island home to coastal walks, an artsy village and the jaw-dropping cliffs of Taejongdae. Busan station and the port area are more than just transport hubs, offering eclectic multicultural districts and a soon-to-be-completed oceanfront opera house. Further north, in the very centre of Busan, youth-centric Seomyeon and Jeonpo pack in more restaurants, cafes and beer joints than you'll ever need.

GETTING AROUND

Trains from Seoul to Busan on the KTX conveniently arrive at **Busan station**, midway between Nampo-dong and Jeonpo. Many buses and Line 1 of the Busan Metro connect Busan station to either district. It's definitely possible (and recommended) to get around Nampo-dong on foot along the pedestrian-friendly roads between Jagalchi Fish Market and Yongdusan Park, site of the Busan Tower. Whether you arrive by bus or at **Jeonpo metro station**, Seomyeon and Jeonpo's bar and shopping streets are adjacent and best explored on foot. Buses to Yeongdo are frequent from the Jagalchi area.

IRYNA MAKUKHA/SHUTTERSTOCK

Nampo-dong (p188)

Take a Stroll through Busan's Chinatown

MAP P182

Hanging red lanterns and Cyrillic signage

Right in front of Busan station, a Chinese-style archway leads to **Chinatown**, the largest Chinese residential area in Busan, also known as Shanghai Street. This is where most overseas Chinese moved during the Korean War, when the US military stationed in Busan built an adjacent **Texas Street** with American comfort foods and entertainment. The **Choryang Modern History Gallery** presents a simple exhibit that documents the quarter's history. It's a nice area to stroll after dark, when red hanging lanterns fire up like bloody persimmons along the grid of alleys packed with restaurants and shops. It's popular for dumplings – expect the *Oldboy* movie *mandu*-type, rather than Chinese *jiaozi*. **Sinbalwon** (신발원), in operation since 1951 and open from 11.45am to 8.45pm, always has a line waiting by the door. The district also surprises with its interesting multicultural mix of Cyrillic and *hangeul* (Korean phonetic alphabet) signs above Muslim-friendly restaurants, sundry shops, massage and karaoke parlours – don't worry, it's not seedy at all – manned by Central Asian and Russian migrants.

BUSAN'S CITY TOUR BUS

With three different loops available, Busan's city tour buses *(citytourbusan.com)* are a convenient way to travel between the area's top attractions. Departing from Busan station, each route stops at 12 different sites nine times a day, Wednesday through Sunday. The red line goes to destinations such as Gwangalli Beach, Haeundae Beach and Shinsegae Centum City; the green line to Huinnyeoul Culture Village, Taejongdae and Oryukdo; and the orange line to Gamcheon Culture Village, Dadaepo Beach and Eulsukdo. For 48 hours, the fare is adult/child ₩20,000/10,000. For the option to transfer between lines, it's an additional ₩5000/3000. You can pay on board.

EATING IN NAMPO-DONG: OUR PICKS

MAP P182

Buyeong Jip: (부영집) Near Jagalchi station, this restaurant specialises in marinated and unmarinated grilled sea eel and sea-eel soup. *10am-10pm* ₩₩

Dolgorae: (돌고래) Serving up tasty standards like *doenjang jjigae* (soybean stew) and *sundubu jjigae* (spicy soft tofu stew). Down a narrow lane; look for the yellow sign. *7am-10pm* ₩₩

Ddoongbo Sikdang: (뚱보식당) Longtime establishment with a lively atmosphere and generous portions of spicy grilled *jjukkumi* (webfoot octopus) and *bossam* (boiled pork). *11.30am-11pm* ₩₩

Jacky's Seafood: Buying a raw-fish dinner is easy thanks to Jacky, the affable English-speaking owner. On the 2nd floor of Jagalchi's main building. *11am-midnight* ₩₩

HIGHLIGHTS
1 Jagalchi Fish Market

SIGHTS
2 Busan Museum of Movies
3 Busan Opera House
4 Busan Tower
5 Chinatown
6 Choryang Modern History Gallery
7 Dakbatgol Mural Village
8 Gwangbok-ro
9 Somang Stairs Monorail
10 Texas Street
see 2 Trick Eye Museum

SLEEPING
11 Dante House
12 Funstay Guesthouse
13 One Way Guesthouse
14 Sohostel

EATING
15 Buyeong Jip
16 Ddoongbo Sikdang
17 Dolgorae
18 Jacky's Seafood
19 Sinbalwon
20 Yeongdeogjib

SHOPPING
see 15 Chungmudong Market

TRANSPORT
21 Busan Station

Stroll Around Yongdusan Park

MAP P182

A tower, pavilion and museums

Yongdusan Park, on the eastern side of Nampo-dong, is particularly pleasant in summer when the grounds are verdant and its 'flower clock' is in full bloom. Stop in at the cafe and take your coffee or tea to go for a leisurely wander around. Scattered about the premises are the Citizens' Bell Pavilion, an artificial waterfall, a small temple, a *hanbok* (traditional clothing) experience centre and statues of famed writer Ahn Huijae and naval hero Admiral Yi Sun-sin.

If the weather is good, buy a ticket to the **Busan Tower** *(adult/child ₩12,000/9000)*, where, from the observation deck, daytime views of container-ship traffic in the harbour provide a sense of the port's scale of operations. If you're in the mood for shopping, there's a duty-free store, or if you're a movie enthusiast, there's the **Busan Museum of Movies** *(busanbom.kr; adult/child ₩14,000/11,000)*. Opened in 2017, it was the first film exhibition and experience centre in Korea. Inside, visitors can partake in different aspects of moviemaking, including storyboarding, acting in an interactive green-screen room, editing and adding their own voiceover in a dubbing studio. The museum's app provides an explanation of the process. The museum is closed Mondays. The **Trick Eye Museum** *(trickeye.com/busan; adult/child ₩8000/6000)* is in the same building and can be accessed by purchasing a separate ticket or an all-in-one ticket.

About a block northwest of the park is the very worthwhile **Busan Modern History Museum** *(free)*. The hour or so it takes to walk through its exhibitions is a fascinating dive into the city's past. The museum, which is closed Mondays, is housed in a Japanese-colonial-era building, with a branch of the popular Casa Busano cafe chain on the main level.

Discover Huinnyeoul Culture Village

MAP P185

Drink a coffee and walk the trails

With the air of becoming a new, less-congested Gamcheong Village, the very scenic **Huinnyeoul Culture Village** on the southwestern coast of Yeongdo island has rows of blue-and-white-painted, cliff-hanging houses that have earned it the nickname of Korea's Santorini. It's pleasant to stroll on a sunny day, stopping for coffee at one of the dozen cookie-cutter cafes, some of which use their rooftops for better ocean views,

BUSAN & THE BIG SCREEN

It's all glitter and glamour in October when the **Busan International Film Festival** (BIFF; *biff.kr*), one of Asia's most important film festivals, takes centre stage. For more than two decades, Busan has welcomed lovers of the cinematic arts and, at times, the city itself has drawn the global spotlight, as seen when it served as a backdrop in Marvel's record-breaking blockbuster *Black Panther* and played a role in the Korean zombie-apocalypse thriller *Train to Busan*. BIFF's screenings are held across six theatres, including **Busan Cinema Center**, a magnificent complex with the world's longest cantilever structure. On the 4th floor of the Double Cone building, there's a free cinema library with more than 44,000 items, including magazines and movie soundtracks on vinyl. Buy movie tickets in advance on the website.

BEST COFFEE SHOPS IN HUINNYEOUL VILLAGE

MAP P185

Firstage Coffee: (퍼스테이지 커피) Exposed bricks and perfect crumble apple pie with ice cream. Out front, swings help enhance the sea views. *noon-6pm*

Yeoul Chaekjang: (여울책장) Try cheesecakes, iced desserts and lattes under book-filled shelves. The terrace has fantastic ocean views. *noon-6pm*

Cafe the Attorney: (카페 변호인) Creatively furnished cafe with indoor and outdoor sections, some that served as locations for the legal drama *The Attorney* (변호인). *noon-6pm*

Healing House Cafe: Well-choreographed cafe with suffused classical music in the large outdoor garden area and lofty, Victorian-style interiors. *noon-6pm*

TOP EXPERIENCE

Jagalchi Fish Market

South Korea's largest fish market straddles the waterfront on the southern side of Nampo-dong. It's popular for its old-world atmosphere, especially outdoors, where many women vendors, called Jagalchi *ajimae*, peddle an astounding range of seafood, from flounder to *daege* (snow crabs), oysters, sea urchins, eels and beyond.

SUCHART BOONYAVECH/SHUTTERSTOCK

TOP TIPS

- Access Jagalchi from the east, where the **Chungmudong Market** (충무동해안시장) is packed with local restaurants and numerous stalls selling a wide range of items, from dried foods to clothing, meat and fish.
- Come in October and you might catch the Busan Jagalchi Festival that takes place here.

Getting There

Busan Metro Line 1 has a Jagalchi station near the market; otherwise, it's a very short walk from BIFF Square or a prominent stop on many bus routes.

Outdoor Market

There's an outdoor market slung along the harbourside outside Jagalchi, with dozens of stalls laden with large seafood – photographers will rejoice, but respect the sellers by shooting discreetly. Simple, no-frills restaurants packed with locals offer the area's most affordable prices. We recommend **Yeongdeogjib** (영덕집), which serves hearty soups and stews from 7am to 7pm.

Market Main Building

The Jagalchi Fish Market proper is housed in a multistorey building. On the ground floor, enter a world of live, slithering creatures floating in water tanks next to humans in shiny plastic overalls. You can buy fish here and bring it to the 2nd floor, where there's a frozen fish market and several restaurants that'll cook it for you. Raw and grilled fish orders start at ₩40,000. The 5th floor has a seafood buffet restaurant.

Sindonga Fish Market

Immediately west of the main Jagalchi building, **Sindonga Fish Market** (신동아수산물종합시장) is in another compound that features numerous seafood stalls at affordable prices and approximately 100 tables. Open throughout the day, it's the spot to try all sorts of raw and cooked seafood.

PRACTICALITIES

- free
- 5am-10pm, closed on the first and third Tuesday of the month

SIGHTS
1 Huinnyeoul Culture Village
2 Huinyeoul Coastal Tunnel
3 Jungni Beach
4 Taejongdae Park
5 Yeongdo Lighthouse

ACTIVITIES
6 Jeoryeong Coastal Trail
7 Jeoryeong Haerang-Gil Trail

DRINKING & NIGHTLIFE
8 Cafe the Attorney
9 Firstage Coffee
10 Healing House Cafe
11 Yeoul Chaekjang

that line the main pathway. Some also offer aromatic footbaths and neck and shoulder massages.

Another reason to visit is to enjoy two parallel scenic coastal walks, connected by stairs for easy access. At the time of research, however, these were closed due to the risk of rockfall. The 3km (80-minute) **Jeoryeong Coastal Trail** skirts the coastline, starting from the base of Huinnyeoul Culture Village along a social-media-incensed **Huinyeoul Coastal Tunnel** to **Jungni Beach**, where there's a red lighthouse atop a breakwater. Up on the clifftop is the less scenic 2km (30-minute) **Jeoryeong Haerang-gil trail**, which runs along the main road, Jeoryeong-ro, from Huinnyeoul Observatory (where the temple of Baengnyeon-sa is located) to Jungni Beach.

Marvel at the Taejongdae Coast

MAP P185

Incredible cliffs and a toy train

On the southernmost tip of the island of Yeongdo, the city's rugged coastline can be experienced along a well-groomed 4.5km walking path in **Taejongdae Park** that follows a circular road. From the main gate, you can set off on foot (about two hours), or buy a ticket for the Danubi Train (a tourist train; *₩3000*), which stops at the geopark's various sights

WAITING FOR BUSAN OPERA HOUSE

Poised to open in 2027, the much-anticipated **Busan Opera House**, the city's next cutting-edge art and cultural offering, is set to rise on reclaimed land on the North Port waterfront, not far from Busan station. It will transform a drab industrial area into one of Busan's prime public culture gateways. Designed by the renowned Swedish architecture firm Snøhetta and Ilshin, the structure features a sculpted, double-curved form that draws inspiration from the Korean trigrams for Heaven, Earth and Water. It will include a public space on the rooftop and entrances from both the park and the seaside. Inside, it will feature an 1800-seat grand auditorium and a 300-seat multipurpose theatre enhanced with cherry-wood panels specifically designed to optimise acoustics.

BEST SHOPPING AREAS IN BUSAN

Gukje Market: West of Nampo-dong, a marketplace selling a staggering selection of items, from leather goods to Korean drums.

Gwangbok-ro: Between Yongdusan Park and Gukje Market, a culture, fashion and street-food area reminiscent of Myeong-dong in Seoul.

Shinsegae Centum City: A shopping complex with seemingly every brand name on the planet, plus a skating rink, golf driving range and Spa Land (p199).

Judies Taehwa: Specialising in women's fashion, this mall is favoured by young people as a meet-up spot in Seomyeon.

Save Zone: Popular discount department store in Haeundae; one of several locations nationwide.

Bujeon Market: An enormous traditional market in Seomyeon packed with produce and knick-knacks.

(except on Mondays). Along the way, you'll pass by pebble beaches with ferry boats, an observatory with cafes and the **Yeongdo Lighthouse**, surrounded by a cultural space and outdoor stage.

At an elevation of about 150m, the rocky cliffs abutted by crashing waves make for a spectacular scene. From the observatory on a clear day, you can see the Japanese island of Tsushima, which lies 56km beyond. To the right of the lighthouse, you'll notice a pair of dramatic rocks: **Sinseonbawi**, said to be the place of immortals, and **Mangbuseok**, a woman turned to stone while waiting for her kidnapped husband. There are also two temples, **Gumyeong-sa** and **Taejong-sa**, the latter reaching the height of its beauty in June and July when its hydrangeas are in full bloom.

Climb the Stairs of Wishes

MAP P182

A slow ride on the Somang Stairs Monorail

If you're looking for a highly Instagrammable spot that's still flying under the radar, check out the **Somang Stairs Monorail** – the so-called 'Stairs of Wishes' connecting the mountainside Mangyang-ro road to Jungangongwon-ro above. You can walk the 192 steps, but the attraction is the two-seater pastel-coloured monorail cabin that glides on a track between them. Built initially for elderly residents (who still have boarding priority) to skip the climb, it also offers visitors a whimsical, easy ride to the top. Bus 190 stops opposite Busan station and gets here in about 20 minutes after negotiating the steep hillsides.

Only 50m below the monorail, via a steep staircase, is the **Dakbatgol Mural Village**. Established in 1953 as a residential area, it joined the mural-village trend in 2010 through the collaborative efforts of artist Koo Bon-Ho and residents, but it remains relatively unknown. There's plenty of mural art for photo ops and, in early spring, it's a favourite photo spot for local cherry-blossom lovers.

Shop & Party with Busan's Youth

MAP P187

A fun-tastic time at Jeonpo and Seomyeon

One of the coolest neighbourhoods in Busan, the Jeonpo-Seomyeon conurbation at the centre of the city is ripe with nightlife, superior shopping and plenty of authentic K-Culture, especially along **Youth Street** (서면젊음의거리), a neon-washed

EATING IN SEOMYEON & JEONPO: OUR PICKS

MAP P187

Sulbing: Busan's beloved dessert cafe puts its spin on *bingsoo*, with shaved frozen milk instead of ice. The original branch is in Nampo-dong. *10am-10.30pm* ₩

Woojung Dolsot Bibimbap: (우정돌솥비빔밥) Basic yet delicious bibimbap in Jeonpo's heart – gruff service and no-frills ambience contrast with the area's glitz. *10am-10pm* ₩

Sol Taphouse: The Seomyeon outpost of this popular pub, with New York-style pizza and pasta on the menu and craft beer on tap. *noon-midnight* ₩₩

Wildcat Brewing: Craft beer, plus pulled pork, sausage and fish and chips, a convenient walk from the subway and train stations. *5pm-midnight Sun-Fri, 4pm-12.30am Sat* ₩₩

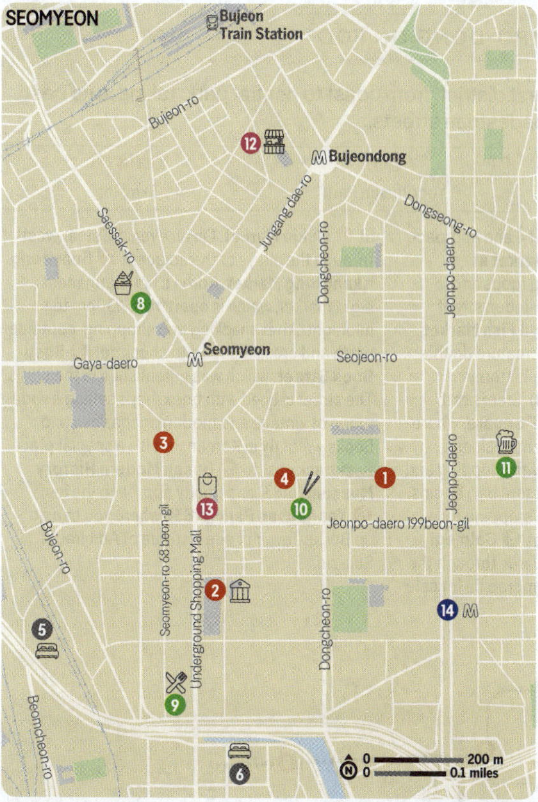

SIGHTS
1 Jeonpo Cafe Street
2 Poopoo Land
3 Seomyeon Food Alley
4 Youth Street

SLEEPING
5 Blue Backpackers
6 Kimchee Busan Downtown Guesthouse

EATING
see 2 Sol Taphouse
8 Sulbing
9 Wildcat Brewing
10 Woojung Dolsot Bibimbap

DRINKING & NIGHTLIFE
11 Beer Shop

SHOPPING
12 Bujeon Market
13 Judies Taehwa

TRANSPORT
14 Jeonpo Metro Station

strip lined with boutiques and photo booths where Busan's young come to strut their stuff. Jeonpo is also an epicentre of coffee culture, particularly along **Jeonpo Cafe Street**, which is packed with dozens of speciality coffee shops. Just a few blocks away is **Seomyeon Food Alley** (서면먹자골목), where many Korean restaurants and *pojangmacha* (street stalls) offer the whole variety of South Korean dishes, including knife-cut noodles and *jokbal*, a Busan speciality of braised pig trotters, with a dedicated area called Jokbal Alley. If you come to Jeonpo with kids, don't miss the very quirky **Poopoo Land** (놀이똥산; *playpoop.com; ₩10,000*) for a laugh. The hilarious kid-focused museum utilises cartoonish cuteness to teach children all about their physiological needs.

EXPLORE NAMPO-DONG ON FOOT

Walk across Busan's oldest district, from coast to central park, taking in its best markets, museums and pedestrian streets.

START	END	LENGTH
Jagalchi station Exit 4	Yongdusan Park	3km; 1hr

Walk out of Jagalchi station Exit 4 and approach the coast from the 1 **Haean Market at Chungmu-dong**. See how dried foods and housewares leave space to fish-laden street stalls all the way to 2 **Sindonga Fish Market** (p184). Complete this seafood-creature double feature with a visit inside the multistorey 3 **Jagalchi Fish Market** (p184). Steer north and cross Gudeok-ro to 4 **BIFF Square**, where Busan celebrates its commitment to cinema, and a pedestrian area packed with shopping and streetside *pojangmacha* (street tent bar) begins. Continue walking north, maybe stopping for a cold glass of Busan craft beer at 5 **Galmegi Brewing Nampo**, and then onwards through the myriad products and K-Pop memorabilia for sale at 6 **Gukje Market**. On an evening, steer west through the alleys of the adjacent 7 **Bupyeong Kkangtong Market**, Korea's first permanent night market, which is open from 7.30pm to midnight. After snacking and shopping, continue north and cross the road to check out 8 **Bosu Book Street**, which was established in the 1950s. The street is lined with bookshops selling a wide range of vintage and modern magazines and books – mostly in Korean, but it's a special place. Backtrack east to 9 **Busan Modern History Museum** (p183) and finally approach the leafy 10 **Yongdusan Park** (p183), where you can go up Busan Tower or see a statue of Admiral Yi Sun-sin.

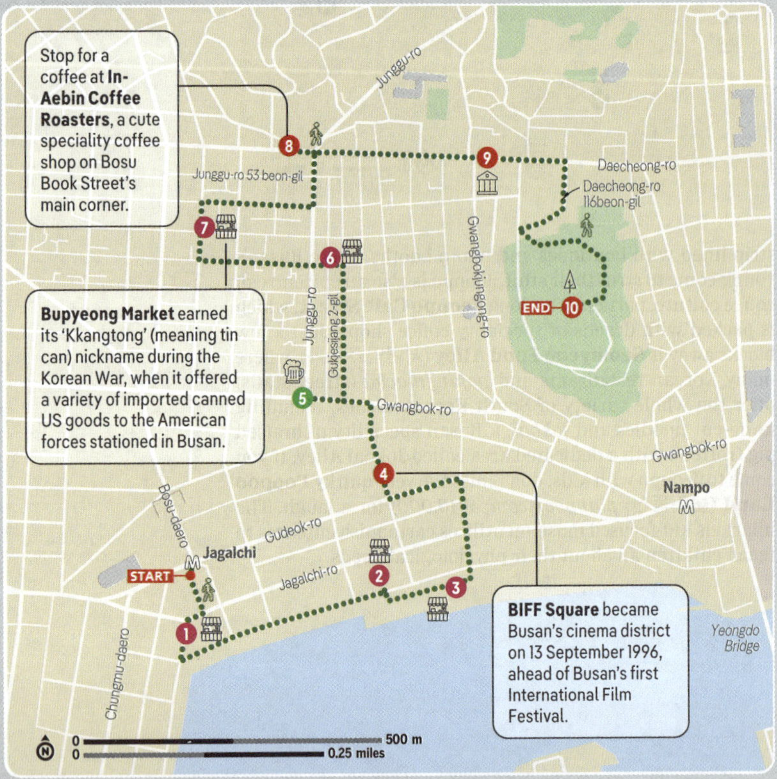

West Busan

PASTEL HILLS AND SEA CLIFFS AT THE CITY'S EDGE

West Busan (Songdo, Gamcheon and beyond), a region of hills cascading to the sea, has long been defined by its port and industrial muscle. During the Korean War, when Busan became the temporary capital after Seoul was captured, this rugged western area is where countless refugees started to settle, especially in the steep, slum-like neighbourhoods of what would become Gamcheon. Today, that gritty history contrasts with West Busan's new reality as both a top tourist draw (Gamcheon Culture Village is now painted, curated, Instagrammed, and one of Busan's top three attractions) and an economic powerhouse, home to major industrial parks, the intercity Seobu Bus Terminal and Gimhae International Airport. Travellers often sleep in other districts, unless they want to enjoy Gamcheon beyond peak tour-bus hours, but West Busan still anchors almost every itinerary, both for what it was and for what it has become.

TOP TIP

For some offbeat sunset views, take the Busan–Gimhae Light Rail to **Daejeo station** before dusk and take a short walk to the **Daejeo Eco Park**'s reed fields to the east. You'll see flaming sunset light on cargo docks, and planes descending over the Nakdong River.

Ride the Busan Air Cruise

Korea's original aerial tramway

Originally launched in 1964 as Korea's first **cable car** (Songdo Marine Cable Car; *en.busanaircruise.co.kr; regular cabin adult/child one way ₩13,000/10,000, return ₩17,000/12,000),*

GETTING AROUND

Even though **Gimhae International Airport**, 27km west of Busan's city centre, no longer has as many international flights as before the COVID-19 pandemic, it remains a prime getaway into Busan, especially for those flying to and from Jeju-do. Gimhae is one of the 21 stations along the Busan–Gimhae Light Rail Transit line. Passengers can transfer to Busan Metro Line 3 and 2, respectively, at Daejeo and Sasang stations – the latter is also where the **Seobu Intercity Bus Terminal**, Busan's western bus hub for destinations in Jeolla-do province, is located. For Gamcheon, the green Seogu 2-2 bus takes approximately 45 minutes from **Busan train station** (p180).

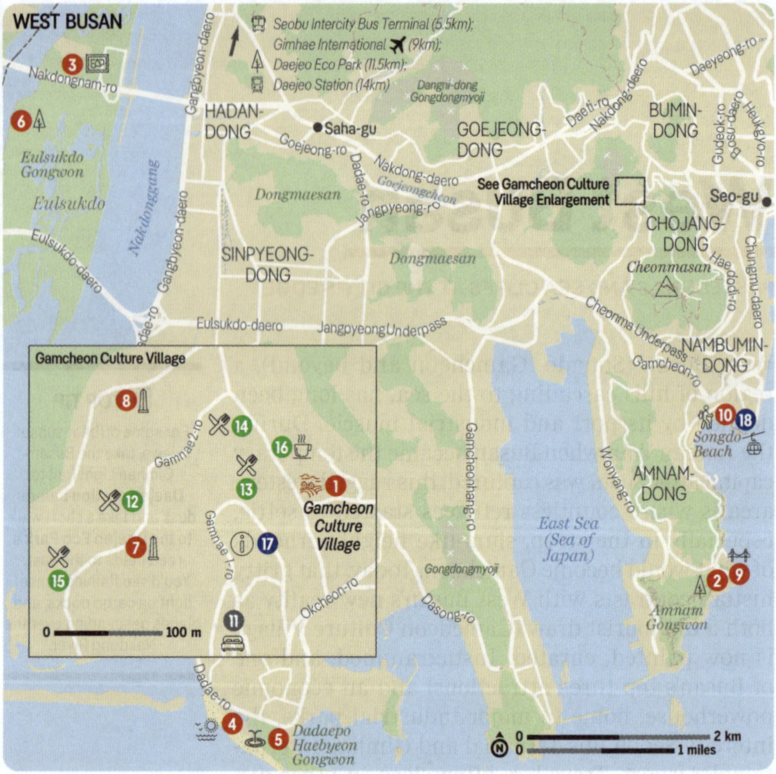

HIGHLIGHTS

1 Gamcheon Culture Village

SIGHTS

2 Amnam Park
3 Busan Museum of Contemporary Art
4 Dadaepo Beach
5 Dadaepo Sunset Fountain of Dreams
6 Eulsukdo Migratory Bird Park
7 Little Prince and Desert Fox Statue
8 Little Prince Statue
9 Songdo Yonggung Suspension Bridge
see 18 Songnim Park

ACTIVITIES

10 Songdo Cloud Walk

SLEEPING

11 Bangga Bangga Guesthouse

EATING

12 Asteroid B612 Cafe
13 Blue House on The Stairs
14 Cafe Wooin
15 The Plate

DRINKING & NIGHTLIFE

16 Gamnae Cafe

INFORMATION

17 Gamcheon Second Information Centre

TRANSPORT

18 Busan Air Cruise

the Songdo Beach attraction reopened in 2017 as **Busan Air Cruise**, measuring a distance of 1.62km – four times its length before its 1988 closure. There are 39 cars – 13 of them with glass floors *(adult/child one way ₩17,000/13,000, return ₩22,000/16,000)* – that traverse emerald waters, offering beautiful views of the hillsides and cliffs.

The one-way or round-trip journey starts from Bay Station next to **Songnim Park** on Songdo's east side, ending at an observatory ('Skypark') at **Amnam Park** in the west. Each station is outfitted with cafes and snack shops. From Amnam Park, you can take the **Songdo Yonggung Suspension Bridge**, which is particularly beautiful at night when it's illuminated, across the sea to the tiny uninhabited island of Dongseom. Pair the cable-car experience with the **Songdo Cloud Walk**, a 365m-long elevated path over the ocean.

Go Birdwatching Among Art

The ecological island of Eulsukudo

On Eulsukdo island in the Nakdong River, visit a variety of ecological sites, from estuary and cultural centres to a **migratory bird park** and an ecofriendly art museum.

Grab a coffee from one of the cafes, view the sculpture park, listen to a performance at the outdoor hall, watch for birds at the observatory, or simply wander the extensive grounds. At the **Busan Museum of Contemporary Art** *(busan.go.kr/moca_en; free)*, there are three levels of exhibition space to enjoy, along with a garden. It's closed Mondays.

Sunset at the Beach

Scenic lookouts at Dadaepo Beach

Famed for its sunsets, **Dadaepo Beach**, formed from sands deposited by the Nakdong River, has shallow waters suitable for children and is a beautiful place to go for a walk as the daylight wanes. Pleasant paths wind through the adjacent park and along the stream, while an elevated boardwalk along the coast provides up-close views of the offshore rock formations. In the forest beyond, narrow trails lead to hidden lookout points. When the sun goes down over the beach from April to October, the musical **Dadaepo Sunset Fountain of Dreams** is also quite a show – as well as being lit with colourful lights, it shoots water to a lofty 55m, forming shapes such as a crane's wings, a rainbow and a sunflower, while a selection of more than 60 songs, ranging from folk to pop to classical, plays in the background.

BUSAN'S BEST CAFE STREETS

Gwangalli Cafe Street: Across from one of the city's best beaches, this row of coffee shops and bars features aquamarine views.

Haeridan-gil: A trending stretch of new cafes and restaurants, north of Haeundae Station.

Oncheoncheon Cafe Street: Oncheon Stream is lined with cherry blossom trees, a cycling path, coffee shops and bars.

Jeonpo Cafe Street: Near Seomyeon and Jeonpo stations, this is a one-time hardware and tools district turned cafe hot spot.

Gijang Cafe Street: Between Imnang and Ilwang beaches, this coastal stretch is dotted with atmospheric cafes and bakeries.

COOL CAFES WITH A VIEW IN GAMCHEON VILLAGE

Asteroid B612 Cafe: Above the Little Prince Statue, this bright-orange cafe has brews, pastries, a photo zone on the 2nd floor and a panoramic rooftop. *9am-8pm* **WW**

The Plate: (더플레이트) Little corner-house cafe for cuppas and brunch (burgers, fish and chips, pasta). Upstairs, tables face large windows with excellent views. *11am-7.30pm* **W**

Cafe Wooin: (카페 우인) Coloured hanging flags lead to a charming balcony to enjoy coffee, smoothies and lattes with views over the hills. *10am-6pm* **W**

Blue House on The Stairs: (계단위푸른집) Grab a drink and sit on this blue house's rooftop to enjoy unobstructed views of the whole village. *11am-7pm* **W**

TOP EXPERIENCE

Gamcheon Culture Village

Once a mountainside shantytown for Korean War refugees who settled here in 1955, Gamcheon Culture Village (감천문화마을) has become one of Busan's top tourist draws after an arty makeover in 2009. The neighbourhood's maze-like alleys wind between terraced buildings spruced up in rainbow colours and filled with cafes, galleries, studios and shops – a historic living community benefiting from tourism.

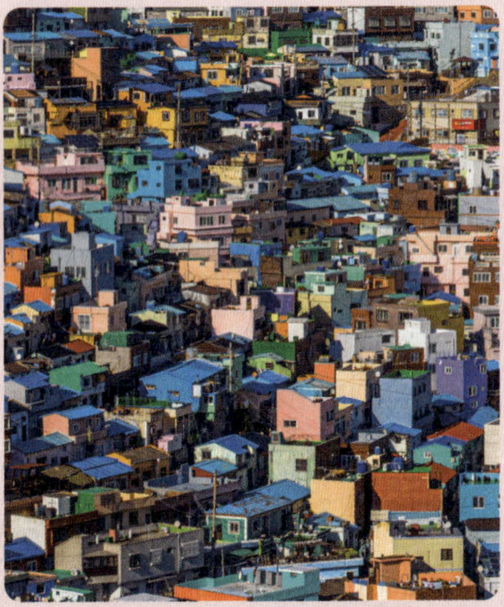

INSUNG JEON/GETTY IMAGES

TOP TIPS

- Parking is available inside the Gamnae Byeolmaru Sports Centre, but come by bus to avoid contributing to the traffic gridlock.
- Avoid crowds by going higher up Tianma Mountain. The bookcase-painted staircase to the right of The Plate cafe (p191) leads to a panoramic trail. Use the maps.me app to follow the path.

PRACTICALITIES

- gamcheon.or.kr
- free
- 24hr, businesses 9am-6pm

Visiting the Village

From Busan train station, the green Seogu 2-2 bus takes about 45 minutes to drop visitors 30m from the village's **second information centre**, where you can buy stamp maps marking establishments supporting local community-welfare projects, such as **Gamnae Cafe** and the **Bangga Bangga Guesthouse**. Free guides meet visitors at the information centre from 10.30am to 2pm (except Mondays) – advanced reservations are required at visitbusan.net.

Tourist Hotspot

Gamcheon is as touristy as it gets, with selfie studios and people in *hanbok* fluttering between picture spots. The two most popular stops have statues of Antoine de Saint-Exupéry's *Little Prince*, whose tale of belief in the power of imagination aligns well with Korean cultural values. The **Little Prince and Desert Fox Statue** faces a most dramatic view of the village cascading towards the sea. The **Little Prince Statue**, seated on a half-moon atop the Gamnae Byeolmaru Sports Centre, is Gamcheon's highest viewpoint. Despite the crowds and long lines for selfies, Gamcheon is large enough to offer anyone a quiet nook with views and atmosphere – use the steep inclines to find your spot and remember that the use of drones is prohibited.

Beaches & East Busan

SURF BREAKS AND SKYLINE BY THE EAST SEA

Of Busan's seven public beaches, the trinity of Gwangalli, Haeundae and Songjeong are the most famous and make up the best part of Busan's central and eastern shoreline. Few metropolises can pride themselves on having such long, beautiful coves right in the city, and it's no surprise that many visitors decide to stay here. Seamlessly connected by public transport, these fine sand beaches have a balmy feel. Gwangalli is 1.4km long, with calm waters ideal for swimming and paddleboarding, and is surrounded by numerous cafes and restaurants. Next east is the 1.5km-long, 30m to 50m-wide Haeundae, Busan's most popular and developed beach, featuring a shallow bay ideal for swimming and able to accommodate up to 120,000 people. At its eastern end, the iconic Blueline Park features a train, monorail and the 4.2km-long Green Railway Trail, which connects to the 1.2km-long, surf-centric Songjeong Beach. It's a short hop from here to Haedong Yonggung-sa, one of Korea's few sea-facing temples.

TOP TIP

Visit Songjeong at night, when the beachfront turns into a quiet after-surf village, best for camaraderie and encounters. Join the locals in damp wetsuits for cheap beers and dried squid by the kerb.

GETTING AROUND

Haeundae has an **intercity bus terminal** that's very conveniently located compared to Busan Central Bus Terminal in the city's north. Haeundae is within walking distance of Haeundae metro station on Line 2, which also connects to Gwangan station for Gwangalli Beach and destinations further west in Nampo-dong and beyond. Buses are another excellent way to hop to and around the beaches. Each beach has a very walkable promenade that also doubles as a cycling and jogging track, and it's possible, albeit long, to cycle between Gwangalli and Haeundae. Coastal walks and trails, particularly the Green Railway from Mipo to Songjeong, offer opportunities for long walks between the central and eastern beach areas.

BUSAN'S BEST CRAFT BEERS

Hyunmi Jung, general manager of Galmegi Brewing, the first American-style brewery in Busan, recommends where to drink. *@_mia_jung*

Galmegi Brewing Haeundae and **Galmegi Brewing Nampo** (p188) are our two main branches. Try our signature beer, Galmegi IPA, or a sour Yuja Gose.

SÜDEN Craftbeer is a good Gwangan pub run by the Turmbrau team, which has a brewery near Osiria metro station.

On Gwangalli Beach's southern side, **Hugus Beer Pub** utilises local Busan ingredients, including honey, carrots, mushrooms and perilla leaves.

The **Beer Shop** in Jeonpo has an outdoor patio to enjoy a large selection from the Gorilla Beer brewery. There's great food, too – try the house's pastrami burgers.

Swimming & Watersports at Gwangalli Beach

MAP P195

City beach for fun and drone pyrotechnics

Located to the west of Haeundae, **Gwangalli Beach** (also known as Gwangan Beach) is a quiet bay with a stretch of sand backed by tall skyscrapers and crossed by **Gwangan Bridge** – an incredible sight when it lights up after dark. Locals come to this happening city beach to jog and cycle. Some bunk by the free thatched umbrellas along the beach, and because of the sheltered bay it's considered the best place to try stand-up paddleboarding in Busan. **Surf Marine**, on the southwestern side of the beach, rents them for ₩15,000 per hour, including a quick lesson to grasp the basics. Skateboarders can use a bunch of compact half-pipes set near the middle of the beach.

Gwangalli is also very popular on Saturday nights for the **Gwangalli M Drone Light Show** *(gwangallimdrone.co.kr/en/home; free)*, the first of its kind in Korea, where hundreds of drones take to the sky to create pyrotechnic light and image shows. The 12-minute performances take place twice a night, at 7pm and 9pm in winter and 8pm and 10pm in summer.

Hop Over to Haeundae

MAP P198

Busan's most popular beach and highest views

Have some fun in the sun at Korea's most famous beach, **Haeundae**, a vast stretch of sand backed by a full-fledged entertainment and dining district. You can partake in any number of water activities, from SUP yoga to snorkelling, go cafe- or bar-hopping along the shore, or simply laze on the sand with a good book and a snack. For a private club experience, check out **ClubD Oasis**, an upscale spa with a rooftop infinity pool and bar.

If the weather's fine, head to 411.6m-high Haeundae LCT The Sharp Landmark Tower, the second-tallest building in Korea, and pay for the prime aerial views at **BUSAN X the SKY** *(adult/child ₩27,000/24,000)*, where an elevator with projections takes visitors up the tower's 98th, 99th and 100th floors. Acrophobes, think twice.

EATING IN GWANGAN: OUR PICKS

MAP P195

Onbap: (온밥) A little restaurant that excels in grilled fish and has a pretty delicious bulgogi. Prices are surprisingly good. *11.30am-3pm & 5-8.30pm* ₩

Ggulggeok House: Simple, superb menu paired with seasonal *makgeolli* (milky rice wine). Takeout bottles available. *5.30-11.30pm Mon & Wed-Fri, 4pm-midnight Sat & Sun* ₩₩

Gogigupneun Namja (Grilling Man) Gwangan: Less greasy, more comfortable Korean BBQ experience at this franchise's beach branch. *11.30am-12.30am* ₩₩

Millak Hoe Town: (민락회타운) Buy fish for around ₩30,000, which can then be prepared into various dishes upstairs. *10.30am-midnight Wed-Mon* ₩₩

SUYEONG-GU & NAM-GU

HIGHLIGHTS
1 Spa Land

SIGHTS
2 Busan Museum
3 Gwangalli Beach
4 Gwangan Bridge
5 United Nations Cemetery

ACTIVITIES
6 Igidae Coastal Trail
7 Oryukdo Skywalk
8 Surf Marine

SLEEPING
9 Gwangan Hound Hotel
10 Hotell

EATING
11 Ggulggeok House
12 Gogigupneun Namja (Grilling Man) Gwangan
13 Millak Hoe Town
14 Onbap

DRINKING & NIGHTLIFE
15 Cafe RicoRica
16 Corduroy Fellaz
17 Happy Monk
18 Hugus Beer Pub
19 SÜDEN Craftbeer
20 Werk Roasters

ENTERTAINMENT
21 Gwangalli M Drone Light Show

SHOPPING
see 1 Shinsegae Centum City

TOP EXPERIENCE

Haeundae Blueline Park

A former section of the old East Sea South Line railway has become one of Haeundae's top tourist attractions (p179). Enjoy a 4.8km section of jaw-dropping coastal scenery from Mipo to Cheongsapo or Songjeong Beach, either by striking out on a walking trail equipped with technological viewing platforms, or relaxing aboard the Haeundae Beach Train or the iconic, pastel-hued Sky Capsule.

PHOTOSEAGULL/SHUTTERSTOCK

Haeundae Beach Train

TOP TIPS

- Haewol Observatory is stunning at night, when LED lights flash it up with striking colours.
- If you only want to go halfway on the Green Railway, exit at **Cheongsapo station** and catch the only bus going to Jangsan metro station, where you can return to Haeundae or continue further west.

Walking the Green Railway

The **Green Railway** *(free)* is a wooden-planked walking trail connecting **Mipo Wharf** to Songjeong. The 4.8km trail offers amazing harbour views and would be a dream to cycle, but it's oddly pedestrian-only – Korean joggers flock here after work.

The trail takes you past two lighthouses and a few viewpoints such as 22m-high **Haewol Observatory** (해월전망대; *free),* a 137m-long oversea U-shaped walking path with crescent-shaped pylons – acrophobes beware.

Further on, you'll pass the 20m-high, 72m-long transparent-floored **Cheongsapo Daritdol Skywalk** (청사포 다릿돌전망대; *free),* also perched above the sea, and the colourful Dalmaji tunnel, featuring several side staircases for plenty of off-path moseying around coastal cliffs. At the end, head to the unbeatable sunset lookout of **Jukdo Park** (죽도공원). If you're up for walking even further, begin with the forest section of the trail, which adds another 5km onto your journey.

Beach Train & Sky Capsule

If you don't feel like walking the entire distance, hop aboard the multistop **Haeundae Beach Train** *(adult/child one way ₩8000/5600, return ₩12,000/8400, pass for all stops ₩16,000/11,200)* at Blueline Park – the 'Blueline' running ground-level alongside the Green Line – or the non-stop, elevated and romantic **Sky Capsule** *(2/3/5 people ₩40,000/45,000/50,000)* that runs on a monorail above.

PRACTICALITIES

- bluelinepark.com
- ride prices vary
- 9.30am-8.30pm May, Jun & Sep, to 9.30pm Jul & Aug, to 7.30pm Mar, Apr & Oct, to 7pm Nov-Feb

Visit the UN's Only Cemetery

MAP P195

A memorial and a museum

See the only **United Nations cemetery** in the world, the final resting place of 2300 men from 11 nations, including the UK, Turkey, Canada and Australia, that supported South Korea in the 1950–53 Korean War. The premises also include a UN Sculpture Park, the Daeyeon Arboretum and the **Busan Museum**, where you can learn more about the city's history and view some of the museum's 45,000 artefacts.

Catch a Wave

MAP P198

Surf at Songjeong Beach

Among Busan's seven beaches, **Songjeong** has gained the reputation of being the city's prime surfing spot – October and November are peak season. Stretching along the shore, you'll see dozens of surf shops, surf schools and surf-oriented cafes and bars. Women looking to learn in a supportive environment should consider signing up for a surf camp organised by **NomadHer** *(nomadher.com)*, the now-global community of women travellers that was first established in Busan. NomadHer's multiday camps are taught by professional women surfers and include only women participants.

Pray at an Oceanside Temple

MAP P198

Seaside mantras at Haedong Yonggung-sa

One of the country's few temples situated right on the coast, **Haedong Yonggung-sa** *(yongkungsa.or.kr; free)* offers spectacular views of the temple grounds and surrounding ocean. Located in the northeastern Gijang-gun district, it gets congested on weekends, but the dramatic vistas, elaborate altars, statues of towering zodiac animals and a giant gold Buddha make the venture well worth it. Take the stairway next to the zodiac animals to reach the dramatic **Sirangdae** wooden observatory deck, the start of a 2.5km coast-hugging trail to Orangdae Park. Get to the temple by taxi, or take a bus from Haeundae or Osiria metro stations and walk up a hilly road lined, in spring, with frothy cherry blossoms.

Once you're done at Haedong Yonggung-sa, the nearby **OSIRIA Tourist Complex** is a fun place to hang out before making the journey back. In addition to the **Lotte World Adventure** *(adventurebusan.lotteworld.com; adult/teenager/child/baby ₩49,000/41,000/35,000/13,000)* theme park and

BUSAN'S SEASONAL FESTIVALS

Samrak Cherry Blossom Festival: Samrak Eco Park turns frothy pink when the cherry blossoms grace the riverside. *April*

Busan One Asia Festival: A *hallyu* (Korean Wave) music extravaganza, with K-Pop concerts at various venues across the festival period. *June*

Busan Sea Festival: Offering cultural events, performances and hands-on experiences at five of the city's best beaches. *August*

Busan International Fireworks Festival: The sky is illuminated with a bedazzling nighttime choreography of light, colour, lasers and music along Gwangalli Beach. *November*

Haeundae Lighting Festival: Haeundae Beach and Gunam-ro Sq glow with millions of glittering lights and lighted Christmas decorations. *December*

COFFEE & DRINKS IN GWANGAN: OUR PICKS

MAP P195

Werk Roasters: Coffee lovers' haven with Scandinavian-style interiors and all the perks to make enthusiasts squirm with caffeinated joy. *10am-6.30pm*

Cafe RicoRica: Loft-like cafe with an unbeatable 1st-floor beach-facing location for great day and night views of Gwangalli and the bridge. *9am-midnight Sun-Thu, to 2am Fri & Sat*

Corduroy Fellaz: Minimalist-chic cocktail bar serving highly curated drinks. Try the whisky-based Coco Celery and Pisco Disco with passionfruit and banana *7pm-2am, to 3am Fri & Sat*

Happy Monk: Beach-facing beer pub with exposed bricks, suitable for happy hours with European beers and finger food, in the thick of Gwangalli. *5pm-3am, from 2pm Fri-Sun*

HIGHLIGHTS
1 Haeundae
2 Haeundae Blueline Park

SIGHTS
3 BUSAN X the SKY
4 Haedong Yonggung-sa
5 Haegwang-sa Yongwangdan
6 Haewol Observatory
7 Jukdo Park
8 Sirangdae
9 Songjeong Beach

ACTIVITIES
10 Cheongsapo Daritdol Skywalk
11 ClubD Oasis
12 Mipo Wharf
13 Osiria Coastal Walk

SLEEPING
14 Coolest Hotel
15 Edge 993
16 Funwave Guesthouse
17 Hotel Hongdan
18 Kimchee Haeundae Guesthouse
19 Paradise Hotel
20 Westin Chosun Busan

EATING
21 Haeundae Milmyeon
22 Haeundae Somunnan Amso Galbi Jip
23 Home Bistro
24 Noran Mahura

DRINKING & NIGHTLIFE
25 Galmegi Brewing Haeundae

ENTERTAINMENT
26 Lotte World Adventure
27 OSIRIA Tourist Complex
28 Skyline Luge Busan

TRANSPORT
29 Cheongsapo Blueline Station
30 Haeundae Intercity Bus Terminal

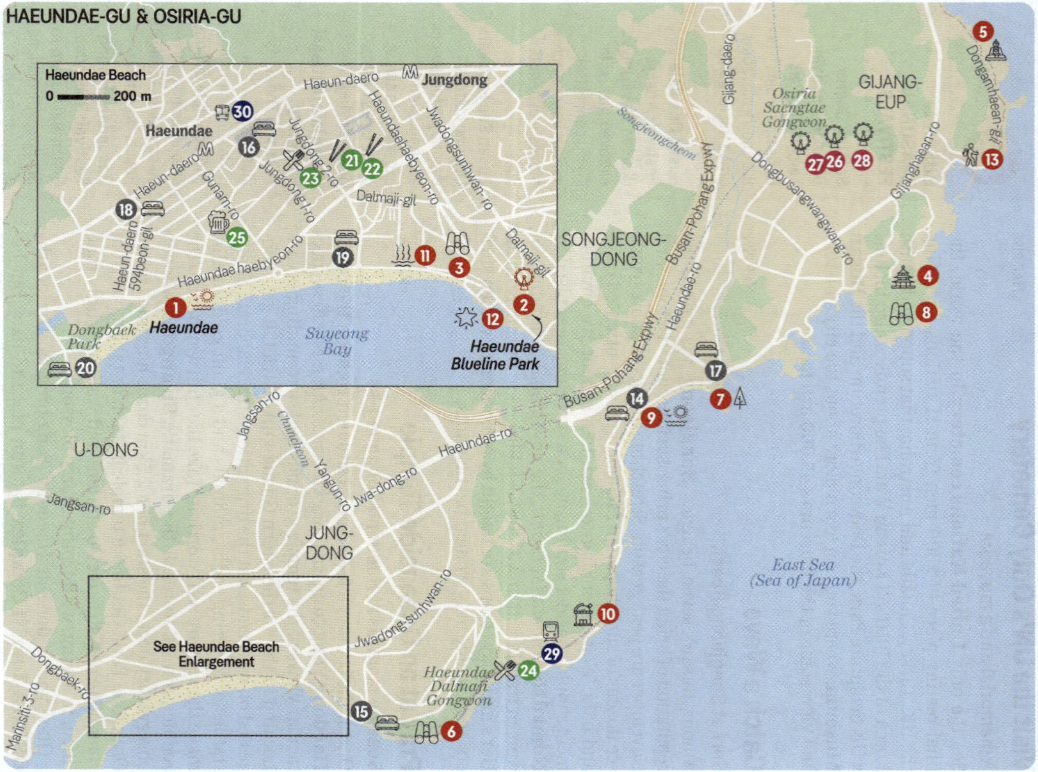

Skyline Luge Busan *(busan.skylineluge.kr/en; packages from ₩31,000)*, the complex is also home to a shopping centre, science museum, golf course and infinity pool. Hikers can strike out on the easy 2.1km **Osiria Coastal Walk**, which takes about half an hour to complete, from Dongam Village, skirting the Ananti Cove resort area and onto Orangdae Park, where the **Haegwang-sa Yongwangdan** temple, built atop a big sea boulder, is a popular sunrise spot.

Take the Igidae Coastal Trail

MAP P195

A seawalk and a skywalk

Ideal for a three-hour stroll, Igidae's 4.7km **coastal trail** goes through forests and over bedrock. Possibly Busan's most popular hike, it offers sweeping views of the Gwangandaegyo Bridge, Dongbaekseom Island and Haeundae beach across the bay. It's one part of Busan's 23-section, 278km-long Galmaetgil Trail. The southern end connects to the transparent-floored **Oryukdo Skywalk**, a 15m-long glass bridge spanning a 35m-high coastal cliff that faces the craggy Oryukdo islets.

Get Steamed at Spa Land

MAP P195

A sweat and a scrub

Across from the Cinema Center and inside the world's largest department store, **Shinsegae Centum City**, **Spa Land** is one of Korea's largest and most luxurious *jjimjilbang*. Enter the building, confusingly marked as 'mall', to find two floors with 22 baths and 13 different types of saunas, nap rooms, a ramen bar and a gaming centre.

FERRY SERVICE TO JAPAN

For ferries to Japan, the **international passenger terminal** is about a 15-minute walk from Choryang subway station. Several companies operate routes to various Japanese ports, including Izuhara (as short as 1¼ hours), Fukuoka (3½ hours) and Osaka (as long as 19 hours). Book online directly with the company (check *panstar.co.kr* for Osaka services), use a third-party site such as Direct Ferries *(directferries.com)*, or purchase tickets at the terminal on the 3rd floor. Remember to bring your passport and any travel documents. With sometimes strong winds and wild waves, the ride to Japan can be rough, so this is not the mode of transport for travellers who are even the tiniest bit prone to motion sickness.

EATING IN HAEUNDAE: OUR PICKS

MAP P198

Haeundae Milmyeon: Try refreshing *milmyeon*, Busan's signature chewy wheat noodles in spicy, icy, meat-based broth. Order a side of steamy dumplings. *10.30am-8.30pm* ₩

Home Bistro: A homey vegetarian eatery serving tasty sandwiches, salads, pastas, pizzas and a good selection of wines. *5pm-midnight Tue-Sat* ₩₩

Noran Mahura: Where people come to watch sunset and unexpectedly stay for sunrise. Meals include grilled *jogae* (shellfish) that tastes even better with soju. *24hr* ₩₩

Haeundae Somunnan Amso Galbi Jip: Cooking exquisite *galbi* (ribs) since 1964. Soak up the drippings with *gamja guksu* (potato noodles). *11.30am-3.15pm & 4.30-10pm* ₩₩₩

North Busan

GREEN RETREATS | MOUNTAIN WALKS | TEMPLE CALM

GETTING AROUND

If coming to Busan by bus, you may find yourself dropped at **Busan Central Bus Terminal**, which is actually in the north of Busan and quite a distance from the city centre – it's an hour from Nampo-dong by metro. North Busan is not the best area in which to base yourself, though Busan's mountainous northern fringes are well connected to the city centre by metro Line 1. Oncheonjang and Bomeo-sa stations are respectively within walking distance of Geumgang Park and the Beomeo-sa.

North Busan (Geumgang Park and Beomeo-sa), along the Gyeongsangnam-do border, feels worlds apart from the city's skyscrapers, art villages and beaches. Here, nature takes centre stage, yet public transport keeps it easily accessible, making it a perfect day-trip destination. Hike Geumgang Mountain's winding trails through forests and ridges, or ride its cable car for a different perspective far from the coast. In the midst of Geumgang Park, Seokbul-sa features a corridor of intricate Buddhist carvings etched directly into the rock face, providing a peaceful spot for a spiritual pause. To its north, the Geumjeong Fortress stands as a reminder of the strategic importance of Busan's mountainous crown, adding history to the scenic surroundings. Quiet paths, sweeping vistas and cultural landmarks combine to make North Busan a refreshing change to the energy of southern Busan, ideal for hikers, photographers, or anyone seeking a breath of fresh air.

Get on a Mountaintop Adventure

A cable car, fortress and temple

Add the **Geumgang Cable Car** *(adult/child one way ₩7000/5000, return ₩11,000/8000)*, set amid **Geumgang Park**, to your list of must-do activities. The view of development coursing through the valleys of verdant mountains is breathtaking and, on a clear day, the Gwangan Bridge is visible. From Oncheonjang station, it's a 15-minute walk, going out Exit 1, heading left to the intersection and crossing the street, following Geumgang Park Rd. The cable car is 150m from the park entrance; look for the 'Ropeway' sign. Also inside Geumgang Park is the **Busan Marine Natural History Museum** *(busan.go.kr/sea_eng; free)*, a folk arts centre, a few temples, patriotic tombs, a botanical garden *(adult/child ₩1000/500)* and a pine tree notable for having grown through a rock. The museum is closed Mondays.

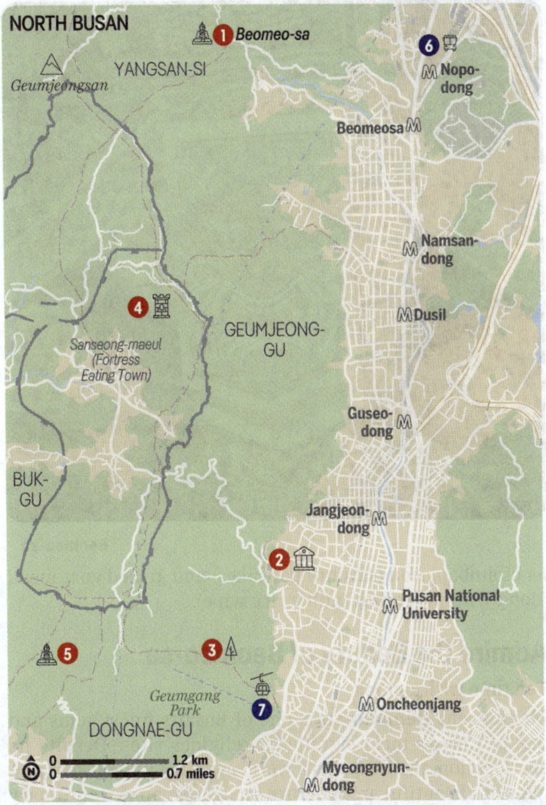

HIGHLIGHTS

1 Beomeo-sa

SIGHTS

2 Busan Marine Natural History Museum

3 Geumgang Park

4 Geumjeong Fortress

5 Seokbul-sa

TRANSPORT

6 Busan Central Bus Terminal

7 Geumgang Cable Car

Atop Geumjeongsan, you're well positioned for a short stroll to **Geumjeong Fortress** *(free)*. Walk to the fortress's South Gate, about 20 minutes from the fortress along marked paths. From here, if you're up for something even more strenuous, you can go onward to the temple of **Seokbul-sa**. The route will take you past a collection of restaurants and a dusty sports court, then down the mountainside along a trail that requires crossing a stream on some rather unsteady rocks.

Way down at the bottom, turn right and walk uphill along the very steep and winding cement road. When you finally arrive at Seokbul-sa, you'll need to catch your breath, for more reasons than one. The hermitage's Buddhist images, meticulously etched into stone, are the kind of work that moves visitors to exclaim 'wow'.

On the way back, you can either keep walking down the cement road from the temple – you'll end up near Mandeok station on Line 3 – or return to Nammun and follow the signs to the cable car, if you've bought the round-trip ticket. The return trek uphill deserves a hearty meal – near the cable-car platform, there are plenty of tables serving food, such

TOP TIP

Base yourself near Oncheonjang and hike to Geumjeongsan's fort walls at sunrise. It's quiet and misty and you'll cross paths only with some local *ajusshi* (middle-aged men) with hiking poles – you'll get one of Busan's most cinematic views without the coastal crowds.

Beomeo-sa

as bibimbap, *jeon* (savoury pancakes) and grilled goat meat, along with *makgeolli* (milky rice wine).

Admire the Beauty of Beomeo-sa

Tea time with a monk

Magnificent **Beomeo-sa** is one of Busan's finest gems and one of Korea's most significant religious sites. Despite its city location, the temple is a world away from the urban jungle, with beautiful architecture set against an extraordinary mountain backdrop. Here you'll find four nationally designated treasures: No 250, a stone three-storey pagoda; No 434, Daeungjeon, the main hall; No 1526, the triad of wooden Buddha statues enshrined in the hall, saving people across the past, present and future; and No 1461, the one-pillar gate, set low to the ground to symbolise the humility one needs to pass through its door.

Beomeo-sa can be a busy place on weekends and holidays, as the path leading to the temple is the northern starting point for trails across Geumjeongsan. Before heading back to the city, visit the *pajeon* (green-onion pancake) restaurants near the bus stop.

ACCESSIBLE TOURISM IN BUSAN

For information on accessible transport, toilets and parking across the city, as well as attractions that offer wheelchairs, contact the **Busan Leisure Activities Support Association for the Disabled** *(wheelbusan.or.kr; 051-783-8308).* The visitbusan.net website provides a list of recommended barrier-free attractions, accommodation options and restaurants, and puts together helpful itineraries for barrier-free tour routes. One takes visitors from Busan station to Busan Aquarium (which offers audio guides for the partially sighted) along the wheelchair-friendly Dongbaek Park Coastal Trail to Nurimaru APEC House, where wheelchairs can be borrowed for free. Another route goes to Songdo Beach and Amnam Park, with accessible paths and facilities.

Beyond Busan

Temples, cherry blossoms, parks and industrial cities scattered between more coastal wonders and inland mountains that hide historical treasures.

Places

Beyond Busan's sprawling expanse, you'll find the industrial city of Ulsan (울산) along the east coast, the mountainous terrain of Gajisan Provincial Park stretching for kilometres to the north and Gyeongsangnam-do's provincial capital, Changwon (창원), to the west. Head to Ulsan for suspension-bridge thrills and a bamboo-forest fantasy in summer, while Changwon's Jinhae Cherry Blossom Festival should command your attention in spring.

In the southern reaches of Gajisan sits a 'Jewel Temple' of Korea, the treasure of Tongdo-sa, and further north unfurls one of Korea's most impressive mountain ranges – what Koreans call the Yeongnam Alps. Make the trek to either, at any time of year, and you'll be rewarded with breathtaking views.

GETTING AROUND

Busan is connected by train and bus to Changwon and Ulsan, and by bus to the Tongdo-sa. From Ulsan, take a bus to Seoknam-sa. Driving by car to Gajisan Provincial Park is best, as it's an easy-to-navigate route north from Busan along the Gyeongbu Expressway or west from Ulsan on the Ulsan Expressway.

Changwon

TIME FROM BUSAN: **50MIN**

Korea's most famous cherry blossoms

Come springtime, cherry blossoms can be found increasingly throughout Korea, as more and more trees are being planted. Yet Jinhae, a district of Gyeongnam's capital city, Changwon, is still known as the quintessential viewing spot, drawing visitors from across the country. At **Yeojwacheon**, the cherry-blossom trees that line the stream give the effect of a flower tunnel. In particular, the Romance Bridge, a filming location for the K-Drama *Romance*, is a popular photo spot, featuring an old train.

Gajisan Provincial Park

TIME FROM BUSAN: **1½HR**

Ascend the Yeongnam Alps

Wedged between Ulsan and Miryang is the gorgeous Gajisan Provincial Park, a stunning sprawl of lush forest against craggy terrain. Part of the Baekdudaegan range, the park's eight peaks are what Koreans call the 'Yeongnam Alps' – and indeed they are impressive. In spring, the mountains are lit by the bright pinks and purples of royal azaleas, and in autumn by swaying silver grasses.

Hikers can choose from the park's vast network of trails, the main entryways of which are anchored by four Buddhist temples: **Seoknam-sa**, **Unmun-sa**, **Daebi-sa** and **Seokgol-sa**. Among them, Seoknam-sa may be the most striking – filled

KOREA'S THREE JEWEL TEMPLES

The Gyeongsangnam-do province is home to two of Korea's 'Three Jewel Temples' – Tongdo-sa in Yangsan and Haein-sa on the mountain Gayasan – with the third being Songgwang-sa in Suncheon, Jeollanam-do. They are so named because each temple signifies one of the three jewels of Buddhism – they enshrine three of the most venerated objects of the faith in Korea. **Tongdo-sa**, representing the Buddha, is said to hold the holy *sari* (crystallised remains) of the historical Buddha; **Haein-sa** (p242), representing the dharma, holds the woodblocks of the Tripitaka Koreana teachings of the Buddha; and Songgwang-sa (p280), representing the sangha, holds the halls of the community of the Buddha, with a long lineage of national preceptors.

INSUNG JEON/GETTY IMAGES

Daewangam Park, Ulsan

with enchanting contours, colours and contrasts – and interesting, too, for the female monks who call it home. To get there, walk 800m from the **park entrance** through heavily wooded forest; the temple is just beyond a fork in the path that is the starting point for a hike up Gajisan, the park's highest peak.

Visit a Jewel Temple of Korea

At **Tongdo-sa** *(tongdosa.or.kr; free)*, the focal point of devotion is the *sari*, a crystalline substance thought to develop inside the body of a pure monk, which is why this temple does not have a Buddha statue in the main hall – a rarity in Korea. The *sari* is enshrined in a fenced area and cannot be seen. Walk the temple compound, stopping by the **Tongdo-sa Museum** (leave your shoes at the front door), which houses a collection of Buddhist paintings with limited viewing hours to minimise light exposure, along with 30,000 artefacts with full-day access, including gongs, roof tiles and wooden printing blocks.

Ulsan

TIME FROM BUSAN: **25MIN**

Cross Korea's longest suspension bridge

At **Daewangam Park**, take in spectacular, sweeping views of the ocean, dotted with delightfully odd rock formations, while walking across Korea's longest suspension bridge. Near the park's entrance, have a coffee or a snack before setting off on the pine-tree trail toward the coast. The 303m-long **bridge** crosses the sea, prone to the wind, making it a scenic, swaying saunter you won't soon forget.

A bamboo forest by the river

Unfurling 4km along the river Taehwagang, the enormous **Taehwagang Bamboo Forest** *(free)* of sky-high trees is a verdant wonderland. Come stroll through the dense forest, then wander around the more than 20 themed gardens full of blooming flowers, from poppies to chrysanthemums and azaleas.

Places We Love to Stay

₩ Budget ₩₩ Midrange ₩₩₩ Top End

South & Central Busan

MAP P182 & P187

One Way Guesthouse ₩ A no-frills hostel with tidy four-person dorms and busy shared toilets, located right next to Busan station's Exit 4. No breakfast.

Kimchee Busan Downtown Guesthouse ₩ This hostel, a two-minute walk from Beomnaegol metro station near Jeonpo Cafe Street, has four- and 10-person dorms, some en-suite rooms and English-speaking staff. There's a common room and shared kitchen.

Blue Backpackers ₩ Dormitory beds or rooms with individual baths, a central location in Seomyeon and a communal sitting area make this hostel a great budget choice. The friendly owner, Jin, is a gem.

Funstay Guesthouse ₩ Perfect location to explore Nampo-dong, this guesthouse has clean dorms and a few en-suite rooms, a friendly owner and homey furnishings.

Sohostel ₩ Another attractive Dong-gu hostel, only 600m from Busan station, with male, female and eight-bed mixed dorms. The common areas and shared kitchen feel futuristic-chic and cosy.

Dante House ₩ Set at the northern end of Chinatown and close to Busan station, this welcoming cafe (where breakfast is served) also has squeaky-clean dorms and a few en-suite doubles.

Beaches & East Busan

MAP P195 & P198

Hotel1 ₩ Featuring all-white-marble finishings, these slick, serene rooms offer stunning views of the beach and Gwangan Bridge. Hip common spaces include a rooftop terrace and 1st-floor cafe.

Kimchee Haeundae Guesthouse ₩ The beach property of this local hostel franchise has an airy lobby and common room, plus serviceable four- and eight-person dorms and en-suite doubles. For non-party lovers, it can get noisy at night.

Funwave Guesthouse ₩ A sparkling-clean, minimal-chic Haeundae hostel with free kitchen and laundry services, close to the beach and, most importantly, quiet for a good night's sleep.

Hotel Hongdan ₩ Clean minimalist rooms at wallet-friendly prices with artistic pops of colour that add flair to a mostly white affair. Its Songjeong location is good for surfers.

Gwangan Hound Hotel ₩₩ A boutique hotel with reasonable prices considering its prime Gwangalli Beach location. There's also a rooftop patio perfect for summer nights.

Edge 993 (엣지993) ₩₩ Perched on the coast by the Mipo Blueline, this coffeeshop-cum-hotel has a cafe with beautiful views on the 4th and 5th floors. The rooms also face the whole Haeundae stretch of coast and beyond to Gwangalli.

Coolest Hotel ₩₩ By Songjeong Beach, this self-proclaimed coolest hotel puts its claim to the test with social-media-worthy decor, sleek floor-to-ceiling windows and a swanky rooftop pool.

Paradise Hotel ₩₩₩ Fantastic service and views of Haeundae Beach make the Paradise stand out, along with luxury amenities such as a casino and rooftop spa pool.

Westin Chosun Busan ₩₩₩ Busan's oldest international hotel gets better with age, with retro hints and modern touches creating a refined sort of cool. A bit removed from the main action on Haeundae Beach.

Ulsan

Remnant Guest House ₩ Central budget guesthouse with well-appointed, adequate rooms at hostel prices. Self check-in, wi-fi and bathtubs in the rooms.

Brown Dot Hotel Ulsan Jangsaengpo ₩₩ Handy harbour location for this modern hotel featuring rooms that feel like mini-apartments, many with balconies with bay views.

Hound Hotel Ulsan ₩₩ East of town on Gangdong Beach, this hotel has large, warm rooms with wooden floors, sea views and little cosy balconies.

For places to stay in Gyeongsang-do, see p251

SAMITDOC/GETTY IMAGES

Above: Bulguk-sa (p228); Right: Hakdong Mongdol Beach (p220) near Geoje-si

Researched by
Marco Ferrarese

Gyeongsang-do

CULTURAL HERITAGE AMID ASTONISHING SCENERY

South Korea's eastern expanse extends from Gangwon-do to Busan's northern city limits, encompassing the country's fourth-biggest city, tiny harbour towns and secluded villages.

Gyeongsang-do, the region comprising North and South Gyeongsang provinces, is resplendent in both natural beauty and heritage sites, including temples, pagodas, rock-carved Buddhas and tombs. A wedge of mountains cascading to the sea, Gyeongsangnam-do packs rolling peaks and the vibe of yesteryear coastal towns not so overrun with tourist development. For a less ordinary Korean experience, board a ferry and go island-hopping across the many verdant islands that comprise Hallyeohaesang National Park, an archipelago breaking south of the charming port city of Tongyeong. Slung between sea and mountains, it has a cable car and a compact city centre surrounded by artsy villages, viewpoints and quiet parks.

PURBELLA / IMAZINS/GETTY IMAGES

In Gyeongsangbuk-do, Gyeongju was the royal capital of the Silla Kingdom for nearly 1000 years. Often called a 'museum without walls', it's a treasure trove of historic sights scattered throughout the city's central, garden-like landscape. The province's major city, Daegu, has a historic centre peppered with old religious and independence-activism sites and a fascinating medicinal-herb market, hemmed in by youth-centric streets packed with dining and drinking options. To the province's north, the ancient town of Andong sits in proximity to Hahoe, one of the best folk villages in Korea, while an adventurous ferry ride off the coast puts you in reach of rugged Ulleungdo island, with endless opportunities to enjoy the spectacular coast.

THE MAIN AREAS

TONGYEONG & HALLYEOHAESANG NATIONAL PARK
A maritime jewel box of island treasures. **p210**

GYEONGJU
Truly Korea's museum without walls. **p222**

DAEGU
Historic centre with modern diversions. **p235**

ANDONG
Korea's capital of folk, arts and old-world villages. **p243**

Find Your Way

Humongous and sliced through with mountains, the parts of Gyeongsang-do outside the grasp of major cities can be difficult and slow-going to reach. Expect long waits for buses and transfers between trains; otherwise, consider driving.

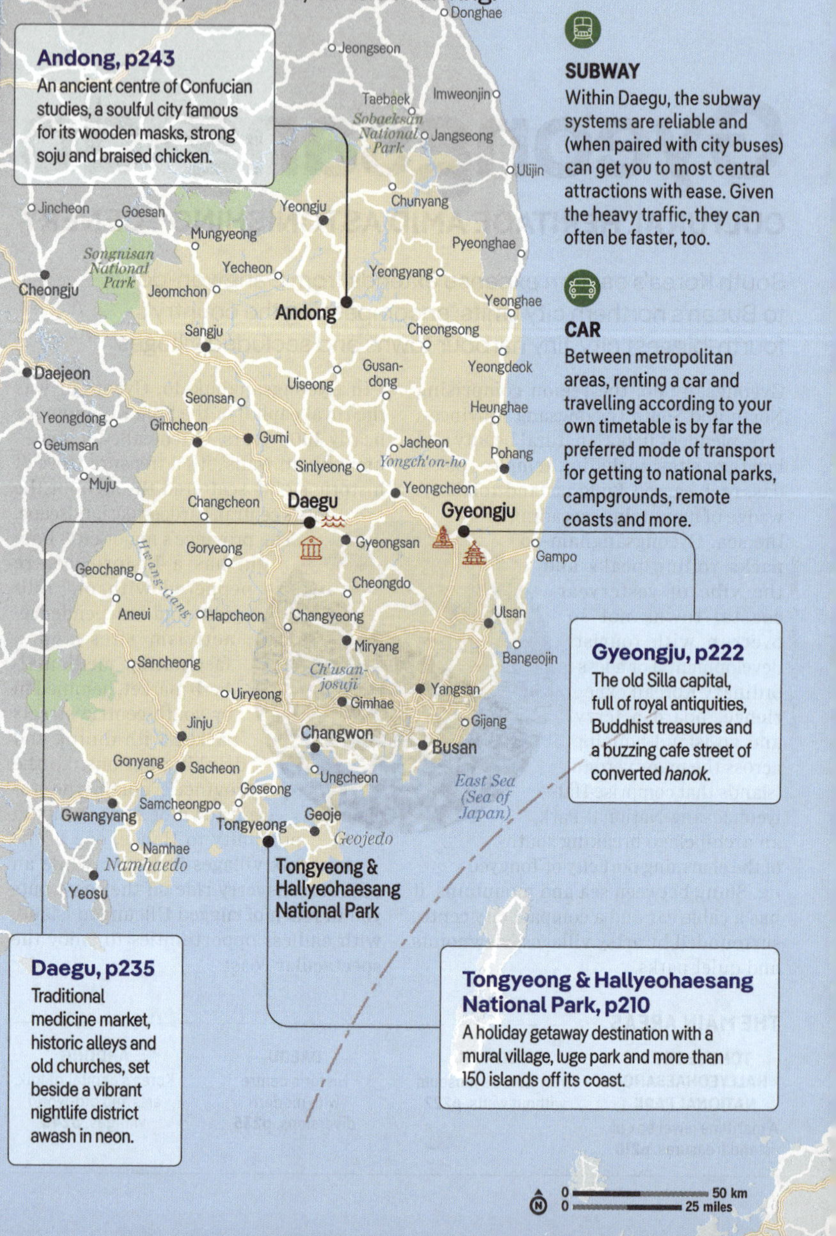

Andong, p243

An ancient centre of Confucian studies, a soulful city famous for its wooden masks, strong soju and braised chicken.

SUBWAY

Within Daegu, the subway systems are reliable and (when paired with city buses) can get you to most central attractions with ease. Given the heavy traffic, they can often be faster, too.

CAR

Between metropolitan areas, renting a car and travelling according to your own timetable is by far the preferred mode of transport for getting to national parks, campgrounds, remote coasts and more.

Gyeongju, p222

The old Silla capital, full of royal antiquities, Buddhist treasures and a buzzing cafe street of converted *hanok*.

Tongyeong & Hallyeohaesang National Park, p210

A holiday getaway destination with a mural village, luge park and more than 150 islands off its coast.

Daegu, p235

Traditional medicine market, historic alleys and old churches, set beside a vibrant nightlife district awash in neon.

STOCK PHOTOS 2000/SHUTTERSTOCK

Daereungwon Ancient Tomb Complex (p226)

Plan Your Time

When in Gyeongsang-do, prioritise its heritage sites and seek out ways to experience cultural practices, from staying overnight at a temple, to clapping along to a mask dance, to buying fresh fish at the market.

A Three-Day Sampler

- Start with a day in **Daegu** (p235), getting your bearings at the **Local History Museum** (p237) and taking a walk through history in the city centre. Then set off to **Gyeongju** (p222) to see **Bulguk-sa** (p226) walk around the **Daereungwon Ancient Tomb Complex** (p226) and shop along **Hwangnidan-gil** (p224). If there's time left over, go to **Yangdong Folk Village** (p231).

A Week in Gyeongsang-do

- Start in **Andong** (p243) for an excursion to **Hahoe Folk Village** (p248) and a meal along **Jjimdak Alley** (p245). See Gayasan and do a templestay at **Haein-sa** (p242), before heading east for a couple of days in the old Silla capital, **Gyeongju** (p22). Get off the tourist trail in Pohang for the **Space Walk** (p232) and some sailing, and finish with a little island hopping in **Tongyeong** (p216).

SEASONAL HIGHLIGHTS

SPRING
In late March to early April, **Gyeongju** (p222) is among the first Korean cities to have cherry blossoms. **Bomun** (p225) lake in particular transforms into a white-and-pink wonderland.

SUMMER
Island hop your way through the shimmering **Hallyeohaesang National Park** (p210).

AUTUMN
In September, the Hwandonghae Cup brings sailors to **Pohang** (p232), and in October, magnificent mask dances take centre stage in **Andong** (p246).

WINTER
Yeongdeok hosts its **Snow Crab Festival** (p250) in February, a chance to shop the crab market and sample crab snacks.

Tongyeong & Hallyeohaesang National Park

HOLIDAY HAVEN | ISLAND HOPPING | SEAFOOD GALORE

> **☑ TOP TIP**
> The tourist information centre, at the southwest end of Gangguan Port, near the passenger terminal, has exceptionally helpful staff and is a great place to store your luggage if needed.

On the southern tip of the Goseong Peninsula, Tongyeong (통영) is a coastal city between Namhaedo and Geojedo that Koreans sometimes like to call the Naples of Korea. Its cerulean seas and small, sleepy port-town feel have attracted a fair share of big-city denizens desperate to get away from the rat race of life – maybe on holiday, or maybe forever. Tongyeong delivers on its dreams with picturesque sights as far as the eye can see, a pretty harbour that seems custom-made for sunset strolls and its endless opportunities to feast on the freshest seafood and sail to an incredible collection of islands.

Tongyeong's section of Hallyeohaesang National Park is often considered the centre of the magnificent 535-sq-km maritime area that extends from Odong Island in the west to Geoje Island in the east, with a vast number of its hundreds of islands concentrated here along the Tongyeong coastline.

Traverse Mireuk Mountain

Ride up, hike down

Ride on the 1975m-long **Tongyeong Cable Car** *(adult/child one way ₩13,500/11,000, return ₩17,000/13,000)*, taking nine minutes to reach near the top of Mireuksan (461m), then walk

GETTING AROUND

There's no train station here, so visitors arrive by car or bus. Coming from Jinju, Busan, Gimhae airport and Seoul, buses depart frequently. The central bus terminal is on the city's northern fringe, with many local buses running south to deposit you in the main port. Once there, this part of Tongyeong is pleasantly walkable, with a bridge even cutting across Gangguan harbour to expedite things. For traversing longer distances, such as crossing south to Mireukdo, buses run regularly (though not always on time), and a taxi is recommended. To get to the islands, ferry schedules are available from the desk inside the coastal **passenger ferry terminal**.

BJARU/SHUTTERSTOCK

Tongyeong Cable Car

up the rest of the way. The bird's-eye view of the surrounding islands of Hallyeo Maritime National Park is jaw-droppingly dramatic, to put it mildly. You can retake the cable car to return to the bottom, but if you're up for a two-hour hike, buy a one-way ticket instead and walk down the north side of the mountain. Following one of several well-marked routes, you'll pass campsites, reservoirs and the beautiful **Yonghwasa Buddhist temple** and hermitage.

Stroll the Gangguan Harbour

Tongyeong's liveliest spot

Gangguan is not the only harbour in the city, but it's the most happening. A busy pier anchored by a promenade with docks, pavilions and picnic areas, it's a popular place for folks young and old to gather. Towards the north end of the port, you'll see replicas of ***geobukseon***, the famed Korean turtle ships used in battle from the 15th to the 18th centuries. Across the street, past the queues to the super-popular **Myeongga Ggulbbang** bakery (명가꿀빵), enter the **Jungang Traditional Market**, where you'll find not only a smorgasbord of fish, but also grannies selling their fruits, veggies and fried snacks out of plastic tubs. On the southern end of the harbour, the 13m-high, 92.5m-long pedestrian **Gangguan Bridge**, opened

continued on p214

YACHTING & SAILING IN TONGYEONG

Koreans sometimes call Tongyeong the Naples of Korea for its picturesque position on the sea, so it figures that sailing is a favoured pastime here, with several marinas hosting clubs and competitions for aficionados. Visitors can also get in on the maritime action, with numerous tour packages available to make it easy. The Sea Explorers of Korea Gyeongnam Nambu council operates sea tours, while the **Tongyeong Yacht Club** runs package sailing programs. Or book through a company such as **Ocean Yacht Breeze**, which offers a variety of cruises, from public to private, including daytime and a popular sunset cruise with sparkling-wine option, with additional activities such as barbecue and fishing.

DRINKING IN TONGYEONG: OUR PICKS

Mireuk Mireuk Beer Hostel: In an old sauna turned hip hostel, with rooms above and a bar on ground level where the congenial owner serves craft beer. *5pm-midnight*

TongYeong Beer Company: (통영맥주) White-tiled brewery retaining its former bathhouse aesthetic, with hightops and barstools beside old showers. *11am-9pm Mon-Fri, noon-10pm Sat & Sun*

Rein Deutsch Brewery: (라인 도이치 브루어리) German brews, fried pork cutlets, burgers and other greasy grub in a seaside locale. *11.30am-3pm & 5-10pm Thu-Tue*

Local Stitch: Industrial-chic art space with large ground-floor cafe and bar, rotating exhibitions on the 2nd floor and chic guesthouse on the 3rd floor. *10am-10pm*

TONGYEONG & HALLYEOHAESANG NATIONAL PARK

SIGHTS
1 Bijindo
2 Chungmu Church
3 Dongpirang Village
4 DPIRANG
5 Gangguan
6 Gangguan Bridge
see 5 Geobukseon (Turtle Ship) Replicas
7 Haklimdo
8 Hansando
9 History Museum of Tongyeong City
10 Jirisan
11 Munhwa-Dong
12 Nammangsan Sculpture Park
13 Oknyeobong
14 Saryangdo
15 Sebyeong-Gyo
16 Seohorakdang hill
17 Seopirang Park
18 Somaemuldo
19 Undersea Tunnel
20 Yeondaedo
21 Yeonhwado
22 Yonghwasa Temple

ACTIVITIES
23 Tongyeong Yacht Club

SLEEPING
24 Jung Seop's Loft Friends
25 Mireuk Mireuk Beer Hostel
26 Motel Mu

EATING
27 Ddungbo Halmae Gimbap Jip
28 Hansan Seom Sikdang
29 Legacy
30 Myeongchon Sikdang
31 Myeongga Ggulbbang
32 O wall

DRINKING & NIGHTLIFE
33 Local Stitch
34 Rein Deutsch Brewery
35 Tongyeong Beer

ENTERTAINMENT
36 Skyline Luge

SHOPPING
37 Jungang Traditional Market

TRANSPORT
38 Tongyeong Cable Car
39 Tongyeong Cruise Ship Terminal
40 Tongyeong Ferry Terminal

continued from p211
in 2025 as part of the city's new Night Tourism Vision concept, connects the port to **Nammangsan Sculpture Park** *(free)*, with open-air installations by 15 artists from 10 countries, via a fibreglass walkway. The adjacent **DPIRANG** digital nighttime art park *(₩15,000)*, closed Mondays, features 1.3km of walking paths illuminated with a magical, mystical effect through lighted digital murals. After dark, even the scenic Gangguan Bridge lights up with colourful LED lights and water fountains cascade off its sides.

Hike to Artsy Villages & a Fortress

Stroll past murals, gardens, shops and history

Set on a hill to the northeast of Gangguan port, **Dongpirang Village** makes for a leisurely – albeit steep – stroll up winding alleyways decorated with brightly painted murals, boutique art shops, casual eateries and cafes. At the top, there's a pavilion with panoramic views of the city and Gangguan (p211) port below. The murals of 'Dongpirang', an amalgamation of *dong* ('east' in Korean) and *pirang* ('hill' in Tongyeong's local dialect), were born out of an invitation by the government to revive this area with public art.

Northwest of the port is **Seohorakdang Hill**, once a disaster-prone area, now transformed into the canola-strewn gardens of **Seopirang Park**. The park's staircases lead to viewpoints and a hilltop pavilion, from which the 1933 hexagonal water-supply facilities of **Munhwa-dong** are visible. Walking down the hill past the maroon-brick **Chungmu Church**, you'll find the **Sebyeong-Gyo** complex, a charming fortress-like series of Joseon-style pavilions and gardens. Across the road, the **History Museum of Tongyeong City** *(free)*, closed Mondays, offers insight into Tongyeong's past maritime prowess.

HUN YOUNG LEE/SHUTTERSTOCK

Gangguan Harbour (p211)

Walk Under the Sea

Take the historic ocean tunnel

Built in the early 1930s, the 483m-long **Tongyeong Undersea Tunnel** connects both sides of Seoho Bay. From the north end, take the cement corridor, stopping along the way to see the historical photographs of its construction. Just out the other side of the tunnel, **Legacy** is a lovely coffee shop with a minimalist concrete aesthetic, serving up financiers alongside its Americanos.

Brave the Skyline Luge

Downhill thrill

This adrenaline-pumping **Skyline Luge** *(tongyeong.skylineluge.kr; 3/4/5 rides ₩33,000/36,000/40,000)*, set on the slopes of Mireuksan south of the cable car's bottom station, offers four twisting, turning tracks that at night are lit up with multicoloured lights. Ride the chairlift up, then soar and swerve your way down 100m of slopes aboard a zero-gravity cart.

COASTAL FOOD: HOE

Along Korea's coast, it's no surprise that fish features prominently in local cuisine. Raw fish, called *hoe*, is a popular food enjoyed with a group of friends, served in slices arranged on a platter, and dipped into *chogochujang* (a sauce made with vinegar and red pepper paste) or *ganjang* (soy sauce) mixed with wasabi. *Hoe* can be eaten on its own like this, or it can be placed on a lettuce leaf (along with rice if desired) then wrapped into a packet and enjoyed in one bite. Most commonly, *hoe* is made with white fish, such as rockfish, flatfish and sea bream. It's customarily followed by *maeuntang* (spicy soup) and often accompanied by soju.

EATING IN TONGYEONG: OUR PICKS

Ddungbo Halmae Gimbap Jip: (뚱보할매김밥집) Serves just *chungmu kimbap*, Tongyeong's speciality of mini rice rolls wrapped in dried seaweed, with spicy squid and radish. *6am-10pm* ₩	**Myeongchon Sikdang:** Some of the freshest, tastiest fish you've ever tasted, grilled whole and accompanied by side dishes, rice and soup. *11.30am-2pm & 5-9pm* ₩	**Hansan Seom Sikdang:** (한산섬식당) Restaurant serving a variety of *maeuntang* and other fish soups that's open early and popular among locals. *6.30am-8.30pm* ₩₩	**O wall:** Offers an impeccable set menu that comes with tapas, salad, pasta, a main, dessert and tea in a quiet part of town. *noon-4pm & 5-10pm* ₩₩₩

HELP ME PICK:

Tongyeong Islands

Designated a national park in 1968 – Korea's first national marine park – the 535-sq-km Hallyeohaesang National Park is made up of six districts that stretch 120km along the country's southern coast: Geoje, Tongyeong, Sacheon, Sangju, Namhae and Odongdo. Among them, Tongyeong is often considered to be the park's centrepiece, its 100-plus islands studding the sapphire sea like emerald gems. From Tongyeong's multiple ferry terminals, many of them are within easy reach.

Where to Go if You Love...

Postcard-Perfect Panoramas

Bijindo Perhaps Hallyeohaesang's most iconic sight, Bijindo is two small islands joined by a spectacular sand bridge. It's a popular getaway destination, with an easy hour-long walk between its two ports and excellent places to picnic along the 550m-long soft sandy beach in between.

Adventure and Activity

Saryangdo Made up of more than 30 islands, only three of which are inhabited, Saryangdo's northern and southern parts are connected by a 530m-long bridge. Many come to the former to hike the six peaks of the Jirisan trail, starting with 368m-high **Jirisan** to the west and ending with 263m **Oknyeo-bong** in the east. Suspended bridges hanging from the peaks give vertigo-inducing views over the bay. Most travellers disembark the ferry and catch a bus to the western side to begin the five-hour hike.

Peace and Quiet

Yeonhwado Remote Yeonhwado has a Buddhist hermitage on its southern edge. At the five-storey pagoda and Goddess of Mercy statue gazing out over the sea, look for Yongmeori, an arrangement of rocks resembling a dragon's head. Or, instead of going south from the ferry terminal, head north and cross a series of bridges linking Yeonhawdo to Banhado to Udo.

Haklimdo Small island with a tiny marina, a seawater pool and a short hike up the central hill for unobstructed views of the coast. Mr Song *(010 44333450)*, who speaks a little English, organises village stays with a shellfish-digging experience.

Historical Significance

Hansando As the site of the Imjin War's Great Battle of Hansan, in which national hero Admiral Yi Sun-sin defeated the Japanese, this island is dear to Koreans and includes a shrine built at the place where the 16th-century naval headquarters once stood.

Family Friendliness

Somaemuldo Waves crashing against sharp cliffs and dramatic rock formations make this island a worthwhile journey. At low tide, you can walk across the land bridge and climb to the lighthouse at Deungdaeseom.

Yeondaedo Known for its black pebble beach, framed by cliffs, Yeondaedo also features a swaying suspension bridge that connects to Manjido and is great fun for kids. In addition, it's a zero-emission island championing ecofriendly waste management, transport and other initiatives.

Bijindo

FROM LEFT: ICEDAMERICANO/SHUTTERSTOCK, JEONG EUN SEO/SHUTTERSTOCK

Somaemuldo

HOW TO

When to go Weekends and summer can be busy and less blissful, and accommodation on the islands can be pricey. Avoid crowds and save money by going in the shoulder seasons or free camping like locals.

Book ahead During peak season, some ferry routes will sell out quickly, so book in advance or have a flexible schedule. You'll need your passport to buy tickets.

Before you go Be sure to pack enough food and a portable cooking set; groceries on the islands can be scant or expensive.

Budget One-way passenger ferry fares range from ₩2700 to ₩19,300. Car fares start from ₩8000.

Transport & Seasons

From Tongyeong's multiple ferry terminals, various passenger and car ferries depart for the islands. Ferries to Hansando (30 minutes), Bijindo (one hour) and Somaemuldo (1½ hours) leave from the **Tongyeong Ferry Terminal** (p210) near Gangguan harbour, while those to Saryangdo depart from both the Tongyeong terminal and the Gaochi terminal, in the city's northwest. To get to Yeonhwado, depart from Tongyeong terminal, Samdeok Harbour or Junghwa Harbour, both on the west side of Mireukdo. Check at the terminal for timetables.

As long as weather conditions are suitable, ferries run year-round to most of the islands. During winter (December to March), when fewer establishments are open, some islands may feel all but deserted, but the emptiness and quietude can make for a peaceful experience. Sitting on the beach or walking on the trails, you may find you're alone.

Another option for getting to the islands is to hire an excursion boat from the **Tongyeong Cruise Ship Terminal**, southeast of Gangguan beside the yacht facility. Depending on the option you choose, the tour will include one or several of the islands, with some routes organised according to theme, such as battle sites. Excursion boats usually only operate in summer and require a group reservation, so be sure to check in advance.

Beyond Tongyeong

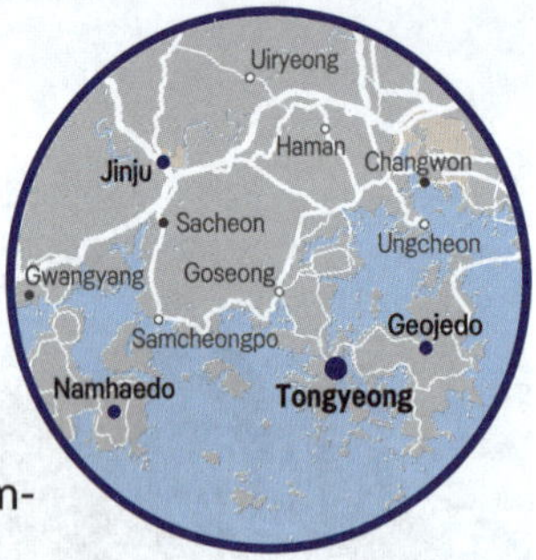

Large islands breaking off Gyeongsangnam-do's coast guarantee days of self-driving exploration. On the way to Jeolla-do, a river fortress town spells memories of battles past.

Places

GETTING AROUND

There are good bus connections from Tongyeong to Geoje and Jinju, from where you can transfer to Namhae. In Jinju, where the **express bus terminal** is south of the river and the **intercity terminal** is north, local buses are frequent and routes are plentiful. On the islands, public transport is not as developed and can involve long roadside waits – renting a car is recommended. Jinju is also serviced by a **train station** on the Gyeongjeon Line; no lines go south.

Eastward, Tongyeong connects by bridge to Geojedo, Korea's second-largest island (which goes on to link northward to Busan). Famous for its shipbuilding and natural beauty, Geoje alternates between pastoral and industrial landscapes, with a surprisingly congested city-centre area. The pace of life slows down considerably in Namhaedo, Korea's fifth-biggest island, west of Tongyeong. The drive around its coast is one of the most scenic routes in Korea: wild sea swells, dense forests and tiny ports unfold kilometre after kilometre along the shore. Meanwhile, north of Tongyeong lies Jinju, a river fortress town known for its role in battling 16th-century Japanese invaders. It's the largest city in the region, yet still quiet and laid-back.

Geojedo

TIME FROM TONGYEONG: **30MIN**

Maritime vistas

About an hour by car from Geoje city centre, the road to the rocky islets and jagged coastline of **Haegeumgang** is filled with twists and turns, along with views so breathtaking that drivers occasionally stop in unusual places to admire the ocean views. Drive with caution. This stretch of the coast forms part of Hallyeohaesang National Park – famous for its life-affirming sunrises and sunsets – along which you'll see fantastic cliffside caves and rock formations such as **Lion Rock** and **Candlestick Rock**. On the way back, make a stop at the picturesque **Windy Hill**, a windmill-topped knoll that is indeed very windy.

A war museum & a monorail

See the **Geoje POW Camp** *(adult/teenager/child ₩7000/5000/3000)* from two different vantage points, first by visiting its modest but worthwhile museum, which provides hard-to-find information about the POW camp experience during the Korean War, and then by riding the **monorail** *(return ₩15,000)* up the Gyeryong Mountain ridge, where you can look down on the remains of the camp from the observation deck. Opened in 2018, the monorail is a 25-minute ride each way.

DRIVING THE NAMHAEDO COAST

Discover Namhae island's villages, beaches and dramatic coastal viewpoints by looping around it on your own wheels.

START	END	LENGTH
Namhae Bridge	DolChanGo Project	115km; 3hr

Start by crossing the bright-red 1 **Namhae Bridge** then looping north to turn onto the coastal Seolcheon-ro road, where you'll pass some 2 **turtle ship replicas** of 15th- to 18th-century Korean warships, docked between the mainland and Namhaedo. At the fork, keep left onto Gangjin-ro. Drive through several small fishing villages, including Munui-ri, Munhang-ri and Jinmok-ri, backdropped by an expanse of itsy-bitsy islands dotting the South Sea. Head back onto Seolcheon-ro and, when you reach the roundabout in Seongsan, turn off on Namhaedae-ro, staying southbound. From there, take Sami-ro eastward and then Dongbudae-ro, coming to the rather unexpected 3 **German Village**, an odd little cluster of out-of-place architecture. Going south, you'll soon spot the 4 **Namhae Treasure Island Observatory**, the 2nd floor of which has the first panoramic glass walkway built in Korea – the Skywalk – and the tiny harbour town of Mijo. Carrying on west, see the 2km of soft white sands and shallow blue waters of 5 **Sangju Beach**. It's a tranquil setting, at least in the off-season. A few more twists and turns down the road and you'll be greeted by the terraced rice paddies of 6 **Gacheon Daraengyi Village**, one of Namhae's most picturesque sights. Conclude with an afternoon latte and dessert at 7 **DolChanGo Project**, a minimalist cafe (open noon to 5pm Thursday to Monday) with views of the surrounding mountains.

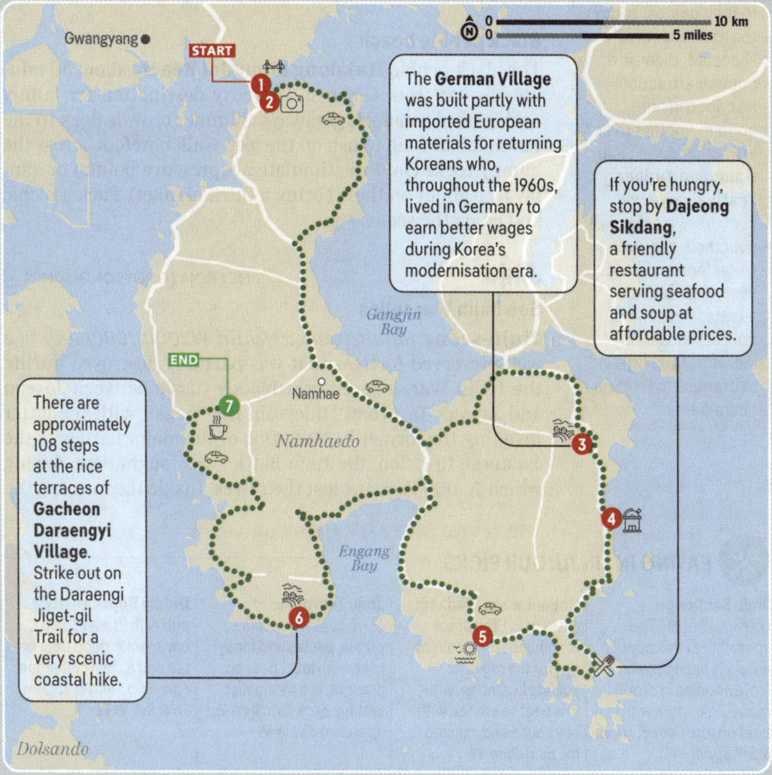

THE RIVER NANGANG, THE LEGEND NONGAE

One of Jinju's most famous historical figures is Nongae, the 16th-century *gisaeng* (trained courtesan) who, according to an oft-told legend, sacrificed herself during the Imjin War in order to kill a Japanese admiral. As the story goes, she lured the enemy to the cliffside at the river Namgang and then grabbed him and jumped, plunging them both to their deaths. Today, the rock from which she leapt, Uiam, is a popular attraction, inscribed in her honour. Another river attraction is the Jinju **Namgang Yudaeng Festival** *(yudeung.com; free)*, a splendid spectacle of glowing water lanterns, held every October. It's a fantastic scene of tens of thousands of lanterns, from tigers to dragons to folktale characters.

ARTYOORAN/SHUTTERSTOCK

Black pebble beach

The black-pebble **Hakdong Mongdol Beach**, about 30 minutes by car from Geoje-si, is a cosy destination for family outings and romantic getaways. Summer crowds flock to the 1.2km-long beach to fish off the pier, walk barefoot across the bumpy rocks (said to stimulate acupressure points) or simply laze about on them (bring a thick blanket). Pack a picnic and enjoy the scene.

Jinju

TIME FROM TONGYEONG: **50MIN**

See Imjin War relics

Jinju-seong *(adult/teenager/child ₩2000/1000/600)* is a well-preserved fortress that was partially destroyed during the Imjin War, a seven-year bloody tussle between Joseon and Japan's Toyotomi Hideyoshi that began with the latter invading the former in 1592. One of the major battles of the Japanese Invasion, the Jinju Battle, was fought here, during which 70,000 Koreans lost their lives. Inside the fortress, the

EATING IN JINJU: OUR PICKS

Jinju Sanhong: (진주냉면산홍) The speciality at this popular eatery is *naengmyeon* (cold noodles in broth) made Jinju-style with raw beef on top. *11am-3.30pm & 5-9.30pm* ₩

Cheonhwang Sikdang: (천황식당) The place for bibimbap. You might opt for the regional *yukhoe* bibimbap, with raw beef seasoned with soy sauce and sesame oil. *8am-9pm* ₩

Jinju Taproom: (진주탭룸) Focaccia pizzas, pastas and fancy fries, with local beer on draught, in a minimalist setting. *6pm-1am Sun-Thu, 3pm-2am Sat* ₩₩

Diddly Bop: Irish-style pub with fish and chips, bar snacks, good beer on tap and a vinyl collection. *6pm-1am Sun-Fri, to 2am Fri & Sat* ₩₩

Bori-am, Namhaedo

Chokseongnu pavilion, Bukjangdae command post, traditional gates and shrines dot the grassy knolls of the heavily wooded park. The small but worthwhile **Jinju National Museum** *(free),* closed Mondays, houses a collection of war artefacts in the Imjin War Hall. Another hall is devoted to relics excavated around Gyeongnam-do, dating from the Neolithic age through the Joseon dynasty, and a third hall consists of 190 pieces donated by a Korean-Japanese businessman. Download the National Museum of Korea app for an English-language guide.

Namhaedo

TIME FROM TONGYEONG: 1HR

Tap into your inner Zen

Behold the beauty of **Bori-am**, a busy Buddhist hermitage on the mountain Geumsan, founded by Monk Wonhyo in 683 CE and famous for its brilliant sunrises and mesmerising vistas over the southern coast and islets.

It's possible to drive to an upper car park in front of the **Bokgok Visiting Information Center** *(entry ₩2000),* only 900m from the temple, but car spaces are limited and waiting times are long. It's best to catch the free shuttle bus from the car park at the mountain base to Bokgok and then walk for about half an hour to the temple, or use a taxi from Namhae bus terminal.

Once at Bori-am, you can take an easy half-hour loop to the summit of Geumsan Mountain (705m) and back to the hermitage. The watchtower by the peak has the grandest view of the coast and islands below.

Gyeongju

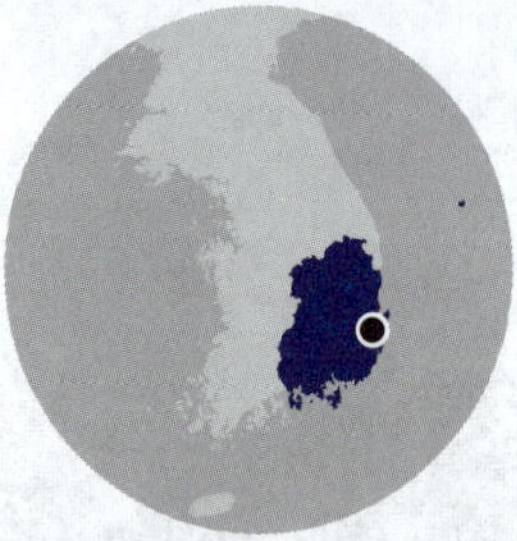

SILLA HERITAGE | ROCK BUDDHAS | HIP HANOK

TOP TIP
Download the National Museum of Korea's app to access an excellent Bluetooth-powered English-language guide to the Gyeongju National Museum.

Known as 'the museum without walls', Gyeongju (경주) is home to more tombs, temples, rock carvings, pagodas, Buddhist statuary and palace ruins than any other place in South Korea. It's a lovely city – the capital of the Silla kingdom for almost 1000 years – and teeming with history. Upon arriving, the first thing you might notice is how low-lying Gyeongju's urban centre is – no skyscrapers in sight – its skyline sculpted instead by the astonishing and substantial round grassy tumuli of the ancient tomb complex and traditional tiled roofs of *hanok* (traditional wooden homes), set against a canvas of green rolling mountains.

Yet as time-honoured as Gyeongju is, it's become very trendy, too. On the hip street Hwangnidan-gil, abutting Silla antiquities and UNESCO heritage sites are some of the hottest restaurants, bars, shops and guesthouses Gyeongju has to offer. Come and move between both worlds – that's the beauty of this place.

GETTING AROUND

Gyeongju is well connected to other major cities by bus or train, though its new **train station** is a bit out of the way, located about 10km southwest of its former location. Of the many bus routes leaving from the train station, buses 50 and 51 stop at the express bus terminal and Jungang market in the city centre in about 30 minutes. Bus 60 is another practical route from the station to the bus terminal, Cheonmachong Tomb, Hwangnidan Gil and Cheomseongdae Observatory.

Gyeongju's compact city centre is pleasant to walk in, even though a bike can be better to whizz between the far-flung sites. The outlying districts contain two not-to-be-missed attractions – Korea's most famous temple, Bulguk-sa and its hermitage Seokguram – within reach of public transport. To maximise time, bus 711 connects the new train station, city centre, Donggung Palace, Wolji Pond, Gyeongju National Museum and Bulguk-sa temple. You can store your luggage for free at the information centre near the bus stop. Bus 710 stops at Bunhwang-sa Temple and Gyeongju World. Gyeongju as a whole covers some 1323 sq km, so if you want to visit some of the lesser-known places, plan on taking taxis or staying for several days.

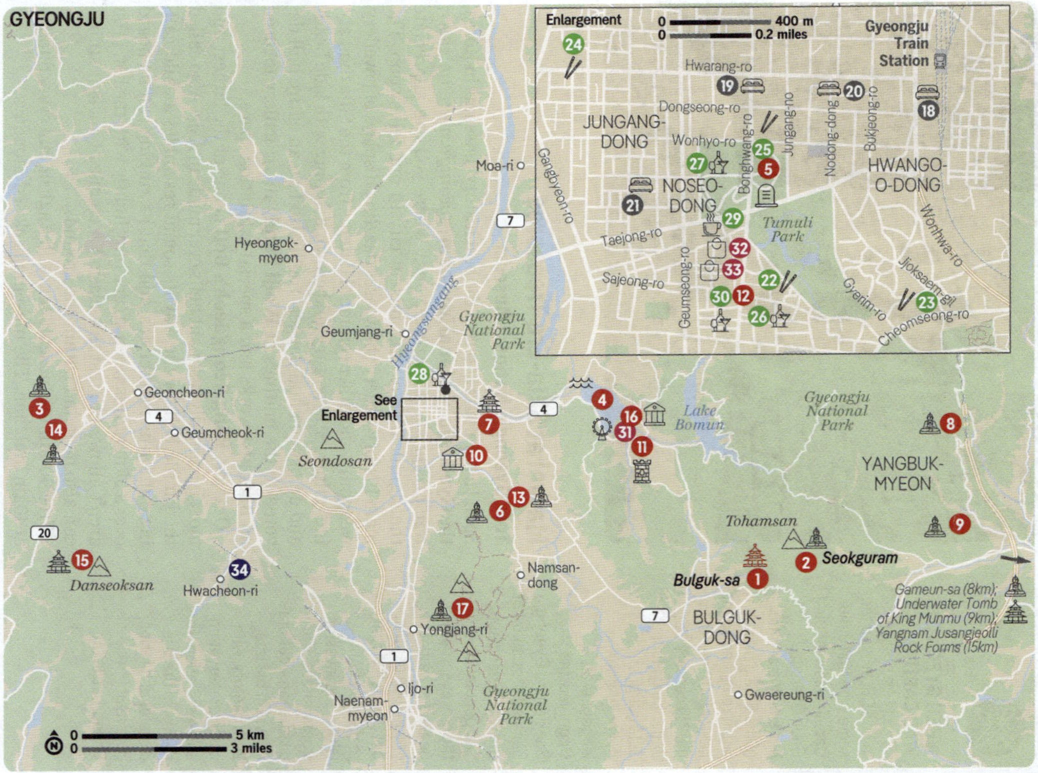

HIGHLIGHTS
1 Bulguk-sa
2 Seokguram

SIGHTS
3 Bokdu-am
4 Bomun
5 Bonghwangdae
6 Bori-sa
7 Bunhwang-sa
8 Girim-sa
9 Golgul-sa
10 Gyeongju National Museum
11 Gyeongju Tower
see 11 Gyeongju World Culture Expo Park
12 Hwangnidan-gil
see 7 Hwangnyong-sa
see 7 Hwangnyong-sa History and Culture Museum
13 Mangdeok-sa
14 Seongnam-sa
15 Sinseon-sa
16 Wooyang Museum of Contemporary Art
17 Yongjangsaji

SLEEPING
18 Blueboat Hostel Gyeongju
19 Doo-baki Guesthouse
20 Friend Guesthouse
21 Pungdengi Hostel

EATING
22 Dosol Maeul
23 Eepungnyeo Kurossambap
24 Hongsi
25 Kisoya

DRINKING & NIGHTLIFE
26 Bar Boon
27 Heu Heu Heu
28 New Orleans Lounge
29 No Words
30 Oasis

ENTERTAINMENT
31 Gyeongju World

SHOPPING
32 Eoseo Eoseo
33 Samdeok Market

TRANSPORT
34 Gyeongju Train Station

WHEN GYEONGJU WAS CAPITAL

In 57 BCE, around the same time that Julius Caesar was subduing Gaul, Gyeongju became the capital of the Silla dynasty, and it remained so for nearly 1000 years. In the 7th century CE, under King Munmu, Silla conquered the neighbouring kingdoms of Goguryeo and Baekje, and Gyeongju became the capital of the whole peninsula. The population of the city eventually peaked at around one million people, but Silla fell victim to division from within and invasion from without. The city began a cultural revival in the late 20th century, with much preservation and restoration work thanks to the late dictator and former president Park Chung-hee in the 1970s.

ALNET/SHUTTERSTOCK

Bunhwang-sa

Marvel at Silla-Era Treasures

Tour Gyeongju National Museum

Spend a few hours at one of the best history museums in Korea, the **Gyeongju National Museum** *(gyeongju.museum.go.kr; free except special exhibitions),* where you can appreciate the significance of this ancient city in one fell swoop. The main history gallery showcases dazzling displays of jewellery, weaponry and other ceremonial items from the Silla dynasty, including a 5th-century gold crown dripping with jade beads and an ornamental dagger. You'll also find an entire hall devoted to the findings at **Wolji Pond**, an art gallery focused on Buddhist works and a special exhibition space.

Outside, **King Seongdeok's Bell** is one of the largest and most beautifully resonant bells ever made in Asia. Also called the Emille Bell for the way its sound resembles a child calling out for its mother, it's said that its ringing can be heard over a 3km radius when struck only lightly with the fist. (You aren't allowed to test this claim.) A couple of ancient stupas can also be found within the grounds.

Free 90-minute museum tours, in English, run every Sunday at 10am and 2pm. The museum is closed Mondays.

Hang Out Along Hwangnidan-gil

Funky cafes, selfie booths and tourists

Gyeongju's hippest street, nicknamed **Hwangnidan-gil** (but technically Poseok-ro) after a famous street in Seoul, is just west of the Daereungwon Ancient Tomb Complex and packs most of Gyeongju's foot traffic. Old *hanok* have been converted into contemporary cafes, restaurants, guesthouses, boutiques, photo studios and more. It's a popular neighbourhood that extends east and west of Poseok-ro, with plenty to taste and photograph for at least a couple of hours. Shop around at quaint and quirky gift stores such as **Samdeok Market** and the well-curated **Eoseo Eoseo** bookshop, then stop for a coffee at **No Words**.

Surviving Stones

The ruins of Korea's one-time largest temple

The ruins of the 6th-century temple of **Hwangnyong-sa** are a sad and desolate sight: once the nation's largest Buddhist temple, it was set in flames by the Mongols in 1238. The temple's standout feature was a nine-storey, 80m-tall pagoda (the world's tallest wooden building at the time), the surviving foundation stones of which can still be seen.

The on-site **Hwangnyong-sa History and Culture Museum** *(adult/child ₩3000/1000)*, closed Mondays, is worth a visit for its model of the enormous temple pagoda as it once appeared and other exhibits related to the former temple. On Culture Day, the last Wednesday of the month, admission is free.

Visit Korea's Oldest Pagoda

See a 7th-century artefact

The large pagoda of **Bunhwang-sa** was built in the mid-7th century during Queen Seondeok's reign, making it the oldest datable pagoda in Korea. It's a rare example of a pagoda made from brick. The magnificently carved Buddhist guardians and stone lions are a feature; the pagoda is unique in that each entrance is protected by two guardians.

Cycle, Paddle & Play at Bomun Lake

A little something for every taste

About 5km east of central Gyeongju, the tourist district around the artificial **Bomun** lake offers a host of diversions. Besides walking, pedalling, paddling and splashing around at the water park, there are fun rides at **Gyeongju World** *(gjw.co.kr; adult/teenager/child ₩36,000/32,000/27,000)* amusement park, art at **Wooyang Museum of Contemporary Art** *(en.wooyangmuseum.org; adult/student/child ₩15,000/12,000/10,000)* and the massive **Gyeongju World Culture Expo Park** *(adult/child ₩12,000/10,000)*. The latter features the 2km narrated **Lumina Night Walk**, circuiting through illuminated Hwarang forest, and an elevator ride up 82m-high **Gyeongju Tower**, built to contain a cutout of the ancient Hwangnyong-sa temple's nine-storey pagoda.

Bomun's shores are suitable for scenic bike rides and long waterside walks. The roads are lined with cherry trees, a sight to behold in early spring when the **Gyeongju Cherry Blossom Marathon**, usually held in April, celebrates the blooming.

MORE BUDDHIST SIGHTS

Girim-sa: One of the largest complexes in the vicinity of the Silla capital, its size compares with Bulguk-sa.

Sinseon-sa: Used as a base by General Kim Yu-shin in the 7th century. It's the site of the Danseoksan grotto containing ancient Buddhist carvings.

Bori-sa: A beautifully reconstructed nunnery set amid old-growth trees.

Mangdeok-sa: One legend says the pagoda of this vast Silla-era temple complex once swayed to warn of a coming rebellion.

Sangseon-am: At this hermitage you'll find lovely valley views and maybe a monk chanting.

Yongjangsaji: A temple with a seated Buddha image etched in rock and a three-storey stone pagoda.

EATING IN GYEONGJU: OUR PICKS

Eepungnyeo Kurossambap: (이풍녀 구로쌈밥) A pleasant place to dine in an area with a lot of *ssambap* (lettuce wrap) restaurants just north of Wolseong-gongwon. *11am-9pm* ₩

Dosol Maeul: (도솔마을) Courtyard restaurant beside the ancient tomb complex, with traditional dinner with an array of mains and sides. *11am-3pm & 5-9pm Thu-Mon* ₩₩

Kisoya: (기소야) A popular chain serving a mouthwatering array of Japanese dishes with a Korean slant, like fried cutlets, sushi and soba. *10.30am-3pm & 5-8.30pm Thu-Tue* ₩₩

Hongsi: (홍시) Traditional *hanjeongsik*-style family restaurant in a stunning *hanok*, with large portions and an ever-changing menu. *11.30am-3.30pm & 5-9.30pm* ₩₩

WANDERING THE DAEREUNGWON ANCIENT TOMB AREA

Go past 1000 years of Silla history by taking a walk across Gyeongju's quiet central gardens.

START	END	LENGTH
Ancient Tombs in Noseo-ri & Nodong-ri	Woljeonggyo Bridge	3.5km, 2½hr

From the north end of the complex, start at the 1 **Ancient Tombs in Noseo-ri & Nodong-ri**, where you'll find the burial mounds of Seobongchong, Geumgwanchong *(adult/child ₩3000/1500)* and Geumnyeongchong, along with the tree-topped Bonghwangdae. Crossing the street south, arrive at the main tomb park, which includes 2 **Cheonmachong** *(adult/child ₩3000/1000)*, the only tomb you're able to enter, Hwangnamdaechong and the Tomb of King Michu. Exiting at the bottom end of the park, you'll soon see 3 **Cheomseongdae**, the stone astronomical observatory that was built between 632 and 646 CE, making it the oldest in East Asia.

Past the flower gardens, on the other side of Wonhwa-ro, are the grounds of 4 **Donggung Palace and Wolji Pond** (p224), built in the era of King Munmu, around which you can make a loop. Heading back west, you'll come to the site of the once-fabled 5 **Wol-seong** (also called Banwol-seong) fortress, the Silla palace of which the only remains today are a Joseon-era stone ice house and surrounding moat. Turn north and walk through 6 **Gyerim Forest**, said to be 2000 years old, passing the 7 **Tomb of King Naemul** and the Confucian school, 8 **Gyeongju Hyanggyo**, nestled near a cluster of traditional homes. Conclude by crossing the spectacular 66m-long, red-and-green 9 **Woljeonggyo** bridge, connecting the north and south sides of Namcheon.

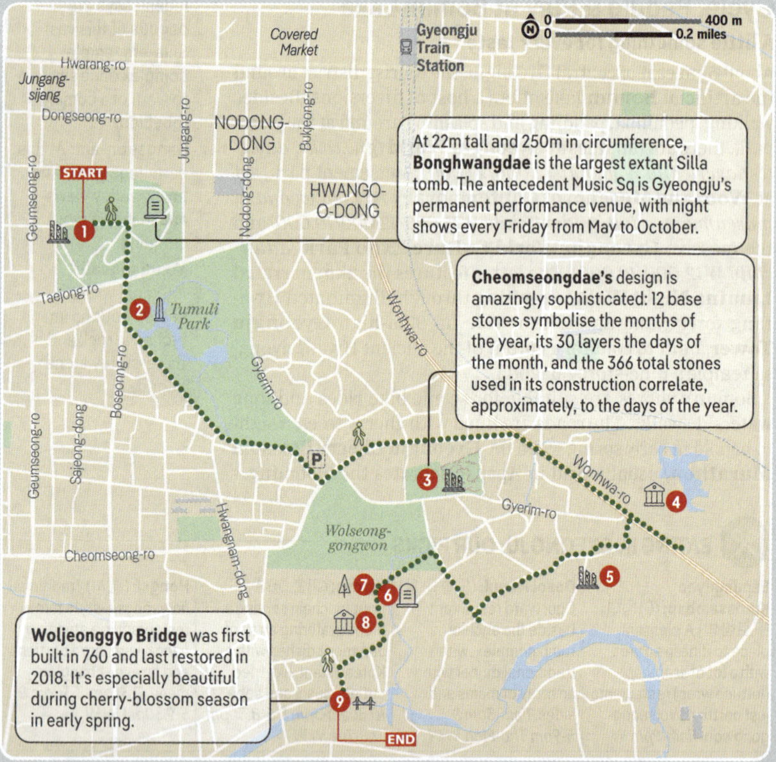

Learn Seonmudo at Golgul-sa

A templestay with martial arts

At **Golgul-sa** *(golgulsa.com)*, a Buddha carved out of solid rock by Indian monks in the 6th century is interesting, but the real draw is *seonmudo,* a Korean martial art that blends fighting skills with meditation. Try for yourself through the templestay program.

Trek to Bokdu-am

Mountain Hermitage

Pack a picnic and set out toward the summit of the thickly forested **Obong-san** (640m) in search of **Bokdu-am**, a beautiful Buddhist hermitage that features a huge rock face with 19 carved niches. The three central niches hold a figure of the historical Buddha flanked by two Bodhisattvas (Munsu and Bohyeon); the remainder house the 16 *nahan* (arhat) monks who have attained nirvana. The carvings are recent and though there's a vacant structure up here, the actual hermitage was burned down in 1988 after an electrical fault started a blaze. There is also a statue of Gwaneum, the Goddess of Mercy, just beyond the rock face.

From the small temple of **Seongnam-sa**, which is about 500m beyond the bus stop in Songseon-ri along the creek, it's an easy hour-long walk to Bokdu-am. From the top of a couple of massive boulders just below the hermitage, there's a stunning view.

Donghae Sights

Underwater tomb and rock formations

Offshore from Gyeongju's east coast, this small rocky island is believed to be the legendary **Underwater Tomb of King Munmu** (661–681 CE), the Silla king and unifier of the three kingdoms who demanded he be laid to rest in the East Sea so he could become a dragon and protect the country against Japanese invasions. An urn containing his ashes is allegedly buried under the islet. Look out for shaman ceremonies and rituals that are performed on mats by the seaside and in the small huts that line the coastal path facing the rock. Down the shore are the **Yangnam Jusangjeolli Rock Forms**, a collection of rare and intriguing columnar rock joints, best viewed from the tall observation tower. Nearby, too, is **Gameun-sa**, the site of an old temple with a pair of three-storey pagodas.

GYEONGJU'S SPECIALITY FOODS

Known for its especially tender beef bulgogi (thin slices marinated in soy sauce, pureed pear and onion, garlic, ginger and sesame oil, and then grilled), Gyeongju's food scene features many *hanjeongsik* full-course menus that serve the meat along with up to 30 *banchan* (side dishes). Pair the meal with Gyeongju's own rice wine, *gyodong beopju*, a slightly sweet, slightly sour alcohol traditionally brewed around Buddhist temples and once the preferred drink of Silla kings. Many *hanjeongsik* restaurants are set in renovated *hanok*, lending a traditional ambience to the dining experience.

DRINKING IN GYEONGJU: BEST BARS

Heu Heu Heu: (흐흐흐) Directly opposite the Noseo-ri tombs, this bar serving craft beer and Korean-style pub grub has an unbeatable view. *4.30pm-midnight*

Bar Boon: Off Hwangnidan-gil with top-shelf cocktails in a cosy wood and concrete styled ambience with traditional touches of Korean decor. *6pm-2am Tue-Sun*

New Orleans Lounge: American bar and pub at the town's north end that's popular among the expat crowd. *7pm-midnight Sun-Thu, to 3am Fri & Sat*

Oasis: Dimly lit and atmospheric wine bar with upscale food and a vinyl collection. *5pm-1am*

JINNIEHOO/SHUTTERSTOCK

Bulguk-sa

TOP EXPERIENCE

Bulguk-sa & Seokguram

On a series of stone terraces about 16km southeast of Gyeongju, set among gnarled pines and iris gardens, is Korea's most famous temple, Bulguk-sa (불국사). The crowning glory of Silla architecture is home to more national treasures than any other Korean Buddhist temple. Together with its nearby hermitage, Seokguram (석굴암), it is a UNESCO World Heritage site.

DON'T MISS

- Cheongungyo and Baegungyo
- Yeonhwagyo and Chilbogyo
- Daeungjeon
- Dabotap and Seokgatap
- Buddha Statue of Seokguram

Accessing the Temple Complex

Leading up to the temple compound are two white stone bridges – actually two sections, set one after the other, of a national-treasure staircase that takes the Korean name for bridge, *gyo*. The lower **Cheongungyo** (Blue Cloud Bridge) is comprised of 17 steps and the upper **Baegungyo** (White Cloud Bridge) of 16 – together, their 33 steps represent the 33 stages to enlightenment. West is another two-section staircase, made up of **Yeonhwagyo** (Lotus Flower Bridge) and **Chilbogyo** (Seven Treasures Bridge). Note that you cannot climb any of

PRACTICALITIES

● bulguksa.or.kr/seokguram.org ● free ● Bulguk-sa 9am-6pm Mar-Sep (from 8am Sat & Sun), 7.30am-5.30pm rest of the year; Seokguram 9am-5pm (to 6pm in summer)

these and instead will need to use the pathway to the right to access the temple from its eastern entrance.

Treasured Pagodas

In front of the main hall are two more national treasures: a duo of pagodas that somehow survived Japanese destruction. The first, **Dabotap** (Pagoda of Many Treasures), on the east side, is of ornate and intricate design – a sensational piece of Silla artistry. The other, **Seokgatap** (Pagoda of the Historical Buddha), on the west side, is much plainer and simpler. When the latter was restored in 1966, it was found to contain a copy of a sutra dating back to the 8th century, making it one of the world's oldest woodblock-printed books. The pagodas are so revered that replicas appear in the grounds of the **Gyeongju National Museum** (p224).

Bulguk-sa's Halls

The main Buddha hall is **Daeungjeon**, which dates to 1765, with the original destroyed in the late 16th century during the Imjin War. Other halls are **Gwaneumjeon** (Hall of the Goddess of Mercy), **Birojeon** (Hall of the Vairocana Buddha), **Geungnakjeon** (Hall of Supreme Bliss) and **Nahanjeon** (where Buddha is flanked by 16 *nahan*, or arhats). Inside Geungnakjeon is the 8th- or 9th-century **Gilt-Bronze Seated Amitabha Buddha of Bulguksa Temple**, while inside Birojeon is the 9th-century **Gilt-Bronze Seated Vairocana Buddha of Bulguksa Temple**, both recognised as national treasures. Within Birojeon's courtyard is the **Stupa of Bulguksa Temple**, said to hold the *sari* (crystallised remains) of a Silla queen-turned-nun – or alternatively of eight monks.

Buddhist Grotto of Seokguram

At 740m above sea level, in the hills above Bulguk-sa, lies its lone hermitage, the world-famous Seokguram. It's a magical place, particularly when it rains and mists envelop the mountaintops. It was a remarkable feat of engineering when it was constructed in the mid-8th century by quarrying huge blocks of granite along a narrow mountain path.

Follow the road past the front gate and bell pavilion and up the stairs. Given the hype, the grotto is a bit of a letdown: the 3.5m statue of the historical Buddha sits far behind a protective glass barrier, gazing out toward the East Sea, surrounded by guardians, disciples and lesser deities such as the 11-faced Gwaneum, the Goddess of Mercy.

Getting Between the Sites

Bus 12 *(₩1700)* departs from the Bulguk-sa bus stop every hour from 8.40am to 4.40pm, arriving at Seokguram in 20 minutes. It returns on the hour between 9am and 5pm (with an extra 5.40pm summer departure). The alternative is using a well-maintained 2.2km hiking trail that's uphill to Seokguram and downhill to Bulguk-sa. We recommend catching a bus to Seokguram, then hiking down and visiting Bulguk-sa.

THE LAND OF BUDDHA

Bulguk-sa means 'Buddha Land Temple', and its temple grounds are laid out to symbolise the kingdom of Buddha, with each distinct area – or hall – representing a separate world inhabited by the Buddha or Bodhisattvas. On entering through the front gates, the visitor is welcomed into this realm.

TOP TIPS

- Stop at the tourist information booth in the car park, near the bus stop, to pick up a helpful map or store luggage.
- Register ahead for Bulguk-sa's popular overnight templestay program *(bulguksa@templestay.com)*, which includes a temple tour, meditation, 108 prostrations and a visit to Seokguram. Due to Bulguk-sa's designation as a UNESCO World Heritage site, participants stay in an adjacent house, a five-minute drive away.
- Not far from Bulguk-sa, the Gyeongju Folk Handicraft Village, with its traditional Korean tiled- and thatched-roof houses, is home to artisans working with metal, ceramic, wood and other materials.
- About 1.4km beyond Seokguram is the peak of Tohamsan, if you're looking to hike.

NAMSAN SAMNEUNGGOL VALLEY LOOP

Hike past royal tombs, rock-carved Buddhas, stone pagodas and mountain shrines to Geumo-bong Peak, the reserve's second-highest, across Namsan's relic-rich valley.

START	END	LENGTH
Samneung Solsup	Poseokjeong car park	6.5km; 4–5hr

Bus 500 and 508 from the city stop at **1 Samneung Solsup** (pine forest) on Namsan's western slopes. Walk 100m to **2 Samneung's Three Royal Tombs**, where the 2.3km ascent to 468m-high Geumo-bong peak starts. After 750m is a **3 headless seated stone Buddha**. Soon after, take the left-hand uphill diversion to a **4 Triad of Carved Stone Buddhas of the Samneunggyegok Valley**. Keep walking to another left-hand diversion to a **5 seated stone medicinal Buddha statue** from the 8th or 9th century. Climb steep stairs to the cliff-hanging **6 Sangseon-am** (p227) hermitage. Rest and enjoy the views.

From here, it's 950m of moderate incline via the spectacular **7 Badukbawi** viewpoint to **8 Geumo-bong**, the second-highest point in the reserve after Gowi-bong. Enjoy a break before looping north on the wide main path, passing 429m **9 Saja-bong**, after which is a platform viewpoint next to the **10 Sangsabawi** boulder.

After about 400m, steer left back into the forest and the **11 Geum-ojeong Pavilion**, soak in the views and descend to its left down a steep path until the **12 Five-storey Stone Pagoda at the Sixth Temple in Poseokgok Valley**, dramatically perched atop 270m Neumbi-bong peak. A couple of hundred metres further down is the simple temple of **13 Buheun-sa**. From here, it's 1.8km through bamboo-strewn forest to the Poseokjeong car park, where you can visit the namesake **14 Poseokjeong Pavilion** or get to the main road to flag any Gyeongju-bound bus.

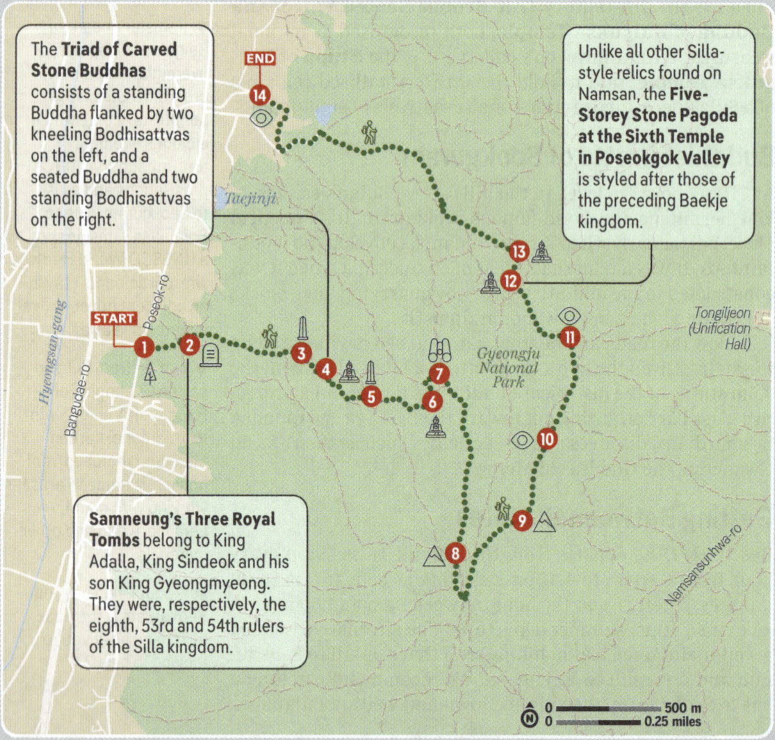

Beyond Gyeongju

Beyond the museum without walls, see more time-honoured treasures, then chase the tiger's tail and an island of mystery.

From Gyeongju, a host of beautiful and historically significant sights awaits, though getting to a fair number of them is a test in patience. To the north is one of Korea's most important Confucian academies, Oksan Seowon, hidden away in the woods beside a rushing stream, as well as the UNESCO-listed Yangdong Village, which is home to the Gyeongju Sohn and Yeogang Lee clans. Seaward lies the silver city of Pohang, home to Korea's largest steel manufacturer, a fact that may overshadow its many coastal wonders, but shouldn't deter you from coming. Then, about 200km east, atop an extinct volcano rising majestically from the sea floor, sits the island of Ulleungdo, offering some of Korea's most spectacular scenery.

Places

Yangdong Folk Village

TIME FROM GYEONGJU: **25MIN**

Step into a traditional clan town

Making your way to Joseon-era **Yangdong Folk Village** *(yangdongvillage.or.kr; adult/teenager/child ₩4000/2000/1500)* can be tricky by public transport (better to go by car or taxi), but you will be rewarded with an intimate look at traditional architecture in an authentic setting. Founded by Sohn So (1433–84) of the Wolseong Sohn clan, the entire village has been designated a cultural preservation area and is replete with stone walls, straw-thatched roofs and green gardens. Set aside a half-day to admire the 180-or-so houses. Some are still inhabited, so you should observe the standard courtesies when looking around; others stand empty and are open to the public.

GETTING AROUND

Gyeongju is well connected to Pohang by train and bus, but less connected to some of its more rural surroundings. To avoid long waits and multiple transfers, renting a car is recommended. Within Pohang, buses are frequent, and the city centre, beach and Songdo Island areas are walkable. It's a 2½- to three-hour boat ride to Ulleungdo. Ferries cost around ₩60,000 one way and leave several times a day from the mainland ports of Gangneung and Mukho Ferry Terminal in Donghae in Gangwon-do, and Pohang and Hupo in Gyeongsang-do. On the island, two local bus lines operate between Dodong and Jeodong, transporting you to popular sites such as Bongnae Falls, Nari and Gwaneum-do. As they don't run late, taxis will be more convenient.

SAILING & WATERSPORTS IN POHANG

Park Haneul, owner and captain of **Sevenstar Sailing**, explains why his hometown is a rising watersports hub. *@sevenstarsail*

Pohang is an excellent place for sailing, diving, surfing and free diving. There's good underwater visibility, schools of small fish, interesting rock formations and some of the best year-round winds in Korea.

Yongil Bay, shaped like a lake, has strong headwinds and, beyond it, the big waves are ideal for surfing, especially at **Yonghan-ri** beach.

The coast from Homigot to Guryongpo-eup and Odo-ri is ideal for diving and free diving, even in winter, when the water is extremely clear.

Every September, we have the **Hwandonghae Cup** *(hwandonghaecup.org)* and the **Fareast Cup International Regatta**, from China to Vladivostok and back via Pohang.

ISEO YANG/GETTY IMAGES

Guryongpo Street, Pohang

Oksan

TIME FROM GYEONGJU: **30MIN**

Visit a riverside Confucian academy

At the base of the hills and next to a gushing stream in the tiny village of Oksan-ri, the Confucian academy **Oksan Seowon** *(free)* is pretty as a picture. Established in 1572 in honour of the scholar Yi Eon-jeok (1491–1553) and enlarged in 1772, it was one of the most important Confucian academies of the time, and one of the few to escape destruction at the end of the Joseon dynasty when *seowon* (Confucian academies) were abolished. However, an early 20th-century fire destroyed some of the structures, so only 14 remain today. From Oksan Seowon, a 10-minute walk up the valley path will bring you to **Doknakdang**, the beautiful and well-preserved private residence of Yi, constructed in 1515 and expanded in 1532. Nearby is the **Thirteen-Storey Stone Pagoda**, part of the now-vanished temple of Jeonghye-sa. Built upon a square base and tapering in stages to its top, it's a unique and very attractive pagoda, dating to the 9th century.

Pohang

TIME FROM GYEONGJU: **40MIN**

Space Walk, then beach walk

Take a stroll along Pohang's central coastline, a lively place of busking, beachgoing and all-around youthful revelry. At the north end, start with the **Space Walk**. Some locals say

EATING IN POHANG: OUR PICKS

Simin Bakery: A famous Pohang bakery, in business since 1949 and selling all manner of doughy delights, including cute turtle-shaped pastries. *9am-10pm* W

Marado: (마라도회식당) By Yeongildae beach, this extremely popular *hoe* restaurant is well worth the wait. *10.30am-3.30pm & 5-9pm* WW

Songnim Tondak: (송림통닭) Local fried-chicken and beer institution on Songdo Beach, perfect to quench a craving for booze, spicy wings and bar food. *2pm-4am* W

Kajung Sushi: (가정초밥) This Hyoja restaurant often has a queue for its excellent sushi sets, rice bowls and udon. *11.30am-3.30pm & 5-9.30pm* WW

the shape of this loopy, curvy, elevated walking structure that cuts through the sky resembles a strange man looming large – and it does – yet it's an exhilarating way to get a bird's-eye view of the city, especially if it's windy. From there, head to the **Yeongildae** beachside walkway, where you can make a stop at the floating pavilion to face the POSCO Steel Plant before going out past the ferry terminal to the long breakwater walkway that leads to a lighthouse at the end.

Chasing the tiger's tail

About an hour away, in easternmost Pohang, off the Homigot coast, is an enormous **right hand** emerging from the watery depths of the sea. It faces its pair, the left hand, towering over the Sunrise Plaza on land. Of course, this is a popular place to pose with arms outstretched in the air for photos. Come for the sunrise, if you can; it's the furthest east you can get on the Korean mainland – Homigot is said to be the tail, if you imagine Korea in the shape of a tiger.

If it's April and the canola flowers are in bloom, the nearby fields will be awash in a lemony yellow glow, with narrow pathways that wind between blossoms taller than you. Otherwise, there's a lighthouse, a lighthouse museum, a gift shop and eateries around.

Japanese colonial quarter

On the southern base of the peninsula's tail is **Guryongpo Street**, a historic Japanese colonial community lined with traditional houses that have been restored and repurposed. While the street is a reminder of a painful history, it's also become a sightseeing attraction, popular among Korean tourists for its interesting architecture and trendy shops, restaurants and cafes. One was the filming site of the K-Drama *When the Camellia Blooms*, and you'll notice the red flowers all around.

Explore Songdo Island

Separated by a narrow canal from the rest of the city, Songdo Island's main attractions are **Songlim Park**, Pohang's only pine forest, with a relaxing walking trail that's set between a **Warship Museum**, housed inside an actual ship, to the east and popular **Songdo Beach** to the west. In the middle of the shore, an elevated staircase viewpoint, opened in 2025, is particularly dramatic at night when it lights up in red tones.

Shop and stroll Pohang's lesser-known markets

A large covered area of intersecting alleys, **Jukdo Fish Market** is the largest permanent market on Gyeongsangbuk-do's east

ULLEUNGDO'S BEST OBSERVATION POINTS

Hyangmok Observatory: Take the Taeha Hyangmok Monorail on a five-minute, 304m ride up a sharp cliff, then walk a 500m trail for a gorgeous vista of the northern coastline.

Samseonam Rock: Some of Ulleungdo's most impressive rock formations, rising like pillars off the northeastern tip of the island, near Gwaneum-do.

Gwaneum-do Bridge: Walk across the bridge to Gwaneum Island for a breathtaking perspective of Ulleungdo from its east side.

Bongnae Pokpo: The primary source of the island's drinking water, this 25m waterfall is spectacular in summer. Nearby is the Cheonyeon Natural Air Conditioner, a cave that maintains a year-round temperature of 4°C.

DRINKING IN POHANG: OUR PICKS

Oh! Bremen: A social-media darling, this cafe features an indoor carousel and rainbow bagels. *10am-10.30pm*

Arabica Coffee Roasters: Minimalist-chic roastery with beautiful, blue ocean views. *noon-10pm Mon-Fri, from 11am Sat & Sun*

Bean & Vino: A casual coffee and wine bar with a friendly owner. Also serves teas, juices and desserts. *noon-10pm Mon-Sat*

XTC Pub: Rowdy 2nd-floor bar by the beach with cocktails, beers and greasy pub grub on the menu. *8pm-2am Tue-Thu, to 3am Fri-Sun*

MYSTERY ISLAND

In Korea, Ulleungdo has long been regarded as a spiritual, sacred island with mystical properties, a place where the energies of yin and yang meet and mingle in harmony. The island is famed for its Yaksu Gongwon, or Medicinal Water Park, where mineral-spring water is believed to have healing powers that offer relief from fatigue, anaemia and other ailments. Old lore has it that the island holds such magic that peaches grew pits big enough to split in half and make into cups, bamboo grew twice as large as on the mainland, and the water dripping from one of its caves was the secret to immortality.

CHO GYO SANG/SHUTTERSTOCK

Haengnam Coastal Walkway

coast. It has fish-tank creatures galore and dozens of small little restaurants where you can try anything from seafood to rice cakes and other fritters. Photographers will love it.

Not far away, the **Yeongildae Bukbu Market** feels even more retro and local. It's famous for *mulhoe,* a cold raw fish *gochujang (*fermented red-chilli paste*)* soup invented in Pohang.

Ulleungdo

TIME FROM POHANG: 2¾HR

Mystical mountain trek

The mystical, mysterious island of Ulleungdo, with **Seongin-bong** (986m) peak at its centre, is a hiker's dream. Its lush forest, filled with ground-cover ferns and Korean beech, hemlock and lime, is a study in green. Of the various pathways to the summit, the two main routes run from the town of Dodong-ri (approaching from the southwest, four to five hours return) and from the agricultural basin of **Nari-bunji** (approaching from the north, also four to five hours return). Better yet, combine the two and do a point-to-point hike. From Dodong-ri, take the main road towards **Daewon-sa**. Just before you reach the temple, there is a fork in the trail and a sign signalling the way to Seongin-bong (a steep 4.1km). It's also well marked going down, where you'll come to picnic grounds and chrysanthemum fields.

Coastal walkway

On arguably Korea's most spectacular seaside scamper, the 4km **Haengnam Coastal Walkway**, let your jaw drop at the surrounding scenery as you make your way around cliffsides and across coves. From the **Dodong-ri ferry terminal**, follow the coastal trail north toward Jeodong-ri. Along the way, you'll pass fantastic rock formations, waterfalls and squid boats with lamps strung like oversized holiday lights, all set amid the dazzling aquamarine swells of the ocean.

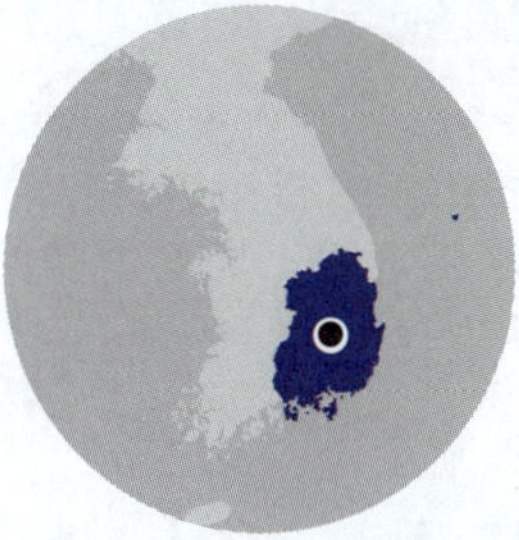

Daegu

INDEPENDENCE ACTIVISM | MISSIONARY HISTORY | TRADITIONAL MEDICINE

South Korea's fourth-largest city, enclosed by mountains and recording Korea's hottest heatwaves, may not be where you want to go in the summer. However, Daegu's (대구) rich history as a centre of traditional Eastern medicine (which the city claims laid the groundwork for the modern infrastructure used to respond to the COVID-19 outbreak in Korea), as well as a hub of grassroots activism during Korea's independence movement, is fascinating to learn about. The city's central area is packed with heritage, old churches and missionary residences, as well as more modern diversions, including some excellent dining, shopping and entertainment options. A draw for exchange students and expat English teachers, Daegu's humming city centre has a young and carefree feel, especially around rowdy Dongseong-ro, where the music plays loud and the neon burns bright. Daegu means 'Big Hill', deriving from the *hanja* Chinese characters 大邱, and the big hill is great fun.

TOP TIP

Check tour.daegu.go.kr for tourist information. The DaeguTrip app, developed by the Daegu Foundation for Culture & Arts, is another helpful tool for planning your time in the city, from browsing attractions, events and restaurants to navigating public transport and booking accommodation and activities. The app also has coupons, wish list and itinerary features.

GETTING AROUND

Travellers arriving by bus will come to one of four terminals around the city: the **Dongdaegu Express Bus Terminal**, located east of the city centre; the **Seobu Intercity Bus Terminal**, southwest of the city; the **Bukbu Intercity Bus Terminal**, northwest of the city; and the nearby **Seodaegu Express Bus Terminal**. Across from the Dongdaegu terminal is **Dongdaegu train station**, serviced by the high-speed KTX. Line 1 connects Dongdaegu to the city's other train station, Daegu, while a second subway line, plus a monorail line criss-crossing the city, make it mostly easy to get around by metro. Local buses are plentiful, but traffic can be slow. Daegu is also serviced by **Daegu International Airport**, about 1.8km north of Line1 Ayanggyo station and 10km from the city centre.

SIGHTS

1 Apsan Park
2 Daegu Local History Museum
3 Daegu Modern History Museum
4 Daegu Yangnyeongsi Museum of Oriental Medicine
5 Dalseong Park
6 Dongseong-ro
7 Duryu Park
8 Gyeongsang-gamyeong Park
9 Kim Kwang-seok Street
10 Suseong Artpia
11 Suseong Lake

SLEEPING

12 Dongseongro Zero Guesthouse
13 Empathy Guesthouse

EATING

14 Bongsan Jjim-Galbi
15 Gaejeung
16 Kyusan
17 Ordinary House

DRINKING & NIGHTLIFE

18 Brewers Brothers
19 Commune
20 Gogo Vinyl
21 Hello Pub

SHOPPING

22 Chilseong Market
see 22 Chilseong Night Market
23 Daegu's Herbal Medicine Market
24 Seomun Sijang

TRANSPORT

25 Bukbu Intercity Bus Terminal
26 Dongdaegu Express Bus Terminal
27 Dongdaegu Station
28 Seobu Intercity Bus Terminal
29 Seodaegu Express Bus Terminal

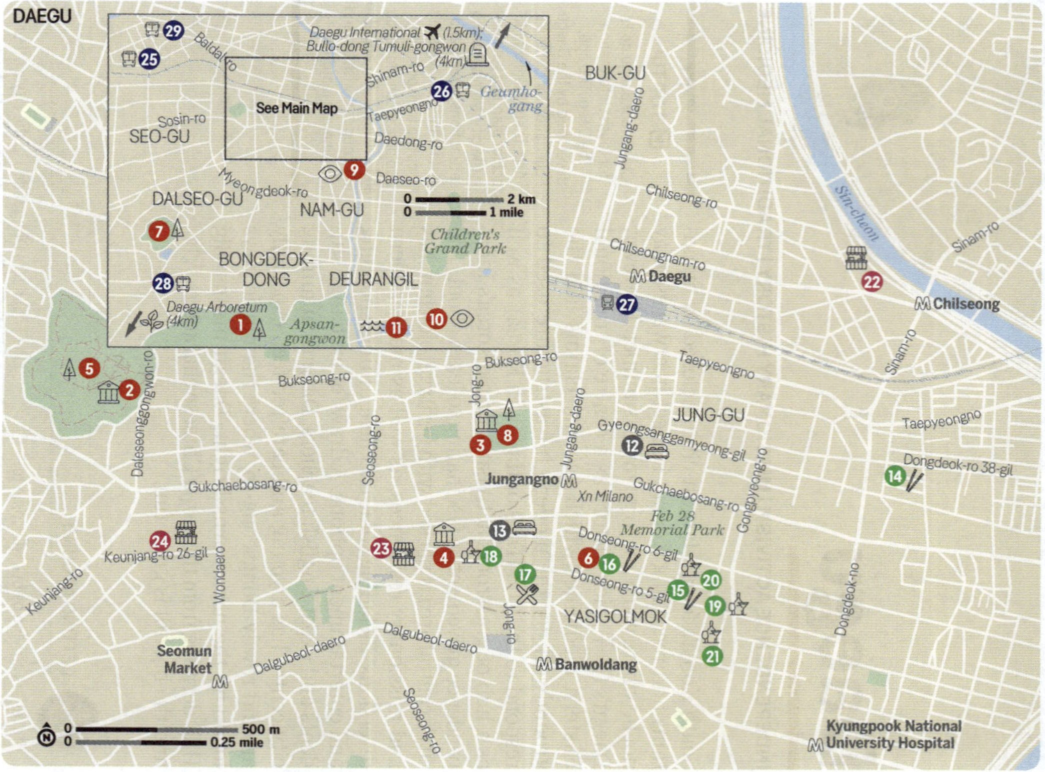

Dive into Daegu's Past

Tour two local history museums

Built on the site of the city's ancient earthen fortification of Dalseong Toseong, now **Dalseong Park**, the **Daegu Local History Museum** *(free)* takes visitors on a journey back through time, starting in the prehistoric age and ending in the 1960s. Exhibitions detail periods such as the Three Kingdoms Era, the Joseon dynasty, the Korean Empire, the Japanese occupation and the 2.28 Daegu democracy movements.

Afterwards, walk about 25 minutes east to the **Daegu Modern History Museum** *(free)*, located within the fabulous former Joseon Siksan Bank building, built by the occupying Japanese in 1932 – check out the old brickwork. Here, you'll learn more about Daegu's 20th-century history, from its contributions to democracy and literary heritage, to its commerce and industry, including the city's most famous home-grown company: Samsung.

Both museums are closed Mondays.

Shop at Daegu's Markets

Hunt bargains at Seomun and Chilseong markets

One of Daegu's most time-honoured traditional markets, **Seomun Sijang** is famous for its cuisine and textiles. Wander through the crowded alleys, stopping at the hundreds of stalls along the way.

After 7pm from Friday through Sunday, the traditional shifts towards the modern, when the place transforms into a lively night market, with a greater focus on fusion foods and various arts and culture events designed to appeal to a younger crowd. On the southern bank of the Sincheon stream, the **Chilseong Market**, founded in 1946, grants another look into Daegu's old-world commerce, with dozens of stalls laden with fruits, fish, flowers, household goods and no-frills restaurants – try the hearty bibimbap on the market's northern side. From 6pm to 10.30pm, except Tuesdays, the **Chilseong Night Market** offers food stalls, street entertainment and performances.

Walk around Suseong Lake

Idyllic waterfront strolls

This **artificial lake**, created in 1925, is a popular spot to see the cherry trees in full bloom in spring and to attend the **Suseong Light Art Festival** in winter. Head to the small

DAEGU'S CITY TOUR BUS

Daegu's circular tour buses are a convenient way to travel between the city's top sites, such as Dongseong-ro, Duryu Park, Suseong Lake and Apsan. From 9am to 5.50pm, buses run between 12 destinations, stopping seven times at each. Purchase an all-day pass on board (₩10,000, cash, credit card or Tmoney card), then hop on and hop off at any stop. Separately available are themed courses, including a night-view tour (Fridays and Saturdays) and a hands-on experience tour (Sundays). Use the **Daegu City Tour** app to see a map of the boarding locations and find information about each stop's surrounding area.

EATING IN DAEGU: OUR PICKS

Ordinary House: Speciality coffee and handmade pastries in a large hall with exposed bricks, wooden tables and a plant-strewn patio out back. *noon-10.30pm* ₩₩

Gaejeung: In business since 1978, serving bibimbap, pork bulgogi, *naengmyeon* and more. This is the main branch; others are located around the city. *11am-9.30pm* ₩₩

Kyusan: This popular restaurant cooks a short menu of excellent ramen dishes. *noon-3.30pm & 5-9pm* ₩

Bongsan Jjim-Galbi: (봉산찜갈비) Located along Jjim-Galbi Street, this restaurant has been cooking up braised beef short ribs for over 40 years. *9am-9pm* ₩₩

DAEGU'S BEST PARKS

Duryu Park: One of Daegu's most beloved green spaces, encompassing Duryu Mountain, E-World, the 83 Tower and more.

Daegu Arboretum: South of town, superb botanical gardens showcase a wide variety of trees and plants.

Gyeongsang-gamyeong Park: Once the residence and office of the Gyeongbuk governor, this urban oasis is a place of birdsong, where young and old alike gather.

Apsan Park: Daegu's largest natural park, home to a temple, skybridge and life-size dinosaur models. Also a cable car and observatory.

Bullo-dong Tumuli-gongwon: On the northeast side of the city, with burial mounds dating from the 2nd to the 6th century CE.

TRABANTOS/SHUTTERSTOCK

Suseong Land *(suseongland.co.kr; three rides ₩13,000)* amusement park, closed Mondays, to paddle a duck boat, ride a bumper car or hop on the merry-go-round. Take a breather with a coffee and a pastry at **Suseongmot Cafe Street**. There are also nice boardwalks that pass through ecological wetlands, where you can spot birds and other wildlife. Art lovers shouldn't miss **Suseong Artpia**, an art centre set 1km east of the lake, equipped with a mega concert hall for opera, ballet, concerts and more.

Learn about Eastern Medicine

Medicinal marvels at Daegu Yangnyeongsi

This market, west of the central shopping district, has a history as vast as its scope. It dates back to 1658, making it Korea's oldest medicine market and still one of its largest, with its stores spilling out onto the street and offering fragrant curiosities.

Next door, the **Daegu Yangnyeongsi Museum of Oriental Medicine** *(free)*, closed Mondays, features a history hall with re-creations of traditional clinics and an exhibition zone showcasing medicinal ingredients and tools, as well as an

DRINKING IN DAEGU: OUR PICKS

Commune: A longtime establishment beloved for its live-music nights and welcoming crowd of regulars. *8pm-2am Wed-Sun*

Gogo Vinyl: Drenched in neon and selling bagged drinks to go, with the added perk of mouthwatering Nazar Kebab nearby. *7pm-3am Tue-Thu & Sun, to 4am Fri & Sat*

Brewers Brothers: Red-tinged corner pub selling different craft beers, fish and chips and pizzas. Enjoy the Brit-pub feel. *5pm-1am*

Hello Pub: (헬로외국포차) A very popular pub with an outdoor seating area, an extensive drinks menu and bar fare. *7pm-5am*

Seomun Sijang (p237)

interactive area with video quizzes that teach about the principles of Eastern medicine. You can also sign up (at least 30 minutes in advance) for various experiences *(₩3000 to ₩5000)*, including footbaths, soap making and lip-balm making.

Sing on Kim Kwang-seok Street

Pay homage to Daegu's activist folk-rock hero

Located near Bangcheon Market, **Kim Kwang-seok St** celebrates the life and legacy of musician Kim Kwang-seok. Born in Daegu in 1964, Kim was a folk-rock singer whose songs struck a chord with the Korean public, as they addressed the social issues of the 1980s and '90s, a time when the country was undergoing democratisation and rapid industrialisation. Kim died in 1996 at just 31 years of age. Today, the street created in his honour, along with its connecting alleyways, is a popular gathering place, featuring many shops, cafes and restaurants, as well as a small amphitheatre. Across the street to the north is **Dongseong-ro**, another favourite shopping and dining street.

MEANDERING THROUGH DAEGU'S MODERN HISTORY

Cross Daegu's city centre connecting past and present on this history-focused walking tour

START	END	LENGTH
Jin Alley	COVID-19 Memorial Museum	1.3km; 1½hr

Begin at **1** **Jin Alley**, a network of pathways decorated with murals that commemorate it as a grassroots site of the National Debt Repayment Movement, which first began in 1907 in Daegu. From the alley, head to **2** **Jongno**, a longtime Daegu commercial centre, and, turning west, follow **3** **Yeongnam-daero**, the Joseon-dynasty road that once led all the way from Seoul to Busan. Across the way, you'll see the original **4** **Jeil Church**, founded by an American Presbyterian missionary in 1898, and housing the Christian History Museum of the First Presbyterian Church of Daegu. Opposite the church, the **5** **YMCA** was a meeting place for protestors, and its leaders Kim Tae-ryun and Lee Man-jip were key figures in the 1 March independence movement. Southwest, the **6** **Old Houses of Lee Sang-hwa and Seo Sang-don** were two other very important activists. Continue to **7** **Gyesan Catholic Church**, an architectural icon of Daegu and one of its first Western-style structures. Go up the **8** **March 1st Independence Movement Road**, the set of steps used by protestors that leads to the impressive **9** **Jeil Church** and **10** **Cheongna Hill**, where you can visit the houses of the missionaries who moved to Daegu in the early 20th century. Finally, for some recent history, there's the **11** **COVID-19 Memorial Museum**, which commemorates Daegu as ground zero of the outbreak in Korea after the virus spread from China.

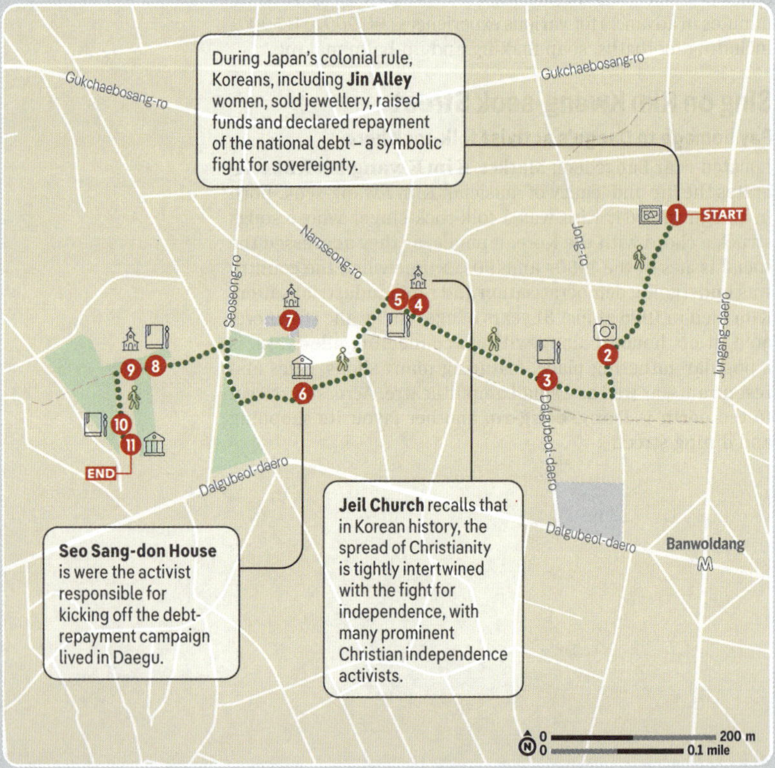

Beyond Daegu

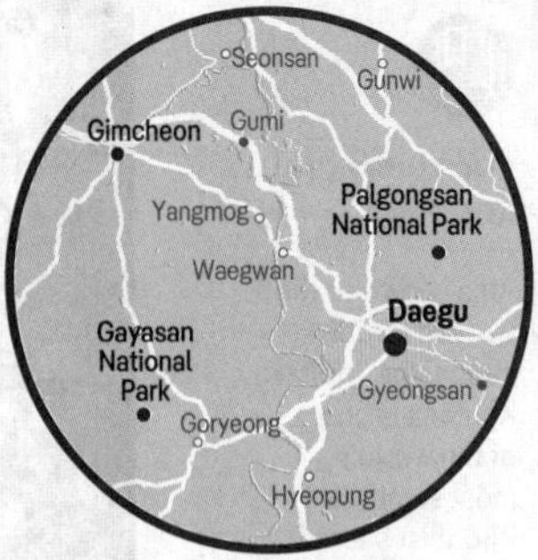

Hike the rocky ridges of Palgongsan and Gayasan and marvel at Korea's most staggering collection of woodblock dharma.

With mountains in every direction, threaded through with rushing streams, Daegu is surrounded by sublime scenery. To the north lies the easily accessible and well-loved Palgongsan National Park, featuring open rocky expanses and thick green vegetation, which was finally upgraded from its former provincial-level designation at the end of 2023. To the west, the emerald beauty of Gayasan National Park might be one of the smallest of Gyeongsang-do's national parks, but it's also one of its most notable, holding the priceless and astounding Tripitaka Koreana at the Buddhist treasure of Haein-sa. In Gimcheon, you'll find one of the loveliest temples you've ever seen, edged in foliage like a photo in a frame.

Places

GETTING AROUND

Buses to Palgongsan National Park are straightforward and frequent, with the red Express Bus 1 to Donghwa-sa departing from several locations around the city. The simplest way to get to Haein-sa is to take an intercity bus from Daegu's Seobu terminal. For Jikji-sa, take a train to Gimcheon station, then transfer to a local bus. For the most convenient rambling about the region, it's best to rent a car and drive.

Palgongsan National Park

TIME FROM DAEGU: 1HR

A cable car and two temples

Make a trip to Palgongsan National Park, the scenic, mountainous and much-loved green space on Daegu's northern outskirts. Its highest peak, **Palgongsan** (1192m), received its name around the end of the Silla period after eight generals who saved Wang-Geon, the founding king of the Goryeo kingdom. From the Donghwa area bus stop near the foot of the mountain, take the **cable car** *(adult/child one way ₩11,000/5500, return ₩14,000/8000)* – a 1.2km, seven-minute ride up. At the top, you can hike to Dong-bong, the east peak, or eat at one of the restaurants with panoramic views.

On the lower flanks of the mountain are **Donghwa-sa**, where templestays are possible, and the Buddhist shrine of **Gatbawi**. The former was built in 493 CE, rebuilt eight times and still features buildings from the 18th century. Don't miss the impressive, 33m-high **Tongil Yaksa Buddha statue**, one of the world's largest stone medicinal Buddha statues, located on the southwestern fringes of the temple complex.

Gimcheon

TIME FROM DAEGU: 1¼HR

Postcard-pretty temple

In a quiet mountain forest setting, **Jikji-sa** is a picturesque temple with an appealing grace. It features delicate paintings on the buildings and several historic stone pagodas.

THE TRIPITAKA KOREANA

Also known as the Goryeo Buddhist canon, the Tripitaka Koreana is one of the world's most significant Buddhist sacred texts, representing the three divisions of Buddhism: the Sutra (scriptures), Vinaya (laws) and Abhidharma (treatises). The original set of blocks, completed in 1087, was destroyed by Mongolian invaders in 1232. A reconstructed set – crafted from carefully selected birchwood that was then soaked in a brine, boiled in salt and dried – was completed in 1251 and is stored at Haein-sa today. Despite the Japanese invasion and fires that destroyed the rest of the temple complex, the repository remained standing with the woodblocks preserved intact.

TOM ROBERTSON/SHUTTERSTOCK

Tripitaka Koreana, Haein-Sa

Of the 40 original buildings, approximately 20 still exist, with the oldest dating back to the 1602 reconstruction. Highlights include the Daeungjeon main hall, containing a triad of national treasure paintings and a ceiling adorned with 330 lotus flowers; the Vairocana Hall, filled with thousands of small Buddha statues; and the **Jikji Museum of Buddhist Arts** *(free)*, with a rotating collection of 2000 Buddhist relics, including a bronze bell and a bronze gong. The museum is closed Mondays.

Gayasan National Park

TIME FROM DAEGU: 1½HR

Woodblock dharma

Set in the hills of Gayasan National Park amid deciduous and coniferous forest, high mountains and rushing streams, the UNESCO World Heritage–listed **Haein-sa** is one of Korea's most stunning and important temples. In a quadrant of four buildings at the upper reaches of the compound, it contains the **Tripitaka Koreana**, a historic and priceless collection of 81,258 carved woodblock scriptures that took 16 years to complete.

The temple's main hall, Daejeokkwangjeon, was burnt down in the Japanese invasion of 1592 and again (accidentally) in 1817, though miraculously the Tripitaka survived. It escaped a third time, during the Korean War, when a South Korean pilot working for the Allied forces refused to allow them to bomb it. The hall is an astonishing sight, with its fabulously carved and decorated ceiling and trinity of Buddhas. The Daebirojeon, or Vairocana Hall, is notable for containing the two oldest wooden images in Korea, both of the Vairocana Buddha.

Hikers will want to climb **Gayasan** (1430m), the main peak in the park, and a pretty one, though the climb from Haein-sa is tough. There are many other temples hidden away among the hills' trees and foliage, allowing for extensive exploration. Be sure to pack water and snacks.

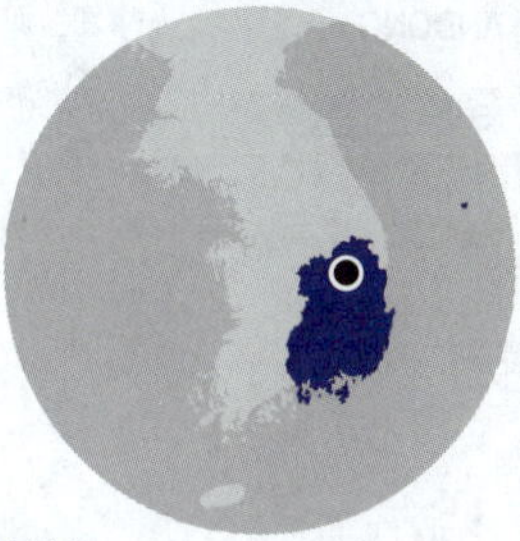

Andong

SPIRITUAL HEARTLAND | RIVER VILLAGE | MASK DRAMA

Andong (안동) is the provincial capital of Gyeongsangbuk-do and, some would say, spiritual capital of Korea – an embodiment of the country's old soul. The city's commitment to preserving its rich cultural heritage, from its Confucian centres to its wooden masks and its particularly strong soju, is to be admired and appreciated. It's because of this dedication to the past that we can immerse ourselves in it in the present. Andong's drawcard, the Hahoe Folk Village (p248), is actually an hour away, but the town has other equally delightful sights, such as Andong Folk Village, an open-air museum of Joseon architecture that can be reached by walking across the dramatic Weolyeonggyo Bridge over the Nakdong River.

Andong's old *hanja* name is 安東 (Peaceful East) – pronounced the same in modern-day Mandarin Chinese – which still holds true today, with the city exuding a relaxed, friendly charm that inspires most visitors to take their time, and some to linger even longer.

TOP TIP

From 9am to 6pm, the 1st floor of the **tourist information centre**, in front of the bus station, features tables, a water dispenser, electric plugs and free wi-fi, making it an ideal spot for travellers to wait for onward buses and trains. The tourist office on the ground floor has English-speaking staff, brochures and the latest bus timetables.

Discover Andong's Old Heritage

Visit the folk village and museum

About 4km east of town, on a hillside across the Nakdong River, **Andong Folk Village** *(free)* is an open-air museum of Joseon-era architecture relocated here from areas submerged

GETTING AROUND

Andong's newer **bus terminal** is around 5km northwest of the town centre, right across the street from where the new **train station** is also located. From there, buses such as 210, 211, 212, 310, 410, 610 and 612 will take you eastward to the **Kyobo Life Insurance building**, roughly at the centre of Andong town. In and around this area, you can travel easily on foot, but to reach attractions further afield by the Weolyeonggyo Bridge, the walk will be long. Some hostels offer free bicycle use.

Local buses serve all the sights, and taxis are readily available. From Andong bus terminal, bus 210 goes to Hahoe Folk Village, and the infrequent 310 bus goes to Bongjeong-sa every two hours. Catch bus 3 to Dosan Seowon.

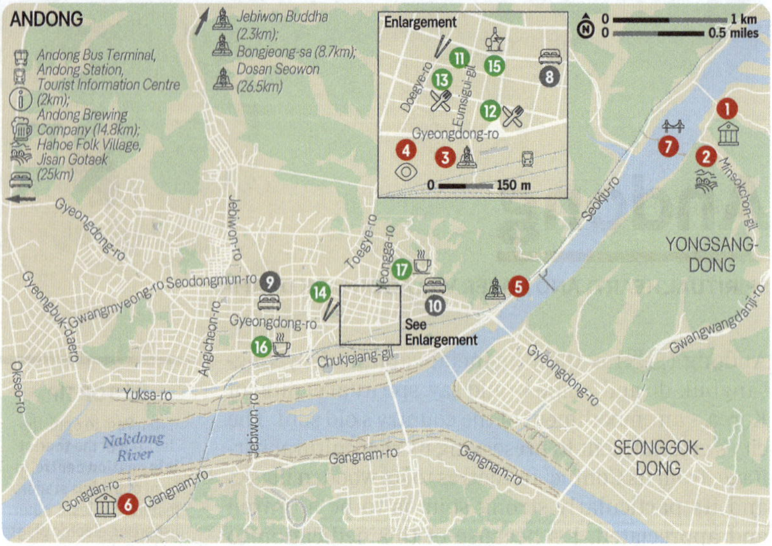

SIGHTS
1 Andong Folk Museum
2 Andong Folk Village
3 Five-Storey Pagoda
4 Kyobo Life Insurance Building
5 Seven-Storey Pagoda
6 Soju Museum
7 Weolyeonggyo Bridge

SLEEPING
8 Gotaya Guesthouse
9 Happy Q Motel
10 Haru the Guesthouse

EATING
11 Andong-Gwan
12 Malcop Burger
13 Mammoth Bakery
14 Sinseon Jjimdak

DRINKING & NIGHTLIFE
15 Daily Beer
16 ThanQ Coffee
17 Zitten

by the construction of Andong Dam in 1976. Take a look around the buildings, which range from peasants' thatched farmhouses to aristocrats' multi-courtyard mansions. There's also a **Folk Museum** *(free)* nearby (closed Mondays), with one large room filled with exhibits focusing on local history, faith, mask culture and traditional clothes.

Get a Taste of Andong's Spirit

A tour of the Soju Museum

Drastically different in flavour from Korea's common Jinro brand, Andong's heady 45% soju may not be to your taste, but its significance has been preserved with its state designation as an intangible cultural property. Located on the grounds of the Andong Soju Brewery, the **Soju Museum** *(free)* features displays with mostly Korean signage that detail the folk liquor's distilling process, drinking customs and ceremonial tables of accompanying foods. You can try a sample of the rice wine, and bottles (some fashioned after Andong's traditional masks) are available for purchase. Located in Andong's south, across the Nakdong-gang, the museum (closed Mondays) is a bit out of the way from the city's other usual attractions, and is best reached by taxi.

Learn About Old Texts & Printing

A walk through a Confucian Academy

Enveloped by mountains and perched over a river 25km northeast of town, the hoary UNESCO-listed **Dosan Seowon** *(andong.go.kr/dosanseowon; adult/child ₩2000/1000)* enjoys a tranquil setting for getting lost in introspection. Built in 1574 in honour of Togye Yi Hwang, one of Korea's most notable Confucian scholars, its quiet, contemplative halls are fronted by a giant willow tree, and the museum within contains a wide range of Confucian texts and philosophical schemata.

Stand Before a Towering Buddha

Ancient religious rock carvings

It's worth travelling 6km northeast of the train station to Icheon-dong, where the body of the standing **Jebiwon Buddha** *(free)*, also called the Maaeyeorae Ipsang, is carved into a granite rock more than 10m high. His 2.5m head is carved out of a separate rock placed on top, a technique typical during the Goryeo dynasty. Emerging from the tall greenery, it's an impressive, stark sight to behold.

Go on a Pagoda Tour

Five- and seven-storey brick structures

Search out the Unheung-dong **Five-Storey Pagoda**, constructed of brick and dating back to the unified Silla period. Hidden away in a small plot, next to a car park near the old train station, it's a most elegant pagoda and in a good state of preservation. Nearby stand the remains of two 2.6m-tall stone pillars that were used to support a flagpole for Buddhist flags. Both indicate this is the site of a long-vanished temple.

The Five-Storey Pagoda is a taster for what's to come – the Sinse-dong **Seven-Storey Pagoda**. Walk east along the river about 25 minutes and you'll come to this beauty, the oldest and largest brick pagoda in Korea. Dating to the 8th century and rising almost 17m in height, the pagoda stands at the former site of Beopheung-sa and is the only surviving part of the temple. Note that the finial – at least the one that is believed to have once topped it – is missing.

THE HISTORY OF ANDONG JJIMDAK

Given Andong's focus on cultural tradition, the city's most famous dish is not as old as you might think. In truth, *jjimdak* has a surprisingly short history, originating in the 1970s when Andong Traditional Market's chicken sellers were brainstorming ways to bring new appeal to their poultry. The soy sauce–based *galbi* grilled ribs sauce came to mind, due to its already established popularity. So they brought the two together, braising chicken in a mixture made with soy sauce, water, sugar, mirin, sesame oil, garlic, ginger and ground black pepper to create the representative dish of Andong we know today. While *jjimdak* restaurants can be found across the city (and beyond), they're clustered along Jjimdak Alley inside Andong Traditional Market.

EATING IN ANDONG: OUR PICKS

Mammoth Bakery: Serving good espresso and pastries, a local favourite since 1974. If the weather is nice, enjoy your treats on the outdoor patio. *8.30am-10pm* ₩

Andong-Gwan: Bulgogi, bibimbap, boiled dumplings and other tasty dishes at a traditional corner restaurant, washed down with soju or *makgeolli*. *11am-8pm* ₩

Malcop Burger: Hip burger joint where the young converge to munch on zesty, well-made Aussie-style burgers with top-quality patties and fries. *11.30am-3pm & 5-9pm* ₩₩

Sinseon Jjimdak: Tasty Andong *jjimdak* along Jjimdak Alley inside Andong Traditional Market. *10am-10pm* ₩₩

ANDONG'S MASK TRADITION

In late September and early October, the **Andong Mask Dance Festival** *(maskdance.com)* takes centre stage, bringing the region's 800-year-old tradition – the commoners' mask drama Hahoe Byeolsingut Talnorii – together with other mask traditions from all over the world. In Hahoe Folk Village (p248), dancers wearing the traditional wooden *tal* put on rousing performances to the awe of crowds. In central Andong, by the old train station, Korean and international dances showcase the cultural diversity and shared humanity of masks, while various contests challenge competitors to delightful 'mask offs'. During the festival, there's also a masked EDM party, fireworks and an opportunity to learn mask dance.

KEITMA/SHUTTERSTOCK

Weolyeonggyo Bridge

Moon Gaze at Weolyeonggyo Bridge

A stunning walk across the Nakdong River

The longest pedestrian-only bridge in South Korea, the 387m-long, partly wooden **Weolyeonggyo Bridge** spanning the Nakdong River features a pavilion at its midpoint. In the daytime, it's a nice route to the Andong Folk Museum (p244) on the far side of the water, but it's a spectacle at night, when strings of illuminated lanterns make it a particularly stunning place to go moon gazing. Weolyeonggyo means 'Moonlight Bridge', after all.

Stand by Korea's Oldest Wooden Building

13th-century architecture at Bongjeong-sa

Andong's largest temple, **Bongjeong-sa**, is most famous for its main hall, the Geungnakjeon, which is presumed to be the oldest wooden building in Korea. Based on documentation discovered during its 1972 reconstruction, the hall dates back to the early 1200s, during the Goryeo dynasty.

DRINKING IN ANDONG: OUR PICKS

Andong Brewing Company: Far west of the city centre, this brewery offers tours to taste its award-winning seasonal and artisanal ales. *10am-noon & 1-5pm*

Daily Beer: Craft beer, good service and bar snacks to soak up hoppy flavours, including – if you're so inclined – deep-fried spam. *5pm-2am*

Zitten: (질은) Ground-floor cafe, basement cultural space and a rooftop with city views – the place where Andong's young come to pursue arts and movie screenings. *noon-11pm Tue-Sun*

ThanQ Coffee: (땡큐커피) Sunlit, wood-furnished cafe with a range of brews and lattes – the vanilla latte with oatmeal, pecan and pumpkin seeds is a house staple. *11am-9pm Wed-Sun*

Beyond Andong

See one of Korea's best preserved folk villages, clamber along a cliff, creep into a cave and find one-of-a-kind ceramic wares.

An hour west of Andong lies its most celebrated sight, Hahoe Folk Village, possibly the best-preserved such village in Korea. Beyond it, past mountains and rivers, before Gyeongsang-do gives way to Chungcheong-do, is Mungyeong, a small city endowed with rich clay soil that led to its heritage as a ceramics centre.

Andong's north and southeast are swathed in pristine parkland – Cheongnyangsan Provincial Park and Juwangsan National Park – the rocky terrain of which makes for excellent hiking routes through gorges, past waterfalls and into caves, while studded with small temples along the way. Often it can feel like you're all alone, but with any luck you'll see an otter, protected Eurasian flying squirrel, or one of the other 900-plus wildlife species that make their home here.

Places

GETTING AROUND

From Andong, it's possible to reach its surroundings by bus, but transfers make the journeys slow and inefficient, and timetables can often be inaccurate. If you can, rent a car – it's two to four times faster to drive. Within Mungyeong's centre, local buses are good. If you want to visit artists' workshops in the countryside, though, drive or take a taxi.

Juwangsan National Park

TIME FROM ANDONG: 1HR

Gorges, caves and waterfalls

Far to the east of Andong, among the Baekdu mountains and reaching almost to the coast, the 106-sq-km **Juwangsan National Park** is dominated by impressive limestone pinnacles that seem to appear from nowhere. Splendid valleys, sublime gorges, caves, waterfalls and cliff walks also feature. Greeting visitors just inside the entrance, like a gateway to the world within, is **Daejeon-sa**, a small, noble temple built in 672 CE and rebuilt 1000 years later.

The popular trail from Daejeon-sa to the 720m peak of Juwangsan takes around 1¼ hours. It can be followed by trekking along the ridge to Kaldeunggogae, from where you can make your way back down to Daejeon-sa (about 1¾ hours) via Hurimaegi (50 minutes), a picturesque valley of trees and a creek straddled by a wooden bridge. On the descent, you can detour to the cave of **Juwanggul**, the legendary place where King Zhou hid – and then was killed. It's accessed by a path that passes the hermitage of **Juwang-am**.

For those wanting to stay overnight in the park, there's a *minbak* (private homes with rooms for rent) village opposite the **Juwangsan bus terminal** with a large number of accommodation choices and a wide choice of restaurants.

If you're a snow bunny visiting in the winter, don't miss **Cheongsong Eoreumgol Valley**, a short drive south from

continued on p250

STOCK FOR YOU/SHUTTERSTOCK

TOP EXPERIENCE

Hahoe Folk Village

A UNESCO World Heritage site, Hahoe Folk Village (하회마을) is the region's most outstanding attraction, located 28km west of Andong. Arrive early in the morning and the mystical beauty creates the illusion that you are in Joseon times. The name Hahoe (하회 – pronounced 'ha hway') means 'River Returning', a reflection of the village's position at a looping bend in the Nakdong River.

DON'T MISS

- Hahoe World Mask Museum
- Mask Dance performance
- Buyongdae Cliff
- Hahoe Marketplace
- Mansongjeong pine forest
- Byeongsan Seowon
- Goddess Samsin Tree

What to Expect from the Village

Some Korean folk villages can seem artificial, but Hahoe, the historic home of the Pungsan Ryu clan, has more than 200 residents, 70% of whom are said to be descendants of the first family members who lived here more than 600 years ago. A place to commune with the traditional fabric of old Korea, Hahoe is a magnificent constellation of centuries-old homes so authentic you'd swear you'd been transported to the Joseon dynasty.

Walk down the dirt roads and be rewarded with a glimpse of enchantment and the gentle rhythms of countryside village

PRACTICALITIES

● hahoe.or.kr ● adult/children ₩5000/2500 ● 9am-5.30pm (last admission) Apr-Sep, to 4.30pm Oct-Mar life. Pass by small garden plots and old pavilions backdropped by mountains, riverbank escarpments and fields stretching to the horizon. Search out the sacred **Goddess Samsin Tree** at the heart of Hahoe, the **Presbyterian Church** with its brick spire on the edge, and the Confucian academy of **Byeongsan Seowon** eastward. You can also wander through the **Mansong-jeong pine forest** along the river, then drive or taxi to **Buyong-dae Cliff** on the other side for a bird's-eye view of the village.

Mask Museum & Mask-Dance Drama

Near the ticket office is the **Hahoe World Mask Museum** *(admission included)*, featuring an intriguing collection of traditional Korean masks. While Andong's variety, carved from alder wood, may be the country's most famous, there are many other regional styles from around the peninsula. The museum's international exhibition also displays masks from around the world.

The Hahoe mask dance, Byeolsingut Talnori, takes place either in the performance hall near the village entrance or at an outdoor area facing the Buyongdae Cliff. Byeolsingut Talnori is a traditional dance drama created by the common folk to satirise the establishment. Characters wear masks representing social classes, including corrupt monks and the rich, some with bulging eyes and crooked mouths. The conflicts among them are portrayed in amusing combinations of popular entertainment and shamanism. Accompanying the dance are the sounds of *nong-ak*, traditional percussive farmers' music.

Performances are held daily from March to December at 2pm, and weekends only in January and February.

Restaurants

Within Hahoe Marketplace, near the ticket office, a selection of small *sikdang* (restaurants) serve food such as Andong's famous *jjimdak* and mackerel. Among the many offering similar set menus, we recommend **Solbat Sikdang** (솔밭식당) for excellent *jjimdak* and *godeungeo gui* (grilled mackerel fish). Try to dine just before or after peak lunch hours, when tour groups flood restaurants en masse.

Overnight Stays

Booking overnight accommodation is a fantastic way to immerse yourself in the village experience, while offering the bonus of being able to enjoy Hahoe's quiet beauty before the crowds arrive and after they depart. See the list of *minbak* on the village's website (reserve by bank transfer), or check Airbnb for the smattering of listings.

The shuttle bus between the ticket office and the village entrance stops departing from the village at 7pm, but from the ticket office at 5.25pm, so if you plan to eat dinner in the marketplace, be prepared to walk the 1km back to your accommodation. Note that if you arrive by taxi to check in after 6pm, when the ticket office is closed, you won't have to pay the admission fee – though you also won't have access to the shuttle bus.

GETTING THERE & AROUND

Bus 210 (₩1500, 50 minutes, 12 daily) runs between Hahoe and Andong. The last bus back to Andong departs at 7.10pm. The shuttle bus between the Andong bus drop-off point, near the ticket office, and the village runs every 10 to 15 minutes along a 1km paved road. At the time of writing, the ferry across the river was suspended; plan on using a taxi to reach the stretches beyond.

TOP TIPS

- Visit an information centre for a handy map. One centre is by the ticket office; the other is at the village entrance.
- Note that Hahoe is a genuine community, with many private residences off-limits. Only visit the ones the information centre circles on the map for you.
- Keep track of your entrance ticket. You'll be asked to present it every time you take the shuttle bus to re-enter the village.
- In the busy warm-weather months, Hahoe attracts large crowds. Opt for the low season (December to March), or if traveling during the high season (June to August), avoid weekends.

GYEONGBUK'S FOOD FESTIVALS

Yeongdeok Snow Crab Festival: Shop the snow crab market and sample snow crab recipes. *February*

Yeongyang Wild Edible Greens Festival: A multiday celebration of foraging for *sannamul* (mountain greens). *May*

Bonghwa Sweetfish Festival: Fish for river *euneo* (sweetfish), partake in water fights and have your catches cooked up. *Late July to early August*

Ulleung-do Squid Festival: In the fishing village of Jeodong-ri, ride squid-catching boats and eat a variety of squid dishes. *August*

Uiseong Garlic Festival: Taste Uiseong's special native garlic, known for being extra spicy. *October*

Cheongsong Apple Festival: At this harvest extravaganza, go apple picking, make apple soap and drink apple alcohol. *November*

Cheongsong Eoreumgol Valley (p247), Juwangsan National Park

continued from p247
the park and accessed from Palgaksan-ro. At this UNESCO Geopark gorge, the temperature hovers around freezing, causing ice to repeatedly form and then melt down the rock face, creating a photogenic effect like white wax dripping down a candle – it's most beautiful when it's gleaming in sunshine.

Mungyeong

TIME FROM ANDONG: **1HR**

Pottering around

Well regarded for its expertly crafted ceramics, with many galleries, workshops and classes tucked throughout the town, Mungyeong is a place every pottery enthusiast will want to visit. The city of 70,000 people is home to a long history of traditional kiln sites that fire *buncheongsagi* (gray-blue celadon ceramics). Visit the **Mungyeong Ceramic Museum** *(free)*, closed Mondays, to explore and learn about this unique art form. Book a tour to see an expert ceramicist at work, or partake in a pottery-wheel experience to try making a piece of your own.

If you can, visit in late April or early May, when the city's provincial park hosts the annual **Mungyeong Chasabal Festival**, a delightful celebration of its famous ceramic tea bowls, with contests, exhibitions, performances and more. Don't leave without sampling *omija*, the delicious, sweet-and-tart berry for which Mungyeong is known. Try it in tea, juice, dessert or wine.

Cheongnyangsan Provincial Park

TIME FROM ANDONG: **30MIN**

Twelve peaks

With tracks wandering along cliff precipices, Cheongnyangsan Provincial Park boasts spectacular views. In addition to the mountain of Cheongnyangsan, the summit of which is Changin-bong (870m), there are 11 other peaks, eight caves and a waterfall, Gwanchang Pokpo. It takes about 5½ hours to complete the 12.7km loop of all 12 peaks. Of the four other routes, the shortest is a 1½-hour round-trip walk to the park's main temple, **Cheongnyang-sa**, built in 663 CE and sitting in a steep valley below the cliffs.

Places We Love to Stay

₩ Budget ₩₩ Midrange ₩₩₩ Top End

Tongyeong

MAP P212

Jung Seop's Loft Friends **₩** Central hostel with clean two-person en-suite dorms, a spacious common area with a little cafe and a balcony. No breakfast is included, and it is often unstaffed, but it offers good value.

Motel Mu ₩ Friendly service and an excellent location make this motel a winner. Some rooms have a view of Gangguan harbour.

Mireuk Mireuk Beer Hostel (p211) **₩₩** Reminiscent of a healing retreat, with a unique Buddha-and-beer concept combining a 1st-floor pub with rooms above, shared bathrooms and a meditation space for guests. The owner is helpful and kind.

Local Stitch (p211) **₩₩** Industrial-chic rooms on the 3rd floor of this art space, with a large cafe on the ground floor and co-working and rotating exhibition area on the 2nd floor.

Jinju

S+ Motel ₩ Funky patterns and vibrant colours that manage to feel 'snazzy', not sleazy. Off the main road by the river, near the fortress.

Gyeongju

MAP P223

Pungdengi Hostel ₩ Just a few blocks from the ancient tomb complex, a high-value hostel with simple dormitory beds or private rooms, a spacious and stylish common area and free breakfast.

Doo-baki Guesthouse ₩ Social hostel run by a Korean motorcycle traveller, with en-suite dorms and private rooms, a large common room and a convivial atmosphere. A good breakfast is included, and a free welcome beer is available at the Doobaki Garage bar next door.

Friend Guesthouse ₩ Spotless dorms in this homey guesthouse run by a kind woman and her super-cute dog. There's a comfy common area, a kitchenette and the complimentary breakfast is substantial.

Blueboat Hostel Gyeongju **₩** Apartment-style hostel with dorm rooms spread around a cosy living room and common area with kitchen, free breakfast and a quiet, homey atmosphere.

Pohang

Chilseong Guesthouse ₩₩ A whole apartment on the 2nd floor of the Sevenstar Sailing headquarters, suitable for larger groups or families and within walking distance of Songdo's forest and sights.

Daegu

MAP P236

Empathy Guesthouse ₩ Run by the Center for North Korean Defectors *(nkpeople.or.kr)*, with part of the proceeds going to resettlement, this is a great place to stay with dormitories and private rooms, a rooftop terrace and a sociable lounge.

Dongseongro Zero Guesthouse ₩ Solid dorms-only hostel option in the midst of Dongseong-ro, the city's food and nightlife area. Within walking distance of the train station.

Andong

MAP P244

Gotaya Guesthouse ₩ Apartment hostel in a nondescript building near the old station, with male and female dorms and a twin room. There's a shared kitchen, a large terrace for relaxation, a simple breakfast included, free bicycles and a washing machine.

Haru the Guesthouse ₩ Set in an alley behind the Haru Hostel, these male and female four-bed dorms with clean en-suite toilets are excellent value. Brit-pop memorabilia hangs on the walls, there's a cosy common room and a kitchenette with a simple breakfast included.

Happy Q Motel ₩ Near Andong's traditional markets, a quality budget option run by a nice couple. Its large rooms feature a TV, computer and mini fridge, with a free basic breakfast until 9am.

Jisan Gotaek ₩₩ Drift off to sleep at this dreamy *hanok*, a registered historic site inside Hahoe, then awake the next day and slide open your mulberry paper door to witness the magic that is a tiny folk village coming to life in the morning.

Researched by
Marco Ferrarese

Jeolla-do

CULTURE, MYSTIC PEAKS & INFINITE ISLANDS

Korea's southwesternmost corner combines progressive, artistic cities with delicious food, ancient mountain temples and more beaches than you can see in a lifetime.

Also known as Honam, the region comprising the South Korean provinces of Jeollabuk-do, Jeollanam-do and Gwangju Metropolitan City has long played the role of Korea's renegade corner because of its recent political history – a possible reason why the region still sees few travellers, despite packing beauty and adventure in spades.

Those who come often just pass by its two main cities: Jeonju, the provincial capital of Jeollabuk-do, which boasts Korea's largest *hanok* (traditional wooden homes) village and is the birthplace of both the Joseon dynasty and Korea's most well-known culinary delight, bibimbap. A short train or bus ride to the south is Gwangju, a sprawling mega-city with a penchant for the arts and a turbulent, rebellious past – the May 18 Democratic Uprising against South Korea's military government in 1980, in which nearly 250,000 people participated. Looming watchful on the city's eastern flanks is 1187m-high Mudeungsan, where hikers flock to see the unique rock formations that earned the national park a UNESCO Global Geopark title.

JEFF1961 / IMAZINS/GETTY IMAGES

Little over an hour to the south, the country's southwestern coast fractures into hundreds of rocky islands and coves, many of which are protected under the largely unexplored Dadohae Haesang National Park. Mokpo and Suncheon are ideal cities to base yourself as you try to make sense of this mind-blowing maritime puzzle.

THE MAIN AREAS

JEONJU
Heritage, food culture and *hanok* village. p256

GWANGJU
Artistic mega-city proud of its turbulent past. p266

SUNCHEON
Quaint garden city hugging a serene bay. p276

JIRISAN NATIONAL PARK
Conquer mainland Korea's highest peak. p282

MOKPO
Coastal hikes, old-world charm and wriggling live octopus. p287

For places to stay in Jeolla-do see p297

PANWASIN SEEMALA/SHUTTERSTOCK

Left: Bibimbap; Above: Suncheon (p276)

Find Your Way

Blocked by the Deogyusan-Jirisan mountain range to the east, Jeolla-do is compact enough to tick off most main sights in a week, but the endless islands breaking off the southern and western coasts deserve a lifetime of exploration.

CAR

Renting a car helps maximise travel time to smaller towns and outlying sights – roads are excellent and GPS navigation works wonders. Use local buses or taxis in cities; parking is limited and expensive.

BUS

Frequent intercity buses connect major cities with outlying sights and even some of the remotest islands. In the countryside, departures are thin on the ground and you'll spend more time planning and waiting for the next connection.

Jeonju, p256
In the capital of Jeollabuk-do, a classy *hanok* village sits amid an amphitheatre of mountains and an array of food choices.

Jirisan National Park, p282
The South Korean mainland's highest mountain sits in the middle of a forested highland wonder that takes three days to hike.

Suncheon, p276
Lose yourself in the Suncheon Bay National Garden, hike across a river wetland and go back in time at a K-Drama film set.

Gwangju, p266
Learn about Korea's student uprising, visit mind-blowing art exhibits, go vintage at Penguin Village and then disappear into the mountains.

Mokpo, p287
Glance down at a Japanese-styled colonial old town as you swing by three coastal peaks on Korea's longest cable car.

SANGA PARK/SHUTTERSTOCK

Penguin Village (p270)

Plan Your Time

Base yourself in a city and hop between surrounding sights by bus or car, as most attractions are within two hours of each major centre.

Three-Day Jeolla Teaser

- Spend a day in chilled **Jeonju** (p256) and stay at a *hanok* home in the **Hanok Maeul** (p258). Next morning, catch a train to **Gwangju** (p266) and hop between museums, galleries and the **Penguin Village** (p270) in the city's southeast. On day three, get to **Suncheon** (p276) as early as possible, stroll the **National Garden** (p276) and catch sunset at **Suncheon Bay Wetlands** (p278).

A Week Between Mountains & Sea

- Don't leave Jeonju without visiting **Maisan Provincial Park** (p262), hiking past three temples and to the top of a 'female' mountain. Spend two days in **Gwangju** (p266), leaving one for the trails and temples of **Mudeungsan National Park** (p269). On your fifth day, see all you can in **Suncheon** (p276) before heading to **Mokpo** (p287) via Boseong's **Daehan Dawon Tea Plantation** (p286).

SEASONAL HIGHLIGHTS

SPRING

Flower festivals (p284) galore around Suncheon, while Seonunsan (p263) is ablaze with camellias. The **Jeonju International Film Festival** kicks off in May.

SUMMER

The weather can reach 30°C and is humid, with significant monsoon rains. The cooler bamboo forests of **Damyang** (p274) attract more visitors.

AUTUMN

In September, the **Gwangju Biennale** (p268) brings the art world to town. In October, check out the **Chungjang Street Festival of Recollection** (p271).

WINTER

Temperatures can reach freezing in most of the region, and December to February means snow – you can take to the ski slopes at **Muju** (p263).

Jeonju

HANOK ARCHITECTURE | FOOD GALORE | CITY WALKS

> **TOP TIP**
> Base yourself in the *hanok* village to be within walking distance of most sights. If you visit Jeonju on a day trip, the **Ohmokdae Tourist Information Centre** in the *hanok* village has free wi-fi, clean toilets, English-speaking staff and a free phone-charging station.

Set at the heart of Jeollabuk-do, provincial capital Jeonju (전주) is well known for its super-duper-touristy, picture-perfect *maeul* (village) featuring more than 700 *hanok* (traditional wooden homes), one of the largest concentrations in the country. It's typically visited as a rushed half-day trip between high-speed train connections to and from Seoul, but this storied city of 1300 years deserves more time – at least to try some of its delicious food.

Birthplace of the bibimbap (a mix of rice, egg, meat and veggies with chilli sauce), Jeonju was declared a UNESCO City of Gastronomy in 2012. If you can splurge, modern re-enactments of the Royal Cuisine of the Joseon dynasty are a deep dive into Korea's most authentic culinary traditions. Don't forget arty-sy villages, pagodas and charming viewpoints – at dusk, the sunset paints the cobblestone lanes and slanted roofs a golden hue as barbecue smoke from the grills curls into the air like magical strokes.

Take a Trip Down Memory Lane

MAP P257

Discover Jeonju's far-reaching history

Most of Jeonju's historic sights are clustered right to the west of its *hanok* village in the southeastern part of the city. The grand **Pungnammun** *(free)* gate, the southernmost of four city gates built in 1734 and restored to its present grandeur,

> **GETTING AROUND**
> Being a provincial capital, Jeonju can be easily reached by direct buses from most Korean cities. The **intercity** and **express** bus stations are a three-minute walk apart and 10 minutes by taxi (or a short bus ride) from the Pungnammun gate that marks the beginning of Jeonju Hanok Maeul. Walking is the best way to get around the main sights. Bus 79 connects the express bus terminal with **Jeonju's KTX train station** at least twice an hour. From here, southbound trains go to Namwon, Guryegu, Suncheon and Yeosu on the Jeolla Line, while northbound trains head to Seoul's Yongsan station via Iksan.

HIGHLIGHTS
1 Hanok Maeul

SIGHTS
2 Cheongyeonru Gazebo
3 Choi Myung Hee Literature Museum
4 Fan Culture Centre
5 Gaekridan-gil Road
6 Gyeonggijeon
7 Gyodong Art Museum
8 Jaman Mural Village
9 Jeolla Gamyoung
10 Jeondong Catholic Church
11 Jeonju Kimchi Culture Centre
12 Jeonju Korean Liquor Museum
13 Omok-dae
14 Pungnammun Gate
15 Royal Portrait Museum
16 Sehoak-dong Art Village

SLEEPING
17 Blueboat Hostel Jeonju
18 Lahan Hotel Jeonju
19 NeaRest Guesthouse
20 Seunggwangje

EATING
21 Gajok Hoegwan
22 Gyeonggijeon Jungang Charcoal
23 Hyundai-ok
24 Namno Galbi
25 Veteran

DRINKING & NIGHTLIFE
26 Cafe Jeokyo Soom Shida
27 Dopamine Ground
28 Haengwon
29 Jeonil Super
30 Jeonmang
31 Kko-ji-tta-ppong Cafe
32 Nomadic Beer Garden
33 Seohak Art Space

SHOPPING
see 26 Vintage

INFORMATION
34 Ohmokdae Tourist Information Centre

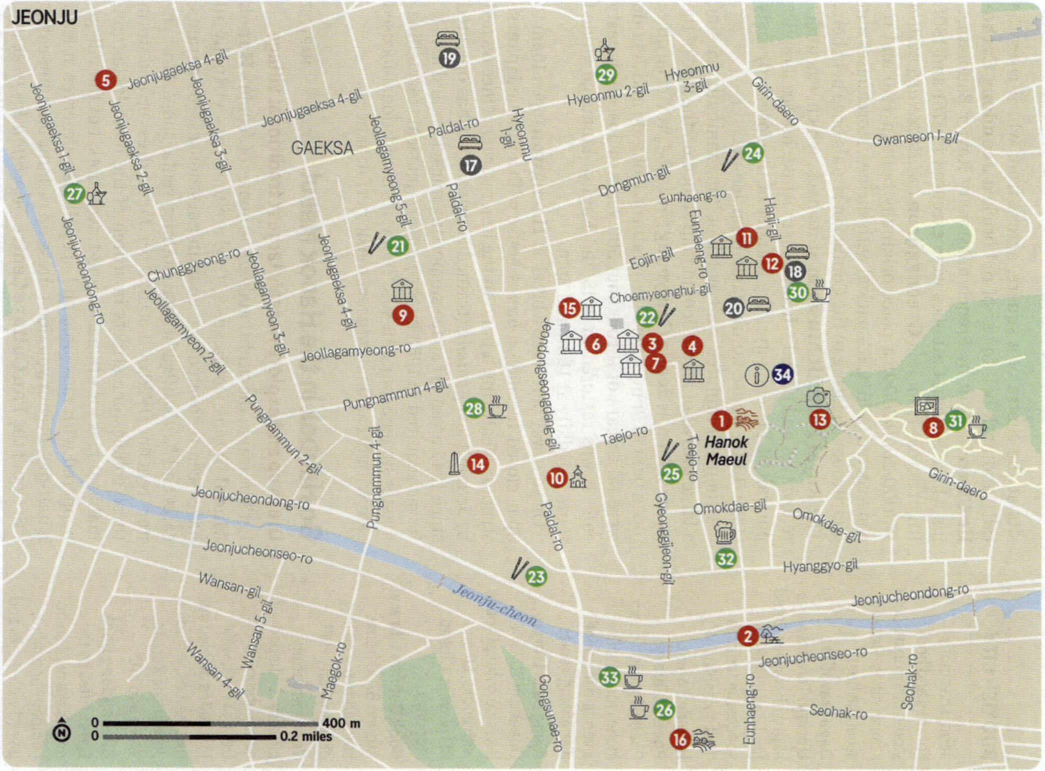

BOOKISH CITY

Jeonju has more libraries and bookstores than most South Korean cities. Here are six of the best.

Daga Travellers Library: Three storeys high with travel-related books and reading spaces, including a 'foot splash' pool.

Haksan Forest Poetry Library: Poetry-focused cabin in the woods with a vending machine dispensing verses.

Ajung Lake Library: Opened in 2025, a lakeside cultural space with books, LP and CD players. Closed Mondays.

Book Column Library: Around 8700 books stacked to the ceiling of Jeonju City Hall.

Yeonhwajeong Library: L-shaped *hanok* library in Deokjin Park, with 1850 titles divided into five themes, including Jeonju, the Korean Wave and art.

Cheongdong Book Cafe: Titles by the namesake publishing company and more, paired with drinks and seating.

sits at the centre of a square, across from which rises the tall, landmark bell tower of red-bricked **Jeondong Catholic Church**. Built by French missionary Xavier Baudounet, it's where Korean Catholics were executed in 1781 and 1801. Right across from it is **Gyeonggijeon** *(adult/teenager/child ₩3000/2000/1000)*, a place originally built in 1410 and reconstructed in 1614. It's packed with shrines, storehouses and guardrooms relating to the Confucian rituals once held here. The **Royal Portrait Museum** at its back, which was under renovation and closed when we last visited, houses a replica portrait of Yi Seong-gye, the founder of the Joseon dynasty (1392–1910), whose family came from Jeonju.

A couple of minutes' walk north of Pungnammun, passing a large **mural** of an old Jeonju map etched on the side of the police station, is **Jeolla Gamyoung** *(free)*, the provincial office (open 9am to 9pm) where the affairs of Jeolla-do and Jeju-do were taken care of throughout 500 years of Joseon-dynasty rule. It was restored in 2018 and English-language guided tours run daily at 11am and 2pm.

On your way here, take a break at **Haengwon** (open 10am to 8pm, closed Tuesday), a *hanok* house with a unique Japanese structure featuring a pond in the inner garden. Once owned by Jeonju's last *gisaeng* (trained courtesan), it has operated since 1942 as an art space supporting musicians and artists. It was acquired in 1983 by the *pansori* (musical storytelling) master singer Seong Jun-suk. Today, it's a traditional-focused cafe with occasional *pansori* music performances.

Go Hanbok in the Hanok Maeul

MAP P257

Dress up and explore Korea's largest traditional village

Let's be frank: the traditional *hanok* homes of Jeonju's **Hanok Maeul** *(hanok.jeonju.go.kr; free)* are touristy – virtually all have been renovated and contain guesthouses, restaurants, cafes and *hanbok* (traditional clothing) rental shops. Most visitors rent one *(₩20,000-30,000 per 3hr)* to dress up and storm these cobblestone streets in search of the most Instagrammable angles for dramatic time-travel shots, but the village, peppered with museums and art galleries, deserves at least a half-day, even if you don't dress up or hunt for a hip cafe.

Seek out the **Fan Culture Centre** *(jeonjufan.kr; free)*, promoting the heritage and cultural identity of traditional fans from Jeonju, the **Choi Myung Hee Literature Museum**

COOL CAFES & BARS IN JEONJU

MAP P257

Kko-ji-tta-ppong Cafe: (꼬지따뽕) Bright-pink and yellow walls, Barbies, a lovely terrace and a life-sized ET doll make this Jaman Mural Village cafe unique. *9.30am-8.30pm* ₩

Jeonmang: The Hanok Maeul's most popular cafe dominates the rooftop of a four-storey building, offering some of the best views and brews in town. *9am-11pm* ₩₩

Nomadic Beer Garden: The only craft brewery in town serves perfect IPAs in a garden setting, plus vegan- and vegetarian-friendly snacks and finger food. *3pm-midnight* ₩₩

Dopamine Ground: Youth-centric bar and restaurant serving good pizzas, cheese platters and Western-style finger food. Live bands on weekends and a summer-perfect rooftop bar. *5pm-3am* ₩₩

JEONJU CITY WALK

Learn about the city's history and contemporary cultural revival on this walking tour in and around the hanok village.

START	END	LENGTH
Pungnammun	Jaman Mural Village	3.4km; 1½hr

Start at the grand 1 **Pungnammun** (p256) gate and go north, where 2 **Haengwon** (p258), a long-standing cultural centre owned by Jeonju's last *gisaeng*, makes for an atmospheric traditional tea break. Walking north, notice the large 3 **mural of old Jeonju** (p258) on the western wall of the Wansan police station as you make your way to 4 **Jeolla Gamyoung** (p258), the former Joseon-era administration hall of Jeolla and Jeju provinces. A short walk west brings you to the impressive 5 **Daga Travellers Library** (p258), stacked to the roof with travel literature and coffee-table books. Retrace your steps back towards the *hanok* village, checking out the orderly stalls of 6 **Nambu-sijang** (p261) before passing by the facade of 7 **Jeondong Cathedral** (p258) and spending some time exploring the pavilions of the stunning 8 **Gyeonggijeon** (p258) shrine. Enter the Hanok Maeul and lose yourself in its small lanes, checking out the 9 **Fan Culture Centre** (p258) and nearby 10 **Gyodong Art Museum** (p260) before making your way to the wooden boardwalk that climbs to the historic 11 **Omok-dae** (p260) viewpoint, where the outlook above the village is splendid, especially at sunset. From here, cross the overpass bridge to the next hill, where the bohemian 12 **Jaman Mural Village** (p260) has fading wall art and a few quirky cafes.

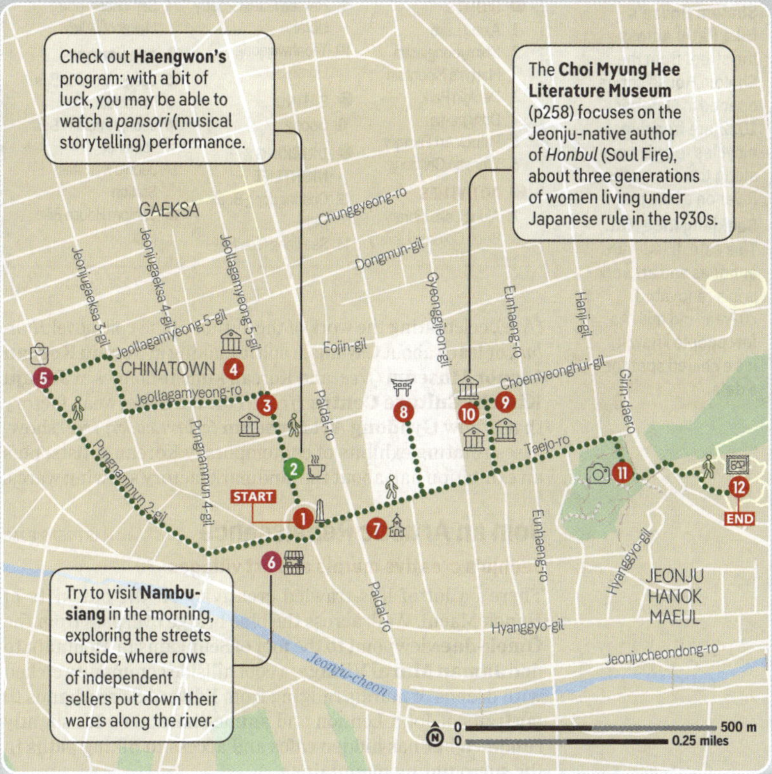

JEONJU'S SECRET HANGOUT SPOTS

Kim Yurim, Jeonju-based flight attendant for Cathay Pacific, names her favourite Jeonju places. *@yes_n_yes*

Jeonil Super: This mini-mart has a seating area where young people flock to order beer, rolled omelettes and grilled pollock. It's different from any other nightlife spot I've seen in Korea.

Shalom House's Bike Path: Across the street from the Shalom House shrine, opened in October 2022, are free rental bicycles to strike out along the Jeonjuchun River on a bike path.

Saekjang Rice Mill: This cafe, filled with antiques and artwork, is in a renovated 70-year-old mill. As few people know it, it's a chilled spot for a date.

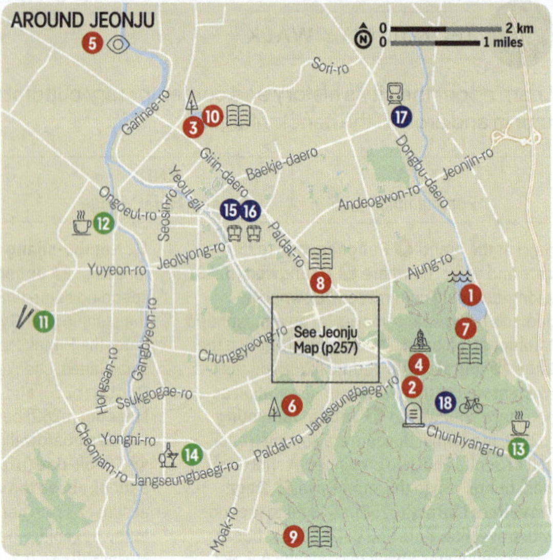

SIGHTS
1 Ajung Lake
2 Chimyeongjasan Martyr's Mountain
3 Deokjin Park
4 Dongga-sa
5 Palbok Art Factory
6 Wansan Chilbong

ACTIVITIES
7 Ajung Lake Library
8 Book Column Library
9 Haksan Forest Poetry Library
10 Yeonhwajeong Library

EATING
11 Goong

DRINKING & NIGHTLIFE
12 Cheongdong Book Cafe
13 Saekjang Rice Mill
14 Samcheon-dong Makgeolli Alley

TRANSPORT
15 Jeonju Express Bus Terminal
16 Jeonju Intercity Bus Terminal
17 Jeonju KTX Train Station
18 Shalom House Bike Path

(free), celebrating the work of the author of the epic novel *Honbul*, or learn about Gayang-ju spirit-making at **Jeonju Korean Liquor Museum** *(free)* and Korean kimchi-nomics at **Jeonju Kimchi Culture Centre** *(free)*. Former underwear factory that is now **Gyodong Art Museum** *(gdart.co.kr; free)* showcases rotating exhibits of contemporary Korean artists, plus an exhibition hall about the landmark factory's sewing wares.

Join an Artistic Renaissance

MAP P257 & P260

Jeonju's creative murals and art villages

There's a lot of less-trawled creativity on the outskirts of Hanok Maeul. Walk across the blue bridge overpass from the **Omok-dae** viewpoint to the foot of Seungamsan Mountain to find **Jaman Mural Village**, a cool hillside community etched with dozens of murals ranging from Edward Scissorhands to portraits of John Lennon and anime characters. It's slightly rundown but has hidden cafes and access to hiking paths in the surrounding mountains.

Walk a bit further south of the Hanok Maeul and beyond the wooden **Cheongyeonru Gazebo** overlooking the river to reach **Sehoak-dong Art Village**. Formerly a suburb for school teachers, these alleys now swell with art galleries, studios and little cafes. Start on Seohak-ro at **Seohak Art Space**, a combination of cafe, art gallery and guesthouse. Then turn south on Seohak 3-gil, the 'village' proper, where painter Lee Jeok Yo runs the side-by-side **Vintage** secondhand shop and the unmissable **Cafe Jeokyo Soom Shida**. This quirky throwback cafe has crackling vinyl, stacks of books and a mean espresso machine, while Lee's studio and gallery are at the back of the shop, which is open 11am to 6pm.

It's also worth taking an hour-long bus detour (numbers 684, 644 and 1002) or a taxi from the Hanok Maeul to **Palbok Art Factory** *(palbokart.kr; free)*, an old cassette-tape factory turned cultural art centre. Exhibits, an art studio and the poplar-tree-lined Palbok Yaho Art Playground make it worth the trek. It's open 10am to 5.30pm (closed Mondays).

Eat Around the Clock

MAP P260

Revel in classic foodie haunts from dawn to dusk

Jeonju's food is praised around Korea for good reason. Get an early headstart at **Nambu-sijang**, a market that opened in 1905 and is a short walk from the Pungnammun (p256) gate. It comprises about 800 stores selling anything from fruits and vegetables to dried fish, silk and general goods. It has dozens of little restaurants tucked among the stalls, mostly open for breakfast. Try the ever-packed and popular **Hyundai-ok** (6am to 2pm), the original Nambu Market shop of this countrywide franchise, dishing up delicious bean-sprout soup since 1979.

For a special experience, Jeonju is the place to try the royal *hanjeongsik*, a full-course, commercialised version of the Goryeo and Joseon dynasties' *baekban* (set meals). **Goong** (noon to 9pm), curated by master chef Yoo In-ja, a disciple of the late Hwang Hye-seong, a court-food expert, is a good choice. Think beef and vegetables wrapped in pumpkin wheat crepes, *duteop-tteok* (a type of rice cake), fermented fish and royal hot pot.

At night, let your hair down at **Samcheon-dong Makgeolli Alley**, where two-person Korean set meals are served with kettles containing 2.5L of *makgeolli* (milky rice wine). Dishes include squid salad, fried pancakes, kimchi and tofu. To browse trendy cafes, go to hip **Gaekridan-gil Rd**, which is also the site for the Jeonju International Film Festival.

JEONJU'S HEALING PLACES

Omok-dae: A hill viewpoint above the Hanok Maeul where a pavilion commemorates General Yi Seonggye's 1380 victory over Japanese pirates.

Deokjin Park: Quiet walking paths surrounding a lake that fills with thousands of lotus flowers in July.

Wansan Chilbong: Garden with deep-pink double cherry blossoms, red azaleas in spring and red maple leaves in autumn.

Dongga-sa and Chimyeongjasan Martyr's Mountain: Hike to a secluded Buddhist temple next to a graveyard for Jeonju's Catholic martyrs, dominated by a cross and a rock resembling the Virgin Mary.

Ajung Lake: Large former reservoir turned outdoor park for relaxed walks, even at night.

EATING IN JEONJU: OUR PICKS

MAP P257

Veteran: Jeonju dining stalwart for delicious *mandu* (만두, dumplings) and noodle dishes such as *kalguksu* (칼국수). *9am-8pm* W

Gajok Hoegwan: (가족회관) Since 1979 three generations have honed their tasty bibimbap recipe in this lovely *hanok*-style eatery. *10.30am-8pm* WW

Gyeonggijeon Jungang Charcoal: No-frills, authentic Korean barbecue joint with floor or table seating, charcoal burners and plenty of hungry locals. *11.30am-3pm & 4.30-9.30pm* WW

Namno Galbi: Specialising in pork *galbi* stew or boiled ribs in sweet-and-sour *gochujang* seasoning and veggies since 1972. *11am-10pm* WW

Beyond Jeonju

A green adventure playground surrounds Jeonju: hike to temple-studded mountains, ski inside a national park and drive to a string of jagged islands.

Places

GETTING AROUND

There is always a bus connecting either of Jeonju's two bus terminals to most Jeollabuk-do towns, but once there, departures to the sights are sporadic and require some tight planning – consider overnighting outside of Jeonju. A rental car is the best option to optimise travel times and see more than one sight a day. In the warmer months, keen cyclists will enjoy moving about on the network of smaller roads and well-developed bike lanes.

Sitting at the centre of Jeollabuk-do province, Jeonju is surrounded by parkland, meaning that if you tire of its old-world charms, food and artistic nooks, you can stretch your legs on any number of fantastic hiking trails. Favourites are the twin peaks of Maisan Provincial Park near Jinan, Deogyusan National Park near Muju (the site of Korea's longest-established ski resort), Moaksan Provincial Park and the gentle hills of Seonunsan Provincial Park. To the west, a sprinkling of islands connected by roads and bridges makes up the green Seonyudo, a bounty of beaches and hiking trails with ocean views. The coast has sandy beaches on the West Sea, from where you can catch ferries to sleepy islands.

Jinan

TIME FROM JEONJU: **45MIN**

Hike a female mountain

The name of **Maisan Provincial Park** (마이산도립공원, Horse Ears Mountain) refers to two extraordinary rocky peaks standing next to each other as they appear from the town of Jinan. The east peak is Sutmaisan (Male Maisan; 678m), which is closed to visitors, while the west peak, equipped with a 1.7km-long boardwalk, is Ammaisan (Female Maisan; 685m). Both 'ears' are made of conglomerate rock, which is rare in Korea.

The best way to approach the park is from its southern entrance, passing by the temple of **Gogeumdang-sa** and a scenic pond with duck-shaped pedal boats for rental. In April, the cherry trees along this road burst into dramatic blossom. A second temple, **Tap-sa** *(adult/youth/child ₩3000/2000/1000)*, open 9am to 6pm, sits at the base of the female ear. It has a sculptural garden of 80 stone towers or pinnacles piled up by Buddhist mystic Yi Kapmyong (1860–1957). Before the Ammaisan climb starts, a third temple, **Eunsu-sa**, is found under the male ear. Note the majestic 15m-tall Chinese pear tree next to it, which is said to be 650 years old – you can strike the giant prayer drum to get well wishes. Near the southern entrance, there's a **campground** *(maisancamp.org; per night ₩20,000, plus ₩3000 per person)*.

To reach the mountain, take a bus from Jeonju Intercity Bus Terminal to Jinan (roughly every 15 to 30 minutes from 7.10am to 9.30pm) and change to a bus to either Northern

PKPHOTOGRAPH/SHUTTERSTOCK

Deogyusan National Park, Muju

Maisan (roughly hourly from 7.40am to 12.30pm, then every two hours until 6.30pm) or Southern Maisan (9.30am, 1.30pm and 5.20pm) entrances.

Muju

TIME FROM JEONJU: 1¼HR

Hiking trails & ski slopes

Deogyusan National Park is a hiker's playground and home to Muju Deogyusan ski resort. Gucheon-dong, a small tourist village, marks the start of the park's best hike. The trail (two hours one way, 6km) follows the river and valley past 20 beauty spots to a small temple, **Baengnyeon-sa**, and finishes with a steep, 1½-hour ascent of 1614m **Hyangjeok-bong**, the fourth-tallest mountain in Korea. Deogyusan is also home to **Muju Deogyusan Resort** *(mdysresort.com; lift and gondola tickets adult/child ₩97,000/78,000)* with the highest altitude and longest slope (6.1km) in the country. A **gondola** *(adult/child return ₩22,000/17,000)* carries passengers up 1520m-high Seolcheon-bong, from where a 600m boardwalk reaches Hyangjeok-bong. Free shuttle buses to the ski resort leave from the **Muju intercity bus terminal**, while Gucheon-dong-bound buses go to the national park's entrance.

Namwon

TIME FROM JEONJU: 1HR

Enter Korea's most epic love story

Originally known as Gwangtongnu, the **Gwanghallu Garden** *(gwanghallu.or.kr; adult/youth/child ₩4000/2000/1500)* by the Seimjin River in Namwon presents a collection of Joseon-era pavilions set amid manicured lawns and water ponds surrounded by ancient trees. The drawcard is **Gwanghallu Pavilion**, built by Hwang Hui Jeongseung in 1419 during the reign of the Joseon dynasty's King Sejong. It's famous

BEST REGIONAL CLIMBS & HIKES

Byeonsan-bando National Park: The only Korean park mixing mountains and sea, with beaches and the dramatic Chaeseokgang Cliff.

Daedunsan Provincial Park: Climb to craggy 878m-high Daedunsan via a 50m-long cable bridge or take a cable car.

Moaksan Provincial Park: Hike in the shadow of 794m Moaksan or pay respects at Geumsan-sa temple.

Seonunsan Provincial Park: Quiet hiking trails surround the 500-year-old Zen temple Seonun-sa and disappear into the verdant forest.

Yonggwolsan Sky Road: This wooden deck staircase is built on the spectacular rock face of 646m Yonggwolsan, with breathtaking views of the Seomjingang River.

THE WORLD'S LONGEST DYKE

Measuring 33.9km in length, **Jeollabuk-do Saemangeum Sea Wall** runs between two headlands to the southeast of Gunsan, dividing the former Saemangeum estuary from the Yellow Sea. Works started in 1991 to create 400 sq km of farmland and a freshwater reservoir. Since then, the South Korean government has spent around US$1.75 billion on construction, an additional US$192 million to strengthen the dyke and US$1.15 billion to transform the tidal flats into agricultural land. Even if there's still plenty of water in the estuary, the enclosure greatly affected 401 sq km of mudflats, contributing to the decline in numbers of migratory birds that once stopped here, causing coastal erosion and yearly red tides inside the dyke.

as the place where Lee Mong-ryong and Lady Chunhyang, two lovers from a well-known Korean folk story, first met. The **Chunhyang-sa**, built in the compound in 1920, houses a portrait of the heroine. Across the road from the southern entrance, the **Seung-Wolgyo Bridge** over the Seimjin River leads to a twin waterfall and the hiking trails, viewpoints and Ferris wheel of **Chunhyang Theme Park**. Cycling enthusiasts can strike along a 32km riverside course.

The garden is open until about midnight and manned from 8am to 6pm. You won't be charged if entering after 6pm.

Gunsan

TIME FROM JEONJU: **50MIN**

Driveable islands

Seonyudo is part of a giant green park of four major interconnected islands (Sinsido, Munyeodo, Bangchukdo and Maldo) in the middle of the Gogunsan archipelago, all tethered by bridges and roads to 33.9km-long Jeollabuk-do Saemangeum Sea Wall, the world's longest sea wall. Seonyudo's main attraction is a long, thin strip of land, **Myeongsa-simni Beach**, where locals take to the surrounding tidal flats to collect shellfish.

If it's all too sedate, the 700m-long **Seonyu Sky SUN Line** *(adult/child ₩20,000/16,000)*, the longest over-ocean zip line in Korea (open 9am to 5.30pm), flies at 45m above sea level to nearby Solsum island. On the beach's northern end are trails to **Mangju-bong**, a low-rise twin peak (152m), and the **Dae-bong trail**, climbing 1km to a viewpoint. To the west, on **Jangjado**, another boardwalk snakes to the top of 142m **Daejang-bong** for incredible views over the archipelago.

For something less strenuous, bikes *(₩10,000 per day)* or scooters *(₩30,000 for two hours)* can be rented near the information booth on Jangjado, while **Saemangeum Cruise** *(sunyoudotour.com)* runs island-hopping boat tours. From Gunsan's train station, take bus 7 or 83 to the **Bieung Port** stop and transfer to bus 99 (every 40 minutes), stopping at Saemangeum Sq, Sinsido, Muyeodo, Seonyudo and Jangjado.

EATING AROUND JEONJU: OUR PICKS

Binhaewon: The country's oldest Chinese restaurant is in Gunsan. Although it looks drab, it serves well-deserved Korean-Chinese delicacies. *10am-9pm Tue-Sun* ₩

Choga Jeongdam: A reputable option for multidish Korean meals near Maisan in Jinan. *9am-9pm* ₩₩

Namdo Bapsang: Popular spot for shellfish noodles, fried flat fish and fish pancakes near the northern end of Seonyudo beach. *10am-7.30pm* ₩₩

Kongsure Tofu: Delicious *sundubu jjigae* (spicy soft tofu and pork stew) in kimchi-based sauce in Muju. Large four-people pots cost ₩39,000. *9am-9pm* ₩₩

MOAKSAN MOUNTAIN TRAVERSE

Cross Moaksan Provincial Park from west to east, passing a historic temple and bagging the 794m-high peak on the way.

START	END	LENGTH
Geumsan-sa car park	Jeonbuk Province Art Museum	8.3km; 4-5hr

Take bus 79 from Jeonju's centre to the last stop (45m) and start walking from the Geumsan-sa car park along a paved road. Grab a map at the information centre, where some English is spoken. After 1.1km, the 1 **Geumsan-sa** temple complex, built in the first year of King Beop of Baekje (599), is beautifully set north of a stream. Continue along the paved road until the small 2 **Shimwonam Hermitage**, 295m above sea level, where the trail to the peak starts. After 1km, make a 100m diversion on a left-hand path to the 5m-tall 3 **Shimwonam Hermitage Three-Storey Pagoda**, built in the Goryeo period. It's another 2.4km along the densely forested ridge to 794m 4 **Moaksan**, open until 4pm. The large building on top detracts from the wild natural feel, but on a clear day, the views extend beyond the Jalaseom Reservoir to the Gimje Plains, Mangyeonggang River and faraway Jeonju. There's a cable-car station, though it was closed when we visited – likely for the foreseeable future. Descend via 670m 5 **Muje-bong**, where you can divert to the small temple of Suwang-sa, and then down to 6 **Daewon-sa**, with a stupa and a five-storey pagoda. After exiting the reserve, consider visiting the 7 **Jeonbuk Province Art Museum**, or relax at one of the cafes along the street. Catch Bus 970 back to Jeonju.

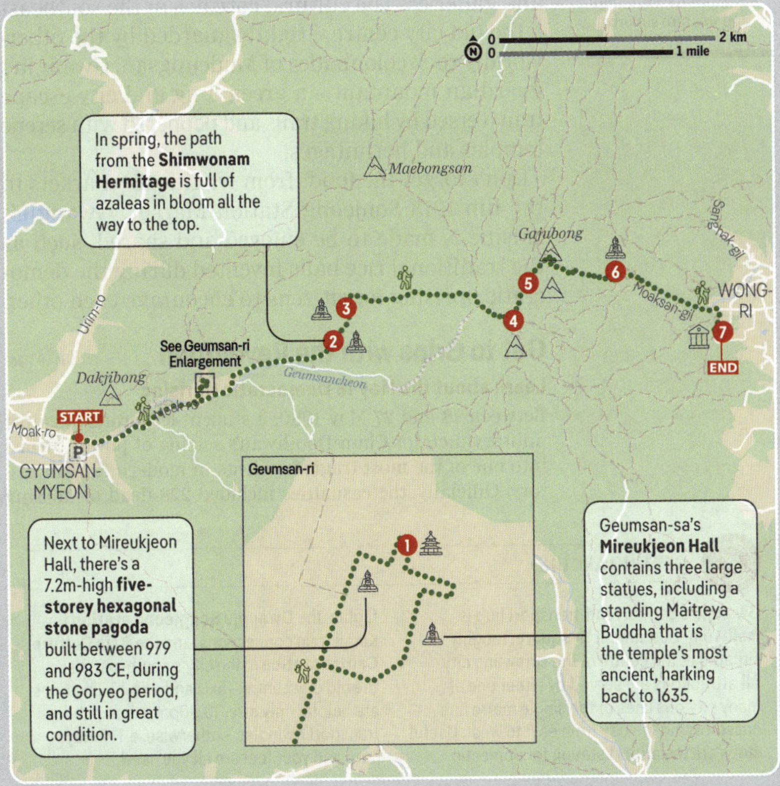

Gwangju

DARK HISTORY | MODERN ARTS | MOUNTAIN ESCAPES

TOP TIP
Base yourself around Yangmin-Dong or Asia Culture Centre to be close to most city attractions and Mudeungsan National Park. It can take up to an hour to get to U-Square and the central sights from the city's southern and western suburbs.

Gwangju is Jeollanam-do province's largest city and Korea's sixth-largest metropolis – a concoction of skyscrapers, flowing traffic and friendly people with an outside reputation as bad as the May 18 Democratic Uprising that brought havoc to the city in 1980. Gwangju has rebranded as a city of arts and culture by playing host to the Gwangju Biennale and Design Biennale and funding many cutting-edge art spaces and galleries. The cultural core lies in the southeast – the old city centre – tightly guarded by the otherworldly rock colonnades of Mudeungsan, Gwangju's guardian mountain – a green lung and city escape transversed by hiking trails and peppered with serene temples and hermitages.

Don't forget the food: from traditional markets to the hip 1913 Sonjeong Station Market, Gwangju's cuisine is made to be enjoyed and shared, such as the traditional rice balls invented during the democratic uprising for citizens to encourage each other.

Get to Grips with the Revolution

MAP P267

Learn about the May 18 Democratic Uprising

Between 18 and 27 May 1980, a student-led protest against military dictator Chun Doo-hwan's seizing of power turned into one of the most tragic incidents in modern Korean history. Officially, the casualties included 228 dead or missing

GETTING AROUND

Gwangju's central road-transport hub is mall-cum-bus station **U-Square**, roughly situated at the centre of the sprawling city. All attractions are served by either one of many city bus lines or the single metro line crisscrossing the city from east to west. Useful stops are the airport station for domestic flights, the **Gwangju Songjeong station** for Korail train connections, and the **Asia Culture Centre station** in the city's southeast, near the old city centre. Taxis and ride-hailing apps are helpful only after 10.30pm, when public transport dwindles – otherwise, a TMoney card and your feet are all you need.

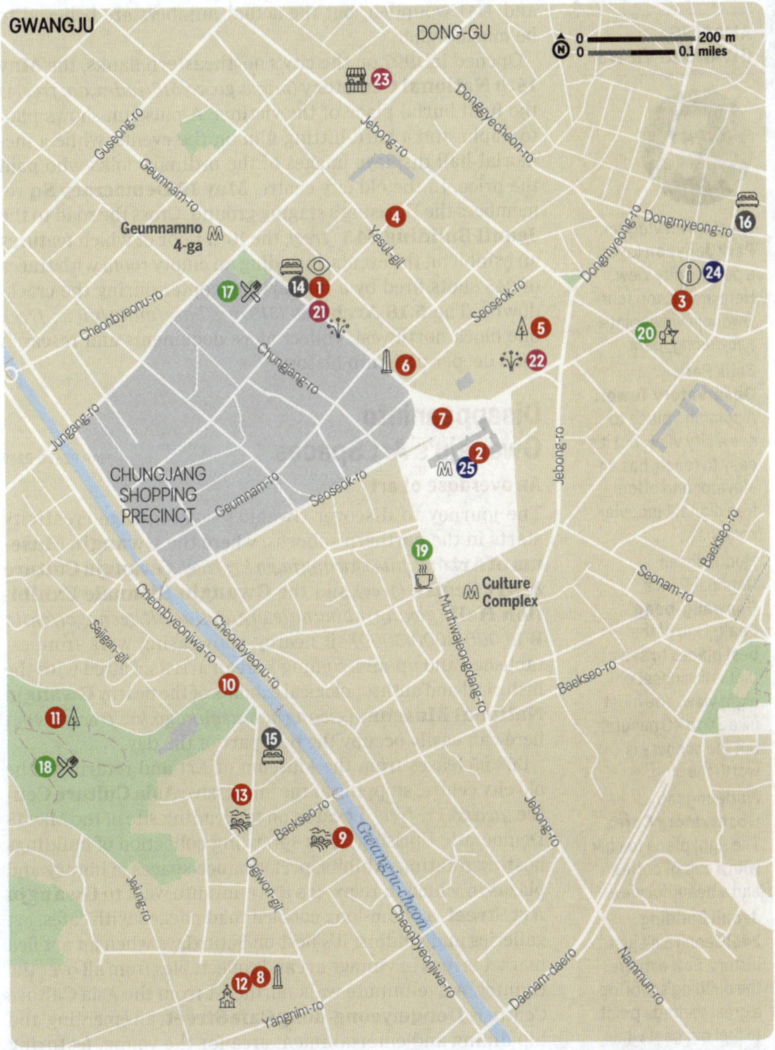

SIGHTS
1 5.18 Archives
2 Asia Culture Centre
3 Dongmyeong-dong Cafe Street
4 Gwangju Art Street
5 Hanul Madang
6 Jeonil Building 245
7 May 18 Democracy Square
8 Owen Memorial Hall
9 Penguin Village
10 Sajik Guitar Road
11 Sajik Park
12 Yangnim Church
13 Yangnim-dong History & Culture Village

SLEEPING
14 ACC Design Hotel
15 Ariene's Guesthouse
16 Oasita Hostel Gwangju

EATING
17 1960 Cheongwon Momil
18 Sajik Tower Cafe

DRINKING & NIGHTLIFE
19 Cafe Museum
20 LP Bar Zeppelin

ENTERTAINMENT
21 Chungjang Street Festival of Recollection
22 Gwangju Busking Worldcup

SHOPPING
23 Daein-sijang

INFORMATION
24 Zip House

TRANSPORT
25 Asia Culture Centre Station

and 4141 wounded, but the actual numbers are believed to be much higher.

Opened in 1997 on the city's northeastern flanks, the **May 18th National Cemetery** *(mpva.go.kr/518/index.do; free)* is the final burial place of the victims. A museum shows photographs and a hard-hitting film on the events, while a memorial hall displays images of the ordinary folks who paid the price. In the old city centre, **May 18 Democracy Sq** remembers the Uprising's staging ground. Cross the road to the **Jeonil Building 245** *(free)*, the 10th floor of which features an exhibit on the events, including an empty room with traces of 245 shots fired by a military helicopter during the crackdowns. The **5.18 Archives** *(518.org/base/main/view; free)*, one block northwest, collect more documents and research for a deeper dive into history.

AMAZING GWANGJU VIEWS

Local travel vlogger **Park Jehyeon** loves a perfect city view. Here are his top four Gwangju viewpoints. *@jeyheong_park*

Sajik Park Observatory Tower: A common place to see a city view, but it's easy to reach, has an elevator and offers free digital binocular screens.

Mudeungsan National Park's **Gunwang-bong Peak:** One of the best places to see a fantastic sunset or night view. You must hike 30 to 40 minutes, but the scenery is worth the slog.

Mudeungsan Observatory Cafe: The right place to chill with a cup of coffee and a beautiful view.

Jeonil Building 245: Jeonil isn't just history. Few explore the building's rooftop, a great vantage point to feel our past while peeking at perfect views of the old city-centre area.

Disappear into Gwangju's Art Spaces

MAP P267 & P269

An overdose of art

The journey to discover Gwanju's cutting-edge creativity starts in the northern suburbs, where the **Gwangju Museum of Art** *(artmuse.gwangju.go.kr; free)*, **Gwangju Culture & Art Centre** *(free)* and the **Gwangju Biennale Exhibition Hall** *(gwangjubiennale.org/en; adult/teenager/child ₩16,000/8000/5000)* sit nearby, showcasing work from established and up-and-coming Korean artists. Paired with the historical and anthropological exhibits of the nearby **Gwangju National Museum** *(gwangju.museum.go.kr; free)*, a visit here can easily occupy the best part of the day.

Bus 95 leaves from the Museum of Art and returns to the old city centre, stopping at the impressive **Asia Culture Centre** *(acc.go.kr; free)*. Located on the leading site of the May 18 Democratic Uprising, it's a sprawling collection of buildings hosting rotating exhibits, performance spaces, a library and plazas in which to relax. It's a five-minute walk to **Gwangju Art Street**, a 300m-long cobbled road packed with cafes, art galleries and studios. It's best on Saturdays when an art flea market brings in vintage art and collectables from all over the country. A five-minute walk northeast from the Asia Culture Centre is **Dongmyeong-dong Cafe Street**, an emerging and hip dining and entertainment area for the young, featuring upscale cafes, restaurants and bars. The district also has **Zip House**, a *hanok*-style information centre where you can store your luggage for free and shop for souvenirs.

EATING IN GWANGJU: OUR PICKS

MAP P267 & P269

Sujata: Run by Buddhist monks, Sujata's all-you-can-eat vegetarian buffet is legendary and a Mudeungsan post-hike must. *11am-2pm* W

1960 Cheongwon Momil: (1960청원모밀) This humble noodle shop, specialising in *momil* (buckwheat noodles), has been in business since 1960. *11am-9pm* WW

Yeongmi: Eighty-year-old *oritang* (duck stew) heavyweight, making delicious stew with ginseng and jujube. *11am-10pm* WWW

Arirang House: Award-winning kimchi and side-dish-based meals at Gwangju's oldest *hanjeongsik* full-course restaurant. *noon-9.30pm* WWW

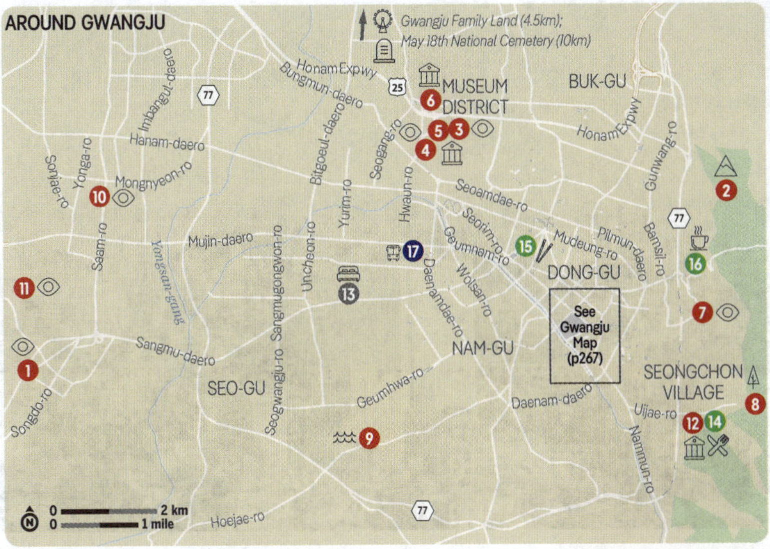

● **SIGHTS**
1 1913 Songjeong Station Market
2 Gunwang-bong Peak
3 Gwangju Biennale Exhibition Hall
4 Gwangju Culture & Art Centre
5 Gwangju Museum of Art
6 Gwangju National Museum
7 Jisan Recreation Area
see 5 Jungwoe Park
8 Mudeungsan National Park
9 Pungam Reservoir
10 Sanjeonggongwon-ro
11 Sochon Art Factory
12 Woo Jae-ghil Art Museum

● **SLEEPING**
13 Pedro's House II

● **EATING**
see 1 Sooks Bakery
14 Sujata
see 1 Sun Bakery
see 1 TTOA Breads
15 Yeongmi
see 1 Yeongmyeong Gukbap

● **DRINKING & NIGHTLIFE**
see 1 Cafe 1913
16 Mudeungsan Observatory Cafe
see 13 Voyagers Cafe

● **TRANSPORT**
see 1 Gwangju Songjeong Station
17 U-Square

Twenty minutes by bus to the east is leafy Unlim-dong Art Street, peppered with art galleries and museums inside **Mudeungsan National Park** *(knps.or.kr/mudeung; free)*. Among the most noteworthy are the **Woo Jae-ghil Art Museum** *(wooart.co.kr; free with purchase from on-site cafe)*, dedicated to the namesake artist as well as being a community-centred art space; the two floors of exhibits at the **Mudeungsan Museum of Contemporary Art** *(free)*; and the **Uijae Museum of Korean Art** *(uijae.org; free)*, displaying works by the late Heo Baek-ryeon (1891–1977), whose penname was Uijae. Other interesting art districts include the **Daein-Sijang** market, revitalised by artists for the 2008 Biennale and now hosting studios and cafes next to traditional stalls, and the **Sochon Art Factory** *(facebook.com/artsochon; free)*, a cultural-regeneration art centre created with containers and offering a solid program of events and exhibits in the western Songjeong area.

BEST PARKS IN GWANGJU

Jisan Recreation Area: The easiest way to conquer Mudeungsan is to ride this thrilling mountainside monorail.

Sajik Park: This quaint city park has a shrine and a free observation tower with binoculars.

Pungam Reservoir: Pavilions and wooden bridges make this quiet lake one of the best spots for walking and jogging in the city limits.

Gwangju Family Land: Jeolla-do's largest amusement park has rides and courses designed for couples, families and children.

Jungwoe Park: This green patch has a children's playground with rides and is used as an outdoor exhibit space for the Biennale.

Historic Neighbourhood

MAP P267

Explore Yangnim History and Culture Village

Tucked between Sajik Park and the the southeastern bend of the Gwanjucheon stream, the **Yangnim-dong History and Culture Village** presents some of Gwanju's oldest remaining architecture, spanning 100 years of Catholic missionary and Korean history. One of the landmark buildings is the reddish, European-looking **Yangnim Church**, built in 1954, which faces the **Owen Memorial Hall**, commemorating one of the first Christian missionaries in Jeollanam-do province. You'll soon bump into the bohemian **Penguin Village**, a junk-art village affectionately named after the cute waddling walk of one senior resident with a prosthetic leg. Upcycled artworks, old frames, wall clocks and memorabilia dot the walls in a bid to revive the historic neighbourhood. There are penguin and cartoonish murals galore, including a portrait of Gwangju-born BTS band member Jung Hoseok. In the evenings, nearby **Sajik Guitar Road** is packed with funky bars hosting live music by local songwriters.

DRINKING IN GWANGJU: BEST CAFES

MAP P267 & P269

Voyagers Cafe: Beautifully bohemian spot blending travel memorabilia, books and vibes from all over. The drip coffee is as great as the rear veranda. *9am-11pm*

Cafe Museum: (카페뮤지엄CM) Three-storey cafe with a drum kit for live bands on the ground floor, art exhibits on the 2nd, and beanbags on the rooftop. *10am-midnight*

Sajik Tower Cafe: The humble cafeteria inside Sajik Observatory Tower has killer 360-degree views of the city and artworks for sale on the walls. *11am-9pm*

LP Bar Zeppelin: Suffused atmosphere with hundreds of vinyl records behind the bar. It'll play your fave earworms when ordering drinks. *6pm-1am, to 3am Sat-Sun*

SANGA PARK/SHUTTERSTOCK

Gwangju view from Sajik Park Observatory Tower (p268)

Celebrate the Old Times

MAP P267

Revel at Gwangju's most important festival

Chungjang-ro, once the city's historic central business district, closes to traffic each October to host the **Chungjang Street Festival of Recollection** *(recollection.kr; free)*, a week-long celebration of past generations, with a main stage for retro music performances, songs from the 1970s and '80s and plenty of old-fashioned games. It's paired with the **Gwangju Busking Worldcup** *(buskingworldcup.com; free)*, an international 'battle of the bands' featuring songwriters and groups from Korea, Asia and beyond, with one stage in May 18 Democracy Sq and one by the grassy **Hanul Madang** on the rooftop of the ACC Creation building at the Asia Culture Centre.

Get on a Hip Food Hunt

MAP P269

Eat and browse at 1913 Songjeong Station Market

Within walking distance of Songjeong Station Exit 2 is the popular **1913 Songjeong Station Market**, operating since 1913 and now evolved into a hip dining district featuring a charming central square with benches and a free wi-fi zone. It's most lively in the evenings.

Among the foods to try are the chocolate pies at **Sooks Bakery** (10am to 6.30pm, to 8pm on weekends), **Cafe 1913's** cuppas, smoothies and tea (9am to 7pm) right on the plaza, and the freshly baked goods at **TTOA Breads** (10.30am to 9.30pm, to 10pm on weekends). For something more substantial, **Yeongmyeong Gukbap** (영명국밥) serves hangover soup and is open 24 hours. At the beginning of the street, **Sun Bakery** (9am to 10 pm) is another popular option for a variety of rolls, breads and cakes.

DIFFERENT FACES OF GWANGJU

Pedro Kim, owner of Voyagers Cafe and Pedro House, suggests different perspectives on his city. *@voyagers_cafe*

Sanjeonggongwon-ro is an area with a diverse mix of people and foods from Central Asia. I like it because it's an example of how immigration is adding diversity to Korean cities, and makes me feel like I'm travelling abroad while still at home.

Since Gwangju is an artistic city, learn about the **Gwangju Folly Movement** *(gwangjufolly.org)*, an urban regeneration project initiated as part of the Gwangju Design Biennale. It engaged Korean and foreign artists and architects to use small, functional architecture to revitalise the city-centre area. Artworks are integrated with daily life, rather than just being showpieces. Spend a day seeking them out as you walk around.

HIKING ON GWANGJU'S GUARDIAN MOUNTAINS

Spend a day hiking the best of Mudeungsan National Park, traversing it from the north to the centre and exiting west to a cluster of art museums.

START	END	LENGTH
Wonhyo-sa	Mudeungsan Museum of Contemporary Art	13.7km; 5–6hr

Take bus 1187 or 1187-1 to the park's northern entrance at the temple of ❶ **Wonhyo-sa**. Trek for 4km through Mudeungsan's dense and rocky forest as you climb towards the centre of the reserve, where the majestic ❷ **Seoseokdae Colonnade** awaits. Its columns are 30m high and up to 2m wide, spread horizontally like a folding screen. Walk towards ❸ **Cheonwan-bong** (1187m), the park's highest peak. (Note that you can only hike up to 1164m ❹ **Inwan-bong** because there's a military installation next to Cheonwan-bong). Descend along the same path and continue south from Seoseokdae until the ❺ **Ipseokdae Colonnade** and marvel at its 40 columnar joints, paying attention to the inscriptions of high-ranking officials of ages past on some of them. Reach the ❻ **Jangbuljae Hill crossing** and, if you have energy and time, make a worthy 1.7km diversion east to ❼ **Gyubongam-sa**, a serene temple in a stunning mountain setting backed by the sheer Gwangseokdae Colonnade. Back at Jangbuljae Hill, start moving westwards to ❽ **Seoin-bong** peak and then descend via ❾ **Yaksam-sa** to join the main path that soon becomes a paved road to the park's western entrance. Stop by ❿ **Jeungsim-sa** temple for one last prayer before hopping on a bus back to the city centre. If it's not later than 5pm, you can also visit ⓫ **Uijae Museum of Korean Art** (p269).

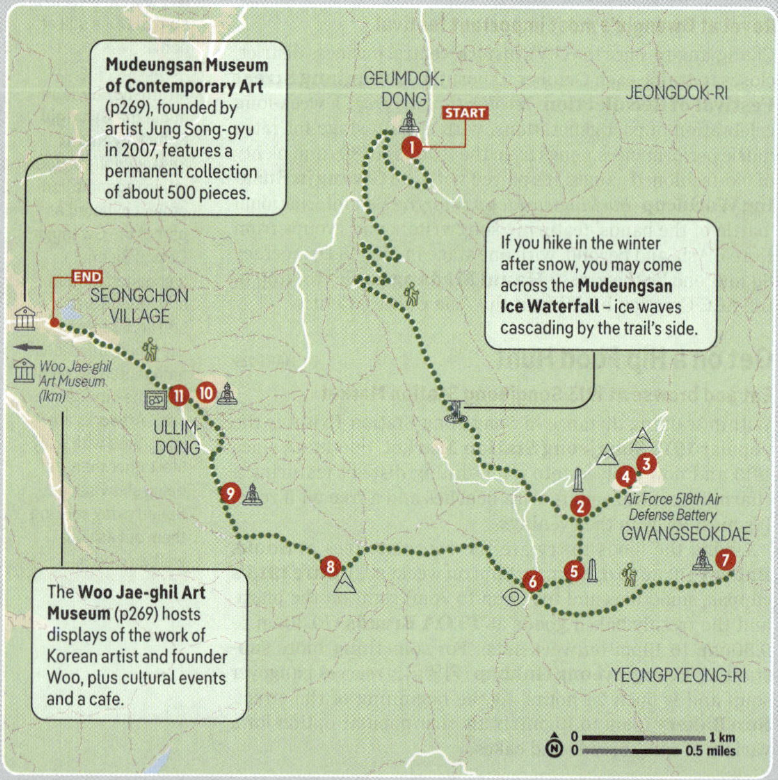

Beyond Gwangju

Leave the big city for the stunning countryside where one of Korea's most significant archaeological sites, an enchanting bamboo forest and wild parkland await.

Gwangju's big-city pulse starts missing beats as soon as the barrage of skyscrapers thins out on the northern city limits. A string of worthy sights fans west to east in nearby towns that make for quick city escapes within an hour's drive of Gwangju's U-Square.

To the west, across the Jeollabuk-do province line, Gochang sits next to one of the world's most archaeologically significant dolmen sites, while just beyond the northern foothills of Mudeungsan National Park, riverside Damyang has plenty of natural attractions, the top of which is Juknokwon, Korea's largest bamboo grove. Further east is Sunchang, famed for its spicy *gochujang* sauce and a vertigo-inducing bridge suspended between two mountains.

Places

GETTING AROUND

Gwangju's U-Square has frequent direct buses to some outlying attractions or, at the very least, to their nearest towns. As they all are within a one-hour drive, stopping at any sight while travelling between Gwangju and Jeonju is sensible, but a rental car is helpful to optimise travel time and see more in a day. Cycling the network of country roads makes for a fun adventure in the warmer months.

Gochang

TIME FROM GWANGJU: 1¼HR

Marvel at prehistoric gravesites

Take a walk in the hills surrounding Gochang to ponder the mystery of a **dolmen site** containing 440 prehistoric tombs from the Bronze and Iron Ages, now registered with UNESCO (along with Hwasun and Ganghwa). At the park's entrance, the **Gochang Dolmen Museum** *(gochang-dolmen.or.kr; adult/youth/child ₩3000/2000/1000)* has information in English on the different uses of rocks in ancient cultures worldwide.

It's a 700m walk to the dolmens, which are scattered around the Ungok Reservoir, a Ramsar site with four hiking trails ranging from 600m to 10.3km. A hop-on, hop-off tourist train *(₩1000)* leaves the museum for the outer dolmen area every half-hour between 10am and 6pm. To return to **Gochang's bus terminal**, walk 800m back to the main roundabout, turn left and hail any of the orange buses passing by. Back in town, the **Moyang Fortress** *(adult/teenager/child ₩3000/2000/1500)* has a 1.6km-long wall from 1453 CE surrounding a complex of reconstructed buildings. It's worth touring if you have a couple of hours to spare.

SPICY VILLAGE

Sunchang is Korea's most famous producer of the fermented sweet and spicy red chilli paste called *gochujang*, with a favourably humid climate to best ferment the paste. It has a special place in Korea, where it's been produced since 1433 as a medicinal food, with its recipes recorded by royal physicians during the Chosun dynasty. A **Gochujang Village** was built in Sunchang in 1997 to support local makers and give them better homes and larger yards to store their fermentation jars. Visitors are welcome to purchase the heavenly paste and learn more about its production methods.

Damyang

TIME FROM GWANGJU: **35MIN**

A world of bamboo

Sandy walking trails wend through **Juknokwon Bamboo Forest** *(adult/student/child ₩3000/2000/1000)*, past pavilions and film locations for Korean dramas. It's one of the area's most popular attractions and can get crowded on weekends, but if you get a quiet moment – enough to hear the wind rustle the leaves – it can be enchanting. Complete your visit with a stop at **Damyang Bamboo Crafts Museum** *(adult/teenager/child ₩2000/1000/700)*, a traditional and modern bamboo-products showroom. Bus 311 and 311-2 depart from the bus stand in front of Gwangju's U Square to Juknokwon.

Majestic tree walk

Planted in the 1970s beside National Road 24, the trees in Damyang's **Metasequoia Land** *(adult/teenager/child ₩2000/1000/700)* are now so high they block out the sun. Every season, a walk here is a different, magical experience and an excellent spot for photography. The best way to arrive here is to walk or cycle along the Yeongsangang riverbank, passing the protected **Gwangbanjerim Forest** *(free)* and the **Dambit Arts Warehouse**. This beautiful cafe, housed inside a former rice warehouse, also features a 100-year-old bamboo pipe organ, the only one in Korea, preserved under glass. Outside, there are gardens filled with statues.

Sunchang

TIME FROM GWANGJU: **45MIN**

Walk in the sky

Opened in 2021, **Chaegyesan Suspension Bridge** *(free)* is a 1.4km out-and-back trail with a section floating in thin air. Boardwalks start from the car park at the bottom of Chaegyesan Mountain, climbing up 538 steps. The impressive suspension bridge is 360m long and 1.5m wide, floating 90m above the ground. The views of countryside peppered with yellow fields of canola blossoms hemmed within mountains are incredible but real torture for acrophobes.

Naju

TIME FROM GWANGJU: **50MIN**

Discover Jeolla-do's historic capital

With half a day, take bus 160 or a train from Gwangju Songjeong to Naju, the former Jeolla-do capital, now known more for its large pears and bone soup than its fine historic sights. The bus gets you closer to the sights than alighting at Naju's train station: from the Catholic Intersection stop, walk to **Geumseonggwan Hall** *(free)*, a large guesthouse and magistrate office rebuilt in 1617 after the Japanese invasion. A five-minute walk west past the **Jeongsulu** pavilion and **Naju Moksanaea Geumhakheon** *(free)* – a *hanok* and former home of Naju's pastor, with a huge hackberry tree – is the **Seoseongmun Gate** *(free)*, a part of the old city walls that can be climbed on. On Naju's eastern edge, the **Kimseongsan Fortress**' *(free)* solitary gate, today used as a roundabout, also recalls the town's former defences. You can catch a bus back to Gwangju from here.

TOP EXPERIENCE

Naejangsan National Park

One of the region's best hiking spots, Naejangsan National Park (내장산국립공원) near Jeongeup is famous for its brilliant display of autumn leaves in October. The rest of the year still offers excellent hiking and views. Besides a cable car on the park's northeastern side, a spider's web of trails crisscrosses the park's three sections, which also offer a most interesting culinary Zen experience.

Baegyang-sa

Main Entrance

The main gate sits on the park's northeastern side. The fastest ascent of the range is by **cable car** *(9am–5pm)*, with an observation deck 300m below the summit. The ridge forms an amphitheatre, and the rim hike is strenuous, rising and falling over six main peaks before Seorae-bong (622m), but views are superb on clear days. Near the park's centre, **Naejang-sa** temple enjoys a stunning setting surrounded by steep peaks.

Alternative Approach from the Namchang Entrance

This quieter western access offers forested streams, ponds and a rewarding hike. From the Namchang parking area, the 4.5km **Ibamsanseong trail** to 641m-high **Gatbawi** rock at the mounaintop passes the namesake Goryeo-era fortress ruins after 2.9km, with only the **north** and **south** gates and leftovers of the **Angku-sa** temple visible. From Gatbawi, you can loop south to Eunseondong junction and return, passing the 5.9km **Monggyepokpo trail** towards the temple of **Baegyang-sa** and the reserve's southern reaches.

Cooking with Monk Chef

Jeong Kwan, a Buddhist nun and chef at Chunjinam Hermitage in Baegyang-sa, gained global attention in season three of Netflix's *Chef's Table* for her philosophical approach to vegan temple cuisine. Templestay guests can join a monthly four-hour cooking class *(adult/teen/child over 10 ₩200,000/160,000/100,000)*. Contact *baekyangsa@templestay.com* or *WhatsApp 010 9037 0434*.

TOP TIPS

- If you're not interested in hiking, choose the main entrance and take the cable car for the quickest access to great views.
- Because of climate change, the autumn foliage season is not as regular as it used to be, sometimes coming as late as early November. Check before you go.

PRACTICALITIES

- knps.or.kr/naejang
- free
- cable car adult/child one way ₩5500/3500, return ₩8000/5000

Suncheon

CITY GARDENS | RIVER LIFE | COASTAL WETLANDS

With its low-rise buildings, wide avenues and relaxed folks, balmy Suncheon is a good choice as a southern Jeolla base and to slow down. Nature lovers may immediately notice that no greener city exists in Korea. After hosting the Suncheonman International Garden Expo in 2013, Suncheon's entire city-centre area transformed into a green patch of flawless manicured gardens, water pools and open lawns where locals thrive and play. On spring evenings and weekends, you'll see locals take to the parks to picnic, listen to live music and just soak up the sun.

There's plenty of fauna, too. Migratory birds flutter above the central gardens and stop by the riverbanks on their way to their resting place at the mouth of the Dongcheong River, where an expanse of reeds plays hide and seek with the shifting tides.

GETTING AROUND

Suncheon is well connected by intercity buses and sits on both Korail's Gyeongjeon Line to Gwangju's Songjeong station and the Jeolla Line between Iksan and Yeosu Expo, which continues to Seoul's Yongsan. Bus and train stations are in the city centre on opposite banks of the Dongcheong River, which bisects the city vertically. Suncheon's extensive gardens lie along the riverbank on the south of the city, and are very pleasant to walk in good weather when trees blossom. You can rely on frequent public buses and affordable taxis to reach further out; renting a car is unnecessary.

A City of Gardens

Into the green heart of Suncheon

Ocheon Green Square is a free, large, grassy meadow with a lagoon on the northeastern side, connected by a bridge to the Dongcheong River. On the southwestern corner are two hill mounds topped respectively by a geodesic dome and a futuristic steel-rod sculpture that can be climbed for bird's-eye views. From spring to autumn, flower beds bloom with the bright colours of tulips, azaleas and more. The square takes an ethereal glow at night when it lights up and, as soon as spring comes, locals start to flock here to relax, picnic and sunbathe.

Immediately to the south is the gigantic **Suncheon Bay National Garden** *(adult/teenager/child ₩10,000/7000/5000, evening ticket after 5pm ₩5000/3500/2500)*, the entry fee for which also includes access to the Suncheon Bay Wetlands (p278), 7km to the south. This sprawling 112-hectare area is planted with a staggering 790,000 trees of 505 species and 3.15 million flowers of 113 species, including tulips, royal azaleas and a large field of canola flowers that create golden waves when blooming in mid-May. The garden is divided by

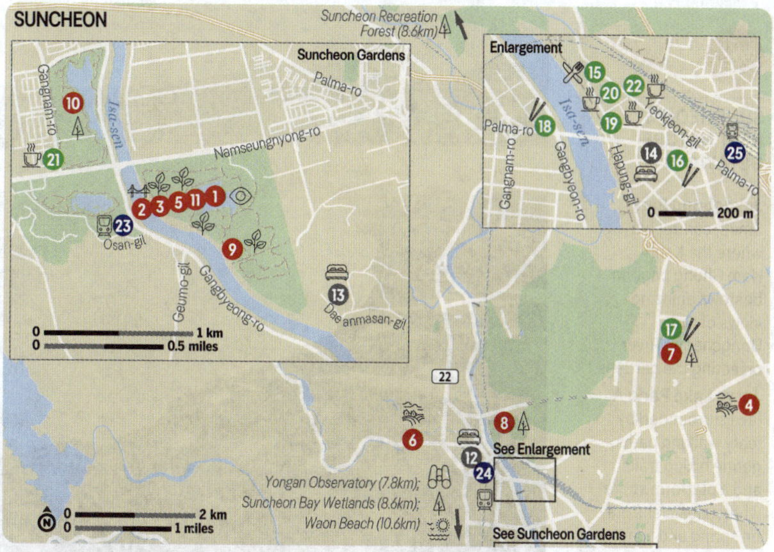

SIGHTS
1 Bonghwa Eondeok
2 Bridge of Dreams
3 China Garden
4 Daldongnae
5 French Gardens
6 Jeojeong-dong Garden Village
7 Jorye Lake Park
8 Jukdobong Park
9 Netherlands Gardens
10 Ocheon Green Square
11 Suncheon Bay National Garden
see 4 Suncheon Open Film Location

SLEEPING
see 19 Baguni Hostel
12 Namu Guest House
13 Suncheon Bay Eco Village Hostel
14 Suncheon Guesthouse 24

EATING
15 Ama Seed
16 Heungdeok Sikdang
17 Shin Kal
18 Uri Restaurant

DRINKING & NIGHTLIFE
19 Basterds Cafe & Pub
20 Brew Works
21 Le Coin Bistro
22 Youth Store

TRANSPORT
23 Sky Cube
24 Suncheon Express Bus Terminal
25 Suncheon Train Station

the Dongcheong River into two areas connected by the **Bridge of Dreams**, which, after sundown, fires up with LED lights and video projections of the wetlands ecosystem.

The eastern bank hosts several country-themed gardens, among which the most notable are the walled **China Garden**, filled with pagodas and water ponds; the **French Gardens**, which cascade into a set of tulip-strewn terraces, and the **Netherlands Gardens**, featuring a life-sized windmill surrounded by a rainbow of tulips. At the centre of the gardens is a lake with a bridge and an inner islet, **Bonghwa Eondeok**, where a circular trail climbs to the top.

TOP TIP
Go to the National Garden in the morning to allow time for exploring the large grounds. Then, hop on the western bank to use the Sky Cube gondola to catch sunset at Suncheon Bay Wetlands.

Become a K-Drama Star

Revel at Suncheon Open Film Location

Stepping into the **Suncheon Open Film Location** *(adult/teenager/child ₩3000/2000/1000)* in Jorye-dong is like taking a trip back in time. The mock-up city contains three movie settings, each built to look like the Korea of the 1960s, '70s and '80s, which served as the sets of several famous K-Dramas, such

SUNCHEON'S BEST NATURE GETAWAYS

Jukdobong Park: Small, central hill where the Kang Nam Chong pagoda bestows amazing views of the Dongcheong River bisecting the gardens.

Jorye Lake Park: A lake surrounded by leafy walking paths, gentle hiking trails and a platform stage where musicians play on spring and summer weekends.

Jeojeong-Dong Garden Village: Urban village garden curated by residents who reflect their personalities with plants and art.

Waon Beach: The southeastern side of Suncheon Bay is a beautiful place to see the sunset as the low tide exposes the coastal mudflats.

Suncheon Recreational Forest: Trails, hiking, camping and a children's water park on the city's northern outskirts.

as *East of Eden* (2008), *Gangnam Blues* (2015) and *Pachinko* (2022). Every detail, from telephone poles, the Sunyang cinema, a police station, a '70s-style disco and small alleys, looks historically accurate. Don't miss the scenic hilltop **Daldongnae**, a set of a poor hillside village in 1970s Seoul, by taking a left turn at the entrance and following the uphill path.

Where the River Meets the Sea

Explore Suncheon Bay Wetlands

The **Suncheon Bay Wetlands** coastal estuary, inscribed on the Ramsar list of protected wetlands, is 7km south of Suncheon Bay National Garden. Walkways span the bay above water and rustling reeds leading up to the **Yongsan Observatory**, a popular sunset viewpoint to catch a bird's-eye perspective above the estuary and bay. Birdwatchers should come on the lookout for rare migratory birds such as hooded cranes, black-faced spoonbills, yellow-billed egrets and swans,

CAFES IN SUNCHEON: OUR PICKS

Brew Works: Dimly lit, industrial-chic cafe renovated from a grain warehouse with ample seating space. *10am-10pm* W

Youth Store: Inside a loft-like space, this collection of hip cafes, bakeries and small restaurants continually rotates and welcomes young entrepreneurs. *11.30am-9pm* W

Basterds Cafe & Pub: On the ground floor of Baguni Hostel, pouring draft beers and coffee. Fills with foreign guests. *9am-11pm* W

Le Coin Bistro: Cafe and French-owned restaurant serving pizzas, wine and a well-executed beef bourguignon. *11.30-3pm & 5-10pm Tue-Sun* WW

NOA_80/SHUTTERSTOCK

Suncheon Bay Wetlands

all of which stop here during their migrations, hungry for the mudskippers and red crabs that thrive in the mud.

Wetland-bound buses leave Suncheon bus station, but the easiest and most scenic way to arrive here is by taking a **Sky Cube** *(skycube.co.kr; adult/child one way ₩6000/5000 return ₩8000/6000)* gondola from Jeongwon station, inside the western half of Suncheon Bay National Garden. It's a scenic 10-minute ride on an elevated monorail track along the Dongcheong River that grants beautiful views of the surrounding countryside. Try to catch an early ride, as the last train back to the gardens leaves the wetlands at 6.30pm. Sky Cube tickets include a free ride on the Reed Shuttle Train, the final stop of which is 2.3km from Yongsan Observatory. If you don't overnight around here, remember that the last Reed Train leaves the wetlands at 6.10pm (5.10pm November to February) to meet the final Sky Cube departure.

SAVING THE BAY

Today, Suncheon Bay is a UNESCO-designated Biosphere Reserve thanks to its diverse ecosystems, but in 1992, things were quite different: the city government planned to mine the bay for sand to use in construction sites. Stern civic-led action halted the project in 1998, opening a new chapter for the world's fifth-largest bay. In 2003, it became a protected area in Korea and, by 2006, it had been accepted by the Ramsar Convention. In 2009, the city council removed 282 power poles and 12km of power lines from the rice fields to attract migratory birds. The bay has become a seasonal sanctuary for 60% of the total population of endangered hooded cranes, which are Suncheon city's proud symbol.

EATING IN SUNCHEON: OUR PICKS

Shin Kal: It's worth getting to Jorye-dong for this noodle joint serving hearty, hot *dak kalguksu* (fermented wheat noodles with shredded chicken). *11am-9pm* ₩

Heungdeok Sikdang: Stalwart *baekban* (set meal) restaurant near the train station, with a popular bulgogi. *8am-9pm* ₩₩

Uri Restaurant: Specialising in *ori bulgogi* (hot-plate-braised BBQ duck), this central restaurant masters one of Suncheon's most famous dishes. *10am-10pm* ₩₩

Ama Seed: (아마씨) Funky, vegetarian-friendly bistro for healthy mains like lotus-leaf-wrapped rice and pumpkin curries. *11am-8pm Sat-Wed* ₩₩

Beyond Suncheon

Flee the garden city for mountain shrines, a charming folk village and a thriving port city where you can walk to an offshore island.

Places

GETTING AROUND

Buses leave Suncheon's bus terminal and travel west to the temples around Jogyesan Provincial Park, the sights of Naganeup-seong and Boseong, while Yeosu is the next stop on the southern KTX Jeolla line. A car is preferred to move freely between sights, avoid relying on the infrequent bus schedules back to the city, and cover more ground between Yeosu and nearby Dolsan island (connected by a bridge).

Leave Suncheon in any direction and you'll bump into some of southern Jeolla's most impressive sights. To the west, the flat city gardens curl into the broad peaks of Jogyesan Provincial Park, guarded by the ancient temples of Seonam-sa and Songgwang-sa. To the north, Gurye is the gateway to hikes in Jirisan National Park, home to mainland South Korea's highest peak. The fortified Joseon-era walls of Naganeup-seong, one of Korea's most picturesque folk villages, lie to the southwest on the way to green-tea county Boseong and the viridian slopes of Daehan Dawon Tea Plantation. To Suncheon's south, the vibrant ocean city of Yeosu beguiles with modern architecture, remote cliff-hanging temples and an over-ocean cable car.

Jogyesan Provincial Park TIME FROM SUNCHEON: 1HR

Zen hiking

Jogyesan Provincial Park harbours a cluster of low, soft-rounded mountains at the outer limits of which are two noteworthy temples: **Songgwang-sa** *(songgwangsa.org; free)* to the west and **Seonam-sa** *(free)* to the east.

Songgwang-sa, considered one of the three jewels of Korean Buddhism, is dramatically set next to a stream and is one of the oldest Zen temples in the country, founded in the 10th century – don't miss the **Stupa of National Master Chinul**, built in 1213, though most other buildings date from the 17th century.

Seonam-sa is a quiet hermitage dating back to 529 CE, where monks study and try to preserve the old ways. Below the temple is **Seungseongyo**, one of Korea's most exquisite ancient granite bridges, with a dragon's head hanging from the top of an arch. Templestays are available at both shrines.

The best way to visit is by walking for about four hours on the moderate and serene 8km cross-park hike connecting the two temples. Start in Songgwang-sa, heading eastbound to Seonam-sa, which has more bus departures back to Suncheon. Roughly midway, a simple shack serves hearty bibimbap lunches *(₩9000)*. Enthusiasts can strike out on a longer 16km hike over the peak of Janggun-bong (884m).

KOREA TOURISM ORGANIZATION - KIM JOON-SEOK

Songgwang-sa, Jogyesan Provincial Park

Yeosu

TIME FROM SUNCHEON: 1¼HR

Marine city

Yeosu's fame skyrocketed after the city hosted Expo 2012. Set on the northeastern side of the town centre, the Expo area has impressive attractions such as the offshore **Big-O Show** interactive fountain, **Aqua Planet** *(adult/teenager/child ₩35,000/32,000/29,000)* aquarium, and one branch of the cutting-edge **Arte Museum** *(artemuseum.com; adult/teenager/child ₩19,000/15,000/12,000)*. The city-centre area develops around **Jongpo Marine Park**, a sea-facing esplanade with dramatic views of Yeosu Marine Cable Car hovering between the **Dolsan Bridge** to the west and the **Geobukseon Bridge** to the east.

A tiny alley climbs from the eastern end of the park to **Gosodong 1004 Angel Mural Village**, a bohemian area with hip cafes, bistros and little guesthouses worth checking out after working hours when the city and bay light up – note that things wind down by 9pm.

Back at the park's western end, a replica of a traditional Jeolla ***geobukseon* turtle ship** *(free)* sits near a statue of its creator, Admiral Yi Sun-sin, in the namesake square. A 400m walk north is **Jinnamgwan** *(free)*, a hall that is Korea's largest single-storey wooden structure (75m long and 14m high), first constructed in 1599, with 68 pillars supporting its massive roof.

Fly above the ocean

Yeosu Marine Cable Car *(yeosucablecar.com; adult/child one way ₩14,000/9000, return ₩17,000/12,000)* starts from **Jasan station** near Odongdo island and travels 1.5km over the ocean to the northern side of Dolsan island. Passengers can choose between standard and thrilling 'crystal' cabins *(adult/child one way ₩19,000/14,000, return ₩24,000/19,000)* to observe the sea below their feet while suspended in midair. Even

continued on p284

HIKES IN YEOSU

Dolsan Coastal Trail: A stunning four-day coastal trek from Dolsan Bridge to the famous cliff-hanging Hyangiram Temple.

Daemisan: Outstanding views on this hike from Musulmok Beach to the 347m Daemisan peak.

Gubongsan: This 388m mountain, which splits Yeosu's urban sprawl down the middle, has a network of well-maintained trails.

Janggunsan: Another of Yeosu's central peaks makes for a moderate hike with rewarding coastal and city views.

Goraksan: In Yeosu's northwestern suburbs, this 335m mountain is clad with remains of two fortresses dating from the Baekje era.

STOCK FOR YOU/SHUTTERSTOCK

TOP EXPERIENCE

Jirisan National Park

Jirisan National Park (지리산국립공원) offers some of Korea's best hiking opportunities. Twelve peaks over 1000m form a 40km-long ridge, including Cheonwang-bong (1915m), the country's second-highest mountain. Although the park straddles three provinces and has three principal entrances, each with a temple, the most accessible and recommended hiking route is from west to east, starting from Gurye in Jeollanam-do.

DON'T MISS

- Cheoneun-sa
- Imgeollyeong Spring
- Banya-bong
- Samdo-bong
- Myeongseong-bong
- Hyeingje-bong
- Cheonwang-bong

The Trailhead

Buses from most Korean cities travel directly to Gurye's bus terminal, where sporadic intertown buses (9am and 2.20pm Monday to Thursday and 8.40am, 10.20am, 2.20pm and 4.20pm Friday to Sunday) travel to the **Seongsamjae Service Area**, the highest point reachable by car in Korea, where the trail starts. There is an Emart here for last-minute provision shopping. With your transport, stop on the way at the mountainside

PRACTICALITIES

- register and book shelter accommodation at reservation.knps.or.kr
- free
- hiking times from Seongsamjae: 3am-4.30pm Apr-Oct, 4am-4pm Nov-Mar

Cheoneun-sa *(free)* temple, set next to a rushing stream. A scene in the 2018 K-Drama series *Mr Sunshine* was shot at the main entrance's pagoda. Templestays are available.

Going Up the Mountain

From Seongsamjae Service Area, the trail goes 2.2km across Jongseokdae peak to the **Nogodan Shelter** at 1540m, where most visitors turn back down and the traverse begins. It's another 3.6km to the **Imgeollyeong Spring** and then 1.3km ascending to **Nolumog**, where the trail swerves north to proceed 900m to 1734m **Banya-bong**, the park's second-highest peak. Hikers descend back to the Banya-bong junction and walk 600m to 1499m **Samdo-bong**, where the three provinces of Jeollanam-do, Jeollabuk-do and Gyeongsannam-do meet. It's another 4.7km east via 1534m **Ttoki-bong** and 1586m **Myeongseong-bong** to the **Yeonhacheon shelter**, where hikers can overnight after the closure of the Baemsagol shelter. The total distance to this point is 17km, which takes between seven and eight hours.

Middle of the Range

The next day, the trail descends for 2km to 1178m **Hyeongje-bong**, with its two peaks that look like stone brothers, and another 1.2km to the **Byeoksoryeong shelter**, a crossroads of multiple hiking routes. The trail ascends towards 1522m **Deokpyeong-bong**, where there's a small eternal spring called Seonbisem, where hikers can stock up on water and wash. **Chilseon-bong** is 1.8km away and boasts seven rocks that, legend says, are seven petrified angels who came from the sky to rest here. It's another 1.5km to **Yeongsin-bong**, a 10-minute downhill walk from **Seseoksam**, the biggest shelter, geared up to host 300 people. Many stay here on their second night, but to catch the sunrise (it's not easy to see it, so don't push your limits), it's another 3km and two more hours to **Jangteomok shelter**. This area is full of royal azaleas in June.

Wrapping It Up

Sunrise seekers wake up at 5am and walk for an hour in the dark to 1915m **Cheonwang-bong**. Sunrise is usually at about 6.40am. Whether lucky or not, the descent to Junsang-ri town starts: it takes about an hour to walk the 1.5km to the temple of **Beopgye-sa**, where there's a Rotary shelter for resting or spending an extra night. The large rock formations of the **Mangbawi lookout** are 1km further down, and 870m later is **Kalbawi**, with even more impressive rocks. A final 2km stretch takes you down to Jungsan-ri, where there's an empty ticket office and a car park where buses depart to Jinju's bus terminal. From there, intercity buses serve Seoul, Gwangju, Suncheon and many other locations.

BEAR COUNTRY

Thanks to a conservation program, the Asiatic black bear population in Jirisan is rising. As of 2023, about 86 Asiatic black bears, including cubs, lived inside the park. Even though the animals tend to avoid humans, mothers with cubs can be dangerous, but don't worry – as long as you stick to the trail, there's minimal risk of encountering one.

TOP TIPS

- It gets cold in the mountains, even in summer. Pack some long-sleeved shirts and a down jacket, and if you don't camp, know that shelters are heated.
- You don't need to complete a full traverse to enjoy Jirisan National Park: take a bus up to Seongsamjae, enjoy the views and take a short stroll towards Nogodan shelter.
- After Nogodan, shelter facilities decrease their standards, so come prepared with an extra inflatable sleeping pad and a light blanket. Carry toilet paper.
- Water is available throughout the route, particularly between Yeonhacheon and Jangteomok shelters, but carry a water-purifying filter or Steripen water bottle.

A NATIONAL HERO

The statue in Yeosu's central square is of Yi Sun-sin, a Korean admiral and national hero whose naval victories were instrumental in the Imjin War (Japanese invasions of Korea) of the 1590s. He's believed to have invented the *geobukseon* (turtle ship), the world's first iron-fortified battleship. After his successes blocking the first Japanese advance in 1592, he was promoted to commander of the entire Korean fleet, but then falsely accused of desertion during a battle and demoted to common infantry soldier in 1597. Yi Sun-sin was reinstated after the Japanese had almost destroyed the Korean fleet, and he soon restored Korea's control of the sea. A stray bullet killed him as he pursued retreating Japanese forces during the last stretch of the war.

continued from p281
if you don't want to ride, take the lift to Jasan station and walk 50m west to an octagonal pagoda and observation deck with a fantastic view of Odongdo and the sea. A staircase descends to the bottom of the hill, where the walk to Odongdo starts.

Walk to an offshore island

Craggy, offshore **Odongdo** is connected to the mainland by a 750m-long bridge that can be walked, cycled or crossed aboard a road train. A boardwalk snakes along the island's southern end, reaching down to the **Dragon Cave** carved into the cliffside.

Around 250m away, amid bamboo forest, is **Odongdo Lighthouse** *(free)*, open 9am to 6pm (closed Mondays). Take the elevator to the top floor for 360-degree views of the port and nearby islands such as Geomundo, Beakdo and Geumodo. Island-hopping boats cost between ₩60,000 and ₩100,000 for four people (add ₩12,000 for each extra passenger).

Cliff-hanging mantras

A Buddhist hermitage with a 1350-year history, **Hyangir-am** *(free)* of the Jogye Order of Korean Buddhism has an enviable location, halfway up a mountain at the tip of Dolsan island, which is connected to Yeosu by a bridge. It's a 10-minute walk uphill from the car park, through stalls selling the local speciality, *gatkimchi* (pickled mustard leaves), and via a stone staircase leading to the main shrine. You'll have to squeeze through tight passages between boulders to the first pagoda, from where the sea and coastal views are stunning, especially at sunset. A 1.7km hike to **Geumo-bong** mountain starts near the temple exit and ends at the Yullimchi car park.

Nagan

TIME FROM SUNCHEON: 1¼HR

Time-travelling village

Among Korea's many folk villages, **Naganeup-seong** *(suncheon.go.kr/nagan; adult/teenager/child ₩4000/2500/1500)* is unique for its setting, surrounded by 1410m of Joseon-period fortress walls, built to protect the inhabitants from marauding Japanese pirates. Using square-shaped stones, it reached 4m in height and 3m to 4m in width.

A walk on top of the fortification offers picturesque views of one of Korea's best-preserved fortress towns, hemmed by hills. It's crammed with narrow, drystone alleyways leading to vegetable allotments and adobe and stone homes thatched with reeds that are still inhabited. Some offer simple yet very atmospheric *minbak* (private homes with rooms for rent) accommodation

EATING & DRINKING IN YEOSU: OUR PICKS

Café Neuf: Speciality coffee, lattes, pastries and cakes near the port. A good place to re-caffeinate after a walk to Odongdo. *8am-8pm* ₩

Wyd Coffee Stand: Arts and coffee inside a hip two-storey house with a rooftop over the bay, in the thick of Gosodong 1004 village. *11am-9pm* ₩

Camellia Sliced Raw Fish: Eat on Odongdo's shores at this popular sliced-fish restaurant as you observe the hubbub across Yeosu's bay. *9am-8pm* ₩₩

Samdaeok: (삼대옥) Popular bakery making strawberry mochi rice cakes and very sweet strawberry ice cream since 1968. *7am-12.30pm* ₩₩

A DAY EXPLORING YEOSU ON FOOT

Make the best of a day in the coastal city, walking from museums to offshore islands, markets and historical mementoes.

START	END	LENGTH
Arte Museum	Jungang Fresh Fish Market	8.2km; 3hr

Get off the train at Yeosu Expo station and check out 1 **Arte Museum**'s (p281) incredible digital exhibits themed after the ocean. Walk by 2 **Yeonigyu Bridge** and follow the coastline until 3 **Yeosu Marine Cable Car Jasan station** (p281). Take the lift up to enjoy views over Odongdo island, then walk down to the island using the staircase and breakwater. Check out the 4 **Dragon Cave** and 5 **Odongdo Lighthouse** for views above the islands of Dadohae Haesang National Park, and return to the peninsula to eat below Geobukseon Bridge at one of 6 **Yeosu Romantic Carriage Street**'s 18 food trucks. Continue east along the coast until 7 **Jongpo Marine Park** (p281) for some of the best views of Yeosu Bay. It's a short walk north to the colourful alleys of hill-hanging 8 **Goso-dong 1004 Angel Mural Village** (p281), where street art, cafes and restaurants have revitalised an ageing seaside district. Walk east along Goso 3-gil until it ends near the historic 9 **Jinnamgwan** (p281) hall. Continue south to 10 **Yi Sun-sin Sq** and the replica of one of the 11 ***geobukseon* turtle ships** (p281) that Yi Sun-sin used to fight the naval battles of the Imjin War. A short walk west along the promenade, stop at 12 **Jungang Fresh Fish Market**, continuing back along the coastal Jongpo Marine Park for more dramatic night views of the bay.

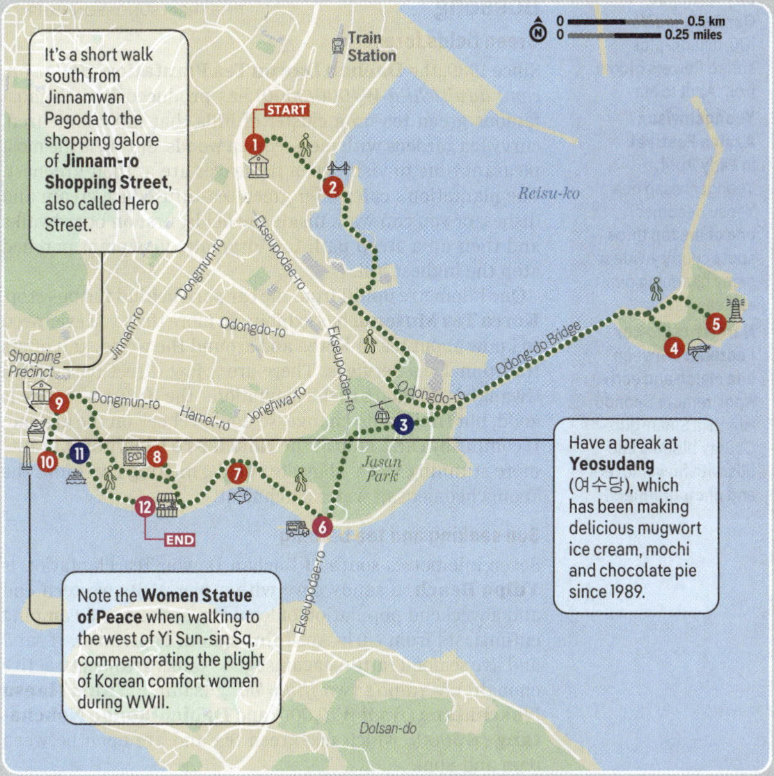

FLOWER FESTIVALS AROUND SUNCHEON

Maehwa Festival: Plum blossoms, or *maehwa*, bloom around Gwangyang town in March.

Gurye Sansuyu Festival: Nine-day event between the end of March and April celebrating the bloom of *sansuyu* (yellow cornelian cherry flowers) near Jirisan mountain.

Spring Flower Festival: Suncheon Bay National Garden's (p276) 100-million-plus spring flowers bloom from April to May.

Yeongchwisan Azalea Festival: In early April, Yeongchwisan near Yeosu becomes one of the top three spots countrywide to enjoy blooming pink azaleas.

Narcissus Flower Festival: Between late March and early April, remote Seondo island in Sinan-gun County blooms and fills with flower lovers and photographers.

BENJAMIN PETER JEARY/SHUTTERSTOCK

Daehan Dawon Tea Plantation, Boseong

unlike anywhere else in the country. If you stay, the **Nagan Minsok Nature Recreation Forest** *(free)*, 2km north of the village, offers quiet trails to the cascading Cheonyeopokpo Falls.

Boseong

TIME FROM SUNCHEON: 1¼HR

Green fields forever

Since 1939, the **Daehan Dawon Tea Plantation** *(dhdawon.com; adult/child ₩4000/3000)* has produced Korea's most famous green tea on a cluster of hills that mix manicured, curvy tea gardens with metasequoia woods. Spring is the most pleasant time to visit, when the leaves are at their greenest. The plantation's cafes offer green-tea-infused ice cream and dishes, or you can walk inside the fields, first on boardwalks and then up a steep path to a dramatic viewpoint perched atop the highest hill.

One kilometre uphill from the car park behind the bus stop, **Korea Tea Museum** has exhibits on more than you ever need to know about tea in Korea and around the world, and offers traditional tea services. There are a few direct buses from Gwangju's U Square to the plantation – the 10.30am service is good, but timings do change, so double check on the ground. If coming by car, a stop at the **Nokcha-ro Viewpoint** grants more stunning views above tea fields, melting away into the Yeongcheonjeosuji water catchment.

Sun seeking and tea bathing

Seven kilometres south of Daehan Dawon Tea Plantation is **Yulpo Beach**, a sandy cove with a pier at its western end and a weekend population of local sun seekers and camping enthusiasts from early April throughout September. If sand and live seafood rattling against glass tanks are not attractive enough, try Yulpo's two *jjimjilbang* (sauna): **Yulpo Haesu Nokchatang** *(from ₩10,000)* and **Dabichikondo Nokchatang** *(₩5000)*, which use green tea and are open between 6am and 8pm.

Mokpo

PORT CITY | OCEAN VIEWS | COASTAL HIKES

Thinking of the sprawling port city of Mokpo conjures three images: seafood feasts, live long-legged octopuses and rides on Korea's longest and highest marine cable car. Set on a small peninsula jutting into the West Sea, Mokpo old town is wedged to the east of three-horned Yudalsan. It's the end of the line for trains and expressway traffic, and a starting point for sea voyages to Jeju-do and the western islands of Dadohae Haesang National Park.

In contrast to many other Korean cities, the architecture of Mokpo's old core has remained steeped in the past, with webs of charming little alleys snaking behind Japanese-colonial-era buildings that rarely soar above three storeys. To the west of the city centre, the coastal Gatbawi Culture District hosts a pack of exciting museums and two iconic rock formations that have become a symbol of the city.

TOP TIP

Visit in the last week of the month to catch the spectacular **Dancing Sea Fountain** (p291) shows in front of Peace Sq in the Gatbawi Culture District.

Soar above Ocean, Mountain & City

Take a ride on the Marine Cable Car

At 3.23km long and 155m high, **Mokpo Marine Cable Car** *(mmcablecar.com; adult/child one way ₩19,000/13,000, return ₩24,000/18,000)* is among the longest and highest cable cars in Korea. It departs from the North Port Terminal and ascends to the summit of Yudalsan, where it rotates 90 degrees

GETTING AROUND

Mokpo's compact and walkable city centre and some of its best accommodation options are within walking distance of **Mokpo train station**, in front of which is a tourist information office with helpful English-speaking staff. It's a short walk to the old town, Yudalsan and its cable-car station. City buses run between the train station and Gatbawi Culture District or the **intercity bus terminal**, 20 minutes away (bus 3 offers the most direct route), with frequent departures to other cities in Jeolla-do and beyond. Two ports at the southern end of town have ferries to Jeju and other nearby islands.

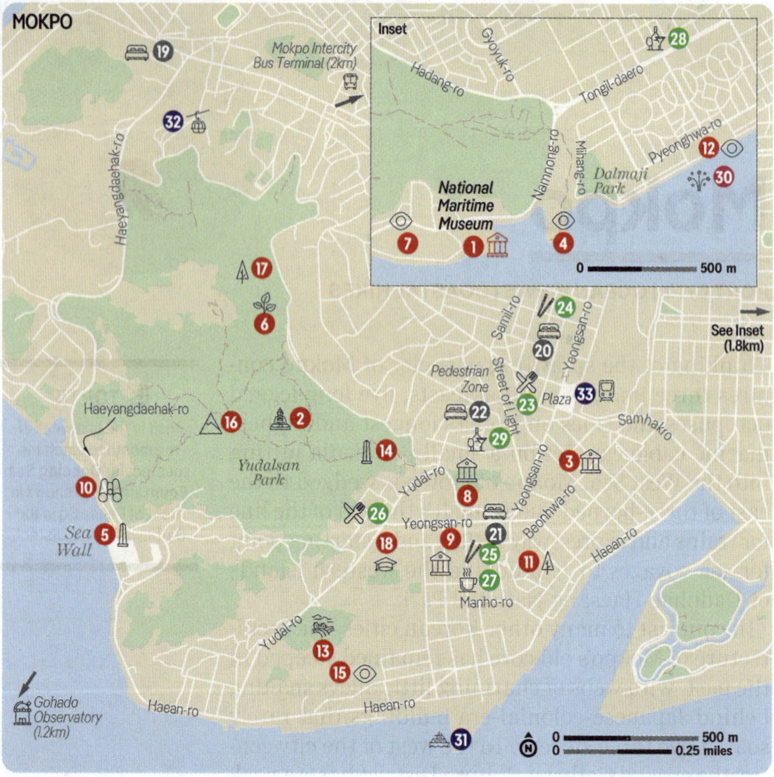

HIGHLIGHTS

1 National Maritime Museum

SIGHTS

2 Dalseong-sa
3 Former Honam Bank Mokpo Branch
4 Gatbawi Rocks
5 Love Statue
6 Mokpo City Specific Native Botanical Garden
7 Mokpo Culture & Arts Center
8 Mokpo Modern History Hall I
9 Mokpo Modern History Hall II
10 Mokpo Skywalk
11 Mokpojin History Park
12 Peace Square
13 Seosan-dong
14 Tears of Mokpo Monument
15 Yeonhee's Supermarket
see 10 Yudal Recreation Area
16 Yudalsan
17 Yudalsan Sculpture Park

ACTIVITIES

18 Yudal Elementary School

SLEEPING

19 Hotel Gabin
20 Picasso Guesthouse
21 Stay Ccassette Player
22 Sudabang Guesthouse

EATING

23 CLB Bakery
24 Dokcheon Sikdang
25 Jeongsong Gimbap
26 Magia Resto

DRINKING & NIGHTLIFE

see 5 Beach Gallery
27 Mano Cafe
28 Moe's Bar & Tattoo
29 OneDoSim Pub & Stay

ENTERTAINMENT

30 Dancing Sea Fountain
see 12 Mokpo Marine W Show

TRANSPORT

31 Mokpo International Ferry Terminal
32 Mokpo Marine Cable Car
33 Mokpo Train Station

to traverse the Dadohae Sea and stops on Gohado island, where you can walk 10 minutes to the curious **Gohado Observatory** *(free)*, made from 13 stacked *panokseon* (the main class of warship used by Joseon during the late 16th century) models. For sea-level views, take the wooden overwater walkway along the island's northeastern side.

A round trip on the cable car takes approximately 40 minutes, with regular and glass-bottom gondolas *(adult/child one way ₩22,000/16,000, return ₩29,000/23,000)* available. At the North Port, Yudalsan and Gohado terminals, there are cafes, restaurants and rooftop gardens.

MORE CABLE CARS

Mokpo fares well, but the **Chuncheon Samaksan Mountain Lake Cable Car** (p382) is Korea's longest at 3.61km. Other scenic cable-car rides are available at **Seoraksan National Park** (p162) and **Yeosu** (p281).

Mountain High

Take a hike to three-horned Yudalsan

Yudalsan is the last peak of the Noryeong range and marks the point where the peninsula halts before the Dadohae Sea. Towering above the western side of Mokpo old town, its three consecutive peaks – Ideungbawi, Lideungbawi (the tallest at 228m) and Madeungbawi – are a symbol of the city.

A web of well-maintained trails covers the perimeter of the massif, at the foot of which are a **sculpture park**, a **botanic garden** and a temple, **Dalseong-sa**. Views from the rocky summit stretch across the coastline, the islands of Dadohaesang National Park and the mountain's peaks. Madeungbawi has two large rock carvings of a Buddha and the King of Great Myeong, etched by the Japanese in the 1920s to promote their school of Buddhism. On the way down Yudalsan's southern flanks towards the car park, there's a **monument** to the song *Tears of Mokpo* by Lee Nan-young, written during the Japanese occupation and playing from a speaker under the walkway.

Enjoy Coastal Views

Stroll and drink at Yudal Recreation Area

Near the western side of Yudalsan (follow directions to Arirang Gogae and Nakjo-dae) is the **Yudal Recreation Area**, featuring a small beach where Koreans come to walk barefoot – a recent health-related trend nationwide. A deck dominated by the **Love Statue** – two giant lovers facing each other while holding a heart – with a stunning background of Mokpo Bridge and a few restaurants is where people enjoy dining and drinking. It's a few metres west of the popular **Mokpo Skywalk** *(free)*, a 54m-long, largely transparent glass viewing platform 15m above the sea.

HISTORIC BUILDINGS IN MOKPO

Mokpo Modern History Hall I: Built in 1900 as a Japanese consulate, now featuring an exhibit examining the Japanese occupation of Korea.

Mokpo Modern History Hall II: This ash-grey, Renaissance-style hall (built 1920) was the Mokpo branch of the Oriental Development Company.

Mokpojin History Park: Two *hanok* buildings stand on the former fort of the Joseon navy, transformed today into a history park.

Yudal Elementary School: This green-roofed building was once the Shimsang Public Elementary School.

Former Honam Bank Mokpo Branch: Mokpo's last colonial-era bank is a modernist structure dating to 1929, featuring rows of tall windows and decorative square designs.

Romantic Artsy Retro Village

Traipse to Seosan-dong and Sihwa Alley

Set to the southwest of Yudalsan and sandwiched along the coast between Bori Madang-ro to the north and Mokpo's fish market to the south, the small fishing village of **Seosan-dong** has beautiful views of the harbour, sea and small villages. The area saw a lease of new life after the Seosan-dong Sihwa Alley Development Project brought artists to spruce up the walls and enhance its 1970s and '80s vibes with vintage artwork. Highlights are Sihwa Alley, a 'poetry road' decorated with verses etched on the walls by residents, and **Yeonhee's Supermarket**, a filming location in the 2017 K-Drama *1987: When the Day Comes*. Bus 1 from Mokpo train station stops at Mokpo Suhyup (목포수협), from where it's a three-minute walk to the village.

EATING IN MOKPO: OUR PICKS

CLB Bakery: The original Colombang Bakery, one of Korea's top five since 1949. Delightful signature cream cheese and shrimp baguettes. *8am-9pm* ₩

Jeongsong Gimbap: (정성김밥) Popular *gimbap* store, famous for its seafood rolls, ramen and a very cosy, modern interior. *11am-9pm Tue-Sun* ₩

Dokcheon Sikdang: (독천식당) Famed long-legged octopus dishes, including *nakji-bibimbap* (octopus bibimbap) with seasoning and vegetables. *10.30am-3pm & 5-8pm* ₩₩

Magia Resto: Near Sihwa Alley, this cosy Western restaurant has all the comfort Caprese, pasta and fries you need. *11.30am-3pm & 5-9pm* ₩₩

TRABANTOS/SHUTTERSTOCK

Gatbawi Rocks

Seaside Walks for Culture Vultures

Take a stroll in Gatbawi Culture District

Four kilometres west of Mokpo's city centre is one of the city's icons, the **Gatbawi Rocks** *(free)*, two sea cliffs heavily eroded into shapes thought to look like two monks wearing reed hats. A walking bridge encircles them over the ocean, offering perfect views.

Ten minutes' walk west is a cluster of museums, the best of which is the **National Maritime Museum** *(mmk.or.kr; free)*. Dedicated to Korea's role in the ancient Marine Silk Road, it exhibits two shipwrecks from the 11th and early 14th centuries, with thousands of priceless Korean and Chinese celadon items, coins and other salvaged trade items, all with English captions.

The **Mokpo Culture and Arts Center** *(art.mokpo.go.kr; free)* houses contemporary art 100m west. Walking east from the Gatbawi Rocks, you get to sea-fronting **Peace Sq**, the place to sit and watch the superb **Dancing Sea Fountain** *(mokpo.go.kr/seafountain; free)* and **Mokpo Marine W Show** *(mokpowshow.co.kr; free)* light up the night sky.

FERRY TO JEJU ISLAND

Most travellers fly from Seoul's Gimpo airport to Jeju island, but once in Mokpo, it's possible to board one of the ferries between **Mokpo International Ferry Terminal** and Jeju. Seaworld Express Ferry operates at least 12 weekly departures, leaving Mokpo at 1am and 8.30am, and reaching Jeju at 5.30am and 1pm. The journey is aboard the *Queen Mary*, a large ferry equipped with a cafeteria, convenience stores, a massage chair area and video games. Economy class doesn't grant seats, only floor space in a futon-equipped area. Ferries return from Jeju at 1.40pm and 4.45pm, arriving in Mokpo at 6.10pm and 9pm.

DRINKING IN MOKPO: OUR PICKS

OneDoSim Pub & Stay: A giant teddy bear passed out by the front door welcomes you to a dimly lit pub with mean cocktails, neo-noir vibes and chic upstairs rooms. *7pm-2am*

Moe's Bar & Tattoo: Reopened in 2022, this is Mokpo's long-established expat and foreigner hangout where people enjoy beers, English chatter and even get inked. *1pm-1am Mon-Sat*

Mano Cafe: Large and welcoming minimal-chic corner-store cafe near the port, with a homey feel, tasty brews and cakes. *10am-8pm*

Beach Gallery: (비치갤러리) Popular Yudal Beach nighttime spot by the Love Statue for beer, burgers, fries and snacks by the sea facing Mokpo Bridge. *10am-midnight*

Beyond Mokpo

Korea's southwestern corner is made of islands, islets and even more islands that break off like breadcrumbs from Mokpo's coast. It's time to take your pick...

Places

GETTING AROUND

Direct buses leave Mokpo bus station to some of the sights, but departures are infrequent and once you get there, it's hard to find connections and explore further. Renting a car is especially useful for driving to the islands of Shinan-gun, many of which are connected to the peninsula by road bridges. In spring, cycling along the well-paved coast and taking ferries to remote islands is a good alternative for those with bags of time and a craving for adventure.

Mokpo is the gateway to the western part of Dadohae Haesang (Marine Archipelago) National Park. Consisting of more than 1700 islands and islets – some inhabited, some just tree-covered rocks – the marine park is divided into eight sections and occupies much of the coast and coastal waters of Jeollanam-do.

A highlight is Shinan-gun, a cluster of 1004 islands, some connected by bridges such as the 7km-long Cheonsa 'Angel' Bridge between Amtaedo and Aphaedo. Haenam County, at the southwestern tip of the Korean Peninsula, has road connections to islands such as Jindo and Wando.

If you tire of beaches, retire east to Yeongam to bag the craggy peaks of Wolchulsan National Park, the smallest national park in Korea.

Shinan Archipelago

TIME FROM MOKPO: **40MIN**

Explore the Purple Islands

The **Purple Islands** *(adult/teenager/child ₩5000/3000/1000, free if wearing purple-coloured clothes)* of **Banwoldo** and **Bakjido**, off the southern coast of Anjwado, are Shinan's most popular attraction. Locals connected three purple walking bridges, painting homes purple and planted fields of lavender. The islands can be explored in two to three hours, usually walking first to Bakjido, where electric golf carts *(₩20,000 for 30 minutes)* go around the island. Popular stops are a **lavender garden** 1.6km to the bridge's southeast, and **Wind Hill**, a viewpoint 200m further south. Cross the bridge to Banwoldo, rent another cart, or walk, and then return to Anjwado. Avoid weekends and holidays, as the islands are usually much more crowded.

The islands are particularly photogenic in the early morning and dusk – difficult timing if you're commuting from Mokpo bus terminal on the infrequent buses 1004 or 2004 to Amtaedo's Namgang Quay (one hour and 10 minutes), where a purple bus continues to Duri Village Wharf (25 minutes) at 8.40am, 9.50am, 11.30am, 1.50pm, 3.10pm, 5.20pm and 6.20pm. Driving a car makes things easier. Otherwise, **Bola Minbak** on Bakjido has large rooms for four people *(₩90,000)* and doubles *(₩70,000)*.

CENTRAL SHINAN ARCHIPELAGO DRIVING TOUR

Leave the city for a cluster of large islands connected by state-of-the-art bridges as you drive to the most accessible heart of Shinan.

START	END	LENGTH
Aphae Bridge	Purple Islands	42.3km; 1½hr

Drive north of Mokpo and take ❶ **Aphae Bridge** to Aphaedo island, appreciating views of the UNESCO World Heritage–listed Getbol tidal mudflats. You'll soon get to ❷ **Cheonsa Bridge**, a stunning 7.2km-long road connecting the islands of Aphaedo and Amtaedo, offering drone-like views of many islets popping out of calm, blue sea left and right.

Continue south along Amtaedo's main road to the ❸ **Gidong Samgeori Perm Hair Mural**, a wall portrait of an elderly couple with real treetops for hair, and then check out the gripping ❹ **Amtae Tenant Farming Struggle Memorial Gallery** (암태소작항쟁 기념 전시관), an art museum inside a warehouse featuring work by the celebrated painter Suh Yongsun. The mixed-mode murals utilise installations of wood, canvas and steel rods to commemorate Amtaedo's turbulent history.

Cross ❺ **Jungang Bridge** to Palgeumdo, the 'yellow island' famous for shrimp and salt farming, and drive across ❻ **Shinan First Bridge** to Anjwado, the birthplace of Kim Whanki, the famous Korean painter who died in New York. A museum should be opened within two years – meanwhile, you can stop by the ❼ **Kim Whanki's Birthplace** (김환기 고택) *hanok*. Proceed southwest to the ❽ **Purple Bridge**, where you can park and cross a footbridge to either of the Purple Islands: ❾ **Banwoldo** (p292) or ❿ **Bakjido** (p292).

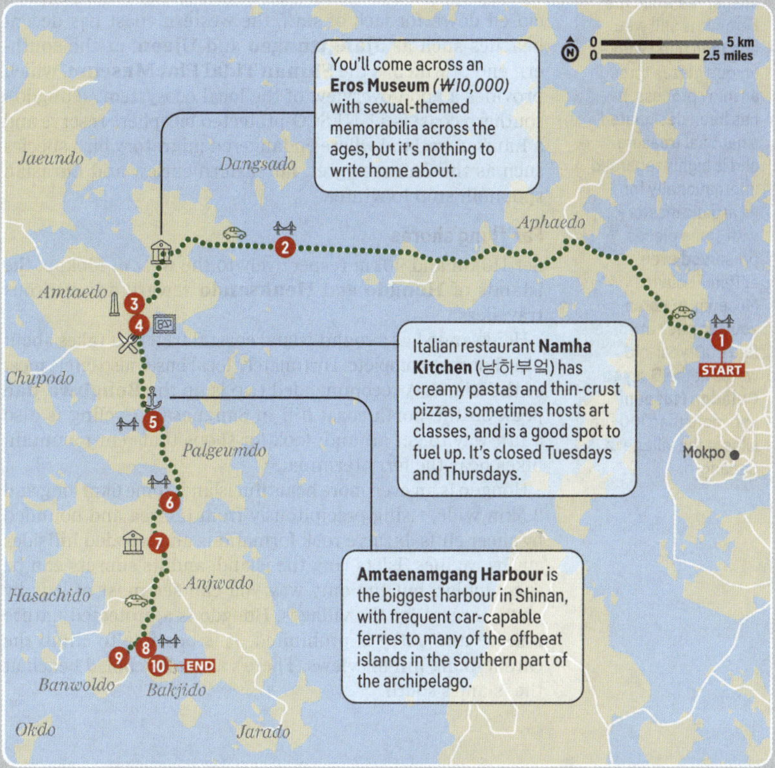

PRIZED JEOLLA CERAMICS

Between the 9th and 14th centuries, the town of Gangjin in Jeollanam-do was the primary production site of celadon ceramics for the Goryeo dynasty. Gangjin's celadon was inspired by the Chinese Yue ware of the Five Dynasties period (907–960 CE) from northern Zhejiang province. Gangjin is specifically famous for etched celadon, in which shallow patterns are carved while the ceramic is still wet, and then filled with unique glazes through an inlay process. It has been designated a national treasure and is highly regarded internationally for its artistic mastery, with some pieces preserved even at Paris' Louvre Museum. In Korea, you can peek at some fine 800-year-old wares at the **Goryeo Celadon Museum** and more than 100 fire kilns in the village of Sadang-ri.

AP TOLANG/SHUTTERSTOCK

Cloud Bridge, Wolchulsan National Park in Yeongnam

Salty island

Jeungdo is an island connected by a land bridge and accessible by car from Mokpo. Even with the Taepyeong Salt Farm, which explained to visitors about this island's main export, closed down for lack of staff, the western coast has decent beaches such as **Jjangttungeo** and **Ujeon**, at the southern end of which is the **Shinan Tidal Flat Museum**, which provides a good overview of the local ecosystem. Jeungdo's southern coast is a UNESCO-protected biosphere reserve and a Ramsar wetland where endangered migratory bird species such as the Chinese egret, far eastern curlew and Eurasian spoonbill stop to winter.

Far-flung shores

Set 110km and 90km respectively to the west of Mokpo, the islands of **Hongdo** and **Heuksando** reward adventurous travellers.

Heuksando has a round-island coastal trail that takes about nine hours to complete. Fortunately, local buses also circle most of the island. A recommended trip is up the **Bonghwa-dae** peak on the north-coast hill in Sangnasan. Cycling is also a fun way to get around; look for shops that rent mountain bikes near the ferry terminal.

Hongdo is an even more beautiful island, some 6km long and 2.5km wide, rising precipitously from the sea and bounded by sheer cliffs, bizarre rock formations and wooded hillsides cut by ravines. Islets ring the island, and its sunsets can be spectacular, but the only way you can see most of it is by boat – except for the villages, Hongdo is a protected nature reserve and entry is prohibited. It is possible to climb the Gitdae-bong hill for views. There's a small pebbled beach at the island's south.

Yeongnam

TIME FROM MOKPO: **45MIN**

Hike in Korea's smallest national park

Though it's just 42 sq km in size, making it Korea's smallest national park, **Wolchulsan National Park** *(free)* has crags, spires and unusually shaped rocks around every corner, as well as an 8m-high Buddha rock carving, steel stairways and a 52m-long steel bridge spanning two ridges. The popular route is the 8km, six-hour hike from **Dogap-sa** in the west to **Cheonhwang-sa** in the east (or vice versa) over the park's highest peak, **Cheonhwang-bong** (809m). Tracks are well signposted, but they can be steep and strenuous in places due to the rocky terrain. Bring lots of water.

If you're not up for a huge hike, head to the more popular Cheonhwang-sa end and hike an hour up a rocky path to a suspension bridge with sprawling views of the surrounding country.

Haenam

TIME FROM MOKPO: **1HR**

Explore Duryunsan Provincial Park

Picturesque views of Korea's southern coastline reward hikers who scale the rocky path up to **Duryunsan Provincial Park's** 630m peak, **Duryun-bong**. The hike begins just behind the temple museum at **Daeheung-sa** and takes 1½ hours. Near the top, it's a hard scramble – it's an easier descent if you follow the stairs down and pick up the trail at the junction of Jinburam. A **cable car** *(haenamcablecar.com; adult/child ₩15,000/12,000)* also heads up to a different peak, Gogye-bong (638m); it does not operate on windy days.

The end of the land

Ttangekkeut (Land's End) Village's claim to fame is its location on the southernmost tip of Korea. The main attraction is the **Ttangkkeut Observation Deck** *(free)*, perched on Sajabong mountain and accessible via a **monorail** *(adult/child one way ₩4500/3000, return ₩6000/4000)*. The views above the island-studded ocean are fantastic.

A **Marine Natural History Museum** *(tmnhm.co.kr; adult/teenager/child ₩5000/4000/3000)* to the north of the village is an excellent stop to see a large whale skeleton. Twenty minutes' drive north, across to Haenam's western coast, is **Songho Beach**, an attractive cove backed by century-old pine trees and with shallow and clear waters for a relaxing swim. The area also retains bragging rights for having Korea's southernmost

BEST BEACHES IN SHINAN

Bungye Beach: This large beach hugging Jaeundo's southwestern cape shelters the old Yeoinsong pine tree.

Baekgil Beach: Another beautiful beach on Jaeundo's southern cape, with a resort in walking distance of the sea.

Hanuneom Beach (Heart Beach): Wide horseshoe-shaped bay surrounded by verdant hills on the southwestern side of Bigeumdo.

Donmok Beach: A beautifully remote beach on the western side of Uido island. Its northern end has sand dunes.

Eomeori Beach: This beach on the southern end of Imjado has tall rock formations and the impressive Yongnangul cave.

EATING & DRINKING AROUND MOKPO: OUR PICKS

Wonjo Jangsu Tongdak: (원조장수통닭) Speciality Haenam restaurant, on the way to Daeheung-sa, serving stir-fried, marinated Korean chicken for over 25 years. *11.30am-9pm* ₩₩

Jeonsama: (전사마) A longstanding seafood restaurant on Wando specialising in abalone served in different ways. *9am-9pm* ₩₩

Haedang 1700: (해당1700) Impressive cafe in a stunning wooden-domed structure surrounded by nature on the south end of Jeungdo's Ujeon beach. *9am-6pm* ₩

Banwol Village Restaurant: (반월마을식당) Complete the Purple Island experience at this Banwoldo spot selling purple-tinged rice with stir-fried octopus and other Korean mains. *11am-9pm* ₩₩

SHINAN'S BEST OFFBEAT ISLANDS

Keunha Kim, a resident of Hongdo island and Shinan Archipelago travel expert, suggests her favourite islands. *facebook.com/keunha.kim.7*

Gijomsoakdo: Pilgrim's Island is the starting point of an incredible religious-themed hike across five islands, each with its own chapel named after one of the Twelve Apostles. The 'sea road' emerges twice a day based on tides. They vary daily, so it's a different experience each time.

Hauido: The birthplace of former President and Nobel Peace Prize winner Kim Dae-jung has great coastal scenery – an islet shaped like a human face makes for fun photos.

Gageodo: Korea's southwesternmost point. It's very remote, with rough waves and difficult to reach, but I still think it has some of the most breathtaking scenery I've ever seen.

SNOWTIGERMAN/GETTY IMAGES

Jindo Miracle Sea Road

temple, **Mihwang-sa** *(mihwangsa.org; free)*, first built in 749 CE on the western side of the 489m-high Dalmasan. It boasts fantastic sunset views over Korea's southernmost sea and unique carvings of sea creatures on a cornerstone inside its main Daeungbo-jeon hall. Templestays are possible.

Jindo

TIME FROM MOKPO: 1HR

Parting of the sea

Jindo, Korea's third-largest island, boasts some of the world's largest tides and is famous for an unusual natural phenomenon – for a few days each year (usually in spring), the tide drops extremely low, exposing a 2.8km-long, 40m-wide causeway that connects Jindo to the tiny island of Modo-ri. Some 300,000 people make the crossing between the islands each year – in tall rubber boots (available for rent, naturally) – coinciding with the **Jindo Miracle Sea Road** festival held annually to celebrate the crossing. From the Jindo bus terminal, catch a local bus bound for Hoedong (one hour, departs hourly) to the festival site; a taxi should cost about ₩15,000 and take 30 minutes.

Wando

TIME FROM MOKPO: 1½HR

Southern beaches

Wando is another island you can drive to. Besides its impressive 76m-high **Wando Tower** *(adult/teenager/child over 6yr ₩2000/1500/1000)* observatory at the top of Dongmangsan mountain, its neighbouring island, Shinjido, is home to **Myeongsasim-ni**, one of the most beautiful beaches on Korea's southern coast. Its golden sand stretches for nearly 4km, backed by a boardwalk and pine trees, with a popular campground with raised platforms for tents and plenty of showers. Buses run here from the Wando bus terminal. For more off-the-beaten-track exploration, a 19.2km ferry trip to small **Cheongsando**, the southernmost island in Dadohae Haesang National Park, rewards with beautiful scenery and a slow lifestyle.

Places We Love to Stay

₩ Budget ₩₩ Midrange ₩₩₩ Top End

Jeonju

MAP P257

NeaRest Guesthouse ₩ Homey backpacker pad with a common room filled with guitars and cosy nooks, a simple kitchenette and clean four-person dorms. Good breakfast included.

Blueboat Hostel Jeonju ₩ The Jeonju branch of this hostel franchise has soothing pastel tones, with dorms and rooms arranged on the two sides of the 2nd-floor's stair landing. Free kitchenette and laundry.

Seunggwangje ₩₩ Humble 75-year-old *hanok* down an alley and owned by Lee Seok, a grandson of King Gojong. Has *ondol*-style (underfloor heating) rooms and photos of royalty in the courtyard.

Lahan Hotel Jeonju ₩₩₩ Midrange business hotel towering above the eastern flanks of the Hanok Maeul. It has a large swimming pool and views over the village roofs.

Namwon

Mua Guesthouse ₩ Perfect budget accommodation in walking distance of the Gwanghallu Pavilion, with squeaky-clean male and female dorms.

Hanok Hotel Namwonyechon ₩₩ It's worth splashing out for the most atmospheric *hanok* accommodation in town, just outside the wall protecting the Gwanghallu Pavilion.

Gwangju

MAP P267 & P269

Pedro's House II ₩ Funky and welcoming guesthouse curated by world traveller Pedro, with comfy dorms and excellent-value en-suite doubles near Ssangchon metro. Free breakfast.

Ariene's Guesthouse ₩ Cosy backpackers right outside the Yangnim-Dong Village, with a bar and lounge on the 1st floor, hostel rooms on the 2nd and a party room on the 4th.

ACC Design Hotel. ₩₩ A collection of superior suites decked in creative, chic details and all amenities in the heart of the old town, curated by Asia Culture Center.

Oasita Hostel Gwangju ₩₩ Swanky boutique hostel inside a refurbished villa in the Dongmyeong-ro entertainment area, with homey and spacious gender-separated dorms and private en suites.

Suncheon

MAP P277

Baguni Hostel ₩ Excellent central, riverside location for this immaculate industrial-chic hostel with dorm beds, en-suite rooms, bicycle rental and annexed Basterds cafe.

Namu Guest House ₩ The dorms at this cosy and clean guesthouse near the bus station are a great budget option, especially for women travellers. Doubles are good value, too.

Suncheon Guesthouse 24. ₩ A valid budget option near the train station, offering dorms and en-suite doubles for added privacy.

Suncheon Bay Eco Village Hostel ₩₩ Quiet, rural, *hanok*-style accommodation near the wetlands, with six-person rooms for ₩150,000 during low season.

Yeosu

Backpackers in Yeosu ₩ Modern hostel with en-suite bathrooms in four-person dorms, plus ample cooking and lounging areas.

Motel Sky ₩₩ Dated but friendly and well-maintained motel near Yi Sun-sin Sq. The 6th floor has the best views.

Mokpo

MAP P288

Sudabang Guesthouse ₩ A very clean guesthouse with dorms, equipped kitchen and a relaxing garden, all within walking distance of the train station.

Hotel Gabin ₩₩ Midrange hotel on Yudalsan's northern side, with well-appointed but straightforward rooms, even though it is quite a trek on foot to the sights.

Stay Ccassette Player ₩₩ Irresistibly hip guesthouse with a vintage-chic theme and retro rooms, conveniently located between the port and the train station.

Picasso Guesthouse ₩₩ Very close to the train station and food options, this midrange option has double and quadruple rooms and a very helpful owner.

Shinan

Banwol-do Purple Pension ₩ Wake up and feel the purple at this simple yet charming pension on the southern flank of one of the Purple Islands.

Yeoin Song Village Pension ₩₩ This hotel's uninspiring exterior belies the quality of its warm, wooden-floored mini apartments, which are set right behind Jaeundo's Bungye beach.

For places to stay in Jeju-do, see p333

PICHIT TONGMA/SHUTTERSTOCK

Above: Yeongsil Trail (p311), Hallasan National Park; Right: Women freedivers (p314)

Researched by
Ann Babe

Jeju-do

CITRUS ISLAND OF WALKING TRAILS

Korea's largest island offers spectacular World Heritage–listed landscapes, beautiful beaches, a unique culture, delicious food and multiple attractions designed for rest and relaxation.

More than 80km south of the Korean Peninsula, Jeju-do (제주도) is Korea's famed honeymoon destination, an island steeped in mythology and forged by volcanic activity. Locally it's known for its stones, winds and fiercely independent women, typified by the *haenyeo* – female freedivers (pictured) who gather seafood from the ocean. Many Koreans come here to hike up Hallasan, the country's highest mountain, or to view the sunrise from the incredible tuff cone Seongsan Ilchul-bong, rising straight from the sea.

Others adopt a slow-travel approach, walking along the Jeju Olle Trails that meander down country roads lined with citrus trees and past jagged coasts dotted with thatched-roof homes made from black lava rock. The ocean is never far away – go diving to view vividly colourful soft corals, or find a lovely beach on which to relax and watch the waves break and clouds drift by. Hop on a ferry to one of the outer islands such as Udo or Gapado for more glorious scenery.

Jeju offers plenty of indoor attractions, too. There are some fine art museums and experiences, including the Arario Museum in the capital Jeju-si and the Bonte Museum in a building designed by renowned architect Tadao Ando. Not least, there's Jeju's delicious food – best experienced in seafood shacks and restaurants with an ocean view, or in the buzzing covered markets of Jeju-si and Seogwipo.

THE MAIN AREAS

JEJU-SI
Historic capital, contemporary art, local cuisine. **p302**

CENTRAL & EASTERN JEJU-DO
Volcanic peaks, stunning coastline, lovely beaches. **p309**

SEOGWIPO
Dramatic cliffs, wonderful waterfalls, artistic street. **p318**

WESTERN JEJU-DO
Tea fields, beautiful islands, art museums. **p325**

Find Your Way

Covering 1833 sq km, Jeju-do is a big island dominated by its central peak of Hallasan. The two main cities are the capital, Jeju-si, on the north coast, and Seogwipo on the south coast.

BUS

Frequent services will get you most places on Jeju. There's free wi-fi on board all buses and at most stops, which have useful screens with live bus information and maps (touch the screen to select English). Invest in a Tmoney card for cheaper fares.

CAR

Driving on Jeju-do is easygoing. Road signs are in English, rental cars come with an English-language GPS system and hire cost is reasonable. Only in Jeju-si will you encounter much traffic. Free parking abounds.

Jeju-si, p302

Learn about the island's geology, history and culture at the capital's museums and historic sites. Check out the Arario Museum in Tapdong.

Western Jeju-do, p325

See the Sanbang-gul-sa Buddhist grotto, explore Hallim's botanical garden and take a ferry to Gapado and Marado.

Seogwipo, p318

Wonder at waterfalls and go diving off the coast. Hike some of the Jeju Olle Trails, stopping along the artsy Lee Jung-seop St.

Central & Eastern Jeju-do, p309

Climb Hallasan, then beach hop your way to the Seongsan Ilchul-bong extinct tuff volcano. Spend a day on the island of Udo.

FOOTAGELAB/SHUTTERSTOCK

Yongmeori Coast (p330)

Plan Your Time

Jeju is a big island and to do its many attractions justice, reckon on spending two weeks here. That said, even on the shortest trip, there's a lot you can pack in.

Long Weekend Jaunt

- Make your base Jeju-do's second largest city, **Seogwipo** (p318). From Seogwipo, you can easily visit the extinct tuff volcano of **Seongsan Ilchul-bong** (p309) to the east, and the Buddhist temple of **Sanbang-gul-sa** (p329) and the **Yongmeori Coast** (p330) to the west. Go surfing around **Jungmun Resort Complex** (p328), stroll to the island of **Saeseom** (p321) and meander along some of the most scenic routes of the **Jeju Olle Trail** (p322)

A Week or More

- Spend a few days in the capital **Jeju-si** (p302) to check out the contemporary art of the **Arario Museum** (p307) and the exhibits at **Jeju National** (p302) and **Jeju Folklore & Natural History** (p302) museums. Climb to the summit of South Korea's tallest mountain, **Hallasan** (p310), then stay at a pension or guesthouse along the northeast coast. On your way back west, stop at the **Jeju Stone Park** (p317) and **Jeju April 3 Peace Park** (p308).

SEASONAL HIGHLIGHTS

SPRING

In March and April, flowers bloom across Jeju-do – from canolas and king blossoms to azaleas. Migratory bird season also means spectacular sightings.

SUMMER

July and August are not only the island's hottest months, but also prime time for typhoons. Keep an eye on weather conditions, and heed government and operator advisories.

AUTUMN

The Tamna Cultural Festival celebrates the ancient kingdom of Jeju-do – along with its mythical demigod founders – in October at **Samseonghyeol** (p303) and venues across Jeju-si.

WINTER

An all-night party is held in Seongsan-ri as people gather to listen to musical performances, see fireworks displays and climb **Seongsan Ilchul-bong** (p309) to greet the dawn of the New Year.

Jeju-si

HISTORIC CAPITAL | CONTEMPORARY ART | LOCAL CUISINE

GETTING AROUND

Jeju-si is a big, hilly city with plenty of traffic. If you're staying in Shin Jeju, near the airport, be prepared to travel by car or bus to reach the old downtown area, home to the bulk of interesting places to see. The old downtown and Tapdong are best covered on foot.

It's possible to base yourself in Jeju-si and travel by bus across the whole island, with the furthest destinations between one and two hours away. Streams of city and round-island buses originate from the **Intercity Bus Terminal** on Seogwang-ro and pass the airport or city hall.

TOP TIP

For easy access to Jeju-si's most vibrant nightlife with the biggest concentration of bars and pubs, aim to get a hotel in the Jeju City Hall area.

Midway along the north coast, Jeju-do's sprawling capital, Jeju-si (제주시), is where you'll first arrive on the island, either by flight or ferry. According to legend, this is where the three ancestors of all Jeju people emerged from the ground. Spend a day or two here to view a handful of historic sites and several good museums, go souvenir shopping, and dine in a legion of hip bars and cafes and delicious restaurants. The city's also a convenient base from which to explore the north side of Jeju.

Along the Tapdong seafront runs a pleasant promenade. This area, reclaimed from the sea in the 1980s, has been the focus of revitalisation in the wake of the opening of the trio of Arario contemporary-art museums. Continue west along the coastal road to Yongduam Rock for splendid seaside views and ample bars and pensions. Some classier places to sleep can be found inland at Shin Jeju.

Dive into Local History & Culture

Visit two museums and a shrine

The fascinating **Jeju National Museum** *(jeju.museum.go.kr; free)* covers the island's history – from its formation by volcanic activity 1.8 million years ago through to the Joseon dynasty. Highlights include an amazing stained-glass domed ceiling featuring a map of the island and an immersive digital gallery screening films that showcase Jeju's natural beauty. The museum is closed Mondays.

The **Jeju Folklore & Natural History Museum** *(jeju.go.kr/museum; adult/youth/child ₩2000/1000/free)*, also closed Monday, has wide-ranging exhibits on the island's varied flora, fauna and geological features. The lobby is dominated by a 12.6m-long skeleton of a fin whale. The folklore halls do a fine job of explaining Jeju's cultural heritage and there's also an interesting section on how the city's old downtown has evolved in recent decades.

DANNI9L/SHUTTERSTOCK

Samseonghyeol

Nearby is **Samseonghyeol** *(samsunghyeol.or.kr; adult/youth/child ₩4000/2500/1500)*, a shrine dating to 1526. Here you can view three depressions in the ground, said to be the holes out of which Goh, Yang and Bu, the mythical demigod founders of Jeju, emerged.

Historic Sites in a Hip Neighbourhood

Explore old and new Jeju

Jeju Mokgwana *(jeju.go.kr/mokkwana; adult/youth/child ₩1500/800/400)* was the island's administrative centre during the Joseon dynasty. Destroyed during Japanese rule in the early 20th century, the compound has been beautifully reconstructed. Outside the main gate is the 15th-century **Gwandeokjeong** pavilion, Jeju's oldest wooden building, once used as a training place for soldiers.

Cross Gwandeok-ro to explore the network of streets to the southwest of Chilseong-no Shopping District, around the old **Hyangsadang** communal hall. Look out for the cute **Urban Brewing** cafe *(@urbanbrewing.official)*, the charming vintage-style stationery shop **Classic Moongusa** *(classicmoongusa.com)*, the retro-chic vinyl-LP cafe and brunch spot **Ummpah** *(@ummpah_)*, and the cheerful and colourful

continued on p306

INDEPENDENT KINGDOM

Jeju-do's history and culture have followed their own trajectory separate from the mainland. Going back two millennia, the island was an independent state known as Tamna, which enjoyed trade and diplomatic exchange with the various kingdoms of mainland Korea as well as China and Japan.

In the 13th century, during the reign of Goryeo's King Gojong, Tamna lost its independence and was renamed Jeju, meaning 'province across the sea'. During the subsequent Joseon dynasty, Jeju was administered as a frontier region where horses were bred and political prisoners exiled. From the 17th century until the early 19th century, Jeju islanders were also forbidden to enter the mainland, reinforcing the island's distinct way of life.

Every October, the **Tamna Cultural Festival** is held in celebration of Jeju's unique culture.

EATING IN JEJU-SI: KOREAN

Dasoni: (다소니) Sit cross-legged at wooden tables at this superb meat-free restaurant. Dishes such as bibimbap use local Jeju produce. *11am-3pm & 5-8pm Mon-Sat* **WW**

Dombedon: (돔베돈) Sample the Jeju speciality of black pig on Heukdwaejigeori (Black Pork St), a street dedicated to barbecue restaurants. *11am-10.30pm* **WWW**

Haejin Seafood Restaurant: (해진횟집) Popular for seafood specialities such as cuttlefish, eel, squid, sea cucumber, abalone etc overlooking the harbour. *10.30am-midnight* **WWW**

Skyview Pocha: Snazzy restaurant at the Grand Hyatt serving street-food faves such as fried chicken, with glittering city views. *7am-1pm & 5pm-1am* **WWW**

★ **HIGHLIGHTS**
1 Jeju National Museum

● **SIGHTS**
2 Arario Museum
3 Arario Museum Dongmun Motel I
4 Arario Museum Dongmun Motel II
5 Art Space IAa
6 Gwandeok-jeong
7 Hyangsadang
8 Iho Tewoo Beach
9 Jeju April 3 Peace Park
10 Jeju Folklore & Natural History Museum
11 Jeju Loveland
12 Jeju Mokgwana
see 11 Jeju Museum of Art
13 Kim Man-deok Memorial Hall
14 Samseonghyeol
15 Samyang Beach
16 Yongdam Valley
17 Yongduam Rock

● **SLEEPING**
18 Bed Radio Dongmoon
19 Brne Stay
20 Goyo Walk
21 Grand Hyatt Jeju
22 Hotel Whistlelark

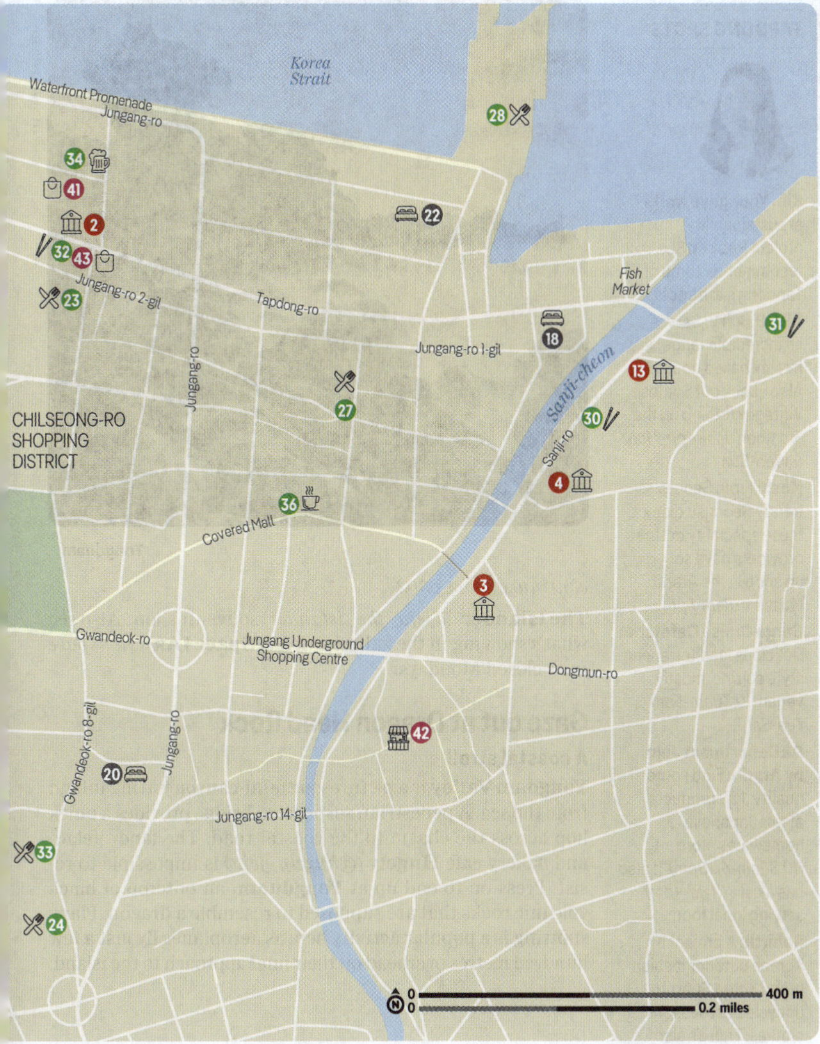

EATING
23 ABC Bakery
24 Bagdad
25 Cargo Cruise Cafeteria
26 Dasoni
27 Dombedon
28 Haejin Seafood Restaurant
29 Hugely
30 Jeokjeom
31 Kim Man-deok Inn
32 Mechin Kitchen
see 21 Skyview Pocha
33 Wardah

DRINKING & NIGHTLIFE
34 Bluebird by Magpie
35 Island Stone
36 Maeumeh On
see 2 Mesh
37 The Taste of Others
38 Ummpah
39 Urban Brewing

SHOPPING
40 Classic Moongusa
41 D&Department Jeju by Arario
42 Dongmun Market
43 Rebirth
44 The Islander

TRANSPORT
45 Jeju Intercity Bus Terminal

TAPDONG SPOTS

Kim Younghye works at sustainability project Rebirth. She recommends some of Tapdong's top spots.

ABC Bakery: Serves an incredible range of freshly baked goods. Also check out Somoso Vintage clothing on the 3rd floor. *8am-4pm Mon & Wed-Sun*

Mesh: From Seoul's trendy Seongsu district, these speciality coffee providers have set up shop in the Arario Museum. *8am-5pm*

Cargo Cruise Cafeteria: Delicious Mediterranean-style cuisine, mostly vegan. *10.30am-5pm Tue-Sat*

D&Department Jeju by Arario: Find some quality Jeju products at this Japanese homewares store *(10.30am-6.30pm)*. It also has a cafe *(11am-4pm)* serving local foods.

Rebirth: A project by Korean outdoor fashion brand Kolon Sport to upcycle past seasons' clothes. There's also an art exhibition space and outdoor-equipment rental. *11am-7pm*

M_CAMERA/SHUTTERSTOCK

Yongduam

continued from p303

The Islander *(@jeju_the_islander)* souvenir shop . Also see what's showing in the galleries at **Art Space IAa** *(@artspace iaa)*, closed Mondays.

Gaze out at Dragon Head Rock

A coastal stroll

Yongdam Valley is a picturesque mini-canyon jutting inland from the sea. A pedestrian suspension bridge provides a quick hop across the chasm to the coastal road. The fancy gelato and bakery cafe **Hugely** *(@hugely_jeju)* is impossible to resist. Press on to end up at **Yongduam**, an outcrop of black volcanic rocks that are supposed to resemble a dragon. Plane spotting is a popular activity here as aeroplanes fly just a few hundred metres overhead on their final approach to the island.

EATING IN JEJU-SI: INTERNATIONAL CUISINES

Bagdad: Classy Indian restaurant. Try its *tandoori* chicken and peanut butter *masala*, with a serving of handmade garlic naan. *11am-3pm & 5-10.30pm* **WW**

Jeokjeom: Scrumptious bowls of pho topped with beef brisket and *cơm sườn* (pork chop and rice) feature at this authentic Vietnamese cafe. *11am-3.30pm & 6-8pm Tue-Sun* **W**

Mechin Kitchen: Lively izakaya-style (Japanese pub) restaurant; sit at the counter and watch the chefs prepare sashimi or sushi rolls. *5.30-11pm Tue-Sun* **WWW**

Wardah: Delicious Yemeni food might not be something you'd expect on Jeju, but with a sizable Yemeni refugee population, it's served at this rustic cafe. *noon-10pm Mon-Sat* **W**

Browsing & Snacking at Dongmun Market

Lobster tails and pork rolls

Covering several city blocks, **Dongmun Market** is well worth a wander to peek at local seafood and stock up on Jeju's citrus. Be sure also to sample the wide range of street food, including black pork rolls and grilled lobsters tails, at its lively night market (5.30-10pm) by Gate 8.

Trio of Art Galleries

Admire top-class contemporary art

The **Arario Museum** *(arariomuseum.org)*, showcasing pieces from an outstanding contemporary-art collection, is split over three locations, all closed Mondays. The former Tapdong Cinema is the largest facility, covering five floors with works that include pieces by Gilbert & George, Damien Hirst and Anselm Kiefer. A short walk away, **Dongmun Motel I** has art by Antony Gormley, Tracey Emin and Issac Julien, while **Dongmun Motel II** is devoted to a solo exhibition of sculptures and installations by Gu Bonju. It's worth buying a pass to visit all three sections *(adult/youth/child ₩24,000/14,000/9000)*.

ARARIO COLLECTION

Kim Chang-il, also known as the artist Ci Kim, is a self-made multimillionaire and owner of one of the largest contemporary art collections in the world. More of his collection is on show at **Seoul's Arario Museum in SPACE** (p67).

Park of Erotic Sculptures

Enter an adults-only zone

Jeju Loveland *(₩15,000)* is an eye-popping erotic outdoor theme park populated with more than 100 sexually explicit sculptures. This adults-only park also features soft-core art galleries, a sex-toy store and a cafe selling genital-shaped bread – some will find it funny, others offended by sexual stereotypes.

Next door, enjoy more mainstream creativity at the **Jeju Museum of Art** *(jeju.go.kr/jmoa; adult/youth/child ₩2000/1000/500)*, which has a mixture of permanent and temporary exhibits of contemporary visual art. The beautifully designed building appears to float on a pool of water. It's closed Mondays.

DRINKING IN JEJU-SI: OUR PICKS

Island Stone: Longtime favourite with a lively atmosphere and friendly staff. It's run by the charismatic Stone, a Jeju local. *8.30pm-3.30am Tue-Sun*

Maeumeh On: Charming *hanok* (traditional home) cafe off the covered Chilseong-no shopping arcade. Try its Jeju green-barley latte, flower teas and traditional sweets. *10am-8pm*

Bluebird by Magpie: Enjoy an excellent range of craft beers brewed on the island and poured at this industrial space. Also serves tasty pizzas and fried chicken. *5pm-1am*

The Taste of Others: Sometimes there are DJs spinning the decks at this intimate, retro-vibes cocktail bar. It offers a whiskey tasting course, too. *6pm-1am*

KIM MAN-DEOK

Jeju's strong-willed women are famous, and none more so than Kim Man-deok (1739–1812), a *gisaeng* (entertainer) who made a fortune as the island's first female trading merchant. She is best remembered for an act of charity in which she used nearly her entire fortune to buy rice for more than 1000 people suffering in the severe famine of 1794. When King Jeongjo heard of Kim's largesse, he was so impressed he granted her wish to visit Mt Kumgang – thus ending the 200-year prohibition on islanders visiting the peninsula. You can learn more about Kim at the **Kim Man-deok Memorial Hall** and also visit a reconstruction of the **inn** that she used to run, which now houses a restaurant.

TRABANTOS/SHUTTERSTOCK

Jeju April 3 Peace Park

Hit the Local Beaches

Bury yourself in black sand

Iho Tewoo, the nearest beach to the city heading west along the coast, has an unusual mixture of yellow and grey sand, which means you can build two-tone sandcastles. It's also bookended by two horse-shaped lighthouses – one red, one white. There's shallow water that makes for safe swimming.

The first beach east along Hwy 1132 from Jeju-si is **Samyang**, which is jet black when wet. In summer, join the locals and bury yourself in the iron-rich sand for a therapeutic sand bath, said to relieve dermatitis, arthritis and athlete's foot.

Repository of Traumatic Memory

Jeju April 3 Peace Park

The **Jeju April 3 Peace Park** *(jeju43peace.org; free)*, 13km southeast of downtown, has a thoughtful and evocative museum that chronicles the events that led up to and followed the April 3 Incident (p398). This most traumatic series of events in the late 1940s and early 1950s, whereby an island uprising was brutally suppressed by government forces, resulted in the large-scale massacre of Jeju civilians – the most casualties in modern Korean history apart from the Korean War. Having digested the harrowing history in the museum, spend some time gathering your thoughts among the sculptures and memorials in the surrounding park.

Central & Eastern Jeju-do

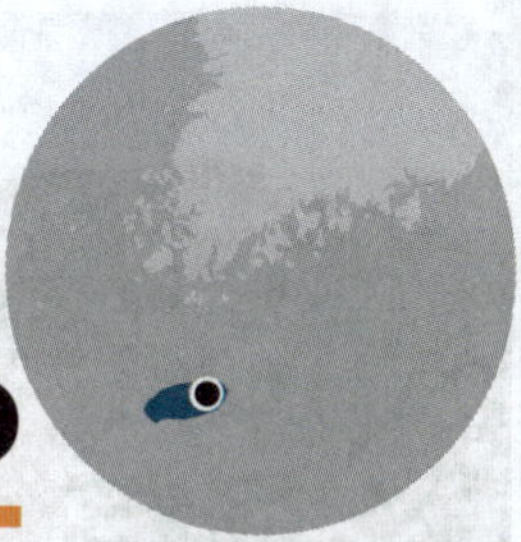

VOLCANIC PEAKS | STUNNING COASTLINE | LOVELY BEACHES

Hallasan, South Korea's highest mountain, dominates central Jeju. The 1950m peak is protected within a UNESCO World Heritage–listed national park. Hiking to the summit is strenuous, but worth the effort.

The coast is what eastern Jeju-do does best. Stretches of pretty beaches, off which the *haenyeo* divers fish, lead you to the island's most impressive sight – the extinct tuff volcano Seongsan Ilchul-bong jutting into the sea. A great little day trip or overnight stay is Udo, a small island with both black- and white-sand beaches, blue waters, and grain and peanut fields.

Other worthwhile sights in this part of the island include Manjang-gul, the access point the world's longest system of lava-tube caves, and the preserved folk village of Seongeup. And just when you thought you'd never want to see another rock, the mystical Jeju Stone Park makes you eat your words.

Climb Castle Mountain

Stand atop Seongsan Ilchul-bong

The majestic 182m-high extinct tuff volcano of **Seongsan Ilchul-bong** (Seongsan is 'Castle Mountain' and Ilchul-bong is 'Sunrise Peak') is one of Jeju-do's most impressive sights and a UNESCO World Heritage site. Shaped like a giant punchbowl, the forested crater rising straight from the sea is ringed by jagged rocks, though there's no lake because the rock is porous. From the entrance, connected to mainland Jeju by a land bridge, the steep stair climb to the crater rim only takes 20 minutes *(adult/child ₩5000/2500)*. Doing it in time to catch sunrise is a life-affirming journey for many – expect plenty of company.

To do the sunrise expedition, you'll have to spend the night in Seongsan-ri, a touristy village filled with motels and restaurants. The steps up the volcano are easy and clear, but if you're concerned, bring a torch. Not an early riser? It's also a popular daytime hike.

GETTING AROUND

Eastern Jeju-do includes the coastal area along Rte 1132 from Gimnyeong to Pyoseon, some inland sites and the ferry to Udo. For full flexibility, having your own set of wheels is best.

Most of the coastal destinations can be accessed by buses 101 and 201 that hug the coast between Jeju-si and Seogwipo via Seongsan Ilchul-bong. Heading inland by bus is a bit more challenging, though the tourist shuttle bus 810 can get you to some sights and back by transferring at one of the Daecheon Transit Center stops clustered around Daecheon Intersection.

TOP TIP

If you plan to hike to the top of **Hallasan** (p310), timing is crucial. Make your wake-up easier by staying overnight at the **campground** (p311) at the Gwaneum-sa entrance, then hitting the trail right when it opens.

Baengnokdam

TOP EXPERIENCE

Hallasan National Park

This 153-sq-km, World Heritage–listed park surrounds Hallasan, South Korea's highest peak. The 1950m volcano, which last erupted some 5000 years ago, can be hiked year-round, though it does get covered with snow in winter, so come prepared. There's a stunning crater lake at the summit, called Baengnokdam, which means 'white deer lake'.

DON'T MISS

- Seongpanak Trail
- Gwaneum-sa Trail
- Eoseungsaengak Trail
- Yeongsil Trail
- Donnaeko Trail
- Seokgul-am Trail
- Eorimok Trail
- Baengnokdam
- Sara Oreum Observatory Deck

The Trails

Of the seven daytime-only trails up and around Hallasan, only Seongpanak and Gwaneum-sa go to the peak. The Eoseungsaengak and Seokgul-am trails are the shortest and least strenuous, but still finish with rewarding sights.

Paths are clearly marked so it's difficult to get lost. Besides, you'll seldom be climbing alone, especially on Sundays. Noted climbing times (one way) are generous. However, set out early – if you don't reach the uppermost shelters by certain times (1pm in summer, 12.30pm in spring and fall, noon in winter), rangers will stop you from climbing higher.

PRACTICALITIES

● visithalla.jeju.go.kr/main/main.do ● 064-713-9953 ● free
● generally 5am-6pm, but varies by season

Seongpanak Trail

This popular route (9.6km, 4½ hours) has the most gradual ascent and a side trail to the **Sara Oreum Observatory Deck** for beautiful views of Sanjeong Lake and Hallasan's summit. With quick access to Rte 1131 and public transport – the **bus stop** is beside the car park – it's a busy place. Shops near the car park sell basic food and hiking supplies.

Gwaneum-sa Trail

This challenging route (8.7km, five hours) is one of Hallasan's most scenic trails. It's also the steepest. While it's most common to hike up Seongpanak and down Gwaneum-sa, consider what your knees can handle.

Reaching the trailhead by bus is not straightforward. Instead, catch a taxi from the Seongpanak Trail car park to the **Gwaneum-sa campground**, where the trail begins.

Eoseungsaengak & Eorimok Trails

The Eoseungsaengak Trail (1.3km, 30 minutes) is an easy hike that begins at the **Hallasan National Park Visitor Center** and finishes atop Eoseungsaeng Oreum, with sweeping views of the Jeju plains and Hallasan's summit.

Adjacent to the entrance of the Eoseungsaengak Trail is that of the Eorimok Trail (6.8km, three hours), which includes a steep climb through a deciduous forest. Halfway up, the dense trees give way to an open, subalpine moorland of bamboo, grass and dwarf firs.

The trailheads are a 20-minute walk from the **bus stop**.

Yeongsil Trail

Covered with boardwalks much of the way, this easy 5.8km, 2½ hour trail offers grand scenery – you'll hike through mixed deciduous forests and dwarf firs, before coming to panoramas of *oreum* (parasitic cone) and pinnacle rocks atop sheer cliffs. It begins with a 45-minute walk from a **park office** (**bus stop** and first car park) to a rest area (second car park), and continues with 3.7km of trails to the **Witse Oreum shelter** (with the option to go further to Nambyeok Junction).

Donnaeko Trail

This southern course (7km, 3½ hours) starts from the **Donnaeko Visitor Information Center**, providing coastal views of Seogwipo and running through a red pine forest. For the best views, it's recommended to climb up Yeongsil or Eorimok and then down Donnaeko.

Seokgul-am Trail

This short route (1.5km, 50 minutes) starts near the Buddhist temple **Cheonwang-sa**, runs through Ahheunahhop-gol (99 Valley) and terminates at the female hermitage Seokgul-am. Though novice hikers may wince at the occasional stretch of steep steps, the end is worth it.

Take bus 240, get off at the **Jeju National Guard stop**, then walk 350m south towards Cheonwang-sa. The trail begins at the parking lot.

RESERVATIONS

Hallasan can be climbed year-round. Only the Seongpanak and Gwaneum-sa trails require reservations *(free)*, which open the first day of each month and can be made up to the end of the following month. Reserve online or by phone. Seongpanak is limited to 1000 hikers per day; Gwaneum-sa to 500. Whichever trail you choose to climb, you're free to descend on the other.

TOP TIPS

- Trails open at 6am (5am in summer) and hikers should be off the trails by sunset.
- Free maps are available from the information centres at the main trail entrances.
- Be prepared for sudden weather changes, wind and rain (snow in winter).
- Mountain shelters are for emergency use only, not for overnight stays. There's a campground at the park's Gwaneum-sa entrance.
- Refreshments are available at the Jindallaebat shelter (1500m) on the Seongpanak Trail and at the Witse Oreum shelter (1700m), the meeting point of the Eorimok, Yeongsil and Donnaeko trails.
- Parking is available at most trailheads.

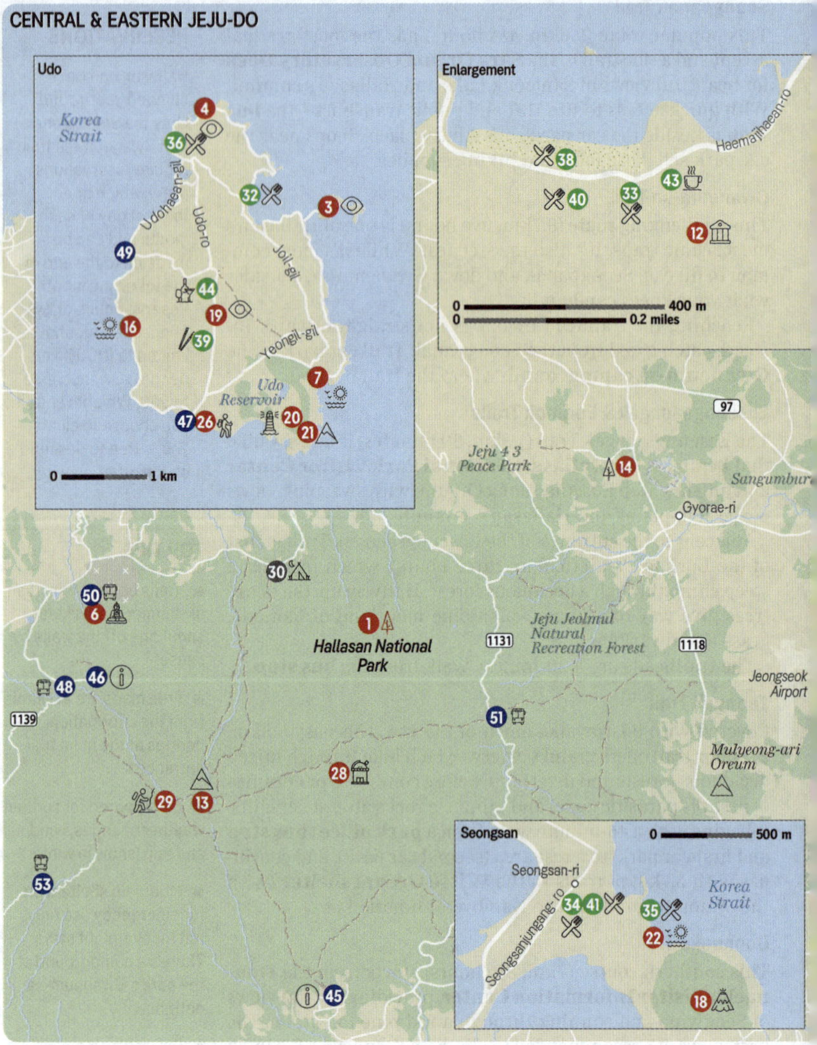

★ **HIGHLIGHTS**
1 Hallasan National Park

● **SIGHTS**
2 Agora
3 Biyangdo
4 Bongsudae
5 Bunker des Lumières
6 Cheonwang-sa
7 Geommeolle Beach
8 Gimnyeong Maze Park
9 Glass House
10 Gwangchigi Beach
11 Hado Beach
12 Haenyeo Museum
13 Hallasan
14 Jeju Stone Park
15 Kim Young Gap Gallery Dumoak
16 Sanho Beach
17 Seongeup Folk Village
18 Seongsan Ilchul-bong
19 Udo
20 Udo Lighthouse Park
21 Udo-bong
22 Umutgae Beach
23 Woljeong Beach
24 Yumin Art Nouveau Museum

● **ACTIVITIES**
25 Aqua Planet
26 Jeju Olle Trail Course 1-1
27 Manjang-gul
28 Sara Oreum Observatory Deck
29 Witse Oreum Shelter

● **SLEEPING**
30 Gwaneum-sa Campground
31 Phoenix Island

● **EATING**
32 Blanc Rocher
33 Dall Cheeze
see 9 Floyeast Bakery Cafe
34 Haeddeuneun Sikdang
35 Haenyeo House
36 HahaHoho
37 Orrrn
38 Seagulls Fam
39 Udoro 93
40 Umteun Delicatessen
41 Umutgae Ilbeonji
42 Yetnal Patjuk

● **DRINKING & NIGHTLIFE**
43 Cafe Hallasan
44 Udo Yunseul

● **INFORMATION**
45 Donnaeko Visitor Information Center
46 Hallasan National Park Visitor Center
see 53 Yeongsil Office

● **TRANSPORT**
47 Cheonjin Port
48 Eorimok Bus Stop
49 Haumokdong Port
50 Jeju National Guard Bus Stop
51 Seongpanak Bus Stop
52 Seongsan Ferry Terminal
53 Yeongsil Bus Stop

REAL-LIFE MERMAIDS

For centuries Jeju-do women have freedived to gather seafood. Working as cooperatives, *haenyeo* use low-tech gear – polystyrene floats, flippers, nets, knives and spears – but no oxygen tanks. They are able to hold their breath underwater for up to three minutes and reach a depth of 20m. While historical records show that men once were divers, factors like war conscription and tax rules led to a women-dominated profession. As of 2025, there are only 2371 active *haenyeo* remaining, and though a handful of young women are joining the fold, over 90% of *haenyeo* are aged 60 or older.

To learn more, read *Moon Tides: Jeju Island Grannies of the Sea* by Brenda Paik Sunoo and *Jeju Island's Haenyeo: A User's Manual* by Joey Rositano.

TRABANTOS/SHUTTERSTOCK

Manjang-gul

Explore a Cape with a View

Aquarium and star architects

At the entrance to the Seopji-koji cape is **Aqua Planet** *(aqua planet.co.kr; ₩44,600),* South Korea's largest public aquarium, stacked with all kinds of marine creatures, from otters and penguins to seals and sharks. Check the website for times of a circus-style acrobatic show and demos by *haenyeo* diving in the aquarium tanks.

Most of Seopji-koji is covered by the **Phoenix Island** *(phoenix hnr.co.kr)* resort. Walking around this scenic location provides wonderful views across to Seongsan Ilchul-bong, plus there's contemporary architecture to admire. Renowned architect Tadao Ando's **Glass House** is home to the bakery cafe **Floyeast**, while his **Yumin Art Nouveau Museum** *(adult/child ₩20,000/17,000)* exhibits French glass works by Émilé Galle and René Lalique. Both buildings are angled to frame Seongsan Ilchul-bong, providing yet more perspectives on the volcano. Mario Botta's geometric **Agora** is the resort's members' club.

EATING IN SEONGSAN-RI: OUR PICKS

Floyeast Bakery Cafe: Having pastries inside Tadao Ando's Glass House is a delight, best during the day to appreciate the views. *11am-9pm* ₩

Haeddeuneun Sikdang: (해뜨는식당) Enjoy seafood stew, grilled cuttlefish or mackerel at this family-run operation at the foot of Seongsan Ilchul-bong. *8am-9pm* ₩

Orrrn: Stylish bakery-cafe in a striking concrete building with superior coastal views. Enjoy your latte and ham-and-cheese croissant at the long glass table. *10.30am-8pm* ₩

Umutgae Ilbeonji: (우뭇개일번지) A bounty of seafood in each bowl of *jjamppong* (spicy noodle soup) and *haejangguk* (hangover soup). *6am-5pm* ₩

Watch Haenyeo at Work

And eat lunch at their restaurant

At the base of Seongsan Ilchul-bong, a long staircase leads down to **Umutgae Beach** a lovely crescent-shaped cove backed by weather-beaten lava cliff walls and boulders. On the left side of the beach, *haenyeo* divers run a **small restaurant** *(8.30am-6pm),* serving delicious abalone, octopus and other freshly harvested seafood, and put on a performance of their skills every day around 2pm.

Haenyeo can also be spotted going about their work off **Gwangchigi Beach**. Running between Seongsan-ri and Seopji-koji, this strip is a unique contrast of colours – mossy-green seaweed-coated rocks, black sand and blue waters, all framed by Seongsan Ilchul-bong.

Black-rock Beaches

Linger in Woljeong-ri and Hado-ri

Woljeong Beach is a fun place to stroll and spend time in the many oceanside cafes and restaurants. You can swim and surf here with a view out to the offshore wind turbines.

Further east along the northern coast, **Hado-ri** has a small attractive beach punctuated by outcrops of black volcanic rock. Hado's **Haenyeo Museum** *(jeju.go.kr/haenyeo; adult/youth/child ₩1100/500/free)* does an excellent job explaining the history and culture of the amazing *haenyeo* divers through exhibitions of their traditional homes, boats, tools and dress.

Record-breaking Lava-tube Caves

Natural attractions and family fun

Set to reopen in spring 2026, following safety inspections and upgrades, **Manjang-gul** *(jeju.go.kr/geopark)* has a main tunnel 18m wide and up to 25m high. You can walk inside this tunnel – part of the world's largest cave system created from flowing lava – for 1km to a 7.6m-high lava pillar. The immense black tunnel with swirling walls looks like the lair of a giant serpent. Take a jacket and good shoes as the cave ceiling drips, the ground is wet and the temperature inside is a constant chilly 10°C.

Nearby is the popular **Gimnyeong Maze Park** *(jejumaze.com; adult/youth/child ₩8800/7700/6600),* where you can wind your way through a puzzle of hedges.

GATE POLE MESSAGES

Jeju-do has traditionally described itself as having no beggars, thieves or locked gates. Instead, in front of homes in the island's villages you'll often see a rudimentary gate made up of two stone pillars drilled with holes to support three long *jeongnang* (wooden poles) between them.

If one *jeongnang* is hung from the gate, it means the residents are away, but nearby. If two are hung from the gate, it means they're travelling far from home but will be back later. If three are hung, it means the residents will not be returning home for a few days. And if all the poles are on the ground, it means 'we're home, please come in'.

EATING IN HADO-RI: OUR PICKS

Umteun Delicatessen: Snack on handmade charcuterie and sausages from a Michelin-starred chef and sip from a bottle of good wine. *noon-7pm Tue-Sun* ₩₩

Cafe Hallasan: Pot plants and vintage odds and ends, including an old rocking horse, add charm to this sea-view cafe serving coffee and carrot cake. *9.30am-9pm* ₩

Dall Cheeze: (달치즈) In a traditional stone cottage with outdoor seating, this appealing cafe serves some Turkish-style food, pizza and local beers. *10.30am-10pm* ₩

Seagulls Fam: Freshly made pizza with tasty toppings such as bulgogi beef or Italian cheeses and rocket. Great seaside location. *10.30am-9pm Fri-Wed* ₩₩

UDO PRACTICALITIES

With a few exceptions, you cannot take a hire car to Udo. Ferries from **Seongsan Ferry Terminal** depart frequently between 8am and 5.30pm, heading for either the port of **Haumokdong** or **Cheonjin**. The crossing takes 15 minutes and you don't need to depart from the same port at which you arrived. Remember to bring your passport.

Many operators at both Udo ports rent bicycles, motorbikes and three-person enclosed three-wheel scooters. An international driver's permit (type B) is required to rent the scooters.

Alternatively, there's a shuttle bus that runs clockwise around the island's coastal road on even-numbered days, and counter-clockwise on odd-numbered days.

See Seongeup Folk Village

Wander through an old Jeju maeul

A former provincial capital, **Seongeup Folk Village** *(jeju.go.kr/seongeup; free)* has benefitted from government assistance that has encouraged the preservation and renovation of its traditional rock-walled, thatch-roofed houses. Though modern intrusions include souvenir shops, restaurants and car parks, most of it still looks fantastically authentic. Unlike other touristy folk villages on the island, Seongeup is the real deal, with people living and working here still.

The core of the village is surrounded by a fortress wall punctuated by ornate entrance gates; Nammun (the south gate) is the main gate. Give yourself an hour to explore and consider having lunch at **Yetnal Patjuk** *(옛날팥죽; 10am-5pm)*, a rustic restaurant serving hearty red-bean porridge.

Photographing the Island's Beauty

Admire the works of Kim Young Gap

The countryside **Kim Young Gap Gallery Dumoak** *(dumoak.co.kr; adult/child ₩5000/3000)* showcases the work of Kim Young Gap (1957–2005), a self-taught photographer whose panoramic images captured the island's wild beauty. Diagnosed with Lou Gehrig's disease, Kim devoted the last year of his life to creating the gallery from an abandoned school. It's surrounded by a lush garden dotted with whimsical sculptures. The gallery, closed Mondays, is on Jeju Olle Course 3.

Day Trip to Korea's Land of Peanuts

Walk or cycle around Udo island

The largest of 62 islets surrounding Jeju-do, **Udo** (Cow Island) is so-called because its shape resembles a sprawled-out cow – the animal's head being the 100m-high peak of **Udo-bong**. Just 3.8km off the coast from Seongsan-ri, it's a lovely, windswept place that attracts throngs of day-tripping tourists, particularly on weekends and holidays. To better experience the island's rugged natural beauty, consider staying overnight.

The best way to explore Udo is on foot, following the 13.2km **Jeju Olle Trail Course 1-1**, which mainly keeps away from the busy coastal road, favouring inland paths. The route takes between four to five hours, starting and finishing at Cheonjin Port.

Udo's largest and most popular beach is gorgeous **Sanho**, which has brilliant white sand stretching out in a crescent on

EATING ON UDO: OUR PICKS

HahaHoho: Enjoy Jeju black pork burgers slathered with Udo peanut sauce, with a sea view and service that couldn't be friendlier. *10.30am-4pm* ₩

Udo Yunseul: If you're staying the night on Udo, this retro-styled wine bar is a fun place to drop by. Snacks include pizza, sausages and cheese nachos. *5pm-midnight* ₩₩

Blanc Rocher: Perched above the rocks, this stylish white-painted bakery-cafe has views across the shallow blue waters of Hagosudong Beach. *11am-5pm* ₩

Udoro 93: Head inland from Cheonjin port to find this modern cafe serving deep-fried coconut or peanut-coated shrimps and tomato udon noodles. *10am-5pm* ₩

TRABANTOS/SHUTTERSTOCK

Dol-hareubang, Jeju Stone Park

the island's west coast between the two ports. **Geommeolle Beach** has black volcanic sand and sits at the foot of dramatic cliffs rising up to Udo-bong, the island's highest point. Offering panoramic views all around, Udo-bong is crowned by a **lighthouse-themed park** with an actual lighthouse and various lighthouse scale models. Other points of interest include **Biyangdo**, an islet connected to Udo by a short causeway (you can camp for free here), and **Bongsudae**, an old stone watchtower on the north coast.

Before you leave, be sure to sample peanut ice cream, peanut *makgeolli* (milky rice wine) or some other specialty made with peanuts, the legumes for which the island is famed.

Bunker for Creative Projections

Immerse yourself in great works of art

A fine rainy-day option (or even if it's not raining) is the immersive art exhibition **Bunker des Lumières** *(deslumieres.co.kr/bunker; adult/child ₩19,000/9000)*. Buried beneath an artificial wooded hill is a 3000-sq-metre bunker that was once used to manage a submarine optical cable system. The concrete walls, floors and ceilings are now the projection screens for imaginative, colour-drenched digital art shows featuring works from the likes of Monet, Renoir and Chagall.

A Park Devoted to Stones

Natural and human-made rock art

Jeju Stone Park *(jeju.go.kr/jejustonepark; adult/child ₩5000/3500)* pairs a museum of extraordinary naturally shaped rocks with beautifully designed trails. Walks here snake past outdoor exhibits ranging from armies of *dol-hareubang* (grandfather rocks) to an enchanting grove populated with 1900 *dongjaseok* (stone tomb guardians). The Seolmundae Halmang exhibition hall showcases the island's mythology, history and folklore. The park is closed Mondays.

GRANDFATHER STONES

Sold across Jeju in all shapes and sizes as souvenirs, *dol-hareubang* are carved basalt statues with helmet-style hat, bulging eyes, a squashed nose and hands on the stomach. Meaning 'grandfather stone', *dol-hareubang* was the official title given to these totems in 1971 when they were designated as Jeju Folk Cultural Asset No 2.

Up to 3m in height, the original *dol-hareubang* are believed to have been carved around 1750 and placed outside the island's fortresses to ward off evil. With their phallic shape, they are also fertility symbols. Folklore has it that women can rub different parts of the statue to increase their chances of conceiving their desired child – the nose for a boy, the ears for a girl.

Seogwipo

DRAMATIC CLIFFS | WONDERFUL WATERFALLS | ARTISTIC STREET

GETTING AROUND

Driving is the best option, and there's plenty of free parking to be found throughout the area.

For walking and cycling, this part of Jeju is no different than the rest of the island in that it can be quite hilly. Safe walking routes abound, not least because Seogwipo is the hub of the Jeju Olle Trail.

If you don't mind spending a bit more time hanging around for services, nearly everywhere is reachable by bus, with 101, 102, 181 and 182 all servicing **Seogwipo Bus Terminal**. There's also a direct route to and from the airport, bus 600.

If you only have a short time on Jeju-do, make Seogwipo (서귀포, pronounced suh-gwee-poh) your base. It has the nicest climate, and sitting pretty on a dramatic volcanic shoreline, also the most striking coastal scenery – dotted with lush parks, a deep gorge and two main waterfalls, plus the spectacular backdrop of Hallasan. Seogwipo's clear blue waters and mild ocean temperatures make it Korea's best scuba-diving destination, and it's also an ideal base for hiking the Jeju Olle Trail, as the site of the network's headquarters.

Seogwipo's compact size makes it easy to walk between most of the sights in town, and at the end of each day, it's likely you'll find yourself back at Lee Jung-seop St. One of the area's most action-packed stretches, it offers some fine art galleries and delicious places to eat, not least the Seogwipo Maeil Olle Market.

A Pair of Pretty Waterfalls

View a couple of cascades

The **Cheonjiyeon Pokpo** *(adult/child ₩2000/1000)* is one of two popular waterfalls in Seogwipo. The 22m-high falls, an easy and relaxing walk from the city centre through a verdant, steep-sided gorge, are also worth visiting in the evening when an illumination creates a romantic atmosphere.

Also not far from the town centre along the coast, the 23m-high **Jeongbang Pokpo** *(adult/child ₩2000/1000)* cascades dramatically into the ocean. The falls are associated with Seobok, a 2nd-century-BCE Chinese scholar and explorer. Legend has it that he landed on Jeju at this spot in search of the elixir of an eternal life – to find out more, drop into the attractive **Seobok Exhibition Hall** *(culture.seogwipo.go.kr/seobok; free)* near the falls.

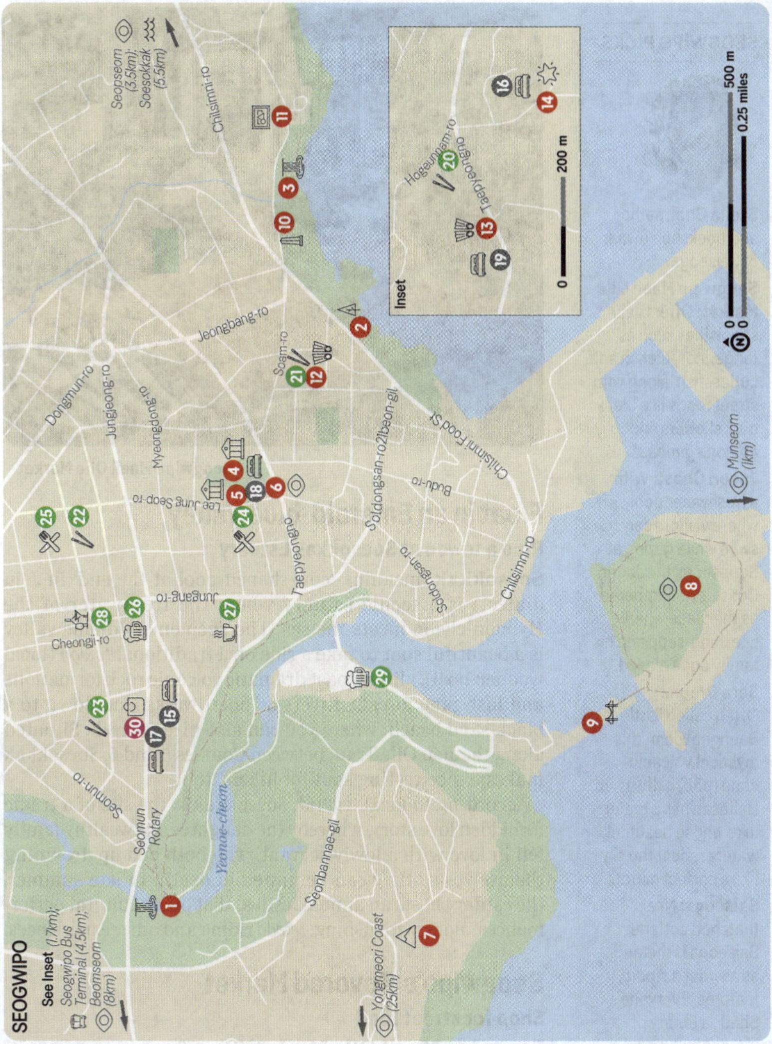

SIGHTS
1 Cheonjiyeon Pokpo
2 Jaguri Coast
3 Jeongbang Pokpo
4 Lee Jung-seop Art Museum
5 Lee Jung-seop House
6 Lee Jung-seop St
7 Oedolgae
8 Saeseom
9 Saeyeon-gyo
10 Seobok Exhibition Hall
11 Walart Museum

ACTIVITIES
12 Big Blue 33
13 MJ Jeju Diving Club
14 O'REVE Hot Spring & Spa

SLEEPING
15 Backpacker's Home
16 JW Marriott Jeju Resort & Spa
17 Olle Stay
18 Saiseoga
19 Seom Studio

EATING
20 Hachi
see 22 Jeok Sim
see 22 Jeseong Bakery
21 Monstera
22 Negeori Olle
23 Negeori Sikdang
24 Pasta Studio Jeju
25 Seogwipo Maeil Olle Market
see 17 Uhmeong Bapsang

DRINKING & NIGHTLIFE
see 6 Cafe Mayb
26 Jeju Beer Fountain
27 Lavarr
28 Mangwoo
29 Rose Marine

SHOPPING
30 Jeju Bonus
see 18 Saiseoga

SEOGWIPO PICKS

Stella Choi, author and bookshop owner of Saiseoga.

Seogwipo Maeil Olle Market: Offers Jeju specialties such as tangerines, tilefish and cutlassfish, along with street foods like black pork skewers and abalone *gimbap*.

Jaguri Coast: With a freshwater pool where visitors can swim while gazing at Seopseom, the Jaguri Coast is remembered as the place where Lee Jung-seop and his family once played.

Sara Oreum: Often called 'Little Baengnokdam', this mystical volcanic cone (p311) halfway up Hallasan has a crater lake whose beautiful waters reflect the sky like a perfect mirror.

Saiseoga: Near Lee's thatched cottage, Saiseoga is themed as a writer's studio. It features 'Everyone's Shelf', a library of life-changing books, and hosts talks, exhibitions and performances.

IZLAN SOMAI/SHUTTERSTOCK

Seogwipo Maeil Olle Market

Float in an Emerald-blue Valley

Ride a tewoo at Soesokkak Estuary

Soesokkak (meaning 'cow-shaped pool at the end' in Jeju dialect) is a scenic estuary where the freshwater of the Hyodon-cheon meets the sea. The deep emerald-blue valley is a beautiful spot to take a ride on a traditional *tewoo* (local wooden boat), gliding past dramatic volcanic rock formations and lush pine forests. Riverside boardwalks lead down to a black-sand beach, where you can also hire a kayak. Situated along the Jeju Olle Trail, between Courses 5 and 6, Soesokkak makes a nice resting spot for hikers, too.

According to local legend, Soesokkak is the site of a tragic forbidden love story, whereby the daughter of a wealthy family fell in love with a lowly servant, who both end up drowning themselves so they can be united in death. In late summer, the estuary hosts an annual festival that offers cultural performances, along with fishing, *tewoo* riding and other experiences.

Seogwipo's Covered Market

Shop for street food

Seogwipo Maeil Olle Market *(11am-9pm)* is an essential stop to browse stalls of delicious fruit, live seafood and souvenirs. You'll want to come to pick up items for a picnic and to dine on local street food.

EATING IN SEOGWIPO: OUR PICKS

Hachi: Book ahead for this classy *omakase* (chef's choice) sushi restaurant with its superb seafood-based banquet using local produce. *noon–9pm* ₩₩₩

Monstera: A charming courtyard garden is the perfect setting for this casual Vietnamese restaurant serving delicious *pho* and spring rolls. *11am-8.30pm* ₩

Negeori Sikdang: (네거리식당) Negeori is rightly beloved for its great renditions of *galchiguk* (hairtail fish soup) and grilled fish dishes. *7am-9.30pm* ₩₩

Pasta Studio Jeju: The friendly English-speaking owner and chef cooks up delicious pasta dishes (some vegetarian) and local craft beers. *11am-2.30pm & 5-8pm Tue-Sun* ₩₩

At the centre of the market are a cluster of places: **Negeori Olle** (네거리올레), specialising in fat deep-fried rolls of black pork, seafood and kimchi; **Jeseong Bakery** (제성제과; *@jeseong_bakery*) for its savoury bread buns; and **Jeok Sim** *(@jeoksim_; 4-10.30pm)*, a sit-down, Japanese-style kitchen bar where succulent chicken and beef patties and vegetables are grilled over hot charcoal.

Discover Two Korean Artists

Follow the Seogwipo art trail

Korean artists have long been inspired by the extraordinary landscapes and light of Jeju. Celebrated in Seogwipo is Lee Jung-seop (1916–56). His distinctive, Fauvist-influenced images are reproduced on walls around town, particularly along the **street** that's named after him. Here you'll find the traditional thatched **house** in which Lee lived and a small free **gallery** (set to reopen in February 2027) displaying some of his art as well as works by other Jeju-based artists.

Lee Wal-chong has been creating art in Seogwipo for more than 30 years. Check out his colourful and charming paintings, ceramics and painted wood carvings in his self-designed **Walart Museum** *(walartmuseum.or.kr; adult/child ₩10,000/6000)*, a distinctive circular building close by the entrance to the Jeongbang Pokpo.

Volcano-shaped Coastline

Stroll to Saeseom; see Oedolgae

One place to aim your ambles in Seogwipo is the area around its tourist port. The attractive **Saeyeon-gyo** cable-stayed bridge, which spans the mouth of Seogwipo Harbour, provides access to the densely wooded island **Saeseom**, around which runs a nature trail. The bridge's distinctive design is based on a traditional *tewoo* boat, with a sail at its centre.

Westward along Seogwipo's coast, look out for **Oedolgae** ('Lonely Rock'), an unusual volcanic basalt pillar rising 20m from the sea that has served as a filming location for a number of Korean dramas.

Returning to the port at night, when the bridge is nicely illuminated, have a drink at the tumbledown **Rose Marine** *(로즈마린; 5pm-2am Mon-Sat)* shack pub, which featured as a location in the K-drama *Extraordinary Attorney Woo*. Order *makgeolli* and *pajeon* (savoury spring-onion pancakes).

TOP TIP

As well as accommodation, Seogwipo's centre has excellent cafes, including **Uhmeong Bapsang** doing all-natural, good-value meals, and gift shops such as **Jeju Bonus** for souvenirs and practical items – socks, bandanas and T-shirts.

LEE JUNG-SEOP

Born into a wealthy family in what is now North Korea, Lee Jung-seop trained as an artist in Tokyo, where he met his future wife, the poet Yamamoto Masako. Nearing the end of WWII, Lee moved his family back to Korea, but on the outbreak of the Korean War, he sought shelter in Busan and then Jeju, where he lived from January to December 1951. While on the island, he refined his painting style and created seminal works such as *A Dream of Seogwipo*. Lee is most famous for his art depicting bulls, but on Jeju he was also inspired by crabs, the landscape and children playing.

DRINKING IN SEOGWIPO: OUR PICKS

Cafe Mayb: Creatively decorated inside, with tables spilling onto the street, this laid-back wine bar is the place to enjoy downtime with a book. *10am-1am*

Jeju Beer Fountain: Seogwipo's best selection of locally brewed ales is a lively pub that also serves pizzas. It has a takeaway branch, too, by the Maeil Olle Market. *4-9.30pm*

Lavarr: An old bathhouse has been transformed into this multilevel cafe-bar, brunch spot and art gallery. Head to the roof for views. *9am-10pm*

Mangwoo: Specialising in *magkeolli* and Korean rice wines, this classy hideaway is also a great spot to sample local food. *5.30pm-midnight*

HELP ME PICK:

Jeju Olle Trail

The Jeju Olle Trail is one of the great success stories of local tourism. In the Jeju dialect, an *olle* is a narrow pathway connecting a house to the main street. Likewise, since starting in 2007, the Olle Trails have been opening up Jeju's culture and scenery to visitors. Choose from 27 routes of between 4.2km and 20.9km in length that meander mainly along Jeju-do's coast (with some inland diversions) and three outer islands: Udo (p316), Gapado (p332) and Chujado.

Where to Hike If You Like...

Beautiful Scenery

Course 1 (15.1km), from Siheung Elementary School on Jeju's east coast down to rocky **Gwangchigi Beach** (p315), where black and white sands swirl together, is a beautiful introduction to the Olle concept. The landscape here is classic Jeju-do: verdant fields grazed by cows and fringed by black basalt walls, sleepy fishing villages beside azure seas and salt flats. The highlight is **Seongsan Ilchul-bong** (p309), a spectacular moss-green-coated tuff volcano rising out of the sea.

One of the network's most stunning sections, **Course 10** (15.6km) goes along the **Yongmeori Coast** (p330), around Songsaksan and past Gapado and Marado.

Gwangchigi Beach

Local Culture

Between Onpyeong and Pyoseon on **Course 3** (14.6km or 20.9km), you'll pass through the village of Sincheon-ri, where there are around 100 murals painted on the sides of houses and walls. One of these murals depicts Jeju's famed female freedivers – the *haenyeo* (p314).

Urban Exploring

The relatively easy **Course 6** (10.1km) finishes at the Jeju Olle Tourist Center in downtown Seogwipo. Before reaching Seogwipo, you'll climb the 95m Jejigi Oreum (parasitic cone). In Seogwipo, you'll walk up **Lee Jung-seop St**, admiring the art of this celebrated mid-20th-century Korean artist, and have a chance to explore **Seogwipo Maeil Olle Market** (p320), a great place to indulge in traditional local eats.

Course 18 (17.1km) starts in the old downtown of Jeju-si, at the **Kim Man-deok Memorial Hall** (p308) not far from bustling **Dongmun Market** (p386), and takes you to the 149m summit of Sara-bong for sweeping vistas of the city.

Remote Islands

There are two trails on Chujado, an archipelago of 42 islands roughly midway between Jeju-do and the mainland. **Courses 18-1** (11.4km) and **18-2** (9.7km) pass through the group's two largest islands: **Sangchujado and Hachujado**. This isolated location offers scenery unlike anywhere else in Korea.

Wheelchair Accessibility

Ten sections of the Jeju Olle are wheelchair accessible, so those with limited mobility can also enjoy the transformative power of the trail. A good example is **Course 10-1** – the shortest trail at just 4.2km – on Gapado. Even at its highest point, this compact island is barely 20m above sea level.

FROM LEFT: JONGHOLEE/SHUTTERSTOCK, STOCK FOR YOU/SHUTTERSTOCK

Course 7

HOW TO

When to go October and November have the best weather. May is also good for spring wildflowers. Avoid July and August when it's too hot.

Festival On the first weekend of November, join the **Jeju Olle Walking Festival** *(₩30,000)* to hike three connected routes between Friday and Sunday.

Getting around Jeju's bus network makes it fairly easy to return to your starting point at the end of each trail. Or hail a cab.

Further information The trail's excellent website *(jejuolle.org)* should be your first port of call. There are 14 information centres around the island, including the headquarters in Seogwipo.

DIY or Guided Tour

Walking all 437km of the Jeju Olle is a physical challenge that will take a month. The network has been purposefully designed to be easy to follow – people aged from five to 90 have completed the trail. Routes are clearly marked by orange and blue arrows on poles, walls and the ground, with similarly coloured ribbons dangling from trees. Orange is for going counterclockwise around the island; blue, clockwise.

You'll also encounter the trail's logo, the 'Ganse', a simplified form of a Jeju pony. The logo's name comes from *gansedari*, Jeju dialect for 'slow idler', and it encapsulates the Olle's philosophy of slow, meandering travel – the perfect antidote to South Korea's stress-inducing *ppalli ppalli* (hurry, hurry) culture.

It's worth investing in a passport *(₩20,000)* to record and remember your time walking on the trails. It's fun to collect the unique beginning, middle and ending stamps of each course (and a fully stamped passport entitles you to a certificate of completion and induction into the Jeju Olle hall of fame). The passport also comes with benefits such as discounts on various accommodation, restaurants and attractions along the routes.

If you register in advance, the Jeju Olle Foundation will set you up with one of its English-speaking walking buddies, who walk Course 6 every Saturday and half of Course 18 every Sunday.

DIVING OFF SEOGWIPO

Kim Kibong is the owner of dive shop Big Blue 33. He shares what makes Seogwipo a great diving destination. *bigblue33.com*

In Korea, there is no better place to dive than here. The seas around Seogwipo have warm water and are perfect for soft corals and tropical fish, but there's also black volcanic rocks and kelp. You can see sea bream all year and sometimes southern bottlenose dolphins and turtles. If you want to go wreck diving, there's a ship that was deliberately sunk just off Munseom for that purpose. For the best visibility, I suggest diving at the end of August, after the typhoon season is over.

THOMAS MCCOMB/GETTY IMAGES

Munseom

Bliss Out at a Spa

Hot springs, saunas and gardens

The palatial **O'REVE Hot Spring & Spa** *(orevespa.co.kr)*, part of the complex at the **JW Marriott Jeju Resort & Spa**, is the perfect place to soothe tired bodies after a day of activity. Thermally heated water has been tapped 2km underground to fill the vast range of pools, including ones in a beautifully landscaped garden where you can soak surrounded by volcanic rocks looking up at palm trees. Inside, there's a floor of various *jjimjilbang* (sauna), including a fragrant cedar-lined room and 'snowroom' where you can go to cool down, and a stylish bar and restaurant.

Rainbows of Soft Corals

Dive beside three small islands

Masses of multicoloured soft corals are what makes diving off Seogwipo so special. The main dive sites are three nearby small islands: **Seopseom**, **Munseom** and **Beomseom**. If you're not qualified to dive, it's still possible to sign up for a non-certified diver program. Operators also run three-day diving certification courses. English-speaking dive guides can be found at **Big Blue 33** *(bigblue33.com; prices vary by course)* and **MJ Jeju Diving Club** *(mjjejudivingclub.co.kr)*, run by Jeong Myeong-hwa and her husband Kim Jeong-ja.

Western Jeju-do

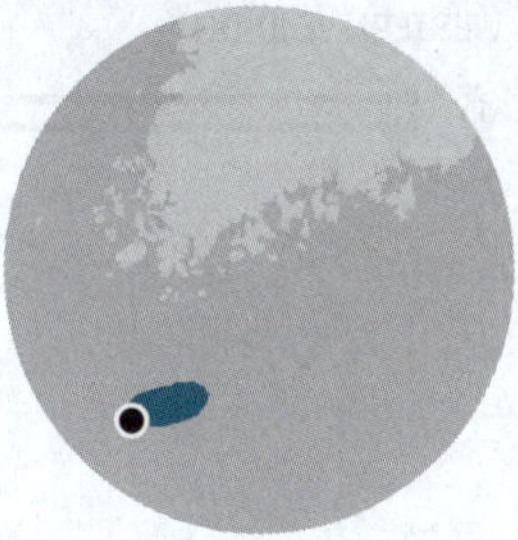

TEA FIELDS | BEAUTIFUL ISLANDS | ART MUSEUMS

The west side of Jeju-do mixes inland cultural treasures of speciality museums and green tea fields with the seaside delights of sleepy beach towns, mountain caves and teeny tiny islands. Along the coast, Hallim and Aewol have found their hipness with restaurants and cafes that lure you in with bright blue-ocean views, while the white sands and crystal-clear waters of its beaches are the perfect grounds for snorkelling.

Other reasons to visit are for the resort town vibes at Jungmun Resort Complex; the quainter Sagye-ri, with its little beach; the imposing outcrop of Sanbangsan, home to a Buddha in a cave; and the spectacular Yongmeori coastal walk. Try to make time too to visit the lovely islands of Gapado and Marado, as far south as you can go and still be in Korea. It takes some exploration to get there, but they promise absolute serenity.

TOP TIP

For booking tickets to the islands of **Gapado** (p332) and **Marado** (p332), don't forget to bring your physical passport to the ferry terminal – photocopies and photos are not accepted.

Hang Ten in Jungmun

Learn to ride the waves

Palm-fringed **Jungmun Beach** is one of the best places to surf on Jeju, both for the waves and for the local surf community. Sign up for lessons from **Jeju Surfing School** *(blog .naver.com/jesurf; starting from ₩60,000 for an introductory*

continued on p328

GETTING AROUND

Western Jeju-do includes the coastal Rte 1132. As always, a car is recommended for maximum flexibility.

For public transit, most of the seaside destinations can be accessed by buses 102 and 202 that follow the coast between Jeju-si and Seogwipo. To head inland, use tourist shuttle bus 820, which goes to the Osulloc Tea Museum, Spirited Garden and other major sights by transferring at one of the Donggwang Transit Center stops clustered around Donggwang Intersection.

For ferries to the islands, check how the weather might affect sailing times before heading to the ports.

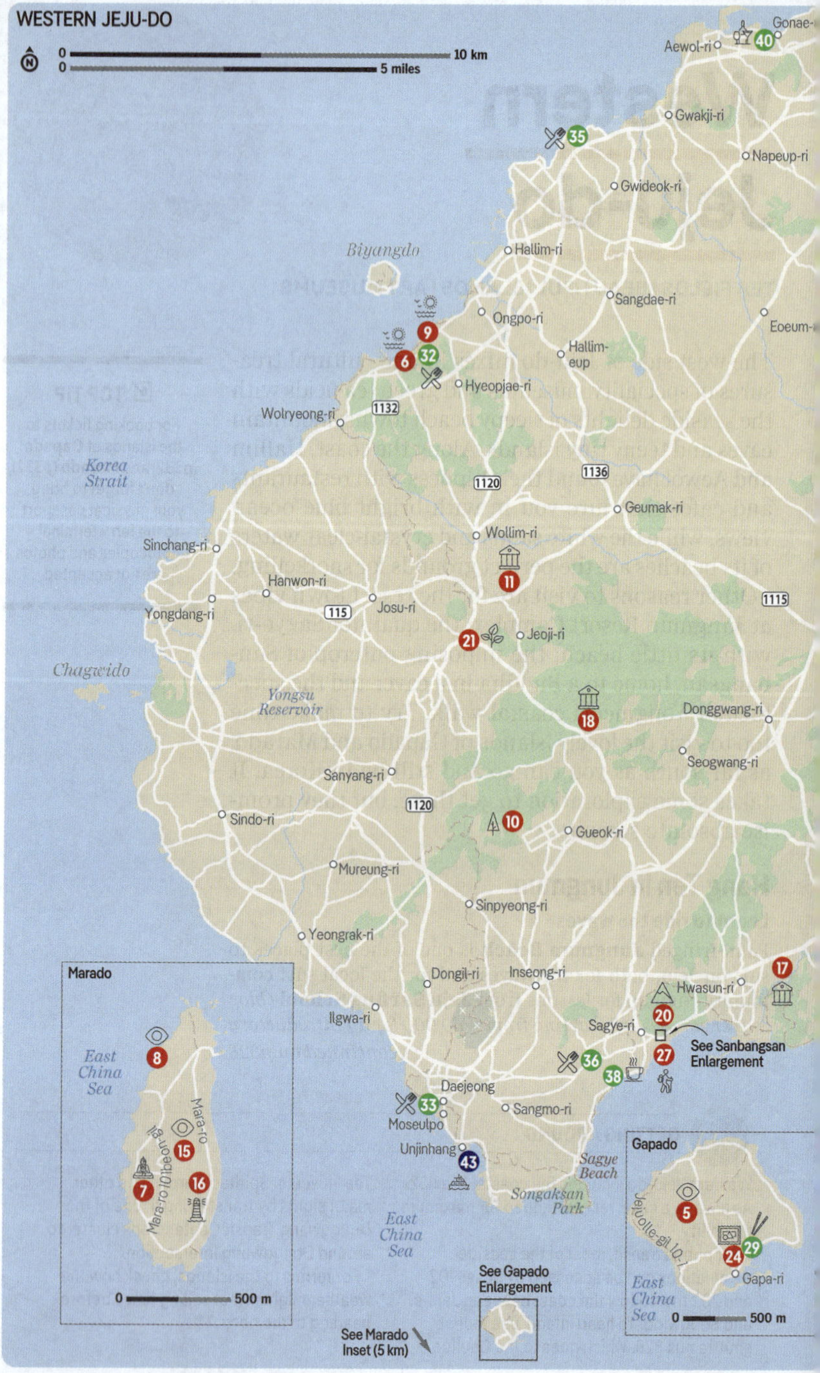
WESTERN JEJU-DO
0 10 km
0 5 miles
Gonae-
Aewol-ri
40
Gwakji-ri
35
Napeup-ri
Gwideok-ri
Biyangdo
Hallim-ri
Sangdae-ri
Ongpo-ri
Eoeum-
9
32
6
Hallim-eup
Hyeopjae-ri
Wolryeong-ri
1132
Korea Strait
1120
1136
Geumak-ri
Wollim-ri
Sinchang-ri
11
Hanwon-ri
Yongdang-ri
115
Josu-ri
1115
21
Jeoji-ri
Chagwido
18
Yongsu Reservoir
Donggwang-ri
Seogwang-ri
Sanyang-ri
1120
Sindo-ri
10
Gueok-ri
Mureung-ri
Sinpyeong-ri
Yeongrak-ri
Marado
17
Dongil-ri
Inseong-ri
Hwasun-ri
Ilgwa-ri
20
Sagye-ri
East China Sea
8
27
See Sanbangsan Enlargement
36
38
Mara-ro
Daejeong
Mara-ro 101beon-gil
15
33
Sangmo-ri
Moseulpo
Unjinhang
Gapado
7
16
43
Sagye Beach
5
Songaksan Park
Jejuolle-gil 10-1
East China Sea
29
24
Gapa-ri
0 500 m
See Gapado Enlargement
East China Sea
0 500 m
See Marado Inset (5 km)

HIGHLIGHTS
1 Sanbang-gul-sa

SIGHTS
2 Bomun-sa
3 Bonte Museum
4 Cheonjeyeon Pokpo
5 Gapado
6 Geumneung Beach
7 Giwonjeong-sa
8 Halmangdang
9 Hyeopjae Beach
10 Jeju Gotjawal Provincial Park
11 Jeju Museum of Contemporary Art
12 Jungmun Beach
13 Jungmun Resort Complex
14 Jusangjeolli-dae
15 Marado
16 Marado Lighthouse
17 Museum of Sex & Health
18 Osulloc Tea Museum
19 Sanbang-sa
20 Sanbangsan
21 Spirited Garden
22 Yakcheon-sa
23 Yeomiji Botanical Garden
24 Yu Yongye Gallery

ACTIVITIES
25 Grande Bleu Yacht
26 Jeju Surfing School
27 Yongmeori Coast

SLEEPING
28 Aloha Jeju Stay

EATING
29 Booseong Sikdang
30 Brunch Concept
31 Cafe Jeju Kiwa
32 Donatos
33 Glagla Hawaii
see 18 Innisfree Green Cafe
34 Jungmun Haenyeo House
35 Mamma Lia
36 Santosha
37 Suksungdo
see 18 Tea Terrace

DRINKING & NIGHTLIFE
38 Delphic
39 Lazybox Café
40 Matilda
41 The Cliff
42 Vadada

TRANSPORT
43 Unjinhang

UNESCO BIOSPHERE RESERVE

Because its geology, topography and nature are so special, all of Jeju-do, plus the surrounding marine areas 5.5km from its shoreline, are designated as a UNESCO Biosphere Reserve. Among the island's most unique natural features are its 368 *oreum*. Also known as secondary volcanic cones, these hills and outcrops range in height from 100m to 700m.

Covering around 224 sq km of the island are *gotjawal*, a local-dialect word for forest biomes where trees, brush, moss and other plants naturally intertwine as they grow from the island's rocky volcanic terrain. You can learn more about this unique type of forest, where tropical northern and southern plants coexist, at the **Jeju Gotjawal Provincial Park**.

VARIOUS IMAGES/SHUTTERSTOCK

Yakcheon-sa

continued from p325
lesson), which has an English-speaking instructor. The school also rents boards *(₩30,000)*, puts on surfing camps and runs the **Aloha Jeju Stay** hostel, located about 1.5km north.

Templestay Near the Sea

Meditate at Yakcheon-sa

Set in lovely open grounds overlooking the sea is the Buddhist temple **Yakcheon-sa** *(yakchunsa.org)*. Constructed in the 1980s to a Joseon-dynasty design, it's one of the island's most impressive buildings. The ornate main hall has two levels of galleries overlooking a 3m-tall statue of Buddha and vibrant murals of scenes from Buddha's life and teachings.

Yakcheon-sa offers several Templestay programs (p41); email *yakchunsa@templestay.com* for details.

Nature at Jungmun Resort Complex

Marvel at the dramatic coastline

A sprawling development of big luxury hotels and kitschy museums, **Jungmun Resort Complex** will not be everyone's cup of tea. The best reason for visiting this area is to view **Jusangjeolli-dae**, a spectacular 2km stretch of coastline known for rectangular rock columns – the result of the rapid

EATING & DRINKING IN JUNGMUN: OUR PICKS

Suksungdo: (숙성도) Get orders delivered to your table by a robot at this premium K-BBQ restaurant with several locations around the island. *noon-10pm* WWW

Jungmun Haenyeo House: (중문해녀의집) Eatery run by friendly *haenyeo* serving just-caught seafood. Get the raw abalone. *8am-6pm* WWW

Brunch Concept: Down a quiet road, this atmospheric spot with a back patio has omelettes, bruschetta and big breakfast platters on the menu. *9am-4pm* WW

The Cliff: An all-in-one entertainment destination featuring a bar, lounge, arcade games, live DJs and its eponymous cliff-side patio. *10am-1am*

cooling and contraction of lava as it poured into the sea. Near Daepo Port, book a luxury yacht tour through **Grande Bleu Yacht** *(brand.naver.com/grandebleu; starting from ₩48,000)* to get a closer view, particularly beautiful at sunset.

For a relaxed perspective on the rocky coastline, drop into **Vadada** *(@vadada.jeju)*, which packs major Ibiza party vibes: think massive white day beds on terraces overlooking the sea, a fake beach shaded by pines and glam-central swimming pool.

At the heart of Jungmun Resort Complex is **Cheonjeyeon Pokpo** *(adult/child ₩2500/1350)*, a three-tier cascade sporting unique basalt columns, tucked inside a forested gorge. Above soars the arched Seonim footbridge decorated with sculptures of the nymphs who served the Emperor of Heaven and who, it's said, used to slide down moonbeams to bathe here. There's an entrance to the falls near the impressive **Yeomiji Botanical Garden** *(yeomiji.or.kr; adult/youth/child ₩12,000/8000/7000)*, which has a huge indoor section with areas that mimic rainforests, deserts and other landscapes.

Art & Architecture in Harmony

Appreciate a collection of beauty

Although admission is pricey, the **Bonte Museum** *(bontemuseum.com; adult/youth/child ₩30,000/20,000/10,000)* is a must-see for lovers of art and architecture. A graceful set of buildings, designed by Tadao Ando and incorporating traditional Korean architectural features, showcases an amazing private collection of both classic Korean arts and crafts, and contemporary works by the likes of Yayoi Kusama and Nam June Paik.

World's Largest Sex Museum

Understand human sexuality

You may be curious to visit the **Museum of Sex & Health** *(sexmuseum.or.kr; ₩15,000)*, around 4km west of Sagye-ri. Standing apart from Jeju's other sex 'museums', this huge complex has extensive sections devoted to sex education and sex culture from around the world (labelling is mostly in Korean). It's laudable for its inclusivity, covering usually taboo subjects in Korea such as homosexuality. There's also a big erotic art exhibition and a library of well-thumbed books and softcore porn magazines, including vintage copies of *Playboy*.

Clamber to a Buddha in a Cave

Spiritual tourism and coastal walks

Sagye-ri is an appealing small port in Jeju's southwest corner. Nearby are several terrific sights, the most obvious being the 395m **Sanbangsan** volcanic outcrop, visible for miles around. Near the foot of the mountain are a couple of prettily decorated temples **Sanbang-sa** and **Bomun-sa**. From here, a short but steep hike up many steps leads to **Sanbang-gul-sa**, a grotto dripping with water and home to a stone Buddha gazing out to sea.

JEJU & SEX

Although attitudes are changing, particularly among the young, Koreans tend to be conservative when it comes to openly talking about sex (and certainly there's a sexist double standard that disproportionately shames and ostracises women for doing so). And yet, Jeju-do has three pretty graphic sex 'museums'. This stems from a time when Jeju was Korea's top honeymoon destination and premarital sex was highly taboo, so many vacationing newlyweds had minimal sex education. Jeju became a socially acceptable place where honeymooners, away from their real lives on the mainland, could learn about sex through sex-themed attractions that were more humourous and playful than outright pornographic.

MORE ANDO

If you're a fan of Tadao Ando's aesthetic of smooth, exposed concrete and use of natural light, also be sure to visit **Phoenix Island**, which has two of his buildings, and **Museum SAN** (p157) in Wonju.

Across the road from the mountainside temples is the start of the **Yongmeori Coast**, a spectacular seaside trail of around 1km with soaring cliffs pockmarked by erosion into catacombs, narrow clefts and natural archways. Yongmeori means 'dragon's head', a name given because of the rocks' resemblance to fabulous beasts.

Botanical Fantasy World

Meditate in a bunjae garden

Displaying a collection of 2000-plus *bunjae* (the Korean style of bonsai), **Spirited Garden** *(spiritedgarden.com; adult/youth/child ₩15,000/13,000/7000)* is a portal into a fantasy botanical world. Basalt-stone pathways lead you through a landscape of pines, palms, lawns, meditative areas, waterfalls and a pond teeming with golden carp. All around, displayed in pots, are the artfully contorted miniature trees and shrubs. Among the prize specimens is a 500-year-old juniper tree.

A few kilometres away, in the artists village of **Jeoji**, is the excellent **Jeju Museum of Contemporary Art** *(jeju.go.kr/jejumuseum; adult/youth/child ₩2000/1000/500)*, closed Mondays. Permanent exhibitions by Kim Heng-sou and Park Kwang-jin are supplemented by regularly changing shows of other artists. The village is dotted with engaging pieces of modern and traditional architecture.

Savour Jeju-grown Tea

Visit the Osulloc fields

Set in attractively landscaped grounds overlooking verdant tea fields, the **Osulloc Tea Museum** *(us.osulloc.com/osulloc-tea-museum; free)* is a place to shop for tea-based souvenirs, and to eat and drink products made from the fresh green leaves. At the **Innisfree Green Cafe** *(9am-6pm)*, try the *haenyeo* brunch basket of seaweed rice balls and salad. And new in 2025 is the **Tea Terrace** *(10am-6pm)*, a noodle bar serving a menu of freshly made matcha noodles, developed in part by Michelin-starred chef Kim Doyoon.

The premium Osulloc tea brand is owned by the cosmetics and beauty conglomerate Amorepacific, the founder of which, Suh Sungwhan, began to create the farms on Jeju in 1979 in an effort to revive the nation's ancient tea-drinking culture. The tea isn't just for imbibing. Green-tea flavonoids are an ingredient in some of Amorepacific's cosmetic products, including

NATURAL WORKS OF ART

The **Spirited Garden** exemplifies Korean pioneering spirit. In 1968, Sung Bum-young, a 29-year-old tailor from Seoul, bought an unpromising piece of land, littered with thistles and volcanic rocks, on Jeju. From this forbidding landscape, he first hacked out a citrus farm while simultaneously nurturing a dream to create a garden showcasing *bunjae*.

You need patience to craft these living sculptures, which can take many decades to come into their prime. As well as growing his own *bunjae*, Sung scoured Korea for others to add to his collection. Since opening to the public in 1992, the garden's reputation has grown and Sung and his son, who now runs the garden, have welcomed dignitaries from around the world.

EATING & DRINKING IN MOSEULPO & SAGYE-RI: OUR PICKS

Glagla Hawaii: Dig into hairtail fish and chips, poke bowls and more at this vibrant Hawaiian eatery facing the harbour. *11.30am-3pm & 5-11pm* ₩₩

Santosha: Delightful cafe specialising in vegan-fermented vegetable dishes served with organic brown rice. *11.30am-2.30pm Thu & Sun, to 6.30pm Fri & Sat* ₩₩

Delphic: In a converted barn just back from the beach, this classy teahouse serves gourmet teas, natural wines and sweet treats. *11am-6pm Tue-Sun*

Lazybox Café: This cute cafe serves fair-trade coffee, freshly squeezed juices and homemade cakes – a nice spot to recover after climbing Sanbangsan. *10am-7pm*

NORTHWEST COAST DRIVE

Rent a car at the airport and head to the coast to bask on the beach, see *haenyeo* dive and admire art.

START	END	LENGTH
Jeju International Airport	Road to Windmill Bakery & Café	62km; 2½hr

From 1 **Jeju International Airport**, drive west to white-sand 2 **Gwakji Beach**. A 40-minute walk west along the coast, following Jeju Olle Course 15-B, is the 3 **Hansupul Haenyeo School**, where you can learn freediving skills from *haenyeo*. In the opposite direction is the 4 **Handam Coastal Walk**, a scenic and easy 10-minute concrete path beside the black rocky coast to the seaside community of 5 **Aewol**. Here you can go sea kayaking and have a drink at one of the many attractive cafes and restaurants along the shore. Jump back in the car and head inland to 6 **Arte Museum**, Korea's largest immersive media art exhibition created by digital design company d'strict in a former speaker factory. Return to the coast and aim for Hallim, where a delicious lunch of deep-fried pork cutlet and udon noodles awaits at 7 **Su Udong**. After lunch, spend an hour or so exploring the lush botanical gardens and lava caves of 8 **Hallim Park** (p332). At Sinchang, the coastal road leads to 9 **Singgyemul Park**, where you can walk up to the base of some windmills, or admire them from cafes such as 10 **Klein Blue**, with its small art gallery, or 11 **Road to Windmill Bakery & Café**. Linger here for sunset, after which the wind turbines become illuminated by LED lights.

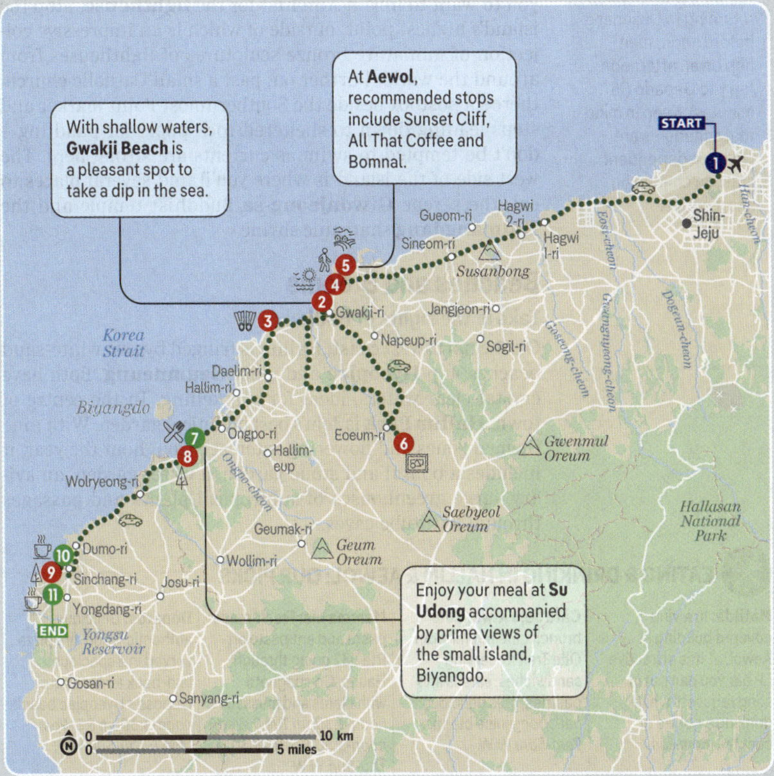

its 'clean beauty' brand Innisfree. It has a skincare shop here, which often sells exclusive-to-Jeju gift sets and other products that you can't find on the mainland.

GETTING TO GAPADO & MARADO

Ferries for Gapado and Marado depart from the small port of **Unjinhang**, near the west-coast town of Moseulpo. Booking in advance is especially necessary during the popular Green Barley Festival on Gapado from April to May.

If you make an early start, it's possible to visit both islands in one day. The best way to do this is to sail to Marado in the morning (30 minutes), returning to Unjinhang before noon, then hop on an afternoon ferry to Gapado (15 minutes). Keep in mind that schedules are weather-dependent and can change on short notice.

Korea's Smallest Inhabited Island

Walk around picturesque Gapado

Even at its highest point, compact **Gapado** is barely 20m above sea level. The best way to see it is by walking the 4.2km Jeju Olle Course 10-1. The trail takes you through the fields of barley for which the island is famous – a **Green Barley Festival** is celebrated here from April to May. You'll also notice a smattering of contemporary architecture that is part of a community arts project.

A good place for a tasty seafood lunch is **Booseong Sikdang** *(@booseong2483)*, near the port on the south side of the island. Also around here, look for the **gallery** of photographer Yu Yongye *(@yu_yongye)*, who is also a *haenyeo*.

Stand at Korea's Southernmost Point

Pack a picnic for Marado

Walking around apple-seed-shaped **Marado** only takes an hour, but there's something about this island that will make you to want to linger. Aim first for the **lighthouse**, atop the island's highest point, outside of which is an impressive collection of miniature bronze sculptures of lighthouses from around the world. Further on, past a small Catholic church, there's a postbox beside the Southernmost Point marker and steps leading down to sheltered rock pools for paddling – don't be tempted to swim as currents are strong here. The west side of the island is where you'll find several places to eat, the serene **Giwonjeong-sa** Buddhist temple and the **Halmangdang** shamanic shrine.

Beaches and Blooms

Take in the sights of Hallim

On the northwest coast, Hallim is fringed by two white-sand beaches: hip **Hyeopjae** and quiet **Geumneung**. Both have crystal-clear waters, ideal for snorkelling. In the centre of town, **Hallim Park** is Jeju's best botanical garden. With nine themed zones and flowering interest throughout the year, it includes a bonsai and stone garden, a water garden, an aviary, large greenhouses of subtropical plants and passages through lava-tube caves.

EATING & DRINKING IN HALLIM & AEWOL: OUR PICKS

Matilda: In a vine-covered building in Aewol, at this attractive LP bar you can put in song requests while drinking a coffee or cocktail. *6pm-1am*

Cafe Jeju Kiwa: Cute brunch cafe not far from Olle Trail 16, serving sandwiches, salads and pastries, plus delicious *hallabong* juice blends. *9am-5pm* WW

Mamma Lia: Fresh-made pasta and antipasto off Rte 1132 going through Hallim. Go spaghetti with clams and mussels. *noon-3.30pm Tue & Wed, noon-3.30 & 5.30-8.30 Thu-Sun* WW

Donatos: Delicious, authentic wood-fire pizza served in a spacious, laid-back atmosphere. Opposite Hyeopjae beach. *noon-3.30pm & 5-9pm Mon & Thu-Sun* WW

Places We Love to Stay

W Budget WW Midrange WWW Top End

Jeju-si

MAP P304

Goyo Walk W Good-value B&B with a convenient central location, a book lounge downstairs and cosy rooms up above.

Bed Radio Dongmoon W Private rooms and dorms, each with their own bathroom, at this friendly Tapdong hostel with a ground-floor cafe-bar.

Brne Stay WW On the coast near the airport, there's a lot going for this guesthouse with a range of stylishly decorated rooms.

Hotel Whistlelark WW Spacious, pleasant rooms with balconies at this full-service hotel on Tapdong's seafront. The outdoor pool is open June to October.

Grand Hyatt Jeju WWW Glitzy luxury hotel with oodles of restaurants, two spas, a fashion mall and fantastic outdoor pool deck.

Woljeong-ri & Hado-ri

Ssari's W A little inland from the coast, this rustic guesthouse has an owner who grows flowers, has an orange grove and breeds peacocks.

Gentleehouse Jeju WW Woljeong Beach guesthouse, a short walk inland from the beach, offering comfortable, clean and stylish rooms.

Seongsan-ri

Hidden Stay W Fab, contemporary-styled hostel ideally placed for a pre-dawn climb up Seongsan Ilchul-bong. Dorms have their own bathrooms.

Bomulseom WW Hilltop pension offering clean, well-equipped self-catering rooms, some with balconies.

Chuidasun WW Chic rooms with soothing sea views, a yoga and mediation program, and beautiful tea room.

Playce Camp WW Artists have decorated each of the rooms at this youthful, contemporary hotel. Has a good bar, cafe and souvenir shop.

Udo

Udo Space 01 W Pleasant modern dorms at this hostel inland from the coast. Has a convivial lounge bar and dive centre.

Hundert Hills WW One of Udo's most upmarket accommodations offers sleek, understated rooms and ocean views.

Seogwipo

MAP P319

Backpacker's Home W Spacious dorms with their own bathrooms. English-speaking staff and a great outdoor terrace for socialising.

Olle Stay W Quality soft cotton bedding elevates these dorms and single rooms above the Jeju Olle Trail Center. Each room door is decorated by a different artist.

Saiseoga WW Stay in the heart of Lee Jung-seop St, with a view onto his thatched cottage, at this private studio located above a charming book cafe.

Seom Studio WW West of central Seogwipo along the coast, the rooms here are creatively designed with a mid-century feel. Yoga and reading are promoted.

JW Marriott Jeju Resort & Spa (p324) **WWW** Outstanding luxury resort offering sea views, arty design and top-class facilities, including excellent restaurants and pool area.

Jungmun

Aloha Jeju (p328) **W** Hang with the surfing crowd at this laid-back hostel a bit south off the main highway through Jungmun.

Seaes Hotel & Resort WWW Gorgeous property where cottages with stone walls and thatched roofs are surrounded by gardens.

Sagye-ri

Sun & Moon Resort WW Spacious and comfortable rooms with floor-to-ceiling views out to sea across the hotel's green lawn.

Zen Hide Away WWW Earthy wood-stone finishes provide a harmony-with-nature theme to the room decor at this small hotel with sea views.

Moseulpo & Gapado

Sodara WW Beautiful tiny-house pensions with Jacuzzis. Steps away from a sandy beach and the ferries to Gapado and Marado.

Gapari 212 WW Rustic cafe on a hill overlooking Gapado's main port, offering a couple of simple rooms should you want to stay on the island.

Andeok

Podo Hotel WWW Designed by Japanese-Korean architect Itami Jun, this architecturally extraordinary property is attached to PINX Golf Club.

Researched by Phillip Tang

Chungcheong-do

UNEXPLORED COAST, HISTORY & LAKE WONDERLAND

South Korea's lesser-visited northwestern and central belt stretches from the long Yellow Sea beaches to the rolling crests and deep aquamarine waters of Chung-ho.

Chungcheong-do (충청도) is Korea's unsung heartland – close enough to Seoul to be convenient, but overlooked enough to feel undiscovered. Split into 'north' (Chungcheongbuk-do) and 'south' (Chungcheongnam-do) provinces, Chungcheong-do is a varied destination where even few domestic tourists visit. Most travellers only glimpse Chungcheong-do's offbeat beauty from the windows of moving KTX trains between Seoul and Busan. Still, this land of coast and islands, ancient historical sites, temple-studded mountains, landmark inventions and a massive lake deserves to be savoured slowly.

For starters, Chungcheong-do holds a royal flush of natural sights. On the Yellow Sea coast to the west, Taeanhaean National Park unfurls kilometre after kilometre of long beaches and islands strewn with paddy fields, quiet hillocks and Korea's oldest pine forests. In the centre of Chungcheongnam-do province, Buyeo and Gongju, the former capitals of the Baekje kingdom, preserve ancient fortresses, multi-storey pagodas and elaborate temples. In Cheongju, the secrets of Jikji – the world's oldest surviving book printed by movable metal type – are unveiled along with the history of Korea's printing and literacy across ages and dynasties. To the east, landlocked Chungcheongbuk-do is peppered with fantastic hiking at Woraksan, Songnisan and Sobaeksan national parks. A fan of mountains surrounds Chungju-ho, an artificial lake that's become one of central Korea's most popular retreats. Chungcheong-do rewards anyone willing to take their time.

THE MAIN AREAS

BAEKJE HINTERLAND
Fortress hikes, royal tombs and meandering rivers. p338

TAEANHAEAN NATIONAL PARK'S COAST
Offbeat coastal paradise between land and sea. p350

CHEONGJU
Arts, fortress and an ancient printed book. p355

CHUNGJU
Korea's lakeland. p361

For places to stay in Chungcheong-do, see p369

TDRC/SHUTTERSTOCK

Left: Jikji (p355); Above: Oksun-bong (p365), Chungju-ho

Find Your Way

Chungcheong-do splits into Chungbuk (nominally 'north' but actually east) and Chungnam ('south', but west). Without a car, expect long waits at small-town bus stations to get around, even though the region isn't huge. Small roads and mountain cordons slow travel but reward patience.

Chungju, p361

Chungju-ho is the lake setting for a host of outdoor adventures, including hiking, camping, boating and more against a backdrop of forested mountain ridges.

Cheongju, p355

Chungbuk's centre of arts and culture, and historical home of the world's oldest book printed with movable metal type and an exciting eating scene downtown.

Taeanhaean National Park's Coast, p350

Hiking and bicycle trails, serene campsites backed by pine forests, and more seafood than you can eat along ribbons of coastline.

Baekje Hinterland, p338

Temples, pagodas, meandering rivers and fortresses abound in South Korea's least-visited historical area where a once-mighty kingdom's legacy is traced in weathered stone.

TRAIN

High-speed KTX trains are the most efficient way to reach the cities. Many stations are far from city centres, making direct buses more straightforward. Book tickets at terminals or online at Korail *(korail.com)*.

BUS

Most towns are well-connected with direct buses to large cities and Seoul. Purchase tickets at multi-language self-service kiosks at terminals. Non-Korean credit-card holders cannot purchase tickets online, but can check times and availability at TxBus *(txbuse.t-money.co.kr)*.

CAR

Four wheels are the best option to explore the region at your own pace and use the excellent car camping facilities on the coast and most national parks. Chungcheong-do offers good expressway connectivity, frequent rest areas and well-maintained coastal bypass routes.

SUNYOUNGYIM/IMAZINS/GETTY IMAGES

Gyeryongsan National Park (p346)

Plan Your Time

Most attractions are within a short distance from each main town, so you can easily take day trips to temples and fortresses before hitting the beaches or downtown museums.

Four Days

- Spend a day in **Gongju** hiking **Gong-sanseong** (p338), visiting the **Royal Tombs** (p340) before settling for dinner by the riverside. The following morning, head to **Buyeo** (p340) to explore the historical theme park **Baekje Cultural Land** (p343). If time permits, catch the sunset at **Gungnamji Pond**. Finally, devote two days to **Chungju-ho** (p364) for hiking and canoeing.

A Week

- Spend two days checking out **Taean-haean National Park** (p350) by car. From Boryeong's **Daecheon Beach** (p348), bus it to **Buyeo** (p340). Stop at stunning **Muryang-sa** (p347), spending three days between here, **Gong-sanseong** (p338) and **Gyeryongsan National Park** (p346). Move on to **Cheongju** (p355) for a lesson in ancient printing, then two days by **Chungju-ho** (p364) and at **Woraksan National Park** (p368).

SEASONAL HIGHLIGHTS

WINTER

Winter blankets the region in snow, perfect for hot springs and tranquil coastal walks – just bundle up. Rural buses continue to run, though infrequently.

SPRING

Spring peak brings mild days and the famous 'blossom snow' to Cheongju and Gongju. It is the best time to explore the ancient mountain fortresses under a pale pink canopy.

SUMMER

Temperatures exceed 30°C with sudden downpours. Get dirty at the **Boryeong Mud Festival** (p348) and admire blooms at **Buyeo Seodong Lotus Festival** (p343).

AUTUMN

The **Cheongju Craft Biennale** (p357) transforms the city into a global art hub. The **Baekje Cultural Festival** (p339) begins in Gongju, featuring parades and early autumn light shows.

Baekje Hinterland

HISTORICAL SIGHTS | MEANDERING RIVERS | SLOW TOWNS

GETTING AROUND

Gongju has direct buses to Seoul Nambu. Isolated Gongju Station on the KTX Honam Line is 23km (or a 25-minute taxi) from the town centre and main sights. An alternative is to go via Daejeon Station and hop on one of the frequent buses to **Gongju's Intercity Bus Terminal**. Seoul Subway Line 1 also reaches Cheonan, from where direct buses leave to Gongju. From Cheongju take a bus to **Gongju Singwan Bus Terminal**, from where frequent buses travel between Gongju and Buyeo, both compact and walkable cities. However buses to outer city sights and surrounding towns are thin on the ground, so rental cars can be a better choice.

The centre of Chungcheongnam-do province may look like a sleepy backwater today, but its rolling hills and meandering rivers, Geum-gang and Baekma-gang, hold great historical significance. Here in Baekje hinterland, the aggressive Goguryeo forced the Baekje (two of ancient Korea's Three Kingdoms) to retreat here in 475 CE, spurring a settlement that lasted another two centuries.

The quiet towns of Gongju and Buyeo, once the capitals of this ancient dynasty, are the area's primary drawcards. Their surprising number of old fortresses, tombs and relics make for an entirely different experience to the big cities of Korea. Gongju sits below the impressive Gong-sanseong, built like dragon scales on a hilltop over the Geum River. It also has a cluster of important royal Baekje tombs.

Buso-sanseong in Buyeo is a sprawling pine-forest hike of temples and pavilions with views over the waters of Baekma-gang and a glimpse of a royal Baekje leisure park.

Hike Gongju's Historic Fortress Walls

MAP P339

Traipse along Gong-sanseong

Slung like a dormant dragon on a hill overlooking the Geum River, stunning **Gong-sanseong** *(baekje-heritage.or.kr; adult/child ₩3000/1000)* reminds us of the time when Gongju was Ungjin, the capital of the Baekje kingdom between 475 and 538 CE. The 2.6km-long fortress walls enclose a large area whose notable structures include **Imnyu-gak**, a banquet hall built initially in 500 CE (the building seen today is a replica); the **Manharu Pavilion** overlooking Gongju's central river Geum-gang, a building that once served twin purposes of defence and recreation; the pavilion **Ssangsu-jeong**, named for a pair of trees that King Injo used to lean against while contemplating the fate of his kingdom, and **Yeongeun-sa**, a temple constructed in the 15th century that once served as a boarding house for warrior monks.

HIGHLIGHTS
1 Gong-sanseong

SIGHTS
2 Geumseoru West Gate
3 Gongbungnu
4 Gongju National Museum
5 Gwangbongnu
6 Imnyu-gak
7 Manharu Pavilion
8 Ssangsu-jeong
9 Tomb of King Muryeong
10 Ungjin Baekje Historical Museum
11 Yeongeun-sa

SLEEPING
12 Hotel N. 25
13 Khai Hotel
14 Stay Onel

EATING
15 Saeihak Garden
16 Sijang's Butcher Restaurant

TRANSPORT
17 Gongju Intercity Bus Terminal

After entering through the grand stone **Geumseoru West Gate**, you can walk along the perimeter and on the old walls, passing numerous pavilions, including **Gongbungnu** and **Gwangbongnu**, rebuilt according to archaeological evidence of their original structures. For the most dramatic views over the river and the rest of the 'new city' that extends beyond its northern shore, hike to the northwest section of the wall. In the evening, the whole (closed) fortress is lit up with floodlights.

Parades, Palaces & Pixels

Family-friendly activities at Baekje Cultural Festival

The **Baekje Cultural Festival** transforms the twin cities of Gongju and Buyeo into an expansive, living museum every September and October. Huge parades, games, traditional music and dancing make for family fun. Unlike the rigid military reconstructions found elsewhere, this event leans into the artistic legacy of a maritime kingdom that flourished 1500 years ago. The true highlight is the Ungjin Night Lantern Display, when thousands of lanterns float on the Geum-gang, mirroring the illuminated fortress walls of Gong-sanseong in the dark water. You can walk across a floating bridge to get a closer look at these glowing figures, which depict everything from ancient

TOP TIP

Avoid visiting on Mondays, when all museums and archaeological sites across Korea stay closed, and hiking around Gongju and Buyeo loses most of its charm.

soldiers to mythical creatures. The scent of roasted Gongju chestnuts fills the air from street stalls nearby.

The atmosphere is a blend of high-tech spectacle and grassroots energy. In Buyeo, the reconstructed Baekje Palace in Baekje Cultural Land (p343) *(bhm.or.kr; adult/child ₩6000/3000)*, closed Mondays, serves as a backdrop for immersive media art that projects swirling patterns onto timber architecture. The daytime streets host massive parades of horses and performers in Baekje-period attire. It's a major destination for families; clusters of children often crowd the riverside to participate in pottery workshops or archer training, making the historical sites feel like an active playground rather than a quiet monument. Between the open-air theatre performances on the river stages and the ritual ceremonies honouring the ancient kings, the festival manages to capture a sense of pride for a culture whose refined, understated style still influences the minimalist aesthetic seen in the region's craft scenes today.

BAEKJE: THE CULTURAL THIRD KINGDOM

The Baekje Kingdom (18 BCE–660 CE) flourished as a vibrant, outward-looking state that defined the era's artistic standards from its capitals in Gongju and Buyeo. During the Three Kingdoms period, Korea was divided between distinct regional powers: the Goguryeo (modern-day North Korea and northeast China) forged a rugged identity through mountain warfare, while the Silla (modern Gyeongju) remained relatively isolated.

In contrast, Baekje leveraged its southwestern coastline to dominate regional trade. It functioned as the primary channel for advanced civilisation, introducing Buddhism, sophisticated pottery and urban planning to Japan. Rather than focusing solely on military expansion, Baekje artisans prioritised an understated elegance that avoided excessive flashiness. This artisanship remains visible in the hinterland's weathered stone pagodas – a stark departure from the brightly painted Joseon-era palaces of Seoul.

A Lesson in Baekje's History

MAP P339

Rounded tombs and National Museum

A 20-minute walk south of the stone arch in front of Gongsanseong in Songsan-ri is a group of six UNESCO-protected Baekje-era tombs, the most important of which belongs to **King Muryeong** *(gongju.go.kr/en/sub02_02_03.do; adult/child ₩3000/1000)*, the 25th Baekje king, discovered miraculously intact and completely by accident in 1971. The king was interred here in 525 CE, two years after his death, and his queen consort alongside him in 529 CE.

The tomb is inside a huge earth mound with a rectangular burial chamber opening into a semi-circular vault with hundreds of moulded bricks decorated with Buddhist lotus-flower motifs and geometric designs. The original tombs aren't open to the public but an on-site museum has models of two that visitors can enter, as well as English-language information about the history of the Baekje dynasty. The **Ungjin Baekje Historical Museum** *(free)* has more exhibits, augmented-reality videos and a tourist office near the entrance.

Roughly halfway along Gwangwangdanji-gil, **Gongju National Museum** *(gongju.museum.go.kr; free)* also provides a comprehensive overview of Baekje's history – including most of the artefacts found in the tombs – among a staggering 41,000 other relics from the Neolithic age to the Joseon dynasty. It's closed on Mondays.

The Ancient City of Sabi

MAP P341

Exploring Buso-sanseong fortress

Built in 538 CE and reconstructed in 605 CE, the walls of the mountain fortress **Buso-sanseong** *(baekje-heritage.or.kr; adult/child ₩2000/1000)* to the north of Buyeo's compact city centre once sheltered the Baekje capital of Sabi on 106m-high Busosan. Today, paved and sandy paths and stairs weave through pine forests past pavilions and temples. On the

BUYEO

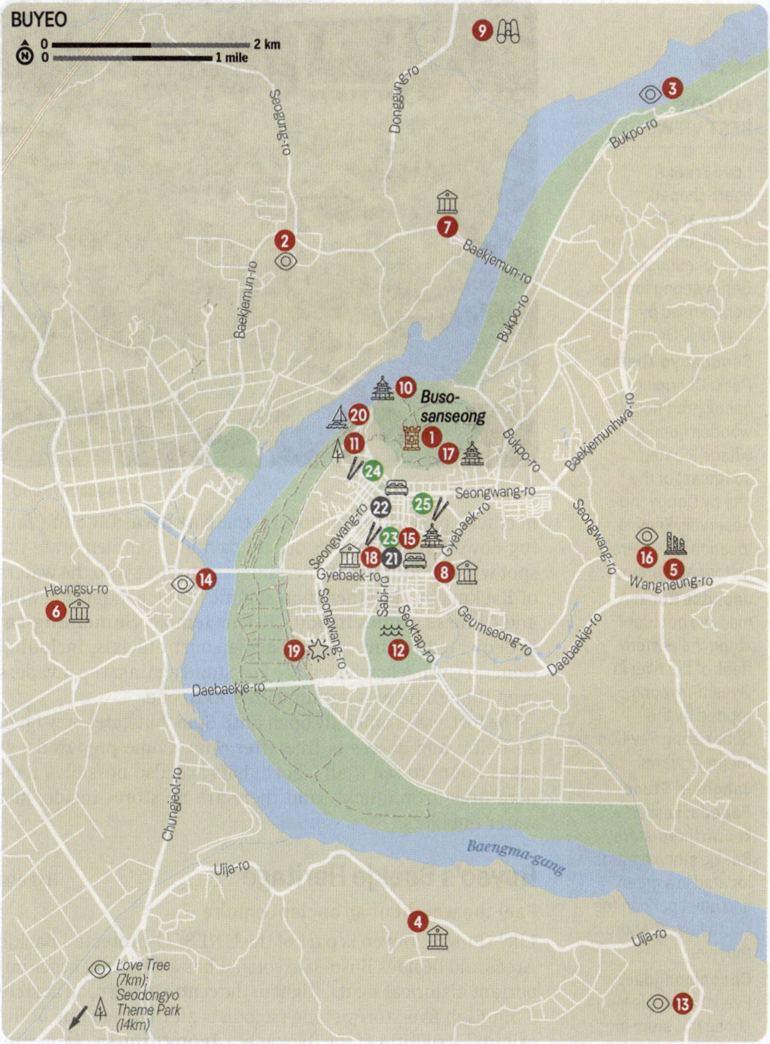

HIGHLIGHTS
1 Buso-sanseong

SIGHTS
2 Baekje Cultural Land
3 Baekje Reservoir
4 Baekje Roof Tile Museum
5 Baekje Royal Tombs of Neungsan-ri
6 Buyeo Ginseng Museum
7 Buyeo Life Museum
8 Buyeo National Museum
9 Cheonjeongdae
10 Goran-sa
11 Gudurae Sculpture Park
12 Gungnamji Pond
13 Jangha-ri Stone Pagoda
14 Jaondae
15 Jeongnim-sa
see 10 Nakhwa-am
16 Naseong Outer City Wall
17 Samchung-sa
18 Shin Dong-Yeop Literary Museum

ACTIVITIES
19 Baekma-gang Leisure Park
20 Buyeo Suryukyangyong Bus
see 10 Goransa Ferry

SLEEPING
21 Healing House Peakjang
22 Su Motel

EATING
23 Gomaru Gamjatang
24 Gudurae Dolssambap
25 House of Baekje
see 20 Jangwon Buckwheat Noodles

ENTERTAINMENT
see 12 Buyeo Seodong Lotus Festival

BUYEO'S BEST VIEWS

Love Tree: A heart-shaped, 400-year-old zelkova tree's canopy inside Seongheungsan's Garim-seong fortress, popularised by several K-Dramas.

Seodongyo Theme Park: Charming *hanok* (traditional wooden homes) village located southeast of the city by Deogyong Reservoir. Filming location for several historical K-dramas.

Jaondae Rock: A massive boulder along the eastern flank of the river in Gyuam-myeong, topped by the Subukjeong Pavilion for great views.

Jangha-ri Stone Pagoda: Lesser-known three-storey Baekje stone pagoda located in a green and quiet park on the southeastern shore of the river.

Cheonjeongdae: Even the Baekje kings chose this stunning riverside viewpoint to offer rites to the heavens before making important decisions.

SOBEAUTIFUL/SHUTTERSTOCK

Gungnamji Pond

northern part of the enclosure, the **Nakhwa-am** cliff ('falling flowers rock') and its ornate pavilion commemorate the spot where 3000 court ladies flung themselves into the waters of Baekma-gang rather than submit to the conquering Silla and Chinese armies in 660 CE. One temple, **Samchung-sa**, is dedicated to three loyal Baekje court officials, including General Gyebaek, who led the last stand against the invaders even though he was outnumbered 10 to one.

The fortress is officially open until 6pm, but gates stay open 24 hours and access is free after 6pm. Come prepared – it takes hours to see it all (short visits are also possible), temperatures drop quickly and there are no stores inside, just water bubblers.

Buyeo's Baekje Heritage

MAP P341

Feel the weight of an ancient empire

Like Gongju, Buyeo is part of the UNESCO-protected Baekje Areas and besides Buso-sanseong, it has a cluster of other important historical sights. Right in the centre of town, an austere 8.3m-high five-storey stone pagoda is all that remains of the original structure of the Baekje-era **Jeongnim-sa** *(jeongnimsaji.or.kr; free)*. A new temple lies next to it at the centre of extensive and well-manicured gardens, often used as a stage ground for yearly cultural events such as the Buyeo Cultural Heritage Night Tour in the middle of April.

Buyeo National Museum *(buyeo.museum.go.kr; free)* an exhibition of some of the best collections of Baekje artefacts, is a short walk away. A highlight is an incense burner from the era weighing 12kg and covered with intricate metalwork, crested with the legendary bonghwang bird. It's closed Mondays.

Set on a hillside 3km out of town are seven **Baekje Royal Tombs of Neungsan-ri** *(baekje-heritage.or.kr; adult/child ₩1000/400)* dating from 538 to 660 CE. The grass-covered tumuli, earthen burial mounds for royalty, are reminiscent of the larger ones in Gyeongju. They are sealed for protection, but visitors can see a reconstruction of the most impressive one painted with the four celestial creatures (dragon, tiger, tortoise and phoenix) guarding the cardinal points. A small museum houses a model of the most ancient tomb, believed to be that of King Sejong.

Halfway between the tombs and the town, the remains of **Naseong Outer City Wall** *(baekje-heritage.or.kr; free)* are among the first of their kind in East Asia. They testify to an 8km-long fortification built to protect the eastern flanks of the ancient capital Sabi.

Reconstructions of the grandiose scale of Baekje's architecture stand north of the river in the historical theme park and museum **Baekje Cultural Land**.

Celebrate Love & Lotus

MAP P341

Taking a stroll at Seodong Park and Gungnamji Pond

Set on the southern side of Buyeo, placid **Gungnamji** is Korea's first artificial pond built in 634 CE by Prince Seodong, who became the 30th Baekje dynasty's King Mu, to celebrate his love for Princess Seonwha. The park's main feature is a circular lake set at its centre: a bridge leads to a beautiful pagoda set over a mound believed to have been constructed here by Mu himself.

The park is beautiful, including at night when floodlights glow in the treetops, making lakeside strolls very romantic. The park fills with seasonal colours throughout the year but gets most scenic in July when thousands of purple lotus flowers bloom inside Gungnamji. It's the time of **Buyeo Seodong Lotus Festival** *(instagram.com/buyeo_lotus_festival; free)*, a potpourri of lotus-focused events and activities – including canoe trips on the flower-studded lake – all over these manicured gardens.

Fun in the River

MAP P341

Baekma-gang cruises and quirky amphibious bus

Hugging the western and northern sides of Buyeo, the Baekma-gang acted as a natural barrier for centuries and contributed to giving the town its green, laid-back character. The whole riverside is a green belt peppered by parks, walkways and the 22km-long **Baekma-gang Cycling Path**.

CHESTNUT CITY

Chestnuts are found all over Korea, but Gongju and Buyeo's chestnut industry is especially well-known around the country. Gongju, in particular, produces 8000 tonnes of chestnuts yearly, accounting for 17% of Korea's total production. Gongju *albam* (chestnut) is renowned for its crunchy texture and savoury taste and is used to produce many things, from nutty and smooth chestnut *makgeolli* (milky rice wine), to creative concoctions mixing chestnuts and meat – *yukhoe bibimbap* (beef tartare bibimbap) uses crushed raw chestnuts. Local restaurateurs are hellbent on continuous research to find even more creative ways to eat the endemic chestnuts: in season, expect most cafes to offer chestnut-based drinks, bread and pies on their menus.

EATING IN GONGJU: OUR PICKS

MAP P339

Sinbulhyang Small Octopus: Restaurant serving delicious stir-fried octopus, iron plate-fried octopus, deep-fried prawns and pork belly. *11am-9pm Tue-Sun* W

Saeihak Garden: Historic Gongju restaurant near the Geum River. Must-try rich beef *gukbap* (rice soup) and the exquisite local chestnut *muk* (jelly). *10.30am-9.30pm Tue-Sun* WW

Sijang's Butcher Restaurant: Judge from the number of shoes stacked by the door how popular this meat-loving barbecue restaurant is. *11am-9pm Mon-Sat* W

Myeongseong Bulgogi: Locals love the raw meat and squid bulgogi at this popular spot south of the fortress. *11.30am-8.30pm Tue-Sun* WW

BUYEO'S BEST MUSEUMS

Baekje Roof Tile Museum: In the Roof Tile Kiln site in Jeongan-ri, this museum highlights unique Baekje roof-tile culture.

Buyeo Ginseng Museum: Established in 2004, this factory offers visual exhibits of the history, cultivation and production of Korean ginseng.

Baekje Reservoir: The tower-like observatory and nearby Geum River Culture Pavillion offer great views and a historical overview of the area.

Shin Dong-Yeop Literary Museum: Birthplace of the nationalist poet who was instrumental in developing lyrical poetry in Korea.

Buyeo Life Museum: A trip down memory lane through exhibits of objects from the daily life of Korea's everyday folks.

CSTRIKE/SHUTTERSTOCK

Baekma-gang cruise

On the southeastern end of the river, **Baekma-gang Leisure Park** *(baekmagangleisure.com; admission free; activities prices vary)* has electric bicycles, garden trains, amphibious electric cart rides and the futuristic, cylinder-shaped **Baekma-gang Observatory** towering above it all for fantastic views of the river – including at night, when it lights up in blue fluorescence.

But it's more fun getting on the water. The **Goransa ferry** service *(one-way/return adult ₩5000/7000, child ₩2500/3500)* between two piers at **Gudurae Sculpture Park** *(free)* and **Goran-sa**, a temple set at the bottom of a steep rocky path leading to Nakhwa-am cliff, departs frequently between 9am and 6pm, gliding for about 20 minutes along nice stretches of the coastal landscape.

An increasingly popular way to take to the river is the thrilling ride on the first amphibious bus in Korea, the **Buyeo Suryukyangyong Bus** *(weekday tour adult/child ¥27,000/21,000)*, which travels on land and water. Starting on land, the bus speeds towards the river and, instead of stopping, plunges in, where it starts acting as a cruise ship to several historical sites along the Baekma-gang. This tourist offering has developed with additional water activities such as canoeing.

EATING IN BUYEO: OUR PICKS

MAP P341

Jangwon Buckwheat Noodles: Popular place by Gudurae Sculpture Park Pier selling bowls of buckwheat noodles. *11am-8pm Tue-Sun* ₩

Gomaru Gamjatang: The speciality is *gamjatang* (pork-bone stew), a hearty and slightly spicy classic. Open all night, a rarity for late-evening drinks in Buyeo. *24hr* ₩₩

Gudurae Dolssambap: Try *dolssambap*, a set meal of hot stone pot-cooked rice with side dishes, vegetables and medicinal plants. *11am-8pm Wed-Mon* ₩₩

House of Baekje: Homey specialities like grilled beef or pork rolled inside *ssam* (lettuce wraps) and *yeonnipbap* (a lotus leaf filled with sticky rice). *10am-9pm* ₩₩

Beyond Baekje Hinterland

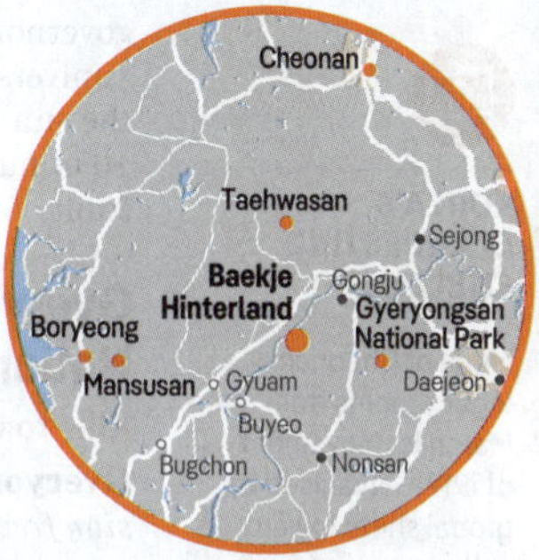

Leave Baekje's capitals for hikes to temples and peaks, a history lesson on Korea's independence and its dirtiest beach party.

Between the Yellow Sea to the west and Chungcheongnam-do's largest cities to the east, the fertile lands on both sides of the Geum-gang boast a bounty of natural and religious sites. The stunning Gyeryongsan National Park and its temples, Gap-sa and Donghak-sa, soar like a mountainous divide between Gongju and the urban areas of Daejeon, Korea's fast-moving fifth-largest city – a whole world away from the quiet of these peaks.

To the immediate west of Buyeo, the sandy coast is home to Boryeong, one of Korea's most famous seaside resorts. Come July, Daecheon Beach turns into the leading site of the boisterous Mud Festival, one of South Korea's most renowned summer events.

Places

GETTING AROUND

Buses go everywhere in Korea, but travelling in Chungcheongnam-do's countryside by public transport is an endeavour that requires patience. Outside large towns, prepare to negotiate few daily departures and long waits for onward connections at basic bus terminals. Renting a car is the best way to get between sights as most of them lie within a very short distance of Gongju and Buyeo.

Cheonan

TIME FROM GONGJU: **1HR**

Learn about Korea's colonial struggle

The **Independence Hall of Korea** *(i815.or.kr; free)* in the countryside east of Cheonan is a worthy half-day detour to understand Korea's colonial history. Hemmed by serene hills, this grand memorial park celebrates Korea's struggle and liberation from Japanese colonisers on 15 August 1945.

It's a short walk from the large, flame-like, towering twin pillars of **Monument to the Nation** *(free)* via a white lotus pond to the **Grand Hall of the Nation** *(free)*, touted as the largest tiled building in East Asia. It protects the park's centrepiece, the imposing **Statue of Indomitable Koreans**. Behind it, six pavilions contain interesting multimedia and interactive exhibits offering a good English-language overview of the history of the Korean people, starting from prehistory to the forming of the Three Kingdoms and focusing on the invasion and colonial subjugation of Korea.

Two pavilions present evidence from the anti-Japanese colonial rule protests of 1 March 1919 and the ensuing years of Korea's patriotic struggle for independence. Outside, on the park's western side, the **Exhibition of the Remains of the Japanese Government Building** *(free)* shows 2400 tonnes of debris from the old building used by the Japanese

KOREA'S CLANDESTINE EMBLEM

Much of Cheonan's legacy stems from the March 1st Movement of 1919. Galvanised by global shifts toward self-governance, activists broadcast a Declaration of Independence in Seoul, igniting non-violent resistance across the peninsula. Though suppressed by Japanese forces, this watershed moment forged a unified national identity and a provisional government-in-exile. The focal point of this defiance was the *taegeukgi* (national flag). Once a clandestine emblem of hope, the flag you see today is steeped in ancient philosophy: the central circle reflects *eum-yang* (cosmic balance), while four black trigrams represent the elemental forces of heaven, earth, water and fire. Today, rows of these flags stand as a vivid tribute to Korea's reclaimed sovereignty.

governor-general of Choson, which was destroyed on the 50th anniversary of Liberation Day. The ruins lie to the west, where the sun and imperialism set. Buses 400 and 338 take about 40 minutes to reach Independence Hall from the bus stop in front of Cheonan's bus terminal.

Gyeryongsan National Park

TIME FROM GONGJU: **30MIN**

Hike to Rooster Dragon Mountain

Gyeryongsan National Park *(gyeryong.knps.or.kr; admission free; parking ₩2000-5000)*, one of the smallest in Korea, rises to the east of Gongju and west of Daejeon. The mountain resembles a dragon with a rooster's head and has three main entrances, each one with a temple: on the east is **Gap-sa** *(gapsa.org; adult/child ₩3000/1000)*, whose main hall has three gleaming Buddha statues and is famous for its striking autumn leaf colours. To the northwest is **Donghak-sa** *(adult/child ₩3000/1000)*, one of Korea's few remaining nunneries, and to the southeast is **Sinwon-sa** *(free)*, where monks perform services for the god of Gyeryong mountain every spring and autumn. Templestays are available at all shrines.

Whichever gate you pick, the park is crisscrossed by a web of well-marked trails that eventually reconnect to the 775m-high **Sambul-bong**, soaring at the centre of the reserve between Donghak-sa and Gap-sa. Boards at the park's entrances suggest six main routes ranging from easy two-hour temple visits to full-day hikes. The most challenging is the advanced 10.2km-long park traverse between Gap-sa and Donghak-sa over a triplet of peaks (740m-high **Yeoncheon-bong**, 766m-high **Gwaneum-bong** and 775m-high Sambul-bong), which takes about six to seven hours to complete.

More accessible routes are the 3.9km-long hike from Gap-sa to Sambul-bong along the Geumjandigogae Pass (2½ hours) and the scenic 2.9km-long hike from Gap-sa's parking lot to 740m-high Yeoncheon-bong and the **Deungun-am hermitage**, set right beneath the peak. Yeoncheong-bong is surrounded by four viridian mountains (**Cheonwang-bong**, **Ssalgae-bong**, **Munpil-bong** and Sambul-bong) and offers views stretching to the **Gyeryongil** and **Yanghwa Reservoirs**. Sunsets here are particularly stunning.

Infrequent bus 320 connects Gongju to Gap-sa's parking lot, while bus 350 goes to Donghak-sa at 9.15am, 10.45am and 4.45pm daily. From Daejeon, bus 107 goes to Donghak-sa every 20 minutes, while buses 340, 341 and 342 run only a handful of times daily to Gap-sa. The best way to get to the park is by private car or taxi.

Taehwasan

TIME FROM GONGJU: **40MIN**

A war-resistant temple

Just 25km northwest of Gongju is **Magok-sa** *(magoksa.or.kr)*, a delightfully ageing temple established in 640 CE. It's believed to protect from war; in fact, it survived both the Imjin War (1592–98) and the Korean War (1950–53) unscathed. Among

BUSAN OPPA/SHUTTERSTOCK

Magok-sa, Taehwasan

its charming ancient buildings are several atmospheric halls, pagodas, pavilions and the Daeungbojeon, a rare two-storey prayer hall. Magok-sa's idyllic setting beside a river would be a valid enough reason to consider the templestay on offer, but three hiking trails also start from the temple and climb to the nearby hills, passing by small hermitages. The most challenging trek is 10km long, conquering two peaks, 414m-high **Nabal-bong** and 423m-high **Hwarin-bong**.

Mansusan

TIME FROM BUYEO: 40MIN

Hike to Muryang-sa

The Mansusan massif west of Buyeo is home to several significant historical sights, including the stunning **Muryang-sa** *(adult/child ₩3000/1000)*, a temple housing six Korean treasures. Destroyed during the Imjin War, Muryang-sa was rebuilt in the 17th century, west of the Mansu-cheon (Mansu stream).

Approaching via the Iljumun Gate and over the river, Cheowangmun gives a great perspective of the temples' centrepiece, the historic two-storey **Geurak-jeon Hall**, fronted by both a **five-storey stone pagoda** dating back to the Goryeo dynasty and an octagonal **seokdung** (stone lantern) believed to date to between the Later Silla (668–935 CE) and

KOREA'S STONE LANTERNS

One of the most common stone structures found at Korean Buddhist temples are lanterns (*seokdeung;* 석등 in Korean). Their body is square or octagonal with four vertical openings topped by a roof cap, and they usually stand before a stone pagoda in front of the main hall. There are about 280 original stone lanterns in Korea, only 60 of which are well preserved. Twenty-four hark back to the Unified Silla period (668–935 CE) when Seon Buddhism spread – stone lanterns represent the spread of Buddha's teachings, the Dharma. It is believed that Korean stone lanterns also travelled to Japan with Buddhism in the 8th century, as few Japanese stone lanterns predate the Kamakura period (1185–1333 CE).

TEMPLE FOOD & DRINKS: OUR PICKS

Toshil's Rice Chestnut Bread: On the way to Gap-sa, this shop has sold this savoury sweet since 1978. *9am-7pm* ₩

Cafe C&D: Gap-sa parking lot's coffee house has decent brews, finger food and smoothies. The upstairs terrace is a nice touch. *9am-8pm* ₩

Cheongnam Garden: Slightly north of the Magokgyo bridge to Magok-sa, this family restaurant has meals to share plus bibimbap and noodles. *9am-7pm* ₩₩

Eunhye Restaurant: The local *hanjeongsik* (Korean-style banquet) type restaurant in the village outside Muryang-sa Gates is famous for its array of side dishes. *9am-7.30pm* ₩₩

HEALING MUD

Back in the early 1990s, muddy Daecheon Beach was not beautiful or a tourist hotspot – to be fair, it wasn't living its best moments yet. The closure of a local coal mine prompted Daecheon mayor Park Sang-don to think out of the box and try to rekindle the local economy by developing mud-based cosmetics after Boryeong's mud was declared the healthiest in the country. The black, mineral-rich mud is believed to have anti-ageing properties. For the past 20-odd years, the Mud Festival has helped popularise it. Today, beauty face masks made with Boryeong mud are appreciated worldwide thanks to their ultra-fine particle powder, making them less irritating and good against acne and scars.

early Goryeo (918–1392 CE) periods. Templestays are available. The mountain also has a series of easy trails and the **Miam-sa** temple *(free)* with a giant outdoor statue of a golden reclined Buddha.

Buses from Buyeo to Boryeong (three daily at 9.10am, 2.40pm and 5.40pm) stop in the middle of Muryang town, a 2km walk from the temple. If taking the first morning bus, it's possible to visit the temple and continue to Boryeong at 3pm.

Boryeong

TIME FROM BUYEO: **45MIN**

Join Korea's dirtiest festival

The **Boryeong Mud Festival** *(mudfestival.or.kr; weekends adult/child ₩14,000/11,000)*, held every July for about a fortnight, has been recognised as Korea's top international festival, with over a million attendees. It began in 1998 to promote the health benefits of the local mud, which is rich in germanium and other minerals. It has developed a reputation for the unabashed, alcohol-fuelled frolics of expats, Korean students and international travellers.

Daecheon Beach, 10km east of Boryeong, is the principal venue. After being baptised in a vat of the oozing grey stuff, participants can enter the 'mud prison' and get doused with

EATING & DRINKING IN DAECHEON BEACH: OUR PICKS

Dubal Cafe & Yokjang Bakery: Have the best pick of local coffee, desserts and cakes near large windows with beach views. *10am-10pm*

La Scala: There's fine espresso here, though the best feature of this expansive cafe are the sea views from every window. *10am-10pm*

Paldogangsan: (팔도강산) Established restaurant for large hotpot seafood soup meals using shellfish, fish and crab. *7.30am-9pm* ₩₩

Mani Mani Grilled Shellfish: Busy restaurant by the beach serving set meals of shellfish, seafood and meat BBQ in a breezy hall. *11am-11pm Sun-Thu, to 3am Fri & Sat* ₩₩₩

ST_TRAVEL/SHUTTERSTOCK

Daecheon Beach, Boryeong

buckets of warmed mud. There's a mud superslide, a mud rain tunnel and many muddy pools where groups run, splash and generally get covered in mud. The festival grounds are just above the beach, where every evening there's a concert or rave, and it's easy to zip out to the ocean for a quick swim or demudding. Many English-speaking volunteers are on hand, and there are free lockers, a campsite and basic clean-up facilities, making this one of the most foreigner-friendly events in Korea – however, accommodation books up months in advance.

Float off to a sleepy island

Floating 13km from Daecheon, Sapsido is a quiet fishing island to escape it all. The largest beach is **Bamseom**, a broad stretch of golden sand on the island's southern coast. A good three-hour hike, about 8km, runs along the southwestern coast, roughly from **Jinneomeo Beach** to the **Bamseom Ferry Jetty**. Ferries run from **Daecheon Ferry Terminal** to one of two jetties on Sapsido in about 45 minutes: **Witmaeul** jetty in Sulttung village or **Bamseom** jetty in Minbak village.

Traverse a tidal bridge

Shifting tides cause a strange phenomenon between September and May that transforms peaceful and pine-clad **Muchangpo Beach** – tucked a scenic 30-minute drive south of central Boryeong – into a pilgrimage site. The lowest tide exposes an S-shaped 1.5km-long rocky road connecting the beach to **Seokdaedo**. You need sturdy rubber shoes and torchlight as the 'Moses road' often only appears well after the sun sets.

From mid-March to April, the **Muchangpo Mystic Sea Road Festival** celebrates this modern-day 'Parting of the Sea' with activities and a bounty of fresh seafood – think shellfish, *gaebul* (fat innkeeper worm) and Muchangpo's delicacy, *jjukkumi* (webfoot octopus) cooked in a variety of styles.

BEST BEACHES IN BORYEONG

Yongdu Beach: At the southern end of Nampo Embankment; more secluded than nearby Daecheon with a pine forest for camping.

Chunjangdae Beach: Nice beach with a gentle slope, pine and acacia trees, and walking paths to nearby islands.

Doksan Beach: Also known as Holmö Beach. A small hill in the middle of the beach gets mistaken for an island.

Jangan Beach: Boryeong's southernmost point hosts the Sohwangsa-gu ecological learning site with a wetland and dunes.

Maryang-ri Camellia Forest: Not a beach but a seaside forest with views of nearby Oryeokdo (Oryeok island) and trees nearly 500 years old.

Taeanhaean National Park's Coast

LONELY BEACHES | SOOTHING NATURE | COASTAL EXPLORATIONS

GETTING AROUND

The small yet sprawling city of Seosan is the region's gateway, with direct bus connections to Seoul Nambu bus station. Intercity buses go from the **Seosan Bus Terminal** to **Taean Intercity Bus Terminal**, from where infrequent buses continue to Sinduri and down to Anmyeondo, where regular public transport across the island is limited. The best way to enjoy the coast and its many beaches is by renting a car. In summer, it's possible to strike out by bicycle, and even on foot, along the well-maintained circuit of trails starting at Sinduri and snaking south along the coast to Anmyeondo and beyond.

The western coast of Chungcheongnam-do province hugs the long and still largely off-the-radar Taeanhaean National Park (태안해안국립공원). It covers 327 sq km of land and sea, 130 islands and islets, over 30 beaches and a panoply of hiking and biking trails. Few travellers make it here, but not because the area lacks infrastructure: surf-friendly Mallipo Beach was one of the western coast's main calling cards until an oil spill disaster painted it black in December 2007 – volunteers from all over Korea scrubbed it clean in little over a year. It's now back to sun, waves and flocks of seagulls.

The park's largest island, Anmyeondo, is Korea's sixth largest and is connected by a land bridge to the peninsula. Expect serene rolling hills, lush paddy fields, wide and deserted beaches, and some of the country's oldest pine forests. Next is small Wonsando, connected to Anmyeondo by the modern Wonsan-Anmyeon Bridge and to Daecheon Beach and Boryeong by a state-of-the-art undersea tunnel.

Korean Sahara

Walk in a desert by the sea

The northern end of **Sinduri Beach**, 17km west of Taean-gun, curls into **Sinduri Coastal Sand Dunes** *(taean.go.kr)*, a carpet of low beachside sandy hills that can be hiked and explored in a few hours. It is believed that they formed around 15,000 years ago, following the Ice Age, as sea winds blew sand towards the coast over thousands of years. The boardwalks make it easy to walk over the fine sand and across an environment mixing beach, shrubs and a backdrop of forest blending into green hills.

To the eastern side of the desert, the land transforms into the **Doowoong Wetland**. Right to the south of the dunes, **Sinduri Sand Dune Center** *(free)* has some simple exhibit panels in Korean, a playground for kids and a rooftop terrace where photographers can enjoy panoramic views of the dunes and the sea.

SONGSUB8 / IMAZINS/GETTY IMAGES

Mallipo

With a day to spare, the 8.6km-long **Baragil Course** starts from Sinduri Dunes via Meodong and Guryepo beach, ending at the **Hagampo campground**. Bus 970 goes to the dunes from **Taean Bus Terminal** (p350), but it's rare. A taxi costs about ₩30,000 one-way.

Mesmerising Gardens

Marvel at Cheollipo's seaside arboretum

Cheollipo Arboretum *(chollipo.org; adult/child ₩15,000/6000)* is among Asia's top botanical institutions, with a collection of more than 13,000 species from over 60 countries laid out with diligent care across 64 hectares of lush coastal property. Only a fraction of them are open to the public, but even that is spectacular – particularly in spring when the arboretum's famous magnolias bloom (early- to mid-April).

The arboretum was founded and built by a man without any formal training: American Carl Ferris Miller was a banker in Seoul when he bought his first plot of farmland in Cheollipo, developing it in the 1970s. He continued to add to it until he died in 2002 at the age of 81. He also relocated several Korean *hanok* (traditional wooden homes) to the nursery to preserve them. You can stay in one; rooms start at ₩100,000 per night. Cheollipo Arboretum is a 20-minute walk from Mallipo Beach.

Surf on the Site of Korea's Largest Oil Spill

Disaster beach

Along with Dacheon, **Mallipo** is considered one of the best beaches on the west coast. It is 250m wide and 3km long, and in addition to bathing, it's a haven for surfers who come here to catch the strong waves. Among the string of surf schools along the road that flanks the beach, long-established **MLP Surf** *(link.inpock.co.kr/mlpsurf)* opened in 2013 and offers beginner lessons for ₩77,000.

Don't miss the **Oil Spill Restoration Memorial** *(free)* celebrating the 'Miracle of the West Coast', a year-long citizen-led

TOP TIP

The best time to visit is in late spring (May) and September to avoid encountering rains or the perpetual Yellow Sea fogs that envelop the coastline.

WHEN MALLIPO WENT BLACK

It's hard to believe looking at pretty Mallipo today, but this very same coast was the epicentre of Korea's most tragic ocean disaster. On 7 December 2007, a Samsung crane barge collided with Hong Kong's crude carrier *Hebei Spirit*, about 9km off Mallipo. Sludge reached the beach in a few hours, and the coast turned black. As soon as the news spread, Koreans sprang to action in what is remembered as the 'Miracle of the West Coast'. Around 1.23 million volunteers from all over the nation came to Taean to help remove the oil sludge, working tirelessly to brush up the coast. The effort was tremendous: Mallipo reopened in June 2008, and finless porpoises returned in 2016.

clean-up operation to restore Mallipo from the largest ocean disaster in Korean history. The memorial has striking photos, videos and English captions about the tragedy and its impact on the livelihood of the Chungcheongnam-do and Jeolla-do regions.

Meet Korea's Oldest Pines

A healing circuit at Anmyeondo Recreational Forest

Since 1978, the centre of Anmyeondo has boasted 115 hectares of Korea's only natural forest pine trees. **Anmyeondo Recreational Forest** *(anmyonhuyang.go.kr; adult/child ₩1000/400)* is home to hundred-year-old red pines with hard, straight trunks that look like tall umbrellas. They were used for building ships and caskets for the royal family during the

HIGHLIGHTS
1 Taeanhaean National Park

SIGHTS
2 Anheung-seong
3 Anmyeon Beach
4 Anmyeondo Arboretum
5 Anmyeondo Recreational Forest
6 Baeksajang Beach
7 Batgae Beach
8 Boryeong Undersea Tunnel
9 Cheollipo Arboretum
10 Cheongpodae Beach
11 Daecheon Beach
12 Doowoong Wetland
13 Ganworam Hermitage
14 Haemi-eupseong
15 Halbaebawi and Halmaebawi
16 Kkotji Beach
17 Korea Flower Park
18 Mallipo Beach
19 Mongsanpo Beach
20 Oil Spill Restoration Memorial
21 Rock-Carved Triad Buddha
22 Sambong Beach
23 Sinduri Beach
24 Sinduri Coastal Sand Dunes
25 Sinduri Sand Dune Center
26 Wonsando Beach

ACTIVITIES
27 MLP Surf
28 Taean Coastal Walk trailhead

SLEEPING
29 Hagampo campground
30 Pinocchio Pension
31 Sand Hill Resort
32 Taean Manripo Feel Hotel

DRINKING & NIGHTLIFE
33 Black Brunch Cafe
34 Cholli Coffee and Dessert
35 Forrenu
36 Sunset Cliff

ENTERTAINMENT
see 17 Taean World Tulip Exhibition

TRANSPORT
37 Seosan bus terminal
38 Taean Intercity Bus Terminal

Joseon dynasty and served as a primary source of timber for the reconstruction of royal palaces in Seoul, including the Secret Garden section of Changdeokgung Palace. Observe them up close on three wooden walkways connecting to a 1km-long looping trail around a forested hill. The large reserve includes a Buddhist temple and walking trails that disappear into the surrounding hills. To its southwest, still within Anmyeondo Recreational Forest, the **Anmyeondo Arboretum** offers more hiking through a pine forest, photo zones and various trails.

Beach Hop Until You Drop

Feeling the sand at Anmyeondo's beaches

Anmyeondo's west coast may have the most beautiful beaches in Taeanhaean National Park. Northwestern **Sambong Beach** is one of the least developed. It has a backdrop of pine trees with walking trails along the **Taean Coastal Walk**, connected to **Baeksajang Beach**, 2km to the north, a quiet speck of sand that sees little traffic, and the famous **Kkotji Beach**, 9.9km to the south, via secluded **Anmyeon Beach**, hemmed by pines and facing a cluster of rock formations, and **Batgae Beach**, which has nice views over a rocky islet and is popular for looking for snails and crabs. Kkotji Beach is more built up because of the popularity of two striking rock formations, **Halbaebawi and Halmaebawi**, that jut off the coast and are most dramatic when backed by red sunsets. To the east of the beach is **Korea Flower Park** *(koreaflowerpark.com, festivals adult/child from ₩9000/7000)*, open only during flower festivals (check website) such as the popular **Taean World Tulip Exhibition** in late April when 2.6 million buds bloom.

OFFBEAT TAEAN

Choi Daeho, a teacher and outdoor enthusiast, recommends offbeat shrines and fortresses.

Ganworam Hermitage: A Buddhist hermitage set on a cliff by the sea.

Seosan Rock-Carved Buddha Triad: In Baekhwasan, trails snake around an old Buddhist temple and a stone Buddha statue.

Anheung-seong: Visit an old fortress castle, with views, in the mountains behind Anheung Port in Jeongjuk-ri.

Haemi-eupseong: A beautifully preserved, free-to-access walled fortress.

EATING & DRINKING IN MALLIPO & CHEOLLIPO: SEASIDE CAFES

Black Brunch Cafe: This humble coffee shop serves the best espresso on Mallipo Beach. *7am-9pm*

MLP Surf (p351): The cafe of this surf school makes zesty bacon cheeseburgers and famous fish and chips. *7am-10pm*

Cholli Coffee and Dessert: Large and luminous cafeteria on the top floor of a shop overlooking Cheollipo Beach for brews and cakes. *10am-8pm*

Sunset Cliff: Stunning cliff-top location among pine trees on the northern side of Mallipo, with coffee, Western and Korean dishes. *10am-10pm*

TAEANHAEAN COASTAL CRUISER

Spend a few days or up to a week exploring Taeanhaean National Park's long coastline on four wheels.

START	END	LENGTH
Taean-gun	Daecheon Beach	150km; 11 hours

On leaving **1** **Taean-gun**, the interstate thins into countryside roads to **Sinduri Beach** (p350), where **2** **Sinduri Coastal Sand Dunes** (p350) offer a slice of the desert by the sea. Before leaving, refuel at **3** **Forrenu** with coffee and dessert by the beach.

It's a short drive to the next headland, where the gardens of **4** **Cheollipo Arboretum** (p351) deserve a lengthy stop. Overnight here or by curvy **5** **Mallipo Beach** (p351), a surf hotspot that recovered from Korea's worst oil spill – learn about it at the excellent **6** **Oil Spill Restoration Memorial** (p351).

Proceeding south towards Anmyeondo, stop at **7** **Mongsanpo Beach**, connected to **8** **Cheongpodae Beach**, to enjoy camping in the pine forest behind it – a set for hit K-Dramas.

Enjoy the lush paddy-field-scenery at **9** **Sambong Beach** (p353), one of the park's least developed, to meet seagulls and crabs.

As you wait for sunset at **10** **Kkotji Beach** (p353) before the twin **Halbaebawi and Halmaebawi** (p353) ('Grandma and Grandpa rocks'), go inland to **11** **Anmyeondo Recreational Forest** (p352) and walk through 100-year-old red pine trees.

Take Wonsan Anmyeon Bridge for a spectacular oceanic crossing to pretty **12** **Wonsando Beach**, which has campsites.

Cross back to Korea's peninsula using the **Boryeong Undersea Tunnel** to hotspot **13** **Daecheon Beach** (p348) – but avoid the Mud Festival's crowds. It's a 1½-hour drive back to Seosan.

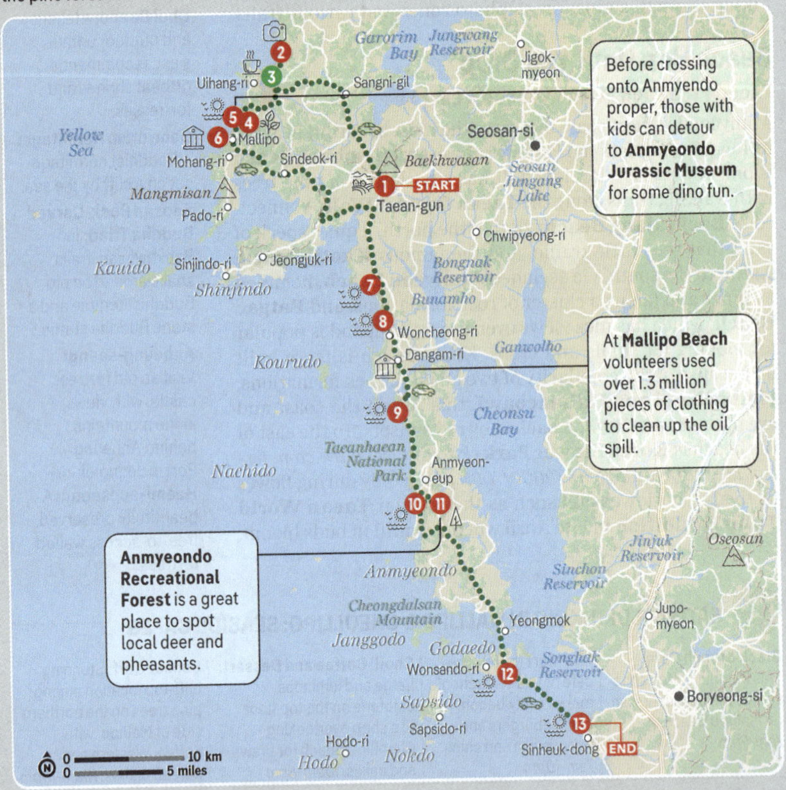

Cheongju

ARTS AND CRAFTS | EARLY PRINTING | FORTRESS HIKE

The capital and largest city of South Korea's only landlocked province, Cheongju (청주) is a cultural centre known for its printing legacy, as the home of the world's oldest book made with movable metal type, creative craft works and artistic spaces.

Though often omitted from many travellers' itineraries, Cheongju is a mid-sized city with a small-town vibe, with friendly people and more than a few reasons to pass through: world-class arts and crafts; a magnificent mountain fortress, and its own twist on *samgyeopsal* (pork belly). Among Koreans, Cheongju is regarded as an educational centre, with Chungbuk National University, Cheongju University, Seowon University and Cheongju National University of Education all located here, which makes for some youthful enclaves of shopping, dining and nighttime revelry. Cheongju is also a place of neighbourhood parks full of elderly people playing *baduk* (ancient board game Go) and swapping stories from the past.

TOP TIP

If you are just passing through Cheongju, the busy bus terminal area has plenty of great-value, spacious love hotels in the quiet, though dark, back streets. It can feel a little characterless but the central location makes getting around easy.

Ancient Printed Book

Learn all about the Jikji

While the Gutenberg Bible needs no introduction, the Jikji languished for many years in relative obscurity, even though it is the oldest book in the world printed with movable metal

GETTING AROUND

Direct buses from Seoul and other cities arrive at Cheongju's **Intercity** (buses to Gongju) or **Express bus** terminals, from where a bus or taxi downtown (south of City Hall) takes 20 minutes. The train arrives at distant **Osong station** or **Jochiwon station**, requiring transfer to a local bus or taxi (40 minutes).

Cheongju is a sprawling city with no metro system and a sometimes inefficient bus service. Downtown is walkable, but to get to the major attractions that are west and south, it may be easiest to take an inexpensive taxi. **Cheongju International Airport** is 18km from the city.

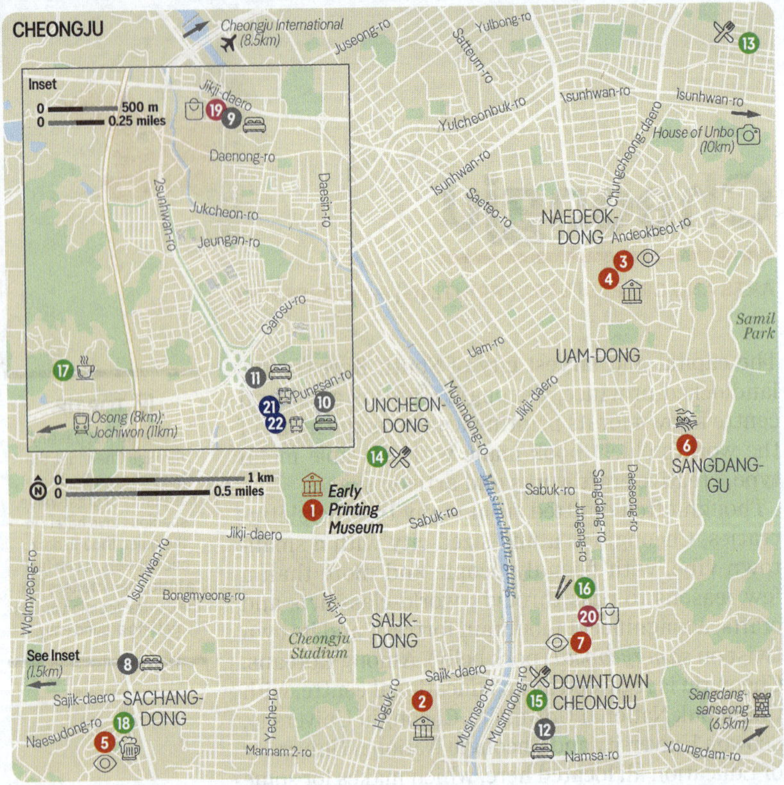

HIGHLIGHTS
1 Early Printing Museum

SIGHTS
2 Cheongju Museum of Art
3 Culture Factory
4 MMCA Cheongju
5 Sacho-dong
6 Suamgol
7 Wondosim

SLEEPING
8 Blanc Hotel
9 Gloucester Hotel
10 Hotel Dictionary Cheongju
11 Joy Hotel
12 Smart Hotel

EATING
13 37.5
14 Manta
15 Samgyeopsal Alley
16 SORORI

DRINKING & NIGHTLIFE
17 Humanitas
see 7 Hyper Market
see 7 Mua Jigyeong
18 Road King

SHOPPING
19 Hyundai Department Store
20 Seongan-gil Fashion Street

TRANSPORT
21 Cheongju Express Bus Terminal
22 Cheongju Intercity Bus Terminal

type. It was printed in 1377 (78 years before the Gutenberg) at the temple of Heungdeok-sa in modern-day Cheongju. Today, the small **Cheongju Early Printing Museum** *(cheongju.go.kr/jikjiworld/index.do; free)* tells you everything about the Jikji, which was admitted to UNESCO's Memory of the World Register in 2001. Sadly the original is not here – it's in the National Library of France – and in its place there's a copy. It's closed Mondays.

The Jikji itself is small: 38 sheets of thin mulberry paper, each one measuring 24.6cm by 17cm. Its full title is *Baegun hwasang chorok buljo jikji simche yojeol* – that is, an anthology of the monk Baegun Gyeonghan's teachings on *Seon* Buddhism (Zen Buddhism), though of the two-volume set, only the second volume remains.

In the mid-19th century it was acquired by a French official in Korea, who took it to France. After it was put on display at the 1900 World's Fair in Paris, it disappeared from the public eye, and it was only in 1972 that Korean historian Park Byeong-seon rediscovered it at the National Library of France. Understandably South Korea would like to see it returned.

A Night Out in Cheongju

Drink with the locals

You can really see how locals let their hair down in three distinct pockets of Cheongju. Follow the on-trend crowd by skipping the fast fashion of pedestrianised **Seongan-gil Fashion Street** (technically on Jungang-ro) and wandering west through a cool emerging enclave in the backstreets of **Wondosim** (Old Downtown). Each night, cool young things (and arty older locals) get dressed up to gather in dozens of laneway bistros, hidden cafes and casual cocktail bars within renovated industrial spaces.

If you want high-energy student vibes, take a 10-minute taxi west to **Sacho-dong** near Chungbuk National University. Here, the *hof* (local pubs) stay loud until dawn with a mix of students and expats. This is where you can pull up alone and speak English with the bar staff.

For something more refined, the bars near the **Hyundai Department Store** offer a chic alternative with wine bars playing light jazz. This new downtown is more upmarket than Wondosim, but on weekends it gets just as noisy with young professionals ordering champagne table-service at late-night lounge bars and clubs.

CHEONGJU'S BEST ART SPOTS

Culture Factory: Former tobacco factory turned cultural complex, with restaurants, shops, craft museum, open library and performance hall. Hosts the **Cheongju Craft Biennale**.

MMCA Cheongju: Contemporary art champ MMCA's Cheongju branch showcases the country's first viewable art collection storage system.

Suamgol: A Korean War refuge has become an amateur mural village with a maze of K-Drama filming sites and rooftop cafes.

House of Unbo: The famous but controversial colonial artist's private home is now a public space, with galleries, workshops and museums.

Cheongju Museum of Art: Modern and contemporary art pieces set within a 'cultural playground'.

EATING IN CHEONGJU: OUR PICKS

Samgyeopsal Alley: At Seomun Market, try Cheongju-style pork belly along Samgyeopsal Alley, marinated in soy sauce before it's grilled. *11am-1am* WW

SORORI: Decked out like a vintage Korean classroom with top-scoring Korean classic stews and crab rice in Cheongju's stylish bistro zone. *11am-8.30pm* W

Manta: Excellent Italian dishes around Unridan-gil, Cheongju's trending area near the Early Printing Museum. *11.30am-9pm Wed-Mon* WW

37.5: Bright brunch spot serving both international- and Korean-style breakfast plates, like eggs Benedict, French toast and kimchi fried rice. *9.30am-4pm & 5-8.30pm* WW

WHY I LOVE CHEONGJU

Phillip Tang, Lonely Planet writer

There's something about turning off the thronging Seongan-gil in Wondosim (Old Downtown) Cheongju and being met by a pocket of calm. Northwest of the main fashion hub, the streets feel deeply intentional and a quiet secret, removed entirely from Cheongju's famous sights. I love this quiet, self-assured district of low-rise architecture and narrow lanes draped in the abundant foliage of overhead trees, softening the lines of the buildings. All my favourite things are here – independent cafes, minimalist bistros mixing drinks and fusion dishes, and wonderfully cramped vintage shops. Quiet laughter is always spilling into the air. The atmosphere is a loud hum. This is Cheongju's most authentic, energetic core.

SOBEAUTIFUL/SHUTTERSTOCK

Sangdang-sanseong

Mountain Fortress Day Out

Hike Sangdang-sanseong

On the slopes of the mountain Uamsan, the sprawling fortress **Sangdang-sanseong** *(free)*, 4km northeast of the city, was originally constructed in the 1590s and renovated in the 18th century. With walls up to 4m in height that stretch 4.2km around wooded hillsides, Sangdang-sanseong's size makes it easy to imagine that it once housed three temples and several thousand soldiers and monks. Today, it offers superb views of farms, mountains and the city, and is a popular place for Korean families to picnic on the fields outside the ornate south gate. A hike around the wall takes about 1½ hours, the easier direction to follow being counter-clockwise. Once you've finished, stop at a restaurant near the bus stop for *jeon* (savoury pancake) and *makgeolli*.

DRINKING IN CHEONGJU: OUR PICKS

Humanitas: Sip premium coffee while gazing across rice fields in west Cheongju from a converted traditional *hanok*. *10.30am-9pm Tue-Sun*

Mua Jigyeong: Retro-cool bar epitomises trendy Seongan-gil with a candlelit, young buzzing crowd scoffing ample soju and *makgeolli* and fusion snacks. *6pm-4am*

Hyper Market: Vast upstairs cafe downtown filled with plants and school chairs for mocktails, strong coffee and desserts like fresh fig or tiramisu. *noon-10pm*

Road King: Foreigner- and solo-drinker friendly pub in the Chungbuk University bar zone where English is spoken and Guinness is served. *6pm-4am*

Beyond Cheongju

Discover the inland escapes, from a presidential villa on the lake to one of Korea's prettiest parklands.

South of Cheongju lies Daecheong-ho, a huge artificial lake presided over by the old presidential summer villa Cheongnamdae, built in 1983 and open to the public since 2003. West, in Boeun-gun, is a gateway to the great beauty of the mountain Songnisan (sometimes also spelled Sokrisan), part of the Sobaek range. Go during any season and you'll be greeted by stunning scene after stunning scene, with each view more breathtaking than the last – from the wildflower-covered expanses of spring, to the burnished bronze foliage of autumn, to the park's many snow-dusted rock formations come wintertime.

Places

Cheongnamdae p359
Songnisan National Park p360

GETTING AROUND

From **Cheongju's Intercity Bus Terminal** (p355), buses depart frequently for **Songnisan Bus Terminal** and take around 2½ hours. Renting a car will get you there about one hour quicker. The village at the main entrance of Songnisan National Park is walkable, with easy access between its hotels, restaurants, markets and trailheads.

Cheongnamdae

TIME FROM CHEONGJU: **45 MINS**

Blue House of the South

Meaning 'Blue House of the South', **Cheongnamdae** *(chnam.chungbuk.go.kr; adult/child ₩5000)*, closed Mondays, is a spacious property, spanning 1825 sq km, whose best feature is not the house itself but its natural surrounds. Hidden from public view until 2003, the grounds were designed to offer total seclusion. The former private summer villa of Korea's past presidents makes for scenic strolling, with walking paths through bright, beautiful gardens and an observatory overlooking **Daecheong-ho**.

To experience the property as the presidents once did, hit the six themed walking paths, each named after a former leader. These trails range from the leisurely **Lakeside Path**, lined with king cherry trees and towering metasequoias, to steeper climbs leading to an observatory that provides a panoramic view of the sprawling lake and the misty surrounding peaks. Unlike the dense urban palaces of Seoul, Cheongnamdae's scale allows for an expansive variety of landscapes, from the manicured **Sunlight Garden** to the **reclaimed golf course** and a massive **fountain** that serves as the property's focal point. The estate functions as a geographical timeline where the walk away from the villa's rigid, high-security architecture essentially leads you backwards through history, transitioning from Korea's strictly controlled political past into the raw, ancient landscape of the rugged hinterland.

CHEONGJU OR CHUNGJU? PRONUNCIATION CHEAT SHEET

Don't mix up the arty city Cheongju with the distant lake-city Chungju. Translation apps often conflate them, so always double-check the Korean script on your tickets. **Cheongju** (청주) begins with 'Cheong-', which almost rhymes with 'lung' in English. Conversely, **Chungju** (충주) uses a 'Chung-' sound that rhymes with the 'oo' in 'moon'. In both, the suffix '-ju' is like the 'jew-' in 'jewel'.

Interestingly, the province **Chungcheong-do** (충청도) derives its name from these two principal cities: Chung (meaning 'loyalty') + Cheong ('clear' and 'pure'). The suffix '-do' rhymes with 'go', not English 'do'.

Also watch out for **Gongju** (공주), which also sounds like 'go'; and **Cheonan** (천안), which can resemble Cheongju when navigating busy bus terminals in a hurry.

SUNG WOO KIM/SHUTTERSTOCK

Maitreya Buddha statue, Songnisan National Park

Songnisan National Park TIME FROM CHEONGJU: 1 HR

The gold Buddha of Songnisan

With forested mountains and rocky granite outcrops, plunging valleys and towering peaks, **Songnisan National Park** *(songni.knps.or.kr; free)* is spectacularly scenic. But the most arresting sight might be the Buddhist temple complex of **Beopju-sa** *(beopjusa.org; adult/child ₩5000/1000),* about 1km from the park's entrance. Dating to 553 CE, the temple is presided over by a resplendent 33m-high gold-plated **Maitreya Buddha statue** (of modern construction). While many of Seoul's grandest statues are made of stone or bronze, this 'Buddha of the Future' is coated in over 80kg of pure gold leaf, creating a reflective glow that seems to shift in intensity with the moving sun.

What sets this Maitreya apart is its sheer verticality and the symbolic weight it carries. Unlike the seated, meditative Buddhas common in city temples, this one stands tall, ready to descend to Earth. It serves as a brilliant visual counterpoint to **Palsangjeon**, South Korea's only remaining five-storey wooden pagoda (rebuilt in the late 1960s). Together, they represent a rare architectural dialogue between the ancient woodcraft of the Joseon era and modern, gleaming metalwork.

To truly experience Songnisan, follow the **Ori-sup Trail** leading to the temple. The towering pines provide a natural windbreak. Along the way, stop at **Jeongipum Pine Tree**, a 600-year-old monument legendary for having its own ministerial rank. You will also find a weather-worn Silla-era **Bodhisattva statue**, a **lotus-shaped fountain** before arriving at the temple's tea house **Dahyang**. Here you can sip *daechu-cha* (jujube tea) while looking out at the golden Buddha silhouette against the granite peaks. Templestays are offered too, if you want to linger.

Beyond Beopju-sa are several hiking trails including the popular 6.6km climb up **Munjangdae** (1033m) and challenging Cheonhwang-bong (1058m).

Chungju

LAKE COUNTRY | K-DRAMA LOCALES | HOT SPRINGS

Chungju's (충주) position in the middle of the Korean Peninsula near a major waterway made it a much desired city, with all three of Korea's ancient kingdoms fighting to control it. Chungju was the administrative centre of the province until Cheongju took over the distinction in 1909.

Today, this mid-sized city is famous for being the place where former UN Secretary-General Ban Ki-moon grew up; for its eponymous lake, a popular spot to vacation, that was created by building its eponymous dam, and for its annual international martial arts festival. Among Koreans, Chungju is also known for its firm, sweet apples – celebrated every October with zeal, which its city hall says are owed to the region's ideal level of rainfall, ample sunlight and large range in daily temperature. Chungju is also a gateway to Woraksan National Park and Suanbo's natural hot springs.

TOP TIP

At Chungju-ho, keep your eye out for a striking stretch of shoreline from **Ageo-bong**, or 'crocodile peak', so named because the view resembles a bask of crocodiles crawling into the water.

The Old Centre of Korea

Stroll Jungangtap Park

Take a walk around scenic lakeside **Jungangtap Park** *(free)*, the site of artistic sculptures, the very small **Chungju Museum** and, most notably, the impressive **Seven-Storey Pagoda**. At 14.5m, this stone monument is said to have marked the centre of Korea during the Silla period. According to local legend, the Silla king sent two men from the north and south

GETTING AROUND

Most visitors to Chungju will arrive at either its **bus terminal**, centrally located, or its **train station**, about 1km south, across the Chungju stream. If coming from Seoul, there is only one direct train to Chungju daily, which runs in the evening, so travellers may find it more convenient for their schedule to transfer at Daejeon, Osong or Jecheon stations. In town, it's fairly simple to get from place to place by local bus, though not often efficient. Alternatively, taxis are easy to order using the KakaoT app and the city centre is walkable.

HIGHLIGHTS
1 Chungju-ho

SIGHTS
2 Bibongsan
3 Cheongpung Cultural Heritage Complex
4 Chungju Dam
5 Geumsusan
6 Jungangtap Park
7 Oksun-bong
8 Oksun-bong Suspension Bridge

ACTIVITIES
see 8 Cheongpung Lake Kayak & Canoe Experience Center
9 Cheongpung-ho Jadeurak-gil
10 Chungju-ho Jongdaengi-gil

SLEEPING
11 Hotel Bali
12 Hotel River
see 12 Station Lodge Hotel

ENTERTAINMENT
13 Cheongpung Lake Monorail
14 Cheongpung Land

INFORMATION
see 14 Jecheon Tourist Information Centre
15 Jongdaengi-gil Information Centre
16 Tourist Information Centre

TRANSPORT
17 Cheongpung Lake Cable Car
see 3 Cheongpung Naru
18 Chungju Bus Terminal
19 Chungju Naru
20 Chungju Station
21 Janghoe Naru
22 Woraksan Naru

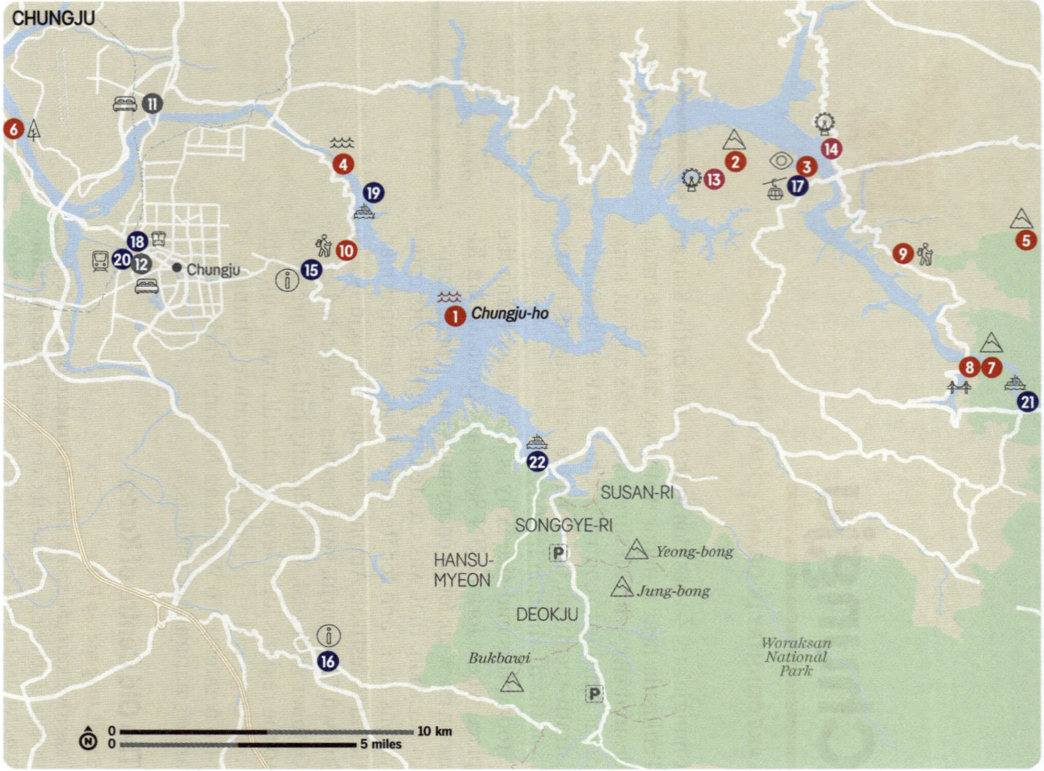

of the kingdom to walk toward each other; they met at this exact spot, leading to the pagoda's construction.

Jungangtap Park has been a filming spot for several K-Dramas, including *Crash Landing on You* and *Vincenzo*, and is a popular place for couples to go, especially at night when the bridge spanning **Tangeum Lake** is illuminated with rainbow lights. You can walk across its nearly 1.5km stretch. At night, the glowing bridge of multicoloured LEDs reflecting off the water creates a romantic backdrop that draws couples of all ages.

By day there are costume stores at the park to rent *hanbok* (traditional clothing) or even vintage 1900s-style school uniforms for a few hours to take photos among the 26 contemporary outdoor sculptures that dot the lawns.

After your stroll, do as the locals do and head to the cluster of restaurants just outside the park entrance. This area is famous for Chungju *makguksu* (buckwheat noodles) often served with a side of crispy fried chicken – a unique local set menu that is almost mandatory for a day trip here.

Alkaline Soak

Dip into Suanbo

Once the favoured retreat of Joseon kings, the tiny town of **Suanbo** is known for its 53°C *oncheon* (hot springs) that are said to have first sprung 30,000 years ago. Since the 1970s, it's been a tourist area full of hotels, saunas, restaurants and cafes clustered across several streets. While much of the town's circa-70s buildings feel a little worn, it's the scenery that's the draw, with lovely mountain views all around. Begin at the **tourist information centre** *(suanbo.or.kr)* in Multang Park, where you can pick up a map.

TAEKKYEON: JOSEON ERA MARTIAL ARTS

While Taekwondo is Korea's famous export, its fluid ancestor, Taekkyeon, remains deeply rooted in Chungju. Strictly forbidden during the colonial era to suppress national identity, it survived clandestinely through a few dedicated masters. Unlike the rigid, linear power of Taekwondo, Taekkyeon is defined by rhythmic '*ik-keu-aek-keu*' breathing (a hiccuping sound that keeps the body flexible) and the *o-geum-jil*, a constant, springy bending of the knees. This creates a deceptive, dance-like flow where 'pushing' kicks and leg sweeps are used to unbalance an opponent rather than strike them. In 2011, it became the first martial art inscribed as a UNESCO Intangible Cultural Heritage. You can witness Taekkyeon displays at the annual Chungju World Martial Arts Festival in September, or for free on some Saturdays at **Jungangtap Park** (p361; check the Performances tab of Korean-language site *taekkyeonwon.com*).

CSTRIKE/SHUTTERSTOCK

Cheongpung-ho Cable Car

TOP EXPERIENCE

Chungju-ho

Human-made Chungju-ho is the largest lake in the country, formed when the valleys around Chungju were flooded after the construction of Chungju Dam, which was completed in 1985. Stretching from Chungju in the west to Jecheon and Danyang eastward, it's a highly scenic area that's become a popular destination for summer retreats, with mountains rising above tranquil waters. In Jecheon, the lake is also called Cheongpung-ho.

DON'T MISS

- Ferry Cruise
- Kayaking & Canoeing
- Jadeurak Trail
- Jongdaengi Trail
- Cable Car
- Monorail
- Cheongpung Land
- Cheongpung Cultural Heritage Complex

Water Activities

For gorgeous views of the surrounding mountains reflected perfectly in the lake's waters, take a cruise across Chungju-ho. The pace is serenely slow, ensuring plenty of time for enjoying the picturesque surrounds. With multiple ferry terminals around the lake – including **Chungju Naru** in Chungju, **Cheongpung Naru** in Jecheon, **Janghoe Naru** (the most popular for scenic surrounds) in Danyang and **Worak Naru** (irregularly used) near Woraksan – there are several companies to choose from, offering a range of options for routes, duration and amenities. One-way tickets start at ₩15,000; round-trip about ₩25,000.

PRACTICALITIES

● chungju.go.kr ● cruise adult/child ₩18,000/10,000 ● hourly ferries 9am-5pm Apr-Oct

For a more adventurous experience, rent a kayak or canoe from Jecheon. **Cheongpung Lake Kayak & Canoe Experience Center** can get you started on an hour-long self-guided paddle (adult/child ₩16,000/13,000) including life jackets and a basic lesson near the picturesque **Oksun-bong** and **Oksun-bong Suspension Bridge**.

Hiking Trails

On the east side of the lake, the seven-section and 58km-long **Cheongpung-ho Jadeurak-gil** is a lovely trail to explore, traversing hills and valleys, and passing villages, a horse ranch and an old fortress wall. From Jecheon, start at the **tourist information centre** and pick up a map. On the west side, there's **Chungju-ho Jongdaengi-gil**, an easy to navigate circular course that goes along the shore to reach a beautiful suspension bridge and cuts through forests up to the small mountain Simhangsan. From Chungju, start at the **Jongdaengi-gil information centre**. Be sure to pack water as there are no shops along the way. Eastward, the mountain **Geumsusan** (1016m) makes for a nice challenging climb. While a fast one-way ascent can take 1½ to 2½ hours, budget four to six hours for a full round-trip.

Cable Car, Monorail & Bungee Jump

In Jecheon, the **Cheongpung-ho Monorail** *(cheongpungcablecar.com; adult/child ₩12,000/9000)* is a quick and fun little diversion along a mountain forest track that emerges to a view of the lake. A 5km drive away is the **Cheongpung-ho Cable Car** *(cheongpungcablecar.com; adult/child ₩18,000/14,000)*, a nine-minute ropeway ride that extends to the summit of **Bibongsan** (531m), offering an even more gorgeous panorama of Chungju-ho enveloped by mountains. Also in this area, across the Cheongpung Bridge, is the adventure sports park **Cheongpung Land** *(cheongpungland.com; single ride ₩18,000)*, with a 62m bungee jump, zero-gravity swing, ejection seat and zip line. Children are not permitted on most rides.

Cheongpung Cultural Heritage Complex

Beside the cable car is the **Cheongpung Cultural Heritage Complex** *(tour.jecheon.go.kr; adult/child ₩3000/2000)*, a key place to visit to better understand the chequered, complex history of this lake. While a much-enjoyed region of relaxation and recreation today, it was also the cause of mass displacement. With the construction of Chungju Dam, an area of 66.48-sq-km was flooded, submerging a number of villages and forcing some 50,000 residents to resettle.

In order to preserve some of the region's rich heritage, dozens of cultural properties, including Joseon-era pavilions, gates and historical residences, were relocated here, along with more than a thousand pieces of pottery and other artefacts. The resulting complex resembles a folk village, named for Cheongpung, the once important Joseon-dynasty town that was absorbed by Jecheon in 1914 and disappeared entirely in the 1985 flooding.

CAMPING AROUND CHUNGJU-HO

While there are many resorts, pensions and hotels around the lake, one of the best ways to experience this beautiful environment is to camp. Campgrounds are abundant, ranging from popular private sites to budget-friendly public areas. For simple traditional camping, bring your own gear and look for first-come, first-served sites, although arriving early is essential. For private campgrounds or popular glamping sites, online reservation is highly recommended, especially on weekends.

TOP TIPS

- Rent a car, as it's the only way to truly be able to see all the looping edges of this lake. Download the Naver Map and KakaoMap apps to navigate. Alternatively, book a long day trip from Seoul.
- There are plenty of restaurants along the main roads, but pack food and water just in case. It's easy to get lost or sidetracked when touring around here.
- For eating at your campsite, many campgrounds operate little shops that sell instant ramen, canned food, crisps, beer and other snacks.
- Have your passport handy, as most ferry companies ask to see it when booking cruise rides.

Beyond Chungju

This is countryside Korea, with tiny towns tucked in winding river bends, dazzling views and daring adventure activities.

Places

Danyang p366
Jecheon p368

GETTING AROUND

Trains run from Seoul's Pangyo station to **Chungju station** (p361), but **Danyang station** and **Jecheon station** are more convenient transfer hubs for the lake. Hopping between scenic landscapes is easiest by renting a car; otherwise, try for infrequent buses. For the lake, bus 301 from Chungju city runs to '**Chungju Naru**' (p364) (30 to 40 minutes) nine times a day. In attractions-filled Danyang, consider a government-subsidised Danyang Tourist Taxi (three hours from ₩55,000).

Settled into the verdant valleys around Chungju-ho are little counties cosied up against soaring peaks, tucked into the bends of the river. This is small-town Korea truly at its most charming, and while you may have planned to simply pass through on your way to the coast, you'll think otherwise when you see it.

The resort town Danyang has everything you could ask for in a setting like this: riverside motels, limestone caves and hiking trails that go through Sobaeksan National Park and past the distinctive, multi-storey Guin-sa (Guin Temple). For adventure, there's Mancheonha Skywalk, a zip wire and more. Next door, Jecheon, blessed with the wild splendour that is Woraksan National Park, is not to be missed.

Danyang

TIME FROM CHUNGJU: 1HR

Mountaintop views

Get your pulse racing by climbing the spiralling walkway up to the **Mancheonha Skywalk** *(dytc.or.kr/mancheonha/89; adult/child ₩4000/3000)*, a glass-bottomed observation deck that offers dizzying views of the slow-flowing Namhan-gang below. After, go under the skywalk to the 120m-high **Mancheonha Zipwire** *(dytc.or.kr/mancheonha/89; adult/child over 135cm ₩30,000)* and be sent rushing across the river, 980m to the other side. For something less stomach-churning, head over to the nearby **Danyanggang Jando Trail** *(danyang.go.kr/tour/1909; free)*, a relaxed and easy 1.2km-long wooden walkway that follows the rock walls along the river.

Rocky beauties

It's said that Joseon scholar Jeong Do-jeon was so taken by the beauty of **Dodamsam-bong** that he chose Sam-bong – 'Three Peaks' – as his pen name. Dodamsam-bong is also the inspiration for Toegye Yi Hwang's time-honoured poetry. Make a trip to Namhan-gang, where the rocky trio rises majestically from the waters, and see the scene for yourself. Framed by misty mountains, Dodamsam-bong – comprised of Janggun-bong, Cheo-bong and Cheop-bong – is an arresting sight indeed, particularly so at dawn when the sun rises over the valley. On the centre rock, you'll notice a pavilion perched atop it, famed as the meeting place of Korean scholars.

KOREA TOURISM ORGANIZATION - KIM JIHO

Mancheonha Skywalk, Danyang

On shore, the **Dodamsambong Tourist Area** offers attractions like cruise ship and sailboat tours, restaurants and cafes. A short walk away is a **stone archway**, a popular picture-taking spot because of the natural frame it creates.

When you're done, with an eight-minute drive southeast following the river and crossing the bridge, you can stop at another rocky beauty, the stunning limestone **Gosu Donggul** *(gosucave.co.kr; adult/child ₩11,000/5000)*, one of Korea's most famous caves. A rabbit warren of slippery metal catwalks and spiral staircases running through 1.7km of dim, dense, narrow grottoes, it's quite an intimate experience, where you can get up close with the rock formations. Stay away if you're claustrophobic.

Hike amid azaleas at Sobaeksan

The views at **Sobaeksan National Park** are astounding, so put your hiking boots on and get ready to take in the sheer beauty of it all. The third-largest of South Korea's mountainous national parks, it's home to the daintily named **Sobaeksan** (Little White Mountain), one of the highest peaks in the country, and the ornate, opulent temple of **Guin-sa** *(guinsa.org; free)*.

The headquarters of the Cheontae order of Korean Buddhism, reestablished by Sangwol Wongak in 1945, Guin-sa is a stately (though largely modern) complex of 30-odd buildings wedged into a valley – to dramatic effect – between steep, forested slopes. Erected on a considerable incline, the temple halls are connected by elevated walkways. From the **Guin-sa bus stop**, the initial clamber up to the temple is heavy going, but it's worth the short and strenuous hike for the vista of the mountains vanishing into the horizon. Be quiet and respectful, as you may hear monks chanting around you.

For summiting Sobaeksan, enter the park from the west at the **Darian Tourist Area**, full of campsites, pensions

CHUNGBUK'S AUTUMN FESTIVALS

Cheongju Jikji Festival: Exhibition of ancient printing techniques, old printed books and traditional music. *September*

Jecheon International Music & Film Festival: Chungbuk's premier film festival and a rousing celebration of music. *September*

Chungju World Martial Arts Festival: Thousands of martial-arts experts from around the world come to Chungju to demonstrate their skills. *September*

Cheongju Organic Life Festival: The largest festival in Korea devoted to agriculture and livestock. *September*

Osong Cosmetics & Beauty Expo: One of Korea's best K-Beauty events, with exhibitions on cosmetics, hair and nail products. *October*

Yeongdong Nangye Traditional Korean Music Festival: Runs concurrently with the Yeongdong Wine Festival. *October*

CHUNGBUK'S SPECIALITY FOODS

Inland Chungcheong-buk-do is known for its freshwater fish and pheasant, which are used to make the region's own local variations of Korean dishes. Fish such as carp, catfish, bullhead and minnow are cooked up in soups and stews, flavoured with funky fermented bean paste or piquant chilli peppers. Or, in a dish called *doribaengbaengi*, tiny barbel fish are oil-fried whole and served with garlic, red pepper paste and perilla leaves. Meanwhile, pheasant, called *ggweong*, is grilled, fried, stuffed inside dumplings, boiled hotpot style or sliced and served raw. Beyond fish and pheasant, Chungbuk is also defined by various regional produce: garlic in Danyang, medicinal herbs in Jecheon, jujube in Boeun and grapes (and thus wine) in Yeongdong.

STOCK FOR YOU/SHUTTERSTOCK

Azaleas, Sobaeksan National Park (p367)

and convenience stores (a good place to pick up a few provisions before heading out). You'll see a sign for the main trail, **Cheondong** (one-way 7km, 2½ hours), which leads you past a waterfall along a well-marked path to the highest peak of **Biro-bong** (1439m). Famous for royal azaleas that bloom in the spring, the views from the grassy mountain top are incredible. From there, you can push on to the peak of **Yeonhwa-bong** (2.5km to 6.8km) if you like.

Jecheon

TIME FROM CHUNGJU: **40MIN**

Summit Yeong-bong at Woraksan

Home to the endangered long-tailed goral, a species of wild goat, **Woraksan National Park** offers fine hiking through forests and past waterfalls, with ancient Buddhist statues and carvings and, if you climb high enough, sensational views that extend all the way to Chungju-ho.

A road conveniently runs through the park, with buses making stops at the villages of **Mireuk-ri** in the south and **Songgye-ri** in the north, and **Deokju-gol** in between them – from which the most popular of Woraksan's hiking routes begins. A gentle path leads past the late Silla-era fortress **Deokju-sanseong**, partly restored, up to the reconstructed temple of **Deokju-sa** *(free)*. The original, which was built at the end of the 6th century and stood a few kilometres distant, was established by, as legend has it, the last princess of the Silla kingdom, Princess Deokju.

At **Deokju-sa** is a handy **tourist information centre**, where you can check out a map for the climb onward. The trail continues for 1.5km to **Ma-aebul**, a rock face with a bas-relief Buddha carved into it, then for another 3.4km, in a very strenuous stretch, up to the summit of **Yeong-bong** (1097m). Allow about 3½ hours to get from Deokju-sa to Yeong-bong. Alternatively, you can approach Yeong-bong from Songgye-ri (4.3km, three hours).

Places We Love to Stay

₩ Budget ₩₩ Midrange ₩₩₩ Top End

Cheongju

MAP P356

Blanc Hotel ₩ A good-value motel in a prime location near Chungbuk National University's party scene. Its budget rooms are a nice place to crash after a night out on the town.

Joy Hotel ₩ Flawless service and, in west-facing rooms, a lovely sunset view over the hills. Doubles are contemporary with comfy beds.

Hotel Dictionary Cheongju ₩ Vast, whisper-quiet rooms near the frenetic Intercity Bus Terminal. Think classy love hotel.

Smart Hotel ₩ Incredible value with suite-like proportions in quiet rooms at budget prices downtown near a park.

Gloucester Hotel ₩₩ This clean, comfortable hotel on the west side of the city is beside G-Well City Mall, with easy access to the Cheongju train station.

Songnisan National Park

Birosanjang ₩₩ Inside the park, on a trail between Beopju-sa and Sinseon-dae, this homey and delightful family run lodging is set beside a gurgling river, with cosy *ondol* (heated-floor) rooms.

Chungju

MAP P362

Hotel River ₩ This budget hotel is set apart by its hearty and filling excellent-value breakfast. There are also rooftop, terrace and *noraebang* (karaoke) facilities on site.

Station Lodge Hotel ₩ As its name suggests, a hotel just a block away from the Chungju train station, with Audrey Hepburn and Marilyn Monroe pop art, a 5th-floor rooftop and tidy basic rooms.

Hotel Bali ₩ North of the Namhan-gang, this wood-accented motel has big TVs and whirlpool tubs.

Danyang

Jungle Guesthouse ₩ Look for the Che Guevara mural and you've found it. Rooms are not big, but there's a friendly vibe in the 1st-floor lounge.

Gongju

MAP P339

Stay Onel ₩ Stylish love motel near Singwan Bus Terminal (from Cheongju) with smart wardrobes to freshen up clothes. Also known as Stay Today.

Khai Hotel ₩₩ Industrial-chic boutique hotel with an unbeatable location between fortress and tombs, a spa, and comfy rooms equipped with high-speed internet PCs and large bathrooms with tubs.

Hotel N. 25 ₩₩ Set right across the river, this midrange hotel has well-appointed rooms with fortress views.

Buyeo

MAP P341

Healing House Peakjang ₩ Close to the bus station and Jeongnim-sa pagoda, this old hotel is as tastefully refurbished and clean as it can be. Has lovely owners and a perfect central location.

Su Motel ₩ No-frills, ageing love motel that's still one of the best options around the bus station. It's a decent central choice for a short stay, but it has no lift.

Daecheon Beach

Day Nice Hotel ₩₩ Located on the beachfront and within walking distance of Mud Plaza, this hotel has large and comfortable rooms with sea views.

Motel Coconuts ₩₩ Attractive updated rooms are big enough for two people. Goldilocks location close to the beach, but without the noise or neon.

Mudrin Hotel ₩₩₩ Picture windows overlook the beach with 24-hour front desk. In the middle of the strip, close to Mud Plaza.

Taeanhaean National Park

MAP P352

Taean Manripo Feel Hotel ₩ Super-clean, modern option 200m from Mallipo Beach. Excellent value with spacious doubles and twins and a friendly owner.

Sand Hill Resort ₩₩ Bungalows fronted by tented gazebos to enjoy Sinduri Beach's views. Pricier because it owns the last scenic spot on the southwestern cape.

Pinocchio Pension ₩₩ Facing the sea are these comfortable cottages with fridges. It's on the slope behind Pino Cafe along the beach's main walking strip.

LEBEDEV/SHUTTERSTOCK

Above: Monument in Pyongyang; Right: Kaesong (p375), tomb of King Kongmin

Researched by
Simon Richmond

North Korea

REPRESSIVE DICTATORSHIP AND NUCLEAR POWER

Officially known as the Democratic People's Republic of Korea (DPRK), this totalitarian state is an unsettling *Alice in Wonderland* world with an appalling human-rights record.

Covering the northern half of the Korean Peninsula and bordered by China and Russia, North Korea has been led since 1948 by the Kim family. It has long attracted curious international visitors, despite being a fearsome dictatorship where basic freedoms, including of association, conscience, information, thought and travel, are denied.

Before the COVID-19 pandemic, when North Korea closed its borders, the country was welcoming, by some accounts, around 300,000 visitors a year, more than 90% of whom were Chinese. Since early 2024, a trickle of foreigners (nearly all Russians) have been allowed to visit specific areas of the country or attend special events such as the Pyongyang Marathon. Most countries continue to advise against visiting (the US and Malaysia ban their citizens from entering North Korea, while South Koreans require special permission from both North and South Korea).

FRENTAN/SHUTTERSTOCK

Concentration camps, executions, state-orchestrated terror and mass control by a vast propaganda machine are the reality for millions here. These brutal facts alone convince many to stay away. The case in favour of tourism is that it is one of the few ways of encouraging openness in the DPRK, of letting people see that the outside world is interested and, more importantly, friendly – not an insignificant fact for a population brought up on a relentless diet of anti-Western propaganda. Tourism also helps provide jobs and money for often desperately poor people.

If you do decide to visit, follow the rules, listen respectfully to the version of history and current affairs given to you by the guides, accept that this is their version and leave any criticism for when you are out of the country. Part of the fascination of travelling in North Korea is trying to divine the real from the fake and attempting to see past the ideology.

FAST FACTS

Capital Pyongyang
Population 26.5 million
Area 120,538 sq km
Official language Korean
Time zone GMT +9
Currency North Korean won (KPW)

North Korea Today

Day-to-day life for the vast majority of North Koreans is austere, with analysts believing that around 60% of the population lives below the poverty line. Fear of arrest or denouncement is constantly present, food is never plentiful, consumer goods remain unimaginable luxuries for most, propaganda is ubiquitous and relentless, work is demanding and often weeks on end will be spent doing physically strenuous manual agricultural work.

North Korea's economic system, which has morphed from communist to black-market capitalist, has created a society in which almost anything can be had for the right price. Non-governmental organisation Transparency International ranks North Korea as the most corrupt nation on Earth on its Global Corruption Barometer. All media in North Korea is under state control. Around 0.1% of the population (about 20,000 people) are assumed to have access to the internet.

Sungbun is the North Korean caste system whereby people are broadly divided into either core, wavering or hostile categories in relation to the regime. The hostile are deprived of everything and often end up in forced-labour camps in entire family groups, maybe for nothing more than having South Korean relatives, or for one family member having been caught crossing into China. The wavering have little or nothing but are not persecuted, while the core enjoy luxuries such as the opportunity to live in Pyongyang and desk jobs. At the top of the tree is the Kim family and its courtiers.

The six-day week (which, even for office workers, includes regular stints of hard labour in the ricefields) makes for an exhausted populace. In turn, Sundays become a real event and Koreans visibly beam as they relax, go on picnics, sing songs and drink in small groups all over the country. Some things do appear to have eased under Kim Jong Un, such as electricity shortages. Once plunged into darkness in most places as soon as the sun went down, a growing number of North Korean households have solar panels that store energy for light and TV in the evening.

For some insights into what contemporary life is like in the country, there are a couple of good essays, including images, at rawinfocus.com – search for North Korea.

History

Between 1910 and 1945, some of the most successful guerrilla warfare conducted against the colonial Japanese took place in the northern provinces of the peninsula. It was here that Kim Il Sung rose to prominence as a resistance leader. Kim escaped to Russia in 1940, where he became a captain in the Soviet Red Army – it was in this role that he stepped back onto Korean soil in September 1945, 11 days after the Soviet Union declared war on Japan. Within a few months, Kim became the Soviets' choice of leader for Korea.

RICHIE CHAN/SHUTTERSTOCK

Pyongyang Metro

The Korean War

The USA, recognising the strategic importance of the peninsula, began to move troops to the country's south. The Soviets established themselves in the north, with both sides stopping at the 38th parallel, a dividing line arbitrarily decided by the US as the temporary division of the peninsula. The intention to have democratic elections across the peninsula floundered on Cold War tensions, and after the North refused to allow UN inspectors to cross the 38th parallel, the Republic of Korea was proclaimed in the south on 15 August 1948. The north proclaimed the Democratic People's Republic (DPRK) just three weeks later, on 9 September 1948.

The brutal Korean War of 1950–53 saw North Korea, under the leadership of Kim, advance deep into the South, followed by a similarly strong counterattack by the US and the UN, which managed to occupy most of North Korea. The tide changed again when China began to covertly help the North by sending in the People's Liberation Army under the guise of 'volunteers'. The North pushed the front down to the 38th parallel and, with two million dead, the original stalemate was more or less retained. The armistice agreement obliged both sides to withdraw 2km from the ceasefire line, thus creating the Demilitarized Zone (DMZ), still in existence today.

The Kims

Kim Il Sung remained North Korea's supreme leader until his death in 1994. He was followed by his son Kim Jong Il who ruled in a similar dictatorial fashion until his death in 2011. Kim Jong Un, next in the dynastic line, was initially considered immature and lacking strategic vision. However, he has

BOOKS ABOUT NORTH KOREA

Nothing to Envy: Ordinary Lives in North Korea (Barbara Demick; 2010) Award-winning book by a US journalist based on interviews with a dozen North Korea defectors.

Without You, There Is No Us (Suki Kim; 2015) Insightful memoir of Kim's time teaching English at Pyongyang University of Science and Technology in 2011.

North of the DMZ (Andrei Lankov; 2007) There are fascinating details about North Korean life in this collection of essays by one of the leading experts on North Korea and based on his experiences as a student in Pyongyang in the 1980s.

In Order To Live: A North Korean Girl's Journey to Freedom (Yeonmi Park; 2015) First-person account of how Park, aged 13, escaped North Korea with her mother, first to live in China and then in South Korea.

The Aquariums of Pyongyang: Ten Years in the North Korean Gulag (Kang Chol-wan and Pierre Rigoulot; 2000). Unflinching account of Kang and his family's incarceration in the Yodok concentration camp.

THE NATIONAL PSYCHE

North Koreans are brainwashed from birth to believe in the god-like status of the ruling Kim dynasty. Publicly there is no questioning of the cult and almost no resistance to it. Even the mildest of jokes about the Kims can land people in prison, or worse. In a 2016 amendment to North Korea's constitution, both the deceased Kims are considered 'eternal leaders' of the country.

There is constant propaganda about how the Korean War was the fault of the US, in addition to which the iniquities of colonial rule under the Japanese are also hammered home. North Koreans have a sense of being hemmed in on all sides – threatened particularly by South Korea and the US, but also by Japan.

After centuries of Confucianism and decades of communism, it should come as no surprise that North Koreans are extremely socially conservative. Despite the equality of women on an ideological level, North Korea remains a patriarchal society.

RICHARD BRADFORD/SHUTTERSTOCK

Paekdusan

effectively silenced his critics with a wave of repression aimed at the nation's elite, alongside calculated brinkmanship via the testing of nuclear missiles. Kim Jong Un also had face-to-face meetings with US President Donald Trump in 2018 and 2019 – something considered a triumph for the dictator, whose father and grandfather had both failed to meet with any sitting US presidents.

In an effort to prevent COVID overwhelming North Korea's poor healthcare system (but also, according to many seasoned North Korea experts, to further increase the regime's control), from early 2020 North Korea was closed to all international visitors. The northern borders were reinforced using expanded fences, guard posts and instructions for border guards to shoot would-be escapees on sight. Halting tourism, diplomatic visits and humanitarian-aid deliveries, the border closure also harmed the informal trade (ie smuggling) that had been conducted by ordinary Koreans struggling to make a living.

In recent years, Kim Jong Un has been rebuilding diplomatic and trade bridges with neighbours China and Russia. Relations with South Korea remain tense and uncompromising.

If You Go

When international tourism to North Korea fully resumes, expect the following. All visits are on packaged tours, which can be private or in a group – this is not a country that permits independent travel. Among the longest-established and best-regarded operators are **Koryo Tours** *(koryogroup.com)*, with excellent local contacts and enormous experience, and Young Pioneer Tours *(youngpioneertours.com)* – both are China-based. Other operators include UK-based **Regent Holidays** *(regent-holidays.co.uk)* and Sweden-based **Korea Konsult** *(koreakonsult.com)*.

There will be restrictions on what you can bring into the country and how you can behave once there, including what you can photograph. You'll always be accompanied by at least two North Korean guides, employed by state-owned companies, and hear a one-sided account of history and current affairs while being bussed from sight to sight.

Detailed itineraries will be available before you sign up for your trip – read them carefully before you commit to travelling. You are very definitely expected to behave respectfully at the statues of the Kims in Pyongyang and most other cities you visit – if that, or any other part of your itinerary, is something you're uncomfortable with, or not interested in, you can ask to opt out. Talk to your tour leader or your North Korean guides – it should be no problem for you to sit out an activity in the lobby or on the bus. Guides have no interest in forcing guests to do something against their will.

Personal relationships with North Koreans who are not your tour guides or business colleagues will be impossible. Men should bear in mind that any physical contact with a Korean woman will be seen as unusual, so while shaking hands is perfectly acceptable, do not greet a Korean woman with a kiss in the European manner. Women should also greet all North Koreans with a handshake, though receiving a kiss from a foreign woman is less of a taboo.

What To See

Prior to 2020, the following locations were the main ones on international visitors' itineraries, and are likely to be so again when tourism resumes.

- **Pyongyang** The showcase capital city, sporting dystopian and outlandish architecture, and monuments.
- **Panmunjom** Experience Cold War tensions at this 'truce village' straddling the DMZ.
- **Paekdusan** The Korean Peninsula's highest peak, this holy mountain has a beautiful crater lake.
- **Chilbosan** Scenically gorgeous corner of the country in which to enjoy mountain hikes and some lovely beaches.
- **Masikryong** North Korea's showcase winter resort.
- **Kaesong** Close to the DMZ, this former capital of the Goryeo dynasty is home to UNESCO World Heritage sites.
- **Rason** Special Economic Zone Beachside port close to borders with China and Russia, where it's possible to shop at the first 'free' market in Korea.

DPRK DOCUMENTARIES

Beyond Utopia (2023) A South Korea pastor assists North Korean defectors. Includes footage shot by escapees.

Closing the Gap (2019) A Canadian director follows the North Korean ice-hockey team as they train for an international match in New Zealand.

Inside North Korea's Dynasty (2018) Four-episode series from National Geographic about the Kim family, who have ruled North Korea for three generations.

Michael Palin in North Korea (2018) Film following the celebrated British actor and travel writer as he celebrated his 75th birthday by travelling around the DPRK.

Under the Sun (2015) An illuminating Russian-produced film in which the cameras kept running between scripted shots to show the extent of the falsification of narrative in North Korea.

Crossing the Line (2006) Tells the incredible, bittersweet story of James Dresnok, an American soldier who defected to the DPRK in the 1960s and died in 2016.

A State of Mind (2004) Two young girls prepare for Pyongyang's Mass Games.

01
01
55
55
30
25
25

Haeundae Sky Capsule (p196), Busan
SUPAVADEE BUTRADEE/SHUTTERSTOCK

TOOLKIT

The chapters in this section cover the most important topics you'll need to know about in Korea. They're full of nuts-and-bolts information and valuable insights to help you understand and navigate Korea and get the most out of your trip.

Arriving

Most international flights arrive at Incheon International Airport *(airport.kr)*. There are also some international flights (mainly to Asian countries) to/from Gimpo in Seoul, Gimhae in Busan, Yangyang near Sokcho, Cheongju, Daegu, Muan in Jeolla-do and Jeju. There are also ferries from five ports in China (including Dalian) to Incheon, and from Fukuoka in Japan to Busan.

Visas

Entry to South Korea for up to 90 days is straightforward, but please check if you need a Korea Electronic Travel Authorization (*k-eta.go.kr*). Fill out the electronic Arrival Card (*e-arrivalcard.go.kr*) at least three days before arrival.

ATMs

Airports have ATMs but not all of them will accept overseas bank or credit cards. There will be money-changing booths, but expect rates to be poor.

Wi-Fi

Free wi-fi is available at airports. While you can get by using free wi-fi in Korea, many travellers buy a local SIM card, international roaming or rent a pocket modem for their visit.

Customs

Visitors must declare all plants, fresh fruit, vegetables and dairy products that they bring into South Korea. Meat is not allowed in without a certificate.

Transport from Airport to City Centre

	Incheon (Seoul)	Gimpo (Seoul)	Gimhae (Busan)
TRAIN	from 1hr **₩4150-4750**	40min **₩3500**	45min **₩2100**
BUS	60-80min **₩5500-18,000**	1hr **₩1500**	60min **₩2100**
TAXI	80-90min **₩50,000**	1hr **₩22,000**	25min **₩20,000**

DOMESTIC AIR TRANSFERS ON ARRIVAL

When booking flights involving a domestic air transfer to a regional airport in Korea, check whether that domestic flight is out of the same airport at which you arrive. For example, if heading to Jeju, you'll likely have to transfer from Incheon International Airport to Gimpo Airport. It takes about 40 minutes using the AREX train (take the commuter service, not the non-stop express train to Seoul). Build time into your schedule between flights to allow for getting through immigration and customs at Incheon first – when busy, it can take up to a couple of hours.

FROM LEFT: FUSE/GETTY IMAGES, GEORGE MDIVANIAN / EYEEM/GETTY IMAGES

Getting Around

Transport in South Korea is reasonably priced, quick and efficient. For land-based travel, services are regular and reliable, but ferries to the islands can be delayed by bad weather.

TRAVEL COSTS

Rental car
From ₩60,000 per day

Petrol
₩1700 a litre

KTX train
Seoul to Busan
from ₩59,800

Pro roadbike/
MTB Rental
Around ₩37,000 per day

Plane

Korean Air (*koreanair.com*) and Asiana (*flyasiana.com*), the two major domestic airlines, offer flights to and from a dozen local airports and typically charge identical yet reasonable fares. Competition is supplied by a handful of budget airlines, such as Jeju Air (*jejuair.net*).

Bus

Long-distance buses whiz to every part of Korea – several times per hour between major cities, and at least hourly to small towns, temples and national parks. Check routes, schedules and buy tickets on *bustago.or.kr*. Express buses link major cities, while intercity buses stop more often at smaller cities and towns.

TIP

Stored-value, touch-and-go cards, such as the **Tmoney Card** (*eng.tmoney.co.kr*), provide discounts on fares on buses and subways.

CYCLING AROUND KOREA

Korea promotes cycling as a green and healthy means of transport. Seoul's metropolitan government has expanded cycling infrastructure in the city, including its own city bike-hire scheme, **Ttareungi** (*bikeseoul.com*), which foreign visitors can use. The website **Korea by Bike** (*koreabybike.com*) provides useful information on long-distance cycling routes, including the 633 km-long **Cross Country Route** (*koreabybike.com/routes/cross-country-route/*) from Incheon to Busan, using four interconnected bike paths, namely Ara, Hangang, Saejae and Nakdonggang.

DRIVING ESSENTIALS

Drive on the right

Stops signs are a red hexagon

.03%
Blood alcohol limit is 0.03%

Train

Although services don't reach as many destinations as do buses, Korea's long-distance rail system is excellent, with clean, comfortable and punctual trains. Check schedules and buy tickets online at *korail.com/global/eng/main*. It's worth considering a KR Pass even for a straightforward return Seoul–Busan trip.

Car

For travels to mountainous or relatively remote areas of Korea, renting your own set of wheels is a good idea. You must be 21 years of age or over and have an International Driving Permit (a driving licence from your own country is not acceptable). Multi-language sat-nav systems are common, or you can use mobile phone apps Naver Maps or Kakao Maps.

Ferry

There's an extensive network of ferries that connects hundreds of offshore islands and the mainland. Services from Incheon's Yeonan Pier connect to a dozen nearby and more distant islands, while other west-coast islands further south can be reached from Daecheon harbour, Gunsan, Mokpo, Shinan Amtaegnamgang Port and Tongyeong Ferry Terminal.

Money

CURRENCY: WON (₩)

Credit Cards

Major international cards such as Visa and Mastercard are widely accepted, with many places – even street stalls – set up for contactless payment. However, there will be times, such as when paying highway tolls or on buses, that your card won't work, so always carry some Korean paper money.

ATMs

ATMs that accept foreign cards are common: look for ones that have a 'Global' sign or the logo of your credit-card company. ATMs often operate from 7am to 11pm, but some are 24-hour. Restrictions on the amount you can withdraw vary, but it's usually around ₩1,000,000 per day.

HOW MUCH FOR...

Subway fare with/without Tmoney card from **₩1200/1250**

Museum entrance **free, or from ₩1000**

Taxi flagfall **₩4800**

Public toilet **free**

HOW TO... Save Some Money

The **Korea Tour Card** *(koreatourcard.kr)*, which is similar to the Tmoney card, costs ₩4000 and is available from airports and convenience stores. As well as using it to pay for transport, the card offers benefits at around 170 tourist attractions. If you're visiting southern coastal Korea, including Busan, Yeosu and Tongyeong, look for the Namhaean Coast version of the card, covering some 210 affiliated businesses.

Changing Money

Money can be changed at banks and moneychangers, which keep longer hours than the banks and provide a faster service, but may only exchange US$ cash.

Tipping

Tipping is not a custom in Korean culture and is not required; you're likely to cause confusion if you try!

TMONEY

The rechargeable touch-and-go Tmoney card is handy for paying for buses, subways and taxis throughout Korea and shopping at convenience stores. For buses and subways, if you have to transfer between services to reach your destination, you'll only pay a single fare if less than 30 minutes elapse between transfers.The card can be purchased for ₩3000 from machines at most Seoul subway stations, as well as bus kiosks and convenience stores, but for ₩4000 at Incheon Airport. Reload it with credit (only cash accepted) at any of the locations mentioned above.

LOCAL TIP

Many Korean supermarkets offer discounts on ready meals and other perishables towards the end of the working day. Also look for two-for-one-type deals at convenience stores.

Accommodation

Backpacker Guesthouses & Hostels

Internationally oriented backpacker hostels are found in major cities and tourist spots across Korea. Ideal for budget-conscious tourists, they usually have staff who speak English. In Korea, the line between a guesthouse and a hostel is often blurred. Both usually offer dormitories and double rooms, some of which have private bathrooms. Free internet and a simple breakfast is typically provided.

Hotels & Glamping

While business hotels are common, luxury hotels are relatively scarce outside major cities, Jeju-do and resorts such as those found in Pyeongchang and Yeongjongdo, next to Incheon International Airport. Online discounts or packages are nearly always available. Glamping is also catching on, particularly in and around the national parks and at seaside resorts.

Motels & Love Motels

Motels and love motels (which have rooms that can be rented by the hour) are by far the most common form of accommodation across Korea. The rooms are always on the small size, but they are packed with facilities and include private bathrooms. Staff rarely speak English and they lack communal areas beyond the lobby, which is not designed for lingering.

HOW MUCH FOR A NIGHT IN A...

Hostel dorm bed
₩30,000

Motel
₩70,000

Pension
₩80,000

Minbak & Pensions

Most *minbak* (private homes with rooms for rent) provide simple accommodation (and usually meals) in rural areas, with a *yo* (padded quilts and mattresses) on an *ondol* (heated floor) and sometimes shared bathrooms. Many people can squeeze into one room – an extra person usually costs ₩10,000. Pensions are more luxurious, with an equipped kitchen for groups of self-catering travellers.

Hanok Guesthouses

A stay in a traditional *hanok* is a unique and memorable experience. Rooms tend to be small and you'll sleep on Korean-style floor mattresses. At cheaper *hanok*, you'll be sharing the bathroom, but many guesthouses do offer en-suite rooms. In Seoul, there are some very luxurious *hanok*. Rates may include breakfast, and traditional cultural experiences may be offered, too.

TEMPLESTAYS

Around 60 temples across Korea provide overnight accommodation via the Templestay program (p41). It's a chance not only to experience the life of a monk, but also to stay in some incredibly beautiful places. You will learn about Buddhist practices such as meditation and the 108 prostrations, and there is usually at least one person who speaks some English. This is an increasingly popular choice of accommodation, with more temples geared towards accepting foreigners, while others will also happily let you stay if you bring along a Korean to help translate.

CLOCKWISE FROM TOP LEFT: GUITAR PHOTOGRAPHER/SHUTTERSTOCK, NEW AFRICA/SHUTTERSTOCK, ANDREY LOBACHEV/SHUTTERSTOCK

Family Travel

Koreans adore children and make them the centre of attention, so travelling with your offspring here is highly recommended. Funfairs and parks can be found in most cities, along with cinemas, video arcades, tenpin bowling, *noraebang* (karaoke), pool tables and board-game cafes. In winter head to the ski resorts, and in summer cool down at water parks and beaches.

Getting Around

Kids under six travel free on subways and buses, while those aged between six and 12, and 13 and 18 years are entitled to different levels of discounts. When purchasing a Tmoney card at a convenience store for kids and teens, bring along their passport as proof of age so the card can be set up to take account of their discount fares.

Accommodation

Hostels, guesthouses and hotels often have family rooms. Also consider traditional Korean rooms at *minbak* and guesthouses, as they're designed for families to sleep together on *yo* mattresses on heated *ondol* floors. Camping and glamping are also fun family-stay options.

Eating

Many Korean restaurants are specifically set up to serve meals family style. Local food options that are likely to appeal to kids are Korean fried chicken, *tonkatsu* (breaded pork cutlets), *ramyeon* noodles, *gimbap* (seaweed wrapped rice rolls) and *mandu* (dumplings). Bakery cafes are another good option for feeding hungry kids. Consider packing small forks and spoons for kids who may struggle with chopsticks.

Infants

Only luxury hotels are likely to be able to organise a cot, but you could always ask for a *yo* (traditional floor mattress). Few restaurants have high chairs. Nappy-changing facilities are more common in Seoul toilets than in the provinces.

FUN WITH KIDS

Everland (p133)
Korea's equivalent of Disneyland is an easy day trip from Seoul with thrill rides, water park and fireworks.

Parks
Seoul has scores of free, city-managed parks with excellent facilities, such as **Seoul Forest** (p94), **Olympic Park** (p117) and **World Cup Park** (p101).

Baseball
Watching Korean fans supporting their teams can be just as enjoyable as following the game.

Cable Cars
The **Chuncheon Samaksan Mountain Lake Cable Car** (p150) is the longest in Korea.

KOREAN MASCOTS

Although not quite as pervasive as in neighbouring Japan, cute animal and fantasy-figure mascots are a feature of Korean life, and looking out for them is a fun way to engage kids. Hechi, Seoul's big pink mascot, is easy to spot around the capital; he's often accompanied by his four tiny guardian mates. Across Korea, you'll also seldom be far from Kakao Friends, originally created as emoticons for KakaoTalk, the most popular messaging app in Korea – merchandise can be found at the company's stores, including flagship ones in Seoul (Gangnam and Hongdae) and Busan.

Health & Safe Travel

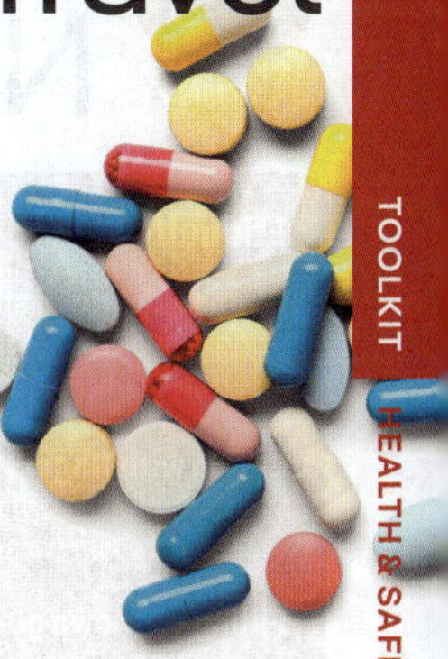

HOSPITALS & PHARMACIES

The quality of medical care across Korea is high. You need a doctor's prescription to buy most medications and it may be difficult to find the exact medication you use at home, so take extra. If the pharmacist doesn't speak English, dial 02-1330 on your mobile phone and ask the interpreter to explain to them in Korean what you need.

Natural Disasters

Check weather forecasts regularly. While the chance of an earthquake is low in Korea compared to neighbouring Japan and China, the country does get hit by typhoons and heavy rains, especially from June to October. In July 2023, at least 40 people died after a weekend of heavy rains caused catastrophic floods and landslides.

Medical Tourism

Medical tourism is a booming industry in Korea. The focus might be on cosmetic surgery – with the highest rate of procedures per capita in the world – but can include anything from cutting-edge cancer treatments to simple check-ups. Health tourism is heavily promoted by the Korea Tourism Organization, with specialised information booths (and even festivals) in Seoul, Incheon, Daegu and Busan.

TIPS

Tap water is fine to drink everywhere.

Download the Emergency Ready App for support in English, Chinese and Japanese.

SEOUL AIR QUALITY

Seoul uses coloured lights on N Seoul Tower to indicate the level of air pollution:

Blue	Green	Yellow	Red
Good	Fair	Bad	Extremely Bad
0~15µg/m³ of microdust	16~35µg/m³ of microdust	36~75µg/m³ of microdust	76µg/m³ or more of microdust

Demonstrations

A protest is still seen as the best way to make one's voice heard in South Korea. In Seoul, you might see police in riot gear streaming out of police buses with their windows covered in protective wire. Student, trade-union, environmental, ferry-disaster and other protests occasionally turn violent. Keep well out of the way of any confrontations that may occur.

EXTREME HEAT

At the height of summer between late June and the end of August, temperatures of 38°C (100°F) in some parts of South Korea are not uncommon. Alongside the humidity, it can be especially draining. Be sure to hydrate regularly and stay alert to the symptoms of heat exhaustion. Also seek out air-conditioned environments such as shopping malls and museums.

CLOCKWISE FROM TOP LEFT: TON PONCHAI/SHUTTERSTOCK, PIXEL-SHOT/SHUTTERSTOCK

Food, Drink & Nightlife

Etiquette

Chopsticks Don't stick your chopsticks upright in a bowl of rice, or pass food from one pair of chopsticks to another.

Eating with fingers Don't touch food with your fingers, except when handling lettuce leaves for *ssam* (wraps).

Filling your own glass (alcohol) Dining companions usually pour drinks for each other – traditionally, never for themselves. It's polite to use both hands when pouring or receiving a drink.

MENU DECODER

Banchan (반찬) Most Korean restaurants include free side dishes, such as kimchi, bean sprouts or cooked vegetables, along with the ordered meal.

Bap (밥) Cooked rice. Also usually included with a meal. If you see this at the end of a menu item (ie bibimbap), it will indicate it's a rice dish.

Bunsik (분식) Inexpensive snack foods like *gimbap* (laver and rice rolls), *ramyeon* noodles, and *tteokbokki* (rice cakes in spicy sauce).

Guksu (국수) or **myeon** (면) Noodles.

Hanjeongsik (한정식) Korean-style banquet characterised by the array of small *banchan* in varied colours.

Chuga (추가) Extra or more, ie cheese *chuga* (치즈추가) means cheese melted atop your main dish.

Guk (국) or **tang** (탕) Soup; another common element of most meals in a Korean restaurant.

Jjigae (찌개) Stews, often spicy.

Mandu (만두) Filled dumplings.

Where to Eat

Restaurants: Occasionally a restaurant may turn away solo diners because it only serves meals in portions for a minimum of two.

Cafes: Bakery and dessert cafes are super popular and good places for breakfast or a light meal.

Bars: Most bars serve good-quality *anju* (snacks such as nuts, dried squid, rice crackers) made for sharing.

Street food: Look for stalls in markets and around areas where there's a lot of bars.

Pojangmacha: These 'street tent bars' act like mini restaurants with food to rival fancier affairs.

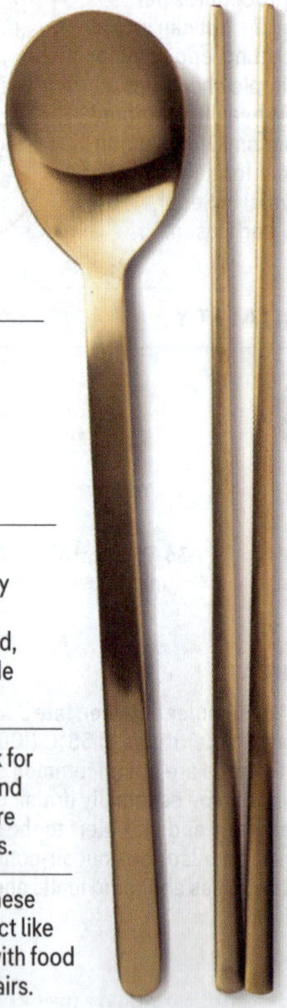

HOW TO... Gogi-gui

Gogi-gui (barbecued meat) establishments are among the most popular types of Korean restaurant. They are often boisterous places where every table has its own small gas or charcoal grill and the main selling point is the quality of the meat and the marinade.

Diners typically cook their own meat on the grill, though servers can assist customers if needed. Some meats, such as bulgogi (beef slices) and *galbi* (ribs), already come marinated in a sauce; others like *chadolbagi* (thinly sliced brisket) or *samgyeopsal* (unsalted pork belly) come as they are.

Having grilled your meats, next make a *ssam* (wrap). Take some lettuce or other green leaves – such as perilla and crown daisy, place the meat on top and add slices of fresh garlic, hot pepper, kimchi and a daub of spicy *ssamjang* (soybean and red-pepper sauce) to your taste. Wrap it all up and eat.

FROM LEFT: NIIK LEUANGBORIBOON/SHUTTERSTOCK, OJKWON/SHUTTERSTOCK

HOW MUCH FOR A...

Apple at a convenience store
₩4000

Barbecue meal
₩50,000

Gourmet meal
₩250,000

Gimbap roll
₩3500

Instant ramyeon
from ₩1500

Draught beer
₩4500

Convenience store soju
₩1300-2000

Coffee
₩4000-6000

HOW TO... Navigate a Korean Restaurant

At some Korean restaurants, you'll encounter traditional floor seating. If so, remove your shoes at the restaurant door or beside the seating area, and sit on floor cushions.

The menu is often posted on the wall in Korean. If an English menu is not on the table, ask for one, as a translation may be available. Some places now have touchscreen tablets at the table with both pictures and English translation. Make your order on the tablet and pay directly with your credit card.

At some cheaper places, such as noodle stalls, you may encounter a vending machine just inside the door. Make your choice, insert your money, take your ticket, hand it to the server and wait at your seat until your meal is ready.

If the table isn't set, look for cutlery (metal chopsticks and long-handled spoons) and paper napkins in the oblong box on the table or in a hidden drawer in the table's side. A bottle of water or weak tea will also automatically be provided along with cups. The spoon is for rice, soup and any dish with liquids; chopsticks are for everything else.

To call a server, say '*Yogiyo*' – it literally means 'here', which may seem rude but is a bona fide way of hailing attention. Tipping is not expected, though high-end restaurants often add a 10% service charge.

Start with Soup

Begin your meal with a taste of soup or stews. This preps your taste buds for the flavourful dishes to come. If something is too spicy, also drink some soup or eat some rice.

KOREAN DRINKING CULTURE

The legal drinking age in Korea is 19. Although it is legal to drink alcohol in public, drunk and disorderly conduct can result in hefty fines and a visit to the police station.

The practice of *hoesik* – a gathering of people, often work colleagues, to eat and drink together – is common. Drinking, and drinking heavily, is the mainstay of Korean socialising, and an evening out can quickly turn into a blur of bar hopping.

The most common poison of choice is soju. The stuff is, more often than not, ethanol mixed with water and flavouring. Drinking too much of it can leave you with a killer hangover. Be especially careful about the infamous 'soju bombs', when a shot glass of soju is dropped into a glass of beer and the two are drunk together.

Helping soak up some of that alcohol will be *anju* (bar snacks; obligatory in some bars). These are likely to be heaped plates of oil-soaked food – French fries, vegetable *twigim* (fritters) or fried chicken. There's even a word for such a combo: *chimaek*, from Korean *chikin* (fried chicken) and *maekju* (beer).

As in other countries, there's a changing attitude to excessive alcohol consumption, particularly among young people. An evening spent in a fancy coffee shop or bakery cafe is the norm for non-alcohol drinkers, while those who are looking for cheap drinks hang out at convenience stores, some of which provide tables for customers to sit down and immediately eat and drink their purchases.

Responsible Travel

Climate Change & Travel

It's impossible to ignore the impact we have when travelling; Lonely Planet urges all travellers to engage with their travel carbon footprint, which will mainly come from air travel. While there often isn't an alternative, travellers can look to minimise the number of flights they take, opt for newer aircrafts and use cleaner ground transport, such as trains. One proposed solution – purchasing carbon offsets – unfortunately does not cancel out the impact of individual flights. While most destinations will depend on air travel for the foreseeable future, for now, pursuing ground-based travel where possible is the best course of action.

The **UN Carbon Offset Calculator** shows how flying impacts a household's emissions.

The **ICAO's carbon emissions calculator** allows visitors to analyse the CO_2 generated by point-to-point journeys.

Shop Local

Visit traditional markets to support local farmers, fishers and craftspeople. Great ones include Seoul's **Gwangjang** (p59) and **Tongin** (p65) markets, **Sinpo** (p137) in Incheon, **Jagalchi** (p184) in Busan and **Dongmun** (p307) in Jeju-si.

Explore Korea by pedal power either for a day, such as riding alongside the Han River in Seoul on a rental bike, or on an extended trip. For more info, see *koreabybike.com*.

Festivals are a great way of experiencing the local culture. They range from the ice-fishing **Hwacheon Sancheoneo Ice Festival** *(January)* and **Jeju Fire Festival** *(March)* to the spectacular **Suwon Hwaseong Cultural Festival** *(October)*.

Slow Travel

The **Jeju Olle Trail** (p322) sets the benchmark in Korea for slow travel. Other long-distance walking trails that enable you to see the country one step at a time include the **Seoul Dulle-gil**, circumnavigating the capital.

Mountain Plogging

Koreans have taken to plogging – picking up trash when they go hiking in national parks such as **Bukhansan**. Rubbish bags are available from the Bukhansan National Park Ui Ranger Station.

CULTURE CLASSES

Sign up for a class during your stay in Korea. Seoul has several great cooking classes, including ones on how to make kimchi and vegan temple food as eaten by monks.

GET OFF THE BEATEN TRACK

Avoid the big cities and head to more remote or lesser visited islands such as Udo (p309), Ulleungdo (p234) and Shinjido (p296), location of one of the southern coast's most beautiful beaches.

Bin it Right!

Koreans take recycling seriously. Rubbish is sorted into separate collection bins for plastic bottles, other types of hard plastic, thin film plastics, cans, polystyrene, glass bottles, paper and cardboard, and food waste.

Discover Folk Villages

Unlike some of the purpose-built tourist folk villages dotted around Korea, **Seongeup Folk Village** (p316) on Jeju-do and the World Heritage-listed **Hahoe Folk Village** (248) are the real-deal living communities.

Secondhand Shopping

Secondhand stores, flea markets and charitable social enterprises such as Aleumdaungage (beautifulstore.org) are great places to hunt for pre-loved items. Stalls on the 2nd floor of **Gwangjang Market** (p59) specialise in vintage clothing.

Volunteering

Opportunities for volunteering in Korea can be found through the **Seoul Volunteer Center** *(volunteer.seoul.go.kr)*, **Seoul International Women's Association** *(siwakorea.com)*, **World Wide Opportunities on Organic Farms** *(WWOOF; wwoofkorea.org)* and **World Friends Korea** *(koica.go.kr)*.

Connect with locals by learning a few Korean words and phrases and observing cultural norms.

See rubbish turned into art at Seoul Upcycling Plaza *(seoulup.or.kr)*, the world's largest space dedicated to upcycling.

Carbon-neutral Korea

Under its plan for a carbon-neutral public sector, South Korea aims to achieve net-zero in carbon emissions across government operations before 2050. Incheon's Carbon Neutrality Strategy has set the target for 2045.

RESOURCES

seoulsolution.kr
Read about Seoul's urban-planning and sustainable-development policies.

wwfkorea.or.kr
Local branch of the World Wide Fund For Nature.

kfem.or.kr
Korean Federation for Environmental Movement.

CLOCKWISE FROM TOP LEFT: CATINSYRUP/SHUTTERSTOCK, CONTES DE FEE/SHUTTERSTOCK, ERMAK OKSANA/SHUTTERSTOCK

LGBTIQ+ Travellers

South Korea has never outlawed homosexuality, but this shouldn't be taken as a sign of widespread tolerance or acceptance. This is a conservative society and sexuality in general is a taboo subject. LGBTIQ+ travellers who disclose their sexual orientation should be prepared for some less-than-positive reactions. Attitudes are changing, however, especially among young people, and LGBTIQ+ travellers should have few fears about visiting South Korea.

Seoul's Gaybourhoods

Seoul's two most famous locations for LGBTIQ+-friendly watering holes and gathering spaces are Itaewon and the Jongno 3-ga area around Nakwon-dong. Itaewon's Usadan-ro 12-gil is where international LGBTIQ+ visitors will feel most comfortable hanging out.

The scene in Nakwon-dong is more discreet and centred on gay Korean men. A bar there that is welcoming to overseas gays is **Shortbus**.

COMMUNITY CHALLENGES

In Korea, same-sex marriage and civil unions are illegal, LGBTIQ+ students face bullying at schools and same-sex couples cannot adopt.

There were recent attempts to block annual Pride festivals in Seoul and Daegu. The situation slightly improved in 2025 with the new liberal President Lee Jae-myung, who allowed the annual Seoul Queer Culture Festival to proceed without incident, even though conservative religious groups still protested.

Chingusai

With its name meaning 'Between Friends', **Chingusai** *(chingusai.net)* has been campaigning for LGBTIQ+ human rights since 1994 and is one of Korea's oldest sexual-minority rights organisations. Its website outlines Korean attitudes to the gay community and provides strategies for South Korean members of the LGBTIQ+ community to successfully come out.

GAY ROLE MODELS

Public LGBTIQ+ figures are rare in Korea. In 2022, Cha Hae-yeong became South Korea's first openly gay elected official. The 35-year-old bisexual woman won in Mapo's 6th electoral district, one of Seoul's more liberal neighbourhoods. In 2020, singer Kwon Do-woon became the first major Korean celebrity to come out on his own terms since actor Hong Seok-cheon did so during a TV interview in 2000.

SEOUL QUEER CULTURE FESTIVAL

The high point of LGBTIQ+ visibility in Seoul is the annual **Seoul Queer Culture Festival** *(sqcf.org)*, usually held in early July. It includes a well-attended gay-pride parade, some 60 booths where you can join in various creative and interactive activities, and the Seoul Queer Film Festival.

Instagram Sites

@queerscoutsbusan LGBTIQ+ community events and news in or around Busan.

@gjqueerfestival Details about LGBTIQ+ events in Gwangju.

@the_nach_barn Jeju-si cafe hosting monthly LGBTIQ+ evenings.

@lesvos_itaewon Yoon Kim Myung-woo, aka Myeongwoo Hyeong, runs Lesvos as a community space for Seoul's gay community.

NITO/SHUTTERSTOCK

Accessible Travel

Facilities for travellers with disabilities in Korea are far from perfect, but are improving. Public transport is increasingly being made more accessible to those with mobility issues. Many museums and tourist attractions offer generous discounts or even free entry for disabled visitors and a helper.

Seoul Subways

Most subway stations have elevators, wheelchair lifts and ramps, accessible toilets and braille tiles to help find directions. In subway cars, there's always priority seating for those who need it.

Airport

Incheon International Airport is equipped with electric vehicles to shuttle passengers with mobility and visual impairments to and from the gates. Escort services are also available before departure and wheelchairs are freely available, too.

Accommodation

Mainly upper-mid and top-end hotels have specially adapted rooms for those with disabilities. It's best to search on rental-accommodation sites such as Airbnb for wheelchair accessible units.

RESOURCES

Korea Wheelchair Tour *(koreawheelchairtour.com)* Travel agency dedicated to those with restricted mobility.

Visit Seoul *(english.visitseoul.net/accessibility)* Information on barrier-free tourism across the capital.

Gwangju Tourist Assistance Center *(jangtour.org)* Helping travellers with disabilities get the most out of their trip to Gwangju.

TabiFolk *(tabifolk.com/groups/south-korea)* Online community dedicated to making travel accessible to everyone.

Visit Jeju *(visitjeju.net)* Search for details of accessible tourism on Korea's largest island.

BRAILLE

Nearly all major museums and tourist sites have descriptions in Korean braille as well as models of exhibits and buildings that the blind and partially sighted can touch.

Accessible Seoul

Danurim Accessible Tourism Center *(seouldanurim.net)* can arrange an airport pick-up service with wheelchair-ramp-equipped vehicles, as well as rental of wheelchairs and shower wheelchairs for your time in Seoul.

Discounts

Those with disabilities as well as people aged 65 and over qualify for discounts of between 10% and 50% on Korean Air's domestic flights. Korail, however, doesn't offer discounts to overseas visitors on train tickets.

JEJU OLLE TRAIL

Several of the Jeju Olle Trail routes (p322), including 1, 5, 10, 10-1 and 14, have sections that are suitable for wheelchairs and strollers, with gentle slopes and wide footpaths.

The **National Museum of Korea** has kiosks where visitors can access voice commentary and use Korean braille keypads to obtain a variety of information. People with hearing disabilities can ask a question in sign language and the kiosk responds through a 3D avatar.

Train Travel

Korea's train network, operated by Korail *(korail.com/global/eng/main)*, mainly connects the major cities and towns. The trains are an efficient and fast way to get around and worth considering if you want to pack plenty of sightseeing into a short time.

Train Types & Facilities

The fastest trains running at minimum speeds of 200km/h are the KTX and KTX-Sancheon trains between Seoul and Busan, Yeosu, Jinju, Donghae, Gangneung and Mokpo.

A grade down are Saemaeul-ho services (also known as ITX), which also only stop in major towns. The cheapest option is the Mugunghwa-ho trains, which are older carriages that are comfortable, slower and stop more frequently. The more modern Nuriro services have replaced them on specific routes, such as the Yeongdong Line and Jungang Line.

KTX and Saemaeul-ho trains typically have a buffet car serving drinks and snacks. If a train is standing-room only, spending time in the buffet car during the journey is the best way to go.

Sleeper Train

If you're after the experience of sleeping on a train, look into the **Rail Cruise Haerang** *(railcruise.co.kr)*, Korea's only hotel-style tourism train. Tour packages of either two days/one night or three days/two nights are available, with accommodation on board the colourfully decorated train ranging from four-bed standard cabins to private suites with a double bed. There's also a bar car and a lounge car. Fares (from ₩1,950,000) include all meals, drinks, transfers, and admission fees to sights along the way.

SR Trains

Run by the SR Corporation, the **Super Rapid Train** *(SRT; etk.srail.kr)* is a high-speed service from Seoul's Suseo station terminating at either Busan or Mokpo. Although the SRT services to Busan are speedier (travelling at an average 300 km/h), in all other respects these are the same trains running along the same lines as KTX services.

Korail Pass

Non-residents of Korea are eligible to buy the Korail Pass. Available either for three or five consecutive days, or two or four selected days within a 10-day period, the pass offers unlimited rail travel, including KTX services, but excluding subways and Korail's tourist trains.

For a travel itinerary such as Seoul–Gyeongju–Busan–Seoul, the pass will save you money over individual fares. It's also handy for spontaneous travel as you can use it to board sold-out trains as a standing passenger. Buy the pass either online from **Korail** *(letskorail.com)* or local tour companies such as **Klook** *(klook.com)*, or at Korail travels centres in Korea.

TOURIST TRAINS

- Korail runs several tourist trains through beauty spots or connecting up sightseeing destinations.
- **Baekdu-daegan Valley Train (V-Train)** A service with retro-1970s-designed carriages that follows a scenic mountain-valley route between Cheoram and Buncheon.
- **West Gold Train (G-Train)** Equipped with a foot-bath cafe and *ondol* floor-heated cars. Runs from Seoul's Yongsan station to Iksan station in Jeollabuk-do and back again.
- **South Coast Train (S-Train)** Travels two routes: one from Busan to Yeosu; the other from Gwangju to Masan. At Hadong station, passengers can transfer from one route to the other.
- **Jeongseon Arirang Train (A-Train)** From Cheongnyangni in northeastern Seoul, via Jeongseon, which hosts a traditional market every five days, and arriving at Auraji.

HELIOPIXEL/SHUTTERSTOCK

Nuts & Bolts

OPENING HOURS

South Korea defies the Asian early-bird stereotypes, as it's not a very early-rising society. Besides traditional markets, most businesses open at 9am or later, but there's always a 24-hour convenience store available nearby. It pays to remember that on Mondays, all public museums and galleries are closed.

Banks 9am-4pm Monday to Friday

Bars 6pm-1am, longer hours Friday and Saturday

Cafes 8am-10pm

Traditional Markets from 6am

Galleries & museums 10am-6pm Tue-Sun

Post offices 9am-6pm Monday to Friday

Restaurants 11am-9pm; many shut between 3pm and 6pm

Shops 10am-8pm

Toilets

There are plenty of free, clean, modern and well-signed public *hwajangsil* (toilets).

Internet Access

There's abundant, fast, free internet access across Korea with decent public wi-fi in cafes, museums and squares.

GOOD TO KNOW

Time zone
GMT/UTC plus nine hours

Country calling code
+82

Tourist helpline
1330

Population
51.67 million

Electricity

220V/60Hz

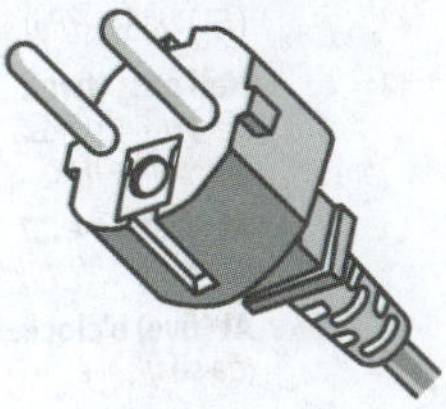

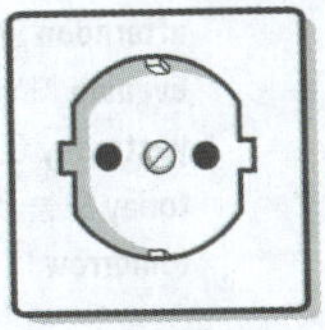

PUBLIC HOLIDAYS

Seollal (Lunar New Year), Buddha's Birthday and Chuseok (Thanksgiving) are set according to the lunar calendar, meaning they fall on different days each year.

New Year's Day
1 January

Seollal 6-8 February 2027; 26-27 January 2028

Independence Movement Day
1 March

Children's Day 5 May

Buddha's Birthday
13 May 2027; 2 May 2028

Memorial Day 6 June

Constitution Day
17 July

Liberation Day
15 August

Chuseok
14-16 September 2027; 2-4 October 2028

National Foundation Day 3 October

Christmas Day
25 December

Smoking

Korea has strict antismoking laws. It's forbidden to smoke in all bars, restaurants, hotels and public buildings. Smoking is also prohibited while walking along the street, or outside subway stations or bus stops.

Language

Korean is spoken by around 80 million people. Its linguistic family is a matter of debate. Some scholars say it's an Ural-Altaic language; others place it with Jeju languages in their own family: Koreanic. Korean script, *hangeul*, is simple and accessible, as each character represents a sound of its own. There are a number of competing Romanisation systems in use today for *hangeul*. Since 2000, the government has been changing road signs to reflect the most recent Romanisation system, so you may encounter signs, maps and tourist literature with at least two different Romanisation systems.

Basics

Hello. 안녕하세요. *an·nyŏng ha·se·yo*

Goodbye. 안녕히 *an·nyŏng·hee*

(if leaving/staying) 계세요/가세요. *gye·se·yo/ga·se·yo*

Yes. 네/예. *né/yé* (Both of these mean 'yes' and they're used about equally.)

No. 아니요. *a·ni·yo*

Excuse me. 실례합니다. *shil·lé ham·ni·da*

Sorry. 죄송합니다/미안합니다. *choé·song ham·ni·da/mee·an·ham·ni·da* (Both expressions are used about equally.)

Thank you. 고맙습니다/감사합니다. *go·map·sŭm·ni·da/kam·sa·ham·ni·da*

You're welcome. 괜찮아요. *gwaen·cha·na·yo*

What is your name? 성함이 어떻게 되세요? *sŏng-ha-mul ŏt-tŏ-ke dway-se-yo*

My name is ... 제 이름은 ...입니다. *je i·rŭ·mŭn ... ·im·ni·da*

Do you speak English? 영어 할 줄 아세요? *yŏng·ŏ hal jul a·se·yo*

I don't understand. 못 알아 들었어요. *mot a·ra·dŭ·rŏss·ŏ·yo*

Directions

Where's a/the ...? ...어디예요? *ŏ·di·ye·yo*

What's the address? 주소가 뭐예요? *ju·so·ga mwŏ·ye·yo*

Could you please write it down? 적어 주시겠어요? *jŏ·gŏ ju·shi·gess·ŏ·yo*

Please show me (on the map). (지도에서) 어디인지 가르쳐 주세요. *(ji·do·e·sŏ) ŏ·di·in·ji ga·rŭ·ch'ŏ ju·se·yo*

Turn left/right. 좌회전/우회전하세요. *jwa·hoé·jŏn/u·hoé·jŏn ha·se·yo*

Time

What time is it? 몇 시예요? *myŏs·shi·ye·yo*

It's (two) o'clock. (두) 시요. *(du)·shi·yo*

Half past (two). (두) 시 반이요. *(du)·shi ba n yo*

At what time ...? 몇 시에 ...? *myŏs·shi·é ...*

At (five) o'clock. (다섯) 시에. *(da·sŏs)·shi·é*

morning 아침 *a·ch'im*

afternoon 오후 *o·hu*

evening 저녁 *jŏ·nyŏk*

yesterday 어제 *ŏ·jé*

today 오늘 *o·nŭl*

tomorrow 내일 *nae·il*

NUMBERS (KOREAN)

1	하나 *ha·na*
2	둘 *dul*
3	셋 *set*
4	넷 *net*
5	다섯 *da·sŏt*
6	여섯 *yŏ·sŏt*
7	일곱 *il·gop*
8	여덟 *yŏ·dŏl*
9	아홉 *a·hop*
10	열 *yŏl*

Know Your Numbers

Use pure Korean numbers for hours when telling the time, for counting objects and people, and for expressing your age.

Use Sino-Korean numbers for minutes when telling the time, for dates and months, and for addresses, phone numbers, money and floors of a building.

DONATIONS TO ENGLISH

You'll find some Korean words are familiar to you, as they are often used in English. Words such as kimchi, ramyeon, soju, K-Pop, hallyu and taekwondo.

Signs

영업 중 Open
휴무 Closed
입구 Entrance
출구 Exit
금지 Prohibited
금연 (구역) No Smoking (Area)
화장실 Toilets
신사용 Men
숙녀용 Women

NUMBERS (SINO-KOREAN)

1 일 *il*
2 이 *yi*
3 삼 *sam*
4 사 *sa*
5 오 *o*
6 육 *yuk*
7 칠 *ch'il*
8 팔 *p'al*
9 구 *ku*
10 십 *ship*

WORD STRESS

Korean pronunciation is pretty straight-forward for English speakers, as most sounds are also found in English or have a close approximation. Korean distinguishes between aspirated consonants (formed by making a puff of air as they're pronounced) and unaspirated ones (pronounced without a puff of air). Syllables are pronounced with fairly even emphasis in Korean.

Emergencies

Help! 도와주세요! *do·wa·ju·se·yo*

Go away! 저리 가세요!
jŏ·ri ga·se·yo

Call ...! ... 불러주세요!
... bul·lŏ·ju·se·yo

a doctor 의사 *ŭi·sa*

the police 경찰 *gyŏng·ch'al*

I'm lost.
길을 잃었어요. *gi·rŭl i·rŏss·ŏ·yo*

Where's the toilet?
화장실이 어디예요?
hwa·jang·shi·ri ŏ·di·ye·yo

I'm sick.
전 아파요. *jŏn a·p'a·yo*

It hurts here.
여기가 아파요. *yŏ·gi·ga a·p'a·yo*

I'm allergic to ...
전 ...에 알레르기가 있어요.
jŏn ... ·é al·le·rŭ·gi·ga iss·ŏ·yo

Eating & Drinking

Can we see the menu?
메뉴 볼 수 있나요?
me·nyu bol·su in·na·yo

What would you recommend?
추천 해 주시겠어요?
ch'u·ch'ŏn hae·ju·shi·gess·ŏ·yo

Do you have any vegetarian dishes?
채식주의 음식 있나요?
ch'ae·shik·ju·i ŭm·shik in·na·yo

I'd like ..., please. ... 주세요.
... ju·se·yo

Cheers! 건배! *gŏn·bae*

짠! *jjan!*

That was delicious! 맛있었어요!
ma·shiss·ŏss·ŏ·yo

Please bring the bill.
계산서 가져다 주세요.
gye·san·sŏ ga·jŏ·da ju·se·yo

Question Words

how 어떻게 *ŏt·tŏ·k'é*
what (object) 무엇을 *mu·ŏ·sŭl*
what (subject) 뭐가 *mwŏ·ga*
when 언제 *ŏn·jé*
where 어디 *ŏ·di*
which 어느 *ŏ·nŭ*
who (object) 누구를 *nu·gu·rŭl*
who (subject) 누가 *nu·ga*
why 왜 *wae*

THE KOREA

STORYBOOK

Our writers delve deep into different aspects of Korean life

Cheonggye-cheon (p76), Seoul

EFIRED/SHUTTERSTOCK

A HISTORY OF KOREA IN 15 PLACES

The present divided Korean Peninsula is mirrored by ancient eras when the kingdoms of Goguryeo, Silla and Baekje jockeyed for control of territory that stretched deep into modern-day China. That powerful neighbour and Japan to the east have both impacted Korea's fortunes down the ages. By Simon Richmond

THE MYTHICAL BEGINNINGS of the Korean nation were in the 3rd millennium BCE, when a legendary king named Dangun founded old Joseon. Real or not, Dangun has been a continuous presence from his time down to the present day, a kingly vessel filled by different people at different times drawing their legitimacy from this eternal lineage. Under its first president, for example, South Korea used a calendar in which Dangun's birth constituted year one – setting the date at 2333 BCE. If the present day's two Koreas can't agree on many things, they can agree on Dangun.

The earliest written histories of Korea were prepared by Chinese scribes about 2200 years ago, but there is archaeological evidence that humans have inhabited the peninsula for at least 8000 years. Around the time of Christ, three kingdoms emerged: Baekje (also spelled Paekche), Goguryeo (Koguryŏ) and Silla (Shilla). By 930 CE, a formidable military leader named Wang Geon unified the country and established a flourishing dynasty, Goryeo, from which came the name Korea. In the early 20th century, Japan colonised the country, while in 1953, at the end of the Korean War, the peninsula was divided into North and South Korea – a situation that remains today.

1. Gochang Dolmen Site

PREHISTORIC TOMBS

Korea's Neolithic people practised agriculture in a settled communal life and are widely supposed to have had family clans as their basic social grouping. They also built stone burial chambers and monuments known as dolmen. There are more than 30,000 examples of these dolmen – the best such collection in the world – scattered across South Korea. The Gochang Dolmen Site in Jeollabuk-do is one of three main clusters of these megalithic Bronze and Iron Age monuments, which collectively form a UNESCO World Heritage Site. The other two clusters are on the island of Ganghwado and at Hwasun, in Jeollanam-do, which includes Korea's biggest stone table.

For more on Gochang Dolmen Site, see p273.

2. Chamseongdan

DANGUN'S ALTAR

Dongguk Tonggam, a chronicle of early Korean history compiled in the 15th century, gives 2333 BCE as the date that mythical leader Dangun founded Korea. The stone altar where he is said to have made sacrifices marking this event is Chamseongdan on the north side of Manisan, the tallest peak on the island of Ganghwado. It's said that the rulers of the Baekje, Goguryeo and Silla kingdoms all offered sacrifices here. The altar was renovated in 1270 under Goryeo's Wang Geon, as well as in 1700 by King Sukjong. A memorial service is performed here every year on 3 October, National Foundation Day.

For more on Chamseongdan, see p141.

3. Gongju

BAEKJE KINGDOM CAPITAL

Gongju became the capital of the Baekje Kingdom in 475 CE. The kingdom controlled western Korea up to Pyongyang. King Muryeong, who sat on the throne from 501 to his death in 523, was the longest-ruling Baekje monarch. In 1971, his tomb and that of his queen were excavated in Gongju. It contained nearly 3000 funerary objects that had not seen the light of day in 1500 years, including remains of the king and queen's wooden coffins, golden diadem ornaments, jewellery, clothing accessories and the king's sword. A small selection of this hoard is on display at Gongju National Museum.

For more on Gongju, see p338.

Baekje artefact, Gongju National Museum (p340)

JOHNATHAN21/SHUTTERSTOCK

4. Gyeongju National Museum

THE GLORY OF SILLA

In the battles between the Three Kingdoms on the Korean Peninsula, Silla emerged victorious in 668 CE. Silla's capital at Gyeongju was renowned as the 'city of gold', where the aristocracy pursued a high culture and extravagant pleasures. To gain an insight into this gilded life, visit the Gyeongju National Museum. Silla's rulers sent many students to Tang schools and acquired a level of civilisation high enough to merit the Chinese designation of 'flourishing land in the East'. Chinese statecraft, Buddhist and Confucian philosophy, Confucian practices of educating the young and the Chinese written language became entrenched.

For more on Gyeongju National Museum, see p224.

5. Haein-sa

BUDDHIST SACRED TEXT

Dating back to 802 CE, Haein-sa is the head temple of the Jogye Order of Korean Seon Buddhism, the largest such Buddhist order in Korea. This beautiful temple houses the Tripitaka Koreana, one of the world's largest libraries of Buddhist scriptures. Throughout the Goryeo period, Buddhism was the state religion, but it coexisted with Confucianism. Buddhist priests systematised religious practice by rendering the Korean version of the Buddhist canon into mammoth carved woodblocks, known as the Tripitaka. The first Tripitaka, completed in 1087, was destroyed by the Mongols in 1232. The reconstructed set, on display today, was completed in 1251.

For more on Haein-sa, see p242.

6. Seoul City Wall

START OF JOSEON DYNASTY

The overthrow of the Mongols by the Ming dynasty in China in the late 14th century provided an opportunity for Korean military men to contest for power. One of them, Yi Seong-gye, overthrew Goryeo leaders and proclaimed himself King Taejo. His new state was named Joseon, harking back to the old Joseon kingdom 15 centuries earlier. King Taejo employed feng shui (*pungsu* in Korean) to select Hanyang (Seoul) as Joseon's capital in 1394. Some 200,000 labourers were mobilised to surround the new capital with a fortress wall that was completed two years later. Around 70% of that wall still stands today.

For more on Seoul City Wall, see p124.

7. Suwon

WORLD HERITAGE-LISTED WALL

In 1762, in one of the more gruesome episodes of the Joseon dynasty, Crown Prince Sado died from starvation and dehydration after being imprisoned by his father in a rice barrel for eight days. Sado's body was moved by his son, King Jeongjo, to Suwon in 1789. Five years later, the king commanded the construction of the Hwaseong fortress to honour his father's tomb and as preparation for moving the capital from Seoul to Suwon. Each year, a procession from Seoul to Suwon, involving thousands of people, was organised for King Jeongjo to worship at his father's tomb. This is why Suwon is known as the 'city of filial piety'.

For more on Suwon, see p130.

8. Incheon

KOREA OPENS UP

From the 16th century, European naval powers began expanding their reach across Asia, opening trade routes and later fully colonising territories. To protect itself, Joseon Korea, like China and Japan, opted for a closed-door policy on trade and diplomacy. However, in the latter half of the 19th century, as European powers, the US and Japan began to demand trade relations more aggressively, that policy changed. Under the Treaty of Ganghwa in 1876, Korea opened three of its ports – Busan, Incheon and Wonsan – to international trade. Overseas traders set up 'concessions' where they built offices, homes and churches in international styles. You can see evidence of this in Incheon's Chinatown and Open Port districts.

For more on Incheon, see p135.

9. Deoksugung

PALACE OF VIRTUOUS LONGEVITY

Deoksugung was a secondary palace until 1897 when King Gojong moved here to be near where foreign legations were concentrated in Seoul at the time. It's unique among the city's palaces in its mixture of Korean and European-style architecture and gardens. Also in 1897, Gojong proclaimed Joseon's new status as the Korean Empire, breaking free from its centuries-old ties to a weakened China. The empire was short-lived, as Korea's powerful neighbour, Japan, had other plans, making the country its protectorate in 1905 and forcing Gojong to abdicate two years later. Gojong continued to live at Deoksugung until his death in 1919.

For more on Deoksugung, see p77.

10. Jeju April 3 Peace Park

ISLAND MASSACRE

The aftermath of WWII was a chaotic and violent time for Korea, particularly on Jeju-do, where as many as 30,000 islanders were massacred by right-wing government forces in events collectively labelled the Jeju April 3 Incident. The terror campaign kicked off when South Korea's first president, Syngman Rhee, declared martial law in November 1948, and ran until the end of the Korean War. For decades the 'incident' was officially censored. The Jeju April 3 Peace Park opened in 2008 as part of reparations for victims, based on the findings of a truth commission into the incident.

For more on Jeju April 3 Peace Park, see p308.

11. Imjingak Resort

ON THE DMZ

This park was built in 1972 as a place of consolation for Koreans unable to return to their home towns, families and friends because of the division of the peninsula into North and South Korea in 1953. The park is on the site of a former railroad bridge spanning the Imjin River – it's known as the Freedom Bridge because it was used by repatriated POWs and soldiers returning from the Korean War. Since the 1970s, the park has grown to include art installations and a cable car that shuttles people over the river for a closer look at the DMZ, the 4km-wide, 250km-long buffer laced with landmines.

For more on Imjingak Resort, see p142.

12. Gwangju

DEMOCRACY UPRISING SUPPRESSED

Between 1961 and 1992, South Korea was ruled by military dictators of one form or another. Political dissent wasn't tolerated,

Deoksugung (p77), Seoul

with many atrocities committed. The worst occurred in May 1980, during the government of Chun Doo-hwan, a protégé of Park Chung-hee, who had been assassinated the previous year. The military brutally suppressed a pro-democracy uprising in Gwangju, killing at least 154 civilians, with another 74 missing, presumed dead. An additional 4141 people were wounded and more than 3000 were arrested, many of whom were tortured. Known as the May 18 Democratic Uprising, its victims are remembered at several places across the city, including the May 18th National Cemetery and Jeonil Building 245.

For more on Gwangju, see p266.

13. Olympic Park

SOUTH KOREA'S COMING-OUT PARTY

Billed as South Korea's 'coming-out party', the awarding of the 1988 Summer Olympic Games to Seoul was seized on as a chance to show to the world how far the country had progressed since the destruction of the Korean War and the turmoil of military rule. The event's most visible lasting legacy is Olympic Park, which helped spur the development of Seoul south of the Han River. The Games also included painful human-rights violations, whereby Korean authorities, desperate to prevent global embarrassment, arrested many unhoused people, disabled people and youth in the area, sending them to vagrant camps.

For more on Olympic Park, see p117.

14. Masudae Grand Monument

EPICENTRE OF KIM CULT

An ideological statement forged in concrete, bronze and marble, Pyongyang is the ultimate totalitarian metropolis. Every itinerary to North Korea's capital includes a visit to the 22m-tall bronze statues of the smiling Great Leader and Dear Leader, the latter in his trademark parka. The first statue was unveiled in 1972 to celebrate Kim Il Sung's 60th birthday, while the second one was added in 2012, following Kim Jong Il's death the previous year. Behind the central statues is a mosaic mural showing a scene from Paekdusan, the sacred mountain of revolution. All visitors to the site, whether locals or foreigners, are expected to bow to show respect.

For more on North Korea, see p371.

15. Cheonggye-cheon

URBAN REVITALISATION PROJECT

The restoration in 2005 of Seoul's Cheonggye-cheon is often portrayed as a triumph of urban regeneration. The stream had been buried beneath asphalt since the late 1960s, with a highway overpass built overhead. Prior to that, the waterway had long been an open sewer. Now encased in a sunken, landscaped promenade, the new Cheonggye-cheon flows with groundwater pumped out from nearby subway lines. Ecologists have attacked the US$900-million project as a fake stream that needs constant and costly maintenance. Nevertheless, it has become one of Seoul's most popular tourist attractions and a place that locals love for the respite it provides in the concrete surrounds.

For more on Cheonggye-cheon, see p76.

CLOCKWISE FROM TOP LEFT: LEOPATRIZI/GETTY IMAGES, IMAGE REPUBLIC/SHUTTERSTOCK, PEKIC/GETTY IMAGES, IMAGE REPUBLIC/SHUTTERSTOCK

MEET THE KOREANS

South Korea is high-tech, high-speed and highly efficient, yet its *ppalli ppalli* culture of ease and convenience belies some hard truths. ANN BABE introduces the Koreans.

ONE OF THE first things visitors might notice about South Korea is how homogenous it is. Korean culture is influenced by Confucianism, which emphasises social order, hierarchy and uniformity. Many Koreans tend to dress the same, wear their hair the same, go to the same places, have the same experiences and mostly try to fit in rather than stick out. To foreigners, this 'sameness' may at times feel challenging to navigate, as if everyone around them is rushing downstream en masse while they swim alone against the current.

Koreans can be incredibly efficient people. Anyone who learns even a few words of Korean knows *'ppalli ppalli'*, which means 'hurry up'. Koreans love to do things swiftly, and they love things that are swift. Korea's internet is one of the fastest in the world, and so is its KTX train. In restaurants, you never wait for service; you call the wait staff over to you, or you order on the touchscreen at your table, and your meal arrives minutes later. Many medical visits are walk-ins that are conducted at an exceptionally quick clip. I have attended weddings that lasted less than a couple of hours from start to finish, including the reception. In any elevator in Korea, the 'door close' button will be the most worn-out button.

Who & How Many

The population of South Korea is nearly 51.7 million, roughly half of whom are concentrated in the capital metropolitan area of Seoul, Incheon and Gyeonggi-do, and about 96% of whom are ethnically Korean.

Tied to the Korean love of speed is the demand for convenience. If at 4.30am you find yourself hungry, don't worry – there's likely to be a 24-hour convenience store close by that offers a full selection of *gimbap* (sesame-oil flavoured rice wrapped in seaweed), sandwiches and other snacks – along with socks, umbrellas, contact solution and beer, just in case you're in the market for any of those items as well. When you order food online or over the phone, the ease of Korean delivery means it can be dispatched not only to your hotel, but to your picnic blanket along the Han River. Forgot to buy your friend a birthday gift? Have one shipped to them right away with the KakaoTalk app. Need a taxi? Hail one using Kakao T.

At the same time, Korea is a consumer society that considers spending power to be a status symbol, and it's a difficult place to live when seemingly everyone is striving, or is told to strive, for the same things. There is immense pressure to keep up, and cut-throat competitiveness to get ahead. There is a harsh divide between insiders and outsiders, often also tinged with ethnocentrism. Amid a widening wealth gap are soaring levels of stress and depression, one of the highest suicide rates on the planet and a happiness rate that, according to the 2025 World Happiness Report, doesn't crack the top 50.

I'M KOREAN AND IT'S COMPLICATED

I was born in South Korea with a Korean name and I grew up in the United States with an English one. That's because, like many, many others, I was adopted transnationally and transculturally from Korea. To date, there are more than 200,000 of us who were separated from biological families and raised in different cultures abroad. In the years since, many of us have come back, on short, long and recurring stays.

While South Korea experiences a persistently low fertility rate – 0.80 in 2025, according to preliminary data, one of the lowest in the world – its population of foreigners is growing. As of 2025, the country is home to an estimated 2.73 million international residents – a record high – comprising international students, international adoptees, migrant workers, marriage visa holders and more. Most of Korea's international population is from China, followed by Vietnam, the US, Thailand and Uzbekistan.

Seoul Marathon (p404)

YASUYOSHI CHIBA/AFP VIA GETTY IMAGES

HIGH ON RUNNING

A global running movement has exploded into a fitness phenomenon in Korea, with runners sporting fashionable attire and fancy footwear. By Jennifer Chang

RUNNING ISN'T THE first sport that comes to mind in a nation whose athletes have swept Olympic medals in archery, short track speed skating and taekwondo. But the trifecta of a global health crisis, hyper-connectivity and a trend-sensitive culture resulted in a widespread adoption of running as a mainstream sport.

Figures Shaping Korea's Running Culture

Few outside of Korea may realise that in 1936, before the country was divided into North and South, two Korean runners travelled from Gyeongseong (name for Seoul during the Japanese colonial period) to Berlin by train, an intercontinental journey of 14 days, to compete in the Summer Olympics. Because Korea was under Japanese colonial rule (1910–45), Sohn Kee-chung and his teammate, Nam Sung-yong, were forced to race under the Japanese flag. But they had a dream – that one day, Korea would be an independent nation and Koreans could run for Korea. Fuelled by an indomitable spirit and a love for their nation, Sohn won the gold medal in the marathon while Nam took the bronze. With Japan claiming the victory, the joy of the win was overshadowed by the sting of shame. But that bittersweet tension found a glorious resolution more than five decades on at the 1992 Olympics in Barcelona. By this time Korea had been liberated from Japan's rule for nearly 50 years, and Sohn, who had dedicated his life to coaching the South Korean marathon team, was in Barcelona to cheer on the runners. When Hwang Young-jo became the second Korean runner to win an Olympic gold medal, Sohn, at the time nearly 80 years old, shed tears of joy. Relishing the historic moment of a dream finally realised, the two heroes of Korea rejoiced in a wholly Korean triumph.

Timely Trend into a Wellness Lifestyle

Despite the colossal achievements of Sohn Kee-chung and Hwang Young-jo, running never quite took off as a mainstream sport in Korea. But in a nation where smart-phones are nearly universal and more than 97% of the population are online, it's easy to see how trends can blow up overnight – sparking a global dialogue of anything from the latest in food and fashion to music, beauty and wellness. While some

E
최하민
18172
E
Wai Shing
23545

trends fizzle others gain traction and keep the momentum going until a cultural shift emerges. And running definitely falls under the latter category. What tipped the scale was the COVID-19 pandemic. Lockdowns and restrictions from gathering meant indoor gyms were off limits, and open-air sports such as golf, tennis and hiking grew in popularity. During this shift, Koreans turned to running. Over the past several years, running crews have exploded in popularity, and the number of marathons and running events held across the country jumped from just 19 in 2020, to 254 in 2024, Nowadays, signing up for a marathon is a bit like winning the lottery or a click war for K-pop concert tickets, with servers crashing and registration tickets selling out within minutes.

Fortunately, those who fail to secure a spot in one of South Korea's major marathons, including the historic Seoul Marathon (formerly known as the Dong-A Marathon), Chuncheon Marathon, and the JTBC Seoul Marathon, can try their luck with one of many other races sprinkled throughout the country. Equally competitive is the ticket for North Korea's Pyongyang International Marathon.

Unlikely Hero

Statistics and data aside, it's hard to talk about the running craze without mentioning Sean, one half of the legendary Korean hip-hop duo, Jinusean. The singer-turned-philanthropist has been racking up kilometres for charitable causes since 2011, documenting his journey on social media. From 2020, Sean has been hosting the 815 Run, an annual event that celebrates Korea's Liberation Day (August 15), where he runs 81.5km, while participants run 8.15km. Funds raised from the event are used to build homes for descendants of Korea's independence activists. He also founded Unknown Crew, a group of runners including actor Park Bo-gum of popular TV shows *Reply 1988* and *When Life Gives You Tangerines* and former professional soccer player, Lee Young-pyo. The members run together daily and often participate in Sean's giving campaigns. In 2025, he fulfilled his dream of building Korea's first care facility for patients of ALS (also known as Lou Gehrig's disease) by raising nearly 24 billion won (US$16.2 million). Harnessing the power of social media to stir up a culture of goodwill and giving, Sean has been at the helm of motivating celebrities and ordinary citizens to get out there and run. With legs of steel and a heart of gold, Korea's third national hero is planning to continue his 'give runs' well into his 100s.

Morning Raves, GPS Art Runs and Sneaker Rentals

With roughly one in five Koreans now enjoying running, luxury fashion and sports brands are cashing in on the hype with coveted products and eye-catching collaborations. Participants of this hip activity get a social 'insider pass', with many tracking (or maybe flaunting) their progress on social media – sweaty selfies stamped with run times, pace and routes. In Seoul, using fitness apps like Strava, Garmin and Nike Run Club to create GPS art has become a popular way to make runs more enjoyable.

Instagram is flooded with posts showing runners who have completed one of several popular routes, including the **sweet potato run** (8km) around Yeoido, which includes the experience of running along the Han River, and the **puppy dog run** (10k), which starts at Gwanghwamun Plaza and passes popular tourist spots like Gyeongbokgung Palace and Bukchon – a popular neighbourhood in Seoul with a large number of traditional homes.

With the ongoing obsession over the sport, New Balance opened a 'Run Hub' in Bukchon, where anyone can rent sneakers and running apparel for two hours for a small fee – making it a great option for tourists to explore downtown Seoul on a run, perhaps creating GPS art for a unique travel keepsake. What was once an affordable and accessible form of exercise for middle-aged and older adults has become a trendy sport for millennials and Gen Zers – referred to as MZ in Korea. These younger runners in their 20s and 30s are driving a cultural change, swapping late-night drinking and clubbing with morning runs and raves, with a refreshing cup of iced Americano in hand.

THE LANGUAGE OF SHARING: HOW FOOD SPEAKS LOUDER THAN WORDS IN SOUTH KOREA

In Korea, food isn't just for nourishment, it's connection made edible: affection measured in small plates and shared bites.
By Esther Carlstone

KOREANS VALUE *JEONG*, a cultural concept that doesn't translate easily into English. At its heart, it's about love, connection and community built through shared experiences. One of the clearest expressions of *jeong* is food – friends and family gathering around a table filled with rice and shared *banchan* (side dishes).

The Origins of Sharing

Korean food culture's emphasis on communal eating stretches back centuries, to when villages were small and isolated, forcing people to rely on their communities for survival. Commerce was limited, so sharing wasn't just neighbourly – it was necessary. Families pooled supplies for harvests, shared ingredients during lean winters and celebrated together when times were good. This collective spirit became woven into the fabric of Korean identity and remains intact today.

You can see it in everyday family meals, when hands reach across to refill someone else's bowl before their own. Or in the now world-famous Korean barbecue, where meat sizzles on the table for everyone to grab while chatting about their day. Eating together is a sacred time to connect in an otherwise busy existence. You'll often hear friends, colleagues and even new acquaintances say to each other *bap gachi meokja,* which literally translates into 'let's eat rice together', but colloquially means let's share a meal and hang out.

Korean mothers are famous for showing love through food. It's not unusual for contemporary adults – including myself – to recall waking to mini feasts: small ceramic dishes filled with glistening *banchan* and a bowl of warm soup to start the day right. Then coming home after school to find mothers armed with homemade snacks, chasing reluctant children around with savoury *jeon* (pancakes) and creamy *gyeran mari* (rolled omelette).

And for centuries each autumn, the tradition of *kimjang* brings entire communities together to make kimchi for winter. In modern times, it's not so much about having enough to survive the harsh winter anymore, but rather about preserving a community tradition and finding time to reconnect in person again. People gather in courtyards *iutgwa hamkke* ('together with neighbours'), sleeves rolled up, hands stained red with *gochugaru* (spicy red chilli powder). After hours of work, everyone shares tender *suyuk* (boiled pork belly) wrapped in fresh kimchi leaves, celebrating not just the food but the bond they've strengthened. Anyone who makes extra

jars passes them along to elderly neighbours or families who could use a little help. It's love, counted out in jars of kimchi.

Even in an age of individual portions and private plates, Koreans maintain rituals honouring this communal heritage. Traditional dining etiquette dictates waiting for the eldest person to lift their chopsticks before anyone else begins – a small gesture that frames the meal as something shared, not something eaten alone.

More Than Just a Meal

Walk into any Korean restaurant, and you'll likely immediately be served *banchan* – those small side dishes some Koreans love more than the main entree itself. Pickled radish, seasoned spinach, spicy cucumber – sometimes half a dozen varieties, sometimes more. Here's the thing: you don't get your own. Everyone reaches into the same small bowls, chopsticks crossing in a delicate dance of shared space. When a dish runs low, servers appear with refills, infinite and free. Taking from the communal pool isn't selfish – it's how Koreans connect.

Korean barbecue takes this even further. The meat sizzles on a grill embedded in the table, and suddenly, dining becomes teamwork. Someone tends the meat, flipping at just the right moment. Someone else wraps a perfect bite in lettuce. Others are dropping cooked meat on everyone else's plates and pouring drinks for all. Hands reach across one another, chopsticks weave through the air, and conversation flows as freely as the soju. It goes beyond just sharing a meal together – it's an essential connection point.

Then there's *son-mat* – literally translating to 'hand taste'. Every cook leaves their unique fingerprint in the food they make. A grandmother's kimchi and *galbi jjim* (braised beef short ribs) tastes different from her daughter's, not because the recipe changed dramatically, but because different hands use their own 'measure from the heart' proportions of spices and ingredients that only they magically seem to know and keep locked inside their heads. When someone makes food for you in Korea, they're giving you something irreplaceable – a piece of themselves measured in labour and love.

Perhaps nowhere is this more evident than the tradition of eating *miyeokguk* – seaweed soup – on birthdays. This isn't birthday cake; it's the soup given to mothers after childbirth to aid in recovery. Eating it on your birthday isn't about celebrating yourself; it's about honouring your mother, thanking her for bringing you into the world. The soup speaks what words sometimes can't: gratitude and love.

Beyond the Family Table

This love language extends everywhere. There's *hoesik* – after-work dinners where colleagues become friends over grilled meat and soju that's practically become an extension of long workdays in Korea. Friends catch up at *pojangmacha*, those street-food tents, over steaming stews and shared laughter. Even casual hangouts at cafes or *bunsik-jip* (snack shops) turn into moments of connection, with shared *tteokbokki* (chewy rice cakes) or fried chicken.

Seoul's streets are full of convenience stores, shelves packed with instant meals meant for one, and delivery motorbikes racing food from restaurant to door are ubiquitous around the big cities. People work longer hours, live faster lives and the kind of long, lingering family meals many grew up with don't always fit the day anymore.

Still, the point hasn't been lost. Those same young Koreans crowd around barbecue grills on weekends. They show up with containers of homemade *banchan* when a friend is struggling. The shape of it changes, but the instinct doesn't: food is still how love gets passed around.

For travellers, learning this doesn't take much. Say yes to the *banchan* pushed in your direction. Reach across the table without apologising. When someone refills your glass, return the favour. In those small, unspoken moments, you're tasting more than what's on the plate. In Korea, a meal isn't just fuel. It's how people say you're welcome here.

Korean barbecue
9919/SHUTTERSTOCK

PSY performing his mega-hit 'Gangnam Style'

PETER PARKS/AFP VIA GETTY IMAGES

K-POP'S GLOBAL MARCH HITS A ROADBLOCK

Three decades after it started, South Korea's most celebrated cultural export has reached a critical fork in the road.

By Marco Ferrarese

IT'S KIND OF ironic that the latest fire to rekindle the global success of K-Pop, Korea's most important musical export and identity, is neither a real idol group nor Korean as the 'K' suggests.

Released on the video-streaming giant Netflix in June 2025, the animated musical film *KPop Demon Hunters* by Seoul-born Canadian director Maggie Kang tells the fantasy tale of Huntr/x – half-girl supergroup, half *mudang* (무당; Korea's female shamans) – who moonlight as demon hunters. In the film, they fight the Saja Boys – literally a boy band from hell – to the last wail.

Produced by Sony Pictures Animation, this USA-produced, English-language film that represents Korean cultural elements with painstaking detail and authenticity became a global success almost overnight. By October 2025, it had surpassed 325 million views, becoming Netflix's most-watched film, beating even the Korean super-hit series *Squid Game*.

A New Era for K-Pop?

The incredible success of *KPop Demon Hunters'* soundtrack has both reinvigorated and challenged the meaning of K-Pop music. By November 2025, eight English-sung tracks by the movie's two fictional groups, Huntr/X and the Saja Boys, had held positions on the US Billboard Hot 100. Huntr/x's *Golden* was also the first K-Pop tune to top the UK's chart in 13 years, following PSY's 2012 mega-hit 'Gangnam Style' – the earworm that sent South Korean pop into the history books by becoming the first YouTube video ever to reach one billion views.

PSY's song had introduced K-Pop to the world as a very localised music genre sung in Korean, featuring lyrics that made fun of the nation's beauty and fame-obsessed society. However, the current success of 2026 Oscar-winning *KPop Demon Hunters* marks a new era for the genre, as it has become increasingly globalised and shaped by foreign capitals and creators – quite a distance from K-Pop's early beginnings.

The Birth of Korea's Pop Tsunami

The term *hallyu* (Korean wave) was coined in 2000 by the *Shanghai Evening Post* after the Korean boy band H.O.T. performed in Beijing for the first time. H.O.T., considered the first Korean idol group, was created by Lee Soo-man, founder of South Korean multinational SM Entertainment, who polled high-school students about their ideal music group. That first international performance in China propelled Lee's

ambitions of conquering the world with a unique South Korean pop-music brand.

SM Entertainment also helped develop the genre from boy bands to large girl groups with the launch of the eight-piece girl band Girl's Generation in 2007. It was followed by Apink in 2011 and another eight-member band, AOA (Ace of Angels), in 2012. By 2014, AOA had found nationwide success with hits such as 'Miniskirt', the video of which possibly offered K-Pop's most sexualised female representation. The song helped AOA debut on Universal Music Japan, first widening K-Pop's reach in North Asia and then to Southeast Asia.

Since 2013, South Korea's biggest K-Pop band has been BTS, a boy group that sold more than 20 million records and became the world's best-selling band in 2021. BTS embodies K-Pop's identity as South Korea's most potent soft-power weapon. The seven-member band was the first South Korean act to top the US's Billboard Hot 100 chart, addressed the United Nations on climate change and COVID-19 in September 2021 and, in 2022, met US President Joe Biden to discuss anti-Asian hate crimes in the US.

K-Pop Crisis

Despite White House visits and being glorified internationally (London's Victoria and Albert Museum hosted a *hallyu* exhibition in 2023), K-Pop may have reached a crisis, at least according to BTS producer Bang Si-hyuk in March 2023.

The commercial explosion of the past decade has diluted PSY's uniquely Korean 'Gangnam Style' into a cloneable standard of young and androgynous beauty, sexualised femininity, predictable refrains and formulaic dance moves – well-honed standards that even AI can reproduce. Formed in 2020, the eight-piece girl band Aespa, another of SM's products, comprises four young women and four digital avatars. MAVE, a girl group created in 2023 by Metaverse Entertainment, is fully digital, featuring avatars created by AI and no live members.

Even the sheer economics seem perplexing. Business is slow and even negative in some markets – a worrying development given that K-Pop has only recently begun to achieve its full global potential. Data from Circle Chart, South Korea's benchmark K-Pop chart, showed zero growth in the US share of physical album sales in 2022, compared with a sharp rise from 2% in 2015 to 17% in 2021, making it K-Pop's third-largest overseas market. Exports to Japan and China, the two largest markets, continued to increase in 2022, albeit at a slower rate than the previous year, while sales declined in every country in Southeast Asia, another key market, except for Vietnam. Album sales continued to fall to 98.9 million in 2024 (down 21.3 million year-on-year), while the industry focused on concert revenue, which, on the other hand, surged 79% between October 2024 and 2025.

New Directions

Paradoxically, BTS's unprecedented success, especially in the US, may have increased K-Pop's dependency on overseas markets and diluted the distinct South Korean identity that helped it take over the world.

By starting to sing in English and collaborating with American artists, BTS helped to transform K-Pop into what sounds like standard Anglo-American pop aimed at the US market. This change is most evident in Blackpink's latest album, *Born Pink* (2022), which is half sung in English and is the first record by a South Korean female act to hit the Billboard 200's top spot.

In Korea, the industry is tapping into new ground by embracing inclusion. Formed in 2025, 1Verse (pronounced 'universe') is an international boy band comprising two North Korean refugees, two Americans and one Japanese member, all focused on showcasing diversity. Another groundbreaking new group is Big Ocean, which uses international sign language because all three members are deaf or hard of hearing.

The announced 2026 return of BTS with a new album and a 65-date world tour after a two-year hiatus to comply with South Korea's mandatory military duties may be what K-Pop really needs right now – even though, after the Saja Boys' hit 'Your Idol' beat BTS' first English song, 'Dynamite', as the highest-charting K-Pop boy-band song in US Spotify history in July 2025, the boys are literally up against some otherworldly competition.

RISING FROM SHADOWS: THE EVOLVING ROLE OF WOMEN IN KOREA

Today's generation of Korean women are redefining what it means to strive for a fair and inclusive society. By Mee Yoo Kwon

FOR CENTURIES, TRADITIONAL Confucian values have significantly shaped Korea's culture and society, particularly gender roles. From the tight grip of neo-Confucian traditions during the six centuries of the Joseon dynasty to today's dynamic and diverse representation in media and beyond, the journey of Korean women is a testament to resilience and change.

Path to Gender Equality

Just over a century ago, women in Korea faced significant restrictions. During the Joseon dynasty, women's rights were low and their presence in public life was minimal. Documents from the era typically only mention women in relation to their roles as obedient daughters or wives, often omitting their names entirely.

In the late 19th century, foreign observers commented on the seclusion of Korean women. Austrian writer and traveller Ernst von Hesse-Wartegg, in his *Korea: A Summer Journey to the Land of Morning Calm,* observed that women, particularly in rural areas, were extremely elusive, often hurrying into their homes and hiding their faces at the sight of an outsider.

Women's roles saw a dramatic shift in the 20th century, particularly after Korea's liberation from Japanese colonial rule in 1945 and the rapid adoption of democratic values. The establishment of the Korean constitution in 1948 marked a significant turning point by introducing legal equality between the sexes. Unlike many nations where gender equality was achieved through prolonged activism and struggle, in Korea these rights were largely bestowed as the country embraced democratic principles. This path to gender equality has shaped the continuing efforts and challenges faced by women in Korea as they strive for genuine social change.

Female Role Model

Many women have been at the forefront of the fight for gender equality in South Korea, among them Lee Tai-young (1914–98), who made history as the country's first female lawyer. Her pioneering career influenced Korea's legal framework, particularly in the areas of family law and women's rights.

Lee dedicated her life to addressing the structural inequalities that plagued Korean society and founded the Korea Legal Aid Center for Family Relations, an institution that provided essential legal support and advocacy for women, particularly those grappling with domestic violence, divorce and other family-related issues.

Lee also led a relentless campaign against the *hoju*, the patriarchal family headship system that designated the eldest male as the head of the family. Her work was instrumental in abolishing this system, paving the way for more egalitarian family laws. Her legacy continues to inspire new generations of women to pursue equality and justice within Korean society and beyond.

Work–Life Balance

Today, women in Korea achieve higher educational levels than men. In 2025, 78.5% of women attended university or higher institutions, compared to 74.2% for men.

According to Statistics Korea, as of 2025, women's labour-force participation rate was 57.2% – the highest since records began in 1963 – with more than 10 million women employed as salaried workers. This marks a notable shift in women's participation in the workforce, indicating a progressive trend towards gender equality in employment.

However, challenges still remain in the professional sphere. The gender wage gap is the most substantial within the OECD, with women earning only 69.3% of what men earned in 2024, underscoring deep-seated economic disparities. South Korea was the only nation in this group where the gap exceeded 30%.

Women's representation in leadership roles is also low. A 2025 report by Unico Search found only 6.5% of executives in Korea's top 100 companies were women, a slight increase from 6% in 2023. This underrepresentation extends to the broader corporate landscape, where structural barriers like the glass ceiling and work-life-balance issues continue to hinder women's career progression.

Despite these challenges, there are luminous examples of Korean women breaking through these barriers. Choi Soo-yeon and Shina Chung lead two of Korea's foremost internet companies, Naver and Kakao, respectively. These leadership roles showcase individual achievements, but also symbolise the slow yet positive change towards gender diversity in the tech industry. Still, such examples are exceptions rather than the norm, with only four women holding CEO positions in the top 100 companies, far below the global average.

While progress has been made towards integrating women into the Korean workforce, hurdles still exist. Achieving a more equitable work environment requires policy changes but also a cultural shift that redefines gender roles in the workplace and at home.

The day for Ji-won, a typical working mother in Korea, begins before dawn as she prepares breakfast and readies her child for school. By 8.30am, after sending her child off to elementary school, she starts her own workday. Having returned from childcare leave to help her child's transition to school, Ji-won also participates in school ceremonies and parent meetings, which are mostly attended by mothers, not fathers. Despite support from her husband, Ji-won predominantly manages childcare and household responsibilities. This scenario is all too common among Korean working mothers, who are often expected to juggle their careers with their roles at home.

Record-Low Birthrates

This work-life imbalance is also contributing to South Korea's low birthrate, 0.80 in 2025, up from its historic low of 0.721 in 2023. This is significantly below the replacement level of 2.1 needed to maintain population stability, and projections suggest a dramatic population decline, potentially halving by 2100.

Factors contributing to this include young Koreans' insecurity about the future, including insufficient income, unstable job market and housing difficulties. Social and cultural pressures, such as the disproportionate burden of household and childcare responsibilities placed on women, and institutional barriers such as inadequate parental leave and childcare systems, exacerbate the issue.

Despite government efforts, including financial assistance for childcare, low-interest financing for first-time parents and expanded healthcare coverage for fertility treatments and high-risk pregnancies, policies remain largely propagandistic. They often focus on incentivising childbirth within traditional heterosexual marriages, neglecting broader needs for family support, gender equality and diversity.

The persistent gender wage gap, long working hours and entrenched societal expectations further complicate the decision to have children, demonstrating a clear disconnect between governmental measures and the actual concerns of young people as the country navigates shifting gender roles and family dynamics.

Portrait of a Woman (c. 1920–40)

METROPOLITAN MUSEUM OF ART/WIKIMEDIA/CC0

Addressing Misogyny

Despite progress in women's rights, South Korea still faces significant challenges related to gender-based violence and deeply ingrained misogyny. As social expectations evolve and women strive for equal footing, some Korean men resist these changes, displaying hostility towards feminism. Misunderstandings about feminism worsens these issues, with some men labeling feminist movements as too radical, creating a hostile environment for women advocating for gender equality or those who defy traditional gender roles. In some cases, identifying as a feminist can even be unsafe.

Lee Tai-young (p411)

JOHN SUNDERLAND/THE DENVER POST VIA GETTY IMAGES

A stark illustration of this hostility occurred in November 2023 when a man assaulted a female convenience-store clerk merely for having short hair, which he associated with feminism, stating that 'feminists should be beaten up'. Such incidents emphasise the urgent need for social change and the enactment of anti-discrimination laws to ensure better protection for all individuals.

The workplace, too, is a battleground for gender equality. Women often face discrimination and backlash for addressing gender issues or being seen as feminists. For example, in July 2023, a female illustrator was abruptly fired from a game company after male users complained about her depiction of a character in a modest swimsuit and the illustrator's public support for a feminist rally via social media. This showcases the harsh penalties women can face in professional settings.

New Pop Cultural Norms

Despite persistent misogyny, changes are unfolding across various sectors of Korean society. The country's rapid economic development, coupled with increased global interaction, has introduced new values and perspectives, challenging traditional ideas and prompting a reevaluation of gender roles that's reflected in popular culture.

K-Pop has seen female idols pushing the boundaries of what is traditionally expected of Korean women. Girl bands such as BLACKPINK, (G)I-DLE and IVE use their music and public personas to portray themes of empowerment and self-reliance, resonating with young audiences and influencing their perceptions of gender.

Once characterised by conservative portrayals, K-Dramas often depicted female characters as cheerful and resilient yet dependent on wealthy, dominant male counterparts. This is changing. Take *Queen of Tears* for example, where conglomerate heiress Hong Hae-in upends traditional gender roles. Unlike the classic K-Drama formula, it's Hong who takes the reins of her destiny, flying a helicopter to propose to her ordinary lover. At the Hong family gathering, sons-in-law, not daughters-in-law, prepare the ancestral ritual food, humorously challenging deep-seated patriarchal norms in South Korean society.

The transformation doesn't stop there. *Extraordinary Attorney Woo* has an autistic female lawyer as its lead character, while *The Glory* centres on a woman seeking revenge against her bullies. *Marry My Husband* features a betrayed wife who time travels to take revenge on her unfaithful husband and friend, reflecting the real-life shift towards independence, career orientation and a lesser focus on marriage among Korean women.

Literature too has seen a surge of female authors exploring themes of feminism, identity and independence. Books such as *Kim Jiyoung, Born 1982* by Cho Nam-joo have sparked national debates about women's experiences in a male-dominated society, highlighting the everyday sexism faced by women and its psychological toll.

It all goes to show that while significant strides have been made through continuous education, legal reforms and evolving cultural narratives, Korea's path to gender equality is ongoing.

Choi Soo-yeon (p413)

SEONGJOON CHO/BLOOMBERG VIA GETTY IMAGES

INDEX

Map Pages **000**

Map Pages **000**

Map Pages **000**

Map Pages **000**

'The first time I saw Taekkyeon (p363), I thought it was a dance intro to the actual martial arts.'

PHILLIP TANG

'As I drove over the Cheonsa Bridge (p293), a dozen islets shrouded by morning mist beckoned at me from a calm, endless sea.'

MARCO FERRARESE

FROM LEFT: METAL693/WIKIMEDIA/CC BY-SA 3.0, GLABB/WIKIMEDIA/PUBLIC DOMAIN

Mapping data sources:
© Lonely Planet
© OpenStreetMap http://openstreetmap.org/copyright

THIS BOOK

The 14th edition of Lonely Planet's *Korea* guidebook was written and researched by Ann Babe, Marco Ferrarese, Simon Richmond, Phillip Tang, Jennifer Chang, Esther Carlston and Charles Usher. The previous edition was written by Simon Richmond, Ann Babe, Marco Ferrarese and Kwon Meeyoo. This guidebook was produced by the following:

Destination Editor Selena Takigawa Hoy

Coordinating Editor Andrew Bain

Production Editor Robin Yule

Image Researcher Ania Lenihan

Cartographer Rachel Imeson

Assisting Editors Liana Cafolla, Natalie Howard, Trent Holden

Cover Researcher Daisy Korpics

Thanks Melanie Dankel, Soyi Kim, Jenna Myers, Darren O'Connell, Kathryn Rowan

FSC
www.fsc.org
MIX
Paper | Supporting responsible forestry
FSC™ C021741

Paper in this book is certified against the Forest Stewardship Council™ standards. FSC™ promotes environmentally responsible, socially beneficial and economically viable management of the world's forests.

Published by Lonely Planet Global Limited
CRN 554153
14th edition – Oct 2026
ISBN 978 1 83869 822 5

10 9 8 7 6 5 4 3 2 1
Printed in Malaysia